Natal and the Zulu Country

Other books by T.V. Bulpin published by Protea Book House

Islands in a Forgotten Sea (2010)
The Ivory Trail (2011)
Lost Trails on the Lowveld (2012)

Natal and the Zulu Country

T.V. Bulpin

PROTEA BOOK HOUSE
Pretoria
2013

Natal and the Zulu Country
T.V. Bulpin

First edition, first impression in 1966 by Books of Africa
Second edition, first impression in 2013 by Protea Book House

PO Box 35110, Menlo Park, 0102
1067 Burnett Street, Hatfield, Pretoria
8 Minni Street, Clydesdale, Pretoria
protea@intekom.co.za
www.proteaboekhuis.com

Editor: Carmen Hansen-Kruger
Proofreader: Danél Hanekom
Cover design: Hanli Deysel
Front cover image: Louis Smit
Illustrations: C.T. Astley Maberly
Typography: 10.5 on 13.5 pt Zapf Calligraphic by Ada Radford
Printed and bound: Paarlmedia, Paarl

© 2013 M.M.M. Bulpin

ISBN (Printed book): 978-1-86919-924-1
ISBN: (E-book): 978-1-86919-925-8

Author's note: Apart from a considerable amount of new material, this book
includes the information contained in *Shaka's Country* and *To the Shores of
Natal* – two works by the author now long out of print.

Editor's note: *Natal and the Zulu Country* was originally written in 1966 and
much of the scenery described by T.V. Bulpin has changed considerably
since then, but the author's account has been left unchanged. The original
place names and measurements have also been retained as in the original
work. Please note that some quotes may contain offensive words. The Editor
has chosen not to alter such words in order to retain the authenticity of the
reprinted work.

Contents

Prelude   7

1. Veil of lost years   15
2. Sands of gold   30
3. The door of night   46
4. Shaka   63
5. Sleepy lagoon   76
6. Black Caesar   88
7. Dingane   109
8. New times   126
9. The Voortrekkers   142
10. Mpande   166
11. The Republic of Natal   180
12. Twilight of the Republic   193
13. The Colony of Natal   207
14. Life in the sunshine   219
15. The settlers in Natal   231
16. Old Durban   244
17. Hunter's moon   256
18. Cetshwayo   278
19. Trading days   288
20. The Valley of a Thousand Hills   302
21. Pietermaritzburg   316
22. Colonial days   329

23. The road to the interior   349
24. Clouds on the horizon   366
25. Thunderclap   385
26. Storm over Zululand   395
27. The thirteen kinglets   414
28. Dinuzulu   428
29. Northern frontiers   443
30. The Drakensberg   458
31. The North Coast Road   480
32. Misty hills   495
33. Down in the South   512
34. Alexandra   526
35. Alfred   538
36. The coast of dreams   551
37. Empire of the trees   565
38. Tongaland   578
39. Natal and Zululand   593
40. Bambatha   611
41. Roads across the wilderness   630

Bibliography   639

Index   643

Prelude

There is a curiously elusive charm to the nature of the fair land of Natal. It was this medley of hills and valleys which the great chief Shaka made into a kingdom for his Zulu people and perhaps it was the blood he shed which helps to make the place so wistful, with a piquant charm, endearing on sight to man, stirring his blood with envy and desire to possess so lovely a prize, and inspiring him to write there a human story full of contention, adventure and intrigue.

There is another subtle characteristic to the nature of Natal. Geologically speaking, the country is so young that its face has an ingenuous freshness and disarming simplicity. The old granites of Rhodesia, the complex rock strata of the Transvaal, are missing from this landscape. Instead, it basically consists of the same colourful masses of Table Mountain, sandstone originally laid down as sediments beneath the sea all along the southern end of Africa. As in the Cape, when these sediments grew too weighty they collapsed into a trough forced into a portion of the ocean floor. The walls of this trough, clamping tight against the load of sediment, folded and raised it above the sea as a child of the African mainland, born beneath the waves from material eroded from its continental parent, and then, 300 000 000 years ago, elevated to bask in the sunshine.

Over the next 100 000 000 years strange things happened on the surface of this sandstone base. The southern hemisphere seems to have been drenched with heavy rain and humid heat. Great freshwater lakes formed and in the mud of their beds (known to geologists as the Karoo System) enormous deposits are found today of plants and coal (the Ecca Series) and above them, in the Beaufort Series, vertebrate fossil dinosaurs and amphibians, and anthracite coal in Zululand. Still another upper layer of sediments – the Stormberg Series of sandstones and shales – abound in the fossil remnants of plants, reptiles, fish and amphibians.

In true science-fantasy "lost-world" style, this age of swamps and monsters ended with an overwhelming flood of lava which buried it all under a 4000-foot-thick layer of basalt known as the Drakensberg volcanics. This mass of crumbling rock still remains the roof of Southern Africa in the high plateau country of Basutoland, washed by the rains and eroded into a wild jumble of dark valleys and rugged mountain ranges. In the east this mass of basalt was attacked with particular violence by the rains. With the Mozambique Current bringing warm, easily evaporated water to the adjoining coast, the rainfall on the eastern edge of the volcanics was heavy. The waters crumbled the lava mass and greedy rivers carried away a huge spoil in debris. The volcanic mass was forced into retreat, leaving behind odd fragments of itself such as the Lubombo range, and revealing below it once more the earlier sandstones and shales which themselves eroded into countless valleys and dales and downlands, and today provide the lovely face of Natal.

One other great change came to this land of Natal. About 100 000 000 years ago the entire southern part of the African continent subsided. The sea flooded over the coastline, breaking against the Lubombo Mountains and drowning such features as the great lagoon formed by the Mhlatuzana and Mbilo rivers (now Durban Bay). Richly fossiled marine deposits (the Cretaceous System) were laid down before the waters retreated again about 60 000 000 years ago, leaving along the coast in Zululand sandy flats covered with shells and with shallow depressions, retaining lakes and lagoons such as Sibaya and St Lucia where the waters of the rivers were trapped.

By this time the face of Natal and Zululand had been fashioned close to its present form. In the west the long escarpment edge of the retreating Drakensberg volcanics presented the handsome spectacle of a mountainous wall. Below this wall a richly fertile and excellently watered downland rolled off to the sea, with vegetation changing from grass to evergreen coastal forest and then giving way sharply to the notably dark golden-coloured sands of the seashore.

Through this wild garden – 125 miles wide and 300 miles long – some 300 rivers find their lively courses down valleys and over waterfalls and rapids, scalloping into the landscape such masterpieces of natural sculpture as the Valley of a Thousand Hills, leaving behind spectacularly isolated flat-topped mountain remnants of older plains and then garlanding the seashore with a chain of palm-girt lagoons. It is the powerfully erosive action of these rivers which is nature's principal tool in modelling the modern face of Shaka's old country. The rich silt of crumbled sandstone which the rivers carry off with them provides the deep gold-coloured sands of the beaches. The prevailing inshore current, flowing counter to the powerful south-moving Mozambique Current only a few miles out, tends to deposit this silt northwards of all river mouths, forming the sandspits which are so characteristic of this coast and forcing the rivers to deflect southwards to avoid the barrier of sand which their own industry is steadily accumulating. The spacious stretch of Durban harbour locked securely in the arms of the land is a fine result of this action of rivers and sea. Durban Bluff, the northern sandspit of the Siphingo River, is the right arm whilst the Point (the sandspit of the Mhlatuzana) is the left arm, with only a narrow gap to provide entrance to the once tranquil lagoon which is now one of the world's busiest harbours.

With an average annual rainfall of 45 inches at the coast, dwindling to about 25 inches inland, the landscape is well grassed, with fine parkland in the areas of heavier rainfall. Wild bananas, the graceful lala palms, wild date palms, tree euphorbias, the *mathungula* with their sweet plum-like fruit, the brilliantly flowering *msinsi* (kaffirboom), the *mthombathi* (black ironwood), the *mdoni* (water myrtle), and many other handsome trees flourish in this pleasant land. Over 120 different varieties of ferns find fertile soil in the shadows, whilst the sunshine is imprisoned in the vivid colours and elegant shapes of such lovely flowers as *Gloriosa superba* (the lily with the petals of fire).

Game animals were as numerous as the wild flowers. The mighty elephant (*ndlovu*) roamed throughout the land. Each river pool had its laze of hippos (*imvubu*), while *ngwenya* (the crocodile) and *mbulu* (the monitor lizard) were common. Through the still nights rumbled the challenge of *ingonyama* (the lion), while *ingwe* (the leopard) lurked in the deepest thickets.

At least ten of the antelope family had their home in Natal. The great eland, *mpofu* (the tawny one) grazed along the face of the Drakensberg. The hartebeest (*indluzele*) was common in the midlands. In the thick bush *unkonka* (the bushbuck) sheltered, frightening away intruders with his curious dog-like bark. The blesbok (*ilinga*) was found with the eland along the mountain slopes where the grazing of red grass was sweet and rich. The lithe oribi (*iwula*), the forest duiker (*ipithi*), the reedbuck (*inhlangu*), and the rhebok (*iliza*), were common all over the land.

Each winter, as well, great migrant herds of antelope from the central plains wandered down the face of the Drakensberg, blazing the first passes as they escaped the cold and lack of grazing of the Highveld. In those halcyon times the black wildebeest (*imbuthuma*), with his quaintly erratic habits, grazed the Drakensberg slopes in countless thousands, even though today little more than one thousand of their kind remain in the whole of Southern Africa, and his presence on the Natal coat-of-arms almost alone remains to remind us of the mighty spectacle of the original herds.

Who exactly were the first human beings to inhabit this land remains unknown. The sandstone caves below the Drakensberg were occupied by people of the Bushman-type in the latter Stone Age and it was there, in fact, and beyond the mountains in Basutoland that this vanished race reached the very height of their culture and prosperity. The sandstone foothills of the Drakensberg were a magnificent home for a primitive hunting people. Free of mosquitoes, the atmosphere cool and invigorating, the streams clear of that great curse of Africa, bilharzia, and the sweet grasslands teeming with game, the Bushmen must have thought themselves as having passed through the gates of heaven when they found this highland.

Some of the finest galleries of rock art known to man remain on the walls of the sandstone caves as a memoral to the Bushmen. Beautifully drawn, with life and vigour and humour, they put to shame the dreary daubs which often pass for modern art, and the skill and love and pleasure of the primitive artists is only too apparent.

The foothills of Giant's Castle were the particular haunt of the Bushmen. It was there in the long red-coloured grass, with crystal streams tumbling down from the heights, that the handsome mountain elands had their home. These great antelope, with the little oribi, provided the most succulent venison in Africa. It was on their tender meat that the Bushmen reached their own ideal of contentment and heart's ease. And it was there and all along the cool land in the afternoon shadow of the Drakensberg that these almost intangible people of whom we know so very little, with the leisure of prosperity perfected their polychrome paintings and their music in the forgotten years just before the dawn of tradition and the beginning of history in Africa.

Milter

Preto

Johannesbu

Vereenigi

Kroonstad

Welkom   Bethleh

Bloemfontein

BASU

ORANGE RIVER

NATAL AND THE
ZULU COUNTRY

Lydenburg
TRANSVAAL
waterval Boven
middelburg
Witbank
Barberton
MOÇAMBIQUE
Lourenço Marques
Lubombo
Mbabane
SWAZILAND
Bethal
Ermelo
Standerton
Piet Retief
usuthu R.
Ponto do Ouro
Kosi Bay
Lake Sibaya
Volksrust
Phongolo R.
Mkhuze R.
Utrecht
Vryheid
Sodwana
Newcastle
Dundee
Lake St. Lucia
Hluhluwe Game Reserve
Harrismith
Umfolozi Gamereserve
Mfolozi R.
St. Lucia Bay
Sandlulana
Ladysmith
Melmoth
NATAL
Empangeni
Mont aux Sources
Colenso
Mkandla
Eshowe
Cathedral Peak
Estcourt
Gingindlovu
Greytown
Thukela (Tugela) river
Giantscastle
Mooi River
Stanger
Howick
Tongaat
Pietermaritzburg
Mngeni R.
Pinetown
DRAKENSBERG
Richmond
Durban
Umzimkulu R.
Ixopo
Amanzimtoti
Umkomaas
Scottburgh
umzimkulu
Kokstad
Port Shepstone
Uvongo
Margate
Port Edward
TRANSKEI
umtata
Port St. Johns
N
W
E
S

ONE
Veil of lost years

Just as distance makes hills so much lovelier, so time spins a veil from all its lost years and the past is obscured by its softness. The passions of men became mellowed; their lives seem much more simple, their problems much easier. The deeper one looks, the softer the vision, the dimmer the outline. In the end only mystery and legends are left, like shadows lingering on the horizon's rim of the secret land of forgetfulness.

The Bushmen, the pioneer settlers of what is now the land of Natal, have vanished entirely and the only knowledge we have of them is from the memories of newcomers who encountered and displaced them. What a fascinating tale could have been recorded if, little more than three hundred years ago, when Europe and the East already had great libraries, even the most primitive of writing could have described the coming of the first Bantu migratory groups, their contacts and frictions with the Bushmen, and their conquest and settlement of the choicest areas of Natal.

Instead, the traditions of the Bantu groups consist of little more than superstitions. To them the first men of the land were simply phantoms. Their voices, legend says, still make the echoes, but nothing else remains save mounds of kitchen debris buried beneath the sands of the shore, Stone Age tools and the paintings on the rocks which bear mute and poignant witness to the vanished race of hunters, the game animals they pursued, and their fights and escapades with encroaching newcomers both African and European.

Tradition does not even provide a clear picture of the earliest of the Bantu migrants, although the date of their advent was not much before the fifteenth century. Tradition only has it that these pioneers, known to later Zulu-speaking migrants as the Lala people, were offshoots of the great Karanga tribe of Rhodesia – small splinter groups and refugees from internecine conflicts who wandered off and found a sanctuary for themselves among the hills and valleys of the south.

Of the lives and personalities of these early settlers little more is remembered than is known of the Bushmen. Even their language is nearly forgotten, and scarcely one hundred words survive. Only at the beginning of the seventeenth century does pure legend and fairy tale transmute into slightly more reliable tradition, for it was then that there occurred a new invasion of an entirely different migratory people who called themselves the abaNguni (people of Nguni), derived from the name of their half-legendary leader.

These newcomers came trudging down the coastal belt from the north. From whence they came is uncertain. They spoke the language we now know as Zulu and by repute were the vanguard, perhaps driven away by strife, of an even larger migratory body which had dallied behind them somewhere in the wilds of Mozambique. This larger host acknowledged as their own legendary leader a hero by the name of Dlamini, and tradition has it that he had led them on their long journey south from their ancient home at a place called eMbo.

The Nguni and the Dlamini people spoke the same language, but in the hundred years while the main body remained in Mozambique they picked up, in some way, a curiously lisping form of pronunciation known as *ukutekela*. Both groups, but particularly the Nguni, incorporated in their speech some of the clicks found in the Bushmen and Hottentot languages. Whether they brought these clicking sounds with them on their migration is unknown, but more likely they had picked them up by contact as they travelled south. Perhaps considering the novel sounds to be smart and fashionable, they accepted them into their own language as a permanent feature.

With their livestock and their impedimenta packed on the heads of their wives, the migrants trudged southwards down through the coastal country of Mozambique, searching for some new land in which to settle. New land where the environment would be more congenial to their pastoral interests, and healthier than the harsh wilderness from whence they had come, where their culture and way of life had been so deleteriously moulded and retarded by the relentless heat, fever, tsetse flies and debilitating bilharzia; the great curses of Africa.

Keeping close to the eastern mountain wall of the Lubombo (the ridge) until it dwindled beneath the flat bush country of northern Zululand, the Nguni people found themselves confronted by a landscape very close to their heart's desire. The coastal flats swept up like a sandy sea breaking on a mass of hills. Well watered and with excellent soil and grazing, these hills offered on their heights and in their valleys a substantial relief from heat and the tsetse fly whose presence was so insurmountable a problem to cattle keepers.

Nguni's following settled there and then broke up. His people dispersed happily over their new homelands. It was then, some three hundred years ago, that the human story of this book really started, for the leader of one of the fragments of the Nguni – simply a handful of people – was a man named Malandela (the follower) who, with his wives, children and a few retainers, wandered off on his own into the countless hills of Zululand and settled in a valley as spacious and beautiful as the dreams of youth.

The valley in which this little group made its home was that of the river named from the strength of its floods, Mhlathuze (the forceful one). It was there that Malandela erected a kraal and to this place, tradition has it, he applied the name of oDwini. There Malandela lived out the days of his life and then died, leaving two sons who founded two tribes destined to play no little part in the story of mankind.

The eldest son was Qwabe. With the principal section of his father's people, he remained at the family centre, and his following, in the fashion of their kind, became known as the amaQwabe (the people of Qwabe). The younger son had received the pleasant name of Zulu (heaven). With his mother and a few adherents, he left the home of his father and wandered off around the hill known as Nkwenkwe (the dried up one); and along the straggling course of the Mfule River to its source on a ridge named Mthonjaneni (the place of the little fountain).

To the north-west, below this ridge with its springlet destined to quench the thirst of many a Zulu ruler, lies a shallow bush-studded basin with the Mkhumbane (river of the hollow) meandering through the euphorbia and acacia trees scattered over its floor. In this basin Zulu settled. It was warm, but the grazing was excellent, the water reliable and the landscape pleasing, with a jumble of hills surrounding the basin like a crowd gathered to view the coming of great events. Over everything loomed the most conspicious landmark in this part of the world, the flat-topped 4715-foot-high Nhlazatshe (the mountain of green stones).

We have no details of Zulu's life in this home of his choice. He made no history other than by his settlement and died in peace. His people, the abakwaZulu (people of Zulu), as was customary, planted a euphorbia tree to mark the site of his grave, ever afterwards revered as *kwaNkosinkulu* (the place of the great chief).

Zulu was succeeded by Phunga, and he by Mageba, and he by Ndaba, and he by Jama. The relics of their villages and graves still linger on the floor of the great hollow while traditions whisper down through the years of reasonably peaceful reigns with only minor raids and fights and the descendants of the original followers of Zulu slowly increasing their numbers through all the hazards of primitive life until, by the middle of the eighteenth century, they had become a clan with a ruler, a son of Jama named Senzangakhona (the purposeful doer). Of this romantic young man, his doings and his product, we shall read much more later. Meanwhile, let us gain some impression of the country as a whole as it was at this almost naive period just before the beginning of great events.

Many other clans had their origin at the same period and in the same manner as the Zulus. The Sibiyas who settled to the east and the Buthelezis in the west were immediate neighbours who came from the self-same stock. Other, later, clans were formed as a result of disintegration of older people, increasing their numbers and then indulging in the normal human distractions of squabbling with one another and fragmenting into contentious elements. Still other clans were formed through romantic convenience. It was taboo to marry within one's own clan, and a chief falling in love with a clanswoman often resorted to the arbitrary device of proclaiming as independent the families of their ladyloves. In such manner there came into existence the Mgazini (in the blood) and the Biyela (the hedged) clan which considered its own origin as scandalous and determinedly remained unmarriageable within the Zulu clan even though proclaimed independent.

Close relatives of the Zulus, and originating from the same migratory movement, were the more numerous Ngwaneni people, who made their home on the southern borders of the Transvaal along the foothills of the mountains later to be named after the chief, Langalibalele. Adjoining them were several other related clans such as the Mabasos. Their namesake chief had settled his followers along the banks of the upper reaches of the river known as the Mzinyathi (the home of the buffaloes). Further down the same river lived more relatives; the Chunu clan, renowned blacksmiths, while the Khumalos made their home in that most beautiful of forests, the Ngome (place of precipitous heights) and found in it a fastness of almost impregnable security.

With these migrants of the Nguni family dispersed and settled in the midlands of the country, there occurred a second and more considerable influx of people. These were the

19

Dlamini people who, in the middle of the eighteenth century, overcame their own inertia and moved south from the sweltering lowlands of Mozambique. It was probably a civil war that caused the movement, for the once cohesive mass disintegrated into fragments. Each fragment went its separate way, but all remembered their old relationship and that, led by the hero-chief Dlamini, they had tramped south from the half-mythical place they knew as eMbo.

One large section of these people from eMbo travelled south until they reached the banks of the river whose name, the Phongolo (like a trough), legend tells us was applied by the migrants when they found it to be so long, deep, and with very few crossing places. The migrants wandered up the river course, through the Lubombo and into the low country on the western side. There one section of the migrants hived off, turned northwards and became the ancestors of the modern Swazis.

The rest of this group of migrants also dispersed. What appears to have been the vanguard went on to the source of the Mzinyathi River where they settled and became the Hlubi tribe. An interesting tradition tells us that it was a section of this group which wandered off into the south and became the ancestors of the great Xhosa tribe. The Bele tribe settled close to the Hlubi in the watersheds of the Ndaka (muddy river) and the iBusi (dominant river), later known as the Sundays and Waschbank rivers, while the Zizi tribe, also a section of the people from eMbo, after all the thousands of weary miles of travelling, settled in the cool foothills of the Drakensberg, the range they simply knew as the Khahlamba (mountain barrier) where they dispossessed the Bushmen of their ancient hunting grounds. These Zizi people traditionally were the earliest of the Bantu to settle amongst the heights and crystal streams of the Drakensberg. They made their homes in the superb uplands where so many of the rivers of Natal have their sources: the Ngwanyane (vigorous one) or Sand River; the Mnambithi (tasty one) or Klip River; the great Thukela (Tugela) itself, and its ingeniously-named tributary the Njesuthi (well-filled dog) or Little Tugela. From this pleasant land the Zizis were tempted to climb the mountain barrier of the Drakensberg and in the eighteenth century they removed entirely into what became known as Basutoland, leaving behind in Natal only a few fragments such as the Tholweni clan who remained at the headwaters of the Mtshezi (brick-red coloured) or Bushman's River, and the Mpofana (little eland) or Mooi River in the shadow of Giant's Castle.

Another section of the people from eMbo, particularly related to the Swazis, found a home on the southern side of the Phongolo around a 2528-foot height whose summit was covered by a dark forest which became the taboo burial ground for their chiefs. These people became known as the Ndwandwes, after their most famous chief, while another of their leaders, Magudu, gave his name to the heights.

The taboo forest on the summit of the heights became a renowned place in African lore. It was reputed to be haunted by malevolent spirits who guarded the graves of the buried chiefs. Many have been the tales of intruders who have there sought to hunt, explore or cut firewood. Instead, they have roused a fury of winds, whispering and shouting around their ears: "Wow! Wow! Who comes here? Do you dare us?" And then, with a great barking of invisible hounds, and a shower of sticks and stones, the intruders have been chased away.

The Ndwandwe folk seem to have been partial to enchanted places. One section of the tribe, led by Gasa, a brother of the reigning chief, made a home at the south-western end of the Lubombo, where the 1736-foot-high Tshaneni (place of the small stone) looks out in silence at the changing world below it.

This Tshaneni Mountain has always been considered a haunted place. Strange lights and flickering fires are said to have often been seen at night around the fissures and crags of the summit. Weird noises and calls have been reported as well, and old Gasa, with his taste for the uncanny, selected the mountain as his burial ground. Since his day each successive chief of the Gasa clan, on his death, has been laboriously carried by the ritual witch doctors up to a cleft between two mighty rocks near the summit and there buried in a taboo cave on this, the so-called "Ghost Mountain".

Many other clans and tribes had their origin as a result of the migration of the people from eMbo. From the original sections, as well, there came in latter days, numerous offshoots. The pleasantly named Langeni (in the sunshine) clan who settled near the Zulus on the upper Mhlathuze River, was one of these sections of the eMbo people. This clan, itself probably the product of some chief's attempt to legalise his attachment to a clanswoman, repeated the same process. In later years, when one of their chiefs loved a clanswoman, he proclaimed her family as independent and named them the abakwaMagwaza (people of the stabber) for he had "stabbed" or taken one of their most desirable daughters.

While all this confused human movement was taking place inland, the earlier Lala inhabitants were still living in reasonable peace along the coast. But trouble was inevitable. The prolific Qwabe people were gradually overrunning the beautiful hill country watered by the rivers known as the Mlalazi (place of whetstones), where the whetstones were obtained for the sharpening of spears, and the old Lala-named Matigulu (the water that scrapes away), so known because of the damage its floods have done to crops.

As the Qwabes increased, so they gradually pushed the Lala people towards the coast and the south. Then, from the north there came trudging a crowd of newcomers. These people, known as the Mthethwas after their most renowned chief, had been a part of the original migration, but they were a very mixed lot, with elements of eMbo, Nguni, Lala and Tonga people in their ranks.

Whatever their exact origin, the Mthethwas travelled southwards, past the source of the river known from its floods as the Msunduze (the one that pushes away) and across the Hluhluwe, so named from the *Dalbergia armata* (thorny monkey-rope), a climber of many coils growing on its banks and used as a purifying charm by murderers or warriors after a killing. The largest and most storied of all the rivers of Zululand is the Mfolozi (the zigzag), so named from its tortuous course and erratic nature. The two great divisions which unite to form the main stream are known as the Mfolozi Emnyama (black Mfolozi) and the Mfolozi Emhlophe (white Mfolozi) on account of some difference in the shade of their mud. It was in the coastlands just south of the united stream that the Mthethwas made their home and became a tribal power of no little achievement and renown.

Before such oncoming hosts the earlier Lala people had an increasingly uncomfortable time. Many started to move away south, while those who remained found themselves compressed into smaller and inferior areas.

Among the Lalas who remained and became vassals of the newcomers, were the abakwaMbonambi (the people of the bad omen) who clung to their ancient lands immediately above the Mhlathuze lagoon. They were famed blacksmiths, skilled at manufacturing spearheads, and great pedlars of their product. One of their most famous blacksmiths was Mabodla of the Sokana section of the clan. By means of the ancient ford across the lower portion of Lake St Lucia, this individual made his way to the spit of land separating the lake from the sea. There the blacksmith settled, took as wife an Indian survivor of a wreck on the coast and became the patriarch of an industrious people.

Around Lake St Lucia, the Cwebeni las' Entlengeni (lagoon of rafts), several Lala and Tonga clans had their homes, defended from the envy of others by prodigious numbers of mosquitoes. Some found sanctuary in the marshlands skirting St Lucia Bay. Others found retreats in the dense forest known as Dukuduku (a place of groping in the dark, trying to find a way). A branch of the Seme people, the Ntlozis, also discovered the shallow ford across the southern portion of the lake and, running the gauntlet of the crocodiles, made their way across and were happily settled when the abakwaMbonambi blacksmiths found them on the wind-blown spit of land between the lake and the Indian Ocean.

Of the Lala clans who made their way southwards, several settled in the colossal valley of the river whose size and flood-power gave it the name of the Thukela (the startling one). In that hot wilderness, with its vast precipices and staggering views, there settled on the south side of the river such people as the allied Hlongwa, Seluku and Phumulo clans, mixed up with elements of the Qwabe people whose tribal boundary lay on the north bank.

Further up the Thukela Valley where the Siwa Samange (the precipice of the vultures) frowns down from the northern side, the oddly-named clan, the Luthuli (people of the dust) made a home on the cool and pleasant heights known as Mpaphala (the open place). From there the increasing pressure of the Qwabes eventually drove them, in the middle of the eighteenth century, to the area around what they knew as Thekwini (the lagoon). There they made new homes in the bush, where the city of Durban stands today, and used the si-Bubulungu (long, bulky thing), the modern Bluff, as their securest refuge.

In the oven-like heat of the Thukela Valley, below the original home of the Luthulis, another Lala clan found sanctuary. These were the Ngcobo people who settled in the bush happily enough, making love and producing as offspring various minor clans to live beside them in the valley. The Malangeni (they in the sun) were one of these offspring. It was one of their number, Nqina by name, who abandoned the sultry valley about 1750 and tramped back north in search of a more salubrious climate. Eventually, he settled in the hills of northern Zululand and, to win mends, so lavishly dined his neighbours that his followers became known as the abakwaHlabisa (people who present beasts for slaughter) and thus gave the name to the magisterial district of today.

South of the Thukela, in the pleasant midlands or what is Natal proper, a great number of Lala clans made their home. The amaPhumulo (people of rest) settled along the banks of the river known as the Mvoti, named after their headman Mvoti Ncashange. The Cele people, related to the Mthethwas and speaking a hybrid Zulu-Lala language, established themselves in the lands between the rivers known as the Zinkwazi (place of the white-headed fish eagle) and the Thongathi (place of *Strychnos mackenii* trees).

As racially mixed as the Cele people, were the numerous clans of the so-called Debe (slit-faced) tribe, so named from their practice of slitting the skin of their faces as a form of adornment. They were basically of Lala origin, but their blood was well diffused with that of the newcomers and they spoke the lisping *tekela* language of the people from eMbo.

Among these Debes was the Dunge clan, living around the headwaters of the Hlimbithwa (muddy water) tributary of the Mvoti. Their relatives, the Bombos, had their homes east of the 4908-foot-high Blinkwater Mountain known to them as Ntaba-kayikhonjwa (he at whom you must never point) on account of a superstition that by pointing at the peak, bad weather would result. Other relatives, the Nyamvus, also lived close to a natural wonder, the huge mass of rock known as esiDum-bini from the number of edible tuber *dumbe* plants (*Colocasia antiquorum*) growing there.

A particular concentration of Debe clans lived in the valley of the river which divides Natal into halves. This river with its tortuous course so full of beautiful waterfalls and rapids was given two names. In its upper reaches it was called the Mso-nginyathi (gatherer of the buffaloes) while lower down where it flowed into the mighty Valley of a Thousand Hills, it was named the Mngeni (river of acacia trees).

Of the Debe clans who settled along its course, the Dla-nyoka people made their homes in the hills just south of the mountain known as Nhlangakazi or Mount Sargeaunt. East of them the Nkulwini people made their homes on the fertile heights known as eThafamasi (the milk producing plain), while still further east, along the banks of the middle Mdloti (river of the bitter wild-tobacco plants) lived the Zelemu clan of uncertain origin and with very odd habits, including a partiality to eating meat raw.

South of these raw-meat eaters, in the shadow of the 2099-foot amaBedhlane (twin breasts) Mountain, dwelt a small clan known as the Ndlovini (they amongst the elephants), from the wild animals who shared their homeland in the Valley of a Thousand Hills. The great valley was itself well settled by Debe clans and the dominating heights of iNanda (the pleasant place) looked down on a patchwork of green fields strung like emeralds on the copper thread of the yellow-brown coloured waters of the river.

At the head of the valley, where the Msunduze (the river that pushes away) joins the Mngeni, the Nyavu people lived, with the tiny Njilo clan to their north on the other side of the river. Dominating their lands and, indeed, the whole valley – a veritable castle of the giants – stood the massive 3143-foot-high, flat-topped Table Mountain, known to the Debes as em-Khambathini (the place of the kameeldoorn trees).

To the people of the valley, this mountain was a natural fortress of a strength and splendour far surpassing that of any man-made castle. From a distance its summit seemed just a level surface. But to those who climbed the pathways providing access up the western slopes, this flat-topped mountain was revealed as one of the natural wonders of the land.

The summit is an undulating meadow, richly grassed with hillocks, valleys and wooded grottoes. The whole atmosphere is that of an island-world of its own, drifting through the ages in a sea made of hills and dreams. From the edges of this island summit there is a view beyond description. The thousand hills of the Mngeni valley lie in a superb jumble all around. Eastwards is a glimpse of the distant ocean; westwards, on the far horizon, lies the Drakensberg, and in between is all Natal.

On the island summit there are many curious natural marvels. On the right of the main pathway to the summit, at the foot of a grassy knoll, there bubbles to life a pleasant little spring where the coolest of waters may always be found. For a hundred yards this streamlet gurgles along and then loses itself in a tangle of ferns and lilies.

Nearby stands a small clump of shrubs and tree ferns. This is the secret entrance to a veritable fairy glen. A narrow gorge, almost hidden by overhanging shrubbery and ferns, leads down through a forest of greenery, mosses, crimson-stemmed begonias, lichens and fungi, until it suddenly opens out on to a natural terrace, a private veranda for some mountain spirit to regard the view.

The main path around the edge of the summit leads on to a grotto from which water springs from a lovely fountain, flows to the edge and then tumbles headlong 600 feet to the forest below. Beyond this grotto the pathway winds round a headland, revealing an ever-changing panorama of the Nyavu kraals scattered over the valley floor far below. Through beds of watsonias the path winds on to a witch's cave lying in a wooded gorge on the eastern side of the mountain. Down this gorge, through a forest of tree ferns, and hidden in a thicket, lies the entrance to the cave. Humans are barred from entry by a chasm across the floor, but for the bats and the spirits the cave burrows on into the mountain, and its end is beyond sight.

Beyond this cave, the path leads through the bracken to a terrace and the so-called Devil's Kloof. Here the mountain has been riven asunder in some past rage of nature and this enormous fissure – the greatest wonder of the mountain – was formed. The terrace leads to a natural bridge made of mammoth rocks wedged and suspended over the chasm's mouth.

From the east side a narrow path leads downwards. To the left, halfway down over big boulders, lies a dense thicket falling away to the valley floor. The path finds a tortuous way through the thicket and leads to a ledge of rock where water drips in silver tears from the overhang. Beyond lies a deep, primeval forest of giant yellow-wood trees, with tree ferns with stems reaching 30 feet high. Ferns in astonishing profusion – maidenhair, silver ferns, flowering ferns and many more – flourish in this secret paradise. Creepers stretch across the path. The shadows and the stillness seem full of enchantment. The intruder stands spellbound by the silence until suddenly some wild creature, a bushbuck perhaps, which, unseen, has been watching in breathless suspense, takes fright and goes crashing off through the trees. Behind, the birds twitter, the wind whispers through the leaves, the intruder sighs, and the forest comes alive again.

West of this Natal Table Mountain, a whole complex of Debe clans made their home in bygone days. Along the banks of the tributary of the Mngeni known as the Mlambomunye (single stream), which Europeans call the Karkloof, the Wushe people lived. The 305-foot-high white beauty of Howick Falls, known to them as kwaNogqaza (place of the tall one) was their proud tribal possession.

South of the Wushe people, in the warm basin below the 4756-foot-high Zwartkop Mountain known as Mbubu (the place of thatching grass), where Pietermaritzburg stands to-day, dwelt the Nqondo clan. Their neighbours to the south and east, along the banks of the river known from its colour and stale taste as the Mlazi (river like whey), were the Mjilo and Cindaneni people with their lands overlapping into the adjoining valley of the emBokodweni (place of round stones), whose name has been corrupted by Europeans into Umbogi-ntwini.

Still further south, towards the deep valley of the Mkhoma-zi (river of cow-whales), lived the Ntshele and Shwawu peo-ple, with the large Ntambo clan across the river in the pleas-ant country drained by the streamlet known as the Lufafa (the fissure), and that oddly-named brook, the eXobo (Ixopo), whose onomatopoetic name comes from the sound of a person squelching across the bog through which it flows.

The jumble of richly-grassed hills forming the south mid-lands of Natal was the home of the Ntozakhe, Gwayi and Mbibi clans. Their villages covered the fertile lands at the source of the river known from its involved course as the Mphamba-nyoni (confuser of the birds), and around the slopes of the 2070-foot-high isiPhofu (tawny-coloured) hill which dominates that most agreeable landscape.

The Mzimkhulu (the great home of all rivers), so named from its size and number of tributaries, marked the southern limit to the pure tribal groups of Natal. South of that river, to the valley of the river whose destructive appetite at floodtime gave it the name of the Mthamvuna (reaper of mouthfuls), there lived a few hybrid clans such as the Xholo and Nzima-kwe people whose tribal relationships were more with the Pondos and Thembus of the Cape than with anybody in Natal.

The same human mixture prevailed on the lower south coast of Natal. People such as the Sushas, whose chief Thonga-si has left his name to one of the rivers, were offshoots of the Pondos; while others, such as the Nyasane clan, were of Thembu blood, making their home in the fertile area where the *amaBedhlane* (hills like breasts) look down on what is still known from the name of one of their chiefs as kwaCekwane, the pleasant area of modern Dronkvlei.

These then, the Lalas, the Debes, the Ngunis and the people from the place called eMbo, were the Bantu settlers who drove the Bushmen away from their ancient hunting grounds and made Natal and Zululand their home. It was a tranquil Arcady in which they lived, full enough of personal squabbles and petty wars, but free for a while of those great disturbances which are the making of history. The early settlers passed their lives in a beautiful and peaceful land, with few events save the changing of the seasons, the alternation of the nights and days with all their moods, and the allotted life and death of each individual, generation after generation, through all those lost years whose details we may only guess.

TWO
Sands of gold

W here the Indian Ocean meets the shores of Natal, the green hills with their secrets and their legends have formed a girdle. It is made up of golden sands; of innumerable sheltered baylets where the sunshine plays; of palm trees whispering with the winds; of blue lagoons sleeping on a beach of dreams; and of an airy spaciousness, exhilarating to mind and eye.

It was in December 1497 that the first Europeans saw this warm and lovely coast. It was then that the illustrious Vasco da Gama, the pioneer Portuguese navigator to the East, made his way along the shores of Southern Africa, and, because his four little ships, originally crewed by only 148 men, were off an unspecified length of the coast on 25 December, he applied to it the name of Natal (Christmas), which later Portuguese mapmakers, with good information to guide them, considered as describing the land from the mouth of the Mthatha River in the Cape to the site of modern Durban.

Da Gama left no description of this coast. The weather was fine, his thoughts were directed towards his great exploratory goal of the East and he did not land or pause in the course of this portion of his journey. What African eyes observed the passing of the Portuguese fleet is also lost in obscurity. Doubtless some Pondo and Lala beachcombers or herdsmen on the hillside must have watched in wonder as the four ships made their way northwards with the inshore current. But African tradition is as silent as European records about this auspicious occasion and only the name of Natal remains as a lasting legacy of the event.

If Da Gama had been a man of prophetic perception he would have painted on the map in the brightest red of danger the whole coastline of his land of Christmas. Camões it was, the Portuguese poet, who wrote of a certain monstrous phantom named Adamastor who haunted the southern end of Africa. His pagan spirit brooded over the sands of gold and the early Portuguese seafarers were certainly destined to find the shores of Natal a perfect home – wild and lonely – for so savage a phantom.

In those days, when navigators had no means of accurately determining longitude, the shores of Natal became a major hazard. Shipping coming in across the Indian Ocean, especially if the pilots took what was known as the outer passage past the southern point of Madagascar, reached the coast of Africa somewhere along the shores of Natal. If they made this landfall at night or in inclement weather, they were apt to continue due westwards and quickly found the golden sands of Natal to cover a malignant line of rocks.

Many of those old sailing ships – so beautiful and brave to the eye – were also singularly rotten inside. Greedy for profits, their owners crammed them beyond capacity with the wealth of the East. With fortunes in cargo and passenger lists made up of some of the noblest names in Europe, many of the ships were nevertheless in ill repair and sailed more by faith and the mercy of Providence than anything else.

One ship after the other came to grief upon the coast of Southern Africa, and it was the survivors of these disasters who were the first Europeans to explore the shores of Natal. The stories of some of these wrecks are remarkable.

The first known wrecks on the coast of Southern Africa were in the year 1552. Two galleons, the *Saint John* and the *Saint Jerome* left Cochin for Portugal. Both were heavily laden and the *Saint John* was the largest ship in the eastern trade of that day.

The two ships sailed in company without event, until they neared the Cape on 11 May. There the pagan spirit was waiting and a most cruel south-easterly gale tore into them. The two ships ran before the storm as though from the wrath of God, with the wind veering to the north-west and blowing at hurricane force. The *Saint Jerome* came to grief just north of the Mhlathuze river mouth in Zululand; and beyond some wreckage dumped upon the beach, she left no survivor to tell the story of her fate.

The *Saint John*, dismasted and damaged, ran before the wind until 8 June 1552, when the crew managed, in a lull, to bring the battered hulk to anchor somewhere in the vicinity of the Mthamvuna River. There they landed and spent three days conveying people and goods to the safety of the beach.

They intended to run the hulk ashore at some selected site and there construct a caravel from the planks and make their way to safety in Mozambique. Instead, the storm returned with renewed fury. The galleon was picked up, as though a straw, and flung upon the rocks. One hundred and ten people were drowned, the galleon broken into fragments, and as the old records have it, "that day merchandise to the value of a million *cruzados* was buried in the sea, as no vessel so richly laden had left India since it was discovered."

The survivors gathered in tents upon the beach, surrounded by such goods as they had contrived to salvage. There they rested and nursed the wounded upon that lonely shore. On the third day, nine Africans appeared on the brow of the hill and for two hours sat and watched the scene below, but then withdrew as if afraid.

About five days later more Africans appeared, leading a cow. They came close to the Portuguese and by signs indicated they would exchange the cow for iron. When the Portuguese offered a few nails, the Africans went wild with delight. Even at that early time the meaning and possibilities of a ship were known to these tribespeople, but by what means, other than by tradition of trade further north, or experience with Arab dhows, is unknown.

Nothing came of this first known barter attempt between European and African in Natal. Bargaining was going on when more Africans appeared on a distant hill and by shouting told their compatriots to withdraw.

Twelve days later the Portuguese left. They divided their number into three companies. There were altogether some five hundred survivors of this wreck, over three hundred of them being Asiatic slaves of various nationalities.

On 7 July 1552, the dilapidated company set off up the beach on the long walk to Mozambique. They started boldly enough, with members of the crew carrying ailing or wealthy passengers who had the means of payment. As they travelled, fording the rivers, pushing through the sand, miserably sleeping in rain and cold and with scanty food, people began to fall by the way. First the sick went, followed by the weaklings and the rich whose way of life had made them flabby and whose fortunes counted for nothing when the hardier sailors became exhausted from carrying them.

So the company passed on up the whole length of the Natal, Zululand and Tongaland coasts. A grim train of camp followers – hyenas and jackals – cleaned up the human debris left behind; and such few Africans as were then in residence in those parts lurked around, snatching whatever pickings they could.

In October 1552, two hundred survivors straggled into the kraal of the kindly old chief, Nyaka, at the bay of Lourenço Marques. The rest of the company, some three hundred in number, remained behind along the beach, to find rest in death or to pour their varied Asiatic and European blood into the veins of such tribespeople as gave them sanctuary.

The survivors at Lourenço Marques, after resting a while, sought to push on up the coast towards Mozambique, the first European settlement. Further up the coast they encountered a hostile tribe which set upon them, and what little they still possessed was forcibly taken from them. Even their ragged clothing was torn off piece by piece.

The captain of the ship, Manuel de Souza de Sepulveda, a noble of refinement and renown, had a young and beautiful wife. She had survived the journey up until then with her children, but her efforts and the care of her husband simply amounted to so much extra misery heaped upon her head. Rather she had died when the ship foundered than cling with such tenacity to a few more months of misery.

There on the beach of Lourenço Marques the Africans stripped her. The records of the wreck tell the story.

"It is said that Dona Leonor would not allow herself to be stripped but defended herself with blows and struggles, as she preferred that the kaffirs should kill her rather than to find herself naked before them. And there is no doubt that her life would then have ended, had not Manuel de Souza begged her to let herself be stripped, reminding her that all are born naked and since this was the will of God she should submit."

So while her children cried around her, she was stripped.

"She covered herself with her hair, which was very long, and made a pit in the sand in which she buried herself to the waist, and never rose from that spot again."

Her husband and children died there around her, for without her they would not move. As for the rest of the company, twenty-two of them reached Inhambane, where the annual coastal trading boat found them naked and miserable the next year, and ransomed them from the Africans in exchange for beads to the value of two pence three-farthings a person.

So ends the story of the *Saint John* and the saga of the first known Europeans to trudge along the sands of gold. The survivors left no record or map illustrating the coast, for nobody with sufficient skill had survived the wreck. It took another disaster to produce the first lasting picture of the south-eastern coast.

Two years later, in 1554, the *Saint Benedict*, overladen with 473 passengers and a vast store of precious cargo, came to grief on what was apparently the south bank of the Mbhashe (Bashee) River on the Cape coast. After sorting themselves out upon the beach, the survivors, on 27 April, set out to walk north to Lourenço Marques. Ninety-eight Portuguese and 224 slaves started the long journey and among their number was a skilled navigator, Manuel Perestrelo. He it was who took some accurate note of the details of their journey.

On 11 May the party reached the site of the wreck of the *Saint John* and discovered there many relics of that disaster. Most of the local African kraals were furnished with souvenirs in the shape of crockery and other salvage.

After rummaging around the site of the wreck for a while, the party pushed on. They crossed the Mzimkhulu, fording it on two rafts and considering it "one of the most considerable rivers on that coast, and which the largest ships can enter."

Beyond the Mzimkhulu, living on the banks of a river, they found a young Indian boy who had been left behind there by the survivors of the *Saint John*. Through his influence, the local Africans received them kindly and traded willingly for food. The Indian boy was tolerably comfortable, and declined to join them on their journey. Instead, when they left, Jorge da Barca, another Portuguese, and thirty slaves, chose to remain with the Indian. There they settled, by the banks of the river, and built a small village for themselves.

The rest of the party plodded on to the Mkhomazi River. At its mouth, "not very wide, but very deep," they stumbled upon a large basket of millet, hidden away in the reeds by some prudent African housewife. The prize was promptly seized by the hungry Portuguese and a row developed when the tribesmen rallied to get it back.

Amid a valedictory shower of sticks and stones the Portuguese forded the river and discovered on the north bank a young Moor named Gaspar who had been left there by the party from the *Saint John*. He was not particularly happy in his African home and decided to join them; his presence as an expert interpreter being invaluable to the party during the rest of the journey.

That night they discussed their plans. At the rate they were travelling they anticipated reaching Lourenço Marques in July, which would be about one month after the scheduled departure of the annual trading craft which called there.

The meeting, accordingly, resolved to send off a flying party to make its way with all haste to Lourenço Marques, in order to intercept the ship before it sailed. Four tough sailors offered to form this party; and with a bonus of one hundred florins each, contributed by their companions, they left the next morning.

The main party followed more slowly. On 27 May they reached eThekwini (the lagoon) at Durban, which the Portuguese named Pescaria (the fisheries) on account of the number of fish traps maintained there by the Bantu fishermen.

At the lagoon they met two former slaves from the *Saint John*, and again the good offices of these people influenced the local tribesmen to trade for fish and other food. The slaves were too happy in their freedom to join the party and saw them leave with mutual regards.

As they left they encountered a crowd of Africans emerging from the bush. Among them was "a naked man with a bundle of assegais upon his back who was in no way different from the rest of them, until, by his hair and speech we found him to be a Portuguese named Rodrigo Tristao." He was a survivor of the *Saint John* party, who had settled on the present site of Durban as its first European inhabitant, and was so tanned by the sun and wind that he appeared to be an African.

Pressing on, they met a man of Malabar living on the north side of the lagoon. He was another survivor of the former wreck and treated them well, but warned them of the hardships to come. On they went. Early in June they reached the Thukela River, which they named St Lucia. At that place disaster struck them. Their wise and kindly captain, Fernão D'Alvares Cabral, who had led them in good order through so much hardship, was drowned when the raft on which he was floating across the river overturned in the current.

They buried their captain at the foot of a hillock, just out of reach of the sea which had treated him so cruelly. They marked his grave with a crude cross, and "with more tears than other funeral pomps" they left him there and persisted with their journey.

The boatswain, Francisco Pires, was elected as their leader; and under him they pressed on. Beyond the Mhlathuze mouth they met Africans who had ivory "which they said they were going to sell at a river which was further on, where there came white men like ourselves." At this information the Portuguese were overjoyed, thinking that Lourenço Marques was near; for as yet Europeans knew not the African, to whom a journey for a pound of sugar and a pinch of snuff could be as long as 20 miles.

Stimulated by the illusion of nearness, the Portuguese pressed on. Just before they reached the present Lake St Lucia, they were battered by a vicious windstorm. The dry, loose sand was blown upon them with such force that whole hillocks seemed about to bury them.

Bowed down before this fury the wretched travellers made their way while, their records say, "the sand beat continually on our legs and such parts of our persons as were exposed, until we were covered with blood."

In such plight they reached the estuary of Lake St Lucia. They called it the Rio de Medaos do Ouro (river of the downs of gold) and this name was applied to many miles of the Tongaland coast, with good reason as their records stated "for it looks like nothing but a down, being of gold-coloured earth as fine as flour, but hard and full of rivulets of water which course through these downs, and the water is yellow, of the same colour as the earth."

They found the Mfolozi mouth running a powerful current. They forded the river higher up and then crossed the estuary of the lake. On the north side they found some Africans who traded goats for pieces of metal, but most of the local tribesmen were keener on robbery than anything else.

So the party went on, tantalised by vast herds of zebra and wildebeest frisking on the adjoining plains. Near Lake Sibayi they learnt that the advance party of four sailors had there come to grief. The Africans had discovered them and, driven by hunger, killed them and indulged in a cannibal feast.

Somewhat disconcerted by this news, the rest of the survivors went on. On 7 July, fifty-six Portuguese and six slaves eventually reached old Nyaka's hospitable kraal at Lourenço Marques; and from there they vanish from our story.

It was as a result of these and other wrecks that the Portuguese king commissioned Manuel Perestrelo, one of the survivors of the *Saint Benedict*, to survey the coast of Southern Africa and find safe shelters for storm-wracked ships.

Perestrelo sailed from Mozambique on this task on 22 November 1575, and spent three-and-a-half months cruising along the coast. On his map he applied the name of Natal to the coast between the Mthatha River and Durban Bluff. He named the Thukela Bluff, Point Pescaria (point of the fishermen), and shifted the name St Lucia up to the present Lake St Lucia. Beyond that point he marked the Land of *Fumos* (smokes) from the endless bush fires of Tonga shifting cultivation, with Cape Smoke off Lake Sibayi. To the estuary of the Kosi lakes he reapplied the old and beautiful name of the Downs of Gold. Ouro Point, just north of Kosi on the present South African-Mozambique boundary, is the last survival of this title of the Golden Sands.

Perestrelo's map was the first reasonably accurate aid to navigation along the South African coast, but it failed to stop the shipwrecks. As an old chronicler says, of what use was navigation when "most or all of these vessels sailed at the mercy of God to save four *cruzados*?"

In March 1589 the *Saint Thomas* foundered at sea off the coast of Northern Zululand. A sorry handful of survivors landed just north of Sodwana Bay, which at that time was known as the river of Simon Dota, an ivory trader who occasionally visited it from Lourenço Marques. From this point the survivors made their way up the coast to safety in the north.

The most remarkable of the Portuguese shipwrecks on the South African coast was that of the *Saint Albert*, a richly loaded vessel which sailed from Cochin on 21 January 1593. The ship sprang a leak off Madagascar. The crew bailed and pumped, and as a last resort threw overboard all their belongings, the cargo and the fitments, until the great galleon left behind it a wake of impedimenta and riches.

By these sacrifices the crew contrived to get their ship to land, and ran it ashore on 24 March, somewhere between the Mbhashe (Bashee) and the Great Kei rivers, with the loss of sixty-two drowned.

On the shore the survivors – 125 Portuguese and 160 slaves – elected as their leader Nuno Velho Pereira. Under him, as a disciplined party, they salvaged what they could; and on 1 April they set out to make their way to Lourenço Marques.

The party marched inland, hoping to find more food and less trouble in fording rivers. Working their way up to the midland belt until they had the snow-covered range of the Drakensberg towering over them, they were the first Europeans ever known to penetrate into the interior of Zululand and Natal.

They crossed the great river valleys of the upper Mzimvubu and the Mzimkhulu, a cool and beautiful flow of water which they named the River of Beautiful Flowers. Through the hot valley of the upper Mkhomazi they tramped, while the Africans, awed by the passage of so large and well-armed a party, showered them with propitiatory gifts and gathered from far and wide to view them, calling from the hilltops: "Come, come and see these men who are the children of the sun and go to seek him."

On 27 May the party forded the upper Thukela and pushed on through the hills of Zululand. Their ocean pilot was their guide and he unerringly, by compass and sextant, navigated them through the centre of the country.

Reaching the Phongolo, they followed it through the Lubombo to its junction with the uSuthu. In the pans of Tongaland they hunted ducks and wild geese and herons and lived well all along their journey on game and on cattle they bartered from the Africans.

At last, early in July, 116 Portuguese and 65 slaves, including two women, reached the bay of Lourenço Marques. There, as reward perhaps for their courage and endurance on this journey without parallel in South African history, they found a trading ship at anchor; and on 22 July they sailed away in it to safety.

Many other noble Portuguese ships came to grief upon the sands of gold: The *Saint John the Baptist* on 30 September 1622, near the mouth of the Keiskamma; the *Sacramento* and the *Nossa Senhora da Atalaia* in 1647 near the Mbhashe; and several others.

Their stories are each as bitter as that of the old *Saint John*, and none so gallant as that of the *Saint Albert*. The number of individual tracks in the trail the survivors tramped along the sands diminished as each successive point revealed to some dispirited traveller a prospect just as endless and hopeless and emptily beautiful as the miles of golden sand behind them.

Behind them each party left no small number of people to merge with the Africans. Each party found, as well, many relics and descendants of the survivors of former wrecks, who were living at tolerable ease among the tribespeople. Many of these settlers were established as rainmakers and witch doctors and were much respected by the credulous local population. About the Mzinto River, known from its damaging floods as *umEnzi weZinto* (the doer of things), there was quite a village of these survivors, particularly between 1600 and 1650, and their houses, square with thatched angle roofs, were remarkable for many years in a society of round-shaped huts.

The various European mercantile rivals of Portugal all added their quota of shipping disasters to the story of the shores of Natal. British, Dutch and French traders all resorted to the coast in search of slaves and ivory; but the scanty population and the natural disinclination of the Bantu to indulge in slaving did not encourage many such visits.

In the early 1680s one of these traders, the *Johanna*, an English ship, came to grief in the bay of Lourenço Marques. The survivors received from the tribespeople thereabouts "more civility and humanity than from some nations I know", as one of the survivors put it; and the distressed party tramped down the whole length of the golden sands in order to find sanctuary in Cape Town.

The survivors gave some account of their journey to the English-speaking world and to the settlement at the Cape, but the coast remained little known, although shipwrecks were numerous. On 9 May 1685, the English slave trader *Good Hope* was wrecked while trying to enter what was then known as the Rio de Natal (river of Natal), the entrance of Durban lagoon.

The survivors scrambled ashore on the Bluff and there they erected a hut and started to build a boat. About six weeks later a small 35-ton trader under Captain Wynnford arrived, and he took four men away with him. The rest completed their boat; and nine men with their captain, John Adams, sailed off to Madagascar to go slaving.

Five men were left in the shack on the Bluff. They had a good supply of trade goods and seven guns. They traded, accumulating about three tons of ivory, exploring the country to a depth of 50 miles and learning the language of the tribespeople.

While the Englishmen were thus engaged, a Dutch trader, the *Stravenisse*, under Captain Willem Knyffe, ran ashore in dead calm weather on 16 February 1686. The captain, who was asleep in his cabin, stamped up on deck in a howling rage, but could do nothing save blaspheme, dive overboard and swim for the shore. The survivors found themselves on the beach somewhere about the mouth of the river known as the Lovu (Illovo), from the mlovu trees (*Cordia caffra*) which have ever yielded their sweet berries in that sheltered and warm river valley.

On the sands the survivors built a shelter. Three days later, 47 of the fit members of the party set out to walk to the Cape. The rest (13 men with the captain) built a rough boat. Within 14 days it was completed. They loaded it up with all their salvaged provisions and tried to put to sea. The first roller swamped them, their boat was broken to pieces and nearly everything they had was lost.

In this extremity they sat down upon the beach and wondered what to do. Then two Englishmen appeared. They were from the wreck of the *Good Hope* at the Bluff. Rumours of the Dutchmen's misfortune had reached them through the tribespeople and they had come to investigate.

They invited the Dutchmen to return with them to the shack on the Bluff and join forces. This was done and the combined party set to work on building a boat in the lagoon of the Rio de Natal.

While they were thus engaged, nine more Englishmen arrived. They were survivors of another ship named the *Bonaventura*, a small 20-ton vessel which had ended on the beach somewhere near Cape St Lucia while cruising along the coast in search of trade.

The combined force busied itself in building a 25-ton boat which was named the *Centaur*. They launched it upon the placid waters of the lagoon and stocked it with 3 tons of corn, 250 fowls, salted beef, 20 goats, 150 pumpkins and 17 half-leaguers of water. Then, on 17 February 1687, eleven Dutchmen and nine Englishmen sailed merrily out upon the Indian Ocean and had no great hardship in reaching the Cape on 1 March.

Four Englishmen and one Frenchman chose to remain at the future site of Durban as they had found the country fruitful and the Africans friendly and compassionate. The tribespeople at that time had the naive idea that white men were not human beings but a product of the sea, on which they travelled in large shells, coming near the shores in stormy weather. Their food was thought to be the tusks of elephants, which they would take from the beach if laid there for them and place beads in their stead, which they obtained growing at the bottom of the sea.

When the *Centaur* arrived at the Cape nothing had been heard of the overland party from the *Stavenisse*. The Dutch authorities at the Cape, therefore, bought the *Centaur* for 400 florins from the Englishmen and fitted it out as a rescue vessel for the missing overland party. On 10 November the *Centaur* sailed on its rescue mission. Near Algoa Bay a headwind fortunately drove the craft inshore and three survivors of the *Stavenisse*, stark naked, were discovered paddling out from the beach.

Nineteen other survivors were found living with the Africans on shore. The rest of the party were either dead or dispersed somewhere along the sands of gold. The *Centaur* then returned to Cape Town to report.

In October of the following year, 1688, the company sent a galiot named the *Noord* along the coast in search of any other survivors and to examine possibilities of trade. The galiot sailed as far as Lourenço Marques. Then, on the way home, it stopped at the Rio de Natal. There, on 5 January 1689, two more survivors of the *Stavenisse*, who had wandered back to the site of their misfortune, were rescued.

Another man was found in Algoa Bay; and on the Pondo coast one old Portuguese sailor was found living with an African wife and a brood of children. He had been wrecked there about 40 years before and declined to be rescued. "He spoke only the African language, having forgotten everything else, his God included," wrote the chronicler in disgust. Still, he was happy enough, and wanted nothing.

Once again, in November 1689, the *Noord* was sent up the coast on a fresh survey and with orders to call in at the Rio de Natal and purchase the place from the local chief. The lagoon was being visited quite often then; the Bluff was known as the English Hut Hill, and the little shack built there became a noted landmark to passing ships, until it eventually fell into ruin.

The Dutchmen concluded some agreement with the local chief and then sailed for home. On the way they were wrecked themselves, just south of Algoa Bay, and only four survivors ever contrived to walk to Cape Town. They had only a hazy idea about the purchase arrangements for the Rio de Natal. Later Dutch visitors made enquiries among the Africans, but the former chief had died and his son knew nothing about it. Accordingly, the whole idea was soon forgotten.

Through the years many other traders visited the coast and there were many wrecks, but mostly they left nothing at all to tell the story of their disaster, save a few pieces of wreckage washed upon the shore.

So the sands of gold claimed their victims through the years. The adventures the unfortunates had upon that lonely beach are legion. They buried their treasures there, hoping some day to return and recover them. They fought the Africans, and fought one another like wild animals when hunger drove them mad. They killed and ate their own companions, sitting around some dancing fire in a ghoulish cannibal feast, and sold wretched scraps of food and drink to their fellows at prices and on promissory notes high enough to have bought substantial farms in Europe.

In some ways these golden sands of the shores of Natal have been like life itself. They stretch away with the beauty of an illusion. From afar they seem a golden road reaching to the land of dreams, but they are soft and treacherous. The going is oft-times wearisome, the gold an illusion. All that is good and bad in human nature has been revealed in the journeys made along them.

Of all those who have started the journey so bravely, some, the loveliest and the best, have fallen by the wayside; some, seeking to be carried on the backs of others, have found their wealth of no avail whatever. Some have made the journey and emerged as men; others have also made it and in the end found that all their ambitions, their intrigues, and all the hopes they had upon the way, have lingered but a little and then vanished like their footprints in the sand, leaving them, as the wretched survivors of the *Saint John*, with nothing at all save the valuation of two pence three-farthings' worth of beads as a ransom for their bodies.

THREE
The door of night

T o the mind of the African, nature is full of prophets.
When nqonqoli rises, the first star of morning, it is said,
as its name means, to "knock at the door" of night as a
warning that the great change of dawn will soon be on hand.

If *ngqungqulu* (the Bateleur eagle) is seen in unusual numbers, then war is considered to be imminent. *Fukwe* (Burchell's
coucal), the celebrated rain bird, is another of these traditional
prophets. When his drowsy song tumbles down the scale, saying so wistfully "*Wafa baba, wafa mame, ngafa, isizunqu-nqu-nqu*"
("My father is dead, my mother is dead, and now I die of loneliness"), then the weather will be fine. But if the scale ascends,
then rain will surely follow.

The early Bantu tribes of Natal and Zululand lived very
close to nature. Every herb and plant had its name, and its
medicinal qualities were known. Every wild creature was observed, its habits remembered and the strange language of its
sounds interpreted. The calls of the birds seemed to have a particular fascination to these primitive tribespeople and many of
their interpretations are beautiful and amusing.

The emerald cuckoo was named *ubantwanyana*, for its rather
plaintive cry was said to be "*Bantwanyana ningendi*" ("Children,
don't get married"). The quaintly serious *uthekwane* (ham-
merhead crane) always staring so intently into the waters of
lagoons and rivers, was humorously thought by the tribes-

people to be looking, not only for food, but despondently at his own reflection, and saying, over and over again: *"Thekwane, Thekwane, nganqimuhle kodwa ngoniwa yilokhu nalokhu nalokhu"* ("Thekwane, Thekwane, I would have been a handsome chap but I am spoilt by this and that and that").

The foolish-looking *insinqizi* (ground hornbill) always amused the tribespeople with his apparent pomposity. There seemed no doubt that the female had good reason for her cry: *"Ngiyemuka, ngiyemuka, nqiya kwabethu"* ("I am going away, going away to my people"). To this the male always replied gruffly: *"Hamba, hamba, kad'usho"* ("Go, go, you have been saying so for a long time").

The old enemy of many an African corn-wife, *ijuba* (the wild pigeon) had a merry, bubbling song, constantly repeating *"Amdokwe avuthiwe"* ("The kaffir corn is ripe"). The mobile carpenter *uSibagwebe* (the woodpecker) sang all day long: *"Sibagwebe, sibagwebe, sibagwebe"* ("Let us prod them, let us prod them, let us prod them"); while the strident voice of *inkankane* (the black ibis or hadeda) echoed down the rivers with *"Ngahamba, ngahamba, ngahamba"* ("I travel, I travel, I travel").

One of the most striking of the bird cries was the song of *inkanku* (the red-chested cuckoo or Piet-my-vrou) who announced the approach of spring with *"Phezukomkhono"* ("On your shoulder"), thus telling the tribespeople to put their hoes on their shoulders and be off to the fields. With the approach of autumn the same bird changed its cry to *"Khawula, khawula"* ("End the work, end the work").

Most wistful of the calls comes from *isikhombazane* (the bush dove): *"Ngibe ngiyazalele lapho, ngithathelwe; ngibe ngiyazalele lapho, ngithathelwe, ngize ngizwe inhliziyo yami ithi to-to-to-to-to"* ("Whenever I lay eggs I get robbed of them; whenever I lay eggs I get robbed of them, until my heart goes to-to-to-to-to").

The birds of the night had their special songs as well with *uzavolo* (the night-hawk) calling *"Zavolo, Zavolo, sengel' abantabakho"* ("Zavolo, Zavolo, milk for your children"). The large black owl *umandubulu* sang *"Vuka, vuka, sekusile"* ("Get up, get up, it has dawned"), while his relative *umabengwane* had a wife who dolefully murmured all night: "*Maye, maye mayebabo*" ("Alas, alas, alas my father"), while her mate tried to sooth her with "*Yini, yini, yini, yini-nje?*" ('What, what, what is the matter?").

Every hill, river, kraal and notable place was given its name, generally very down to earth, for the early African settlers were less interested in romance than the presence in the area of such things as edible or medicinal herbs and plants, the location of drinking water, or the impressive power of a river when in flood.

Fairy tales and legends were improvised in rich profusion and they linger for ever over this land of hills like the last misty relics of the magic clouds of the past. Water sprites and *utokoloshe* (poltergeists) haunted the deep pools and waterfalls of every river. The waters of such rivers as the Mthamvuna were said, like the waters of the sea, to hate an unclean person. Any traveller attempting to ford such rivers had to confess his sins, otherwise the angry waters would sweep him away.

The whole coastline of Natal and Zululand was haunted with mermaids, and odd spirits of the sea danced upon the golden sands in the moonlit evenings and left strange tracks for mankind to see.

Many of the mountains were reputed to be particularly enchanted. Looking down like a silent sentinel upon the colossal valley of the Thukela River, stands the 3696-foot-high mass of iTshe lika Ntunjambili (the rock with two openings), known to Europeans as Kranskop. It is a veritable guardian of a land of myths, and the stories which cling to its own heights are singularly fascinating.

This almost inaccessible castle of rock is capped with a crown of trees and linked to the precipice edge of Natal only by a natural bridge, 80 feet long and 12 feet thick. A giant tunnel pierces the rock beneath the bridge and legend tells of a second cavern, now collapsed, which gave the mountain its name of the rock with two openings.

Within this sentinel mountain, the tribespeople said, there dwelt a spirit whose siren song could be heard coming from the caverns. It was fatal for a traveller to pause and listen to the song or to watch the entrance of the caves. The song of the siren drew humanity into the mountain and many stories are told of people lost in those sinister caverns where the bark of the baboons echoes through an eerie stillness. It was even said that if any human being approached the mountain with the prayer "iTshe lika Ntunjambili, let me come into your house," the great rock face would open like Aladdin's cave. Girls, weary of carrying water up from the Thukela were reputed to have often asked the mountain for sanctuary and their sighs for freedom ever more linger around the precipice face.

The greatest omen of change which the eyes of the superstitious tribespeople could have seen would have been the passing of the ships of Vasco da Gama and then the successive parties of shipwrecked Europeans tramping up the golden sands in their search for sanctuary in the north. All these were symptomatic of new times and legend has it that it was a mysterious white man who, in about 1805, really stimulated the beginning of the period of change.

It was inevitable, of course, that of the patchwork of Lala, Debe, Nguni, or clans of the people from the place called eMbo, one would develop ambitions of conquering its fellows, and the first stirring in this ominous direction came from the Mthethwas. At the time, the chief of these people was an individual named Jobe. This chief had a younger son, named Godongwana who, more ambitious than prudent in his desire for his father's power, was driven away from his homeland with a spear lodged in his back.

It is at this stage in the story of Natal and Zululand that legend and pure fairy tale start to transmute to more reliable tradition. Godongwana, we are told, after healing his wounds in the bush, joined a party of Tonga pedlars, the itinerant traders of old Zululand. With loads of trade goods – cloth, beads, pieces of unworked metal and sundry herbs and magic charms

– these enterprising individuals bartered their way along the network of footpaths which covered the face of the land like a fallen spider's web.

Godongwana accompanied some of these pedlars on their journey from kraal to kraal. On the way he discreetly changed his name to Dingiswayo (he who is banished) and, when he reached the area of the upper Mzinyathi River, found a sanctuary for some years as a lowly cattle herdsman working for the Hlubi chief.

At this stage the mysterious white man appears on the traditional stage. Precisely who he was, is unknown. In the early 1800s he rode into this land of petty clans, dazzling the inhabitants with his marvellous possessions – a horse, clothes, gun and retainers from a foreign people.

This white wonder who has left such a deep impression on local tradition, was, some think, a Doctor Cowan or a member of a party of exploration led by that gentleman, which set out from the Cape about this time and was never heard of again. Whoever he was, this traveller engaged a number of Hlubi men to act as guides and servants, and among the party was Dingiswayo. The explorer continued on his way and in the land of the Qwabe people encountered disaster. The hut in which he was sleeping was set alight one night and he was burned to death. What precise part Dingiswayo played in this affair has been discreetly forgotten. All that is remembered is that he collected the larger part of the loot of the white man's possessions and when next heard of was on his way home, magnificently riding the only horse in the country, firing the only gun, and supported by his late master's foreign retainers.

Back in his old home, Dingiswayo found that his father had died and his brother Mawewe was established as chief. The horse, gun and foreign retainers soon changed this position. Dingiswayo established himself as chief of the Mthethwa people and commenced a career of far-reaching consequences to the human patchwork of clans and tribes inhabiting Natal and Zululand.

Dingiswayo was an enterprising man, full of projects and ambitions. He examined his tribe of some 4000 people and organised an army. At the same time he turned his attention to local industries. The Mthethwa, having in their veins much Lala blood, were inclined to the manufacture of baskets and pots, the carving of wood, dressing of leather and other activities. This industry was encouraged by Dingiswayo and when local activity produced an exportable surplus, he organised a pedlar trade to the neighbouring tribes.

Trade was even commenced with the Portuguese in Lourenço Marques. Regular parties of porters were sent north along the arterial path winding across the humid flats of Tongaland. Ivory and skins were carried up to the Portuguese traders and all manner of goods and novelties brought back, including a European-type table and chair which were carefully copied by the local Mthethwa craftsmen, who carved their furniture from solid blocks of wood.

Thus established, Dingiswayo looked for fresh worlds to conquer. His army of perhaps 500 men was organised in the conventional way of his people, with individuals of similar age groups collected together into what were called *amabuto* (enrolments) for the sake of convenience in sundry ceremonials such as the now extinct circumcision guilds which started to fall out of favour at this time. These *amabuto* each had a name and distinguishing decoration and were the equivalent of regiments in a European army.

With his 500 warriors, Dingiswayo set out to conquer the approximately 75 000 people who, at that time, made up the population of modern Zululand and Natal. Each neighbouring clan and tribe was attacked separately by war or intrigue, and tradition informs us that by 1816 Dingiswayo had contrived to subjugate no less than thirty of the Zululand tribal groups. All the people along the coast and in the midlands bowed to the rule of the Mthethwas, and tradition tells us that it was enlightened, mild and humane. By binding these diverse groups together Dingiswayo was well on the way to the creation of a kingdom for himself: a "Mthethwaland", in fact, instead of a Zululand, but as we shall see force of events brought him to a most bitter defeat long before he reached the goal of his ambitions.

It was at this interesting stage that, for the first time, there appeared in the traditional limelight one of the most remarkable individuals ever known in Africa. In the Mthethwa army, in the enrolment known as iziCwe (the Bushmen), barracked in a kraal named eMangweni (the place of the steep incline), there served for some six years a warrior of intelligence, courage and renown. His name was Shaka and his shadow, although he never knew it, was destined to cover Africa from the great lakes to the Cape of Good Hope, while the strength of his personality was to bind a patchwork of insignificant clans into a nation of martial renown worldwide and leave them a legacy of pride based largely on the glamour of his name.

Shaka's personal story started one sunny day about the year 1785. On that auspicious day a merry group of youths of the tiny Zulu clan were whiling away their time on the banks of the Mkhumbane streamlet which flowed across the floor of the bush-covered basin in which their forefathers had made a home.

Among this carefree company was Senzangakhona, the youthful Zulu chieftain. While he and his companions hunted and staged mock combat among the thorn trees, a group of maidens came along the path. They were girls of the neighbouring Langeni clan going to visit nearby relatives, and among them was Nandi (the sweet one), the daughter of their chief.

Beside the gurgling streamlet the young people met, and again the next day when the girls were homeward bound. Flirting and fun which wasn't so innocent followed, and then the girls wandered off on their journey home. Three months passed, and the pleasant encounter was but a hazy memory to Senzangakhona, when a message reached him that something unfortunate had taken place.

There was a hasty consultation among Zulu dignitaries. "Go back," they eventually told the messenger, "and tell the girl she is mistaken. The cause of her trouble is that she is simply harbouring an intestinal beetle" (*ishaka* or *ikhambi*). Nandi suitably digested this diagnosis of her condition, but it failed to help her. Six months later she and her little Shaka were deposited in the Zulu kraal with some shame and no festivity; she as a minor and not much loved third wife, and he, the little beetle, as an unwanted son.

In the years that followed, Nandi and her Shaka were not happy. She had one other child with Senzangakhona, a daughter named Nomcoba, but Nandi, by all accounts, was a masculine and savage woman with a tongue like a rasp. Shaka was not much loved either, and traditionally he is said to have been the cause of the eventual break in his parents' marital state.

One afternoon Senzangakhona's pet fat-tailed sheep was found dead in the bush, and Shaka, as herdboy, was blamed for negligence. A quarrel between his parents followed and resulted in Nandi and her children quitting the Zulu valley and going back home to the Langeni clan 20 miles away on the middle Mhlathuze River, among the high hills that look so blue when you see them from the Nkandla-Eshowe road.

At this place the exiles settled and Shaka found misery. He was not liked. He was turbulent and moody and his extraordinary intelligence made the older boys jealous. They tormented and irritated him day and night, and planted in his brain a seed of hatred for them which was destined to sprout one day and yield them a terrible crop.

Until he was about fifteen, Shaka remained with the Langeni. Then, around the beginning of the nineteenth century, there came the drought and famine known as *Madlantule* (eat and still want). Nandi and her family wandered on in search of relief and shelter. For a time they lived at the source of the Matigulu River. Then, destitute and unwanted, they wandered down to the coast to the land of the Mthethwa tribe. There, under the kindly rule of the headman, Ngomane, they settled, and Shaka for the first time found happiness in those rolling downlands between the Nseleni and Lower Mfolozi rivers. There he grew up and in time was called to join the army of Dingiswayo. Those were stirring times. Dingiswayo, as we have seen, was forging for himself a kingdom, and his army, cloaked in the glory of the victories he gave it, was a magnet and a mecca for many young men who yearned for a chance of personal fame in a setting of adventure and combat.

In this Mthethwa army Shaka rapidly became a hero. His exploits were the start of the legendary thread of his life which spun itself into one of the epic tapestries of human history.

Those were the days of easy-going African warfare, when opposing armies, seldom more than a few hundred a side, spent more time and laid greater store on ceremony than on battle. Victories would often be won solely by a verbal dual waged between rival bards bawling out the *izibongo* (praises) of their chief and people from adjoining hilltops. At most the battles generally ended in a display of javelin throwing from safe distances and casualties were few.

Shaka changed this. It was he, tradition tells us, who at this time designed the short, murderous stabbing spear. He carried his idea to the greatest of the Mthethwa blacksmiths of his day, and there, upon a forge hidden deep in the forest, the first weapon was hammered and doctored with human blood.

Shaka henceforth used this weapon, charging down upon the astonished foe, offering personal combat, and delighting in the battering, clashing battle of stabbing spear and club.

One other exceptional incident came to spread his fame still further. In the ward of Ngomane, the kindly patron of the destitute Nandi and her family, there appeared a crazy giant, maddened by some mental warp and an excessive love of smoking dagga (hemp).

This madman, Lembe by name, established himself on a hilltop fastness and from there raided cattle and women at will, and generally terrorised the neighbourhood. Time after time some challenge was made to this bandit. Single heroes and whole armies sallied out against him, but only to their own cost.

In the end it was Shaka who rallied to the aid of his stricken patron. With some companions from his regiment he made his way to Lembe's hill. At the foot the party stopped and diverted themselves by shouting insults to the madman. With a howl of rage he came pounding down the hill. Shaka's companions fled, but he stood firm, and with his stabbing spear, his shield and club he fought it out with the madman in a wild clash of savagery and muscle.

In the end it was the madman who fell and choked away his life with a spear in his throat, while Shaka went home to be fêted as the greatest hero of his day.

This fame of Shaka's did not fail to reach his father. Senzangakhona and his Zulus had become very minor vassals of Dingiswayo. It was their overlord who summoned Senzangakhona to his presence sometime about 1816 and asked an explanation for the exile from his homeland of one who was the star warrior and the greatest favourite of the Mthethwa people.

Senzangakhona explained it away as best he could. Nervous and confused in the presence of his tributory lord, he met Shaka for the first time in twenty years. He saw in him a young man of boundless courage, ambition and resource, with but scant respect for his father and no love at all for the chosen heir to the Zulu throne, a half-brother named Sigujana.

Senzangakhona went home to his Zulus, an anxious and sick man. He died about the same year and wandered dejectedly away from history, down the valley of the shadows to forgetfulness, with naught save a euphorbia tree and a lingering tradition to remember him in the land and story of his tribe.

Down in Mthethwaland Shaka soon heard the news of his father's death and the assumption of the chieftainship by his rival. The situation was soon altered. Shaka despatched a crony of his, a half-brother named Ngwadi, to the Zulu valley. Posing as a refugee, this Ngwadi, the son of Nandi and her second husband, asked sanctuary from the Zulus. When his request was granted, he repaid the kindness by sticking a spear into the ribs of the new Zulu chief while he was bathing in the Mkhumbane stream.

Shaka then arrived to claim what he considered to be his own. Escorted by a detachment of his regiment kindly loaned to him by Dingiswayo, Shaka trudged over the hills and down to the valley. There the stunned Zulus, including several other half-brothers, had no alternative but to accept him with his overwhelming force. So Shaka became a chief in his own right of a tiny clan which at that time counted for nothing at all in the local way of life.

Shaka, however, was a rare bird in the African aviary. He was a character who made things hum, and the process must have caused much complaint and scandal in the privacy of not a few African huts. First Shaka built himself a new capital. In the Zulu valley near the right side of the Mhodi tributary of the Mkhumbane he selected a site and there had his subjects build a kraal. This he named kwaBulawayo (the place of the man who was killed). This name referred to himself, for Shaka considered himself to have been much afflicted in former years almost to the point of death by ill-treatment and persecution.

With a new capital recently completed, Shaka then needed an army to garrison it, for what is a capital without military show? He gathered together the manhood of the Zulu clan, and to his professional eyes, after his years in the Mthethwa army, they must have looked a sorry crowd of knock-kneed youths and married men run to seed long years ago.

Shaka sorted them out. Those beyond 40 years of age were sent about their business. The married men from about 30 to 40 years were banded together into a regiment named the ama-Wombe (battlers), and to house them a barracks was built on the Nolele stream and named Mbelebeleni (the place of persistent worries).

A second regiment was formed out of the men of 25 to 30 years of age. The first section of this regiment was named

Dubinhlangu (ignorers of the bushbuck), also jocularly called the Ntontela (tears on the face) for they were all young men who had received permission to marry from the late chief, but were now ordered to remain bachelors. They were sent to garrison Senzangakhona's former isiKlebe kraal on the right bank of the Mkhumbane.

To join this group Shaka sent a second section of men of similar age group who were still waiting for permission to marry. This section he called the uDlambedlu (eaters of impatience), and among them was Shaka's half-brother, Dingane. Together with the Dubinhlangu they henceforth constituted the Zimpohlo (bachelors' regiment).

Finally Shaka banded together all the youths around twenty years of age who presented the promise of being hammered into his best troops. These he named uFasimbe (the blue haze). They garrisoned Bulawayo itself and became his favourite regiment and special pride and bodyguard.

Then, with an army to play with, Shaka, like many other powers who have invested in armaments, found that the occupation of an army is war, and if you have one, then sooner of later it will fight. With Shaka it was a case of the sooner the better. He had many scores to settle, so first of all he wiped out everybody in his own tribe who had ever done him or his mother an ill in former days.

Then Shaka turned with some glee on his mother's tribe, the Langeni, who had proved so churlish in their hospitality to the refugees. Up over the Mthonjaneni ridge, where the Zulu chiefs traditionally secured their drinking water, Shaka led his brand-new army to its baptism of blood and the first of its foreign conquests.

The Langeni folk, living tranquilly beside the middle Mhlathuze, had long since forgotten Shaka. The reminder was painful. He surrounded their capital kraal and impaled upon the spikes of the enclosing palisade all against whom he had some score to settle. Then, for good measure he roasted a few other unfortunates to death in order thoroughly to cow the Langeni.

The Langeni folk were absorbed into the Zulu pouch as vassals, and a military kraal was erected to govern the new territorial acquisition. This first of many outposts Shaka named Ndlamathe (the place where he swallowed his spittle), in satisfaction of having had his vengeance.

The Langeni had put up no effective resistance whatsoever. The very ease with which they had been conquered and the readiness with which their young men were absorbed into his army was a stimulant to the ambitions Shaka had for foreign conquest. He looked for a fresh foe, and alighted upon the Buthelezi tribe who lived around the eastern slopes of the 5265-foot-high mountain landmark named Babanango (father, there it is), a term describing a prominent object.

This Buthelezi tribe had long been accustomed to bullying its weaker Zulu neighbours; so when the Zulu army appeared over the horizon they laughed and poked fun, expecting a few javelins to be thrown at them from afar, and then for the Zulus to retire precipitately the way they had come. It didn't work out that way. While the Buthelezi warriors were preening themselves before their admiring womenfolk, a horde of Zulus poured down upon them like wolves on the fold. Warriors, women, beer already brewed for victory, all went by the board. Their chief, Phungashe, didn't stop running till he reached the sanctuary offered by the great Ndwandwe tribe, whose chief, Zwide, then received his first certain information so far about the up-and-coming Shaka.

With these victories and some voluntary submissions by the small people who always hasten to attach themselves to a rising star, Shaka began to be a man of some consequence. He and his now heterogeneous following, however, were still vassals of the great Dingiswayo and subject to military servitude. In the winter of 1818 they were summoned to join the Mthethwa army in the attack on the Mangwaneni tribe of the chief Matiwane.

This campaign did not last long before victory came. As was customary, the warriors then dispersed to their various homes

58

to be fêted and dined by their womenfolk. However, with the winter military season still far from closed, Dingiswayo resolved on a second campaign, this time against the doughty Zwide.

Once more the army was summoned to support its lord, but this time the crop reaped was disaster. Made careless by success, Dingiswayo, without waiting for his entire force to mobilise, ran into a trap. He was taken prisoner, and Shaka with his Zulus, hastening to support his lord, arrived on the scene only to learn of Dingiswayo's death and the retreat of the Mthethwas to their homeland.

Shaka withdrew to the Zulu valley and did some hard thinking; but whatever decision he might make, his destiny was inevitable. Fight the victorious Zwide he must, if only because Zwide would attack him in order to consolidate his first victory and establish himself as the paramount power of the land.

The clash soon took place. The Ndwandwe army travelled through the bush of the Zulu valley like a black battering ram. Shaka led his army out to hold the strategic door at the hill known as kwaGqokli, just south of the White Mfolozi River. There the armies met and fought each other to a standstill. No less than five Ndwandwe princes, including the heir, died that day on the slopes of kwaGqokli. Then the Ndwandwe general withdrew his army, like a savage beast, to lick its wounds and consider future strategy.

Shaka also did some thinking. He may have stopped the Ndwandwe host in the first head-on collision, but the cost had been high. Never was he more aware of the smallness of his Zulu clan and the fact that the Ndwandwes were at least twice as numerous. Accordingly, he made his plans and dispositions in a manner well in keeping with the classic strategy followed in similar predicaments by wise generals the world over.

When the Ndwandwe grand army came hotfoot back for vengeance and Shaka's head, the warriors found the Zulu valley completely deserted. All crops had been destroyed and every living thing had vanished, with the women, children and livestock safely hidden away in the Nkandla forest.

The bewildered Ndwandwes searched around for somebody to fight. Flitting about on the Mthonjaneni heights they discovered a few Zulu figures. In hot pursuit they set off after the decoys and were led a merry chase up hill and down dale until their tongues were hanging out like terriers who chase a bird from tree to tree.

In the end the exhausted Ndwandwes made a camp at a place called kwaNomveve, close to the Mhlathuze River. There they laid themselves down to sleep, and in the darkness the Zulu army crept upon them. It was a wild night at kwa-Nomveve.

When the dawn came, the relics of the Ndwandwe host crawled out of a mixture of mud and their own blood and ran for home. Behind them the exultant Zulus idolised their chief for the victory his cunning alone had given them.

The Ndwandwes subdued for the season, Shaka looked around for military occupation. First on his list was the Qwabe tribe, living around their chief Phakathwayo's capital kraal, Mthandeni (the place of love), to the south of the middle Mhlathuze. The fight, such as it was, took place on the Mhlathuze River itself, near the bridge on the Eshowe-Melmoth road. It ended with the defeat and death of the Qwabe chief, and Shaka found himself richer by the spoils and his army the larger by a further impressment of conquered subjects.

All through the next summer Shaka and Zwide prepared for what both realised would be the decisive battle of their lives. Zwide dug deep into his pocket of tribal manpower, and when the winter of the year 1819 came, he had gathered an army representing his total strength. Its general was Soshangane, the then chief of the Gasa section of the Ndwandwe tribe, and he led the army like the shadow of a thunder cloud through the bush and the hills to the valley of the Zulus.

Once again Shaka had cleared out his valley. All women,

children and livestock had sometime since been sent far off to safety across the Thukela and up into the heights, where the wattles grow today, around Kranskop.

The Ndwandwes allowed themselves to be decoyed once more as far as the Thukela River. There they decided to call the Zulus' bluff. They retired up the Nkandla heights once again and encamped themselves upon a carefully selected site by the oSungulweni hill, just south of the forest. There they dug their heels in and waited for the expected Zulu "surprise" attack.

But Shaka was up to all the tricks. He knew just what his enemy expected. Instead of waiting until evening, he sent his youngest and most vigorous men to the Ndwandwe host. All day they worried them, lurking around the fringes of the grand army, cutting down stragglers, but always slipping away when the enemy attempted a charge.

In the darkness the Ndwandwe, not thinking their hill site as good as they had anticipated, retired down into the Mhla-thuze valley in order to stave off a repetition of their previous disaster.

In the wilderness about the upper reaches of the river, near its Mvuzane tributary, the Zulus found them the following morning. There Shaka tried his strength and threw the full weight of his army upon them. In the brown waters of the river they fought it out, while the crocodiles for miles down its course slid gently off their sandbanks and moved upstream, following the ever-increasing stain of blood.

It was a desperate and bitter fight. The Ndwandwes were more than holding their own when Shaka sent his last reserves secretly up the river. They crossed it and then went down behind the Ndwandwe grand army where they were stubbornly presenting the Zulus from gaining a footing on the north bank of the river. Taking the army in the rear, they surprised it and started a rout. The once arrogant Ndwandwe army disintegrated into a mass of panic-stricken individuals, each seeking a personal escape. The Mhlathuze River saw a sad slaughter that day.

In order to make his victory complete, Shaka rushed off some of his fleetest young men for Ndwandweland with instructions to capture Zwide. By night they approached the kraal in which he was residing, and as they drew near they sang the Ndwandwe national song in order to make the occupants think that their own army was victorious and returning. This stratagem fooled a few women, who were killed for their mistake, but Zwide was too sly a fox to be trapped in such a manner. With the remnants of his once mighty host, he fled.

So the great Ndwandwe tribe bit the dust and scattered. Some accompanied their defeated general, Soshangane, up through the wilds to Portuguese East Africa, where he forged the so-called Gasa empire, and returned again to his proper home only as a corpse, furtively carried by night and buried in the secret cave in the heights of Ghost Mountain. Others fled with their chief Zwide and found a home of sorts in the Eastern Transvaal.

Like Soshangane, Zwide never saw his ancient land again. In his death he, once mighty lord of the land, had to be carried by stealth, at night and along strange paths, in order to be buried with his ancestors in the taboo forest on the top of the Magudu Mountain.

FOUR
Shaka

The great human disturbance around the coming to power of Shaka and his Zulu clan was something like an explosion in a quiet pool, with ripples running red to the furthest edges.

The first of the neighbouring tribes to feel the impact of the upheaval in the future Zululand, was the Ngwaneni people. Under their chief Matiwane they were then living peacefully enough beneath the northern Drakensberg. In two successive years they were totally despoiled; first in 1818, when Dingiswayo and his Mthethwas attacked them, and then by the Ndwandwes. Destitute and half crazy with anguish and famine, they turned on their own neighbours in an effort to replenish losses of cattle and corn.

The Hlubis were the first to feel the impact of the Ngwaneni people. One night their chief and all his principal courtiers were surprised in their village and slain. The whole Hlubi tribe promptly buckled up. Abandoning their possessions, they clambered up the face of the Drakensberg and fled into the highveld plains leaving the Ngwaneni to burn and destroy until the grey mountain wall of the Drakensberg each night reflected the red glow of flames.

The Ngwaneni people looted their way down the length of the mountains through the lands of the Bele and Zizi tribes. Eventually they reached the beautiful jumble of sandstone foothills between the Thukela and Njesuthi rivers. There they settled down for a while to digest their booty and an uneasy peace came to this portion of the world.

Meanwhile, Shaka was very busy expanding his control over the future Zululand. Since the defeat of Zwide there was no remaining major power to challenge Shaka's progress. The once insignificant Zulu clan within the space of four tumultuous years had taken giant strides towards nationhood. Each of its neighbouring tribes and clans had been absorbed by direct attack or peaceful dismemberment when their people put discretion before valour and tendered allegiance to Shaka.

The Zulu leader's appetite for conquest was insatiable. He reached further and further afield. In 1820 he attacked and defeated the Thembu clan then living along the banks of the Buffalo River near the mountain known as Hlazakazi. The Thembus, with sundry allies, were forced to flee. Like a flood they poured over the hills and valleys of Natal, destroying peace and gathering to themselves a horde of refugees.

The Debe clans of the Mngeni River suffered particularly badly from this human flood. After looting them, the Thembus, led by their chief Ngoza, moved on through the midlands of Natal and into the lands of the Pondo tribe of the Cape, where they received a welcome more than hostile.

While the Thembus fought for living space, Shaka elevated a renegade named Jobe to the chieftainship of such of the clan and their relations, the Sitholes, as had clung to the old homeland. These survivors at least kept their lives as Shaka's vassals and they became herdsmen to some of the enormous booty of cattle which the Zulu army was steadily accumulating.

The Thembus were the first of the Natal clans to flee to the south. The idea of flight in that direction came easily to these people. Their whole migratory history had always been a retreat from pressure in the north, and in 1821 the Chunu clan, also uprooted by their blood relations, the Zulus, fled with their chief Macingwane in search of sanctuary in the Cape. Before they left, the Chunus systematically attacked their own neighbours in the once happy highlands of the Mvoti. Most of the original residents there were driven south while others cast in their lot with the Chunus on a vast plundering expedition. Among these recruits was a crowd of Wushe people led by one Madikane who abandoned his proper home on the 3120-foot-high Otto's Bluff (kwaKhwela) and set out with the Chunus to loot the small clans before the Zulus could reach them.

Madikane and Macingwane, between them, were largely responsible for uprooting all the remaining clans of the midlands of Natal. Macingwane eventually came to grief through his own success. Shaka heard that he had paused at kwa-Cekwane (Dronkvlei) to enjoy his loot. A Zulu punitive regiment found him there one night. Macingwane, after a futile resistance and a desperate flight, ended in the securest of all hiding places, the stomachs of a band of Bele cannibals who found him poverty-stricken and alone.

The disruption the Natal clans experienced affected them in devious ways. Most fled southwards, but some, the more stubborn of their kind, clung to the old hills and valleys they knew so well. Bereft of cattle and with agriculture ruined by the constant passage of refugees or raiding groups, these survivors were in a desperate plight through lack of food. In the uplands especially, where cannibalism had traditionally lurked from ancient times, when great famines had given many people an appetite for human flesh, there was little hesitation in returning to this gruesome habit.

The Bele people, disrupted by the very first of the Natal disturbances, when the Ngwaneni tribe attacked them, became notorious as cannibals. Most of their people were driven south into the Cape; but the survivors clung to the hills and fastnesses of their former home like wolves, and there, under leaders such as the notorious Mahlaphahlapha, they resorted to hunting men for food.

The familiar 5700-foot-high mountain landmark of eLenge (the precipitous one) known to Europeans as Job's Kop, became a particularly odious resort of these man-eaters. There Mahlaphahlapha governed his cannibals with conspicuous success. Eventually, after an ogre-like, if prosperous reign, he made a cardinal error for a cannibal king. Instead of allowing his success to run to his head Mahlaphahlapha allowed it to go to his stomach. In the course of time he grew too fat and his followers too tempted – so they ate him.

Another renowned cannibal leader of those times and parts was Luphalule, who had his principal stronghold in the area now contained in the farm Freiburg. At this place there stood a large rock known as *iTshe lama Zimu* (the rock of the cannibals). Victims were taken to the top of this rock and hamstrung to prevent escape. While they waited to be cooked, the cannibals' children – sweet things – amused themselves by pitching rocks at them.

Below this cannibals' pantry was a large flat stone on which, tradition tells us, the victims were slaughtered. The marks where spears and knives were sharpened can still be seen; while under this butcher's block lies what an English butler might refer to as a snuggery, a cosy sheltered place where Luphalule whiled away his time in between meals.

The activities of these cannibal bands, the passage of one refugee tribe after another, and the ominous rumours of the explosive events in Zululand, unsettled all the remaining Natal tribes. After the passage of the Chunu people in 1821 many chiefs did some hard thinking and, towards the end of the year, one after another of the clans uprooted themselves. Travelling together in a loose sort of alliance a crowd of mid-land clans started off on a journey to the south.

The whole of inland Natal was thrown into turmoil by this movement; and a flood of hopelessly mixed humanity rolled down across the upper Mzimkhulu and into the Cape, where the refugees fought among themselves for years, with occasional Zulu raids to rake the coals of their hatred and misery into flames. To this horde, despised alike by Zulus and the great tribes of the south, were given various names such as the amaMfengu (the destitute people) or the amaBaca (the people who hide).

Some of the clans sought to find new homes for themselves in the southern reaches of Natal, preferring the threat of Shaka to the pandemonium in the Cape. The Ntlangwini were one of these groups. After wandering all the way from their old homeland at the junction of the Thukela and Mooi rivers, and taking part in the uproar in the Cape, they returned to the valley of the upper Mkhomazi and there, under their chief Fodo, built a new capital for themselves which they named Mdumezulu (where the heavens thunder), and later commenced a profitable business in ivory hunting.

The coastal tribes were also involved in the mass mix-up and exodus to the south. The Thuli tribe, at Durban lagoon, rode out the storm by using the Bluff as a sanctuary and hiding in its bush; but they did so at the expense of all their property and livestock. They were reduced to living on shellfish, roots and insects, while some of them turned cannibal. An old tradition tells of a Zulu raiding band, rummaging about one day in the bush of the river known as the Mhlathuzana (forceful little one) which flows into Durban lagoon.

To their hungry nostrils was wafted a delicious odour. The Zulus followed up the cooking smell at a run and stumbled upon a forest glade, with a merry party of Thulis gathered around some pots in the centre. The Thulis scattered and the Zulus gleefully dived at the banquet. Opening the pots and grabbing at the stew, they were horrified to find a hideous mixture of scraggly feet, arms, heads and thigh bones. In disgust they overturned the pots and fled the place.

The year 1822 saw most of the coastal tribes uprooted. In that year the Hlongwa people, one of the oldest of the Lala clans, packed their impedimenta on their wives' heads and made their way southwards. After trudging around, fighting with all concerned for a while, they settled at the place known as the Mzumbe (bad kraal). At this place the Hlongwa people set up shop in a small way as brigands and, under the direction of a ruffian by the name of Lukulimba, made a living by robbing the passing stream of refugees. Another section of the clan moved some few miles up the coast to the area of the river which now carries their name (the Hlongwa).

Other sections of the Hlongwa tribe settled along the south coast. The Lange clan settled at Mzinto, while the Lulekos built their huts near the mouth of the Fafa (sprinkling or sparkling) River.

The old Maphumulo clan also came to grief and fled southwards into the Cape in 1823. Like most of the others, this clan infiltrated back into Natal and one member of the Seleku branch of the clan, Dumisa by name, apprenticed himself to the Bushmen of the Drakensberg and, under their expert tutorship, for some years studied the art and science of elephant hunting.

Eventually Dumisa passed out as being expert himself, his Bushmen masters informing him of the fact that his student days were over by presenting him with a fly-blown piece of meat to eat. Suitably insulted, he abandoned their company and wandered down towards the coast, where he built for himself and his followers a kraal named iziMpethwini (among the maggots), nearby the Mzinto, and there he commenced a profitable elephant-hunting business for himself.

Many other members of the Maphumulo clan such as the Shingas, the Ndelus and others, also established themselves at various times along the south coast, especially around the Mzimkhulwana (little Mzimkhulu), at the Lovu River and by the banks of the river known as the Mthwalume, from the *thwalume* (what it carries must stand upright) trees which grow there and are, as their name indicates, used as a standard specific for dysentery.

In 1824 the Zulu army invaded the area immediately south of the lower Thukela and the whole north coast of Natal was thrown into uproar. The Cele tribe, who lived between the Nonoti and the Mdloti rivers, was then divided into two contentious factions, completely preoccupied with fighting each other. Shaka settled their quarrels by giving them a common trouble in the shape of himself.

The one faction, led by Magaye, with headquarters at the sources of the Mhlali River, promptly submitted and thenceforth became the devoted vassals of the Zulus.

The second section, led by Magaye's rival brother, Mande, put up some resistance, and for its pains was driven into the coastal bush between the mouths of the Mdloti and the Thongathi. There the refugees lived a precarious bandit existence, hiding in the shadows by day and stealing out, like shadows themselves, when the nights came, to allow them to raid the herds and crops of what the Zulus considered to be the better half of the Cele tribe. Mande was eventually killed in a clash with passing refugees, and his people were dispersed down the ever hospitable south coast.

Most of Mande's Celes found sanctuary in the bush along the lower reaches of the river known as the Siphingo, from the intertwining, thorny shrub of that name (*Sentia indica*) growing there. Magaye, Shaka's favourite, was later wiped out by Dingane. His portion of the Celes then also made tracks for the south, and eventually some of them settled on the Hlongwa, while others settled at the Mzimkhulu and at the place called eShongweni (the place where the *Xysmalobium* shrubs grow), where the Durban municipal water reservoir lies today. A minor section of the Cele clan, the Ngangeni, settled further up the Mlazi in the broken hills that climb from the coastlands to the Drakensberg.

The Debe clans of the Mngeni River nearly all, at some time or other, removed themselves to the safety of the south; where they still live scattered about among the pleasant rivers and hills of the coast of Natal. Only a few clung to their ancient homeland like phantoms. Of these many turned cannibal as the only way of existence when all Natal was ruined.

The beautiful Mngeni valley, with its thousand hills, became a place of a thousand terrors. On several occasions in 1821 and 1822 Zulu raiding bands swept through the valley, destroying and then burning the ruins of anything that was left. Only a pack of man-eaters, led by an ogre named Mdava, a sorry relic of the valley's former peaceful occupants, managed to hide themselves in that wilderness of hills.

The Nyavu clan fortunately had the great Natal Table Mountain as their especial stronghold. They hid on the summit and were among the very few to survive the Zulu scourge. Many of them were scattered, and those who clung to Table Mountain had but a miserable time of it; for the man-eaters of the Valley of a Thousand Hills pestered them like a nightmare and hunted them down with packs of savage dogs.

There is a story that the cannibals once surprised a whole group of Nyavu women and children, furtively trying to cultivate a field in the bush. All were taken captive. Among them was Nomsimekwana, the youthful heir to the chieftainship.

The wailing group of prisoners was driven off towards the cannibals' stronghold. On the way they passed along the banks of the Msunduze. Nomsimekwana saw his chance and made the most of it. Diving suddenly into the water, he swam underneath the surface into a patch of reeds. Trusting to luck with the crocodiles he sat in the water, with only his nose reaching up to the air, until the cannibals grew tired of searching for him and went on their way with their prisoners. The site of the escape is still remembered as Nomsimekwana's Pool.

The Nyavu people were almost unique. In all the uproar of Natal they were among the very few to retain any individuality, and they can be found today, still residing in their ancient home. For the rest, hopeless confusion was the only lot. Scattered members of their peoples may still be found all over the length and breadth of the fair land of Natal. Curiously enough, nearly all claim to be Zulus; a pathetic legacy from the past, indeed, when the human wreckage takes on the name of the overwhelming storm and has no pride in any earlier origin than the catastrophe that crushed them.

As the epicentre of all this human upheaval, Shaka and his Zulus were flourishing with success. By 1823 the whole of Zululand and most of Natal was in the possession of these abakwaZulu (people of the man named Zulu), a mere minor clan which, five years earlier, had been considered insignificant. Now they had become the centre of gravity of a martial nation, and in the winter of 1823 Shaka began to erect for himself a new, more central and far more imposing capital from which to administer his brand-new kingdom.

The first Bulawayo was abandoned. It was rebuilt with the same name on a carefully selected site overlooking the Mhlathuze valley on a hill slope some 17 miles from the modern town of Eshowe, just off the main road to Empangeni.

The old Zulu homeland of the Mkhumbane valley was left without population, but was by no means forgotten. Guardians were appointed to watch over it, for it was sacred ground and dear to the hearts of every Zulu. All the original kraals, such as kwaNobamba, had been built in this valley and their sites were well remembered. All of the early chiefs, Shaka's ancestors, were also buried in the valley, with each grave taboo and marked by a buffalo thorn tree, the *umlahlankosi* (that which buries the chiefs), or an *umhlonhlo*, one of the large tree euphorbias, specially planted over the site.

The guardians of the valley were under orders to protect it strictly and no hunting or trespassing was allowed. Game animals, birds and snakes had the run of the place, no grass was ever burnt, no trees were cut and any human being travelling through the valley would carry all his sticks in one hand and not dare to spit or to point at anything other than with a closed fist.

In times of national stress the Zulus would always resort to this valley of the Mqangqatho (ridge). It was the national sacred place and there they would pray to the ancestral spirits to intercede for them with the power of nature, to relieve a drought, or aid them in war. Black oxen would be slaughtered there and the tribal songs would be sung. Before each grave in turn the army would pray, and the thunder of the voices of the warriors would echo through the valley as one regiment followed the other to each grave, shouting out their prayers and the grim salute to dead chiefs: *"Ngathi, impi!"* ("Because of us, war!")

It was from this valley that the power of the Zulus radiated over the land and the shadow of Shaka reached out across the mountains and plains until distant African mothers whispered his name as a bogeyman, and people spoke of him as a god, or a demon.

All manner of fables and traditions became attached to his person. Wherever he walked, even though thousands had been there before, Shaka's was the footprint that remained in the ground, and innumerable place names came into being simply because of some deed or word of his left behind in man's memory long after his passing.

Looking down, for instance, upon the great Thukela Valley, there is a flat-topped mountain by the name of iSabuyazwi. A typical Shaka legend tells how it received the name.

On a certain day, Shaka with two of his regiments was travelling past the slopes of this mountain. As they tramped along, the regiments sang war songs, whistled and chanted the praises of their king, while the game animals scurried off before them and hid in the darkest depths of the forest.

When they arrived at the foot of the mountain, one of Shaka's servants shouted out for a man whose task it was to milk cows for the king. The servant shouted, "Hey, so-and-so!" and his voice echoed back from the mountain.

Shaka heard the echo and laughed, and his laughter also echoed back from the listening mountain. Then, to praise their king, the regiments shouted: *"Bayede, Zulu"* ("Hail, Zulu"), rattling their shields and whistling; and the sound travelled down the long files of men and was reflected and echoed by the mountain.

"So," said Shaka, "this mountain is iSabuyazwi (the returner of sound)," and the regiments thundered out their appreciation of the name and the wisdom of their king in bestowing it.

As with the beds in which Queen Elizabeth slept in Britain, the number of bushes in Zululand and Natal under which Shaka is reputed to have rested is legion. In the Lembe hills near modern Vryheid there grows one such a tree with the pretentious name of isiHlahla sikaShaka (the bush of Shaka). In the shade of this old tree, legend tells us, Shaka was fond of sitting, and from it there was a grand view of a hill which the king admired so much that he expressed a wish that he could remove it bodily to Zululand.

Accordingly, the story goes, his ever loyal warriors, eager to fulfil his slightest wish, gathered around and dug away at the base of the hill until the amused Shaka ordered them to desist. The marks of this mammoth effort at excavation made by about 20 000 men are still pointed out and give a curious shape to the hill known as Mkhuphane (where the digging took place).

An even more famous story of Shaka concerns the Lala people who lived in the valley of the Thukela. As with their Karanga forebears in Rhodesia, these Lalas were skilled miners, and the immense valley of the Thukela provided them with many exposures of metal which, although patchy and chemically refractory, could sometimes be profitably worked by their primitive methods.

Iron was the metal these Lala miners sought most eagerly. The making of spears, hoes, tools and battle axes brought great profit to those with the skill to manufacture such items, and the people engaged in this activity were much respected and known as iziNyanga zokuKhanda (doctors for beating).

Other, rarer metals were also mined and worked into decorative devices and it is of such an industry that this story is concerned. Somewhere in the valley, a group of Lala miners had discovered deposits of silver, gold and copper. With these materials they specialised in the manufacture of articles of jewellery, including silver armbands of striking design.

These armbands were greatly admired by the Zulus, and Shaka so ordered matters that only he had the right of distribution to such of his people who deserved distinction. Unfortunately for the manufacturers, some obscure skin complaint affected certain of the individuals wearing these armbands. The diviners consulted to discover the cause of the affliction accused the Lala metal workers of spreading poison by this ingenious method among the Zulu nobles in vengeance for the killing of so many of their own kind.

Shaka reacted violently to this accusation. He gathered in every item of jewellery made by the Lala people. A regiment was ordered to carry this treasure back to the Thukela Valley. There, in the very pits from which the metal had originally been mined, the jewellery was buried. The unfortunate Lala metal workers were rounded up with all their relatives. They were killed and their bodies thrown on top of the jewellery so that their spirits might act as guardians of the buried hoard. There they lie to this day, their art and skill forever lost, their product a legend and themselves only a poignant memory to haunt the stillness of the Thukela Valley.

From the period of this event, iron was the only metal mined in Zululand. Whenever a shortage threatened of iron implements, a regiment would be detailed to go and mine ore. A site on the upper Mhlathuze River, known as eMtasheni (place of the mine) was the principal source of ore.

At that place the regiment would camp while the warriors dug out ore. The results of their labours would then be carried to the forests of the Nkandla, where another regiment would take over duties. Under the guidance of an expert, great fires would be lighted by twirling sticks from the *uluzi* trees. Secret medicines would be placed in the fires and then the metal would be melted from the ore.

When the fires died down, skilled blacksmiths took the blobs of metal from the ashes and set to work, hammering out spears, knives, hoes, eating forks, axes and bangles. The completed tools were generally taken to the Nsuze River to be sharpened on the whetstones found there.

But now, enough of legends and tradition. The fact was that at this period in the 1820s Shaka's personality and ambitions weighed heavily in the thoughts of every human being in Zululand and Natal, and it was at this interesting period that tradition finally gives way to history proper in the recording of the tangled events of this troubled portion of the globe.

FIVE

Sleepy lagoon

Of the gems and novelties which cram the scenic jewel-lery box of earth, there is none which was wilder or lonelier, more secret or lovelier in its natural splendour, than that vast land-locked lagoon which the Portuguese called the Rio de Natal, for it seemed to them that it must be the mouth of some mighty river whose source lay far in the interior. It was an airy and spacious sheet of blue-brown water in those past years. A million ripples danced like fairies upon its languid surface. The seabirds, flying, sped swiftly up and down its length. In the midday heat it was still and lazy; at sunset it was bathed in sensuous colours; at night moonlight laughed upon its waters, while shadows flirted with reflections, and ripples like those of an enchanted lake chased one another to the shore.

Knowledge of the existence of this solitary place was general in the world of ships. Occasionally some passing trader would anchor at its entrance and send a ship's boat nosing in for food and drinking water from those streamlets which fed it, such as the merry little Mbilo (the bubbler).

Occasionally, too, these ships would leave behind a deserter or a trading party, or maroon there some turbulent soul. Thus, in 1699, the English ship *Fidelity* left three of her crew behind to trade for ivory and never returned for them. Six years later one of them, Vaughan Goodwin, was still living there with two African wives and seven children. His two friends were dead, but he was sufficiently happy to refuse to leave when the Dutch galiot, *Postloper*, visited the place in search of timber for the Cape.

Thirteen years later, in 1718, an even stranger character made his home there. This was a penitent pirate who, the old record tells us, "sequestered himself from his abominable Community and retired out of Harm's way". How long he stayed there remains unknown. If he had lived for another hundred years the outside world would still not have caught up with him. In all that time little more than the winds and the rains and the seabirds lingered at the River of Natal.

It was not until 1821, at the time when Shaka was forging his Zulu nation, that destiny decided to weave a spell over the lagoon of the River of Natal. The British had recently occupied the Cape of Good Hope, and in London the Lords Commissioners of the Admiralty, for strategic reasons decided to investigate the whole coast of Southern Africa in order to discover if there was any harbour there which some hostile power could exploit as a base from which to disturb the passage of British merchantmen to the East.

For the purpose of this survey, two ships, the *Leven* and the *Barracouta*, were fitted out and placed under the command of Captain W.F. Owen. On 13 February 1822 the two ships sailed from England and safely reached Cape Town on 7 July. There they completed their equipment and, among other things, shipped aboard 13 natives from various parts of the coast and Madagascar to act as interpreters. Seven of these men, including a man named Jacob, were taken from the Robben Island political prison, where they were in banishment for sundry frontier disturbances in the Eastern Cape.

Then the naval men began their survey. To the *Barracouta*, under Captain William Cutfield, had been given the special task of surveying the coast of Southern Africa. For this purpose the ship sailed from Table Bay on 3 August and made her way up to Lourenço Marques, where she had a rendezvous with the *Leven* again. Only half of her task had been accomplished, for bad weather along the Natal and Zululand coasts had forced her to remain well at sea.

At Lourenço Marques the two ships busied themselves in surveying the place, overawing the Portuguese and negotiating with the local tribespeople for a possible cession of the place to Britain. While all this work was going on, the mosquitoes were also busy. No less than half of the seamen of the vessels and two-thirds of the officers came down with fever and most of them died.

The rest made all haste to leave the place. In company they sailed south and track-surveyed the whole length of the Tonga and Zululand coasts. As they mapped the coast they systematically named all points of interest, and most of the coastal place names in use today hail from this survey.

At Lourenço Marques they had tried to secure some information as to the interior of Zululand from sundry refugees who had fled to the place from the activities of Shaka. Included in their information was a hazy idea of the existence of a river known to them as the *omKosi*, a badly distorted version of the name of the Mkhuze River which flows into Lake St Lucia. On their journey down the coast they searched for this river. They discovered nothing more resembling its mouth than the estuary to the chain of lakes in northern Tongaland. They accordingly marked this place on their maps as being the mouth of the Kosi River, and so perpetuated the erroneous place name of Kosi, applied only by Europeans to the four lakes.

The point on the coast opposite the lakes they named Boteler Point, after Lieutenant Thomas Boteler. Cape Vidal, opposite Lake St Lucia, was named after Lieutenant Alexander Vidal; Morleys Bank took its name from the shipmaster, William Morley; and Point Durnford was named after midshipman Durnford.

Below Point Durnford they ran into bad weather and, abandoning the survey, they sailed straight for the Cape to refit and recruit their loss of human complement.

At the Cape sundry local trading concerns heard with interest the details of the coast given to them by the naval men. Two different companies immediately decided to commence a trade with the coast. One interest, H. Nourse & Co., fitted out two vessels, the brig *Mary* and the sloop *Jane*, and sent them up to Lourenço Marques to trade for ivory. Aboard the *Jane*, as super-cargo, was a young man named Henry Francis Fynn, whose name was destined to become part of the history of Natal.

The second interest consisted of Lieutenant George Francis Farewell and Lieutenant James Saunders King, in conjunction with various merchants. They fitted out the brig *Salisbury* and the sloop *Julia* and planned to visit Lake St Lucia and attempt to develop an ivory trade with the Zulu people.

Owen gave this last party, led, as it was, by two ex-naval men, much advice and some of his interpreters, including Jacob, the convict from Robben Island, and in return asked King, the master of the *Salisbury*, to survey for him the bay of Port Natal, of which he had heard a rumour, and Lake St Lucia, both of which places he had been prevented from visiting on account of bad weather and pressure of time.

The *Mary* and the *Jane* went up to Lourenço Marques and did a reasonably successful trade. Lieutenants King and Farewell sailed up to Lake St Lucia. They found the estuary to the lake completely blocked by sand. They attempted to land by using surfboats. Farewell was almost drowned when his boat was upset by the rollers. Then A. Thompson, one of the merchants with the party, tried to land. His boat was overwhelmed about a mile from the beach and three men were drowned. The rest managed to swim for the shore, and among them was the interpreter, Jacob.

In the squall the ships had to leave the survivors of the disaster on shore for some days. While wandering about waiting for rescue, Thompson and Jacob had a row. Thompson hit Jacob and threatened to have him thrashed when they returned aboard. Not liking this prospect, Jacob slipped off into the bush and made his way to Shaka. There his glib talking, foreign travels and general experience secured him a post in the Zulu court as a sort of adviser on all matters concerned with Europeans. He was known to the Zulus as Hlambamanzi (the swimmer).

The rest of the trading party abandoned St Lucia in disgust and sailed down the coast searching for a suitable landing place in the various river mouths. In this way they eventually found themselves off that Rio de Natal of which rumour had whispered strange tales for the last two hundred years.

At that stage a squall began to blow. The ships were in immediate danger, for they were anchored close to the shore. The traders decided to take a chance. With a bump and a roll they gaily sailed in across the bar of the Rio de Natal and there they found a sanctuary upon the broad and tranquil waters of the land-locked bay.

Their anchors dropped with a splash that sent the fish darting through the waters and the ripples spiralling to the shore. From the decks the human interlopers to this wild and lonely place looked around them in amazement.

The great sheet of water, in its setting of primeval forest, was dreamy with the sunset. Trees of strange shape, many clad in vivid flowers, looked down in vanity at their own reflections, while ferns and shrubs in remarkable variety pushed behind the water-edge trees like a milling crowd.

To the south, the Bluff stretched off as a mysterious background. In the trees birds called and monkeys twittered. As the evening came, moonlight laughed upon the waters and strange thuds and cries in the bush came from the world of wild animals.

There, among the hippos and countless thousands of waterfowl, the two little ships lay at anchor for a space and King busied himself in doing a thorough survey. The place was only too obviously an ideal base for a trading venture. Everybody was enthusiastic. An abortive effort was even made to reach the Zulus overland, but lack of guides and fear of the unknown turned the party back only six miles from the lagoon.

On 3 December 1823 the party sailed back to Cape Town. King was wild with excitement at the results of his survey. As soon as possible he sailed to England with his chart. Farewell busied himself in Cape Town organising their projected attempt at the establishment of a trading base which, they hoped, would short-circuit much of the trade of Lourenço Marques.

In England, King hastened to lay his chart before the Admiralty. He was tremendously proud of his work and expected substantial promotion as a reward. Instead, to his astonishment, the Admiralty would have none of him. They sent King about his business. Had they not recently undertaken a costly survey of the coast, and did its numerous reports and charts make any mention of a worthwhile harbour in all that area? King returned disconsolately to the Cape, with the reputation of being a humbug. Captain Owen's omission in not visiting the River of Natal was destined to influence an entire policy, and for some time leave the British officially convinced that there was no such thing as a worthwhile harbour on the whole coastline of Natal and Zululand.

Farewell, meanwhile, had proceeded apace with plans for the settlement. The Cape Government officially gave its blessing to the project, on the distinct understanding that it was to be an entirely private enterprise. Men and means were enlisted for the venture and among them was Henry Francis Fynn.

This Henry Francis Fynn, who was destined to leave his mark so indelibly on old Natal, was 21 years of age at that time. He had been born and educated in London and then journeyed out to the Cape to join his father, who was a hotel-keeper and ocean trader there. He was at heart more of an explorer and pioneer than a trader, and such achievements as were to be his were not to be counted in terms of cash or personal wealth.

In May 1824 Fynn sailed up to what was now known as Port Natal. With him, on board the 25-ton *Julia*, went a mixed company of three builders, half-a-dozen servants, interpreters and associates to the total number of 26 persons. The idea was for Fynn to lay the foundations of a settlement and, if possible, secure an introduction to the Zulu nation and its renowned monarch Shaka.

The *Julia* anchored in the harbour somewhere near the mouth of the Mbilo where the settlers spent a wet night ashore, pestered by rain and hyenas. The next day they explored the area and Fynn eventually selected a campsite "opposite the present church of St Paul's in Durban, where the present railway station stands". There they chopped down bushes, and the following morning the craftsmen, under a man named Henry Ogle, set to work building a house, 12 feet square, of wattle and daub.

While the men were busy, Fynn and his interpreter wandered around the bay in search of inhabitants. For some time all they found were footprints in the sand. Only the next day did they observe a few miserable-looking people grubbing about after shellfish on the Bluff beach. Fynn rowed across to them in a small boat. The beachcombers promptly fled into the bush. Fynn patiently displayed a few beads and an individual named Mahamba appeared. He was one of about 60 persons, remnants of the Luthuli clan, living in the bush of the Bluff. Fynn tried to question him about the Zulus and their famed chief Shaka. The only response was terror. The Zulus had almost wiped the Luthulis out and made them what they were: half-starved refugees hiding in the bush.

Fynn made friends of them by means of presents and assurances. Then, a few days later, he set out to walk up the north coast to Zululand, which he imagined was about 10 miles away. For 12 miles he plodded through the sand, followed by his servants, and then sat down to rest. They lighted a fire to brew coffee, and while waiting for the water to boil Fynn saw a sight given to few Europeans to see.

Looking down the beach, he discovered the Zulu army trudging towards him like a black avalanche. As far as his eye could see, an immense and seemingly endless mass of men was marching along. Fynn stood in petrified amazement as they approached him.

The leading officers examined him in similar astonishment. Then one of them pointed to some beads in a necklace. With that the army appeared content. Fynn had been identified as one of the rare species of bead-trading humans. The army trudged onwards, each one of its 20 000 members staring him out of countenance as they passed in their orderly and disciplined regiments.

Fynn collected his servants, who had scattered into the bush. They slept the night at that spot on the beach. The next day they followed the well-beaten path of the army as far as the Thongathi River. There they found a small kraal whose owner made them welcome for the night. Another vast mass of Zulu soldiers tramped past the place that afternoon and night. They were part of Shaka's grand army returning from a great raid into Pondoland.

The headman of the kraal, Siyingila, advised Fynn not to proceed further until Shaka made his wishes known. For some time, therefore, Fynn remained at the kraal. Messengers passed between the kraal and Shaka, inquiring who he was and what he wanted. Gifts of cattle and ivory were showered upon him.

After fourteen days came a message from Shaka, along with a gift of forty head of cattle and seven large tusks. The message told Fynn to wait a while as the Zulu army had just returned from a most arduous campaign and Shaka wanted it to rest before giving the visiting Europeans a ceremonial reception.

In the delay Fynn returned to the settlement, where he found that Farewell and a second party of thirty people had arrived in the ship *Antelope*, with cattle and eleven horses. There was a pleasant reunion and a holiday was declared. Two small cannon were fired and the British flag hoisted as a sign that possession had been taken of Port Natal, with all its surrounding unoccupied country.

A few days later came the expected summons from Shaka to attend his court. Farewell; his hard-swearing Dutch father-in-law, Petersen; Fynn and the interpreters then set out on a hazardous and fantastic journey along a path drenched in blood.

Shaka was determined to impress his visitors. They were led by their guide, Mbikwana, along a rambling route past all the various regimental barracks, where they were carefully shown the full mass of Zulu manpower. Many ocular demonstrations of Shaka's power in summary executions and smellings-out were staged for their instruction, so that they might reach the capital suitably awed by the strength and ruthlessness of the Zulu nation. That first visit of the traders from Port Natal to Shaka cost the local Africans dear, for Shaka saw that the journey towards Bulawayo led along a path well paved with corpses, and the culmination was in the capital itself.

After 13 days of travelling they at last saw the great kraal of Bulawayo, a vast pattern of several thousand huts, full two miles in circumference, lying on a gentle slope, with a superb view over the immense and misty beauty of the valley of the middle Mhlathuze. There, a mile from the capital, the visitors halted in the shade of a euphorbia tree, watching the commotion going on around the kraal and waiting for a message from Shaka. At last a messenger came and requested Farewell and Fynn to enter the capital, leaving Petersen, the servants and baggage under the euphorbia. The two men entered Bulawayo. They found drawn up before them in the vast cattle kraal 12 000 men in their war attire, with at least double that number of women and servants standing around the outskirts.

Fynn was requested to gallop within the circle, and the whole vast company shouted their praise at the marvel of a horse. Then the two men were led to the head of the kraal, where a dense mass of people stood. Standing before this throng, the induna guiding the Europeans delivered a speech. While he spoke, Fynn examined the mass of faces, and soon picked out Shaka, superbly dressed and a king indeed. He pointed him out to Farewell, and the king, seeing that they recognised him, smiled and wagged his finger at them.

Two elephant tusks were laid at their feet, and Shaka then

raised the stick in his hand and waved it to the right and left. The whole mass of people broke from their position and formed into companies, each moving to an alloted place.

Into the vacated area 10 000 girls then trooped, each holding a thin stick in her hands. For two hours this company danced and sang in honour of their king.

For hours there was a grand parade of countless thousands of cattle. Each herd was sorted into its own particular colour, and with their drovers and the multitude of people dancing, the spectacle was like a restless sea with its waves first breaking and then receding.

Fully 80 000 Zulus were engaged in that overwhelming spectacle. In the midst of it the two white men sat and marvelled, while Hlambamanzi, to the astonishment of his old employer, Farewell, acted as their guide and interpreter and in the name of Shaka made them feel at ease.

Late in the afternoon the spectacle ended and the white men were shown to their appointed huts, where food awaited them in the form of corn, cattle, sheep and beer.

The next morning came the first reception and discussion. The Europeans found Shaka seated beneath a tree, surrounded by about 200 men. He was superbly dressed in a variety of carefully selected and tastefully arranged skins and feathers. For some time vast herds of cattle were driven past the king. Each herd was sorted into its own special colour, and the regiment which acted as its drovers was armed with shields of a similar hue and pattern.

Only in the evening was Shaka ready for a discussion. Then the three white men, with Jacob as their interpreter, spent some time, mostly with Shaka questioning Fynn on the medical skills which he had displayed in curing a sick woman on his way up to the capital.

They slept while the vast assembly of Zulus slaughtered cattle and sat gossiping around the campfires which were sprinkled over the surrounding country like a continuation of the Milky Way.

The next day Farewell gave Shaka his presents, a lavish and well-chosen selection of every article which the ivory traders would be able to trade for tusks. Blankets, beads of many sizes and colours, brass bars, sheets of metal, military uniforms, and even a few pigeons, a pig, and some cats and dogs.

All that day the dancing and cattle display continued, with fresh regiments and animals constantly arriving from distant parts of the country. In between the various spectacles Shaka questioned the white men about their origin, intentions and hopes. Occasionally, as a final touch to his plan of impressing his visitors, Shaka would point his finger at some unfortunate standing by, and the individual would immediately have his neck broken by those near him.

The effect this had on the Europeans was definite. Old Petersen there and then decided to dissolve his partnership with Farewell and quit Natal immediately. The others shrugged it off. Prospects of trade were too good and Shaka too favourably disposed to them. They would remain.

The next day Farewell and Petersen returned to Durban, while Fynn remained at Bulawayo at Shaka's request, for his skill as a doctor had impressed the king. He and Shaka became particularly friendly. He spent some days there having long conversations on such topics as the respective merits of Zulu and European arms and the advantages or otherwise of having a white or black skin. Shaka, being Shaka, won all debates and arguments. It was mutually agreed in the end, for instance, that the only reason Europeans wore clothes was to hide the ugliness of their white skins. Again, the idea of imprisonment was a horrid torture. If a man was guilty, why not punish the deed with death? So reasoned Shaka in the long and nightly discussions.

Then one night, in the midst of a torchlight dance, some would-be assassin attempted to kill Shaka. In the press of the dance a spear was driven through his left arm and into his ribs. The national festival of welcome was immediately transformed. The people, already worked up to an emotional pitch by the occasion, now became hysterical. They moaned and cried and many killed one another in a frenzy of accusation and counteraccusation that individuals were not showing enough grief.

For five days Fynn tended Shaka with such medical skill and materials as he possessed. Then the king recovered. Regiments meanwhile had been scouring the countryside in search of the would-be assassins who were thought to have been sent by Zwide. Three men were eventually caught and killed. Their bodies were dragged near the capital, and there the whole vast human assembly filed past, each individual throwing a stick at the bodies until they were completely buried from view.

Fynn had sent urgent messages to Farewell informing him of the attack. Farewell returned to the capital post-haste and arrived in time to find Shaka recovering. The Zulu monarch was deeply grateful to Fynn for his medical aid and touched by the concern of Farewell. There and then Shaka presented to Farewell and company all the land around Port Natal for 100 miles inland and about 35 miles along the coast, roughly between the rivers known as the Mdloti (place of wild tobacco) in the north, and the Mbokodweni (place of round stones) in the south. This historic document was signed on 7 August 1824 and it recognised Farewell as being chief of what is substantially the land of Natal.

Hugging this document to his breast, Farewell, with Fynn, returned joyfully to the River of Natal, to build their shacks and commence a trade in skins and gum and ivory, the foundation and very beginning of the great commercial city and harbour of Durban which today leads a bustling life where once only the birds, the game animals and the shadows of the clouds moved along the banks and over the waters of a lonely and sleepy lagoon.

SIX

Black Caesar

Shaka's sivivane.

T he day after their return to Port Natal, Farewell, Fynn and their companions formally took possession of the place in the name of King George IV. Guns were fired, toasts drunk and, being a cheerful and energetic crowd, they began forthwith to establish their settlement and explore the country which Shaka had so generously presented to them.

Fynn was a particularly restless and inquiring man and he set out to explore the south coast which, from the sea as he had sailed past it, looked so inviting, with its green hills and golden beaches. He soon found that such tranquillity as it possessed was confined entirely to its scenery. The whole area was in a state of terror and destitution following the great Zulu raid against the Pondos.

The poverty of the coast, indeed, presented a major difficulty to any traveller. There was no food at all to be obtained. After tramping along the beach for about 40 miles, Fynn gave up and returned to Port Natal.

A few weeks later Fynn again tried to explore the south. This time he took two companions: W.H. Davis, the master of the *Julia,* and a sailor named Joe. He had a good store of food carried by five Africans, also two horses and two cows. By easy stages the explorers made their way down the whole length of the south coast. All along the way they encountered only half-starved and completely demoralised survivors of the Zulu raids. Food was so scarce that nearly all they carried was stolen by the time they reached the Mzimkhulu or, as they called it, the Bloody River.

Suffering considerable privation, they penetrated into the Pondo country and investigated ivory possibilities before returning to Port Natal. Fynn had found his explorations of absorbing interest. Not the least fascinating of his discoveries were stories among the tribespeople of the wreck of the *Grosvenor* on the Wild Coast of Pondoland and of the adventures of the survivors.

One of these survivors, a man who was apparently handy with tools, had remained behind at the scene of the wreck and made a living as a blacksmith for the tribes. Under the name of Mbethi he had lived among the tribespeople for years, in later times settling among the Xholo people on the banks of the Mzimkhulu and exploring that river by means of a canoe.

By permission of Faku, the Pondo chief, Fynn set up an ivory trading station in Pondoland and remained there for nine months. Back at Port Natal, meanwhile, the settlement was busy and energetic. There were many comings and goings. Farewell's father-in-law, old Petersen, with most of the other more nervous members of the party, had left the place as soon as possible. The murderous reputation of the Zulus disturbed their sleep at night and they preferred the comforts of the Cape. Those that remained found themselves carefully watched. A Zulu military garrison was established by Shaka at a post jocularly named uKangel' amaNkengane (watch the vagabonds). This garrison kraal subsequently gave the name of Congella to a suburb of Durban.

At first there were not many vagabonds for the garrison to watch. Farewell was left at Port Natal with Henry Ogle, Joseph Powell, John Cane, and a 14-year-old boy named Thomas Holstead. They were completely isolated and their situation was made even more precarious when their ship, the *Julia,* sailed for Cape Town on 1 December 1824 and was never heard of again, save in a rumour passed up through the bush that the coastal Africans had seen "a white man's house on fire, going along the sea".

Lieutenant King, in the meantime, had sailed from London in command of the brig *Mary*. On the way to the Cape he stopped at St Helena to unload goods for a local merchant named S. Solomon. When he sailed for the Cape again, King took with him a 17-year-old Jew by the name of Nathaniel Isaacs, a nephew of Solomon's who was weary of island life and wanted to seek his fortune in travel.

At Cape Town, King learnt of the troubles of the Natal settlement and the disappearance of the *Julia*. He raised some local support and, on 26 August 1825, he and Isaacs sailed for Port Natal to relieve the settlement.

On 1 October they arrived off what was known as Cape Natal (the end of the Bluff). There was a stiff breeze blowing and the little *Mary*, being contrary by nature, became unmanageable. King tried to save her by running before the wind into the bay; but she struck, lost her rudder, and the crew had to take to their longboat.

It was a sad arrival. On the beach a few tribespeople watched their misfortune, and presently a party of eight men appeared and planted a Union Jack on a small hillock on Point Fynn (the Point).

The shipwrecked men rowed to the shore. The official welcome consisted of Thomas Holstead, clad in tattered European clothes, with a cap made of catskins, which he doffed elegantly enough, and a Hottentot woman named Rachel, dressed in a dungaree petticoat. Five naked African men and one woman, covered in a piece of bullock hide and a mass of horrible scars, completed the party.

All the other ivory traders were away. After an abortive attempt to get their ship off the rocks, the newcomers removed to the ivory traders' settlement. At that time it consisted of Farewell's house, a barnlike structure made of wattle and plastered with clay. It had a thatched roof, no windows, and a door made of reeds.

Next to Farewell's house was the shack occupied by Cane; and beyond that Ogle had erected for himself a so-called *hartbeeshuisie* – a triangular affair of thatch which looked like a roof placed directly upon the ground, with one end open to serve as a door. A couple of African huts completed the settlement, although Farewell was in the process of building a commodious fortress for himself on the flats nearby.

The newcomers resolved to build a ship for themselves. They searched around for a suitable spot and eventually selected a site on the southern side of the bay, sheltered by the Bluff and just opposite the eastern point of the island they called King's Island after Lieutenant King. The smaller island was known as Farewell's Island.

This position was selected because it was near good timber for shipbuilding and had deep water for launching. They named it Townshend, after Lord James Townshend, and there the shipwrecked crew set to work on the laborious task of constructing a vessel in which to rescue themselves.

On 14 October, at sunset, John Cane arrived back home with a number of cattle, and the next day Fynn trudged in after his solitary months of ivory trading with the Pondos. Fynn presented a classic picture of a Port Natal ivory trader.

He was a tall, powerful man. "His head was partly covered with a crownless straw hat; and a tattered blanket, fastened round his neck by means of strips of hide, served to cover his body, while his hands performed the office of keeping it round his 'nether man': his shoes he had discarded for some months, whilst every other habiliment had imperceptibly worn away, so that there was nothing of a piece about him." His face was matted with beard and he was surrounded by about one hundred Africans who practically adored him as their chief.

Five days later Farewell returned from a trading visit to Shaka and there was a joyful reunion of old friends, with yarning and gossiping going on until the early hours.

Shortly afterwards came a peremptory summons from Shaka. He maintained a most efficient secret service and his spies had informed him of the arrival of the newcomers. It was necessary that they present themselves at his court. Salvaging such trappings as they could from the wreck to serve as presents, King, Farewell and Fynn, with two seamen and 40 African bearers, set off to visit Shaka, leaving Isaacs at Port Natal with the rest of the sailors so that the building of the ship could proceed with all possible speed.

Shaka received the newcomers kindly and spent the evening listening to their adventures and ridiculing the power of their firearms. He always loved such an argument. The next afternoon there came an opportunity for putting their guns to the test. A troop of elephants had ventured close to the royal kraal. Shaka peremptorily ordered the Europeans to prove the merit of their much-boasted weapons, and, with some reluctance, they set out, for none had ever shot an elephant and their bullets were made of lead.

Two miles from the capital they found the 16 elephants. They had hoped for little more than to scare the animals and drive them away, but one sailor, who fired quite by chance, sent a bullet through the ear of a sizeable bull and dropped him with a thud which shook Shaka's belief in the superiority of spears over guns.

That night they celebrated their success. The Zulus danced in their honour, while they replied with an entertainment consisting of a lusty bawling out of "God Save the King" and a few popular ditties.

After some days' delay consequent upon the death of Shaka's grandmother, the party was given final audience and then returned to Port Natal. Back at the lagoon, Isaacs listened to their tales of Shaka with fascination, and resolved to go up on a visit himself. Mounted on a dilapidated, one-eyed horse which had carried Fynn on many a lengthy journey, he rode up to the Thukela to fetch back a quantity of ivory accumulated there by Farewell. From there he went to Bulawayo, and reached the capital on 3 December 1825. Shaka, as usual, made him welcome and allowed him to roam at will through the great kraal, with its labyrinth of huts and endless activity.

Isaacs had a fascinating time exploring the place and meeting the fantastic crowd of courtiers, freaks and jesters who crowded around the person of Shaka. Among these oddities, according to Isaacs, was an individual named Ngqengelele, who held the unique position of intsila yeNkosi (the king's dirt). His task was to be in constant attendance to Shaka, even sleeping at his feet as a sort of footrest, and at all times receiving on his person the royal spit, which he disposed of by rubbing into his clothing or skin, in order to prevent any hostile witch doctor from obtaining it as a powerful medicine.

This Ngqengelele, despite the extreme lowliness of his position, seems to have done his duty so conscientiously that Shaka rewarded him with some power and wealth. In the solitude of the bush of Northern Zululand he was allowed to establish a kraal. There his son, Mnyamana, took up residence and gathered together the scattered remnants of the former Buthelezi tribe. This kraal, the first in that wildest of valleys, was named Mbekamuzi. That name attached itself to the valley, destined to become one of the most famous of all the big-game hunting areas in Zululand.

Another individual of interest at Bulawayo was a Portuguese trader who had tramped there from Lourenço Marques in search of cattle. Shaka amused himself by trying to play the two Europeans off against each other. He very much wanted to see two people fighting with guns, and for some time his conversation was of the "let you and him fight" variety. It took much diplomacy to keep the peace between Portugal and Israel.

Shaka enjoyed these visits by Europeans. He received from them a strange variety of presents. All sorts of odd ornaments and flamboyant uniforms were given to him. The figurehead of the ill-fated *Mary* was carried all the way to Bulawayo to amuse him, and patent medicines were his particular delight. These he dosed wholesale to his indunas or concubines in order to observe the effects, while the rest of the gifts he played with for a while, like a child with a toy, and then gave them to his women or his friends.

He loved to hold long discussions with his visitors or his soldiers. Sitting around him at night, when the cool breezes swept up the great Mhlathuze valley from the sea, they talked of ghosts and gods and of the universe. White man's novelties always fascinated him, and any description of European weapons of war was always listened to with the most intense anxiety.

By day, dances and reviews of his different regiments and herds of cattle beguiled him. He delighted in doing his toilet in public. Three boys carried water to him in relays. This they poured over him while he stood casually chatting to his courtiers. When the bath was finished, his servants rubbed red ochre and fat into his skin until he was sleek and shiny.

Trials of criminals and offenders occupied much of his time. His court was always surrounded by supplicants and people either awaiting trial or sentence. Many would have to lurk around for days or weeks, awaiting their judgement for some offence. All such people dreaded the arrival of European visitors, for then it was that Shaka not only always had available an impressive concentration of his army, but he loved to order a batch of unfortunates off to sudden death as a means of impressing his guests.

He was a most contrary monarch, kindly and sympathetic one moment, despotic and bloody the next. Killing people was a matter of indifference to him. Thus we find him seated one day, talking to one of his regiments and to Isaacs. Shaka asked if King George had as many fighting men as he. Isaacs told him as many as all his men, people and cattle put together.

Shaka was impressed at this. He remarked that if King George attacked the Zulus they would lose all their cattle, and perhaps their lives as well. "The warriors," wrote Isaacs, "would not heed the king's apprehension, but said they were willing to try it, because they were confident they should be able to repel any invader of their country. This caused great arguments with the king, and ended by his killing eight of them."

The army was generally happier when it was busy killing others than being caught up itself in the capriciousness of its monarch. For some time there had been peace in Zululand, but early in 1826, to the army's delight, trouble blew up over the horizon.

Zwide, Shaka's old enemy, had died about 1824 in the Transvaal. After the usual fighting over the succession, his one son, Sikhunyana, had become chief of the Ndwandwes. This prince was ambitious of leading his people back to their former home, and for months there were rumours in Zululand of a coming invasion.

Shaka mustered his grand army and summoned his vassals, including the ivory traders of Port Natal, to aid him. The Europeans came rather unwillingly, but go with Shaka on this campaign they must, if they were to retain his goodwill.

In October 1826 they set out. The whole army, with its following of small boys as mat-bearers and girls carrying beer, numbered according to Fynn about 50 000 people. Covered by an appalling cloud of dust, they made their way first to the royal graves at kwaNobamba. Then, after the customary prayers for aid from the ancestral spirits, they set out on the long march to the enemy.

For days they tramped through the thorns and heat and dust of north-western Zululand. They slept in the veld, each man finding what shelter he could, such as the great cave known as iNqaba kwaHawana (the fortress of Hawana), some 20 miles from modern Utrecht. This cave had once given refuge to the rebel chief of that name, and now provided sleeping accommodation for some of Shaka's men.

At last they reached the Ntombe River and encamped there in a forest, close to the hill known as Ndololwane (the elbow). On this hill the Ndwandwe army was lying ready for the coming battle. The next morning Shaka reconnoitred from the top of the adjoining Ncaka hill and made his plans. Then, in the afternoon, he gathered his army around him and harangued them until their loyalty reached fever pitch, when one after the other, they rushed out to *giya* (a self-adulatory dance) and promise their king that they would bring him glory in the coming battle or die for him.

At dawn the next morning the armies were ready. The Zulus advanced up the hill, and Jacob commenced the battle by firing three shots into the ranks of the Ndwandwes. With a tumultuous yell, the armies clashed. One charge after another followed, for over an hour. Then the Ndwandwe army broke and fled.

All afternoon and night the Zulus hunted down their beaten enemy, and by the next morning the country was littered with corpses. Men, women and children, all who had hoped to return to their homeland, were butchered around their mountain of ill-fate. Sikhunyana, their chief, escaped with a few cronies by hiding in an elephant pit. They sat there silently, staring ever upwards, while the searching Zulus thrashed about in the surrounding bush, until darkness came and allowed them to flee far off into Swaziland and the lands of Soshangane.

With this pleasing victory to digest, Shaka turned for home. On the way he passed the darkly-forested range of Ngome, and the sight galled him. Living in the forests there was a certain famous character by the name of Beje. This Beje was a petty chief of the Khumalo clan, and Shaka had a grudge against it. Back in 1822 a rather brash young man, Mzilikazi by name, a member of this clan and employed by Shaka as commander of a raiding band, had tried to embezzle some cattle seized in a raid. Mzilikazi had fled into the Transvaal and with his so-called maTebele (refugees) was actually setting himself up as a rival robber baron to the Zulus.

This Beje of the Ngome forest was also a man of resolution and stubbornness. In his forest stronghold he had established himself so securely that both Zwide and Shaka had several times failed to dislodge him. A proverb, "Beje is in the bush," had even found its way into Zulu lore and was used to describe any act of pronounced stubbornness.

Once again, then, Shaka detached a portion of his army in

another unsuccessful attempt to beat this notorious Beje from the bush, while the king went on back home to celebrate his recent victory. During Shaka's absence a new capital had been built for him south of the Thukela, on the site of the present town of Stanger. This city of huts Shaka named kwaDukuza (the place of he who was lost), and there at the end of 1826, he settled down to enjoy the lavish supplies of beef, beer, adulation and women which were the portion of a Zulu king.

From this capital, as a sort of house-warming, Shaka despatched the bulk of his army on a mass raid, up through Swaziland and the Transvaal bushveld as far as the uBalule (Olifants) River. Shaka was left at his ease, surrounded by women and courtiers to flatter him and sing the songs he loved, such as the well-known

Thou hast finished off the tribes.
Where wilt thou wage war?
Yes, where wilt thou wage war?
Thou hast conquered the kings.
Where wilt thou wage war?
Thou hast finished off the tribes.
Where wilt thou wage war?
Yes, yes, yes! Where wilt thou wage war?

The ivory traders from Port Natal, meanwhile, were busy on their adventurous occupations. Plodding along the tangled footpaths of Natal and Zululand, searching for ivory or carrying presents up to Shaka, each man covered hundreds of miles a month.

Their adventures on these journeys were legion. They forded flooded rivers dressed only in their birthday suits, while Zulu matrons crowded around to view them occasionally in the crush pushing one of their number into the water and at all times loudly shouting comment or admiration at what they saw to less fortunately situated ladies in the rear.

All manner of marvels were to be seen along those tortuous paths. As though Africa was not full enough of game animals,

Isaacs heard of one chief who claimed to possess a unicorn. With much excitement Isaacs had the man produce the animal. While it was being fetched, Isaacs had fleeting dreams of the renown he would win among the naturalists of the world for this strange discovery. Unfortunately the animal was a one-horned billy goat!

The Port Natal settlement was slowly gaining in strength. The sailors were still busy on their ship, but the isolation of the settlement was relieved in April 1826, when the naval sloop *Helicon* visited the bay to see if all was well. King sailed to the Cape aboard this vessel and busied himself in trying to raise capital and support for the traders. When he returned aboard the *Anne* in October he brought with him Farewell's wife, who became the first European woman to settle at Port Natal.

There was little support from the Cape for the ivory traders. Apart from Mrs Farewell, mail, supplies and lavish presents for Shaka (including a handsome brass crown), King brought no great augmentation of strength. Instead, the Cape visit resulted in a grave weakening, for King and Farewell fell to arguing over what should have been and the whole settlement was soon partisan and at loggerheads.

From thence on, Farewell and King followed different paths. King and Isaacs commenced trading on their own joint account, with Hatton and George Biddlecombe as assistants. They concentrated on the area north of Port Natal and even contemplated a complete break from Farewell's influence, by establishing a port of their own at the mouth of the Mlalazi River. With Shaka's sanction, possession was taken of this area in January 1827. The Union Jack was hauled up there and a couple of guns were fired in salute, sending the hippos and crocs diving for the deepest water while the ivory traders toasted the latest venture.

King and Isaacs were also interested in the possibilities of the Mhlathuze lagoon, for it was a long tramp for porters to Zululand from Port Natal and a more convenient harbour was attractive.

Farewell and Fynn, on the other hand, concentrated their

activities south of Port Natal. On the hilltop dominating the southern approaches to the ancient drift across the lower Mzimkhulu River (Batstone's Drift) Fynn established a trading centre which was named by the Africans kwaNomnyali (the place of the one who licks up), for he was said to gather or "lick up" the refugees from the Zulus and give them shelter and protection.

By then, each of the ivory traders had gathered around his person a following of Africans. Innumerable refugees hiding in the bush made haste to attach themselves to the persons of individuals who were considered to be both generous and protective. Around Fynn, in particular, there gathered many people. He named them the Nsimbini and they were most devotedly attached to him, for he was a kindly and intelligent man.

All of Natal and Zululand was scoured by the ivory traders in search of elephant tusks, hippopotamus teeth and rhinoceros horns. They trained African hunters, supplying them with guns and then sending them off into the bush in search of elephants. Fynn developed profitable relations with several groups of Bushmen who lived in the uplands of Natal. One party, under a leader named Hele, who lived in the wilderness of the middle Mzimkhulu, were particularly active hunters and long supplied ivory to the traders, until they eventually wandered off across the Drakensberg to avoid European settlers.

Most of the hunters and supervisors used by the ivory hunters were Cape coloureds, and these were inclined to be troublesome at times, stealing liquor and interfering with Zulu girls. Two of them, by forcing their attentions on the daughters of a chief, brought the whole settlement into hazard early in 1827. In order to atone for the affair, Shaka demanded that a party of riflemen be sent up to aid his army, who were still trying to prise Beje out of his bush.

Isaacs, Cane and several sailors volunteered for the job. They tramped up cheerfully enough to the Ngome range and there joined the Zulu regiments which for three months had been trying to find the elusive chieftain. Guns soon had their effect. Beje became so impressed by the Europeans potshotting his followers every time they showed their persons as a target that he sued for peace and, by means of surrendering his livestock and ten pretty girls, got himself admitted into the Shakan fold. But he still remained in the Ngome forest.

The Europeans resumed their ivory trading, and, ragged adventurers as they were, they contrived some astounding travels. One 15-year-old youth named John Ross actually walked all the way up to Lourenço Marques in order to buy a few pounds' worth of medicines. Accompanied by an escort which Shaka provided, the youth did the journey with little trouble. The Tembe chief, Makhasane, and the Portuguese treated him with great kindness. The Portuguese, in fact, loaded his bearers with all the medicines and comforts they could carry, and then refused payment when he left on the twenty-day walk back through the flats of Tongaland to Port Natal.

At the beginning of October 1827 there occurred one of the most renowned of all events in Zululand's troubled story. Shaka had been hunting elephants about 60 miles from his Bulawayo kraal. Fynn, King and some of the other Europeans were with him, although all but Fynn left him as he worked his way up the Mhlathuze valley towards the old capital. Presently came messengers reporting that Shaka's mother, Nandi, was seriously ill.

More and more messengers came panting in each hour, reporting the worsening of her condition. Shaka then decided to go to her. After a gruelling six-hour tramp through the bush, Shaka, Fynn and their following reached Nandi's Mkhindini kraal, about three miles west of Bulawayo, at three o'clock in the morning of 10 October 1827. Fynn went in to see Nandi immediately, and had to practically fight his way into her hut, for it was jammed with herbalists, diviners and nurses.

Fynn took one look at the old woman and saw that she was dying of dysentery. He reported accordingly to Shaka. The king heard the news in silence, and then sat quietly among his indunas for about two hours until word was brought that Nandi had expired.

Then began a fantastic display of mass hysteria. Fynn thought that the Zulu nation had gone mad. "As soon as the death was publicly announced," he wrote, "the women and all the men who were present tore instantly from their persons every description of ornament. Shaka now appeared before the hut in which the body lay, surrounded by his principal chiefs in their war attire. For about twenty minutes he stood in a silent, mournful attitude, with his head bowed upon his shield, and on which I saw large tears fall. After two or three deep sighs, his feelings becoming ungovernable, he broke out into frantic yells, which fearfully contrasted with the silence that had hitherto prevailed. This signal was enough. The chiefs and people, to the number of about 15 000 commenced the most dismal and horrid lamentations."

All day and night more and more people poured into the kraal from the surrounding countryside. By noon of the next day about 60 000 people were gathered there, and their cries were indescribably horrid. Then Shaka formed them into a circle to sing the war song. At the end he ordered several men to be executed on the spot, and no further orders were needed.

"As if bent on convincing their chief of their extreme grief," wrote Fynn, "the multitude commenced a general massacre. Many of them received the blow of death while inflicting it on others, each taking the opportunity of revenging their injuries, real or imaginary. Those who could not force more tears from their eyes – those who were found near the river panting for water – were beaten to death by others who were mad with excitement. Towards the afternoon I calculated that not fewer than 7000 people had fallen in this frightful, indiscriminate massacre. The adjacent stream, to which many had fled exhausted to wet their parched tongues, became impassable from the number of corpses which lay on each side of it, while the kraal in which the scene took place was flowing with blood."

Only when the sun set did this bloodshed cease. Then, two days after her death, Nandi was entombed in the customary sitting position, and ten of the best-looking girls in the kraal were buried alive with her, to act as her attendants in the spirit world. Twelve thousand men were allocated to guard her grave for the next year, while other regiments scoured the whole country, butchering anybody who was considered not to have shown sufficient grief.

It was strange that Shaka, who killed so many others without concern, should make such a fuss about the death of his mother and be so concerned at his own grey hairs. He was not old by any means, but the fear of death pressed heavily on his mind. Back during the campaign against the Ndwandwes, Shaka had seen Fynn writing a letter with black ink and had enquired whether there was no preparation which would keep hair black.

Fynn, in an ill-considered moment, told him that Rowland's Macassar oil was said to produce that effect, and this idea, planted in Shaka's mind, grew to a mania. All he wanted was Rowland's Macassar oil to keep his hair black and, as a consequence, give him eternal youth.

He hunted elephants with great energy, and on 30 April 1828 when the little home-made schooner, the *Elizabeth and Susan*, which had taken two years to build in Port Natal, eventually sailed for the Cape, it carried, besides a party of the ivory traders, three Zulu ambassadors to King George and instructions to obtain some of the wonderful Macassar oil. As a sort of under-the-counter instruction, the ambassadors were also to thoroughly spy out the strength and prosperity of the Europeans. This they did to the extent of reaching Port Elizabeth, drinking grog at Government expense for three months, and being interviewed occasionally by Major Cloete, a minor bureaucrat dressed in gold braid in sufficient quantity to make the self-conscious ivory traders feel like real Robinson Crusoes. They were all dressed in home-made clothes – Isaacs had only a dilapidated pair of trousers and a leopard skin cap – and a more sunburnt and rugged crowd could scarcely be imagined.

Back in Natal, six months after his mother's death, the time had come for Shaka to stage the ceremonial hunt which always marked the ending of a period of mourning. The quarry was usually game; but Shaka preferred men, and he resolved on a great raid against the Pondo and Xhosa tribes. Early in May the Zulu army, with Shaka in personal command, tramped down through the bush of the south coast, leaving behind a trail of blood and death indelibly marked in the traditions of the African residents.

Shaka, as we have already seen, was always a prolific source of legend and place names, and this south coast promenade was a classic occasion. Innumerable were the rocks and trees under which he is supposed to have rested; and so many pools are scattered around the country into which, legend tells us, he threw condemned persons, that there would hardly have been people enough in all Natal to supply the victims.

In such manner the traditional account of the passage of the Zulu army down the south coast is rich in incident. Led by renegade Thembu guides, the army followed a path at first somewhat inland from the coast. At the hill known as isiHluthankungu (the plucker of the mists), Shaka rested, while his army occupied itself in looting the surrounding country between the upper Fafa and the Mthwalume rivers.

From the camp at the hill the Zulus, after ruining the pleasant area known as the Cabane (open plain), pushed down towards the sea. On their way, following the ancient pathway leading towards the Mzumbe (the bad kraal) – so named from the cannibals living there – they bivouacked for a night on the saddle, separating the Cabane from the coastal lands.

At this spot Shaka picked up a stone between his toes, took it in his hand, spat on it, and deposited it beside the pathway on the summit of the ridge; a superstitious gesture considered by Africans to ensure good luck on a journey into a strange or hazardous area. The Zulu army emulated Shaka, and this *sivivane* (accumulation) of stones became one of the most famous of its kind in all Natal.

If it was a fight the Zulus hoped for, the *sivivane* soon gave them that. They had not encountered much resistance to their passage so far, but now the local Bele tribe, under chief Ngcwanguba, attempted to defend their homes and livestock. A fierce battle took place between elements of the Zulu army and the tribesmen. The local people had little chance and were driven southwards to the river known as the Njambili. There they were cornered and practically wiped out. After the fight, the body of Ngcwanguba was found by some survivors and buried beneath a tree on the hill ever afterwards known by the name of the ill-fated chief.

The Zulus crossed the Mzimkhulu by the old Batstone's Drift. Fynn, who was in residence at his kraal there, was about the only coast dweller to make them welcome, and Shaka decided to remain in the vicinity. He encamped at a bush near modern Marburg, known as isiHlala sikaShaka (the bush of Shaka), and there spent his days gossiping with Fynn and lazing in the sun.

The army had been divided into two sections. The largest, under the renowned commander, Mdlaka, went down the coast to tackle the Pondos. The second division, under Manyundela, swept inland, with orders to liquidate the Thembus and other tribes. The armies were to meet on the Msikaba River.

It was a bitter time for the border tribes. Rumours of the approach of the Zulu army threw them into a blind panic, and even the British down in Grahamstown heard the news and sent an army forth to chase the invaders away.

The Zulus looted their way down to the Cwanguba forest, south of the Mthatha River. There they encamped and busied themselves in ruining the surrounding countryside. Both the Pondo and Bomvana tribes vanished into the bush, but 30 000 of their cattle were rounded up. With this booty the army returned to the Mzimkhulu, leaving behind a destitute country for a belated British army to search one month later.

Shaka received his army with mixed feelings. He had instructed his commanders to proceed as far as the Xhosas, but instead they had come back, content with their loot from the

Pondos. For four days he refused to see them and let it be known among them that his displeasure could best be dispelled if they volunteered to march immediately the whole length of Natal, Zululand and Swaziland and attack Soshangane's people. The army agreed to do this. They were then purified by the doctors and ceremoniously washed in the sea near the mouth of the Mzimkhulu River.

They began the march home. With Fynn keeping them company, they followed the coast all the way back to Shaka's capital kraal of Dukuza.

The usual string of traditions was left behind as they travelled. Fresh water for drinking was always in demand on these tiring marches and, with most of the rivers salty from connection with the sea, there was a great shortage along the coast.

At the mouth of the river known as the Mphambanyoni (the deceiver of birds), tradition informs us that Shaka's attendants discovered for him, on the south bank, a spring of fresh water known as umThombo kaShaka (the well of Shaka). At this place he is said to have relaxed for a day or so while his army rested and sported on the beach making mock attacks against the waves where the holiday makers from Scottburgh swim today.

Moving on, the Zulus forded the next large river and were fascinated, tradition tells us, to see the female whales lying with their calves in the shallow water. UmKhomazi (the river of cow-whales), was the name Shaka then applied to it, while another version, umKhomo Manzi (the whale waters), is also sometimes used.

Still further north, the army reached a certain river. Shaka's personal attendant filled a calabash with water from this stream and carried it to his master. Shaka, resting in the shade of an umDoni tree, sipped it tentatively and was pleased. *"Kanti Amanz'a mtoti"* ("So, the water is sweet"), he said, delicately using the *hlonipha* (respectful alternate) word for the taboo name of his mother, Nandi (the sweet one). The army, as usual, acclaimed his saying, and the pleasant little river was henceforth known as aManzamtoti (the sweet waters).

The army returned to Dukuza with its vast booty in cattle straggling behind and gradually being dispersed among the military kraals of Natal such as Ndabankhulu (the great affair), near the site of modern Bellair.

Three days after its own arrival at Dukuza, towards the end of July 1828, the army, with some ominous mutterings, set off on the long raid north. Tramping right up across Swaziland, the warriors reached the lands of the Pedi and had what they considered to be an enjoyable time, seizing corn, cattle and women from their rightful owners.

Then they roamed down the uluSapha (Sabie) River, through the present Kruger National Park and into Portuguese East Africa. There Soshangane received them as warmly as his much smaller army allowed him, and after another month of looting they returned homewards, leaving many of their number behind as casualties of war, malaria or dysentery. Down through Tongaland they tramped, back into their own familiar maze of hills and forests. There, by the banks of the great Mfolozi, tidings reached them of one of the most momentous events in all Zulu history.

Shortly after the army's departure, Shaka's ambassadors to King George had returned, reaching Port Natal on 17 August. They had experienced a frustrating time. Distorted rumours of the recent Zulu raid had travelled down the bush telegraph to Port Elizabeth and caused a general alarm. An invasion was expected; the ivory traders were regarded as renegades, and Shaka's ambassadors suspected as spies.

After three annoying months, King had returned with Shaka's three ambassadors aboard the HMS *Helicon*, leaving the rest of the traders to follow on the *Elizabeth and Susan*.

King returned mortally sick from dysentery and a bitterly disappointed man. He retired to bed in his hut at the place he had named Mount Pleasant on the Bluff. Isaacs had to tramp up to see Shaka with the returning ambassadors and a bundle of presents sent by the Cape Government.

So far as Shaka was concerned, the whole venture had proved a fiasco. Instead of visiting England, his ambassadors had been detained in Port Elizabeth all these long months. To make matters worse, in the general disappointment the all-important Rowland's Macassar oil for which Shaka longed so much, had been forgotten as but an insignificant item.

After venting his spleen on Isaacs, Shaka summarily instructed John Cane to walk down to the Cape to secure the precious oil and complain to the government about the treatment of his ambassadors. The ivory traders cursed Fynn for a fool for ever having indulged Shaka in his belief that in Macassar oil lay that fabulous elixir of life for which alchemists had searched so long. None of them knew what to say to him. How could they explain that there was no chance of a handful of ragged ivory traders succeeding, when all science had failed to find the marvel?

Cane trudged off into the bush with much bad language. In Port Natal, King lay dying of dysentery. Isaacs and Fynn doctored him as best they could from Buchan's medical work, but nothing availed. They tried to get Farewell to aid them, or at least to visit his old friend, but he stubbornly refused.

Hutton, Fynn and Isaacs stayed with King to the end. On the evening of 7 September 1828 he died while his faithful African followers howled and wailed around his hut. It was a miserable night for everybody.

They buried him near his hut and piled stones on his grave to keep the hyenas away. Then, on 14 September, Isaacs and Fynn went up to see Shaka to tell him of the death. The Zulu king genuinely regretted the news.

Death seemed to be weighing heavily on Shaka's mind, but if he looked to Rowland's Macassar oil to protect him from it, it was because he knew not from which direction the old man with the sickle would strike.

It was towards sunset on 22 September 1828 that a party of Tswanas arrived, bringing Shaka a tribute of crane feathers. Seated in a small kraal named Nyakamubi (the bad year), close to Dukuza, Shaka received them and impatiently demanded to know why they were so late.

One of Shaka's courtiers, Mbopha, suddenly jumped up and drove the men away, hitting at them with an assegai and feigning annoyance at their excuses. Shaka stood up from his seat in surprise, and as he did so the servants at his feet scattered in terror.

Into the kraal behind Shaka strode two men, Mhlangana and Dingane, both half-brothers of the king.

Shaka turned in surprise. He saw spears in their hands and death in their eyes. "Ye children of my father," he wailed, "what is the wrong?" They made no answer, but advanced with menace upon him. He turned to flee and tripped across the kraal gate. There they caught him and, while he sought to stagger to his feet, they stabbed him, his blood turning the dust into mud. All night his body lay there, while a pall of silence hung over the kraal. The next morning some menials rolled him up in a black oxhide and bundled him and his personal possessions into an empty corn pit. There were no tears, only numbness in the minds and hearts of his people. Death had put the most final of full stops to the end of a strange chapter in Africa's story.

Ltd F.G.Farewell

SEVEN
Dingane

Manyosi the glutton

The Black Mfolozi chooses its ferrymen for victims. So say the Zulus in an ancient proverb, and certainly if anybody ever died at his trade it was Shaka, for his trade was death, and the price of it was his own murder.

Dingane had been an oversight on the part of Shaka. Any really prudent African chief of that day would have systematically destroyed all his brothers as a preventive measure against just such a catastrophe as Shaka experienced. This lapse cost Shaka his life and the Zulu nation its spirit. Without him it slowly subsided from the peak of its power and slid gently down into the dark valley where the ferrymen from the Black Mfolozi waited to take them over the river of defeat into the shadows of death.

Dingane (the needy one), then about thirty years old, commenced his reign with caution. Messages were sent off with all speed to the neighbouring dependencies, including the Europeans of Port Natal. All were informed of the change and assured that the new monarch was inclined towards peace and would do them no harm.

Then Dingane waited for the grand army to trudge back from the north. In the two months of suspense he rampaged around, murdering all the more ardent aristocratic supporters of Shaka, who still remained in Zululand. His brother and ally,

Mhlangana, he also murdered when the two quarrelled about who was most entitled to the vacant throne.

Nearly every Zulu of military age was away in the army. In order to provide some support for himself and to serve as executioners of his immediate enemies, Dingane rummaged out all the menials and herdboys, Natal men who were used as semi-slaves by their Zulu overlords. This heterogeneous collection Dingane organised into a home guard regiment, which he called the uHlomendlini (that which is armed at home). There were two companies to this regiment, the younger men being grouped into the Mnyama (black) section, and the older men in the Mhlophe (white) section.

Thus fortified, Dingane met the returning Zulu army. The warriors received the shattering news in stunned silence. Dingane promised them peace, a life of ease and the enjoyment of their booty, with a general right to get married. To the common troopers this was something to conjure with. Only the grandees could weigh the political implications. Of these, most accepted the inevitable and bowed to Dingane. Mdlaka, marshal of the army, objected to the whole business, but the majority were against him. He was strangled in his hut shortly afterwards, and so the Zulu nation lost its leading star and its strongest arm in the same disaster. Ndlela succeeded him as general of the army.

Dingane soon abandoned the labyrinthine hut-city of Dukuza with its evil memories. He withdrew all the way back to the traditional Zulu valley, where the Mkhumbane stream still tinkled down as pleasantly as ever. There, on the gently sloping ridge which lies above the stream, he erected a new capital for himself, and this he named Mgungundlovu (the secret plot of the elephant) referring to his own plot to assassinate Shaka.

At this place Dingane settled himself down comfortably to enjoy life. The flower of Zulu womanhood, the best of food and drink, were his for the asking. He grew fat and sleek and sluggish. A host of idle courtiers surrounded him; all manner of individuals sought to win his favour by adulation.

Dwarfs and freaks and jesters sought to entertain him. One notorious fat man became his particular joy. Manyosi Mbatha was the name of this man, and he was a glutton beyond compare. An entire goat could vanish as a single meal down Manyosi's cavernous gullet, and end with a request for more. Dingane often showed him off to friends. The Zulus envied him his life of pampered ease. To the curious stool-shaped mountain which looks down upon the Zulu valley from the north, some wag jocularly applied the name of isiHlalo sikaManyosi (the seat of Manyosi). So he found his fame, grew presumptuous in the nature of his kind, said something out of place one day, and Dingane had him starved to death. The Zulus shook their heads at this. "Even Manyosi died," some coiner of proverbs said, and in that saying, strangely enough, Manyosi lives for ever.

Dingane was not unduly brutal by nature. He killed people – that was expected of him – but not quite with the reckless abandon of his brother. It was perfectly normal for the Zulu king to sentence people to death; that was the only known way of punishing criminals, and forbearance in this respect would have been construed as weakness.

Accordingly, although the hysterical mass killings of Shaka's time ended, the executioners were still kept tolerably busy, and the vultures, whose delight it was to dispose of the debris, were still well fed. They perched on the kraal fence and watched the trials with discernment. Then they would accompany the condemned person and the executioners to the execution hill, flopping along around the party; repulsive, ghoulish things, their feathers clotted with blood and emitting an evil stench.

Beyond these judicial killings, Dingane's life was one of feasting, dancing, ceremonial military parades and displays of cattle. Increased prosperity actually came to Zululand. The army settled down at home for a while to enjoy the fruits of its victories – a country bulging with looted cattle and captured women, who were set to work to till the fields and produce military reinforcements.

The ivory traders at Port Natal, meanwhile, had heard the news of Shaka's assassination with all the shock of mankind suddenly confronted by the unknown. As a precautionary measure, they collected at Townshend and discussed the future. Most of them were completely dissatisfied with the development of their settlement. The persistent refusal of the Cape Government to regard them as being anything but a collection of ragged adventurers and, as such, having no claim to protection or support, had particularly galled them.

Farewell, Isaacs and a few others agreed that the precarious life at the place was not worth living, and they decided to leave. They set to work packing their belongings and preparing the little *Elizabeth and Susan* for her voyage.

Dingane, meanwhile, sent them frequent protestations of his peaceful intentions. If anything, the security of Port Natal was improved by Shaka's murder, especially when Dingane abandoned the old Dukuza kraal and withdrew deep into Zululand to his new capital of Mgungundlovu.

On 1 December 1828, however, Farewell, Isaacs and the other dissatisfied traders sailed out of Port Natal and headed for the joys of civilisation. The first joy they found was when the authorities at Port Elizabeth promptly seized their homemade little ship as having no register, and the traders lost almost everything they had, for it was never returned to them.

Back at Natal, Fynn, Cane, Ogle and Holstead remained at the port. Other traders soon came to join them, including two of Fynn's brothers, William and Francis. Life returned to normal. The country was at peace and, one by one, the traders journeyed up to Dingane to pay their respects and make themselves known.

Several visitors arrived in the country as well, for all the uproar about Shaka had given the place much publicity. In February 1829, Dr Alexander Cowie, a former surgeon of the Albany

district of the Cape, and Benjamin Green, a well-known Grahamstown merchant, arrived at Fynn's hut at Port Natal. Their
intention was to explore Natal, journey to the Drakensberg
and discover the source of the Orange River.

Reaching Port Natal, they were entertained by the ever-
hospitable Fynn, and with him went up to see Dingane on 18
February 1829. There, at the Nobamba kraal, they met a party
of about forty half-caste Portuguese traders who had visited
Dingane with a view to reopening trade. Talking to these people Cowie and Green became interested in visiting Lourenço
Marques.

Fynn therefore arranged for Dingane to give them supplies
and the use of Jacob as an interpreter. Leaving their wagons
behind with Fynn, the party set off on 6 March and tramped
up through the bush on the western side of the Lubombo
Mountains.

Just beyond the Phongolo they climbed to the top of the
Lubombo, and then dropped down the eastern slopes into the
vast wilderness of Tongaland. On 14 March they were camped
near the junction of the Phongolo and the Ngwavuma rivers.
From there they hunted and roamed down the banks of the
Phongolo, finding it to be a veritable river of adventure, with
its gorgeous forest-clad banks and its teeming river life of crocs
and hippos, at constant war with the men who sought to cultivate land beside the riverbanks.

They explored the great, shallow lakes, sailing across them
to shoot the hippos by means of the Tembes' dugout canoes.
Each lake seemed more fascinating than the last. Near the junction of the Maphuto and Phongolo rivers, on the Portuguese
side, they camped beside one such of these lakes, about four
miles long by 350 feet wide, its waters "fresh and translucent
as glass; the haunt of the alligator, hippo, and an innumerable
diversity of fish, it is garlanded around by splendid shrubs, approached by a lawn of the most verdant grass." Game abounded all around, and, as is the nature of these lakes, death lived
there as well, for the mosquitoes sang all night.

The travellers pushed on, through sand and bog, to the shores of the bay of Lourenço Marques. There Jacob, afraid of the slave trade, left them. On 24 March 1829 the Portuguese Governor sent his boat to transport them across the bay to Lourenço Marques town. There, for seven days, they were royally entertained. Then they pushed on north to their deaths. On 4 April, Cowie was taken ill. He bled himself, made his will, and with everything arranged as neatly as possible, died that night.

Their coloured servant, Platje, died the next day, and three days later the heartbroken and weary Green followed them in their travels down the silent glades of death. Only Jacob and one of Fynn's servants, loaned to the travellers, managed to return to Natal with news of the tragedy.

Down in the Cape meanwhile, Farewell had felt his old ties with Port Natal tugging at his heart. He raised fresh capital and determined once again to establish trade. With several wagons loaded with goods, accompanied by John Cane and two would-be explorers, Messrs Thackwray and Walker, he set out in September 1829. On the journey up the coast they encountered the lawless refugee Qwabe tribe under the chief Nqetho, near the Mzimvubu River. Farewell, Thackwray and Walker visited the chief and were all stabbed to death in their tent that night. John Cane slipped into the bush and lived to tell the tale. In this wretched manner died Lieutenant Francis George Farewell at the age of 38, one of the founders of Port Natal who all seem to have had nought as reward for their toil save a miserable end in the loneliness and savagery of the wilderness.

Another disaster happened at Port Natal in January 1830. A Portuguese slave-trading ship, the *African Adventure*, was deliberately run ashore by her crew after being blown about for three weeks in a violent storm. A total of 130 of her load of 160 slaves had died of thirst. The Portuguese crew had survived by the simple expedient of throwing their slaves overboard in order to conserve drinking water. Aided by the Fynns, the survivors were sheltered and guided overland up to Dingane who, although abhorrent of their slaving, provided an escort to take them to Lourenço Marques.

Like Farewell, Nathaniel Isaacs had also found himself drawn back to the great lagoon of Natal. To the surprise of his old friends, on 31 March 1830, he arrived at the bay as supercargo aboard the American brig, *St Michael*.

The Fynns welcomed Isaacs back with pleasure and he entered into partnership with them, while Cane and Ogle took over Farewell's old business. It seemed as though they were in for a new and prosperous epoch of trade under Dingane. The chief was the height of courtesy to them all and, although Isaacs considered him to be "deliberative and calculating", he was certainly not nearly as predatory or bloodthirsty as Shaka and he actively stimulated trade.

"Look around," he once said expansively to Isaacs, "see the mountains and forests: their extent and their production. They are all mine. They contain innumerable elephants, and my rivers the hippopotami. I have given up going to war. I mean to cultivate peace and live on terms of goodwill with all my neighbours, as being more congenial to my feelings and more conducive to the welfare of my people. I shall then hunt the elephant and the hippopotamus, which will be an amusement for my subjects and enable me to remunerate my friends."

All this, as Isaacs translated it, sounded very grand. It neatly overlooked the fact that, in that very month, Dingane had packed the Zulu army off on a major raid against Mzilikazi in the Transvaal. On its homeward journey the same army swept through the Ngome forest. Drumming their shields with heavy *kerries*, the warriors searched the bush for days until poor Beje, who had clung to his beloved forest for so long, was stampeded out with his cattle and was seen in Ngome no longer.

Still, to the traders Dingane seemed to be a paragon of African virtues. He presented them with 16 head of cattle and 20 hides in exchange for their rifles, and gave his blessing to a new joint trading venture launched by Fynn and Isaacs. Henceforth the two divided Natal and Zululand between them.

While Isaacs traded with the Zulus, Fynn busied himself in the south. Especially in the middle and upper reaches of the Mkhomazi, where the Ntlangwini tribe lived, did he develop a most profitable trade. This tribe had learnt elephant hunting from the Bushmen, including the secrets of the use of the bow and poisoned arrows, and they scoured all Natal in search of tuskers. In Bushman fashion, when they killed an elephant the whole tribe would camp around the carcass until they had totally consumed it. Then they would secrete the tusks and move on in search of another victim. Later, they would gather the tusks and exchange them with the traders, at the rate of a cow for a tusk.

Other ivory traders, such as Biddulph, Collis and Oughton, were attracted to Natal by the general prosperity, and everything seemed fine. Not only were the numbers of Europeans increasing, but every day some African refugee from Zululand or elsewhere would reach the settlement and attach himself for protection to one or other of the traders. Each European was regarded as a chief in his own right and had the power of life or death over his subjects. Gardens were made, fruit and vegetables planted and an entire community grew up around the growing port of Natal.

Fynn and Isaacs established their headquarters around King's old house at Mount Pleasant. They spent most of their time roaming around the country, returning periodically with the results of their trade. Indunas were appointed to control their following of Africans, but the Europeans remained at all times judges, chiefs and doctors to their people. Regular trials were held in African fashion. Medical treatment was handed out with the aid of Buchan's old-fashioned home doctor. Fynn, on one occasion, even managed to amputate the accidentally shattered arm of one of his hunters with its aid.

The other traders lived in similar style. Their houses were

scattered about the site of the centre of modern Durban; while the old coloured woman, Rachel, had made her home in Farewell's never finished fort, where broken walls and two or three rusty cannon marked the ruination of his hopes.

A fair amount of rivalry grew up between the traders. Newcomers, such as Collis and Biddulph in particular, found it hard to establish themselves. The older traders had long-standing agreements with the ivory-hunting tribes, precluding sales to strangers. Some of the newcomers returned disgruntled to the Cape and there spread a story that Fynn and Isaacs owed their success to large-scale sales of gunpowder to the Zulus.

A story promptly filtered back to Port Natal through the bush, that the government was fitting out an armed force to punish the traders. This news was treated by them with some hilarity, but the rumour found its way to Dingane in the even more distorted form that the expedition was aimed against him.

Dingane had pondered much on the question of firearms and Europeans, and he held many lengthy discussions about the matter with his warriors and his visitors. Thus, on one of his trading visits in 1830, Isaacs saw a group of warriors mustering at the head of the kraal. "I went thither and seated myself among them. Dingane talked to us, as in the morning, on the subject of fighting with the white people. It was the chief's opinion that the Zulus could conquer Europeans by attacking in the night. They said: 'When the white people discharge their muskets, we could go and spear them before they reload!'"

Isaacs contended against this idea. There was much discussion, with one induna boasting so much about what he could do to Europeans that Isaacs grew annoyed. "I told him to get his shield and spears, and that I would get my weapons and meet him on the hill, where the king might have an opportunity of witnessing our combat and decide who were victorious."

The induna declined and tendered an apology. Later Isaacs gave the warriors a demonstration of the penetrative force of bullets by firing at tree trunks. Dingane had other opportunities of studying firearms in action. On another trading visit, Isaacs found that the king had as prisoners two of the wives of the Qwabe chief, Nqetho, who had murdered Farewell on his journey in the Cape. Now Dingane and his army were awaiting an entertainment with pleasant anticipation.

Isaacs was expected to execute the two women in vengeance for the murder of Farewell. When he refused, one of his servants took the gun and shot the women. Dingane was very impressed. "He at once acknowledged it to be his opinion," wrote Isaacs, "that no power he had could combat with another that used firearms; but added, he did not believe any people could conquer the Zulus excepting Europeans."

Dingane pondered much on this prospect of a clash between his people and the Europeans. He resolved to send a mission down to the Cape to arrange good relations between himself and the British. As ambassador he selected John Cane, and ordered Jacob (Hlambamanzi) to accompany him.

On 21 November 1830 the mission reached Grahamstown. Cane presented four tusks to the Civil Commissioner and gave him the message that Dingane wished to live in peace with his neighbours, that he wished to encourage trade and would protect traders, and that he desired a missionary.

While this message was still being digested by the government, Cane hastily sold his own supply of ivory, given him by Dingane for sustenance, and then returned homewards, being fearful of the rains making the rivers impassable for that season. With Thomas Holstead, who had accompanied him, and the seven Zulus of the mission, including Jacob, he reached Port Natal on 10 March 1831. There he loitered around on his private affairs, contenting himself in sending up to Dingane just the goods and presents the king had wanted.

Jacob and the Zulus, however, returned to the king. Jacob had much to say. He and Cane had quarrelled nearly the whole length of the journey. Now he had his vengeance by stressing the negative results of the mission. In his haste Cane had not even brought an official acknowledgement from the British

Government, and his failure to report was the last straw to the annoyed Dingane.

He mustered a regiment forthwith and sent it hurrying down along the path to Port Natal. Before dawn on 18 April it raided Cane's house. Cane was too spry an individual to be caught asleep. When the Zulus got there, they found his house deserted. They had to content themselves with burning the place down and seizing a few stray cattle.

The rest of the Europeans, not knowing what was happening, thought that the entire settlement was being attacked, and fled forthwith into the bush. There they hid until messengers came from Dingane explaining the matter. Henry and William Fynn then went up to see him, with eighty carriers following behind them loaded with a vast store of beads, brass bangles, iron pots, rugs, cloth and what-not, including eleven muskets, which Dingane was most desirous of obtaining.

Reaching the capital, the Fynns found it a seething mass of mistrust and ill-feeling against the British. Jacob had spun a whole series of stories. He had reported, wrote Fynn, "that as he was going to the Colony he had met a Frontier Kaffir, who told him he wanted to find a home with the Zulus, as there was no living so near the white people; that at first the white people came and took a part of their land, then they encroached and drove them further back, and have repeatedly taken more land, as well as cattle.

"They then built houses (i.e. missionary establishments) among them for the purpose of subduing them by witchcraft; that at the present they had even got as far as the amaMpondo; that lately no less than four kings had died, and their deaths were attributed to the witchcraft of the *abeLungu* (Europeans), as all the *iziNyanga* (prophets), had predicted it; that during his stay at Grahamstown the soldiers frequently asked what sort of a country the Zulus had; if the roads were good for horses; if they had plenty of cattle; and had said: 'We shall soon be after you.'"

With information such as this, no wonder Dingane was in a panic. He had marshalled all his forces, and, to Fynn's astonishment, he had even induced the Portuguese to send a company of coloured soldiers from Lourenço Marques to support him against the anticipated invasion.

Fynn attempted to pacify Dingane by contradicting Jacob, but it was useless. On his way back to Port Natal he was warned that Dingane planned to kill the ivory traders and was busy devising an excuse. The information seemed authentic and the whole settlement bolted.

The American trading vessel *Saint Michael* fortunately called at the bay at this crisis; and on 24 June, Isaacs, then only 23 years old, left the place aboard her and no longer played any part in the story of Port Natal.

The rest of the traders sought the safety of the bush. The Fynns gathered their numerous following and wives and made off down the south coast for the sanctuary of the Cape.

On the seventh night of their retreat the Fynns slept in the bush on the south side of the mouth of the river known as the Mbilanhlola. At dawn the next day they were attacked by one of the Natal garrison regiments, commanded by Sotobe, who considered that they were running away with the king's cattle.

There was a vicious fight in the bush. The Fynn party broke up and scattered. The three Fynn brothers all had narrow escapes. Frank Fynn was actually trampled upon by the Zulus in the dark. Henry Fynn made off along the beach, and escaped with his personal servant, Andries Fakaya, only by shooting the leader of the Zulus sent to pursue him and by swimming through the sea from one rocky outcrop to another.

Henry Fynn's eldest son, Frank (known as Mpahle), the child of an African woman named Nombaca, a princess of the Langeni tribe, was separated from the rest of the party with a small following of his own. Hotly pursued by the Zulus, they were eventually cornered some miles to the south, at a curiously-shaped, mammoth sand dune, which dominates the country thereabouts and is known as isaNdlundlu (that which is shaped like a hut). The whole party was killed and the dune has ever since been known as Tragedy Hill.* The rest of the Fynns eventually reached safety at the Bunting Mission Station in Pondoland.

The whole affair was really the result of a false alarm. Fynn's informant had been a liar. Dingane was certainly alarmed but, after some time spent in hiding in the bush, John Cane plucked up enough courage to see the Zulu king and discuss the matter with him.

The whole quarrel was ironed out. Dingane pointed out that after hearing Jacob's story, he could not have acted in any other manner than to marshal his army for the defence of the country. He had done so, however, with the mental reservation that if within six months no British invading army appeared, he would call Jacob to account. Those six months had now passed. Jacob had also overplayed his hand. A man cannot be dishonest in one thing only. He spoiled his case by stealing some of Dingane's cattle. For that offence alone his death was inevitable. In January 1832 Dingane ordered Cane to kill Jacob, and Henry Ogle for a fee of five head of cattle shot him with pleasure, for he had caused much trouble.

The ivory traders gradually trickled back to Port Natal after their alarm. Some newcomers arrived as well: C.J. Pickman; the three deeply religious Cawoods – Samuel, James and Joshua; and several others also journeyed up by wagon from the Cape and settled with their families around Port Natal.

The Fynns came back as well, although they were very nervous. Frank Fynn, known as Phobana, contented himself with making a home on the lower south coast, by the banks of the Boboyi River.

Frank Fynn, like most of the other ivory traders, had married African wives. His principal wife was Vundlase, and on his death, about the year 1840, his following – known as the

---

*This is the version told by the descendants of the Fynns. A Zulu version states that a party of Pondos was killed at isaNdlundlu, and the Fynns were killed near the Mbilanhlola River.

iziNkhumbi (locusts) – remained under her charge. She removed to the Mthwalume area, at a place known as Nyangweni, and on her retirement in 1882 was succeeded by Frank's heir, Charlie Fynn. On his death in 1911, the tribe broke up. One section, in the area of iziNgolweni (the place of wild cats), fell under a brother of Charlie named Tom Fynn, whose grandson, Wilson Fynn, controlled their destinies at the place called eNqabeni (the stronghold).

Henry Francis Fynn returned to Port Natal, and for some time endeavoured to get Dingane to compensate him for the loss of his livestock and property. All his efforts were in vain. In disgust he left Port Natal and returned to the Cape, to secure a post in government service and thenceforth follow new trails.

His African followers, the Nsimbini, remained under the care of his brother and Vundlase until his second son and heir, Duka Fynn, grew old enough to become their chief. This young man married Susan, daughter of the renowned hunter, Hans Lochenberg, and built a kraal named kwaNobamba (the place of the catcher) on the banks of the Boboyi. His son Willie succeeded him, and his grandson Percy Fynn controlled the tribe from his "capital", named iNyandezulu on account of the snakes of that name found there.

The row between Dingane and the ivory traders, meanwhile, had again given Natal much publicity in the Cape. The Government decided to make some investigation into affairs there and, in January 1832, a well-known explorer of the day, Doctor Andrew Smith, travelled up from the Cape with a Lieutenant Edie. Henry Fynn acted as their guide.

They were well received and Dingane was his old hospitable self. He entertained them royally, parading the beautifully dressed girls of his harem for their diversion, and leading his warriors in dancing. All the glory of the Zulu nation was there as Fynn had first seen it, with the army undergoing preparation for a raid against Mzilikazi, to be launched at the end of June of that year. The country was peaceful, green and beautiful.

Travelling with Smith was a Cape farmer named Willem Berg. He was in raptures at what he saw. All he could talk about was what his countrymen would do when, on his return to Cape Town, he told them of what he had seen.

The raid against Mzilikazi passed off successfully. Mzilikazi was almost a perennial subject for raids. He was such an energetic looter of cattle himself that no matter how often the Zulus visited him they could always rely on a good fight and a rich bag of livestock. In 1833, however, Dingane decided to give the Matebele a breathing space and accordingly in April, he sent his army sneaking down along the long wall of the Drakensberg with orders to attack the Pondos and other border tribes in the rear.

The raid was not particularly successful. The Pondos could hear a Zulu coming even if he was carried by the winds. They vanished into the bush with their herds, leaving the Zulus to thrash around the country, rifling what they could. In the process, some of their scouts came across a party of eight coloured hunters from the Cape, busy shooting hippos in the Mzimkhulu River. The seven adult members of this party were wiped out, while one youth was taken prisoner and brought back to Zululand.

Distorted rumours of this affair reached Port Natal by means of the bush telegraph along the coast. The ivory traders were told that a party of Europeans had been murdered. They jumped to the conclusion that two of the traders, James and Joseph Cawood, who were operating somewhere on the border, must have been the victims. In a rage the traders collected their force. When the hungry and tired Zulu army came tramping up homewards in June 1833, and aggravated things by looting some of the traders' cattle, the Europeans opened fire, killing over two hundred Zulus and driving the rest away in confusion, for the warriors had explicit instructions not to fight with white people.

The next day the ivory traders abandoned Port Natal in great haste, fearing retribution from Dingane. But Dingane had nothing against them. On the contrary, news of this clash infuriated him. He killed most of the scouts concerned in the murder and had the eyes of their captain put out for being unable to distinguish anybody like a European. Messengers were sent to the ivory traders inviting them to return, and all Zulu garrisons were withdrawn from Natal in order to restore confidence.

By the end of the year several of the ivory traders and some newcomers had returned to Port Natal. Business was re-established, although the Portuguese had profited by the long disruption of British competition, and had flooded Zululand with their trade goods. Still, the traders came back, and to their ramshackle little settlement there also journeyed some interesting visitors.

Dr Andrew Smith and his companions had been most enthusiastic about Natal on their return to the Cape. Willem Berg, especially, had boasted about the greenness and fertility of the place. As a result, early in 1834, the farmers of Uitenhage and Grahamstown organised a so-called "commission trek" to visit Natal and obtain information about the prospects of settling there.

Twenty-one men and one woman, with their servants, travelled in this commission. Using fourteen wagons, they followed Dr Andrew Smith's well-described trail up the coast. The border chiefs welcomed them with surprising kindness. Hintza, the great Xhosa chief entertained them royally. When the leader of the commission, Petrus Lafras Uys, told him they were in search of land, Hintza considerately gave them the land between the Tsomo and Mzimvubu rivers.

Uys rode up forthwith to inspect the area. He found it consisted of the Pondo tribal lands. Faku, the Pondo chief, received them there kindly and also offered to give them land. Uys was a bit cautious by now. "What land?" he asked. Faku graciously offered him the area between the Mbhashe and Ntina rivers (Hintza's domain). Uys declined with regret and rode up to see what Dingane would offer.

At Port Natal the ivory traders greeted the visitors with pleasure. Among the traders there was a 22-year-old Englishman named Richard King, who had first come to Natal in 1828 as a servant to the ill-fated travellers, Cowie and Green.

The commission picked King up as a guide and went on to the mouth of the Mvoti River, where they pitched a laager. From there they cautiously sent King up to Dingane to ask for land. Dingane received the request with interest and suggested that the commission members visit him in person.

King returned to the laager and found Uys down with fever. Each of the other men seemed to have a different excuse for not visiting the Zulu king. At length Johannes, younger brother of Uys, rode up on his own. He found the Thukela in flood and impassable. The only contact he had with the Zulus was by means of messages shouted across the water. The youth eventually returned to report that Dingane had indicated that Natal was vacant and available for European settlement.

With this information the party gleefully turned for home. They travelled inland on their return journey, exploring the beautiful Natal midlands. In their imaginations they selected farms for themselves, and carried back to the Cape stories of fertility, of tumbling streams and waving grass, of soft winds and cloud castles, of flowers and game, of an uninhabited garden of God contained between the sea and the purple mountain wall which they knew as the Drakensberg.

isaNdlundlu
or Tragedy Hill

EIGHT
New times

A t Port Natal, the ivory traders were completely una-
ware of the profound interest with which their country
was being regarded by the farmers in the Cape. They
continued their habitual lives; trading and roaming about in
a carefree, careless sort of existence, dressing as they pleased,
and doing pretty well as they felt.

Their trading activity, if nothing else, had given the Zulu
people a whole convention and fantasy about beads. Beads of
each colour were given a particular name and meaning. White
beads were called *ithambo* (bone) and were said to represent
love; pink beads were called *ubumpofu* (poor ones) and represented poverty; black beads, in later years, were called *isiti-
mane* (shadows) and meant grief through absence.

Green beads were *obuluhlaza* (new grass) and represented
feeling; blue beads were *ijuba* (the dove), for faithfulness; red
beads were *umgazi* (blood) and represented tears, while yellow
beads were called *incombo* (young corn) and meant wealth.
Striped beads were called *intotoviyane* (the striped grasshop-
per) and represented doubt; brown beads were *umlilwana* (a
low fire) and indicated disappointment.

With the so-called language of the beads thus established, it
became the practice for girls to send bead love letters, known
as *incwadi*, to their young men. The successive colours in a
string (read from the fastening) or the colours in a small orna-

mental square (read from the outside inwards) conveyed the message of their affections. In this pretty way the old ivory traders founded a curious memorial to themselves in the very items they principally bartered to their customers.

The first indication of the coming of new times to the life of the traders was on 29 December 1834, when into their startled community came a dynamic and restless character by the name of Allen Francis Gardiner, a 41-year-old ex-commander of the Royal Navy, who had been more than badly bitten by the bug of religious zeal on the death of his wife eight months previously. He had sworn at her deathbed to devote his remaining years to missionary activity, and Zululand was the field of his choice.

James Collis, the senior ivory trader at that time, made the newcomer feel welcome, gave him advice, and saw that he was provided with a new wagon; for in his enthusiasm Gardiner had pushed on so rapidly that his own transport was some hundreds of miles behind him.

Gardiner went on to Zululand forthwith. All the rivers were in flood, but one of the traders, John Stubbs, helped him across. At the Thukela he was forced to leave his new wagon, for the river was a raging torrent and he was able to cross with his interpreter, George Cyrus, only by the aid of a party of traders encamped there, with a rudely constructed skin canoe. They ferried him across and then watched him disappear into the hills of Zululand with amazement, wondering whether he would ever come back.

It was on the afternoon of 10 January 1835 that Gardiner had his first view of Mgungundlovu, a vast circle of huts lying like a strange, savage gem in the traditional valley, with the ten thousand hills of Zululand all around as a tranquil setting.

Gardiner was given a hut and supplies of sugar cane and beer. Then Dingane summoned him, and he was told to sit a short distance from the fence surrounding the King's private quarters.

"After a little pause, the bust only of a very stout personage appeared above the fence, which I was soon informed was the despot himself. He eyed me for a considerable time with the utmost gravity, without uttering a word. At last, pointing to an ox that had been driven near, he said: 'There is the beast I give you to slaughter.' And on this important announcement he disappeared."

Later the potentate came out himself, "clad in a blue dungaree cloak relieved by a white border and devices at the back. The train swept the ground, and, although tarnished and worn, well became his height and portly figure." Seating himself on a chair, Dingane asked Gardiner who he was and why he had come. Gardiner tried to explain his religious venture, but had hard work of it. Dingane soon became bored. Where were his presents? Gardiner had to explain that they were in the wagon, back at the flooded Thukela. Dingane then made him describe each present in minutest detail. If he could have bitten into them to test their genuineness he would have done so. The meeting then ended.

For several days Gardiner loitered around the capital, being somewhat indifferently treated, for by overlooking his presents, he had distinctly undershot Dingane's hospitality. Occasionally the king spoke to him, examining a Bible and asking pertinent questions about God, where He lived, and how.

The usual entertainments of dancing and singing passed the hours at Mgungundlovu. The women were even more fantastically beaded than in olden times, and Dingane viewed their sleekness as a sign of the prosperity of his reign. "Are we not a merry people?" he asked Gardiner. "What black nations can vie with us? Who among them can dress as we do?"

The inevitable trials and smellings-out added interest and horror to Gardiner's visit. The army was also being fitted out for the next season of campaign, and Gardiner saw the regiments come for their new shields. The capital was the great shield manufactory, for more cattle were killed there than in all the rest of Zululand, and two shields were made from every hide.

The men of the capital were almost exclusively engaged upon this industry and vast stores of shields were accumulated. One after the other the regiments called to receive their set. They would wait outside until permission was granted for them to enter. Then they would rush in and seat themselves around the king. His military adviser, Dambuza, would then relate everything that was bad about the regiment, while they sat nervously listening. Their own colonel would then stand forth and rebut the charges, miming and gesticulating, while every now and then one of his men would run forth to *giya*. If the balance of evidence was in favour of the regiment, Dingane would grant them permission to select shields, and there would be a great rush to the storage huts, with much sorting out and thumping as the shields were tried.

Feeding these regiments was a major task. Most of Dingane's mornings were spent in selecting cattle for slaughter. The army was entitled to two main meals a day, with beer and meat in the evening. The meat was generally stewed in large earthern bowls, and was so tough that the sound of mass-mastication in the evening lingered over the capital like the sighing of the wind.

A final big dance in the evening would round off the day. Dingane, despite the fatness which had come to him through luxurious living, was a renowned dancer, and he invariably led the performers dressed up until he was a sight for sore eyes. In the moonlight and firelight he would sometimes be carried away by the excitement while every now and then one of his praisers would rush out to eulogise him, dressed like a lion or leopard, with the hollowed-out head over his own and his eyes glaring through the sockets.

After a month, Dingane at length gave his reply to Gardiner's request for a mission site. For the present it was a refusal, unless Gardiner would agree to teach the Zulus how to use the *isibamu* (musket). As Gardiner declined to teach them this, Dingane recommended him to expend his energies on the Natal tribes. Gardiner returned to Port Natal a bitterly disappointed man.

At the Port the ivory traders did their best to cheer him up. They had long felt that their rough-and-tumble community needed some sort of moral stiffening. Most of them were young men and, so far removed from civilisation, they had hitherto found it distressingly easy to forget their loneliness in the arms of Africa and strong drink. Perhaps they needed a missionary more than the Zulus!

Accordingly, on 14 March 1835, Gardiner received a letter signed by eight of the traders, asking him to commence missionary work at Port Natal. He was delighted. The following day he held his first service under the shade of two trees, before a congregation of thirteen of the ivory traders.

Then he searched around for a mission site. He selected a position on the northern end of the long hill overlooking the lagoon. This he named the Berea, after that place mentioned in the Acts of the Apostles, whose people had received the word more gladly than those of Thessalonica.

There Gardiner commenced his first school, in a tent, with six Zulu children as pupils. These he clothed in "a piece of printed calico, that they might appear decently dressed," and, while he built a house and church, looked around him at this settlement of Port Natal.

It was a wild and solitary place at that time. Of the ivory traders, Collis was the only one who lived in any style. He had a European-type residence made of reeds and mud. The rest lived in huts. There were about 30 Europeans and their 2500 African followers, living in widely scattered homes hidden in the bush, like a buccaneers' stronghold.

The Africans were the agriculturalists. The Europeans depended entirely on hunting and their trade, obtaining meat and hides, horns and tusks. They roamed about the country like wild men. In his travels Gardiner came across one of their typical encampments.

It was occupied by four Europeans, dressed in leather trousers, with torn woollen frocks, home-made bonnets and rough shoes with the toes sticking out. Their African servants and some coloureds from the Cape made up the rest of the party. They lounged around, watching a campfire dancing in the night; their camp strewn with muskets, powder horns, skins, fats, venison, dogs, carcasses and tusks; the Africans singing and the hunters yarning.

Gardiner took the settlement under his wing and tried to reform it. He soon found that he had responsibilities. Each year, when the Zulus started their winter military season, alarms reached Port Natal that the traders were to be the objects of attack. In time the traders had become used to these rumours. They were indifferent, saying they would simply take to the bush if things got tough, for they had so little to lose there was nothing worth defending.

This year, 1835, the rumours were particularly persistent. On 25 April the ivory traders held a meeting and asked Gardiner to visit Dingane, to arrange some sort of treaty which would give them greater security of existence. With a heavy load of presents Gardiner journeyed up to Zululand, while the traders speculated on the outcome.

Dingane, at the time, was staying at his kwaKhangela (place of the watcher) kraal some eight miles on the Empangeni road from present-day Eshowe. Gardiner travelled up to him; his wagon rolling along, following the tangle of paths through long, sweetly scented grass as high as his head. The missionary forded the Thukela, with the water lapping over the floor of the wagon, the goods meanwhile supported high on bundles of sticks and the oxen desperately floundering as they strained to keep their hooves on the bed of the river and their noses in the air.

Dingane, still clad in his favourite blue cloak, received Gardiner kindly, the more so as this time his visitor brought a vast

store of presents with him. Naval epaulettes, ladies' gilt brace-
lets, silk sword belts, coloured engravings, a telescope, and
other gew-gaws delighted the heart of the monarch.

Then they settled down to talk. Dingane was pleased at the
idea of a treaty. He had no fear of the ivory traders. They had
never been a threat. Accordingly, on 6 May 1835, he signed a
treaty with Gardiner. In it Dingane guaranteed the lives and
property of all individuals, white and black, in Natal. On their
part, the Europeans undertook to harbour no more refugees
from Zululand, for the ever-increasing numbers of Zulu deserters and runaways had long been a sore point with Dingane.

For Gardiner, Dingane had a special gift: the much desired
permission to establish a mission in Zululand. Everything
was dependent on the Europeans refusing to harbour any
refugees; and as a sign of good faith, Gardiner had to return
to Durban, secure a number of recent runaways, and return
them to Dingane.

New times seemed to have come. Gardiner returned jubi-
lantly to Port Natal and took four of the wanted men back to
Dingane himself, hoping to save their lives by a personal plea.
Dingane kindly obliged by sentencing them to be imprisoned
without food in a hut. Their necks were wrung as soon as the
missionary left, which was perhaps a kindness.

The mission site granted by Dingane was between the Matigulu and Thukela rivers, in the area garrisoned by the Hlo-
mendlini regiment. On his way back to Durban, Gardiner inspected the area and selected as site a hill of moderate height
skirted by the Msunduze stream. He named the site Khulula
(to set free) and arranged to have some huts built for accommodation.

On the strength of their new security the ivory traders, on
Tuesday, 23 June 1835, held a meeting to lay out a proper town.
It was a motley company of ragamuffins who gathered there.
After agreeing on the desirability of a town, they all poured
happily out to inspect the ground.

Gardiner was in their midst, striding along impatiently with the others, "some walking, others seated on the floor of a wagon without either tilt or sides, which was drawn at a stately pace by ten oxen. Short pipes, an indispensable accompaniment, were in full action on all sides. Being the winter season, it was a sort of reunion of hunters, who, tired of chasing sea-cow and buffalo, were now sighing for townhouses and domestic cheer. The appearance of any of these forest rangers would have gained the medal for any artist who could have transfigured his *tout ensemble* upon canvas.

"At length a pause was made. 'This'll do,' cried one – 'That's the spot,' exclaimed another. After some minutes of such-like random conversation, the whole party compactly collected, and the business at length entered upon and conducted in a rational manner, every proposition being subjected to the votes of those who were present, and carried or negatived accordingly.

"It was in this impromptu manner that the town of D'Urban was named – its situation fixed – the township and church lands appropriated – and, in short, as much real business gone through as would have required at least a fortnight's hard writing and debating in any other quarter of the globe."

The ivory traders certainly had big ideas. Each of the traders was entitled to a building lot in the projected town and each man undertook to erect a proper house (no African huts allowed) within 18 months. A town committee was to be appointed each year on 1 July, and a first committee was elected, consisting of Captain Allen Gardiner, F. Berkin (who had travelled up with Gardiner), J. Cane and H. Ogle.

Three thousand acres were set aside as an endowment for a Church of England clergyman. More land was allocated for a school and hospital, and a town fund was formed to clear the bush, the inhabitants contributing either cash or their voluntary labours.

The infant colony was named Victoria in honour of the then princess, and a petition was drawn up to the Governor of the

Cape, Sir Benjamin D'Urban, soliciting the protection of the British flag. Besides Gardiner and the elected Town Committee, the responsible ivory traders who signed the petition were C. Pickman, F. Kew, J. Francis, J. Mouncy, G. Cyrus, C. Adams, R. Wood, T. Carden, R. Fourcraft, G. Duffeys, J. Wynkaardt, T. Holstead, J. Pierce, R. King, D.C. Toohey, R. Biggar, C. Blanckenberg, J. Stubbs, R. Russell, G. White, M. Michau, C. Ferris, J. Jones and J. Snelder. At that time there were about forty Europeans living in Natal. Three thousand Africans and a few hundred Bushmen formed the rest of the population.

Everybody was very optimistic. Then three days later, Thomas Holstead returned from a trip to Zululand with the shattering news that Dingane had banned all trade and stated that only Gardiner was to be allowed across the Thukela in future.

Gardiner immediately rode off to find out what had happened. Dingane, now back in Mgungundlovu, was as friendly as ever to him. He complained bitterly that Holstead and another trader named John Snelder had themselves broken the agreement by misconducting themselves. They had persuaded some young Zulu girls to run away with them, as well as used the king's name to induce people to trade.

Speaking in the royal hut, a mammoth affair with a roof supported by three parallel rows of posts, Dingane told Gardiner that he expected him to stop such abuses. When the missionary expostulated that he had no power, Dingane replied, "You must have power. I give you all the country called siBubulungu. You must be chief over all the people there."

They went into details about the matter. It seemed logical to Dingane that, as he had recognised the virtual tributary independence of the whole area from the Thukela to the Mzimkhulu and from the sea to the Drakensberg, there should be a supreme chief over the place. He appointed Gardiner to the post forthwith, and informed him that in future he would allow no European into Zululand from Natal unless he had a permit from Gardiner, or any other individual placed in authority by the British Government.

Gardiner accepted the offer but he was awkwardly placed. He knew well that the traders were too rugged a crowd to accept a missionary as their government. Accordingly, he returned to Durban (as the place name was written) and without delay set off down the south coast, in order to visit the Cape Governor and ask him to take over Natal.

At the Mzimvubu the interminable tribal wars turned Gardiner back to Durban, hoping to find some ship there, but the little sloop *Circe*, which normally supplied the lagoon, had vanished with all hands, including Berkin, and was seen no more.

Gardiner then prepared to travel inland, cross the Drakensberg, and journey to the Cape by a detour round the troubled areas. With two wagons driven by Dick King and Henry Ogle, assisted by G. Cyrus and J. Wynkaardt, he left Durban on 24 September. A few hours after they left, J. Collis, his infant child and two servants were all killed when 1500 pounds of powder kept in a magazine accidentally exploded.

Gardiner's party followed a tangle of footpaths and the wagon tracks of the recent Cape Farmers' Commission, as straight due west as they could. It was a tedious journey, with the wagons constantly slipping and sticking; but the scenery enthralled them. Game was plentiful, especially eland, hartebeest and other antelope. Lions were also seen.

With the Drakensberg steadily looming nearer, they forded the middle Mkhomazi at the Mdumezulu kraal of the Ntlangwini tribe. From there they moved up towards the mountains, making towards the peak now known as Hodgson's Peak, but then named by Gardiner the Giant's Cup.

They made a laborious exploration of the mountain valleys, hoping to find some practical pass, but without success. Then they moved down the face of the mountains, hoping to find a break. In this way, on 17 October, while tortuously circumventing a precipice, Gardiner was "at one time, quite startled at the appearance of a rugged mountain which I have named the *Giant's Castle*. As seen over an intervening hill its resemblance to Edinburgh Castle, from one or two points, was so striking that, for the moment, I could almost fancy myself transported to Princes Street." This was the mountain now known as Garden Castle.

On all this portion of their journey they saw no human beings at all. Like Robinson Crusoe, they found some tantalising traces of man – a broken hoe, and footprints in the sandy bank of a stream of two persons accompanied by a dog.

Hartebeest, eland and wildebeest were numerous: but there was no sign of a pass. Day after day they searched. Once they stumbled upon a fine cave, with a well-trodden path leading to it. It consisted of a huge slab of rock jutting out, with the inside partitioned off by tree trunks into four separate rooms. Old fireplaces were apparent and remnants of mats, cooking bowls, and broken armlets. Traces of horses seemed to indicate the cave's use as a hunters' resort, but by whom was uncertain.

At this place, named Cavernglen, on 23 October, Gardiner finally abandoned his search for a mountain pass; and the wagons jolted their way down to the Pondoland coast, leaving the unrelenting Drakensberg to vanish into the blueness of distance. Fortunately the travellers discovered that the recent tribal disturbance had ended and the road was open again to the Cape.

At Port Elizabeth, on 3 December 1835, Gardiner met Sir Benjamin D'Urban and told him of all the developments in Natal. The Governor was sympathetic – perhaps the naming of the new town in his honour pleased him – and on 5 December he wrote the first official letter to Dingane, welcoming good relations and promising to send a representative soon to be in authority over Natal.

Also in Port Elizabeth were three American missionaries, sent out by the American Board of Commissioners for Foreign Missions to establish a mission in Zululand. They were Newton Adams, Aldin Grout, and George Champion and they were preparing to sail to Durban in the *Dove* to visit Dingane.

Gardiner gave them much friendly advice, and when they sailed D'Urban's letter to Dingane was taken on the same ship by the merchant Benjamin Norden, then on his first visit to the Zulus. Gardiner, meanwhile, rode on at breakneck speed to Cape Town, covering some 80 miles a day on horseback, and sailed to England on 19 December in order to induce the British Government to take over Natal and to obtain support for his Zululand mission.

The American missionaries reached Durban on 21 December 1835, and promptly proceeded to read the ivory traders a Christmas lecture on morals. If they must marry Africans, then must they marry so many? The traders sheepishly excused themselves by saying that they were regarded as being chiefs, and chiefs had to have many wives.

The missionaries went on to Dingane. As usual he was pleasant to them, although he was somewhat engrossed in the annual ceremony of the first fruits and had little time for visitors. Nevertheless, Gardiner's letter pleased him, but he recommended the Americans to establish their mission in Natal. This they agreed to do and, while Grout and Adams returned to Port Elizabeth to collect their families, Champion selected a mission site on the lower Mlazi River and on 7 March 1836 commenced work there in a school under a shady tree, with a sandy floor convenient for use as a blackboard.

Dingane, at that time, was busy preparing for the new military season. No great foreign raid had been planned for 1836. The services of the army were needed at home, for in the wild country around the Biggarsberg (known simply, like the Drakensberg, as uNdi [the heights] to the Africans) the four tribes of cannibals who lived there were getting troublesome.

The Zulus had always controlled these cannibals through the medium of Jobe, chief of the satellite Sithole tribe. This Jobe acted as a sort of warden of the Zulu western approaches, and for years he had wielded a big stick on the backs of the cannibals.

Of late, however, the man-eaters had become more truculent. Supported by packs of vicious dogs, they were hunting down and eating many of Jobe's followers. As a result, the Zulu army was that year to teach them a salutary lesson. The whole country around the Biggarsberg was thoroughly ransacked and every human being, cannibal or otherwise, was wiped out. From thence on Jobe was left untroubled. Vast herds of cattle were sent into the area by Dingane and the Sithole tribe acted as herdsmen. Jobe had his principal kraal in the rugged country of the valley known as Nhlanyanga (the dwelling place of the doctor), dominated by the 5200-foot-high bulk of iLenge (Job's Kop).

The return of his army, with its mission accomplished, put Dingane in a good mood. To complete the military season he planned a short campaign against some Swazis who had raided his cattle. The ivory traders were summoned to supply a rifle contingent for this campaign, and 30 of them, led by John Cane, rode up to the Phongolo River to aid the Zulus who were commanded by Ndlela.

On the return of this expedition the army was feasted and disbanded for the year. Everything seemed to be peaceful and under firm Zulu control. Accordingly, in July 1836, when the American missionaries revisited him, Dingane gave them the much sought permission to establish missions in Zululand. As a result one mission named Nginani (I am with you) was established in the area Gardiner had selected for his Khulula station. At this place, on 26 September 1836, George Champion settled and commenced work as the first resident missionary among the Zulus.

A second mission was established on the left bank of the Mhlathuze River in July 1837. This station was named Themba (trust), and was occupied by Henry Venable and Alexander Wilson, who had come to Zululand after an unsuccessful effort at starting work among the Matebele in the Transvaal.

Apart from these American missionaries, there were a few other Europeans resident in Zululand. Deserters from British army elements garrisoning the Cape accomplished prodigious journeys into the interior in those days. On 23 December 1836, for instance, two of these wanderers arrived at Champion's mission after walking for 23 days across the Drakensberg from Thaba Ntsho in the Orange Free State. In May 1837 two more of these wanderers arrived at Mgungundlovu and were hospitably received by Dingane. They had also crossed the Drakensberg, following the footpaths first blazed by migrating game and then by the Bantu.

Most of these wanderers settled with the Zulus and turned native, although some took service with the missionaries. Dingane used them in an effort to teach his soldiers something about Europeans' weapons and to supervise shopping expeditions sent to Lourenço Marques to buy guns. Richard Lovedale, Robert Joyce and J. Clark were three of these odd characters, but the names of the others are lost, like themselves, in the silence of the ages.

On 24 May 1837, Gardiner returned to Durban. He had had a disappointing time in Britain. During his long absence he had struggled to persuade Britain to accept Dingane's present of Natal, but the high authorities considered it would yield them no profit, only trouble. Gardiner, accordingly, returned with only the meagre status of a JP [Justice of the Peace] over the British residents.

In the religious field he had been more successful. The Church Missionary Society had agreed to establish a Zululand mission and the Reverend Francis Owen was appointed to the task. Gardiner planned to settle personally at his Berea station in Durban and he brought with him his second wife and children. He found the ivory traders in their usual chaotic condition.

The always precarious relations between Dingane and the ivory traders had taken a sharp turn for the worse. A fresh flood of refugees from Zululand, the result of Dingane liquidating a few offending tribal elements, had sought sanctuary under the traders, and their disinclination to return them according to treaty had irked Dingane. The usual mustering of the Zulu army for the new campaigning season had also thrown the Europeans into their annual state of doubt as to who was to be the target for the attack.

Dingane had attempted to pacify matters by swearing his peaceful intentions and packing his rowdy army off on a long raid across the Transvaal, into the rich herds of the Matebele. Gardiner's presence also eased the tension, but the frustration of his hopes of government intervention had left him without real influence in the affairs of this uproarious part of the world.

He did attempt to establish his scanty magisterial authority. On 1 June 1837 he called a meeting and disclosed his appointment as a JP and would-be ruler of Natal. The ivory traders shouted him down. Led by a truculent character named Alexander Biggar, they would have none of Gardiner. His opinions of their moral status, freely expressed in England before the House of Commons Select Committee on Aborigines, had somehow got back to them, and after their kindness to him in the past they considered this as being rather churlish. Many trading quarrels they had with Dingane were also considered to be due to his lingering influence.

Gardiner gave them up in disgust. He packed his bags, abandoned the Berea, and removed to an idyllic site on a hillock about one mile from the mouth of the Thongathi River. There he established a new mission which he named Hambanathi (go with us) and thenceforth left politics to others.

For some time the ivory traders expended their tempers in letters to the Cape newspapers and in petitions that Natal be taken under proper British control. In the midst of the uproar the Reverend Francis Owen arrived in Durban in August 1837. After a few weeks there he went up to Zululand with Gardiner, who introduced him to Dingane. A site at Mgungundlovu was granted to him for his mission and there he settled with his wife, daughter, and a few servants and interpreters, making a curious little outpost of civilisation in so savage a place.

The Americans were also expanding. Reinforcements to their number had come and with their arrival the Americans opened one new mission in Natal under the Reverend Daniel Lindley, at a site named Mfume (the damp place), on the headwaters of the river known as the Mngababa.

In such manner, then, did new times steal upon the ivory traders of old Port Natal, as unobtrusively as early dawn came each morning to the waters of the great lagoon. Like the stage of a theatre, the beautiful land of Natal had been arranged by the stage manager – Destiny – into a certain order; and its human characters, with their conflicting emotions and hopes, were drawn up in full array, ready to play their parts in the next act ... of tragedy.

Allen Gardiner

NINE
The Voortrekkers

It was in September 1837, when the Zulu army returned from its raid against the Matebele, that Dingane received his first positive information about the activities and prowess of the Voortrekkers, the Dutch pioneers of the interior. Before that, rumours had reached him and the American missionaries had told him something of the defeat inflicted by the trekkers upon the Matebele. It took his own army, however, to give him all the details for, along with vast loot in cattle, they brought some prisoners and Matebele renegades who told Dingane of the murderous effect the massed firearms of the trekkers had upon warriors armed only with spears.

Almost simultaneously with the return of his army, there came an urgent message from Jobe, the guardian of the royal herds in the west. The message told Dingane that a few days previously when Kentethe, a grandson of Jobe, was out supervising the herd-boys, a force of strange men, mounted on horses and carrying guns, had swept down from the Drakensberg and commenced rounding up cattle.

Kentethe objected and was shot dead for his pains. The herd-boys had run to Sandlovu, father of Kentethe, to report. They said the raiders had constantly shouted that they were *maBhunu* (Boers). Sandlovu had promptly followed the tracks of the raiders back up the passes of the Drakensberg. There, on the heights, he learnt that the strangers were not Boers but followers of the well-known Tlokwa chief, Sigonyela, trying to cloak their rustling activities under somebody else's name.

Such was the news sent to Dingane, and a few days later came another panting runner. The dust of horsemen had been seen on top of the Drakensberg and rumours had whispered across the veld of a vast concourse of people travelling towards the mountain passes. Jobe immediately ordered the herdsmen to disperse their livestock into the vastness of the Nhlanyanga valley, as a precautionary measure. He then retired to watch proceedings from his kraal on the overlooking mountain known as iLenge (the precipitous one), or Job's Kop. At Mgungundlovu Dingane pondered on the news and, while his army rested from its arduous raid, he awaited developments. They soon came.

Great events had been taking place on the central plains. The mass exodus of farmers from the Cape had been going on for months. On the Vet River in the Orange Free State, over a thousand wagons had congregated, and the leaders spent bitter weeks arguing the toss about where they should go. Some wanted the Transvaal; others, with Piet Retief at their head, wanted Natal.

The Transvaal was further from the British, but it had no port and fever was bad. Of Natal everybody had heard. Every visitor to the place had praised it to the heavens as a land of perpetual summer, where three harvests could be reaped a year and the rivers were always flowing.

The disadvantages of Natal to the trekkers were: the crossing of the Drakensberg, for the commission trek had, like Gardiner, seen only the forbidding southern section and reported it as uncrossable; the presence of British at Port Natal; and the attitude of the Zulus.

In the midst of the argument, with tempers so high that challenges to duels were common, Retief effectively settled the first problem by sending five men on 4 July to explore the Drakensberg. They came back laughing 24 days later. The Drakensberg they had seen was child's play. They had found no fewer than five places where wagons could cross simply by following the tracks of the seasonal migrations of game.

Still, the majority of the trekkers were dubious of Natal. What of the British and the Zulus? Eventually only 54 of the thousand wagons followed Piet Retief to the edge of the Drakensberg. On 7 October 1837 they reached the vast, flat-topped and curiously stately mountain which they named the Kerkenberg (church mountain). There they were rallied and drawn up in formation by their laager commandant, Abraham Greyling, while Retief with fourteen men and four wagons went on ahead to reconnoitre Natal.

On 7 October Retief arrived at the very edge of the Drakensberg and for the first time saw the fair land of Natal spread out below him, like a relief map of infinite detail and exquisite colour. "From the heights of these mountains I saw this beautiful land, the most beautiful I've ever seen in Africa," he wrote, and for some hours he and his men gazed spellbound at the sight: the green fertility; the glistening rivers; and the purple wall of the high Drakensberg stretched out on their right. They named the place on which they stood Blijde Vooruitzicht (the joyful prospect).

From this place an easy pass led down to Natal. The pass, thenceforth, was known by a variety of names: Oudeberg (old mountain) or Step Pass; but properly it was The Pass of Pieter Retief, and down it the fourteen men went.

It was a tough, 90-hour journey to drag the four wagons from the mountains to Port Natal, but the trekkers were well rewarded when they reached the place. The Englishmen welcomed them with pleasure. Flattering addresses were exchanged and the hours were pleasantly spent in yarning and hunting hippos in the lagoon.

Retief was serenely happy. The second objection of the trekkers to Natal – the attitude of the British ivory traders – was dispelled by their friendliness. The political implications of the arrival of the trekkers was a matter of some dispute among the traders. All welcomed the arrival of more Europeans to Natal, for it would naturally strengthen their own security; but the idea of becoming subjects of a sort of farmers' republic, which would be not only independent but foreign to their own country, was naturally not easily acceptable.

Retief was unstintingly supplied with all information regarding the Zulus and the settlement. He thus learnt that Natal had already been given to the Europeans on several occasions and all that was really needful was for him to pay the customary courtesy call on Dingane and secure his formal permission to settle.

Retief, therefore, sent a letter to Dingane on 19 October 1837, expressing peace and friendship and telling him that he would be coming up to Mgungundlovu to discuss the question of land.

Owen translated this letter to Dingane and told him what little he knew of the matter. Gardiner had sent him a private letter informing him of Piet Retief's arrival in Durban after the arduous trek across the Drakensberg, and that Retief and his fourteen companions formed a commission, sent in advance of a larger party which had remained on the central plains waiting for them to explore the country and, if possible, secure possession of it. They planned to settle there and establish a government of their own. On this project the ivory traders were of divided opinion. Some welcomed it, others were strongly against it and all were for calling on the British Government to recognise their settlement as a proper colony.

Dingane considered the matter carefully. Then on 31 October he dictated a reply. The contents astounded Owen.

"The purport of this letter," the missionary noted in his diary, "does credit either to Dingane's honesty or to his policy or to both. It was to say that some sheep which had been captured from Mzilikazi (in number 110) belonged to the Dutch, and that he was anxious to return them to their proper masters; that hundreds had died on the road and many more had died since their arrival here, the skins of which he sent."

Three days later Dingane dictated a letter to Gardiner, asking him to come and advise him respecting the territory to be assigned to the Dutch. "He said," noted Owen, "that they were desirous of settling in the country which he had already given to Captain Gardiner, and he did not wish to displease him by asking him to relinquish it, but he had rather that they go and settle in the country near that from whence Mzilikazi had lately been driven."

From Durban, meanwhile, Retief sent two of his men back to the main trek party with samples of the fruits of Natal and a letter. In it he told his followers waiting on top of the Drakensberg that everything was fine and they could come down. Most of the ivory traders had welcomed him heartily and had made it clear that Natal was already theirs by cession from Dingane. They welcomed him as a neighbour and potential customer. The only need he had of visiting Dingane was the customary courtesy call.

Retief, accordingly, rode up to see Dingane. Seven of his men were left at the Thukela while he, with Thomas Holstead as interpreter and five other trekkers, went on to Mgungundlovu. Dingane welcomed them on 5 November with customary hospitality. Like Shaka, he sought to impress the newcomers with his power and the glory of the Zulu nation.

William Wood, interpreter to Owen, has described Mgungundlovu as it was then:

"The form of Dingane's kraal was a circle, it was strongly fenced with bushes and had two entrances. The principal one faced the king's huts, which were placed at the furthest extremity of the kraal, behind which were his wives' huts. These extended beyond the circle which formed the kraal, but were also strongly fenced in. On the right-hand side of the principal entrance were placed the huts of Ndlela (Dingane's captain) and his warriors; and on the left, those of Dambuza (another of his captains) with his men.

"The kraal contained four cattle kraals which were also strongly fenced and four huts erected on poles which contained the arms of the troops. At a short distance from the entrance was the trunk of a large tree which was in a state of decay, and which no person was allowed to touch, being the tree under which Dingane's father died, and which he valued very highly. Near this tree grew two other trees, which are called by the Zulus, milk trees. The other entrance was from that part of the kraal behind Dingane's wives' huts; and this was considered private."

The principal feature near the kraal was the hill of execution, a barren and befouled eminence, covered with loose stones and stunted shrubs and the resort of a horde of fat-gutted vultures and filthy hyenas. It was littered with human bones and each path passing in the vicinity had piles of luck stones (*isivivane*), deposited there by superstitious passers-by. This execution hill was generally named kwaMatiwane, for the chief of that name had recently been executed there and he was the best known of all unfortunates to have come to grief upon that evil spot.

Behind the execution hill was a height known as the Hloma maButho (mustering place of the conscripts), where the army was always marshalled. The huts occupied by Owen and his mission stood outside the capital, on their own and facing the execution hill. On the other side of the capital stood one giant euphorbia tree, looking out tranquilly over the teeming activity of the kraal. Beneath this tree Dingane was wont to sit at ease and consider policy with his courtiers. There he would judge his subjects and, in the comfort and coolness of the shadows, pass sentence of life or death.

The Voortrekkers found Dingane to be a robust, fat man, but well proportioned and with the regular features of a well-bred Zulu. There was nothing at all forbidding in his appearance. He was always smiling and was scrupulously clean, being well scrubbed every morning by some of his women in the royal bath, a depression in the ground near his hut.

He was shaved every day as well. He hated hair on his head, and one of his women kept him as bald and clean-shaven as a newborn babe, by means of an exceedingly sharp axe. After this toilet, and being well rubbed with fat, he generally spent his day sitting in an armchair attending to business, drinking beer and playing with any gew-gaws some European visitor might have given him, such as a telescope to watch his people around the kraal, or a magnifying glass to burn holes in the arms of his servants.

In the afternoon he took a nap. Then, when it got dark, he retired into his hut, where his women assembled to amuse him with songs and conversation. Servants held up thin strips of lighted wood, replacing one after another from a bundle as they burnt out. About 9 p.m. the king retired to rest, lying on his mat in Zulu fashion, with a blanket to cover him and his head pillowed on the conventional wooden rest. Usually a woman kept him company, for, like Shaka, he had a large harem of the most attractive girls in Zululand, although he married none of them and any offspring were strangled at birth as a safeguard against their ever forcibly displacing him from the throne.

Retief was well pleased at Dingane's manner. "Dingane received me with much kindness," he wrote to the Grahamstown *Journal*, and indeed the travel-weary man was almost overwhelmed by what he saw. Dances and feastings and sham fights passed the time. On the first day 2000 of the young warriors danced. On the second day 4000 of the elders performed.

"In one dance," wrote Retief, "the people were intermingled with 176 oxen, all without horns and of one colour. They have long strips of skin hanging pendant from their foreheads, cheeks, shoulders, and under the throat, which are cut from the hides of calves.

"These oxen are divided in twos and threes among the whole army, which then dances in companies, each with its attendant oxen. In this way they all in turns approach the king, the oxen turning off into a kraal, and the warriors moving in a line from the king. It is surprising that the oxen should be so well trained; for notwithstanding all the shouting and yelling which accompany this dance, they never move faster than a slow walking pace."

Dingane's smallest herd consisted of 2424 oxen, all red in colour with white backs. His palace was the last word in huts, for it was 20 feet in diameter, supported by 22 pillars inside, each entirely covered in beads, and with a floor as smooth and polished as a mirror.

In this environment the trekkers talked land with Dingane, while Owen or Holstead acted as interpreters. Dingane told Retief of the recent cattle raid by mounted men shouting that they were Boers. Retief denied all blame. "It can be no other than Sigonyela who has done this," he said. "He is the only kaffir who has horses, and some of his people are clothed as we are."

Dingane shrugged. "If it was Sigonyela and you are innocent, you must first prove this. I will make the herdsmen accompany you and also one of my generals. Go back to your people; give my herdsmen a free opportunity to seek amongst the cattle of your people. If none of my cattle are there, then go and show my herdsmen where their cattle are, and get them back for me."

So far as land was concerned, Dingane would discuss the matter when the cattle were returned. If the Boers were innocent of the theft he would grant them land. Owen remonstrated at this. In front of the Boers he taxed Dingane with his prior grant of the land of Natal to Gardiner. Dingane replied that he would discuss the matter further when he recovered his cattle.

At the mission huts Owen also discussed the matter with Retief. He stressed the prior grant of the territory. Retief acknowledged this but avoided the issue. He said that he would recover the cattle in order to clear the good name of the trekkers. Then he and his people might settle further north. With that the trekkers rode away.

A few days later, on 9 November, a letter came to Dingane from Gardiner. In it the missionary remonstrated over the king's promise to give the same land to the Boers as he had already given to Britain. He advised Dingane not to give the land until he had heard from the British Government.

Once again Dingane shrugged at this. He had never said he would give the land about Durban to the Dutch, he told Owen. He meant them to occupy Mzilikazi's old lands which the Zulus had just conquered.

Owen couldn't quite see daylight in the matter. He struggled on with his mission, endeavouring to get the Zulus to understand the complex ideas of sin and salvation, while they in turn thought him to be mad. The weeks passed.

The two messengers sent from Durban by Retief, Coenraad and Piet Meyer, had meanwhile ridden back up the Drakensberg carrying with them the samples of the fruits of Natal. The trekkers' camp on top of the mountains practically exploded with happiness when these messengers reached them on 11 November. The people danced and sang and talked excitedly around their fires all that night, while the rock face of old Kerkenberg looked down upon them in surprise.

The next day was Sunday, and the 57th birthday of Pieter Retief. It was a day of thanksgiving, and Retief's 22-year-old daughter, Deborah, wrote her father's name upon a rock with green paint: a little memorial which still survives, surrounded by a number of more recent names.

The next day the trekkers broke up their camp and removed to the edge of the mountains. On Tuesday, the 14th, the descent of the Drakensberg started.

"In the morning," wrote Erasmus Smit, the schoolteacher, in his diary, "we inspanned twenty-three wagons to descend the high Drakensberg. After much difficulty, using brake chains on the wheels, we came with eighteen wagons at sunset to the bottom. Only one wagon, that of our friend W. Prinsloo, overturned at the beginning of the very difficult descent. A set of chairs was broken but nothing else."

The next day six wagons descended, on Thursday thirteen, on Friday thirteen, and on Saturday sixteen more came bumping down the successive terraces which make up the pass. By Sunday 66 wagons were gathered at the bottom of the Drakensberg. Only two had overturned during the descent and the *disselboom* had broken on a third. The scouts who had discovered the pass, and Abraham Greyling who had been in charge of road-making, had all done their work well.

News of the favourable events in Natal was carried with all haste to the bulk of the trekkers, still on the central plains. Wagon after wagon was hastily inspanned and the *voorlopers* headed the oxen towards Natal. Uys and his followers also descended the Drakensberg by Retief's Pass; but the rest of the trekker parties used other passes.

Maritz and Potgieter led their followers down the two easiest of all the mountain passes; the one then named Potgieter's Trek Road but now known as De Beer's Pass from H.S. de Beer who had a farm in later years at its foot; and the other then named the Quagga Pad, from the quaggas who used it in their annual migrations, but now known as the Bramhoek Pass. Other parties used what is now known as Middledale Pass, which descends the Drakensberg down the slopes of the bulky, flat-topped mountain named Thintwanyoni (the toucher of the birds). Still others used the pass now known as Bezuidenhout's Pass, after Daniel Bezuidenhout who farmed at the foot of the road in later years.

It was a colourful, animated spectacle, all those people descending the Drakensberg. Everybody enjoyed the adventure of the journey into their new homeland. The women and children walked and helped to drive the livestock, and good humour was the order of the day. They laughed at one another when they slipped, and shouted admonishments and advice. Pretty girls were suitably helpless and the young men were gallant.

On 27 November Retief rejoined the trekkers at the foot of the Drakensberg and reported the result of his visit to the Zulu king and the necessity of an expedition against Sigonyela. Retief remained resting at the camp until 24 December, while reinforcements poured down the Drakensberg. Then, with a strong party, he rode back up his pass to settle the matter of Sigonyela.

The Tlokwa chief did not prove very difficult. The trekkers knew him well, having negotiated right of transit for themselves from him on their journey across the central plains. Pretending to have to see him again, they returned to his lands and met him in the garden of the missionary there, the Reverend Mr Allison. Daniel Bezuidenhout walked up to the chief and produced a pair of handcuffs. He offered to show the chief how to wear these new ornaments – and Sigonyela found himself a prisoner.

The trekkers questioned their captive. He admitted having stolen 300 head of cattle from the Zulus. The trekkers forced him to surrender 700 head of cattle, 63 horses and 11 guns as restitution and punishment. Then they let him go and rode back to the wagons at the foot of the Drakensberg.

From the camp, towards the end of January 1838, Retief and 69 of his adult followers, with some youths and 30 servants driving Dingane's cattle, set out for Mgungundlovu. In Natal, Gert Maritz was left in charge as acting leader. Completely confident, the trekkers were dispersed over a wide expanse of country, with the men riding about tentatively selecting farms for themselves.

The main body of Retief's followers, under Abraham Greyling, had their 78 wagons in an open formation at a place they had named Doornkop (thorny summit). Another hundred wagons under J. du Plessis were scattered closer to the Drakensberg and Hendrik Potgieter also had his followers there.

Near the site of the present town of Estcourt, Maritz had his laager, while Sarel Cilliers, with five families, was close to the banks of the river they had named the Boesmansrivier (the Mtshezi). Many other small family groups were scattered along the banks of the river the Africans knew as the Msuluzi (the disappearing one), but which the trekkers had named the Bloukrans, from the bluish colour of its cliffs.

At Mgungundlovu, meanwhile, a letter had arrived from Retief on 2 January 1838. It informed Dingane that on December 24th, the day on which the letter had been written, the trekkers were leaving to recapture his cattle. It also told Dingane that the trekkers had defeated Mzilikazi with heavy loss to him but none to themselves.

Of this battle Dingane had already been well informed by his spies. He often discussed the matter with Owen.

"It is not without apprehension and a lively interest that we trace the course of the Dutch," wrote the missionary, "and wonder how it will terminate, especially in what way the Zulus themselves, if they are not extremely cautious of offending or giving just provocation to this powerful body, may be affected by them."

Dingane was still perplexed and, as usual at such a time, he was receiving a barrage of conflicting advice from all manner of people. On 13 January, John Cane sent him a letter, advising him to draw a line from the iLovu to the Thukela and about 20 miles from the sea. The trekkers could live on one side and the British on the other.

On 22 January came a second letter from Retief. Sigonyela had been easily captured. He had admitted stealing 300 head of cattle from the Zulus. He had given up 700 head, 63 horses and 11 guns to the trekkers as restitution and punishment for having impersonated them.

Retief promised to bring Dingane's cattle with him, the rest had been distributed among the trekkers. Dingane slept on the matter. The next day he dictated a letter requesting the horses and guns as well.

Dingane spent hours discussing developments with his courtiers. Each day spies brought him news and he was well aware that even before Retief had returned to the Drakensberg, his followers, cheered by the messengers from Durban, had poured down the mountains and ridden over the country selecting farms.

153

Now, Dingane was a man possessing all the attributes of the savage just emerging from the darkness of his own nature and balancing between the extremes of ferocity and reason. His whims were capricious, his dislikes violent, his reactions always definite.

He was frightened of the trekkers. They were a tough crowd; of their prowess he knew, and the descent of the Drakensberg showed him that they cared but little for his consent. Accordingly he made his plans.

On 3 February 1838, Retief and his men, driving Dingane's cattle, arrived at Mgungundlovu. It was a great day. Dingane had mustered his army for the occasion and the trekkers put on a big show, staging a sham fight and firing their guns into the air. Dingane sat huddled in his armchair and watched their magnificent horsemanship and the deadliness of their fire.

The next day was Sunday. The Zulus sang and danced all day. The trekkers attended church service and then Retief and Dingane settled down to discussion. At the end the following cession was written down.

"Umgungundlovu,

4th Feb. 1838.

Know all men by this – That whereas Pieter Retief, Governor of the Dutch emigrant South Africans, has retaken my cattle, which Sigonyela had stolen; which cattle he, the said Retief, now delivers unto me. I, Dingane, King of the Zulus, do hereby certify and declare that I thought fit to resign unto him, the said Retief, and his countrymen (as reward of the case hereabove mentioned) the place called Port Natal, together with all the land annexed, that is to say, from Thukela to the Mzimvubu river westward, and from the sea to the north, as far as the land may be useful and in my possession. Which I did by this, and given unto them for their everlasting property.

Signed,

The Mark of Dingane."

Witnessed by three Zulus and three Boers.

That night the trekkers yarned and laughed around their fires, dreaming of the farms they soon would have. At dawn festivities started afresh with a farewell entertainment of beer drinking, dancing and singing. In the midst of it Dingane sat in his armchair and chatted idly to the trekkers around him.

On the hill nearby Owen listened to the noise. Something in the air disturbed him and his people. William Wood, his young interpreter, even tried to warn the trekkers, but they laughed at him.

In his dairy Owen tells the story of that day:

"A dreadful day in the annals of the mission! My pen shudders to give an account of it. This morning as I was sitting in the shade of my wagon reading the testament, the usual messenger came with hurry and anxiety depicted in his looks. I was sure he was about to pronounce something serious, and what was his commission! Whilst it showed consideration and kindness in the Zulu monarch towards me, it disclosed a horrid instance of perfidy – too horrid to be described – towards the unhappy men who have for these three days been his guests, but are now no more. He sent to tell me not to be frightened as he was going to kill the Boers."

Owen gathered his people and they prayed and wept. "Dingane's conduct was worthy of a savage as he is," wrote Owen. "It was base and treacherous to say the least of it – the offspring of cowardice and fear. Suspicious of his warlike neighbours, jealous of their power, dreading the neighbourhood of their arms, he felt as every savage would have done in like circumstances that these men were his enemies and being unable to attack them openly, he massacred them clandestinely."

The massacre itself was soon over. Dingane started from his armchair suddenly and screamed out: "Seize them!" There was an overwhelming rush. Thomas Holstead, the trekkers' interpreter, cried out, "We are done for," and added in the Zulu language: "Let me speak to the king!"

Dingane heard him but waved him away with his hand. Holstead then drew his knife. With it he ripped open one

Zulu's stomach and cut another's throat. Then he went down under a mass of warriors. One or two of the trekkers also cut up a few Zulus, but, with their guns stacked outside the kraal, there was nothing really which they could do.

Owen and William Wood, his interpreter, watched the tragedy from the mission. "The farmers," wrote Wood, "were dragged, with their feet trailing along the ground, each man being held by as many Zulus as could get to him, from the presence of Dingane, who still continued sitting and calling out *'Bulala amaTagati'* ('kill the wizards').

"He then said: 'Take the heart and liver of the king of the farmers, and place them in the road of the farmers.' When they dragged them to the hill of execution, they commenced the work of death by striking them on the head with knobbed sticks; Retief being held and forced to witness the deaths of his comrades before they despatched him. It was a most awful occurrence, and will never be effaced from my memory."

Then Dingane and his officers discussed plans for a few hours, while the army was mustered. With the shadows of afternoon the Zulu army left; like an assassin's dagger, slipping stealthily up through the bush of the great Thukela Valley, heading for the dispersed wagons of the trekkers in the land of Natal.

For them there was no premonition of danger. One rumour only reached the Voortrekkers that something was wrong. A lone African voice shouted from a hilltop, telling them that Retief had been massacred, but nobody took any notice.

The trekkers went to bed on the night of 16 February in untroubled contentment. Daniel Bezuidenhout has recorded the wild adventure which followed.

"It was about 1 o'clock in the night, and there was no moonlight. Our camp stood on a rough hillock, near thorn trees. We had three or four bold savage dogs that would tear a leopard to pieces without difficulty. I heard the dogs bark and fight, and thought that there was a leopard.

"I got up, having no clothes on my person except a shirt and drawers, and went to urge on the dogs: and when I was about three hundred yards away from the wagons I heard the whiff of assegais and shields, and perceived we had to do with Kaffirs, not leopards; and with the Kaffirs the dogs were fighting.

"I shouted to my brother, 'There are Kaffirs here, and they are stabbing the dogs,' and I ran back towards the wagons to get my gun, for I was unarmed. But the wagons were already encircled by three rows of Kaffirs. Still I strove to push with my hands, and struggle, in order to pass through the Kaffirs to get at my gun.

"When I had in this way got through the three lines of Kaffirs, I found that there was still a number within the lines closely surrounding the wagons. As I was still advancing I heard my father say, 'Oh God!' and I knew from the sound that he was suffocated by blood. He had a wound in the gullet, above the breast.

"Roelof Botha had fired three shots, and there lay three Kaffirs, struck down by his shots; then he too, cried, 'Oh Lord!' I heard no more, and then I tried to make my way back away from the wagons, through the three rows of Kaffirs. Then I received the first wound from an assegai on the knot of the shoulder, through the breast and along the ribs.

"A second assegai struck the bone of my thigh, so that the point of the blade was bent, as I found afterwards when I drew it out. The third struck me above the left knee – all the wounds were on my left side. A fourth wound was inflicted above the ankle, through the sinews, under the calf of the leg. Then I found myself among the cattle, and stood a moment, listening. I heard no further sound of a voice – all were dead; and the Kaffirs were busy, tearing the tents, and breaking the wagons, and stabbing to death the dogs, and the poultry."

So it went on that night. The De Beers, the Liebenbergs, and many other family groups were completely wiped out. Some people had fantastic escapes. Mrs Heila Robbertse, whose husband was with Retief, was awakened by shots. With her son and daughter she had just time to catch three horses and gallop away. A party of Italian traders, who had accompanied the trek from the Cape in three wagons, also saved themselves on horseback; and one girl, Therese Vigliome, did her best to warn the people before she reached safety at Doornkop.

The small stream, known ever afterwards as the Moordspruit from this murderous night, was a particular scene of tragedy. The Bothmas were camped along this stream. They defended themselves with great resolution and made a fighting retreat to a flat hillock, where they were eventually overwhelmed when the Zulus drove a herd of cattle through their ranks. Sixty-five trekkers and many Zulus died on that hillock.

At the top of the Rensburg Spruit the Van Rensburg family retreated to the summit of a hillock and held the Zulus at bay. The noise of the fighting served to warn the parties camped further westwards. Laagers were hastily formed and skirmishing parties under Cilliers, Rudolf and Maritz, rode out to meet the Zulus and slow down their advance.

The Zulus were already weary after their long march; and the arrival of the skirmishing parties soon turned them to retreat. The massacre was over, and with the dawn began the melancholy task of gathering in the wounded and the dead. The whole area was littered with death and destruction, and vultures in enormous numbers were flocking for the feast.

Relations and friends had the bitter task of searching for victims, often guided by vultures to some spot in the bush where a wounded trekker had crawled to die. A few had escaped by hiding under the bodies of others, while some had hidden in the bush or climbed into trees, where again many had been stabbed. Some 41 trekker men, 56 women, and 185 of their children had died, as well as about 250 of their servants. About 500 Zulus had also been killed. The whole area looked like an abattoir.

In the rear laagers terror and misery prevailed. Everyone was missing a relative or friend, and the wounded were being crudely treated with such medicines as were available. The Zulus had also retreated with 25 000 head of the trekkers' cattle. Although Maritz tried desperately to recover them, the Zulus managed to drive the vast herd safely into the Thukela Valley, leaving the Voortrekkers despondent.

The Voortrekkers naturally had no clear picture of what had happened. Only the next day did Dick King trudge in, sore-footed, from Durban, trying to warn them in time that news had reached the traders of Retief's murder.

The reason for the treachery eluded the Voortrekkers. Some bitterly blamed the ivory traders or the missionaries, thinking that they must have turned Dingane against them. The real reasons – that Dingane feared them after their victories over the Matebele; that he was frightened of the numbers who had poured down the Drakensberg without prior consultation with him; that he was confused by the counterclaims to Natal of trekkers and traders; and that he regarded treachery as a legitimate counterweapon against guns – eluded the Voortrekkers at that time of isolation and unhappiness.

In Zululand, Owen and the American missionaries had fled from their stations in horror. Dingane made no effort to stop them. On the contrary, he gave them every facility. Such possessions as they left behind were scrupulously respected until the wind and rain dissolved them into ruin. Even the personalities and efforts of these early missionaries have been so completely forgotten that not the slightest tradition of them or their teachings survives.

At Durban there was a panic as great as any in the laagers. All the ivory traders collected at the port, except one or two who were hunting inland and joined the trekkers in their laagers. The missionaries – Gardiner, Owen and the six Americans – joined the traders. Fortunately, a small brig, the *Mary*, arrived at this critical time and provided a safe sanctuary at her anchorage in the lagoon. The island known as Salisbury, in memory of the brig Lieutenant King had sailed into the lagoon, was also a refuge secure from any possible Zulu attack.

The Voortrekkers, meanwhile, reorganised themselves as hastily as possible. An immediate punitive expedition was essential, if only to try to retrieve some of their livestock. Urgent messages were sent far and wide to gather reinforcements. Piet Uys and Hendrik Potgieter, who were still in the process of crossing the Drakensberg, hastened to join them. A patrol was also sent down to Durban, and the ivory traders resolved to make common cause with the trekkers against Dingane and launch a joint attack.

From the first, the Voortrekkers were hamstrung by quarrels among themselves. Three hundred and forty-seven men were gathered for the attack, but no strong man emerged as leader to replace the unfortunate Retief. Maritz, Uys and Potgieter were all jealous of one another and each wanted the leadership. Eventually, after much argument, a gathering was held on 28 March and it was decided that Maritz would become head of the government and remain with the laagers, while Uys and Potgieter would each command a section of the punitive force and have joint discussion of tactics.

With this unfortunate division among themselves, they rode out on 6 April; some excited and confident of victory, others despondent. They rode in the direction of Dingane's kraal. On the third day they sighted a group of Zulus and for two days they were decoyed on until they were eventually led to a battlefield which the Zulu commander, Ndlela, considered most favourable to himself.

The battlefield consisted of a basin set within mountains, with deep gullies criss-crossing it, hindering the horsemen and providing cover for the Zulus. Overlooking the basin was the bulk of a mountain known as eThaleni (the place of the shelf), and on its slopes the Zulu army of about 6500 men, in two divisions, stood waiting to receive the trekkers.

The two trekkers' divisions – 1347 mounted men altogether – separated, each intending to attack a section of the Zulus. Uys commenced the action. With his men, he rode up and dismounted about 20 yards from the Zulus and prepared to fire. The Zulus were sitting down taking snuff. They promptly sprang up and charged, but a couple of volleys of bullets turned them on their heels.

The trekkers set out in pursuit and immediately found themselves in an ambush. Seven of them were killed as they fought their way out, and Uys received a spear in the loins. He pulled the weapon out and even managed to take another man, who had lost his horse, in the saddle behind him.

Within a few minutes, however, Uys fainted through loss of blood. Recovering again, he was helped along by two men on either side of him. Then, feeling his end approaching, he said: "Here I must die. You cannot get me on any further, and there is no use to try it. Save yourselves, but fight like brave fellows to the last, and hold God before your eyes."

With that they left him. A few hundred yards away his 14-year-old son, Dirk Cornelis, turned and saw the Zulus closing in on his father, while the dying man lifted his head to watch them. This was too much. Dirk turned his horse and galloped back. He shot three Zulus and then died beside his father.

In the meantime Potgieter had sallied out towards the Zulus and then retreated nervously back into the valley where he remained inactive. The Zulu general soon perceived this indecision. He suddenly sent his men charging down the hill, shouting and rattling their shields.

Potgieter and his men fled. For two hours the Zulus pursued them, capturing all of the trekkers' 60 spare horses, their baggage and ammunition.

Ten of the trekkers had been killed and about 650 Zulus.

On 12 April the trekkers were back at their laagers, having taken one day to cover the same distance it had taken four days to travel on the journey out. Ever afterwards this commando was known as the Vlug (retreat) Kommando.

The ivory traders had been quarrelling among themselves just as much as the trekkers. They could not decide what to do. Eventually they chose the easiest and most attractive course –

they would raid cattle. This idea attracted much support and the traders rallied their followers. The Reverend H. Hewetson, who had arrived at Durban to join Owen in the midst of the excitement, has described a section of this army of the ivory traders.

"March 11th 1838. I fell in with a strange set of warriors. About 400 Zulus came bellowing a war-song. It sounded exactly like the noise of angry bulls. No one could mistake its meaning; its tone was that of gloomy revenge. The words in English were: 'The wild beast had driven us from our homes; but we will catch him.' They were headed by a white man, who had an old straw hat on, with an ostrich feather stuck in it. He had on his shoulder an elephant gun, covered with a panther's skin, and walked quite at ease at the head of his party, who went on with this dismal song, except that occasionally they all whistled the Zulu charge.

"They had flags flying, on one of which was written: 'IZU-NKUMBI' (the locusts), on another: 'For Justice We Fight'. They did not fatigue themselves with jumping or shouting, but the monotonous howl could be heard for at least two miles. In front they drove the cattle for slaughter; in rear, the degraded wives carried Indian corn, pumpkins, etc., all of which passed so quickly by me that it seemed like a frightful dream."

The traders led their following up through the hills to Kranskop (Ntunjambili). On the way two factions, led by Cane and Ogle, quarrelled over some supposed rights of precedence and came to blows. Ogle's followers got the worst of it and swore vengeance.

At Kranskop they found that all the Zulu males were away fighting the trekkers. The traders had a glorious time. They seized over 4000 head of cattle, along with 500 women and children. Then they returned to Durban to share out their loot. Endless quarrels took place. John Cane caught one of his headmen in the act of stealing a portion of the loot and shot him dead without argument.

In the midst of the row Robert Biggar returned from a journey to the Cape. Keen on striking a blow against Dingane for his brother who had been killed with the trekkers at Bloukrans, he organised a second raid. There was much disagreement about this. Ogle and several of the other traders refused to go; but eventually 18 traders, 30 coloureds, and 3000 of their African followers set out; a miscellaneous collection, including some old men who could hardly walk, but hobbled off on sticks to get their share of loot.

This army went up the coast to the Thukela River. On the northern side they saw a small force of Zulus. After the usual arguments as to what to do, they decided to attack. They forded the river and proceeded to the kraal named Ndondakusuka, surrounding it at daybreak on 17 April. The whole kraal was destroyed, all its people killed and the huts burnt down.

The Zulu army, meanwhile, was dangerously near. Commanded by Nongalazi, it numbered close to 7000 men and they were flushed with the recent victory against the trekkers. They also wanted vengeance for the Kranskop cattle raid. They attacked with great resolution.

The traders were drawn up near the ruins of Ndondakusuka and they did much destruction. Then, at the height of the battle, Cane ordered a party of Ogle's followers, who had accompanied the army, on a special task. Still keen on revenge, however, they seized the chance and slipped away across the river to Natal. The sight of the traitors running, spurred the Zulus on. They clambered over their own dead and attacked again. Cane fought throughout with a pipe in his mouth. He died, covered with wounds, with his pipe still between his teeth. Bob Joyce, a deserter from the 72nd Regiment in the Cape, put up a terrific battle and managed to shoot his way out. Of the rest, John Stubbs, Robert Biggar, Thomas Carden, Robert Russell, Richard Wood, William Wood, Henry Bott, John Campbell, Thomas Campbell, Richard Lovedale, Charles Blanckenberg, John Kemble, J. Clark and W. Bottomley, all died. Besides Joyce, only Dick King, Richard Duffy and Joseph Brown escaped. Six hundred of their African followers also died.

All over Natal there was mourning and panic. At Durban the missionaries prepared to sail away aboard the *Comet*. Few of them were ever to come back, Gardiner dying a wretched death from starvation while establishing a mission in South America on Tierra Del Fuego. In Natal the missions were either looted or burned to the ground by the Zulus and all their work was trampled in the dust.

At Durban only Alexander Biggar, Henry Ogle, Daniel Toohey, Charles Adams, Robert Dunn, Dick King, Bob Joyce and a few others decided to remain. They took shelter on Salisbury Island while, in the last week of April 1838, a vengeful Zulu army ransacked the whole area around the bay, destroying every house and living thing they could find. From the anchored *Comet* the Europeans watched the flames of destruction and saw the army looting their houses, with warriors ludicrously attired in women's clothing.

On 11 May the *Comet* sailed, and the remaining traders were left to their fate. Whatever their former opinion, they now had no choice. Either they must join forces entirely with the trekkers or die, for there was certainly no support anywhere else.

In the laagers complete despondency prevailed after the series of defeats. Many faint hearts started to abandon Natal. After twelve days of recrimination Potgieter and his entire following went back across the mountains in high dudgeon, for many people had blamed him for the disaster at eThaleni. His departure was actually a relief to the trekkers, for he was a great dissentient and always quarrelling.

Carel Landman became the provisional leader of the Natal trekkers, while urgent messages were sent all over, appealing for reinforcements and aid. On 16 May, Landman rode down to Durban with a strong patrol, and by arrangement with the traders he annexed the port to what was then known as the United Laagers. Alexander Biggar was appointed *landdrost* of the place; William Cowie, who had accompanied the trek from the Cape as a mechanic, settled nearby on the hill dominating the old track to the north still known by his name, and became a field cornet.

Then throughout Natal a period of rest began; of patient reinforcement and preparation. The whole tragic sequence of events had been like a vicious slap in the face given by a fickle mistress to her swain. Gone was the high excitement of the Drakensberg crossing. Now Natal was stained with the blood of the Voortrekkers and they were stoically determined to make it their own. The slap in the face would be returned with interest, but it took time to mount the blow.

TEN

Mpande

Blood River

In the weary month of waiting the trekkers divided themselves into two great laagers; one known as Maritzlaager, being on the upper reaches of the Little Thukela; while a smaller laager of about 290 wagons was encamped on the upper Bushman's River, at a place named Gatslaager, because it lay in a hollow surrounded by high hills.

Altogether there were about 640 men, 3200 women and children, and some 1260 of their African servants, divided among the two laagers; along with 300 000 sheep, 40 000 head of cattle and 3000 horses. With plenty of venison also readily available, the trekkers lived reasonably well, and at both laagers fields were ploughed, water furrows dug, and food crops planted.

Dingane left them severely alone until August 1838. Then he sent a few regiments probing about to find out what was happening. This army came upon the Gatslaager. It was under orders not to launch a major attack, but simply to feel out the trekker strength and raid their cattle. The Gatslaager was found to be wedge-shaped, its base resting on the riverbank and a small cannon at its point.

The Zulus encircled the laager in daylight, firing off guns captured in the previous engagements but taking good care to keep well out of the trekkers' range. One trekker, Hans Froneman, was taken by surprise away from the laager. He jumped into a pool and tried to hide under floating grass, but the Zulus probed him out with their spears and killed him.

166

The Zulus then occupied themselves in rounding up the trekkers' livestock. At sunset they withdrew to a safe distance and lighted great fires, around which they sat like phantom figures – feasting on the captured animals – while the trekkers lay beside their guns all night.

The next morning the Zulus again approached the laager. They hurled spears wrapped in blazing grass at the wagons but declined to rush them. All day they skirmished, keeping the trekkers tightly bottled up while they rounded up livestock. Then, that night, the Zulus set the grass alight around the laager. Leaving the trekkers battling with the flames, the Zulus slipped away like shadows, taking vast booty in livestock with them.

This cattle raid was a sad blow to the trekkers. For the sake of security the Gatslaager, or Veglaager as it was now called, was broken up as soon as the Zulus had gone. The whole affair was removed to a site close to the Maritzlaager and the passes over the Drakensberg. After this last setback, even hope seemed to be running out; and at this lowest ebb in trekker fortunes their one leader, Gerrit Maritz, after months of sickness, finally died on 23 September, and left them to their sorrow.

From this point onwards trekker fortune started to improve. Reinforcements reached them in a steady trickle and confidence returned. Men such as Jacobus Boshoff, clerk to the Civil Commissioner of Graaff-Reinet, journeyed up privately to give them advice, and Boshoff drew up a detailed constitution for their much longed-for republic. They even decided upon the site of their future capital, a central area known as the Boesmansrand, where, on 23 October 1838, they resolved that when times were good they would lay out a town.

Then, on 28 November, a new leader, Andries Pretorius, rode cheerfully into camp with 60 men and a bronze cannon. Pretorius was a big, brawny, successful farmer-type of man, aged 39 at the time, and of a Cape family noted for its pride and authority. Under him the trekkers were mustered and prepared for the settlement of accounts with Dingane.

Down in the Cape, meanwhile, the British Government had heard the news of the trekkers' misfortunes without surprise. Such troubles, indeed, were not peculiar to Southern Africa and were only to be expected when one emigrating body attempted to lodge itself in any area already settled, or within the orbit of older people. The fact that treachery had been used was also not exceptional in the history of relations with primitive peoples, for they regard its employment as a normal weapon.

To the British Government, the whole trek had been a straightforward act of aggression against the African tribes of the interior. It seemed to them that it was time to intervene and prevent further bloodshed. They then decided to at last occupy Port Natal in order to stop any further flow of illegal immigration or trade in ammunition.

Like a python, the British Empire had already swallowed so much of the world that a period of administrative digestion had been taking place, during which all ideas of fresh territorial acquisitions had been repudiated. Because of this, the British had persistently refused to support the ivory traders of Port Natal. Now, however, the trek had forced their hands. Confronted by the prospect of endless trouble in Natal, caused by what were legally British subjects, they had no alternative but to act.

On 14 November 1838, Sir George Napier, the Cape Governor, issued a proclamation announcing the seizure of Port Natal "in consequence of the disturbed state of the Native tribes in the territories adjacent to that part, arising in a great degree from the unwarranted occupation of parts of those territories by certain emigrants from this colony, being Her Majesty's subjects, and the probability that those disturbances will continue and increase."

Napier's plan was to reclaim the trekkers as British subjects, to establish peace, and, seeing the die was cast, to establish the settlement in Natal on a proper basis. Major Charters, who was selected to command the British force sent to Durban, was instructed to land his 80 men, reconnoitre the harbour, and establish some sort of fortification.

He was to obtain what information he could about both Boers and Zulus, and on no account was he to open fire unless fired upon. Maintenance of peace was his primary objective. He was to protect both trekkers and Africans from one another. Medical aid and stores were to be furnished in case of need.

With these instructions Charters and his men sailed up to Port Natal, and on 3 December 1838 they commenced to land at the Point, without any opposition or incident. Two storehouses there were commandeered from their owners, Robert Dunn, and J. Owen Smith of Port Elizabeth, and in these buildings the soldiers bedded down in comfort and good spirits. The transports landed ample food and the men were completely sure of themselves.

They found a few of the ivory traders living around the bay. Ogle, King, Toohey, Steller and others, together with about 25 Boers, were settled at Congella. Most of the male population, however, including Robert Joyce and E. Parker, had gone off with Alexander Biggar to join Pretorius's commando against Dingane. Charters hastily sent two African messengers to the trekkers, informing them of the British occupation and ordering Pretorius to desist from any further warlike adventures and to place his followers under British protection.

The messengers reached the laager after the commando had left. At about the same time that Charters was landing his men at the Point, Pretorius had ridden off with 464 straight-shooting followers ready for battle. Retribution against Dingane was the desire of every man, but each one had a lurking pang of fear. The Zulus had a reputation exaggerated by their previous successes and the trekkers were badly conscious of their own small numbers.

Still, they rode on resolutely enough. Pretorius and Charl Celliers discussed the prospects soberly, and it seemed to them that unless the God of hosts and battles was with them, they would be overwhelmed. Accordingly, they resolved to make a promise to the Lord, which they would explicitly fulfil.

On 7 December, therefore, the men were rallied around a gun carriage at one of their laagers. Celliers, who was deeply religious, addressed them.

"My brethren and fellow countrymen. At this moment we stand before the Holy God of heaven and earth, to make a promise if He will be with us and protect us, and deliver the enemy into our hands so that we may triumph over him, that we shall observe the day and the date as an anniversary in each year, and a day of thanksgiving like the Sabbath in His honour; and that we shall enjoin our children that they must take part with us in this for a remembrance even for our posterity."

Thus, with frequent prayers, hymn singing and talks, the leaders heartened their men and they rode on. There were few events on the journey. Crossing the range which the trekkers had named the Heuningberg (honey mountain), the cart which Biggar was driving fell over in a bog and the range was henceforth referred to as the Biggarsberg. For the rest, Pretorius led his men with great care and prudence through the old grazing grounds of the Zulu herds, so green and beautiful with the summer rains that the hearts of the farmers longed for it.

All the fat Zulu cattle had vanished, but in a mealie field the commando surprised a grandson of Jobe, hiding with one of the herdsmen. The two were pressed into service as guides and from this event the Zulus still regard Jobe's people as renegades.

On 15 December the commando arrived at the banks of a river known as the Ncome (praiseworthy one), from its plentiful water and green banks. Beside this river the commando pitched a laager, for their scouts had discovered signs of a major Zulu force ahead.

Charl Celliers has described the laager site in his journal. "I cannot omit to bring to the notice of all how the Lord in His holy providence had appointed a place for us, in which He had determined that the fight should occur. On the west there was a ravine which discharged itself into the river, and the bank close to the edge of the camp was 14 feet high and could not be scaled.

"Then there was the river, which had a sea-cow-hole (deep river stretch) at least 1400 yards long, on the eastern side. So that the camp, by God's mercy, was protected on two sides. On the other sides the encampment was on open ground."

Dawn found them at this place on 16 December, and as the shadows of night slipped away, so 10 000 Zulu warriors came down upon them. Of the battle itself Charl Celliers wrote: "They came down on the camp with great courage and, if I am not mistaken, endeavoured four times to take it by storm. Each time they were driven back. We could both hear and see their commander, who wished to repeat the attack, but the men refused to do so."

The laager was quite unassailable by the Zulus. Daniel Bezuidenhout described it: "Between the wagons we had fastened long ladders, and skins of oxen were stretched over the wheels. At the back of each wagon there were little heaps of gunpowder and bullets, and when the battle was fought, and the Kaffirs in thousands were no further than ten paces from us, we had scarcely time to throw a handful of powder into the gun and then slip a bullet down the barrel, without a moment even to drive it home with the ramrod.

"Of that fight nothing remains in my memory except shouting and tumult and lamentation, and a sea of black faces; and a dense smoke that rose straight as a plumb line upwards from the ground."

"When the attack was wholly discontinued," wrote Charl Celliers, "there was a considerable number at the edge of the sea-cow-hole who, being unable to cross the water, lay down under their shields; and we, clearing the edge of the encampment near the water, and reaching the spot by a direct course, fired on and killed them. And when the other Kaffirs saw that they would all be killed, they fled, but with great loss."

The trekkers always kept their horses saddled up in battle – either for pursuit or retreat. Now they jumped into the saddles and rode out. The Zulus offered little resistance.

"We were on their right and left, and they were huddled together. We were animated by great courage, and when we had got in front of them, the Kaffirs lay on the ground like pumpkins on a rich soil that had borne a large crop.

"When they saw that there would be no escape, as we were driving them towards the sea-cow-hole, they jumped into the water and were among the rushes at the river's edge. I believe that all were killed, that not one escaped. I was witness to the fact that the water looked like a pool of blood – whence came the name of *Blood River*."

About 3000 Zulus died that day beside the banks of the once pleasant little river. Of the commando only four had been wounded; and that night they celebrated their victory in prayer, jubilation, and the narration of individual exploits and adventures. If Weenen (the place of weeping) was a place name crying of the Zulus' triumph in that first wild night of killing, then the name of Blood River ever afterwards recorded the price they paid for their first success.

The next day the commando advanced on Mgungundlovu and reached the place on 20 December. They found the great capital entirely deserted, a place only of ghosts and fearful memories, with no living soul to be found in all those 2000 huts. Dingane's great hut was in flames, but the rest of the place was intact. The commando pitched a laager in the vicinity and searched around until the men found the remains of their lamented leader Piet Retief and his comrades.

"We found the corpses about 1200 yards from Dingane's dwelling," wrote Charl Celliers. "They had been dragged in one direction. Their hands and feet were still bound with thongs of untanned hide, and in nearly all the corpses a spike as thick as one's arm had been forced into the anus, so that the point of the spike was in the chest. They lay with their clothes still on their bodies. No beast of prey or bird had disturbed them."

It was a dreary and lamentable business. Nearly each man had a relative or friend to search for among that putrifying heap. On Retief's body they found his leather shoulder bag intact. In it, among his papers, was the treaty signed by Dingane, describing the territory given to the trekkers.

A common grave was dug and the bodies buried. Then, with tempers roused, the commando searched around to find the Zulus. The whole countryside seemed deserted, but presently their scouts came across one solitary Zulu flitting about in the bush. They seized him and led him to the leaders. His name was Bongoza. The Zulu army had dispersed, he told Pretorius, and Dingane had fled into the wild country over the White Mfolozi River.

The Zulus' cattle, Bongoza continued naively, were hidden in the White Mfolozi valley, and he offered to lead the trekkers to them. Pretorius was nervous. If the Zulu army, as yet only half beaten, wished to lure the trekkers away from their invulnerable wagons, then this plausible story of Bongoza seemed an ideal trap.

Still, the trekkers hungered for cattle, for it was urgent that the catastrophic losses in livestock inflicted on them around the upper Thukela should be made good. Pretorius cautiously moved his laager, on 26 December, to the commanding point of the Mthonjaneni ridge, from where the rugged valley of the White Mfolozi was in clear view. The trekkers could see the Zulus' cattle moving about in it.

Early on the morning of the 27th, 300 trekkers, with 75 Africans led by Alexander Biggar, sallied out on a cattle raid. Pretorius was suffering from a wound received at Blood River. He remained behind in the laager with 160 men, while Carel Landman took command of the raiding force.

Bongoza acted as guide. He led the men into the great ravine, known as oPhathe from its flattened sides, which leads from the ridge down towards the valley of the White Mfolozi. The going was terribly tough. They scrambled down, leading their horses.

A few hundred Zulus were seen, but these fled so ostentatiously that the trekkers became nervous of being led into an ambush. They proceeded with great caution. Suddenly a mass of Zulus materialised from what the trekkers had thought to be a herd of cattle.

The trekkers found themselves cut off. Zulus were appearing on all sides and they were in a serious trap. Bongoza slipped quietly off into the bush, his work so well done that ever afterwards the Zulus had a saying around his name: "Do you think I am Bongoza?" whenever they were suspected of treachery.

The commando had split into two sections. Landman made his own men tie their horses into a circle, intending to fight it out. The second section was under the command of Hans de Lange. He was averse to the idea of a major battle in such a place. He galloped to Landman and held a hurried conference.

In the end they decided to shoot their way out. The two sections galloped off towards the White Mfolozi, with De Lange in command. The Zulus were nonplussed at this, for they had concentrated their main strength between the trekkers and their laager.

With only minor resistance, the trekkers reached the White Mfolozi. They swam the river, splashing through the mud and scrambling up the far bank. Behind them the Zulus were in hot pursuit and a running fight took place, with both sides dodging through the bush. It was a nightmare journey but presently the trekkers reached an open place where they could gallop and put distance between themselves and the Zulus.

Another division of Zulus now appeared and sought to cut them off. Fifty trekkers went to turn them while the main force continued their retreat.

They rode on quickly, intending to recross the river higher up and turn back to the laager. Occasionally some Zulu, faster than the others, would overtake them, only to be shot. Once, a Zulu galloped right into their ranks before he was killed. His horse was found to belong to one of the men in the party who had lost it in the ill-fated Vlug Kommando.

Many of the cattle looted from the trekkers were also grazing in the vicinity among the Zulu herds. These animals seemed to recognise the Europeans by the smell. They lowed a welcome and stampeded off with the retreating party.

The trekkers forced their horses into the river in a panicky mass of animals and humans. It was a difficult ford, with steep banks and mud. Six of the Europeans were killed there, including Alexander Biggar. Seventy of his Natal natives also died there, mostly through being shot by mistake by the trekkers.

There were many hairbreadth escapes among individuals. Then reinforcements reached them from the laager, and at sunset Landman and the bulk of his party reached the wagons. A second party, which had tried another ford, stumbled home at midnight. Bongoza had baited the trap well, but the jaws had failed to close.

For three more days Pretorius remained in the laager to rest the exhausted horses and in the hope that the Zulus would attack the wagons. Then they burnt Mgungundlovu down and rode away. On New Year's Day they were at the Nieuwejaars Spruit, and a few days later they were back at the Natal laager, with about 5000 head of cattle as booty. From thence on this commando was known as the Wen (victory) Kommando.

Jubilation at the victory spread over the land of Natal like green grass after the rains. The laagers broke up and the wagons rolled gaily over the country, the people relishing their new freedom and security and finding the land more fair than they could ever have dreamed. Especially around the river they named Mooi (beautiful) the grass was green and gaily speckled with colourful flowers.

At Port Natal, meanwhile, Major Charters was still in control of a two-mile area around the high-water mark. Beyond this confined area, however, British influence was negligible. Charters and his 22-year-old interpreter, Theophilus Shepstone, left the place on 20 January 1839 and rode overland to see Faku and reassure the alarmed border tribes that they would not be attacked by the trekkers. At Durban Captain Henry Jervis was left in command of the garrison, and he busied himself in trying to patch up peace between the trekkers and Dingane.

For the next few months the trekkers and the Zulus looked at each other uncertainly over the ten thousand hills. Dingane had withdrawn to a hillslope overlooking the river known as the Vuna (the reaper) from its habit of washing away crops in flood-time. There he proceeded to rebuild his Mgungundlovu kraal, while he considered future policy.

The trekkers, meanwhile, were well aware that a decisive third round with the Zulus was inevitable, for as long as Dingane was in power they would always live under a threat. Also, there was the matter of the vast herds of their cattle which he still retained.

In February Jervis despatched a message to Dingane suggesting that the Zulus send an intermediary to discuss peace. On 26 March the Zulu and Boer delegates met in Durban and terms of peace were discussed. The Zulus returned to their king with the terms: the Thukela was to be the boundary and Dingane was to return all looted cattle; and to this he readily agreed.

On 13 May a peace treaty was signed in Durban, in which the Zulus undertook to return 19 000 head of cattle, along with horses, guns, sheep and other goods. William Cowie, J.A. van Niekerk and J.P. Roscher rode up the next month to Dingane's new capital on the Vuna River and received a first instalment of 1300 head of cattle, 400 sheep, 52 guns and 43 saddles. Peace seemed assured.

The trekkers busied themselves in establishing their republic. Their capital at the Boesmansrand was laid out by Piet Greyling during March 1839, and named Pietermaritzburg in honour of the two dead leaders, Pieter Retief and Gerrit Maritz. This became the meeting place of the trekkers' government, the capital of what they called the Free Province of New Holland in South East Africa.

At Durban, Captain Jervis was left with little to do now that peace had returned. He took a lively interest in the country, and the British traders, especially Daniel Toohey, gave him many accounts of deposits of minerals. In March 1839 the captain sent a specimen of coal to the Governor of the Cape and reported it as being common in Natal. This report, forwarded to London, produced the first real interest in Natal the British Home Government had shown. Careful investigation was ordered "as such a resource might prove of the utmost importance to steam navigation in the adjacent seas."

In March the ship *Mazeppa* brought back to Natal Dr Adams, the American missionary, on a reconnaissance to find out what was happening. Discovering that everything was peaceful, he returned to the Cape, and on 12 June, he and Daniel Lindley came back with their families and re-established their old mission on the lower Mlazi River.

Also aboard the ship, *Mazeppa*, had been a Swedish naturalist named Wahlberg, and a French naturalist named Adolphe Delegorgue, who busied himself for some time in thoroughly exploring Natal and most of Zululand. Several other ships also came into Durban to trade, and the successful establishment of the Republic seemed assured as soon as the British should abandon Port Natal.

Dingane, meanwhile, considering his southern frontier safe, set about extending his territory to the north. For the winter military season of 1839 he mustered his army and sent it off into Swaziland, where the warriors spent some months in thoroughly ransacking the country in the most devastating raid the unfortunate inhabitants of that part of the world ever experienced.

One result of this raid was to prove disastrous to Dingane. Living in the south of Zululand, on the Matigulu River, was a younger half-brother of his, named Mpande (the root). He was a simple, easy-going, lazy sort of man, and so fond of the ladies that Dingane held him in great contempt, considering him to have the heart of a woman.

When the army was marshalled for the Swaziland raid, Mpande received the usual summons to report for service, but at the same time someone whispered to him that Dingane meant to kill him. Accordingly, Mpande remained at home during the course of the Swaziland raid and pleaded sick. If Dingane had any intention of killing him before, it now became a certainty. He sent a peremptory order for Mpande to present his person at the new Mgungundlovu.

Mpande promptly packed his impedimenta. With about 17 000 followers he fled, helter-skelter, south across the Thukela to the Thongathi River, where he built himself a kraal named Mahambehlala (the runaways' rest).

News of this influx into Natal threw the entire country into alarm. The well-known Hans de Lange happened to be hunting in the vicinity of the Thongathi River at the time and he met Mpande. The refugee presented De Lange with 180 head of cattle as a peace offering to the Europeans and told his story to the hunter.

De Lange decided to take the refugee to the newly founded capital of Pietermaritzburg. There, on 15 October 1839, the chief was interrogated before the Volksraad. He answered his questioners frankly and impressed them as being a man of peace who had genuinely fled from Dingane and might be a useful ally for the future. He was therefore granted permission to settle in the area between the Mvoti and Mhlali rivers, until he should be able to live on the other side of the Thukela in safety.

Then, on 26 October 1839, an embassy of 28 trekkers and others, led by the *landdrost* of Congella, travelled up to see Mpande in his new home and officially set him up as head of all refugee Zulus in Natal.

They found Mpande in an improvised hut in his newly erected village. The whole place was jammed with Zulus who stared the European visitors out of countenance in friendly curiosity. The Europeans crowded into Mpande's hut, shook hands with him, and exchanged presents. They liked him. He was quiet, and a gentleman, middle-aged but of good figure and appearance, with a superb body, only just beginning to show signs of his later obesity.

A marquee was pitched next to the new village and, on 27

October, a treaty was signed establishing Mpande as "Reigning Prince of the Emigrant Zulus", with his successor to be chosen according to tribal custom, but to be confirmed by the trekkers. Mpande also undertook to stop witchcraft and smellings-out. Before about 6000 Zulus he repeated his assurances, first given in Pietermaritzburg, of peace, friendship and alliance.

The next day a big feast and dance celebrated the new alliance. In the midst of it Mpande's followers beat to death one of his newly appointed councillors, a man named Mpangazitha, whom they suspected of being a spy of Dingane's. Apart from this disturbance, the alliance seemed to bode much good for the Europeans, if only Mpande could be manoeuvred into the position of ruler of a completely subservient Zululand. But before this could be contrived, the British would have to be induced to leave Natal.

The British position, actually, was fundamentally weak. According to proclamation, the garrison had been sent up to maintain peace and prevent the Republicans from importing armaments necessary for further war. Peace was now in the land; and so much ammunition had already been smuggled to Natal from the Cape that the Republicans never worried about any blockade at Durban.

All the garrison was doing was eating its head off, gambling away its pay, and getting very drunk. Governor Napier had no permission to do anything else with the troops so, accordingly in November 1839, he sent orders for the garrison to evacuate Durban. There was glee among the Voortrekkers. On Christmas Eve the British left aboard the *Vectis*. From the beach the trekkers waved them a real soldier's farewell and gaily ran their flag up – a standard of three red, white and blue triangles, with the base of the white forming the outer edge. The Republic of Natal was at last a living thing. The future seemed full of promise for the trekkers, and trouble for Dingane.

ELEVEN

The Republic of Natal

In Pietermaritzburg, on the departure of the British, the Republicans made as merry as circumstances allowed. The town, by then, was an inconsiderable affair; no more than a camp of palisades, mud huts and wagons, still cautiously arranged in defensive formation. All around it rolled the green hills of Natal, while the high escarpment of the Boesmansrand enfolded the place in a warm and sheltered sleepy hollow, where the Voortrekkers found it easy to dream of future prosperity, and a pleasant town with snow-white houses drowsing in the shade and streamlets playing along the sidewalks like children laughing home from school.

But before such pleasant dreams could come true, the trouble with Dingane had to be settled, livestock losses recovered, and the ever threatening cloud of Zulu power wiped away from Natal's blue sky. So reasoned the trekkers; and with the departure of the British they made ready for the final settlement.

It was easy to pick a quarrel with Dingane. He had fulfilled his treaty obligations of returning livestock as eagerly as a person losing teeth in a dentist's chair. Accordingly, the trekkers sent a demand for the immediate surrender of 19 000 head of cattle. In reply Dingane hastily sent along his courtier, Dambuza, as ambassador, with a minor chief named Khambazana and 200 oxen.

The trekkers promptly arrested Dambuza and his associate on grounds of complicity in the Retief massacre and, on 4 January 1840, resolved to muster their full force in order to demand 40 000 head of cattle and to take them by force if necessary.

The Thukela River, between the sites of modern Colenso and Winterton, was fixed as the rendezvous for the commando. There it was mustered under the command of A.W.J. Pretorius, and on 21 January the 350 men rode off for Zululand.

There was a mixed crowd in the commando. Most of the trekkers regarded it more as a holiday outing, for they felt that they now had the measure of the Zulus and victory was a foregone conclusion. Accordingly they enjoyed themselves, exploring and hunting as they travelled, reading the Bible at big gatherings, and passing the time in jokes and games.

Mpande accompanied the commando as a hostage, while his own army, commanded by Nongalaza (the same general who had defeated the ivory traders at the Ndondakusuka battle) invaded Zululand from the Kranskop area. The plan of campaign was for the two armies to converge on Dingane like a nutcracker closing. Runners kept the two commanders in constant communication.

The captives, Dambuza and Khambazana, travelled as prisoners in the commando, while the French naturalist Delegorgue went as well and provided for future generations a pertinent, and sometimes acid, commentary on proceedings.

The commando followed roughly the trail of the old Wen Kommando. As it travelled, minor tribes and chiefs hastened to pay homage, for approaching disaster for the Zulus was very much in the air. The petty chiefs, Matuwan and Jobe, made their bows in the vicinity of modern Ladysmith. There Matuwan's followers paid their tribute in so lively a fashion that the site of the laager where the event took place (later a great railway marshalling yard) was known as Danskraal, from the way the tribesmen danced.

From Danskraal, the commando crossed the Biggarsberg and rode on past the site of the modern town of Dundee.

Nearby Delegorgue discovered many surface traces of coal, and the name Steenkoolspruit (coal stream) was applied to a rivulet there.

On 29 January the commando reached the old Blood River battlefield, and in memory of it they decided to hold a trial. Mpande acted as accuser, while Dambuza and his associate were the accused. Delegorgue was a cynical onlooker.

Dambuza freely acknowledged the accusations made against him. He had been one of Dingane's principal indunas and, as such, had played his full part in the unhappy tragedy of the Retief massacre. He sought to protect the minor chief who was his companion, but the trekkers were in vengeful mood.

Both Zulus were sentenced to death. Delegorgue watched them being shot, with a mixture of admiration for their stoicism and painful feelings at the manner of their trial. To his mind the two had been ambassadors and, although Retief had been most treacherously murdered, the fact remained that another evil hardly made the first one right.

From the Blood River, the commando rode on to the site of present-day Gluckstadt. There, on 1 February, a runner arrived to tell them that on 30 January Nongalaza's men had met Dingane's army under Ndlela on the hot *maqongqo* (ridge) on the Mkhuze River, ten miles above the present irrigation scheme near Magudu.

In the battle Dingane's men had been gaining the upper hand, when a cry was heard that the Boers were coming. Dingane's men had then lost heart. They had fled into the bush towards the Phongolo River and Mpande's army was victorious.

Pretorius, with 250 men, immediately left the main camp and rode as fast as possible to try and intercept Dingane. They found few of their old enemies. Dingane's men had attempted to rally, for their defeat by Mpande's renegades galled them, but news of the approach of the commando sent them scurrying off into the bush.

After scouring the countryside, the commando, on 8 February, reached the Phongolo River between Magudu and the present Phongolo irrigation dam. They had found no trace of Dingane, only many rumours had reached them of his destitution and flight. At the Phongolo, incessant rain and horse-sickness obliged Pretorius to abandon his ideas of further pursuit. The commando, therefore, turned for home, driving 10 000 head of cattle with them as booty.

On 9 February, dripping wet from the rains, they arrived at a campsite on the Black Mfolozi River on the farm then named Wagendrift. At this camp, on the next day, the overjoyed Mpande was proclaimed King of the Zulus. Standing on top of a large rock, he swore alliance with the trekkers which was to last as long as the rock on which he stood.

After a few days of general celebration and mutual congratulations the commando, on 13 February, set off for Pietermaritzburg. In Mpande they felt that they had a strong and faithful ally. They were jubilant that the victory had been won at the cost only of their support of the new Zulu king. Even the pouring rain failed to dampen their gaiety. The commando dispersed in Pietermaritzburg, after a mass distribution of the 31 000 head of cattle they had collected on their ride through Zululand. From this rich booty the commando was ever afterwards known as the Bees (cattle) Kommando.

Dingane, after his defeat, had ordered the immediate death of his general, Ndlela, and then fled north across the Phongolo. Perhaps he had heard the ancient jingle, "There is no winter on top of the Lubombo," for towards that fertile and pleasant part of the world he headed.

Living on the summit, so cool and green both in summer and winter, were a number of minor clans and petty tribes of various origins. Principal of these were the Mngomezulu clan of Sotho extraction, who lived mainly north of the Ngwavuma River; and the Nyawo tribe, of the same blood as the Zulus, who lived mostly between the Phongolo and Ngwavuma rivers.

It was in the tribal lands of the Nyawos that Dingane sought sanctuary. Disregarding them entirely, he made his way to the beautiful Hlathikhulu (great forest), some ten miles south of the present magistracy of Ngwavuma.

If Dingane disregarded the Nyawos, they could not afford to overlook him. There were many furtive consultations in their kraals. Then, early one morning, their chief, Silevana, his son Sambane, Zulu Nyawo, a Swazi named Nondawana, and a few retainers, silently surrounded Dingane's unfinished huts. With a rush they overwhelmed them. Dingane was caught, wounded, questioned, and then stabbed to death. And there they buried that ex-despot, planting three stones to mark his grave, beneath a large wild-fig tree.

Back in Zululand, Mpande was busily engaged in erecting for himself and the Zulus a brand-new capital. Leaving the traditional Zulu valley, and the black ruins of Mgungundlovu, he chose as the site of the new kraal the vast basin in the hills known as Mahlabathini (place of white sands), from which the White Mfolozi drew most of its light-coloured mud.

In this place Mpande built his capital, and rather vaingloriously named it kwaNodwengu (place of the irresistible one). There he settled down to a long reign of peace and prosperity. Not that he didn't kill people – that would have been asking too much – but he was most moderate in his executions.

As was to be expected, however, he consolidated his power by liquidating the most ardent supporters of Dingane. His only half-brother, Ggugqu, was also prudently disposed of in 1843, and at the time of that event most other dissident elements abandoned Zululand in a mass exodus, led by an aunt of Mpande's named Mawa.

This resolute old woman, with a large following of persons politically odorous to Mpande, settled on the bank of the Mdloti River, around a rocky, rounded knoll about a mile and a half from the sea. This place, known as kwaHoqo, became a place of refuge for all who fled from Mpande. There old Mawa, whose crossing into Natal became a Zulu historical landmark, lived and, in her time, was buried where the green ocean of sugar cane waves today.

Beyond this "crossing of Mawa's", Mpande's reign was one of feasting rather than fighting. Only one military campaign was undertaken. It was a half-hearted sort of raid against the Swazis, launched more as an exercise than anything else. Known as the ukuFunda kukaThulwana (learning of the Thulwanas); its purpose was less to wring loot out of the Swazis than to show the young men, including Mpande's heir, Cetshwayo who was in the Thulwana regiment, how to conduct military affairs. Just how well Cetshwayo learnt the lesson will be seen later.

The liquidation of the Zulu threat brought complete joy to the Voortrekkers. For weary months they had been living a nervous, cramped sort of life in their laagers; dreaming always of scattering into odd and personally favoured corners of the land with that abandon which made their communities loosely knit and fragmentary.

Delegorgue summed up the Voortrekkers' ideal of life well when he wrote:

"To pass away their time in frequent meals of meat, to sip their coffee at every hour, to have a wife who may beguile the dreariness of the evenings, to please themselves with the sight, by day, of large herds of various colours, shining in their fatness and enamelling the green meadows, and at times to follow the chase – an employment at once profitable and refreshing to their limbs – such is the ideal common to them all, their notion of the comfortable and called by them *lekker leven* (a pleasant life)."

In pursuit of this unfettered life – a free one with themselves as their own masters – the Boers had trekked, and the cramped living in laagers had been a sad climax to a thousand miles of travelling. Shortages of firewood, water and grazing had plagued the great encampments. The unpleasant penalties of so gregarious a life had been emphasised to them on 3 June 1839, when a candle overturned by a servant girl had started a fire. Huts, wagons and belongings had gone up in smoke, along with a store of gunpowder. Nine trekkers had been killed, twelve injured, and the effects of 29 families totally destroyed. Eyes had been fixed with redoubled longing on the open hills after that catastrophe.

And now, with the defeat of Dingane, the thunderclouds had vanished. The skies were blue and the veld was free. Like children cooped indoors during rain, they poured outside the moment the sun shone and scattered to their chosen farms. The Zulu cattle made good their former losses, and some thousand Zulu children captured during the raids were distributed among them as "apprentices"; a conveniently camouflaged form of free labour.

Every trekker who had come to Natal before the beginning of 1840 was entitled to two farms, and one erf in any of the villages. Those coming later received one farm. For government, a Volksraad (people's council) was elected with 24 members. They were to meet on the first Monday of January, April, July and October, and a new chairman (or president) was to be elected at each meeting.

There was hardly any civil service. The civil list was probably the smallest ever known to history. Its total was under £500 a year for all services, including £45 a year given as pension to the faithful but ailing old schoolmaster and amateur minister, Erasmus Smit.

The quarterly elected president, with a few other Volksraad members living conveniently near the capital, carried on the administration as a so-called "Commissie Raad" until the next Volksraad session; while each year the field cornets or honorary district officers, who acted as JPs over the twelve wards into which the country was divided, collected papers from all the burghers on which were written the names of their two desired Volksraad representatives.

It was a rural democracy of extreme simplicity, and every adult man in good standing was entitled to discuss momentous affairs at public meetings with the Volksraad, using the most violent language, if he wished, in stressing a point to the head of the state.

Public revenue came from customs duties, harbour duties of 3d. a ton on all vessels dropping anchor, court fines, transfer dues, and a tax of 18s. a year on all 3000-morgen farms. Life was easy and simple; isolated not only from the luxuries but also from the cares of a civilisation of which the trekkers knew little and cared less.

In this simple setting Pietermaritzburg grew up as the capital. J.A. Wahlberg surveyed the place in detail in 1840 and a powder magazine, prison, houses and shops were built, while all around more and more farms were handed out as fresh settlers trekked in across the Drakensberg.

The characters of this old republic were a stalwart and rugged crowd. Their personalities still seem to linger over the green hills of Natal in some indefinable way, all these long years after they have gone. Philip Rudolph Botha, who settled on the hill by the roadside between Pietermaritzburg and Durban, was one of those who left his name behind for ever on the maps (Botha's Hill), while the son of his second son was destined to be the famous Louis Botha, one of the giants of South African history.

Pieter Uys, who settled in the thorny basin henceforth known as Uys Doorns, was another trekker who had his home by the old arterial wagon track that linked Durban to the Drakensberg. Of early tradesmen there were Gert Rudolph, who opened the first butcher shop in Pietermaritzburg; Ouma Retief, who started the first bakery; and Doctor Poortman, who was the first to establish a medical practice.

Besides Pietermaritzburg, two other towns were planned. At Port Natal one George Cato, who had come to Natal in March 1839 to trade with the trekkers, was appointed to lay out a plan of a town along the north-east beach. In June 1840 the first public sale of plots was held. Plots fetched from £18 for big 100 x 700-foot erven to £3 15s. for smaller sites in less favourable situations. Some 121 plots were sold, and in the course of time 40 families took up residence around the bay, with the majority concentrated in what was known as the village of Congella.

The second new town was laid out in the same year as a centre for the uplands of Natal. It was established on a farm granted to James Howell the previous year, among the rather bleak mixture of thorn trees, erosion and broken hills of that part of the land. It was there that the Bushman's River, after winding an erratic course through miles of rugged wilderness, suddenly swung round a bend and almost stopped in surprise; for before it lay a flat and shallow basin set in the hills, like the bottom of a frying pan.

Through this basin the river flowed lazily, as though resting a while on its journey. Beside its banks the trekkers laid out a straggling little town which they named Weenen (weeping) in memory of that wild night of death when Dingane's army had attacked them in the nearby valley of the Little Thukela.

A picturesque townlet grew up there, full of the music of water running down furrows, of tall trees, of bridges, neat streets, and irrigated fields like a patchwork quilt of many colours. A scattering of cottages and shops completed a village which still retains some of the atmosphere of those quiet days; for little has come to change it save a quaint narrow gauge railway, puffing along importantly, not so much linking Weenen with the outside world as insulating the place from it.

Weenen was never on the main highway, even in the days of its foundation. The old arterial wagon road leading down from the Drakensberg passes ran some miles west of the village. It crossed the upper Thukela on the farm Kleine Waterval, and with some minor twists and turns made its way straight down to the so-called Alleman's Drift across the Mngeni River, just above the waterfall of *kwaNogqaza* (Howick). From there it went to the outspan place of Kettlefontein on the farm Groenkloof, and then down to Pietermaritzburg over World's View. To Durban the road, with steeper gradients, followed substantially the same route as the modern road; first along the edge of the Valley of a Thousand Hills, then clinging to the course of the Mhlathuzana River and reaching Durban where South Coast Junction lies today.

With the practical details of their republic established, the trekkers turned to more abstract matters. Upon the recall of the British force from Durban they had considered their independence as having been completely recognised.

Their constitution provided for a president, but no such individual was elected and there was no more permanent a head of state then the chairman of the Volksraad, elected every four months.

Pretorius held the rank of head commandant and had aspirations to the presidency, but politically he was not a strong personality and he had many enemies. Stephanus Maritz and Jacobus Burger, particularly, opposed him, and the quarrel expended itself on all manner of minor issues. Pretorius and Maritz went to law and the whole of 1840 was notable for bitter feelings, with many people quarrelling over such matters as shares in the Zulu cattle and the allotment of farms. Trekkers were always good quarrellers, for it was a cheap form of entertainment and there was little else to do.

Towards the end of the year the arguments started to wear themselves out; the cattle were all divided, farms allocated and the trekkers were feeling more at home after the release of pent-up emotions. Pretorius remained as commandant. The presidency was left vacant by tacit agreement, while the government generally was strengthened by the arrival of the original architect of the trekkers' constitution, Jacobus Boshoff. He had been lately dismissed from British Colonial Service for his support of the trekkers; and now he journeyed up to Pietermaritzburg to become its *landdrost* and provide a cultured and educated brain to assist in solving the problems of the Republic.

The British, meanwhile, had been enraged, unbeknown to the trekkers, by news of the attack on Dingane; the seizure of the 1000 Zulu children as "apprentices" (which meant that they had to work for nothing until they reached the age of 21) and the killing of the two chiefs; all taking place as soon as their backs were turned. In June 1840, Napier was summarily instructed to re-occupy Port Natal and re-establish "the influence of the British name in a country which is devastated by the reckless proceedings of the Queen's subjects."

Napier received this instruction in the midst of frontier disturbances which occupied all his available force. Also, he was kindly disposed towards the trekkers and wished rather for a peaceful settlement with them than an enforcement of British rule.

Accordingly, when they wrote to him on 4 September 1840, asking for peace and acknowledgement of their freedom, he was fain to correspond with them and see if conciliation could not settle the problem. Negotiations followed and a happy conclusion might have been reached but for the intervention of a most unfortunate episode.

From the beginning of their occupation of Natal the trekkers had been plagued with stock thefts. First the Zulus, and then the Bushmen from the Drakensberg swept down at night and played havoc with their herds. There is no surer way of raising hell in a farmer's heart than to rob him of his cattle; and the trekkers were not notably restrained in such matters as vengeance and rage.

After much quarrelling among themselves as to what to do in the matter, the hotheads among the trekkers decided on a punitive expedition. In December 1840, Pretorius led 190 men on a raid calculated to liquidate the cattle thieves, whoever they might be.

They swept down the length of the Drakensberg and found all the signs indicating that the cattle raids were engineered by Ncapayi, the chief of the Baca people. In January 1841, therefore, the commando attacked this erring chief and had no difficulty in wiping him out, for his following at that time consisted of little save a group of professional bandits, their hands already stained by the blood of quite a few murders.

The commando recovered many of the stolen animals in Ncapayi's kraal. After seizing a number of other animals as compensation, they rode back to the republic.

Faster than the commando rode, rumours of this punitive raid travelled southwards as each alarmed tribesman shouted a greater distortion to his southern neighbour. By the time the British heard of the event in their frontier outposts the raid had grown into a full-scale invasion of the peaceful Pondo tribal lands.

The British were enraged. For years they had sought to lull the inflammatory border into some sort of dependable peace, and now, living up to the worst anticipations, the trekkers were apparently wrecking the whole political edifice with their irresponsible adventures. In the same month the British hastily sent up Captain Thomas Smith with a small mixed force from Fort Peddie to a strongpoint on the Mgazi River, from which it was calculated that he would be able to repel the threatened trekker invasion of the border tribes.

So far as negotiations between the Republic and the British over independence were concerned, the Ncapayi raid was the death-blow. Even the Pietermaritzburg Volksraad had sensed that a major blunder was being made. At the time of the raid the eighth article in the treaty of independence they were negotiating specifically stated "that this Republic engages never to make a hostile movement against any of the native tribes who reside between the boundary of the said Republic and that of the Colony of the Cape of Good Hope without first giving notice thereof to the representative of that government here, or to the governor..."

Negotiations came to a sudden end. After months of silence, the British Governor wrote, on 10 June 1841, that he "could not enter into negotiations or further communication with them until they distinctly acknowledge their full and entire allegiance as British subjects."

While the Volksraad engaged in bitter recriminations over this awkward Ncapayi raid, a fresh trouble disturbed them. When they had first reached Natal they had found it practically depopulated of Africans. Accordingly, the trekkers had shared out Natal among themselves, with no thought at all of complications with aboriginal inhabitants.

Now, after the defeat of the Zulus, the trekkers learnt just why Natal had been so inviting a no-man's-land. A horde of tribespeople who had fled the country in fear of their lives 20 years before, in Shaka's time, now started to troop happily back from sundry points of refuge in foreign lands. Overnight, whole parties of people would appear on farms, mostly allotted to trekkers but as yet unoccupied, squat contentedly down on their old kraal sites, and erect huts.

This influx drove the trekkers almost to distraction. After lengthy deliberation they decided, on 2 August 1841, that all the returned tribespeople should be forcibly collected, removed and settled in one vast location between the Mzimvubu and the Mthamvuna rivers. The classic policy of complete segregation could then be followed, with a convenient deviation which allowed each farm to retain five families of African squatters as a labour force.

The major fault with this policy lay in the fact that as soon as news of it spread abroad, Faku, the Pondo chief, sent screams of panic to the British, informing them that the proposed republican native location incorporated the whole of his, and some other border chieftains' tribal lands.

The official British hair stood on end at this development. At the same time came news that an American brig, the *Levant*, had crossed the bar at Port Natal in August, anchored in the lagoon and traded as much merchandise to the trekkers as they had money or ivory to pay for. This news put the Cape merchants into a panic and a chorus of protest was levelled at the Governor. A foreign power was entering the British trade preserve of Southern Africa and something had to be done, or a strategic threat on the sea route to India might result.

On 2 December, the British proclaimed that the rumoured seizure of Faku's lands as a location would be resisted; and reinforcements were despatched to Captain Smith to enable him to march up to Durban where, without interfering with the civil government of the trekkers, he was to establish his force as an effective antidote to any military adventures, frontier disturbances, or intrigues with foreign powers, which might disturb the all-important British trade route to the East, or the political balance along the borders of the Cape Colony.

TWELVE

Twilight of the Republic

If dawn and sunset are the most colourful portions of a day, then the beginning and ending of the Natal Republic were well in keeping with nature's convention. Born in an ominous red glow of treachery and strife, the Republic had a stormy career and then died in a bonfire of shooting, hard riding, quarrelling and sheer adventure, which are so typical of the story of Southern Africa.

In the Republic, news of the unfavourable turn of British feeling had revived old quarrels, and each sect was blaming the other. In the Volksraad a motion of censure was moved on Pretorius for his part in the Ncapayi raid, but the affair was talked out.

Rumours of the British military movements in the south stirred up war fever like a stick in a bees' nest. Guns were oiled, gunpowder dried and horses conditioned. News that the British intended to remain on the Mgazi River soothed jagged nerves somewhat. The trekkers relaxed into their private quarrels with relish, for land occupation was a hopeless mess. The whole of Natal was covered with farm claims and counter-claims and the Volksraad was dominated by the endless quarrels of rival claimants.

The resident ivory traders were also involved in the general bickering. The Republicans were highly suspicious of them. They well knew that the traders had accepted the Republic only through necessity and their allegiance remained with England. Accordingly, at the first sale of erven at Port Natal, the ringleaders of the traders had been forbidden to buy as the trekkers hoped this would drive them out of the country.

William Cowie, a Voortrekker himself, was suspended from his office as a field cornet for airing his opinions too freely, the trekkers having a suspicion that he was writing pertinent comments on their behaviour to the Cape newspapers.

With these and other grievances to irritate them, the ivory traders and some of the British trekkers were far from satisfied with the Republic. In the midst of this welter of disaffection and quarrelling, on 24 March 1842, a strange vessel, the *Brazilia*, slipped into the harbour of Port Natal, and dropped its anchor with a splash which sent ripples spreading as far as Cape Town and the British Foreign Office in London.

The ship was owned by a firm in Holland, J.S. Klyn & Co., and its story was romantic. In Holland news of the great trek had aroused much sympathy, and to many it seemed that the time had come for a rapprochement between the home country and its former colonial offspring.

An individual named George Gerhard Ohrig was particularly interested in this movement from a commercial point of view. He exerted himself to form an association to trade with the Natal Republic and published a pamphlet recounting the former attachment between Holland and the trekkers and extolling their courage and qualities. This pamphlet, *The Emigrants at Port Natal*, was widely read, but the sympathy it aroused failed to produce any cash from Dutch investors, for they were nervous of a possible clash with Britain.

Ohrig then induced his own firm to build and send out the *Brazilia*, under a Dutch captain named Cornelius Reus and with a super-cargo named Johan Smellekamp.

At Port Natal the two men were received with enthusiasm by all save the ivory traders, and were taken up to Pietermaritzburg. Some distance from the town a large party of young men met them, unyoked the oxen from their wagon and drew it in themselves, with the honoured visitors proudly seated inside.

The whole of Pietermaritzburg was gay with bunting; even items of underwear, it is said, were used to make up a shortage of supply. As was natural in people living so isolated a life, the trekkers picked up rumours with great facility, and news of the arrival of the little trading ship had been easily exaggerated into full-scale Dutch intervention in South African affairs.

In their troubles and isolation the trekkers seized on this unexpected event like a drowning man a plank. The Volksraad formally welcomed the visitors as representatives of Holland. There were religious services, "and strong men were observed to shed tears when a distribution was made of a number of Bibles and books of devotion which had been sent out as a present by Mr Jacob Swart."

For eight days public meetings, feastings and discussions enlivened the usually tranquil Pietermaritzburg days. Ohrig's pamphlet was read again and again by people who had hitherto read nothing other than the Bible, and this merchant's manifesto was thought to be as truthful as the Holy Book.

If the traders had not originally intended to be deceitful, they now found themselves almost committed to live up to their reputations as saviours of the threatened Republic.

Smellekamp was furnished with funds, and on 30 April he left over the Drakensberg for the Cape, in order to return to Holland and secure a treaty of assistance and supplies of scarcities – including ministers, schoolteachers, and 500 Dutch settlers.

At Swellendam the unofficial ambassador was arrested under an old law prohibiting foreigners from travelling without a pass. He was sent on to Cape Town on 25 June 1842 as a prisoner. After a couple of days of questioning in gaol in the mother city, he was released and allowed to return to Holland.

Back in Port Natal, the little *Brazilia* disposed of as much of her cargo as the trekkers could buy. The spectacle of this public auction in the old preserve of the ivory traders; the truculence of the Hollanders; and the atmosphere of enthusiastic hope of Dutch intervention against Britain, infuriated the few Englishmen still resident there.

Just before the *Brazilia* sailed on the next stage of her voyage to Batavia, George Cato and a friend of his, J. Douglas, carried off the official flagstaff as a sign of their annoyance. Skipper Reus and his men observed the insult from their ship. They promptly rowed ashore, caught Douglas and soundly thrashed him. Cato escaped in the bush, to commiserate with his fellows on the mortification of seeing Holland apparently supplant England as the owner of the old traders' settlement.

In the midst of the ivory traders' chagrin, an African messenger came tramping through the south coast bush with a private message for them. Captain Smith and his soldiers in Pondoland were to march up forthwith to Durban – would the ivory traders support them? The reply can be imagined.

On 1 April 1842, Smith marched off from the Mgazi River for Durban. He started with 263 men, their families, and 60 wagons; but this establishment was increased slightly during the course of the journey. One Joseph Brown, bugler of the 27th Regiment, graphically described the journey in his letters home.

With the lusty singing of "We Fight to Conquer" they plodded off gaily enough, but it was a hard journey.

"We were three days marching through Faku's territory. The same night Mrs Giligan was delivered of a son, and the next day the commissariat issuer's wife was delivered of a beautiful daughter. On the morning of the 9th, we arrived on the sea coast, where we took breakfast, and every man had a good swim in the salt water, and had great eating of oysters and many other varieties of shellfish.

"Our march chiefly was along the S.E. coast the whole way, until within a few days of Natal. We came across many pieces of wrecks belonging to unfortunate vessels, and skeletons of whales; and many curious shells, and many other things, were picked up by the men and the officers, as we went along.

"The men caught three brown bucks, and gave them to the officers. We saw a great many sea-cows, and came across the spoor of lions and elephants in the woody parts along the coast. We suffered much from marching in the sand; it got into our boots, and cut our feet to pieces; and the sun, reflecting from the sand, burned our faces. In like manner, the men had many fatigues in repairing the roads every four or five miles they went along.

"… we crossed 122 rivers, and most of them we had to swim over; some of them extending across 600 and 700 yards in breadth, they are the largest and greatest rivers I ever saw in my life. We stopped two days and part of the third at the Um-komaas River. During our stay here, we had to muster, parade, and Articles of War."

From this point the force proceeded with great caution, for Smith had no idea of what sort of reception awaited him from the trekkers. As they neared Durban, however, the ivory traders came down to meet them, all heavily armed with swords, pistols, and double-barrelled elephant guns; and they brought the news that the trekkers would be hostile but would certainly not attack without prior discussion of the position with Smith.

At the Mbilo River a trekker spokesman, Jan Meyer, met them and officially protested at the British occupation, but there was no resistance.

At about 4 p.m., on 4 May 1842, the soldiers bivouacked on a hill adjoining Robert Dunn's old Sea View estate. The next morning Smith inspected the environment of the bay and hauled the Union Jack up in place of the Republican flag waving over the Point. On 6 May the troops set out for the selected site of their encampment.

All this time the trekkers had hardly shown a sign of interest. Congella was almost deserted, for the men were mustering under Pretorius a few miles inland.

"We marched through the town," wrote the bugler, "and came to our camp ground at eleven o'clock; but such a place for bad water I never saw in my life; it is as black as ink, and full of different insects, and stinks into the bargain."

Nevertheless, it was there that they camped, at the Old Fort site of Durban, and while they built a rough stronghold the men slept in their accoutrements in case there was any attempt at surprise.

Captain Smith was a middle-aged officer whose years in the regular army had revealed him as a conscientious man, but without much talent in anything save administration. His government had not sent him to Natal with his pocket army to indulge in heroics or conquests. The visit was intended as a demonstration of British authority, to warn the trekkers of the consequences should they disturb the peace by any future interference with the border tribes. Before the soldiers reached Durban it had already been decided to withdraw them once the gesture of authority had been made.

After the troops had passed through Congella, Pretorius and his men reoccupied the place. Smith sallied out with his men to meet Pretorius at a rendezvous near the village. The troops were drawn up at ease and stared at Pretorius curiously as he rode up for the meeting. "He is about six feet high, and has a belly on him like the bass drum," mused the bugler.

Captain Thomas Smith had no great authority. He had been told to impress upon the trekkers that they were responsible to Britain for their behaviour and were legally still British subjects. The trekkers' deputation somewhat took the wind out of his sails, by telling him that they were in treaty with Holland. Still, he tried to overawe them with such examples of the pomp and power of the Queen, as his person and his force presented. The trekkers were not much impressed. They outnumbered the British three to one and well knew that they were better shots and fighters than any professional soldiers with stereotyped, parade-ground training.

The meeting broke up. Days passed in an uneasy unofficial truce. The soldiers were busy building their little fort and the trekkers were all bustle and preparation at Congella. Several times the trekkers tried to negotiate with Smith but, like all army officers, he was nervous of departing from the strict letter of his instructions, and he would have nothing to do with them unless they acknowledged themselves to be British subjects.

The soldiers were short of rations from the start. They had hoped to obtain supplies of food in Natal, but the farmers boycotted them entirely. Fortunately two small ships, the *Mazeppa* and the *Pilot*, arrived with some stores; but there was no fresh food of any sort.

Smith started to commandeer provisions, and the trekkers immediately retaliated. One night they swept down and rustled away Smith's 600 draught oxen, thus leaving him stranded with his 60 wagons.

Smith was in a fury. Like most of his kind, he suffered from the professional fallacy that the enemy is always a contemptible amateur for whom, as a point of honour, there must be nothing but scorn. It was a professional weakness which had in the past caused much grief among British widows – and it was destined to cause much more.

At 11 p.m. on the night of 23 May, Smith sent his force marching silently down to the bay, along a path which was later Aliwal Street. From there, one section of the force set out along the beach in an effort to surprise the trekker encampment. Another section loaded a howitzer into a boat and became the navy for a while; the idea being to row the piece within range and then open up a devastating surprise bombardment.

The trekkers could hear a tax collector or a British soldier coming from as far away as Cape Town, let alone from Smith's little fort and accompanied by a squeaky gun carriage. They lay entrenched behind the mangrove trees and waited for the soldiers to present the best possible target.

The fight was short and sharp. Standing hopelessly exposed on the beach, the soldiers tried to make a stand, until someone with some sense told them to run for home. Within three minutes 17 soldiers were killed, 31 wounded, and 3 missing. The trekkers chased them to the fort and spent the rest of the night peppering the place with bullets. One trekker had been killed during the whole operation.

Smith and his men were in a sad way. Short of food, and quite unprepared for such a contingency, the future looked pretty bleak in their solitary fort. While he considered what to do, Smith secured a 24-hour truce in order to bury his dead and succour the wounded.

The only chance of survival seemed to be to obtain reinforcements. But how? Smith discussed the matter with some of the traders during the day, while the soldiers hastily used the period of the truce to strengthen the camp with an additional trench.

That night, one of Smith's confidants, the trader G.C. Cato, went quietly aboard the anchored *Mazeppa*. On it was sleeping Dick King, whose charmed life and extreme toughness was already part of the story of Natal. Cato shook him up and told him of the trouble and their decision. Somebody had to ride, by hook or by crook, to Grahamstown and report the disaster.

King asked no questions. He was a taciturn sort of man. He went ashore and woke his 16-year-old servant Ndongeni. Two good horses were available although, thinking King would ride alone, only one set of saddle and stirrups was provided, an omission which was to mean misery for the young Zulu.

It was at midnight on 25 May that the two set off from the Point. Two rowing boats ferried them across the bay. In them George and Joseph Cato, Peter Hogg and John Douglas tugged at the oars, while King and Ndongeni held the reins of their horses which were swimming behind.

On Salisbury Island the two men landed. There they whispered good-bye to the others. Then they made their way through the mangroves and waded across the narrow channel to the further shore.

There they mounted. Dodging moonbeams; they started their ride. They climbed the Bluff, to Mnini's kraal, and asked him to obliterate their trail. Then, down the coast they went, to the mouth of the Mlazi. They swam across, avoiding the ford which they knew was picketed by the Republicans.

On they went, riding hard but silently, even the horses seemingly aware of the urgency of the journey.

At dawn they swam the Lovu and hid in the thick bush near the mouth for the day, drying their clothes and eating. Ndongeni, wearing only a shrunken *mutshi* and an innocent expression, slipped out to reconnoitre the land. He met a party of Republicans who told him Dick King had been shot during the night in Durban Bay.

With darkness the two resumed their journey. In the blackness they swam the Mkhomazi River. There some friendly Africans, who knew all about the adventure through the bush telegraph service, warned them that the Republicans were on their trail.

They raced onwards, across the Mphambanyoni close to the sea. At dawn, cold and grey, they were at the Mzimkhulu. From there on they felt safer and could ride in daylight. On down the coast they went, as far as the Mthamvuna. There they swung more inland to the old military post on the Mgazi River, and to the various mission stations, where they secured fresh mounts.

At Mgazi, Ndongeni, suffering intensely from chafing, was given a saddle and stirrups; but the relief came too late. "My legs had almost been jerked from their sockets by them," he said. He struggled on a bit further with his master, but then King told him to return. He rested at the Mgazi camp for a while and then walked back to Durban. Later he was rewarded with a piece of land, called Ndongeni, after him, on the north bank of the Mzimkhulu, where today he lies buried.

Notwithstanding a two-day delay through illness, Dick King reached Grahamstown, 600 miles and reputedly 122 rivers from Durban, ten days after leaving the besieged camp; and his tale of disaster stirred the military there as never before.

In Durban, meanwhile, at dawn on 26 May, the trekkers sprang a surprise attack on the Point. Creeping stealthily along the beach from the mouth of the Mngeni River, they pounced out of the bush on the guards at the diminutive Fort Victoria which protected the port. Two soldiers and one trader, Charlie Adams, were killed.

Sixteen other soldiers were taken prisoner, along with G.C. Cato, F. Armstrong, S. Beningfield, J. Douglas, J. Hogg, H. Ogle, H. Parkins, D. Toohey, F. McCabe and B. Schwikkard. The *Mazeppa* and the *Pilot* were also captured and well looted, but their crews were left aboard. The rest of the prisoners were removed, first to Congella, and then to the gaol in Pietermaritzburg.

The trekkers settled down to the process of starving Smith and his men into submission. They surrounded the fort and erected at suitable spots the few guns they had captured. With this artillery they commenced a desultory bombardment, which resulted in 651 shots being thrown into the fort by 25 June.

Before they settled down to really serious siege operations, the trekkers, on 1 June, considerately sent a flag of truce into the fort with the Reverend Mr Archbell, a missionary who had come up from the Cape with Smith. They stated that they would allow women and children to leave the fort and go aboard the *Mazeppa*, where they would be out of danger.

Smith naturally was only too pleased to rid himself of so many non-combatant mouths to feed. The women and children were courteously escorted on to the ship by the Republicans and the siege continued with all energy.

On the ship Christopher Joseph Cato considered the position carefully and decided to take a chance. On 10 June a brisk south-wester sprang up. With the aid of the crew he cut the cable. The seven women and eighteen children helped the twelve members of the crew to hoist the sails and they slipped out to sea. The Republicans peppered the little 90-ton schooner with shots from their elephant guns, but mattresses were fixed up along the bulwarks and no serious damage was done. With a cheer they cleared the bar and sailed off safely to Lourenço Marques hoping to find there a British warship.

At Durban, Smith and his men received great encouragement from this escape. With two chances of news being carried to the outside world it was now merely a matter of waiting for aid.

As sieges go, it was not an unduly severe affair. Some of the British traders, such as William Cowie, managed to smuggle a few head of cattle to the fort; and at worst rations were reduced to half-a-pound of dried horseflesh a day, some biscuits, and forage-corn ground into meal. An occasional skirmish broke the monotony of proceedings, but beyond that the Republicans were content to take things easy and this certainly suited the British. During the whole siege eight soldiers and four of the trekkers were killed.

News of the discomfiture of Smith and his men spread throughout Southern Africa in a remarkably short space of time. Far off – on the central plains, in the farmsteads of the Cape and around remote hunters' campfires in the bush – rugged characters discussed the affair with concern or jubilation, as their prejudices allowed.

So far as the British officially were concerned, the news Dick King brought them of the firing of the first shot settled the fate of Natal. The Government may have decided to abandon the place and leave the trekkers to their own devices, but a defeat of a British force involved delicate matters of prestige. News of the affair had already given stimulus to rebellious leanings in the Cape and it could not be tolerated. One dead soldier settled the fate of a Republic!

At Port Elizabeth, a company of the 27th Regiment under Captain Durnford was sent post-haste aboard a small vessel named the *Conch*, under Captain Bell. Bell knew Durban harbour well, as he had traded there, and accordingly had offered the services of himself and his boat.

While news of the affair was hastily carried on to Cape Town, the *Conch* sailed up to Durban. Nearing the Bluff, on 24 June, the soldiers were packed down below and the little ship sailed to an anchorage with almost a smirk of innocence. After some delay, a boat came from the shore with two men aboard. One was Edmund Morewood who had been appointed Port Captain by the Republicans and the other was an overdressed military secretary to Pretorius.

Both clambered importantly aboard and promptly discovered the soldiers, packed like sardines, grinning up at them from the hold. Morewood went visibly pale around the gills, and a vision of being hanged as a renegade swayed through his mind like a noose in the wind.

The two men, however, were sent back with a letter to Pretorius, asking permission to land a doctor and a letter for Captain Smith. That night a stream of rockets was fired into the air, while the besieged men in the fort cheered and laughed in the knowledge that relief was at hand.

All the next day the *Conch* lay at anchor, waiting for the reinforcements which must be coming from the Cape. That evening the frigate *Southampton* arrived, loaded with troops under Lt Col A.J. Cloete, and a hurried consultation was held over plans for landing.

On shore, the Republicans made one last effort to take the fort but failed. In the morning the *Southampton* sent some broadsides into the Point bush and by noon the time was ripe for landing.

The *Conch* was crammed with soldiers, protected by shields of planks and blankets run around the sides. With a string of the *Southampton*'s boats tied behind, she sailed boldly in across the bar. A hail of bullets welcomed her, killing three men and wounding five others, but the Republicans soon lost heart. The boats made for the shore and the Republicans vanished into the bush with the soldiers in full cry after them.

A second party of troops under Major D'Urban made a landing on the ocean beach. The force combined and, with scant resistance, the men marched in to relieve the fort at 4 p.m. that afternoon, 34 days after the commencement of the siege. The welcome they received can be imagined. The fort was a sad wreck; every wagon and shelter was riddled with bullet holes and an evil stench pervaded the whole place. The only horse still alive was sitting on its hind quarters like a dog, struggling weakly to rise.

The next day Cloete marched on Congella. There was no resistance. The village was deserted by all save two Germans and two others, and the 20 houses were left to the mercy of the troops. The Republican force had retired to the bush twelve miles away.

Cloete relieved the village of such food as it contained and then abandoned it. Fresh food was his immediate preoccupation; and the need to recoup the loss of Smith's transport animals, which had been rustled by the Republicans. Accordingly, he asked the local tribespeople, who had watched these military operations with great interest, to secure as many cattle for him as possible. The convenient excuse for looting they accepted with relish, and much trouble did they cause to the farmers – and to the British, when the Republicans subsequently blamed them for starting off a series of raids and murders.

There was no more fighting. After assessing the strength and determination of the British force, the trekkers withdrew to Pietermaritzburg, where they fell to quarrelling with one another over who was to blame and what was to be done.

There was complete pandemonium in the town. In the general excitement one hothead, Jacobus Snyman, went to the gaol, stuck a gun between the bars, and fired into the cell containing the British prisoners captured at the Point. At this they started such a clamour that Pretorius came himself and released them. The hothead was arrested and placed in the stocks himself to cool off, while the former prisoners were given their guns and a wagon and told to clear off.

On 14 July, Cloete went up to Pietermaritzburg to talk things over. After a stormy Volksraad meeting, Boshoff, Pretorius and Landman (the three leaders) induced their fellows to agree to a provisional peace, which involved recognition of the sovereignty of the Queen and restoration of all looted property. In return, Cloete announced a general amnesty to all save four men and then went back to Durban.

Apart from the usual shouting and argument, it seemed that the days of the Republic were over. Pending political solution of the problem, Cloete left the Republican administrative institutions in power and then sailed for the Cape with his men on 21 July. Smith, who was made a major for his work, was left as temporary military commandant of Natal at Durban, with a garrison of 350 men to maintain order and protect the trekkers from any raids by unruly tribespeople.

The Union Jack looked at its own reflection in the waters of the romantic old River of Natal, while behind it the crimson sky at the setting of the Republican sun gradually faded into the darkness of a few men's despair.

The "Conch", crossing the bar.

THIRTEEN
The Colony of Natal

With the departure of Lt Col Cloete, there was a lull in the affairs of the Republic of Natal. Major Smith sat pompously in Durban as Commandant of Natal; but the trekkers were left very much to their own devices, while the British Government made up its mind what to do with the place.

It was not an easy decision to make. Sir George Napier, the Governor of the Cape, had for long strongly favoured the occupation of Natal, if only to stop further migration and the slow draining away of the best farmers from the Cape.

The British authorities, however, had never agreed with him over this question. Before they received news of the clash at Durban they sent to him, on 25 August 1842, categorical instructions to withdraw Smith's garrison as soon as the flag had been shown and then to abandon Natal. They saw no sense in extending boundaries to overtake a people who were likely to migrate still further and thus force another unprofitable annexation.

Napier had to sit on this last instruction and wait for his superiors to digest the news of the fight. Meanwhile, Natal was left to seethe with unrest and intrigue. Hotheads all over the colony planned fresh wars and schemed to kick the British out.

Smith, at Durban, had a warm time of it during the months of uncertainty. The trekkers despised him and he had little control over the situation. He was constantly plagued with rumours of coming upheavals, which threatened to box him up in Durban even more effectively than in the past.

At last, on 18 December 1842, the British Government made up its mind. Napier was instructed to send to Natal some suitable individual to act as commissioner. He was to communicate with the trekkers, confirm the terms of Cloete's peace treaty, and examine the country in detail. Then he was to find out the number of farmers and obtain their opinion as to how they would like to be administered. Slavery was to be abolished which meant the ending of the convenient apprentice system; there was to be no legal distinction between colours or creeds; and no aggression tolerated against local tribes.

By the time these instructions reached Napier it was May 1843. On the 12th of that month he issued a proclamation, announcing the incorporation of Natal into the Empire as a British colony and the appointment of the Honourable Henry Cloete, a barrister brother of Lt Col A.J. Cloete, to be Her Majesty's Commissioner.

On 5 June, Cloete arrived at Durban to commence his task. He sent a message up to Pietermaritzburg, announcing his arrival and calling a public meeting. He then asked Smith to provide him with a suitable escort – but that worthy had still not grown out of his subaltern days and refused any assistance whatever, as he had received no instructions.

Cloete rode up to Pietermaritzburg and arrived there on the 8th. He found the little town boiling with excitement. For long the trekkers had been hoping that Smellekamp would return from Holland with assistance. To their delight the *Brazilia* had actually sailed into Durban the previous month (8 May) but Smith had refused permission for anyone to land. The ship had sailed away again, leaving only rumours that Dutch warships would soon be at hand; and the idea of a last-minute rescue of the Republic had unsettled everyone.

The day after his arrival, Cloete addressed a meeting of about 450 people in the court-hall. He then explained his mission, while the crowd listened attentively. Then Anton Fick stood up and announced that he wished to read sundry resolutions passed by a public meeting a few days back.

Cloete objected, but he had no choice. The resolutions protested at the treatment given to the *Brazilia*; and then went on to present a long statement prepared by the trekkers' wives, detailing their past suffering and appealing to the people not to recognise Cloete's authority.

This was too much for the Commissioner. He left the hall, leaving the meeting to its own devices. In his report on proceedings he considered that there were many people sympathetic to the British, but they were frightened of coming forward without adequate protection.

Certainly, the amount of abuse and threats against any traitors in Pietermaritzburg was impressive. Messengers were also riding off, carrying news of proceedings to the Voortrekkers settled in the central plains, and things looked ominous.

Cloete prepared some posters, calling upon occupiers to present claims for the ownership of their land – but the signs were promptly defaced or destroyed. British residents and a few other foreigners registered claims, but of the Boers only a small minority made any effort, and they did so furtively, as though ashamed.

It seemed to Cloete that law and order would have to be effected before anything could be achieved. In his report he asked for 200 troops to garrison the town – and he suggested that Johan Zietsman, the present *landdrost*, be supported in power, for he was disposed to be friendly.

For the rest of his stay, Cloete tried to learn as much as possible about the Republic. Then, having arranged for a special Volksraad meeting on 7 August, the Commissioner returned to Durban.

Acting on Cloete's advice, the British sent up 200 reinforcements to Durban and empowered Smith to despatch them to Pietermaritzburg. A first-class row immediately developed between Cloete and Smith. The major reckoned that the 200 men were hopelessly inadequate, and he refused to send them to the capital for fear that they would be cut off with no cavalry to support them and no lines of communication.

Cloete was in an awkward position; but fortunately a letter arrived from the leaders of the trekkers, giving assurance of personal safety and requesting him to come on his own to avoid any danger of a clash.

Cursing Smith for a fool, Cloete had to ride off to Pietermaritzburg, while Smith glowered after him and muttered his disbelief that a civilian interloper could do any good with such a treasonable crowd.

Cloete rode up through the superb scenery, his mind beset with doubts as to the nature of his reception. To his surprise, he was met three miles out of the town by a mounted party of about 75 men, who escorted him into Pietermaritzburg with great civility. Perhaps it was just as well that Major Smith and his men had remained in Durban. The trekkers were in an ugly mood, but they would not take it out on any one individual.

Cloete found Pietermaritzburg jammed with people, gathered for a meeting which they all felt would be the most momentous in the history of the Republic. The trekkers' political arrangements had always allowed their fellows from the central plains to take a full part in their deliberations and, of the 650 heavily armed men who thronged the little town, some 200 were a particularly wild and freedom-loving crowd who had come from beyond the Drakensberg, under a tough leader named F.G. Mocke.

Mocke and his men intended to dominate the Volksraad proceedings. A most stormy and unruly meeting was held, with the number of Volksraad representatives enlarged to 36, to include men from beyond the mountains.

Feeling that they were in a minority, Mocke and his men declined eventually even to nominate any members. For the rest of the proceedings, they confined themselves to standing in the body of the hall, shouting abuse and threats to those taking part in the meeting.

The Volksraad quarrelled until late that night. Several of the best-known members, such as Pretorius and Zietsman and Joachim Prinsloo, advised moderation, for they knew what the Republic was up against. No decision could be reached. The meeting adjourned and the rumpus travelled out of the Volksraad building, spreading over the town like a breeze, arguing and murmuring and quarrelling with itself until morning.

The next day the representatives of the outer areas withdrew from the Volksraad entirely, leaving the matter to the Natalians. Whatever Natal decided about itself, they would retain their independence on the central plains.

Natal's mind was largely made up by a letter received overland from Lourenço Marques. It came from Smellekamp. After Smith had refused landing permission to the *Brazilia*, the ship had sailed up to the Portuguese port. In his letter Smellekamp regretfully informed the Republic that Holland would not support them, for fear of a clash with Britain.

Instead of military support, Smellekamp now could offer only trade and the comfort of a schoolteacher and a licentiate preacher, who had come out from Holland with him to join the Republic.

All day the Natalians weighed up the situation. Cloete stayed in a house nearby and waited for a decision. Constant deputations and messages from the Volksraad kept him occupied all day.

One of the deputations consisted of a most aggressive party of women. They stormed into Cloete's room and told him that, in view of the hardships they had shared with their husbands, they felt they were entitled to a voice in affairs. The Volksraad had sent them about their business, so they had come to tell Cloete of their fixed determination never to yield to British authority. They would rather walk barefoot back across the Drakensberg.

Cloete tried to reason with them, but feelings soon became raw. Cloete irately told them that as married ladies, they boasted of a freedom which even in a social state they could

211

not claim, and that, however much he sympathised with their feelings, he considered it a disgrace on their husbands to allow them such a state of freedom. The interview broke up in disorder.

Towards the approach of evening on that stormy day, a deputation came from the Volksraad and presented their declaration of unconditional acceptance of the British annexation of Natal. Twenty-four of the twenty-five members of the Volksraad had signed the declaration.

Cloete was jubilant. He reported his success to the government that night, and recommended that the boundaries of Natal should be those laid down in the famous Piet Retief treaty with Dingane. Garrisons at Durban and Pietermaritzburg would easily keep the country under control; while a third force stationed at Daniel Bezuidenhout's farm at the foot of the principal Drakensberg pass, would seal off the unruly element beyond the mountains.

These men from the central plains were bitterly disappointed at the course of events. Most of them went back dejectedly across the mountains the next day. Others lurked around Pietermaritzburg for some time, roaming the streets at night and throwing rocks on the roofs of the houses of those they considered to have betrayed the Republic. There were so many complaints about this behaviour that the reluctant Smith was eventually persuaded to march 200 men to Pietermaritzburg. On 31 August 1843 he hauled up the Union Jack on a hill slope overlooking the town, and commenced work upon a fortification which was named Fort Napier, after the Governor of the Cape.

With Smith at Pietermaritzburg to watch over affairs, Cloete decided that his immediate duty was to journey up to Zululand to see Mpande and inform him of the changes in Natal. As Smith still refused to supply him with even an interpreter, let alone a military escort, Cloete obtained the services of three of the traders – Joseph Kirkman, Henry Ogle and D.C. Toohey –

while Commandant Rudolph of the Republicans accompanied him as escort.

Mpande received Cloete with his habitual politeness on 30 September. News of events in Natal was listened to with interest, and the boundary lines were then confirmed in writing by both, as following the Thukela River to its junction with the Buffalo, and then up that tributary to the Drakensberg.

After five days of conversation and entertainment, Cloete rode off to examine the renowned Lake St Lucia, which the Republicans had considered of great potential value as a future harbour. Cloete was disappointed in both it and the Mhlathuze lagoon.

Lake St Lucia was too shallow, and the bars of both made it too obviously impracticable at the time to develop them into harbours. Nevertheless, as a precaution against any foreign power ever seizing Lake St Lucia, he induced Mpande to cede it to Britain in the treaty of peace signed by the two on 5 October 1843. Cloete then rode back to Natal, satisfied that Zulu affairs were well under control.

In Natal there were many problems for the energetic Commissioner to solve before the place could be considered satisfactorily launched upon its career as a British colony. Land ownership was in a particularly horrible mess. The Republic had entered all applications for farms provisionally into their books, pending future investigation. Boundaries of farms were often hazy, and beacons were remembered vaguely as being, for instance, at a place where some person had once shot a buffalo; and in at least half the cases the same farm was claimed by more than one person.

The usual land sharks had jumped gleefully into this confused picture. Individuals such as Commandant G.J. Rudolph claimed to own 40 farms; while other land racketeers, such as F. Collison and S. Benningfield, managed to have some twenty-nine 6000-acre farms registered between them.

Topping even the claims of these ambitious individuals was one for the whole of Natal. This claim was made by the widow of Lieutenant Farewell, on the strength of the original cession by Shaka. It was fortunate perhaps that Lieutenant King, Nathaniel Isaacs, J. Collis, Captain Gardiner and a few other pioneers didn't put in like claims, for all, including Piet Retief, had received at various times equally embracing grants of the fair land of Natal.

Cloete had a nightmare task sorting out all these claims. Bona fide occupation of land was made the touchstone by which he recognised the rights of title; but very few of the Republicans were in that happy state. Of the 365 families then in residence in Natal, most had clung to the towns until recently, in apprehension of any Zulu troubles or war with the British; and only preliminary development work had been done on the farms.

Seven hundred and sixty people claimed ground when Cloete asked them to register. Of these, 260 were ruled out on technical grounds, many of them claiming farms for which others already held title deeds or documentary proof of possession from the Republic.

One hundred and ninety-eight people could prove bona fide occupation of their farms for twelve months prior to his arrival, while another 173 had been in occupation for shorter periods. To the first group Cloete granted 6000-acre farms. A total of 389 people lost their claims entirely and much ill-feeling consequently arose.

As his final act, Cloete, on 6 January 1844, rode up to examine northern Natal. Like the Republicans, he considered it the finest part of the whole colony. "It is by far the most healthy part of the country for cattle," he wrote, "and coal is so abundant that in every river or stream the strata lie exposed, and every shower of rain, by filling these streams, throws off fragments which are picked up in the beds of the rivers."

Then, having done his job both diligently and patiently, Cloete left Natal at the end of April 1844 to report to Governor Napier in Cape Town. Cloete recommended a most liberal treatment of the Republicans, both in land distribution and political control. Napier was inclined to agree with him that in that way lay the making of contented subjects, but their recommendations had to go to London for assessment and approval.

In the long delay that followed before the final fate of Natal was known, life there proceeded as though under an uneasy truce. The Republicans had not much hope of regaining their independence. As a last chance, four young men – Joachim Prinsloo, Gert Rudolph, Cornelius Coetzee and young Bezuidenhout – had ridden all the way to Lourenço Marques in December 1843.

They had found Smellekamp still there, but the schoolmaster, L. Marliman, had died and the wife of the licentiate minister, P.N. Ham, had passed away in childbirth. Smellekamp informed the young men that the Dutch government had refused to have anything to do with the Republic, as the British had asserted sovereignty right up to the twenty-fifth degree of latitude, and any foreign power meddling in that area would do so at grave risk. All Smellekamp could do was suggest that they move north, across the twenty-fifth degree of south latitude, and open trade with him at Lourenço Marques.

Disappointed most bitterly, the young men turned for home 24 hours after their arrival at the port. It was a long path they followed. Coetzee died of fever on the way and Prinsloo died two weeks after reaching home. The other two could report only disappointment to their fellows, and the last hopeful gleam in the eyes of the stricken Republic faded into a memory.

People tried to adapt themselves to the new times, but conditions were against settlement. As the months passed, all manner of conflicting rumours were rife as to the ultimate intentions of the British Government. Meanwhile, Major Smith was the sole sign of British authority. Apart from sitting in one of his two forts, he did little to reassure the people, although he was kindly enough.

During the delay many of the farmers started to drift out of Natal. It was not only hostility to the British which caused this. Bushmen stock-rustlers were very busy raiding cattle, and their haunts in the deepest fastnesses of the Drakensberg defied discovery.

The apparently lush Natal grasslands had also proved something of a disappointment. The sheep farmers, particularly, found there were many stock diseases in Natal. In company with the cattlemen, their thoughts turned to the fine, sweet grazing of the central plains, and many abandoned the green but sour grasslands of Natal as not worth the trouble they were having to get possession of them.

There was at least some development in the towns. The first newspaper, *De Natalier*, started in Pietermaritzburg early in April 1844, under the control of one whom Major Smith referred to as "an unprincipled Frenchman of the name of Boniface".

A few business enterprises commenced. Tradesmen wandered in from the outside world and opened up a handful of shops, and some effort at entertainment took place. A Pietermaritzburg Turf Club held a meeting of sorts on 8 July 1844, while the Natal Turf Club at Durban followed suit on the 22nd of the same month. A few dances, play-readings and romances also whiled away the days.

Everybody felt restless during the long wait for news from London. Feelings varied month by month. The Volksraad remained in civil authority over the country; and in September 1844, when new representatives were elected and all refused to take the oath of allegiance to the Crown, the old Raad had to remain in office while a new election was arranged. Thus it lived on for a while – but only in name.

At last, in February 1845, came the long-awaited news: Natal was to be annexed as a district to the Cape settlement as from 31 May 1844. The recommendations of Cloete and Napier about administrative control were considerably watered down. It was not considered practical to treat Natal as a completely separate colony. It was too remote, and as yet had to be regarded as a poor relation of the Cape.

Legislative power, therefore, was to be in the hands of the

Governor and Executive Council of the Cape, and a Lieutenant Governor in Natal, aided by an Executive Council of five members. Local bodies or municipalities were to be formed, with powers of district taxation and legislation, while the Supreme Court of the Cape was to have supreme judicial power. British settlement in the area was to be positively encouraged.

The land recommendations of Cloete were substantially accepted, and the urgency of the matter was recognised by the prompt appointment of a Surveyor General, in the person of W. Stanger, with four assistants. To him was given the immediate task of deciding on boundaries and preparing a trigonometrical survey of the whole colony.

The various towns had also to be laid out, the problem of locations for the tribespeople looked into and, of course, all farms had to be accurately surveyed at a cost of £11 10s. to each farmer. Quitrents of £4 on a 6000-acre farm were also to be imposed and these were to be redeemable at 15 years' purchase.

To the Republicans the whole affair was a disappointment. They had at least hoped to be given some voice in their government, but now all that was given them was a control of municipal affairs. One by one they started to abandon their farms.

A few more months slipped by. Major Smith and his 27th Regiment left Natal at the end of August 1845, after being relieved by the 45th Regiment under Lt Col Boyes. While the new Commandant of Natal was settling down, a new series of ordinances and proclamations was issued by the British, describing the personal details of the new government of Natal.

There had been some difficulty in obtaining suitable officials for the new colony. It was a lonely and not very important place, and salaries were small. Accordingly, officials had to be appointed from junior members of the Cape Civil Service, and there was little enthusiasm for the transfer.

Still, for better or worse, the office of Lieutenant Governor was given to Martin West at a salary of £800 a year, which was a little more than his former position as Civil Commissioner of the lower Albany district had yielded.

Henry Cloete, the late Commissioner, was appointed as Recorder, or Judge, of Natal, at £600 a year; Donald Moodie became Secretary to Government at £500 a year; Walter Harding was appointed as Crown Prosecutor; and Theophilus Shepstone (the government agent at Fort Peddie) became Diplomatic Agent with the tribespeople in Natal, at a salary of £300. In that position he was destined to win more renown than the rest of his fellows put together.

Lieutenant Governor West arrived in Durban to the thuds of a 13-gun salute on Thursday, 4 December 1845, and was respectfully welcomed by the inhabitants. From there he went up to Pietermaritzburg as grandly as he could, seated together with his wife in an ox-wagon. On 12 December the capital received him pleasantly, with addresses of welcome, firing of rifles, and a regimental dinner; as *De Natalier* put it, "in admirable style, with great taste and judgment, with every luxury of the season, and wine in abundance."

Toasts were drunk, speeches were made, there were cheers, the regimental band played nobly, the British were gay and the Republicans were sad; for, in the nature of life, the death of the old had seen the birth of the new, and cheers for the future covered a sigh for the past.

FOURTEEN

Life in the sunshine

L ife in the sunshine of the old Colony of Natal was an
affair made insular and self-centred, if only through the
very isolation of the place. Few ships called, and those
that did were only small coastal traders from the Cape. There
was little business, and such agriculture as was practised was
tentative and exploratory; for none knew what crops the land
could most profitably yield, or what manner of livestock would
flourish best.

There were not more than 3000 Europeans in all the land at
the beginning of 1846, and there seemed to be greater incen-
tive for people to leave the country than to come into it. When
Lieutenant Governor West landed in Durban, he found 400
Voortrekker families resident in Natal as subjects. But twelve
months later all but 60 of these had wandered away, back
across the Drakensberg to Republican freedom in the vastness
of the central plains.

West did what he could to make the Voortrekkers satisfied
with the new administration. He was deluged with complaints
about the allocation of farms. Everybody in Natal seemed to
fall into one of two plaintive groups: either they had received
no land, or what they had received was too little. It was a nightmare task trying to please everyone, and the British Government to which he was responsible, was not very sympathetic.
Prejudiced by the European type of small, fertile, well-watered

farm, it was hard for them to understand a man in faraway Natal who complained of receiving only 2000 acres.

Another great trouble confronting the new authorities was the ceaseless cattle rustling of the Drakensberg Bushmen. Nearly every night livestock disappeared from some farm or other, and many people were forced by these night raiders to abandon their homes entirely. Nothing seemed to subdue the enterprising little thieves, and the harassed authorities, in February 1846, were forced to send Lieutenant C.J. Gibbs of the Royal Engineers, along with Colonel Piper and Stanger, the surveyor, off on a tour of the most troubled areas, in order to find suitable sites for military outposts.

The problem of the returning refugee tribespeople was also urgent. A special commission of inquiry went into the matter and, on 29 May 1846, it recommended that the only solution was to apportion a number of locations to house these people. It particularly recommended for this purpose the area south of the Zwart Kop Hills, and around some of the mission stations established by the Americans.

Of these missions, the most suitable were Groutville, established by Aldin Grout on the lower Mvoti in June 1844, and the area on the south coast between the Mlazi and Lovu rivers, where the Mlazi Mission was in full swing. The next year, 1847, the Reverend J.C. Bryant re-established the old Imfume Mission there and Adams commenced a new work on the upper aManzamtoti (*Adams Mission*).

The extent of the problem of these returning refugees was alarming. The 3000 tribespeople the trekkers had found in the area had grown to over 100 000, all determined to remake their homes now that the Zulus had been defeated.

The task of controlling these people was immense. It took years to shepherd them into the areas allocated as their new homes. As fast as one area was cleared of squatters, newcomers would arrive, like mushrooms springing up overnight. Shepstone, the young diplomatic agent among the tribespeople, had the task of arranging this mass reshuffling of humanity;

and his subsequent immense reputation sprang directly from his efficient, trouble-free management of the whole business.

Within ten years over 2 200 000 acres had been settled by the returned tribespeople. Over each area Shepstone appointed headmen and chiefs, for the government had no funds to support European officials and it was certainly preferable to have tribal law rather than anarchy. The Lieutenant Governor was appointed supreme chief, while Shepstone had the status of principal induna and did all the actual administration.

Shepstone certainly accomplished a mammoth task with conspicuous success. Through his administrative pyramid of tribal elders, headmen and chiefs he managed, with neither police nor military, to control all those tens of thousands of mixed people in tolerable peace, and with a firm kindliness which made the tribespeople extremely loyal to the Government. They paid their tax of 7s. a hut without murmur and busied themselves happily in re-erecting the structure of their ancient way of life, in conditions and security radically different from the murderous days of Shaka and the Zulu raids.

For purposes of European administration, Natal was at first divided into two magistracies. On 23 July 1846 these two magisterial districts of Pietermaritzburg and Durban were proclaimed, with Walter Harding holding dual authority as magistrate over both areas simultaneously.

This arbitrary partition of Natal was purely a temporary measure. In December of the same year the Lieutenant Governor appointed a commission to investigate the whole matter of future magistracies. William Stanger, Theophilus Shepstone and Lieutenant C.J. Gibb busied themselves in their spare time for the next twelve months in planning out the future of Natal, and an interesting time they must have had, visualising districts and choosing sites for villages and towns.

In their report, produced on 29 December 1847, they recommended that Natal be divided into eight magisterial districts. Apart from Durban and Pietermaritzburg, the six new districts were named after the principal river of the area concerned, for want of any better system of name-giving. The new districts were visualised in some detail. Umvoti was the name given to the first of the new divisions. This division lay right down the Thukela, from its middle reaches to its mouth. One village was planned at the mouth of the Thukela, while the seat of magistracy was to be at the old wagon ford across the Mvoti River, which gave its name to the district.

The second new district was named Impafane, from the Mpofana (Mooi) River. Its capital was to be at the ford across the Bushman's River, with ancillary villages at Weenen and the Mooi River Drift.

The third new district was to be known as Upper Tugela, with its centre at the Commando Drift over the Thukela River. Villages were also to be founded at Lombard's Drift, over the Thukela; and at Venter's Spruit, under the Drakensberg, near Bezuidenhout's Pass.

The fourth new district was to be called Umzinyati. A site for the capital of this district had already been selected by the late Volksraad. It was on the farm occupied by Andries Spies, on the Sunday's River. A village was also planned by the Commission at the foot of De Beer's Pass.

The two other new divisions were purely tentative and were left as unsurveyed reserve areas south of the Mkhomazi River. In the older division of Durban three new villages were planned: at the wagon ford over the Thongathi; at the wagon ford over the Mdloti; and on a stream flowing into Sterkspruit, below the farm of that name.

In the Pietermaritzburg division a new village was planned at Alleman's Drift, above the Mngeni waterfall, and on the Mlazi River near Van Der Schyff's farm.

All told, it was a comprehensive picture of a prosperous colony. The only thing wrong was that there were so few civilised inhabitants, and to remedy this, the Commission recommended extensive immigration from Britain.

The trouble about immigration was to provide some attraction for immigrants. At that time hardly anything was known of Natal in the outside world. There were not even any detailed maps of the place available, and the only information about Natal in newspapers and books dealt largely with sensational stories of Zulu raids and massacres – hardly the type of propaganda which would attract immigrants.

Month after month, the European population of Natal tended to decrease instead of increase. By January 1847 there were only 40 of the original Voortrekker families still living in Natal, and many of them were dissident.

Most restless of these remaining families were those living in the choice grazing lands between the Buffalo and Thukela rivers. The trekkers had always been more partial to this Klip River area than any other part of Natal. While many of their fellows elsewhere were abandoning their homes and wandering off across the Drakensberg, the Klip River settlers lingered on.

They were very uncertain about their future. With no newspapers, they were an easy prey to rumours that the area was to be given back to the Zulus; that it was to be turned into a location by Shepstone; or parcelled out to British immigrants.

Eventually, tired of all this uncertainty, four of the Klip River settlers – Andries Spies, the old *landdrost* of the area, Lodewyk de Jager, and G. and I. van Niekerk – rode up to see the Zulu king. Mpande denied that he had ever ceded the Klip River area to the British. The deputation then asked for permission to occupy the land, and this Mpande readily granted.

Indunas were sent to fix a boundary along the Buffalo River; and on 7 January 1847 a formal treaty was drawn up and signed by Andries Spies, Piet Uys, Johannes de Lange, the renowned hunter, and Mpande. In it the settlers received possession of the area, although Mpande reserved the right of military passage for his army.

All the settlers in the area contributed towards a purchase price of 1000 rix-dollars, and in return became burghers of what was proclaimed as the Klip River Republic. Andries Spies was elected Commandant, his brother Abraham became Registrar of Lands, and Lodewyk de Jager became Field Cornet.

News of this interesting political development first reached the British in May 1847. Lieutenant Governor West was incredulous at first. As a precaution he sent a letter up to Spies's farm, requesting information and informing the would-be Republicans that the frontier of Natal extended right up to the Buffalo, and the Klip River area was thus a part of the Colony.

The settlers were much excited at this news. Spies was away in Zululand at the time, but the African messengers sent by West returned to the Governor with the news that all the Republicans who had read the letter had stated that they would cross the Drakensberg if the British interfered.

Captain Kyle and John Shepstone were sent up to see Mpande to remind that forgetful monarch that the treaty signed with Commissioner Cloete set the boundary line with the British along the Buffalo River. Mpande acknowledged the older treaty without much hesitation. He had merely been confused, he stated, as to whether the boundary was final or just provisional.

All that remained now was to induce the little Republic to lie down quietly and proclaim itself dead. To officiate in this political burial the son of a missionary, young Archbell, was sent up on 28 June 1847. The young man could do little. He surreptitiously distributed a number of proclamations concerning the boundary in places where they would be discovered only after he had safely left, and then returned to the Governor with the news that the settlers regarded themselves as subjects of the Zulu king and the Republic declined to be buried.

On 3 August, West rode up himself to try to settle the matter. He encountered no resistance. The settlers just ignored him. He camped about eight miles north of the Klip River and tried to gather the settlers for a meeting, but they made a distinct detour around him if they even happened to come into his vicinity.

West returned nonplussed to Pietermaritzburg. A few other government representatives were sent up at different times, but they experienced like treatment. In the game of patience, however, the settlers were the first to weaken. They started to panic and quarrel among themselves. Eventually J. Uys rode down and asked West to send up an officer and enquire into the whole matter.

Walter Harding was sent up to Spies's farm and, on 27 September, 40 of the settlers met him there. Harding read out the details of the various treaties and soon convinced them that they had no legal title to the ground.

Spies defended their bid for independence on the grounds of the complete absence of government authority or protection in the area. He asked that the whole affair be forgiven and forgotten, that farms be registered and government properly established, instead of the old conditions of complete exposure on a dangerous frontier.

Harding was sympathetic. He reported to the Governor and, on 18 October, it was decided to appoint a magistrate over the area and establish a military post on Spies's farm as soon as circumstances permitted.

Full pardon was offered for all who took the oath of allegiance. J.M. Boshoff was appointed as the first magistrate. He arrived at Spies's farm on 16 November and soon found that, far from signing the oath of allegiance and settling down, most of the Republicans were packing their impedimenta and preparing to leave.

The whole district was in a fine flurry of nerves. Rumours that Mpande intended to invade the country and kill anybody who signed the British oath of allegiance had been spread by some of the more resolute Republicans. As a result, the whole district was rapidly being denuded of its population. Boshoff could do nothing. A small military force of 140 men, under Captain Campbell, was sent up as far as the Bushman's River on 28 December 1847 in an effort to reassure the country, but it did little good. The site they occupied was that originally selected as a frontier post against the Bushmen by Colonel Piper and Lieutenant Gibb, and for some time occupied by Cape Mounted Riflemen.

In the midst of all the disturbance Sir Harry Smith, the Governor of the Cape, rode down the Drakensberg on an official visit to Natal, after a somewhat uproarious tour of the central plains.

At the foot of the pass the Governor found about 450 trekkers preparing to leave Natal. He listened to their complaints of Zulu scares and frontier hardship and was touched. He promised immediate investigation and relief and rode on hastily to Pietermaritzburg to learn the official position.

The picture he saw on his journey was depressing. "From the Drakensberg to Pietermaritzburg the whole country is entirely deserted," said the *Natal Witness*. "Mr and Mrs Gregory, formerly of Cape Town, and one other family, are said to be the only residents at Weenen."

The whole fair land of Natal seemed to have more complaints in it than human beings. Sir Harry arrived in Pietermaritzburg on 9 February 1848, and immediately issued a series of proclamations which he hoped would remedy the position.

The proclamation demanding the oath of allegiance was repealed and he pledged himself for the loyalty of the people. Good farms of 2000 morgen each were to be granted immediately to all original emigrant subjects, and a commission was appointed to effect distribution with a minimum of fuss.

About thirty families of Voortrekkers returned to Natal after Smith's proclamation, and immediately a new stream of complaints came from them. The farms they had abandoned recently had been promptly occupied by tribal squatters. Shepstone was hastily sent up in May to warn the squatters off, leaving one reserve only for Jobe and his people at the junction of the Thukela and Buffalo rivers.

With all this confusion going on down below them, the Bushmen of the Drakensberg were reaping a rich harvest in stolen livestock. In 1846 they were particularly bad, and many of the Natal farmers were almost ruined. With limited military forces and the farmers' exodus in full swing, the government could do little.

As there was a faint chance that the Bushmen would listen to reason, J. Uys and a small party of men were sent off to discover the strongholds of the rustlers, and if possible negotiate peace. Uys met some of the Bushmen and brought two of their leaders back to Pietermaritzburg. They were loaded with presents and sent home on 4 November 1846, with promises of future peace. Exactly one month later, however, another serious raid took place; and the whole endless process of retaliation and bloodshed continued. Nothing seemed to stop the little men. A few parties of Cape coloured soldiers were scattered over the country as garrisons, but these did little except dice away their pay, and each night the Bushmen raided on.

In the midst of this disturbance a few individuals were struggling to lay the foundations of Natal's future prosperity. In Pietermaritzburg a few tradesmen and businessmen had wandered in. Among them was a young former reporter of the Cape Town *Mail* named David Buchanan. He travelled up with a supply of old type and a half-worn-out hand press, given to him as a parting present by his former employer.

This mixture of youthful energy and old scrap became the *Natal Witness*, which first saw the light on 27 February 1846. It succeeded the old *De Natalier*, originally brought out by Charles Boniface, which had had a circulation of about 40 and had been printed on a strange variety of paper, ranging from newsprint to wrapping and blotting paper, according to supply. When the *De Natalier* had gone broke, a sheet named the *Patriot* had taken its place for a brief spell, before it too had vanished and left the ground clear for Buchanan.

The *Natal Witness* was a perky little paper in its early days. It was published weekly, and to secure distribution the enterprising Buchanan organised the first regular connection with Durban. This, the *Natal Witness Express*, consisted of a Zulu runner who left Pietermaritzburg at 2 p.m. on Saturday, 18 April 1846, for the first time, and thereafter conducted a weekly service, carrying papers to the coast subscribers and letters at the rate of 6d. a sheet. He left Durban on his return at 10 a.m.

on Wednesdays, took about twelve hours, rain or shine, to do the journey, and was very proud of his punctuality.

The paper was largely dependent upon government proclamations and notices. In what space was left Buchanan held forth, often with some effect. On 25 February 1848, for example, he published some remark about a current perjury case which the court was unable to digest. Buchanan was arrested and lodged in gaol, pending trial for contempt of court. As the paper was a sort of one-man band, with Buchanan doing everything except print, he had to turn his cell into an editorial office, and for some issues the address "Pietermaritzburg Prison" graced the pages of the journal. He was eventually fined £25 and released.

The pioneer commercial activity in the infant colony consisted of the export of ivory, skins, some cattle, butter, beans and maize, sent largely to Mauritius. For the rest, there was much experimentation as the few enterprising settlers who did arrive tried to discover a profitable crop. Whatever this crop was to be it obviously had to be suitable for export, for there was no local market at all.

Tobacco was grown in small quantities, but it was not very good. Flax was tried without conspicuous success. Pawpaws were introduced from Brazil in 1850 by Dr Henry Bowen and his wife, while other fruits, like red bananas and pineapples, were brought into the colony by William Middleton and Mark McKen.

Indigo was also tried, and was championed by men such as W.R.S. Wilson (Indigo Wilson). It flourished well, but the development of synthetic dyes overseas robbed the plant of its value. Arrowroot was introduced from Mauritius by E.F. Rathbone, but there was such a limited demand it was hardly worth growing.

Coffee was introduced from Réunion Island and Mauritius by S. Benningfield and William Lister respectively, and grew well, especially on Lister's farm Red Hill, until the deadly leaf and bark disease and the borer came and wiped the plantations out entirely. Lister also introduced avocadoes and mangoes to Natal.

Tea was another crop tried by the pioneers. An individual, aptly named Robert Plant, brought out a few plants from Kew Gardens; and George Jackson and James Brickhill, at later dates, also managed to grow some Chinese and Assam tea, but there was no spectacular financial return.

It was cotton which was the first crop to offer any great promise and attract a substantial number of immigrants. Cotton seeds were first introduced by the American missionary, Dr Adams, while men such as D.C. Toohey imported seed from experimental plantations at the Cape.

Two recent settlers, Hippolyte Jargal, a Frenchman, and P. Jung, a German, formed a joint stock company, the Natal Cotton Co., in March 1847. J. Bergtheil was Managing Director and its aim was to cultivate cotton on a big scale. The company obtained 22 750 acres on the Mdloti River and settled 28 British immigrants there, but the venture proved a disappointment.

The company also bought an estate from Edmund Morewood and a handyman named Brooker was occupied in proving to the directors' satisfaction that cotton of the Sea Island variety would grow there. Prospects looked so bright that more land was obtained and the 15 500-acre estate was named Westville, in honour of the Lieutenant Governor.

It was a beautiful estate, lying on the line of road between Durban and Pietermaritzburg, and the company conceived the idea of settling German immigrants upon it. For this purpose Bergtheil proceeded to Germany and, after some hard talking to convince the stolid Germans that they were not meant as food for cannibals, he secured 35 family groups (183 individuals altogether) as settlers.

The ship *Bertha* sailed from Bremerhaven on 19 November 1847 with the immigrants, the first large party to come to Natal directly from Europe. After a four months' voyage they arrived safely in Durban, where they were welcomed by Walter Harding and given their deeds, granting each of them a five-year lease, with rights of renewal, over 200 acres for cotton and ten acres for vegetables and a homestead.

Free seed and aid in buying livestock were given to the settlers, in return for a contract under which they agreed to pay one third of all future crops to the company, with the exception of vegetables.

The cheerful noise of these settlers building snug homes for themselves was the best thing heard in Natal for many a long year. A cotton pack-house with a defensive palisade, a comfortable dwelling for the manager, and a neat chapel for their pastor, the Reverend Mr Posselt, were soon erected, and the farmlands were tilled and energetically worked. As a cotton-growing enterprise, however, the settlement soon disappointed its originators. The settlers found vegetables yielded better returns for less trouble, and market gardening in this, the so-called New Germany, soon became the general activity.

Apart from these German immigrants, there were a few other sources of settlers. A few soldiers from the garrison, whose time had expired, were induced to remain in the country by the grant of allotments and, in 1846, a number of dissatisfied settlers from the Cape wandered up overland. These people consisted of a community of 74 Europeans and 52 of their servants, from the village of Butterworth. They had been driven out of their homes by the hostility of the local tribespeople. Some resettled at Buntingville in Pondoland, while others travelled up to Natal. There they formed a welcome addition to the population of some 3000 Europeans, hardly more than that of one English village, who at that time lived a lazy life in the sunshine of the fair land of Natal.

FIFTEEN
The settlers in Natal

The early years of the Colony of Natal were so quiet economically that only a few hardy and ingenious individuals flourished.

Several speculators, however, had considerable faith in the future of Natal. Men such as Edward Chiappini and J.C. Zeederberg bought up farms, at not much more than a penny an acre, from Republicans abandoning the Colony. The immense tracts of land these speculators acquired were simply left idle, while the owners extracted exorbitant rents from African squatters and waited for values to increase as a result of the labours of others on the few farms worked.

Some of these land speculators, finding the natural course of development to be too slow, decided to promote immigration themselves in order to dispose of their land holdings. Times were certainly favourable for immigration from Britain. The "hungry forties" were in full swing; unemployment and depression were rife. People were sailing off to a more hopeful life in the colonies and America as fast as they could take ship. The only thing which had hitherto prevented an influx of immigrants into Natal was the complete ignorance prevailing about the place.

This ignorance was regarded by some of the speculators as almost an asset. It left the field wide open for propaganda of the most extravagant kind. James Methley, in his booklet *The*

New Colony of Port Natal published in 1849, was typical of these propagandists.

"You look around over your own broad acres," he wrote, "and see your corn bending to the breeze and your herds grazing over what was a short time ago a wilderness, and what has now become, by your own exertions, a smiling spot in the landscape. Every work you have accomplished is a source of comfort; each new undertaking is to you prospective wealth; each hardship is a care past and gone; each day, as it glides away, leaves its blessing; you eat and sleep in comfort, you rise and toil – but it is for yourself – for your family; the sweat does not drop from your brow for the benefit of the tax-gatherer, you are not haunted by the fear of the returning rent-day. You want no licence to take the venison which bounds across your path. It is as much your own as the oxen pasturing before your door. You do as you like, go where you like and when you like; you cannot trespass."

With material like this to digest, it was no wonder that the Briton, ground down by poverty and all those irksome inhibitions consequent upon a large population, screwed up his eyes at the prospect of an escape to the broad acres of Natal.

Francis Collison was one of the absentee landlords who exploited the current mood of escapism. He had acquired 14 farms in Natal (some 84 000 acres) at an average price of 8¾d. an acre. From his office in London he advertised allotments of 100 acres for £100, including an ocean passage for two to Natal. As the ocean passage was worth about £15, this left £85 for the 100 acres which had cost Collison £3 13s.

To the fanfare of much publicity such as "the appearance of a nobleman's park", "covered with fountains and streams", "no preliminary labour needed in clearing land", the first buyers fell into the trap, and on 29 August 1848 the first immigrant ship, the *Gwalior*, sailed from England.

These first immigrants had much to learn. The propaganda which had attracted them to Natal made no mention of the complete absence of communications or markets and the prevailing uncertainty as to which crops would flourish.

When they landed they were left to their own devices in a strange land. Fortunately, the few remaining Republican families were hospitable and kind. People such as the Boshoffs, Ottos, Prellers, Wolhuters, Zeederbergs and Zietsmans at Pietermaritzburg; the Nels, Bothas, Scheepers' and Jacobus Uys in the Mvoti district; Stephanus Uys at Mpolweni; and the Landmans, Labuschagnes and Adendorffs in the north, became pillars of support for the newcomers, and their friendly advice and old experience saved many a callow newcomer from bankruptcy.

The dodge worked by Collison gave many other people ideas. Among them was a plausible, well-dressed character by the name of Joseph Byrne. This individual had spent his life knocking around the world, speculating when any opportunity came his way.

The financial possibilities of exploiting immigration attracted Byrne. He borrowed money and opened an office at No. 12 Pall Mall East, with an ornate sign proclaiming his "Natal Emigration and Colonisation Office".

His office, like his person, was large and impressive. It held a green baize table, deep armchairs, and its walls were covered with pictures of smiling Zulus and the fair land of Natal. Seated there, he answered all enquiries with the advice that faith and cash be lodged with him, against issue of a receipt of most reassuring appearance.

In Natal, the services of John Moreland were obtained as surveyor and local representative. The whole affair was largely financed by the shipowners, Marshall and Edridge, who hoped to organise passengers and freight for their ships.

Two farms, Vaalkop and Dadelfontein, were bought from Collison and, with other properties, were surveyed into 20-acre allotments. Government land was also available to promoters of immigration, against a deposit of £1000 for 3000 acres; the deposit being returnable after immigrants had been successfully settled.

The shippers wanted £6 17s. 6d. a passage for an adult to Natal. It was planned to offer this steerage passage and 20 acres of land for £10, with intermediate passage at £19 and cabin class at £35. The scheme was an immediate attraction. On 22 January 1849, the brig *Wanderer* sailed with the first 15 immigrants, while on 17 April the *Washington* followed with over 70 settlers; and thereafter regular sailings carried one party after another to Natal.

Many other speculators engaged in similar activity. Jonas Bergtheil operated a scheme on land near Pietermaritzburg; while Richard Hackett sent out 129 immigrants in 1850, on terms of £16 for a passage and 40 acres near Karkloof. George Murdoch was another speculator who tried to profit out of the idea. He offered 20 acres on the Mdloti River, together with a passage of sorts to South Africa for £10. John Lidgett and James Methley, jointly, ran another organisation. Their settlers were located mostly around places known as Lidgett's Town and Caversham, and experienced a fair measure of success in those parts.

Another man who became involved in the immigration business was William Josiah Irons. When a number of distressed fellow Methodists started looking for a way of escape from England, he occupied himself on their behalf, as it seemed to him that he could combine a charitable act with the making of some slight profit for himself.

Irons organised an affair called The Christian Emigration and Colonisation Society, and secured the patronage of the Earl of Verulam for his schemes. Some 400 immigrants altogether were gathered and handed over for despatch to Byrne, who paid Irons a commission of £1 a head for everybody he could enrol.

Most of these Methodist settlers were sent to the Mdloti River area where, on 13 March 1850, a handful of houses and shacks on a hillslope running down to a bend in the river were planned as the nucleus of a village named Verulam, after the noble patron of the movement.

These Verulam settlers were comparatively fortunate. The area selected for them was intensely fertile, and all the known crops of Natal, together with fruit and vegetables, flourished there. The settlers also arrived with a few comforts. On the barque *King William* they brought out seeds, some funds, a large marquee tent as a communal shelter, and a blue banner with the name, Verulam, in gold letters.

Ox-wagons took them up from Durban to their settlement: large, cheerful bundles of humanity, singing hymns and then yelping with excitement when they saw some wild animal bounding across their path.

The country was still alive with game, and every settler had some adventure to relate. Mrs Fynney at Verulam, while her husband was away, heard a disturbance in the cattle kraal one night. With a storm lantern and an African servant carrying a gun, she went out to investigate. They discovered a lion in the cattle kraal. "Shoot it," hissed Mrs Fynney. The African lifted the gun, closed his eyes and pulled the trigger. It was a clean hit – right through the head of their best cow! The lion promptly seized the corpse, jumped the fence, and vanished into the bush.

Times were certainly picturesque. On weekdays stalwart pillars of the church could be seen weeding their gardens in top hats. On Sundays vigorous church services were held at a central hall, while a giant mimosa tree stood patiently outside, holding the settlers' horses tethered to its trunk. In the hollow trunk of this old tree some bees had residence. It is on record that an argument developed once between them and the horses. The horses lost. They headed for the horizon, and many a churchman walked home that day.

The immigrants who came to Natal were of all types and classes. Cotton spinners, out of work owing to world shortage of materials; railway workers, hard hit by the slump in construction; small tradesmen, farmers and craftsmen, squeezed out of their homes by taxation and depression, were all in search of a better life beyond the seas.

One after another, the immigrant ships disgorged their human cargoes at Port Natal. Because of the shallow bar, the ships had to land most of their cargoes and their passengers by means of lighters, and the immigrants with their impedimenta would be packed like sardines into dark holds, battened down for a last spell of seasickness and discomfort as they crossed the bar.

Jammed together on their last sea journey, they must have looked but a sorry crowd, with hope as their most treasured possession. For months they had endured a miserable ocean passage, crammed together, with poor food and blank monotony to remind them of just how many thousands of miles they were sailing from the land of their birth. Quarrelling amongst one another; making future friends and bitter enemies; the inevitable pilfering of belongings by sneak-thieves; the kindness of some ships' officers, and the harshness of others – all these must have provided the last memories of the voyage behind them as the rusty lighters carried them into the great harbour of Natal.

Landing on the Point beach, the immigrants would eagerly scramble up the sand dunes, full of curiosity to see their new homeland. Unlike Mr Byrne, it was not a reassuring picture: a line of bleak, shrub-covered sand dunes, a few shacks, and a rough barracks put up to shelter the newcomers. Durban was two miles way in the bush, and was not much of a place anyway: just a few sandy streets, with one or two wagons and some half-naked Zulus lolling in the sun.

In the barracks, there would generally be a few leftovers from the previous ship who would hand on, like a contagious disease, their complaints of delay, neglect, useless allotments and refusal of the locals to cash Byrne's cheques.

For those who landed with some means, things were not too bad. But for those who had little, or had entrusted Byrne with their all, conditions were miserable. A harassed John

Moreland, with no funds or support, could only try to get them off in ox-wagons to the land allotted to them and then hope for the best. For these people only their own hardihood and the kindness of older inhabitants, who gave credit and loans, stood between them and misery.

The wagon journey to the allotments was the final disillusionment for many. None knew exactly where or how far they were going. The wagon drivers generally spoke only Zulu and the few maps were useless. From the silver sheet of the bay the wagons took them through a virgin wilderness, with mammoth trees and mysterious bush, full of elephants and leopards, wild boars, porcupines, antelopes and wildcats; while at night came the lonely cries of the bushbabies.

In this fair wilderness with its empty acres, the settler was very much like a child putting his hand into a barrel and reaching for a lucky packet. None knew what he was to receive; and having received it, few knew what to do with it, or they dissipated their energies by envying others.

Like Verulam, many of the areas chosen for the settlers were good. On 16 May 1850, Byrne purchased 31 000 acres at four shillings an acre on the upper Lovu River, where the old wagon track to the Cape found a ford. This area, known as Tafelberg to the Republicans, was already thinly settled by such stalwarts as Philip Nel (on the subsequently famous dairy farm of Nelsrust), Lucas Meyer, Jacobus Hamman, J.C. Breytenbach, G. Rudolph and Servaas Breda; and these had proved it to be a first-class agricultural area.

John Moreland surveyed Byrne's purchase into allotments and laid out a village on the banks of the river. This village was first named Beaulieu, after the seat of the Duke of Buccleuch in Richmond, for a batch of some 40 immigrants from his estate arrived in Durban on 9 May 1850, to settle at the place under his patronage.

A pleasant village grew up at the site, with thatched cottages made of stone and green brick and surrounded by vast gardens, gay with flowers, fruit trees, rose bushes and murmuring streams. The place became notable for its enterprising settlers. Big, burly John Bazley, formerly a railway engineer with George Stephenson, came out with his tools and skill and his family in May 1850, on the *Edward*, to escape from the slump.

In July he settled at the new village as its first inhabitant, built a mill, dug a watercourse, and generally became the mechanical life of the place.

Anthony Pigg, the wheelwright, was another settler from the *Edward*. He became the lay reader, started a Sunday school in the village, and planted its oak trees. Robert Aiken was another settler there who was destined to make his name; while C. and J. Dacomb opened the first store in the village and Sam Strapp opened an inn.

With all these practical settlers, the tongue-twisting name of Beaulieu didn't stand a chance. By September the name was being corrupted by so many English dialects, from Cockney to Yorkshire, that a public meeting was held on the 23rd to end the confusion. Very wisely, the more easily pronounceable name of Richmond was selected, for it still honoured the memory of their patron, and by that name the village has ever since been known.

Near Richmond a second settlers' town was laid out and named Byrnetown. Unlike Richmond, the site of Byrnetown was miserable to a degree. It was destined to receive settlers aboard the ship *Minerva*. This vessel arrived at the Durban roadstead on 3 July 1850, and was blown ashore and wrecked on the Bluff. Nobody was drowned, fortunately, but the immigrants lost all their belongings and had the further misfortune of receiving wretched allotments when they were themselves in a wretched condition.

Settlers such as C.M. M'Leod and Robert Ralfe went to Byrnetown and did their best, but the place never became anything and boasted of little more than a thatched chapel in the place of public buildings.

G.H. Mason was one of the settlers who drew an allotment in Byrnetown. His experiences were common to many other emigrants. Keen to see his allotment and irked by the delays in getting a wagon, he walked up to Pietermaritzburg from Durban; a long walk, but with grand scenery and a sprinkling of little houses of accommodation to provide shelter at two shillings a night.

Pietermaritzburg was bulging with people. "Hundreds of fresh emigrants arrived each week," wrote Mason. "The market place was dotted over like a fair with many-coloured tents, wagons and carts, piles of furniture, bales of merchandise, and open-air dinner parties. Dogs, Hottentots, untidy women, neglected children, laughing Africans, cooking utensils, bedding, and smouldering fires lined the broad, open streets, or occupied the vacant and deserted erven of the expatriate Boers."

From Pietermaritzburg, Mason walked to Richmond. At that time it "could boast of only a single house – which, by the by, was a good stone one, and a house of accommodation – although there were upwards of fifty substantial African huts inhabited by emigrants, each standing in an enclosed and fresh dug garden."

Mason put up in the Richmond Hotel. It was hopelessly, but cheerfully, overcrowded with people who, like him, had come up only to discover their allotments were useless. The whole company sat down at one long table "to a smoking hot dinner, consisting of huge beef pies, rounds of boiled beef, with stewed pumpkin and other vegetables."

Tobacco fumes, wine, spirits, a blazing log fire, songs and old English newspapers combined to cheer the hearts of the emigrants. After a convivial evening they all retired to sleep, making their beds all over the floor and in the ramshackle outhouses.

They had just bedded down and the lights were out when the landlord woke everybody up by bawling out: "Gentlemen, who has the bellows?" When silence and snores answered his query, he became angry. A few hearty oaths shook up even the snorers. Translated, the oaths indicated that either the landlord got the bellows and a missing baking-pot, or there would be no breakfast in the morning. After some search, the bellows were found in use as a mattress and the baking-pot as a pillow. The house then relapsed into sleep.

The biggest blow to the emigrants came at the beginning of 1851, when Byrne went bankrupt. His last immigrant ship, the *Bernard*, arrived in Durban on 18 February with 54 settlers, who brought the total number of persons Byrne had sent to Natal up to about 2500. They had paid Byrne £30 262 altogether; but he had paid out £30 310 to shipowners and others as the costs of his scheme.

The profit he expected from the return of his deposits by the government when his emigrants were settled would be real enough, but he had slipped up in expecting quick returns to cover his shortage of capital. When long delays in surveying and endless quarrelling with the emigrants made the government more than usually slow in refunding his deposits, he simply went bankrupt. His name is buried in history beneath a mound of abuse, but at least his scheme had served to give Natal its needed flow of settlers, even if it had caused them hardship.

Many of the emigrants were ruined by his bankruptcy. Individuals had handed their all over to Byrne for forwarding to Natal, to avoid danger of theft on the journey; and now they found their drafts were useless. Stranded in a strange land, they tackled their problems with remarkable courage. Tinkers, tailors, cobblers and bakers, they each started up some little trade and struggled to earn a respectable living.

To add to the emigrants' troubles, there was the usual crowd of landsharks and other antisocial human rubbish who feed on distressed persons. Plausible gentlemen offered to sell land at reasonable rates to make up for bad allotments, and then withheld transfer on some pretext or other. Eventually, they would turn the unfortunate buyer away, after they had already built a house or effected improvements to the land.

In the face of all these troubles, many of the emigrants abandoned Natal in disgust and either returned home or wandered off to the Australian goldfields. Some of them couldn't have cared less where they went provided that it was out of Natal. Paul Ainstie was one of these. After battling to establish the Belvedere Flour Mill, he went bankrupt. The last heard of him was that he had sailed from Simonstown under an alias, "quite indifferent whether the boat went to Mauritius or India or anywhere else."

The majority of people, however, stuck it out with fortitude and patience. Some took to transport riding, and many a ragged wagon-man spoke with an Oxford accent. Others found employment with the earlier colonists. George Lamond had all his money stolen on the voyage out from England. He landed at Durban with hardly a sixpence to his name, but found a job with Morewood on his farm, Compensation. In time he did well for himself.

William Hartley secured a position as tally clerk at the Point for 4s. 6d. a day. He saved his money and then opened a store in Durban. He struggled on until 1854, when the ship *Ariosto* was wrecked on Durban beach with a cargo of pepper. Edward Snell bought the wreck and Hartley bought the soggy, stinking mass of pepper from him for little more than a song. He salvaged some one hundred tons of pepper, dried it, sent it to London, and from the sale laid the foundation of his future fortune.

All over Natal the genuine farmer-type of settlers faced conditions as they found them. With the wishful promise to their families that things would be better later, they built crude shacks and set about tilling the soil with resolution and fortitude. At least, in one way, they had the better of the earlier trekkers. Natal was reminiscent of Britain in many respects, and the livestock and seed which the settlers brought out with them often took to the pasturage and soil with greater facility than those which had been brought up from the Cape.

This similarity between Natal and Britain gave many of the settlers a touch of nostalgia. All over Natal, whenever some landscape evoked a memory of home, they applied a place name which reminded them of past days in the old country. Thomas Fannin, from Dublin, went to Natal in 1847. He bought the farm, Buffels Bosch, in the lovely district which he named The Dargle, on account of its resemblance to the country of the Dargle stream, south of Dublin.

David Gray, a Scottish weaver, was another to bring a place name to South Africa from his former home. After a spell of running a roadside inn at Weston on the Mooi River, he moved up to the Drakensberg and settled on a farm he named Cathkin, after Cathkin Braes near Glasgow. In time, this name attached itself to the great mountain peak which stands guardian over the farm.

Dalton was another name brought out to Natal, as a reminder of someone's home in that small, East Riding village. York was the settlement of a group of Yorkshire farmers who immigrated in a co-operative venture, organised by one Harry Boast. Two hundred and sixteen immigrants came out in this venture, in October 1850. They were duly settled on their 20-acre allotments, but with so much confusion and argument that Boast died of a brainstorm while trying to untangle the matter. The trouble was never straightened out. By 1863 York consisted of just a blacksmith's shop. Today it is only a memory.

There are many other memories of those old British settlers: memories of successes and bitter disappointments. If success came their way it did not come easily. For every bit of happiness they earned, they toiled full measure for those hard taskmasters – hope and ambition.

From the beginning of 1849 until the end of 1852 about 5000 immigrants entered Natal. These newcomers joined with the older inhabitants to give the colony a total European population of 7629 persons, according to the first census taken in 1852. As all the immigrants came from Britain, it meant that the European population of Natal was now dominantly English-speaking. Over the next few years their numbers were still further reinforced. Independent settlement, combined with a government scheme of assisted immigration for persons nominated by friends already settled in Natal, served to increase the population.

By 1865 another 2000 British settlers had arrived. Their labours and schemes fused with the hopes and disappointments, experiences and adventures of the earlier immigrants; and the total made up the fundamental character and spirit of those foundation years of the fair land of Natal.

SIXTEEN
Old Durban

D urban, at the time of the coming of the British settlers, was little more than a village. Its streets were sandy, its houses shacks, and the green forest crowded all around, patiently seeking to reclaim that which had once been its own.

This forest was at one time both a menace and an attraction to Durban. Hunters revelled in its dark jungle, still teeming with game, while the settlers feared it. Many were the stories of elephants roaming among the trees. One settler, returning from work in his fields, came upon an elephant cow who neatly tossed him to the top of a mimosa tree. Another settler woke up at night to find an elephant's trunk reaching through the window trying to pull his blanket off.

The bush of the Berea was particularly dense and was infested with elephants. The paths the elephants tramped, indeed, were the only means of penetrating this forest, and the hunters who ventured along them did so at some hazard. More than one party was chased out of the Berea bush quicker than they had ever gone into it.

Theophilus Shepstone, the Native Administrator, had the narrowest escape of his life in this bush. In his youth he had been a keen hunter. His well-known African name, Somtseu, had been applied to him on this account. Before coming to Natal, he had been Agent General for the tribes on the Cape border. There he had spent so much of his time scouring the landscape in search of game animals that the Africans, half-jocularly, named the 19-year-old youth Somtseu, after a renowned Xhosa hunter who had flourished some years before Theophilus had been born in 1817.

When Shepstone first came to Natal as interpreter to Major Charters, in 1838, he sallied out into the Berea bush with a party of hunters, in search of the notorious elephants. Passing along a track, one of their dogs dashed into a thicket and began barking furiously.

An elephant bull promptly charged out. The dog ran for the hunters, with the elephant after it. The party scattered. The dog ran to Shepstone for safety and the two went flying through the bush with the elephant trumpeting shrilly close behind them.

Just as Shepstone was thinking his end had come, another elephant crossed the path ahead of him. The new terror saved his life. He was forced to jump aside and bury himself among the thorns in some bramble bushes. The elephant bull hurtled past without noticing him. Shepstone lay in the thorns panting, until his friends came and rescued him. The shock had been so great that never afterwards would he go near even a tame elephant in a circus. As for Somtseu's hunting days – they were over!

The elephants of the Berea lingered on for several years, gradually being shot or driven off. Eventually only two were left. These wandered up to a ravine near modern Pinetown. There John Field shot them, and their bones were later used by surveyors when they ran short of iron pegs.

Durban harbour, before the settlers came, was a very quiet place indeed. The first vessel to come direct from England, with a cargo exclusively for Natal, was the 158-ton brig *Sarah Bell*, which arrived on 18 February 1846. Since business was so dull, it was only natural that harbour facilities were primitive. For signalling there was nothing but a small flagstaff on the Bluff. As the man in charge could be in any of four conditions:

at home, away, asleep, or drunk, it meant that communication was hazardous.

Ships would arrive, anchor in the roadstead and, after hours of delay, both inexplicable and irksome to the passengers, at length manage to signal their desire for a tender to the harbour authorities. A boat manned by a parcel of retired cutthroats would then make its way out to the ship and enquire: "Where from and any sick?"

Hours more would pass, while the authorities digested the information. Then a lighter or cargo boat would come, rusty and full of smells. The women and children would be lowered into it in a variety of chair made from a cask, while the men and boys would scramble down a side ladder.

Stowed away in the lighter's hold, the passengers would be ferried to the shore. Crossing the bar was the final irritation. The hatches would be put on "to keep yer things dry, in case any water slops on board".

Then, in darkness, they would be tossed around until they thought they were standing on their heads. Children howled, people vomited, water swirled – a final thud and then cheerful sunlight streamed from the opened hatchway as the lighter sailed safely into the calm waters of the harbour, where a few tiny trading vessels rested close to the shore.

Durban harbour in those days was shallow, and thick grass-like seaweed covered part of it like an ocean meadow. Innumerable odd creatures used the place as a sort of grazing ground; shellfish, crabs and birds of great variety made the place their home. The mangrove forests on the islands were the roosting places of these birds at night. In the daytime, the calm and brilliant waters at the head of the bay were studded with wild fowl. The delicate colour of flamingoes and the grotesque forms of the pelicans were conspicuous, while the snow-white plumage of the cranes stood out like stars in a deep blue sky.

At the Point stood the nucleus of a harbour: a few stakes and stones, a wooden cottage, a customs house with a soldier on guard outside, a warehouse and G.C. Cato, "a short, sharp, clean-shaved, American-looking man in white clothes and a large manilla hat worn at all angles on the head, according to the humour of the hour." He was the general factotum.

To this harbour establishment the passengers were ferried from the lighters on the backs of grinning Africans – and were dumped by them upon the shores of Mother Africa to make their homes and fortunes.

Durban's future fortune as a harbour depended entirely on the problem of the bar. This bar, or barrier across the entrance to the harbour, was formed by a combination of debris carried out from the lagoon mixed with sand accumulated by the natural current drift along the coast. The depth of water over this bar varied unpredictably and was of as vital interest to the local merchants and visiting sailors as temperature is to a sick man. Like a sick man, praying to be rid of his temperature, so Durban longed to be rid of its bar.

As long as this bar remained, the great harbour was closed to shipping of any size above the smallest coasting vessels. Any ship of larger size had to be content with a precarious anchorage in the roadstead and, in a hopelessly exposed position, subject to sudden gales and having no possible shelter anywhere, this anchorage soon gave Durban the reputation of being a ships' graveyard.

According to an abstract of wrecks, published in the Departmental Reports of the Natal Harbour Board for 1886, no fewer than 66 large ships were blown ashore on Durban beach between 17 December 1845, when the *Suffren* was wrecked, and 12 December 1885 when the *Sea Nymph* was stranded.

To owners of a certain type, Durban acquired a reputation of having excellent facilities for the losing of well-insured ships. Wrecks could be contrived there with a maximum material loss but minimum loss of life. Only about 35 men were drowned in the wrecks of 60 ships; and the people of Durban became so accustomed to the business that it was quite accepted for shipping intelligence to list vessels as "in port", "outer anchorage", and "on the beach".

The problem of the bar exercised the ingenuity of many minds, both professional and amateur. Innumerable letters were written to newspapers, proposing ridiculous schemes. Endless arguments were waged on the highest technical levels; but no satisfactory solution could be found, although over £200 000 was used up in various schemes.

John Milne, known as "Old Mortality", a tall, gaunt man who loved his job, was one of the first really to tackle the problem as an engineer. He proposed that two symmetrical stone moles should be built, one from the sandy point on the north side of the harbour entrance, running in a direction nearly parallel to the north side of the Bluff, and the other from the end of the Bluff, on the south side of the harbour entrance, running in such a direction as to allow an entrance at the outer end of the two moles.

This scheme was estimated to cost £77 743. The plans were approved and work began in 1849. For seven years Milne struggled on against the sea. Then rivalries and dissident opinions as to the value of his work first slowed it up and then eventually stopped it.

A second plan was then drawn up by James Abernethy and Captain Vetch, hydrographer to the Admiralty. This plan proposed that a breakwater be run out from either side of the harbour entrance. The two breakwaters were to converge to form a new entrance. The new scheme cost £165 500. A loan was floated to finance it and work went on for some time, until it eventually foundered in the stormy seas of incompetency and insinuations of embezzlement.

In all this time the bar had remained the capricious mistress of Durban harbour. In 1855 it had a low-water depth of 9 ft 4 in. and, although high tide added an extra 5 ft of water, crossing it was dangerous even for the small traders. On 21 February 1856 for instance, the 200-ton barque *Annabella* ran aground as she was crossing and eventually sank, leaving her name on the long-vanished, but in its day notorious, shipping hazard of the Annabella Bank.

In 1860, despite the efforts of man, the bar depth had actually decreased to a hopeless 4 ft 3¼ in. In desperation Captain Vetch, in the period of 1861 to 1864, planned the creation of an entire artificial harbour, but the seas washed away all his works almost as fast as they were built. Sir John Coode, a harbour engineer of some reputation overseas (which he largely lost in Natal) was then employed to study the problem. In 1870 he at last furnished a report, and for the next few years his findings were argued, modified and alternately condemned and approved. His scheme also visualised the construction of breakwaters out to sea, at a cost of some £500 000.

Innumerable experiments were made by people such as Edward Innes, C.W. Methven, and other experts employed by the Harbour Board to study the problem. After 30 years of argument, however, all Durban had got for its money were some interesting ruins for the waves to laugh at each time they tumbled over them in their game of head over heels.

Eventually, dredging and the narrowing of the entrance channel from 1500 to 800 feet to increase the tidal scour, contributed towards the defeat of the bar. The dredger *Octopus* arrived in 1895 and the *Walrus* soon joined it. By 1897 the dredgers had removed 9 928 348 tons of spoil from the channel and lagoon. By 1898 the depth of water over the bar had been increased to 18 ft 7 in., and thenceforth Durban as a harbour has never looked back.

Strangely enough, the elimination of the bar marked the start of the slow deterioration of Durban beach as a holiday resort. The ocean currents were disturbed by the work at the harbour entrance. Steady erosive reaction set in along the beach, materially reducing the expanse of sand available for holidaymakers and provoking almost as much argument and expense in the search for a cure as had the original problem of the bar.

Durban itself, when the 1850 settlers came, was a miserable place. After the final British occupation Stanger had thoroughly surveyed the town and laid it out properly. The streets, although there were few houses, were all named after the celebrities of the day. Smith Street was named after Major Smith; West Street came from Martin West, the first Governor; Aliwal Street was named in honour of Sir Harry Smith's great victory at Aliwal, in India; Gardiner Street took its name from Captain Allen Gardiner; Field Street was named after William Field, the first Collector of Customs and Resident Magistrate; Grey Street was named after Earl Grey, Secretary of State for the Colonies; Russell Street was named after Lord John Russell, the British Premier; and for good measure George Street and Andrew Street were named after the saints.

There were hardly any edifices worthy of the name of buildings. The centre and commercial hub of the place was a wattle-and-daub thatched store, run by Cato. It sheltered beneath some magnificent trees, where wagons outspanned and auctions were held. From nearby came the tinkling of a forge, where C.C. Griffin and C. Hovenden had a smithy. Dick King had a thatched butcher's shop, with a large kaffirboom acting as a slaughterpole outside, in what was called King's Street. A Wesleyan chapel and mission house were buried in the trees, while a few other ramshackle structures were scattered about. There was nothing else.

Trade consisted largely of imports to supply the inland republics and Zululand. The principal exports were meat, butter, maize and beans sent to the sugar plantations of Mauritius. Hides and ivory sent to England, principally from Zululand, gave Durban its most colourful activity.

There were chronic shortages of nearly everything. Clothes were scarce and shoes so hard to come by that they were generally replaced by home-made veldskoen. Luxuries, such as dates and sugar, were imported from Mauritius. Dried fruits, wines and flour came from the Cape, while groceries were all imported from England. Local food supplies, fortunately, were both varied and numerous. Beef, venison, pythons, young monkeys, cane rats, porcupines, iguanas, fowls, pumpkins, mealies, beans and milk were all standard articles of diet, cheaply obtained from the tribespeople.

Wages for workmen were generally from six shillings to eight shillings a day. Most of the public works were done by the men of the garrisoning 45th Regiment – a crowd of hard cases. They built barracks, quarters, dug ditches and were often loaned out to private contractors on works of public importance.

There were no entertainments save grog shops, where the military gentlemen brawled and diced away their pay. A few so-called hotels grew up to meet the demands of the settler influx. They were shabby places at first, made from the usual wattle and daub. Besides human guests at five shillings a day, a variety of ants, bugs, snakes and other creatures stayed in them for nothing.

The settler influx soon changed Durban. Many of the newcomers were persons of considerable enterprise. Jeremiah Cullingworth arrived on the *King William*, carrying a small printing press among his baggage with which he intended to ventilate his opinions. In August 1851 he started publishing Durban's first newspaper, the *Natal Times*. On 25 November 1852 this paper was changed into volume one, number one, of the *Natal Mercury*, with George Robinson as its editor. Ever since, it has voiced itself in no hesitant manner on affairs in general.

Social life naturally increased with the size of the population, which, by June 1854, amounted to 1204 people. The women, particularly, made the most of things. In so ramshackle a place, the wife of even a down-at-heels gentleman in England was nevertheless a person of consequence when she migrated to Natal. Ridiculous social snobberies became rampant among those with nothing better on their minds.

Apart from gossip, there were at first few pastimes, but this state of monotony was steadily overcome. In 1853 a Mechanics Institute was formed to provide a library. A Glee Club was also organised by a set of young fellows. They rented a house in Union Street and upset the neighbourhood by spending their nights sitting on top of the corrugated-iron roof, bawling out ballads and hymns. While they sang they beat time with their heels on the tin roof!

A more musical association was the Durban Philharmonic Society, organised in 1853 to form a band. Bishop J.W. Colenso, who arrived in Durban on 30 January 1854 to familiarise himself with Natal before commencing work there, attended one of the first concerts, which the local newspaper referred to as occasions of "refined enjoyment."

"The music hall," wrote the Bishop, "was a large store, fitted up ingeniously for the occasion with flags and evergreens. But I was rather amused when, in the middle of the performances, the ladies were requested to step aside for a few minutes while part of the roof was taken off to cool the room!" A band of about twelve performers presented, to a very full and attentive audience, a programme of Handel, Rossini, and Beethoven.

As early as 18 April 1848, a Natal Agricultural and Horticultural Society had been formed. This association acquired the ground originally occupied by John Cane and his tribe of followers, and this was slowly developed into the famed Botanical Gardens.

Hypolite Jargal, a French settler of means, was the first president of the society. It organised its first show in Durban on 9 August 1850, but this was a failure. The society was then reorganised and, on 1 August 1851, a second show was held in the grounds of the Botanical Gardens. Farmers from all over the colony attended this event, camping out, exhibiting their garden produce and staging picturesque ploughing competitions.

Horse races were occasions for other social gatherings. The first proper Durban race meeting was held on 14 and 15 January 1852. The course was among the bushes, between the road to the Mngeni River and the old swamp across the present race course. Cape coloureds were the jockeys, while a bugler from the 45th Regiment acted as starter. A cheerful and animated crowd of settlers gathered for the occasion, together with a vast crowd of curious Africans. For the latter, a foot race over one mile was organised to end the proceedings. As an epilogue to the whole business, a stick fight developed when some of the losing runners caught up with the winner at a beer drink.

Another occasion for social gatherings came when public executions took place. With so small a population, there was naturally not much crime. Three European and some African constables served to keep order, while a cottage fitted out with stocks acted as a gaol. The Chief Constable, William Harrison, a prim and corpulent man, rode his rounds in a leisurely manner on a snow-white pony as decorous as himself. Some wag broke into the animal's stable one night, led the horse out, and painted it with black zebra stripes. The horse was found the next morning wandering disconsolately up West Street looking, it was popularly supposed, for a barber's shop.

The law, despite its apparent leisureliness, was harsh to a degree to any malefactor it caught. Floggings and hangings were all conducted in public. They were well attended, as something in the nature of entertainments, and the onlookers certainly received full value so far as sentences were concerned. On Saturday, 2 July 1853, for instance, a soldier named Desmond received 50 lashes on the market square, for having received stolen property.

A very celebrated execution took place on Saturday, 28 July 1853. A beachcomber by the name of Samuel Harris (better known as Jemmy Squaretoes, from the loss of his toes through frostbite) had been living a dissolute life in a slovenly kraal on the back beach. He had with him a coloured woman named Flatta, a mixed gang of African cut-throats, and a runaway sailor named Frederick Cooper.

When sober, Squaretoes was tolerable, but when drunk he was impossible. His associates decided to get rid of him. They throttled him one night and threw his body into a swamp with the idea that the police would think it was an accident. This opinion they duly reached, reporting him as "drowned while drunk, poor devil".

Then one of the murderers was arrested for carrying a gun. In gaol he boasted of the murder, the story spread, and the whole gang was arrested. There was a sensational trial, at which they were all found guilty and sentenced to be hanged at the site of their crime.

At 7 a.m. on the appointed day practically the whole of Durban turned out to watch the spectacle. Stolid German families from New Germany, determined to have a good view, journeyed down in carts the previous day. They camped out around the gallows in cheerful social groups, brewing coffee and anticipating the coming show with relish, while the young folk flirted with one another.

The newspapers waxed lyrical over the scene, and the whole affair was described in toothsome detail for readers kept away from the proceedings by having something better to do.

The five condemned were all hanged together. Two ministers comforted them with a lengthy funeral service, during which the crowd reverently uncovered. The prisoners were then asked if they had any last words. Cooper was in repentant tears and spoke of his mother in England, but the Africans seemed indifferent. The executioner, a moron named Wardle, then pulled white nightcaps over their faces, lit a clay pipe, let the ministers have their last say, and then stamped upon the trapdoor lever.

"For a few minutes no one moved or breathed," wrote George Russell, one of the spectators. "A wailing of native women broke the silence. My limbs refused to obey the impulse of my mind; my eyes were fixed on the swaying bodies as the ropes began to untwist, and I have an indelible recollection of that pipe-smoking hangman reaching out and tenderly steadying first one, and then the other."

Events such as this provided topics of conversation for months. Another favourite story of the time concerned a certain pig, involved in one of the most unusual accidents ever known. This pig was first observed by an African who was delivering bread. Leaving his cart outside, he entered the yard of a West Street dealer. As he did so, he noticed a particularly well-filled and contented looking pig making its way outside.

The African was delivering his bread when suddenly there was a violent explosion outside. There was a general rush into the street. Where the bread delivery cart had stood there now was only ruin, while the horse was in full gallop down the street. What had happened was at first a mystery.

Then an individual crawled out of the gutter. He had been a spectator. Walking down the street, he had noticed the pig come out of the yard, waddle up to one of the cart's rear wheels and start to scratch its back on the axle. The pig had then exploded.

The problem, of course, was why the pig should have blown up. The answer came after much investigation. In the yard of the dealer was a quantity of storm-damaged junk awaiting disposal. Among it was a carton of dynamite. The pig had found the soggy dynamite palatable and supped well, if not wisely. The back-scratching process had detonated the tasty meal and caused the explosion.

All these events and stories belonged to Durban's toddler days. Once the sandy little village had matured into a town, it became more decorous and conventional. Plans for a municipality were mooted as early as 1851, but lack of money made it apparent that the village could not afford the luxury at that time.

Several boisterous public meetings were held to discuss the matter over the next few years. Meetings were considered to be one of the few forms of amusement. They were always well attended, whether they were called to protest against rumours that Natal was to become a convict settlement; to celebrate, with as much pomp as the place allowed, the Queen's birthday; or to wrangle over the question of a municipality.

The whole issue was eventually settled in 1854. On 15 May of that year Durban was proclaimed a borough of four wards, each returning two councillors. On 2 August the first council was elected and three days later G.C. Cato was elected first mayor. Thenceforth, the face of Durban started to change. The carefree laughter of childhood vanished and the cares of commerce, trade and depression put wrinkles on its brow. Soon little was left of those early days except, perhaps, a twinkle that still lurks in the civic eye.

SEVENTEEN
Hunter's moon

In Zululand, while Natal was slowly changing, Mpande remained king and white men could do no wrong. They had made him king and he was grateful. Being easy-going by nature, his gratitude combined with his temperament, and the result was that white men could do very much as they pleased. All Zululand lay open before the adventurers. It was a honey-coloured moon that lit the ten thousand hills in a golden age for hunters and traders and wanderers.

Across the Thukela an eager company travelled to explore a wonderland of scenery and game. Their wagons rolled onwards through the bush and the grass, with the crisp air of the early morning breezes wiping the last memory of their dreams from the travellers' thoughts. Every tree and blade of grass would be covered with countless dewdrops, glistening with rainbow colours in the rays of the rising sun.

Now a bushbuck would go crashing through the tall grass, crossing the track and vanishing again into the undergrowth beyond. Then a herd of frisky antelopes would scamper away over the distant hills, turning round with an inquisitive look and a whisk of their tails before they disappeared over the summit.

Flocks of pigeons wheeled overhead, and beautifully coloured birds sailed from bush to bush with their plumage flaming and flashing in the rays of the sun. Here and there a troop of monkeys would peep down from the tops of the trees, while hawks and vultures hovered high in the air, and the great crested eagles blinked and plumed themselves on the decayed branch of some bare trunk.

All day the adventurers hunted and traded and explored. It was a carefree, careless kind of life, full of excitement and surprise, and the nights were a delight. Then, beside some friendly campfire, the wanderers lazed beneath the stars. There they yarned and swopped their tales of triumphs and disappointments, with the air full of the smell of tobacco and the African night, their faces ruddy in the fire glow, and the tongues of the hunting dogs hanging red in the light.

Then it was easy to forget all troubles, prosaic inhibitions, wars, peace and politics. Was not the world as vast as the night? Were not the heavens but the product of all the smoke of all the campfires that were ever burnt, with the stars a few lingering sparks? So they would yarn and roll over and sleep until the first morning star, *nqonqoli*, came to knock at the door of night and wake them up. Then the bustle and the packing and the hasty eating would start all over again, so that with Venus, the second star of morning, *ikhwezi* (the lifter up of the shadows and sleepers from the ground) they were ready and eager to be off.

Around these wanderers there lived an animal world of surpassing variety and number. The huge, formidable buffalo, *inyathi*, would come out of the bush and stand in the trails watching the wagons and the straining oxen with interest and amusement.

The Zulus say, "The buffalo is enquired about from those ahead." It is a proverb of prudence, meaning "forewarned is forearmed". And, truly, such is the courage and resolution of *inyathi* that the hunters found in him a character to be reckoned with and more than one disturber of the peace of the animal world came to grief on his horns.

Thomas Duff, who was one of the hunters of the 1850s, has described a typical buffalo adventure. With his party he came across a herd of a dozen drinking at a pool in a narrow, open valley. "From a fringe of bush at the side we fired our guns at them, and in a minute the herd all scrambled up the valley into the bush. Without waiting to load my gun, I thoughtfully hurried down to the side of the pool to look if I could not see any blood spoors and, hearing a rush in the bushes a little way up the valley, I raised my eyes to see a big buffalo rushing down towards me.

"Turning around, I took long strides down the valley, running for my life, but on glancing behind I saw the angry beast was gaining on me and felt that in a minute or two I would feel his big horns against my back. At that moment a thought providentially struck me. I sprang aside around a clump of bushes and ran up the bank and got into a forked tree. The enraged animal rushed past me for about fifty yards down the valley, then wheeled round, raised his head and looked about disappointed, but at once galloped back the way it had come to join its fellows."

Another animal character of Zululand well able to look after himself was the rhino. *Ubhejane* (the vicious one), the Zulus call the irritable black rhinoceros, and his reputation as a doughty and most dangerous opponent was in curious contrast to that of his close but rarer relative, *umkhombe*, the so-called white or square-lipped rhinoceros, whose nature is more docile, although his bulk, as his name indicates, is considerably larger.

The white rhinoceros was first observed by William Burchell in the year 1812. Wandering through the area around Kuruman, in the southern Kalahari, he encountered this species and named it *Rhinoceros simus* although it became more generally known as the square-lipped or Burchell's rhinoceros. The species was well distributed all over Southern Africa in those days. Some years later, when a party of Boer hunters found it in the vicinity of the Vaal River, they called it the *wit* (white) rhinoceros, for no known reason apart from the possibility that the first specimens they saw might have been plastered with whitish mud from some wallow.

Like the buffaloes, the rhinos have always been partial to mud, for, despite the thickness of their hides, they are much pestered by gadflies, and ticks also manage to establish themselves. The rhino bird, *inhlalanyathi*, removes most of the ticks, but he generally does so with the taste of a connoisseur, picking out only the nice fat ones and leaving the others to feed for a while to fatten in a sort of tick fool's paradise.

The rhino's fearsome reputation is known only to man. With all other animals he lives in peace. At waterholes the most cantankerous of black rhinos nevertheless drinks with all comers. Knowing no fear for himself, he tolerates a troop of lions within yards of the muddy mess he is making of the water as he wallows and splashes around like an overgrown, armoured pig.

The most timid duiker will drink unafraid beside some battle-scarred old rhino bull that stands rooting the ground into furrows, an action which man interprets as an erratic display of savagery, but the animal world knows well is just the black rhino's idea of personal hygiene in the burying of its dung.

But rhinos are unpredictable things. In the 1850s a party of Tongas were one day threading their way through the tangled tapestry of the bush. Among the party was one woman with a baby on her back. Suddenly a black rhino hurtled out of the bush. There was a wild scatter for trees. The woman, in a panic, made for the wrong tree, found it unclimbable, and the rhino caught her.

He tossed her in the air. She fell unconscious to the ground, with the baby on her back screaming its head off. The rhino went up to the woman, sniffed the squalling baby, licked it, and walked quietly away. The woman escaped with bruises and a broken rib.

Another peculiarity of the rhino is his hatred of campfires. Whether nature has appointed him an irate conservator of the bush, or whether he suspects that the fire may be destined to roast him, is unknown, but many are the hunters' stories of their camp being attacked for the sole apparent purpose of stamping the fire out.

W.H. Drummond, who hunted around the 1870s, tells how he and his companions were camped at a waterhole nearby the Black Mfolozi. They were lolling around their fire roasting venison – congenial task – in the late evening after a strenuous day of adventure.

Drummond was just in the act of cutting off the first slice of meat with his knife, his comrades watching him with hungry eyes, when they were startled by an ominous succession of puffs, almost like a train starting. They were all old soldiers at that camp. Within three seconds everybody was sitting in a tree. Within ten seconds a black rhino had scattered the fire into the mud, stamping his feet and squealing with rage in the process. The venison roast was deep in the mud. Blankets and clothing were mixed up in a smouldering mess with the relics of the fire. The whole camp was a wreck.

Eventually Drummond recovered his wits. He grabbed a rifle one of the Zulu hunters had carried up the tree. Taking a potshot, he planted a bullet somewhere in the rhino's hide. The giant fell with a thud. He picked himself up, grunted, and hurtled off into the bush, leaving the camp in ruins behind him.

Generally the hunters' camps were pretty secure. They were invariably in large parties, for hunting was a business, and their camps were more in the nature of temporary settlements scattered about the bush like tiny islands of companionship in a sea of solitude.

Generally some tall and shady trees, wild fig or mimosa of the giant umbrella type were selected as the centre of the camp. These served as shade and shelter, and wet buffalo hides would be festooned upon the branches to form a rainproof roof. Around the trees a rude but strong fence of thorns would be erected for protection. Inside, each man would select a corner for himself, cut reeds to make a mattress, and otherwise make himself at home.

From this encampment hunters would sally out each morning, scattering to all corners of the horizon. Some would have the task of keeping the camp supplied with meat, but the majority attended solely to the business of hunting elephants for ivory.

In the evening the hunters would trickle back. If unsuccessful, they would return in silence. If successful, they all, white and black, would always have the tail of the animal they had killed hanging from their belts, and the Zulus would sing a hunting chant.

Provided it wasn't raining, these hunting encampments would be merry places in the evenings, with venison being grilled and a host of anecdotes of the day's adventures being swopped and innumerable fascinating observations being made on Africa's natural history.

Imagine a night just such as this. It was warm and breathless, and around the camp a myriad of insects twittered, the bullfrogs grunted in their deep bass voices, and high overhead came the lonely cry of some nightbird flying. Marrow bones and buffalo tongues had filled many hungry bellies and snores came from all sides. William Baldwin, one of the best known of the hunters of the 1850s, was just snuggling down into bed when he was aroused by one of the oxen bellowing and the dogs barking.

He rushed out into the dark with his gun. He found his wagon-boy precariously seated on the top of a temporary grass hut six feet high. Baldwin joined him.

In the dark they could hear an ox coughing out its life and the quarrelling of a pride of lions gathered for the feast. The lions were only about 14 yards away. It was tolerably light; there was no moon, but the stars looked down brightly enough upon the scene.

Seeing the shape of the ox upon the ground, Baldwin fired at it. His driver joined him, and they blazed away at random. But the lions paid no heed.

Suddenly the darkness seemed to condense into a single shape hurtling out of the shadows at them. It was an infuriated lioness. "I was aware for a single instant only that she was coming," wrote Baldwin, "and the same moment I was knocked half-a-dozen somersaults backwards off the hut, the brute striking me in the chest with the head."

Baldwin scrambled through the grass to the wagon. He found it choked with Zulus. All his Zulu hunters who couldn't get inside were sticking like monkeys to the sides, with the wagon-boy sitting on the rooftop. How he got there so quickly from his former position beside Baldwin was a mystery.

There was complete pandemonium in the camp. In the midst of it the five lions went on with their quarrelling and gorging. They were complete masters of the situation until the dawn came and drove them away. Then the wagon-load of shivering humanity crawled back to bed and slept it off.

The lion, *ingonyama*, whose name means "a wild beast of prey", was one of the few animals who sometimes gave the hunters a run for their money, and often gave them a very great scare.

Drummond tells of one of his hunters who was following the trail of a herd of buffaloes through a thicket.

"Suddenly a male lion rose out of a clump of bush, and, sitting on its hindquarters, snarled at him. He had hardly seen it when another, about three-quarters grown, showed itself within a few yards on one side, while from behind he could hear the low, rumbling growl of a third.

"Partly turning, so as to watch them all, he saw that the latter was a lioness, and that three cubs, not much larger than cats, were following her. He had, unawares, got into the centre of a lion family. Unfortunately, one of the cubs saw him and, without exhibiting the least fear, it ran up to him; whereupon its mother, in terror for her offspring, rushed up, and, as he afterwards described it, fairly danced round and round him, springing to within a yard of him, sideways, backwards, and in every way but on him."

The man was petrified with terror. He stood dead still and thereby saved his life. Eventually the cub tired of nipping his feet and gambolled off into the bush, followed by its parents.

Lions, indeed, like rhinos, are contrary things. Sometimes an old and toothless lion would attack human beings through inclination, but generally it was interference which first provoked it. If undisturbed, they were invariably reasonable.

For food the lions were most partial to the plumb zebras, *idube* (stripes), as the Zulus called them, and apparently they made particularly toothsome meals. They were hard to catch, however, for long persecution by lions had made them uncommonly wary. The buffalo was much easier to catch, but infinitely harder to kill, so as a stop-gap hungry lions turned to such alternative dishes as *inkonkoni*, the blue wildebeest (brindled gnu), whose mixed-up appearance has inspired his alternative name of *imbuzimeshe* (the goat like an ox).

Other dishes for the lions in Zululand were *impofu* (the tawny one), the eland; *impala*, the sprightly little antelope; his bigger relative, *inoni* (the fat one), the sable antelope, whose horns were traditionally used to make the signal horns of the Zulu army; *unkonka*, the shy bushbuck; *iphithi* (the erratic one), the tiny forest duiker; *inhlangu* (the one of the reeds), the reedbuck; *inyala* (the shifty one), one of the most beautiful of antelopes; and *umgankla*, the kudu, whose meat was traditionally disliked by Zulu maidens and whose name was always applied to any undesirable young man.

The great, tough-skinned giraffe, *indlulamithi* (he who surpasses the trees), was also common to old Zululand, along with a host of smaller animals such as *isimbamgodi* (the hole digger), the ant bear; *umhlangala*, the mongoose; *inungu* (the thorny one), the porcupine; *isinkwe*, the bushbaby (Garnett's Galago), whose shrill voice is often heard in the early hours; the quaint warthog, *intibane*, whose shape and tusks have inspired an alternative descriptive name, *indlovudawana*, (the miniature elephant) and *iqaqa*, the polecat, concerning whom there is an apt Zulu proverb: "There is no polecat that ever smelled its own smell."

The monkey, *inkawu*, was also well in evidence, along with his larger cousin, *imfene*, the baboon. Like the wildebeest, *imfene* has a second name, *imbuzimawa* (the goat of the precipices) and about him there is also a legend. Baboons were once people, the Zulus say. They belonged to a lazy tribe known as the Thusis. They did no work, and from sitting on their hoes all day the shafts grew into their bodies as tails, and the weeds in their gardens covered them as hair.

The daring leopard, *ingwe*, is another of Zululand's animal characters who has gathered to himself a variety of legends and proverbs. "The leopard does not sleep with the goat," the Zulus say if two people are incompatible; and, again, "The leopard devours his master," when somebody returns evil for good.

The crocodile, *ingwenya*, also has his place in Zulu lore. Aptly enough, his name indicates "a lawless criminal" and is also the name for one's tonsils. "The crocodile devours in the strong current," say the Zulus as a warning to keep away from bad company, and the evil presence of iNgwenya has often driven man away from some formerly well-used ford. Whole pathways have fallen into disuse and diversions have been tramped to some other crossing point when a particularly vicious crocodile has made a ford his haunt and challenged the passage of all comers.

The hyena, *impisi* (the ugly one), was another animal character with an evil descriptive name. *Nswelaboya*, the Zulus called him, meaning literally "the hairless one", but in its usage indicating a murderer of the worst possible kind, a witch doctor who resorts to ritual murder and the production of magic from human fats.

The jackal, *impungushe* (the grey one), has ever played his allotted role of clearing up the debris of the great hunters, and during the years of large-scale elephant shooting he must have fattened much on a rich harvest. The elephant, *indlovu*, has a name which means "the trampler". Of him the Zulus say in one of their proverbs: "iNdlovu has fallen and the tribes have gone to cut off pieces," which means that when the mighty fall the little men all take advantage of them.

In the days of the great hunters, *indlovu* fell in countless thousands. In the vast Mbekamuzi valley, a renowned hunting resort full of memories of campfires and hunters' yarns, Johannes de Lange once trapped an enormous herd in a dead-end valley. He slaughtered so many of them there that the whole valley stank for months afterwards. Among this unfortunate herd was its leader, a famous elephant known from his size as iNdlulamithi (he who surpasses the trees), who possessed, besides unusual height, a sagacity and length of tusk which had made him legendary.

Peter Hogg, a large-scale professional hunter of the 1850s, came across a herd of some 1500 elephants once in 1858. They were trekking for water in the neighbourhood of the Sabie River in the area of the present Kruger National Park. Within two hours he and his Zulu hunters had killed 95 of the giants.

The ivory from this bag whetted their appetites. A runaway slave from Lourenço Marques told Hogg of the marvellous hunting in the land of Soshangane. Hogg sent two of his men with the slave up to Soshangane with presents and a request for hunting rights.

In February 1859 this party returned with a favourable reply. Hogg then invested £1500 in fitting out a mammoth hunting party in Durban. The best Zulu hunters available were enrolled, and, delirious with joy at the prospect of fortunes in ivory, they set out in May 1859.

Hogg went with his party as far as Swaziland, where fever sent him back to Durban. His party of 400 trained and heavily-armed men went on to Gasaland. There they scattered to commence hunting, and were hunted themselves. A rival hunter, annoyed at the intrusion, spread a rumour that they were an advance guard of a Zulu invasion. Soshangane wiped out the entire party of 400 men in one murderous debacle. Hogg was ruined, and he abandoned hunting altogether after that.

One of the best known of the earlier hunters was "Elephant White". He had received his nickname not from the elephants he hunted, but rather from his own prodigious size and strength. In company with Peter Hogg and William Proudfoot he ran a joint ivory hunting business in the 1840s. They hunted mostly in the area between the Phongolo and uSuthu rivers and around Lake St Lucia.

Koos van Staden and his partner, James Brody, a deserter from the British 45th Regiment, were also active in those times and parts. Ivory was fetching around five shillings a pound then, and with elephants extremely numerous, the profits of hunting were large.

Each of the hunting parties was generally organised on a large scale, with wagons, ample supplies of spare oxen, guns and provisions. Each group would secure from Mpande the hunting rights for a specified area, and if one group poached on the other's preserves there was always trouble.

In their allotted area the hunters would systematically ransack the bush in search of tuskers. On killing an elephant, the normal practice was to make their mark upon it – generally cutting a distinctive pattern into the ear – and then leave the carcass to rot. Later they would return, the tusks being easier to extract when the body was putrid.

The hunting parties all trained and armed considerable bodies of Zulu professional hunters, and these roamed far and wide all through the year. They generally received one-third of their spoils, and were considered to make good money, although their lives were arduous and exceedingly dangerous.

The adventures these hunters had were legion. Three of the Zulu professional hunters were once returning to their masters after a season in Tongaland. They were following the old path which led through the Lubombo Mountains along the banks of the Phongolo River. In this pass, in the reeds around a shallow lagoon, there lived a renowned old lion. He was no man-eater, but he was prone to attack any human who disturbed his haunts, and in this manner he had already killed two wayfarers and scared several others out of their wits.

The three hunters had been warned of this lion, but, confident of their guns, they went their way. Suddenly, without warning, the lion charged them. He sprang upon the leading man and crushed him to the ground.

The other two hunters made for the trees, but, hearing their companion shriek, they turned to aid him. Walking forward together, they were on the point of firing, when, with a roar that almost paralysed them, the lion charged.

Beneath this fury one man went down. The survivor jumped for a tree and escaped with inches to spare. Then, from an uncomfortable vantage point in a thorn-tree, he experienced the horror of watching the lion return to its victims.

The first man was already dead. The lion took the second victim up in its mouth, dropped him, tossed him from paw to paw as a cat does a mouse, and then crunched his life out between its jaws.

Then the lion came back to the tree. He looked up at the human being in a complacent manner, aware that though he might be unable to reach him for the present, patience might still prevail. The lion stretched himself out lazily, and after licking the blood off his hide, closed his eyes as if to sleep.

The thorn-tree – one of the larger acacias – had two stems, which separated about six feet from the ground. Into this fork, some feet below him, the man had jammed his gun in his struggle to climb the tree.

A quarter of an hour passed without the slightest movement from the lion. The gun was a yearning temptation to the hunter. At length he determined on reaching it. Quietly he descended the tree, foot by foot, until at last all he need do was to stoop to reach the prize. All the time he was watching the lion.

Everything was still. He was in the act of stooping when he saw an involuntary tremor of excitement run down the lion's body. The man straightened himself with a jerk, and the lion's violent spring ended in a disappointed howl of rage.

Furious at this setback, the lion returned to the corpses of his two victims, dragged them together, and lay down in triumphant regard. This was his mistake. A minute later a six-pounder bullet put daylight between his ribs, and he bounded away to his private sanctuary to reflect, maybe, that a bird in a tree was worth two on the ground.

The hippopotamus, *imvubu* (the fat one) was almost as much hunted as the elephant. His teeth also supplied high quality ivory, and his body fats and skin were all of value. Lake St Lucia was the greatest hunting ground for hippos, and each year parties of hunters encamped there.

Elephant White was a particularly regular visitor, although not always successful. One of his hunting visits to the lake became famous and its story is part of the tumultuous bittersweet history of Zululand.

In 1849, when Elephant White returned from a hunting trip, he stated that he thought there was a navigable entrance to Lake St Lucia and he intended developing it as a convenient means of shipping out ivory and skins.

Late in December 1851 he set off overland for the lake with a boat carried on the top of one of his wagons. With him went a party made up of some of the most famous hunters Zululand ever knew. Charley Edmonstone was there, as well as E.R. Price, son of a wealthy London banker, C. Arbuthnot, Monies, McQueen, Gibson, White and William Baldwin, who had just come out from England in search of sport and adventure.

They travelled on across the Thukela into Zululand, hunting and adventuring. At the Black Mfolozi they halted their wagons and sent the oxen 20 miles back to graze in an area safe from the tsetse fly. Then they launched their boat on the turbulent waters of the river and planned that half of the company would sail it down to the lake, while the others walked along the bank.

It was a hot and rainy season. "The mosquitoes were so

dreadful on the riverbanks," wrote Baldwin, "that we lighted cow-dung fires in every pot we had and put them inside the now empty wagon, and all turned into it, and had the choice of two evils – to be worried by the mosquitoes or almost stifled with heat and smoke in the wagon."

On 24 January 1852, Monies and Gibson set off in the boat, while Price, Arbuthnot and Baldwin started their journey overland. The rest of the party had gone to see Mpande to get permission for the venture and present him with the usual gifts.

The boat party soon came to grief. Crocodiles were so numerous, attracted especially by the dogs carried in the boat, that they crowded around and soon smashed both oars and rudder. The men had to abandon the boat on a sandbank and walk to the prearranged rendezvous with the overland party.

The bulk of the party then returned, made oars, declared war on the crocodiles, and rowed down the Mfolozi to St Lucia. There they commenced blasting away at the wild life – ducks, hippos and buffaloes – until the lake had a fair percentage of blood on its surface, and the crocodiles, big, fat, gorged and insolent, lay on the sandbanks and dreamt the sweet dreams of the glutton.

The party sailed up the whole length of the lake and eventually made a camp on some high land overlooking the bay, directly opposite the mouth of the Hluhluwe River. There they built a so-called *hartbeeshuisie* (a triangular-shaped affair made of two slanting roofs of reeds). Big reed sheds were also made to store tusks, meat, oil and their own provisions.

They hunted the hippos from their boat, generally keeping near to the shore. The carcasses would be retrieved by the local tribespeople who crowded around the hunters to enjoy free meat. They formed long chains going out into the water, the one holding the hand of the other and pulling the carcasses to the beach.

On shore the Africans stood respectfully by while the tusks were removed, together with the best of the meat for salting, the skin for sjamboks and leather, and the inside fat for rendering down into oil in big, sooty pots, which were kept constantly on the boil.

This process of commercial dissection finished, the rest of the carcass would be "declared an open season" to the tribespeople. A seething mass of humanity would pounce upon the carcass and literally rend it to pieces with bare hands. What remnants that were left, together with the general slaughterhouse stench, attracted lions and hyenas to the place like a plague, and the nights were hideous with their yammerings.

By 11 March the party had killed 55 hippos and one elephant. Everybody was feeling slightly sick, so they decided to abandon the venture for the time being. They packed up and quit the place, returning to their wagons and setting out for Natal.

The change in temperature put the finishing touch to the fever in their veins. Arbuthnot was the first to die, then Monies gave up the ghost, and McQueen followed him when they were at their last camp, only a few miles from Durban. E.R. Price only had a boy with him in his wagon when he felt death approaching. He called the boy to him. "I'm going to die," he said. "It's not a sight for you to see. You can come back presently." The boy withdrew into the bush for half-an-hour, and when he returned Price was dead.

Three other of Elephant White's hunters died that year in Zululand. Gibson, Edmonstone and Baldwin recovered, but it had been a bad year with at least 14 known European hunters dying of fever. The white man had to learn through bitter experience that when *umsinsi*, the kaffirboom (*Erythrina caffra*), *umhlaba*, the giant aloe, and *inkalane*, the small aloe, cover themselves with their deep red flowers each spring, it is nature kindly showing mankind the warning colour of danger, telling him that fever is coming once again and the bush should be left to brood in solitude through the months of heat and rain and singing mosquitoes.

Other individuals opened up Lake St Lucia as a point of export. The cutter *Haidee* was later sent up by sea from Durban and it had no difficulty in entering the great lake. They found the bar 50 ft wide, with about 12 ft of water over it, and the lake itself had an average depth of 9 ft.

Regular seasonal visits were thenceforth made to the lake and it was thoroughly explored. In July 1853, the cutter *Liverpool*, under William Rider, sailed up and spent five months cruising around the lake, hunting hippos, exploring the islands, and even sailing for 30 miles up the Mkhuze River.

The knowledge that summer in Zululand was fatal for the European soon became generally known. No one had the least idea that the mosquito was the carrier of the dreaded disease, and ideas of cures were fantastic. One favourite specific consisted of an emetic made of a large teaspoonful of mustard and hot water, and then a large teaspoonful of Stockholm tar three times daily. If the patient wasn't dead by the next morning, he was considered to be out of danger from the disease. Whether he was out of danger from the medicine was another matter.

Some hunters had remarkable escapes from fever. In July 1855 Charles Barter, later magistrate of Pietermaritzburg, was hunting in the region around the upper part of Lake St Lucia. He went down badly with fever. His Zulu hunters took the news to his sister, who was with the wagons at the base camp in the hills 45 miles away. She unhesitatingly walked to her stricken brother and had him carried back to comfort on a rough stretcher. He recovered, but never hunted in Zululand again.

The renowned Elephant White had a hide so tough he seemed to be impervious to mosquitoes. He knocked around in Zululand for many years, and then eventually went off to the Australian goldfields.

William Baldwin had been White's partner during his last few years in Zululand. White traded for cattle in Zululand, while Baldwin remained on a farm in the iNanda and occupied himself in fattening the animals and then reselling them on the Natal market. It was a dreary life, but he enlivened it by regular winter hunting trips across the Thukela.

In April 1854 he planned his annual trip to Tongaland. Travelling entirely on his own, he wandered into the vast green flatness of the land of the lakes. The Tongas treated him with pronounced hospitality and a large crowd of camp followers attached themselves to him for the sake of free meat.

Baldwin carried strings of *umgazi* beads with him for trade, and a few of these always secured him fowls, eggs, nuts, rice, beer or palm wine. The Tongas had no cattle. As a sort of negative defence from raids, they prudently kept nothing to arouse the cupidity of the Zulus.

As a curious by-product of this lack of cattle the Tongas lived on good terms with the lions; they even asked Baldwin not to shoot any of the animals. They said they were so fond of meat and it was so hard to come by, that they often shared the repast of the lions, for after a kill the Tongas would beat the jackals and vultures to the spot and seize such delicacies as the lions had left.

Tongaland was alive with game. Eland, buffalo, nyala, wildebeest, waterbuck and impala were everywhere. The rivers and pans were the homes of countless numbers of ducks, geese, pidgeon, cranes, waders and divers. Baldwin roamed about in complete contentment. He was a rough sort of chap who loved the wilderness for itself, and so long as he could obtain food and make enough profit to grubstake another trip, he was content.

Each Tonga clan vied with its neighbour in showering him with gifts as an inducement to remain with them for a while as a tribal meat provider. The Tongas hunted largely with pitfalls, and travelling was risky unless a sharp lookout was kept at every footstep. Despite these traps, however, the Tongas caught little game and the animals normally led their lives with but little disturbance.

Elephants browsed in the bush, vast troops of enormous creatures flapping their ears lazily in the warm air, breaking off boughs and pushing trees over to get at the marula berries and tender shoots.

Baldwin found the Phongolo and uSuthu rivers to be magnificent waterways in their settings of luxuriant vegetation. They abounded in hippos and swarmed with so many crocodiles that the wonder of it was how all the brutes found enough to eat.

The Tongas at least had plenty of food while Baldwin was with them, for he was an expert shot and nearly every day he would provide them with a hippo. They would drag it to the shore for him and then courteously stand aside while he took his choice. "But as soon as I delivered over the carcass to them there ensued an indescribable scene of confusion. The Tongas rushed at the beast with assegais, knives and picks, hallooing, bellowing, shoving and fighting in a manner that no one would believe who had not seen them. Occasionally the captain ran in and laid about him with a rhinoceros sjambok in every direction. The strongest of the savages got at the beast, cut off pieces and hurled them over their heads to their accomplices outside, who dashed at them and ran with them, each to a separate heap, where he deposited his piece and where no one meddled with it."

Baldwin lived like a king. His sort of life was miserable enough at times, in excessive rain or heat, but its delight was in wearing what you liked and doing pretty well as you pleased. For food, when he tired of the veal-like taste of undiluted hippo meat, he had a recipe of his own concoction, viz.: Take 1½ lb. of breast of hippopotamus, well stewed and cut up small; about three tablespoonfuls of inside fat rendered down as white as snow; a few red peppers; salt; a handful of rice; a handful of fine flour; a couple of pickled walnuts and a few sprigs of thyme or some such herb. Serve piping hot beneath the stars of an African night somewhere in Tongaland.

From the uSuthu, Baldwin returned to his shack in Natal. Each time he returned there he found it in a greater state of dilapidation. The white ants undermined its foundations just as the monotony of settling down anywhere undermined his happiness.

His stock was stolen, his fields overgrown, until eventually all he had left was a ruin, one solitary cock, which always fled for the bush in fear of its life when he returned, and a wonderful little pig which always kept itself in good condition, defended itself against all the attacks of wild animals, and had a strong attachment to the place where it had been brought as a suckling.

Although Baldwin seemed to live a ramshackle sort of life, he made money enough from his knocking about. When he returned to England a few years later, after wandering about Southern Africa as far as Lake Ngami and the Victoria Falls, he had saved enough from ivory and skins to be tolerably well-to-do.

Some hunters made sizeable fortunes in Zululand. George Shadwell, another well-known character of the time, bagged 150 hippos and 91 elephants in a single season in 1853. John Clark, Henry Paxton and Septimus Sanderson were other large-scale hunters who made money from their adventuring, while men such as Peter Hogg, William Mayer and Johannes Strydom, who later died of fever at Lake St Lucia, all specialised in guiding parties of overseas dude hunters through the land of game animals.

Whilst most of these hunters did little for Zululand save denude it of game in the process of enriching or entertaining themselves, it was given to a few of them to be of real service to the people. W.H. Drummond was one such an adventurer, for he it was who relieved north-eastern Zululand from the oppression of the country's most celebrated man-eater.

In the early 1870s this man-eater commenced his vicious career along the banks of the Phongolo River, to the west of its pass through the Lubombo Mountains. For several years this animal reigned supreme in the land. Many villages were entirely deserted, for his strength and cunning became legend. No fastenings seemed of use against him, for his immense strength allowed him to force an entrance through stockades and huts.

Like a human brigand, a man-eater depended for his success on his own daring, and this lion had more than his fair share of resolution and courage. He was cunning as well, and usually confined himself to killing one individual out of each kraal. "A man only stabs one of his herd when he is hungry," the Zulus say, and verily this was true of that bloodthirsty lion, for he never spoilt his hunting by preying too much in the same area.

The tribespeople, in the manner of their kind, after some ineffective resistance to the lion, at length came to the conclusion that witchcraft was at the bottom of the business. They accordingly made no further resistance save magical incantations, smellings-out and hiding their heads under mats and blankets when they slept.

Drummond often hunted in the area and was often requested to do something about the lion. At times he tried tracking the brute, but the animal was inordinately cautious and no one could ever find his lair.

At last came a season of rain, with the earth soft and tracks easy to follow. Drummond was sheltering in a village from the very storms which were moistening the earth. Lying drowsing in his hut one night, he was aroused by a sudden clamour from the village. While he sat bolt upright in the darkness wondering what was happening, there came "such a blood-curdling yell of mingled pain and despair as I hope I may never hear again and which haunted my dreams for many a month after."

He peered out of the hut entrance, while his two Zulu hunters who shared his hut crouched in a far corner, shivering and afraid. It was inky black. The whole village was now like a tomb. There was no movement or sound and no indication as to what had caused the sudden alarm. Such had been the speed of the attack and the infectious atmosphere of horror and fear and self-preservation in the presence of the man-eater, that the entire village was subdued.

In the morning they tracked the animal. The victim had been a young married woman, a relation of the chief, Thegwane. They found her remains about 200 yards away. From there the track went on to a stream a mile away, which the lion had befouled when quenching his thirst.

The whole village rallied around Drummond and his hunters and all able-bodied men set out in search of vengeance. They tracked the lion to the Mbeka bush, a jungle of thorn and shrub on the side of a hill. At that place nearly five hundred men were mustered and sent in to beat the bush.

The men took terror with them as they entered the forest fastness. Each man had a deep fear of this notorious lion. Bawling out hunting songs to revive their spirits, and constantly crying out encouragement to one another, they pushed steadily deeper into the thorns.

Suddenly there was a chorus of shouts from the extreme left. All congregated in that direction. The lion had shown himself for a brief moment.

Drummond and his hunters concealed themselves thereabouts and the beaters slowly converged upon the spot. Suddenly there was a tense "There he is!" The lion had come out. He stood in the dark shade of a tree, with his head turned towards the oncoming beaters, uncertain as to which direction to take.

Then he made up his mind. He turned straight in the direction of the waiting hunters. At 60 yards one of them fired. Over went the lion like a rabbit, performing a complete somersault before he regained his legs. The whole line of hunters rose with a shout.

The lion bolted. He made for a small tree and with his back to it stood at bay. The hunters approached, with the beaters coming up behind to cheer them to the kill.

From a distance the hunters opened fire. The lion charged like a thunderbolt, roaring horribly. Nothing seemed to stop him. The hunters emptied their guns and then scattered before him.

The beaters, once cheering but now silenced, stood in a petrified line. The lion charged up to within ten yards of them.

Then, awed by their numbers, he slowed and walked slowly up and down like a sergeant-major on parade before a terrified crowd of recruits, growling and showing his teeth and looking a very noble animal with his heavy mane floating around him.

One of the beaters, bolder than the rest, suddenly flung a spear and a curse at the lion. The spear just grazed him. The lion immediately sprang. He struck a six-foot shield, and while he tore at it, the warrior stabbed him in the chest with his double-edged stabbing spear.

At this the whole line of beaters closed in around the lion like a sprung mantrap. That was the end. One man was killed by the lion, and the warrior who had originally thrown the spear was badly mauled, but in the crush the lion had no hope. Hundreds of spears were embedded in his body. Drummond counted the holes in his skin afterwards and found between five and six hundred. Six bullets had also struck him; in the jaw, eye, the chest, and two in the neck, while one had travelled the entire length of his body.

Like most man-eaters, this lion was an old fellow with badly decayed teeth. But, like Mother Africa herself, although old and wrinkled and scarred by innumerable fights, he possessed an ageless savagery, an iron resolution and a desperate courage which asked no quarter but carried him fighting on to his last charge and his final breath.

EIGHTEEN
Cetshwayo

The days of Mpande's reign over Zululand were remarkably tranquil so far as the Zulus were concerned. He was easy-going and fat, and too good-natured to indulge in any large-scale killings or wars. This was so unusual for the Zulus that, like a person with ever increasing blood pressure, they sooner or later had to find relief. For want of foreign adventures, they started blood-letting among themselves.

Mpande, although so supine in most matters, had managed to raise a family of more than respectable proportions. As the days of his 32-year-long reign stretched out, this family grew up and the sons, as is the nature of princes, became impatient for their inheritance.

After some shuffling about, the question of succession to the Zulu throne eventually became an issue between two of Mpande's sons: Mbulazi and Cetshwayo, who was born about the year 1830. Mpande sensed the antagonism between the two but could do nothing about it except endeavour to keep them separated as much as possible. He appointed Mbulazi to live with his mother on the Mfaba hills and allocated him some adherents who were known as the iziGqoza.

Cetshwayo (the slandered one) was sent to live with his mother Ngqumbazi at the old Mthethwa military kraal of eMangweni, where Shaka had served as a trooper. Cetshwayo's followers were known as the uSuthu and feelings between them and the iziGqoza steadily became worse.

Meanwhile, over this developing volcano, the European hunters and traders continued to swarm across the country, while missionaries were also seeking permission to settle. One of the most persistent of these was the Norwegian, H.P.S. Schreuder. From 1843 onwards he had tried to get permission to found a Zulu mission, but constant refusal eventually disheartened him so much that he removed to China. Later he returned to Natal and in 1850 he established the mission of Mphumulo (place of rest).

But Zululand remained his goal and eventually fortune favoured his persistence. While on a visit to Mpande he managed to cure the king of an ailment. As a reward Mpande, in December 1850, gave his permission for the establishment of a Zululand mission and the following year the Norwegians erected a station on the banks of the stream known as the em-Pangeni (place of *Treema guineensis* trees) from which his mission took its name.

This was the first mission in Zululand since the ill-fated attempts of Owen and the Americans. It was a rough sort of establishment but with a good heart. William Baldwin, the hunter and trader, visited it a few years after its opening and has described a church service there.

"*June 3rd.* I went to church and saw such a medley as I should have thought a mortal would never have the chance of seeing. The side walls were built of mud, and, with the help of wooden posts, supported a zinc roof. To windward the walls had fallen in, leaving the building airy and open. From the beams hung Kaffir ropes, the tent and sides of a wagon, loads of mealies, old saddles, yokes, neckstraps, and all apparatus for wagoning, old hats and bridles, and part of a splendid leopard skin.

"In the midst of all this and ten times more, rose a pulpit, the cushions and hangings of which bore marks of a great deal of service; and in the pulpit a tall, bushy-whiskered Norwegian missionary, in a black coat buttoned to the throat and reaching to the heels, with spectacles of course, held forth.

"About thirty Zulus, men and women, squatted on a mat on their hams, huddling close together two under one blanket, hunting the borders for lice, and cracking heaps of them, or taking thorns out of their feet with wooden pins, unseen by the pastor, who held forth for more than three hours."

It was near the site of this mission that Cetshwayo lived, and perhaps Mpande had hoped that the presence of the pastor might moderate the ambitions of his son. If this was the case Mpande was disappointed, for the ill-feeling between the two young rivals steadily worsened and at last came to a head.

All through the year 1856 the air in Zululand was electric with the approaching storm. Blacksmiths were busy hammering out spears and the two princes were rummaging around gathering supporters. In November Mbulazi started to panic. His spies told him that Cetshwayo had collected almost four times as many warriors to his cause than had Mbulazi.

Mbulazi then resolved to make a move. Gathering his supporters, he marched down to an old kraal established by Dingane, on a site overlooking the main drift across the lower Thukela River. At this kraal, named Ndondakusuka (slow to move), Mbulazi left his followers while he forded the river into Natal. There he saw the British border agent and asked for aid. When this was refused he attempted to raise a force of mercenaries from the various peoples, African and European, who had sought sanctuary on the Natal side from the very evident approaching troubles.

Of these people about three hundred Africans were attracted to Mbulazi's side by promises of liberal reward. Several European traders who were gathered there also became involved in the business through Mbulazi's offer. Among them were J. Waugh (Matyonga), J. Rathbone (Ngqelebana) and John Dunn (Jantoni).

Of the three adventurers John Dunn was destined to become the best known. He had been born in England in 1884, the son of a respectable couple who had immigrated to Durban in 1836. There they had lived happily enough on their farm of

Sea View until 4 September 1847 when Robert Dunn (John's father) was trampled to death by an elephant. Four years later Mrs Dunn died and young John, then 17 years old, took to wandering around the country.

Dunn was a man who was particularly fond of his gun and, in his youth at least, led a solitary life. After an unfortunate period of employment by a transport rider who defrauded him of his hard-earned wages, saying he was too young to have money, Dunn had found society irksome and wandered off into Zululand. There he had hunted and adventured and worked for the well-known and eccentric border agent, Captain Joshua Walmsley, until the year 1856, when he decided to rove off again on his own. Hunting in the great valley of the Thukela River he had been disturbed by reports of the impending clash and had withdrawn to the border at the drift. There Mbulazi found him and induced Dunn to support his cause.

About 7000 men were gathered at Ndondakusuka with Mbulazi. After two days of preparation Cetshwayo arrived on the scene with his uSuthu faction which numbered about 20 000 men. Things looked grim for Mbulazi, but he sallied out at sunset on 1 December 1856 to meet his opponents. A few shots were exchanged before darkness blanketed the contentions of man in sleep.

The following day – a raw, cold, drizzly morning – the fight began. The uSuthu, exploiting their numerical superiority, set out to surround Mbulazi's army. Dunn soon saw the battle was lost. He gathered his hunters and charged his way through one of the encircling wings without much trouble, for the Zulus were overawed by his horse and the few gaspipe firearms of his followers. The two other Europeans also decided to clear out.

Behind them there was a sad slaughter. The severest fighting took place on the banks of a streamlet which to this day is known by the name of Mathambo (the place of bones). The iziGqoza were completely routed. No less than six of Mpande's sons, including Mbulazi, were killed that day.

The battle ended with a general stampede towards the Thukela River. A final slaughter occurred along the banks and in its waters, which resulted in hundreds of corpses being carried downstream and deposited by the ocean along the beaches on either side of the river mouth.

A mass of struggling and drowning humanity spread over the face of the river like ants floating on water, each one trying to escape by trampling on his fellow. The one small ferryboat, manned by an excited ferryman, did its best to save as many as possible, but hundreds were drowned. When John Dunn rode into the water, so many people grabbed hold of his horse hoping it would tow them across the river that the unfortunate animal couldn't move. Dunn jumped off, stripped, and swam for it, holding his gun in one hand. His horse managed to kick itself free and followed him.

When the slaughter was over, Captain Walmsley happened to be walking along the riverbank on the Natal side. He heard a child crying. He approached the place in the reeds and found a woman lying face downwards, dead. On her back was a child of about three years of age, crying bitterly, and with little more than its head above water.

Walmsley took pity on the child. He removed it from its dead mother and carried it home. The child was a girl. Walmsley's wife was French, a lonely woman in that solitary border post. She adopted the child and brought it up as her own. She educated it, taught it French and, apart from its colour, it became to all intents and purposes a European miss in manner, taste and behaviour.

Then, at the age of 17, this young girl fell in love with a Zulu living in a kraal nearby. The Zulu was completely primitive and the Walmsleys were both shocked when the girl told them of her desire to quit European society and revert to her own people. Argument and not a few tears from Mrs Walmsley were of no avail. The girl was in love and go she must.

Walmsley, knowing the customs of the Africans, accordingly demanded very heavy *lobolo* (bride price) for the girl, as only by this means would the Zulus really evaluate her social standing.

The lobolo of a chief's daughter was therefore demanded and duly paid. Then the girl was married in Zulu custom. She took off her European clothes and went back to her own kind, to live with them happily and never more to return to European society. The Walmsleys henceforth only spoke of her by her Zulu name. They later gave the lobolo cattle to her as a present.

The victory at Ndondakusuka established Cetshwayo as the dominant personality in Zululand and the heir to the throne. As a sign of his triumph he erected a military kraal about twelve miles away to watch over an area which he henceforth regarded as being peculiarly his own. This kraal he named Gingindlovu (the swallower of the elephant), for it was said that by defeating Mbulazi he had eaten up the greatest opponent to his ambitions.

Immediately after the battle Cetshwayo's followers rounded up all cattle in the neighbourhood as booty. Among these cattle were about one thousand which were owned by the various traders who had fled for sanctuary across the river. Some effort was made to recover these cattle by H.F. Fynn, but to no avail. Then John Dunn decided to make an attempt.

Dunn made his way into the heart of Zululand as though on a hunting trip. Leaving his party in the bush he rode to Mpande's kraal to see the old king. Mpande was so dominated by Cetshwayo that he was afraid to talk in public. He arranged a meeting in the centre of a cattle kraal so that nobody could overhear. There he asked Dunn to give him a full description of the battle and with tears in his eyes he thanked Dunn for having aided his dead sons. So far as the cattle were concerned Mpande told Dunn to go to the eMangweni kraal where Cetshwayo would return them.

Dunn made the journey with some diffidence, but Cetshwayo greeted him hospitably. He well knew of Dunn's partisanship on the side of Mbulazi, but he never mentioned the fight. Without demur he handed over the cattle, which were at the Gingindlovu kraal, and with them Dunn returned to Natal. There the traders gave him a reward of £250 and received their cattle back.

Dunn then returned to Zululand to trade with goods bought with his £250. On several occasions he met Cetshwayo. A friendship developed between the two and presently Cetshwayo suggested that as he wanted a white man for a friend, to live near him, advise him, and write and answer letters, Dunn should remove permanently to Zululand. The suggestion was to Dunn's liking. He sold such impedimenta as he possessed in Natal which might hinder his project and then crossed the Thukela into Zululand for good.

Cetshwayo allocated Dunn a portion of land near the Matigulu River. He selected for his residence a site near the forest known as the Ngoye (secluded), about 80 miles from Cetshwayo's eMangweni kraal. It was an almost totally uninhabited area, but abounding in game, and while Dunn built his house he would occasionally take a potshot at a buffalo whose curiosity had brought it to see what all the hammering was about.

With his house constructed, Dunn married a girl named Catherine Pierce, daughter of a white father and a coloured mother. She was installed in the house and when, as fancy led him, he married 49 Zulu wives, they were each given a hut for themselves. There they were well fed, clothed and tolerably happy. Indeed, a close friend of Dunn's, Colonel Sparks, reckoned that the 50 women "were all faithful". This must have taken some doing on Dunn's part.

Dunn became Cetshwayo's confidant, adviser and English interpreter. He spent his time dabbling in Zulu politics, hunting, and accumulating a comfortable wealth in cattle. Many Natal tribespeople and Zulus joined him, acknowledging him as their chief, for he was a strong personality and a kindly, hospitable man at the same time.

Dunn's following soon developed the proportions of a sizeable tribe and to cope with numbers he obtained more land nearer to the Thukela. There, five miles from the river, he built a village named Mangethe (place of rugged country). This became his principal seat, where his chief wife Catherine lived, while the older establishment at the Ngoye forest was still retained and was known as Thwayo Nduku (carrying the stick).

Dunn rapidly developed his power and standing in Zululand, until he was generally recognised as being second only to Cetshwayo, with the old king, Mpande, wedged between them.

Cetshwayo was also consolidating his power. He kept his father completely beneath his thumb. In 1860, when the old man seemed to be showing an undue partiality to one of his wives named Nomantshali, Cetshwayo struck hard. An armed band was sent up to liquidate her and her sons. They found her absent but one of her sons, Mpoyiyana, was there. He was seized and dragged to the Nodwengu kraal.

Mpande was sitting in the sun. When he saw the party arrive, he stood up and sought to intervene, but Cetshwayo's men had brought their victim to the kraal with the deliberate intention of showing Mpande his own impotence. The old king was brushed aside and the terrified boy hustled away to his death beneath Mpande's own tree of execution, while his father was left weeping behind them.

Then the mother was ferreted out of a neighbouring kraal and killed. Her other two sons, Mtonga and Mgidlana, managed to escape with two headmen. They slipped over the northern border and found sanctuary with some Boer farmers near Utrecht. Two other half-brothers of Cetshwayo, Sikhotha and Sikhungu, also saw the signs of the times and slipped away into Natal.

Cetshwayo was particularly irked at the escape of Mtonga and Mgidlana. He got in touch with the Boers and after some negotiation signed a document on 28 March 1861 promising to give them a slice of land which would extend the Utrecht Republic to a line from Rorke's Drift up to the Phongolo River.

In return for this cession the Boers acknowledged Cetshwayo as heir to the Zulu throne, gave a few head of cattle to seal the bargain, and handed over the refugee Zulu princes. Cetshwayo promised to spare their lives and this promise he kept.

The Boers immediately started beaconing off their new boundary. The Zulus, however, refused to acknowledge the promised-land cession of Cetshwayo. Cetshwayo never properly ratified the agreement either and Mpande refused to countenance it. The Zulus returned the cattle and war between them and the Boers seemed imminent, hanging in the air like a thundercloud in a drought-stricken land, occasionally shedding some threatening drops.

Cetshwayo continued to live at the eMangweni kraal for some little time. Then a season of floods precipitated a bad plague of mosquitoes and the whole lowland area of Zululand was stricken with malarial fever. Cetshwayo became alarmed at the deaths among his following and in 1860 he announced his intention of removing to the cool and breezy heights known as eShowe.

This hilltop plateau of eShowe was a pleasant place. Many a Zulu in the sweltering valley of the nearby Mhlathuze had murmured with a sigh the old saying, "It's always cool at eShowe," meaning that there is always an escape from oppression somewhere. The name of the height, indeed, is said by some to indicate a place where the cool, early morning sea breezes blow through that stately forest known as the Dlinza (the grave-like place of meditation). This may be, although it is more likely that the name is derived from the vast number of *Xysmalobium* shrubs growing there which the original Qwabe inhabitants knew as iShowe or iTshowe and the Zulus nowadays call iShongwe. From early times this height had been a noted harvesting place for these little milky shrubs. Their bitter juice, rubbed on eggs, deters dogs from raiding the nests of sitting hens, and when smeared on hides or skins left to tan in the sun, effectively prevents any hungry animal from chewing them.

At all events, Cetshwayo removed himself close to this desirable spot. On the banks of the Mlalazi River he erected a brand-new kraal which he named eSiqhwagini (the abode of robbers); a reference, once again, to the defeat of Mbulazi and Cetshwayo's forceful assumption of the position of crown prince.

When he moved, Cetshwayo suggested to the Norwegian missionaries at Empangeni that they move with him, and this they were pleased to do. Empangeni remained as an out-station, but Ommund Oftebro, the missionary, established a new station on a most commodious site at Eshowe, granted to his church by Mpande. This new mission became known as the kwaMondi mission, for that was the nearest the Zulus could get to saying the "Place of Ommund", the Christian name of Oftebro.

Other mission stations were also being established in Zululand about this time. The first Church of England mission in Zululand, among the Magwaza clan at kwaMagwaza, was founded by Robert Robertson in the same year, 1860, as the kwaMondi station. A few years earlier, in 1858, the German Hanoverian order had founded a mission under F. Volker at a place called eMbalazi, near John Dunn's establishment.

Generally the last years of Mpande's reign, despite the impatient ambitions of Cetshwayo, were a pleasant Indian summer to the halcyon days of trade and hunting and roaming around which had been ushered in by the defeat of Dingane.

John Dunn

CHAPTER NINETEEN
Trading days

The upheaval between Cetshwayo and Mbulazi hardly disturbed the European hunters and adventurers who roamed through the bush of Zululand. Some traders took fright and fled into Natal for a short while, but most others were scarcely aware of the affair. William Baldwin was tramping back to Natal from one of his hunting trips at the time of the Ndondakusuka battle. He travelled in perfect safety and was surprised as he approached the Thukela to discover the countryside littered with corpses.

"The whole air was tainted with dead bodies for the last twelve miles," he wrote. "They were lying in every possible attitude along the road – men, women, and children of all possible sizes and ages." The darkness made it even worse. A vast horde of hyenas and jackals were engaged in clearing up the debris. All night they howled and yammered and squabbled, chasing one another and fighting madly for the choicest morsels. Baldwin passed on with a shudder.

The whole business was soon forgotten. There was too much to do in Zululand in those adventurous days for people to have long memories. From the first glimpse of the country across the Thukela it was as though the traveller was entering wonderland. Thomas Duff has described how he looked down on the vast Thukela Valley from the heights beyond the Mphumulo mission.

Immediately below he saw "an immense herd of more than a hundred elephants enjoying themselves in the deep valley. It was a grand sight to look down upon them from the bush-covered rocks above while they were breaking down the tall tree branches to eat, squirting the water from the pools in the stream over their big bodies with their long trunks and raising up and down their big flabby ears like sails, while the younger elephants were sporting around them."

Duff lay on his stomach and watched the giants for hours until they moved off, following one another in single file along an elephant path and fording the river into Zululand. The tracks the elephants followed were almost as old as the hills and valleys through which they wound. One of these tracks, thousands of years old, led all the way from the interior of Zululand down to the favourite elephant forests on the hill now known as the Berea, at Durban.

Many of these elephant trails had been developed by the tribespeople into pathways, for the animals had unerringly found the most direct and convenient routes between points, as well as the most reliable fords across the rivers. The traders, in their turn, enlarged the footpaths into wagon tracks and in this fashion the first highways of Zululand came into general use.

The best known of these highways was the one generally known as the "Zulu Traders' Road". This road forded the Thukela at the lower drift and twisted up north through the undulating and acacia-covered flats of the Zulu coastlands.

After fording the Mhlathuze River the road divided into a loop. The lower part of the loop continued up northwards to the Hluhluwe River and then veered westwards to rejoin the other arm of the loop which, meanwhile, had climbed up the hillsides to Mpande's kraal, Nodwengu, and then dropped down again to meet the lower loop at a place known as Ngammanya.

From this junction the reunited road wandered on through northern Zululand, visiting innumerable kraals to trade, until it eventually reached the Ngwavuma River. It then followed the Ngwavuma through the Lubombo and off across the Tonga wilderness of forest and swamp until it ended in the sandy streets of Lourenço Marques.

At the junction of the Ngwavuma with the uSuthu, an "Elephant Hunters' Track" branched off from the Zulu Traders' Road. This track followed the uSuthu right up through the Lubombo. It crossed the Swaziland flats and forded the Phongolo in its upper reaches. From there it wound down to the Buffalo River and eventually poured its quota of adventurers into the old Voortrekkers' Road, just below Bezuidenhout's Pass, across the Drakensberg.

These roads were just unmade tracks worn by the rolling wheels of the wagons, but they were good enough to carry the trade of Zululand for years and along them moved a whole cavalcade of romance and adventure, of traders, hunters and of wanderers.

These European pioneers in Zululand, as we have seen, were of great variety. The itinerant traders were the most numerous. With their lumbering wagons, loaded to the roofs with some 7000 lb. of goods, they wandered over the country bartering blankets, knives, umbrellas, Salampore cloth, tobacco, snuff and beads in exchange for hides, horns, ivory and cattle.

For months on end they led a gypsy sort of life, completely isolated in a wilderness they considered a home and, although often all alone amid the mass of Zulus, they travelled unharmed. Through all those years of trade in Mpande's reign there is no record of any European suffering the slightest harm, so long as he behaved himself as a gentleman.

These traders were a rough crowd, but mostly good-natured, generous and daring. They knew little and cared less about what went on in the outside world. Few of them read books, and newspapers were unknown. Many of them had forgotten how to write a letter years before and some had almost lost the use of their own language. All of them spoke Zulu fluently and amongst themselves they often carried on conversations in the language of the land in which they lived.

With strangers these traders were silent and uncommunicative. Occasionally, however, their track would cross that of a crony. Then, somewhere in the bush, beside a fire, they would spend a jolly evening swopping yarns, with the last man out from civilisation giving all the news, as they dined on some African delicacy such as the heart of an elephant – very tender and good – or its foot, baked in an antheap oven, turned into a glutinous dish not unlike brawn, and considered the prince of hunters' dinners.

The traders had plenty of yarns and excitements to recount over their campfires. Among their own fellows there were many hard cases and tough guys whose doings provided food for scandal. Two of these characters, for instance, Paul Dupré and a desperado named Pierce, set themselves up about half a mile on the Zulu side of the lower Thukela ford and announced that they had been appointed customs agents by Cetshwayo.

Surrounded by numerous coloured offspring these two characters settled down to a lazy life, supported by the toll claimed from all traders. Cetshwayo, indeed, was entitled to his tax, being the power of the land, but the amount extracted by his self-appointed agents became infamous. They claimed to be guarding the ford as well, and all Zulu refugees attempting to flee the country would be stopped and held by these highwaymen, unless they could pay a bribe. Eventually the partners became too generally detested. On the night of 10 May 1865, Captain Walmsley waived international law, slipped across the border and made for the rogues' lair. He found Pierce dying of fever, but Dupré was arrested and Zululand knew their racketeering no more.

Hunting adventures were legion in the Zululand of that day. Almost every man had some pet story of a narrow personal escape or record bag. John Dunn, who was a particularly aggressive hunter, was a renowned raconteur. In common with many of his kind, he found the bush around the Hluhluwe River to be an ideal hunting ground, and one of his most oft-told adventures occurred there.

Dunn was walking along a path when he heard a grunt behind him. Before he had time to turn, a buffalo tossed him up through the thorn bushes to land spreadeagled on top of a mimosa tree. For an hour the buffalo tried to reach him, standing on its hind feet and, as a last resort, trying to unseat him with its file-like tongue.

At last the buffalo seemed to tire. It wandered off into the bush and Dunn tried to scramble down to retrieve his gun, but the buffalo came hurtling out of a thicket from where it had been watching him. Once more Dunn skyrocketed to the top of the thorn tree and once more the buffalo retired into the bush.

Dunn did some hard thinking. His seat in the thorn tree was intolerable; in fact he was unable to sit down comfortably for months afterwards. Thus, literally spurred on, he took his life in his hands. Suddenly jumping down from the tree he grabbed his gun, turned and fired, dropping the charging buffalo when it was only 20 feet from him.

The doings of the dude hunters who flocked to Zululand also provided the professional wanderers with both gossip and employment. The dudes came from all parts of the world: English aristocrats and army officers; French counts; American millionaires; and innumerable other types with little in common save a burning desire to blot out as much of Africa's animal life as possible.

The professionals found much employment as guides and couriers to these usually overdressed and overequipped parties. Not all of the tours were successful. Early in 1851 a party of five of these tourists arrived in Durban. They engaged two of the professional hunters, Peter Hogg and William Mayer, as couriers and in March 1851 they set out.

The party headed for the upper end of Lake St Lucia. Leaving their wagon about 14 miles from the lake, they walked down to the shore and commenced hunting hippos. Something was also hunting them. One after the other the party went down with fever. Even the Zulu attendants started to die and the healthy individuals bolted in fright.

Eventually only Hogg and Mayer were left alive. Hogg went down in delirium one day. When he recovered he found himself quite alone in a camp of death. Mayer had abandoned him, fearful of death himself. Hogg lay among the corpses for two days. Then he regained strength somewhat and dragged himself for many weary miles, until chance led him to the camp of another party of dudes, guided by Hendrik Strydom. They cared for him until he was strong enough to walk to Durban. There he stayed with the Strydom family to recover and eventually married one of Hendrik's sisters. In this way he obtained a wife from his adventure; while the dudes, instead of the trophies they coveted, found a common grave for their bones when Hogg revisited the scene of the disaster some time later and buried them in a porcupine burrow.

Quarrels and feuds between rival traders often occurred, although generally they tried to keep aloof from one another in a trading preserve of their own. The Zulu elephant hunters they employed, however, often came to blows. Many died in shooting affrays in the bush when one band poached in territory regarded by someone else as a private preserve.

One of these quarrels ended in the shooting of the leader of a hunting band, a man named Dukusa, among the most famous hunters of his day. The rest of his band bided their time, waylaid the culprit, tried and condemned him, and the relatives of Dukusa were allotted the task of execution. This they performed with relish. They exhumed the corpse of Dukusa, tied the condemned man to it face to face, and threw both of them into a crocodile pool.

With events such as that to gossip about, no wonder the traders could sit up so late at night; one story leading to the other, with the Zulus listening in rapt attention and adding their own quota of tales of faction fights and hunts, until it was time for the last pipe and cup of coffee. Then off to bed, with a healthy frame and clear conscience perhaps, but not always to sleep. Baldwin tells us how, on one of his trading trips, his camp followers – Zulus; coloured men; women and children of all sorts, colours and sizes – "having got possession of a case of gin that Gibson had in his wagon, spent the most noisy, quarrelsome, abusive night I ever witnessed." But that was infrequent. The nights were heavy and languid. Man slept, only the shadows moved, and each camp seemed as lonely as the furthest star.

Trading was a strenuous life. David Leslie was one of the wanderers and his career was typical of many. He went to Natal when he was eleven and by the time he was fourteen he was appointed Zulu interpreter in the law courts. In February 1858, when he was nineteen, he set out on his first trading trip to Zululand. He had but little capital and, for want of a wagon, he walked; leading, safari fashion, a string of Zulu porters, each with a load of trade goods on his head.

It was heavy going. "Such hills!" wrote Leslie. "I never perspired so much in my life as when toiling up them, and my eyelashes were fringed with drops."

He tramped from kraal to kraal, trading two blankets for a beast and it was hard work, with talking and trading going hand in glove. "I rose in the morning," he entered in his diary once, "and after getting something for my hungry Kaffirs, I set to work to buy from the induna Gaon. The first beast he brought me was a small one. He began by asking two blankets for it. I said no! He brought up another, and wanted seven bunches (about £1 worth of beads) for it. It was a good cow and I offered him 12s. worth. There we were, bargaining and bargaining, on into the afternoon, till I was thoroughly disgusted. I never in my life had such a day's talking, and all for nothing."

He roamed on, hunting elephant and buffalo in between trading and having all manner of adventures. The paths through the bush of Zululand led to all manner of surprises. At Luhungu's kraal near the Thukela River, for instance, there dwelt at this time a dwarf two-and-a-half feet high, with no arms, his hands growing straight out of his shoulders.

Nearly each kraal possessed some odd character or relic which the inhabitants were pleased to show to a visitor. Especially after the battle of Ndondakusuka, all Zululand was alive with stories of the fight, of old grievances settled or new ones made, of heroism and cowardice, of torture, humanity and atrocity, and each kraal had some souvenir.

Leslie records how he slept at one kraal, "the owner of which was covered with scars gained in battles. He had a shot in his thigh; it came out at his groin, struck his knee, and fell to the ground; he had a scar across his head from the butt-end of a gun; these he got from the Boers. His shoulder was all scarred from an encounter with a lion. His thigh was pierced by a buffalo. His knee was laid open by an assegai in the battle between Mpande and Dingane. He had a gash down his back, and another through his arm, and last of all, he had his arm broken by a shot at Ndondakusuka."

The Zulus treated the visiting trader with kind hospitality, and their womenfolk especially took a lively interest in the traders' persons, toilets and general activities. The traders would always be invited to any beer drinks and more than one misguided European staggered back to his wagon feeling as though his skin was far too small to contain him.

Especially at the beginning of each year these great beer drinks were numerous. Then it was that the ceremony of the first fruits would be staged; a period of mystic ceremonial, of dancing and singing. At this time, the days of the *ukuNyathela* (preliminary harvest festival) and the *umKhosi* (royal festival) the whole nation would meet at the capital to pass greetings and, with mass hysteria, fortify the national spirit of love of their king.

Then it was that the national song, the Ngomankulu, would be sung and danced in a fever of excitement. A black bull would be slaughtered by the young men with their bare hands; the king would be doctored and reinforced with sundry medicines, including seawater and water from all the principal rivers of Zululand.

At that time the night would be dramatic. "The whole countryside was full of people," wrote Leslie, "and the noise, day and night, was incessant – chattering at night and dancing during the day. At night the fires on the hills, and the figures of the Zulus passing the light, imparted a weird character to the scene which would have made a famous study for a Gatti or a Van Schendal."

In an atmosphere such as this the wandering trader found himself in a world apart and anything seemed possible. Strange fears and superstitions haunted the countryside. Not satisfied with the vast array of wildlife, the Zulu imagination added a whole genus of magical creatures of incredible variety, but with at least one thing in common, their malignancy towards human beings.

One of the most popular of these bogey creatures was the so-called *isiDawane*. This ingenious creature was supposed to be about the size of a hyena. It lived by choice upon the brains of people. To obtain its food the bogey creature usually resorted to the stratagem of knocking or calling at a hut door at night until somebody came out. The victim would then be whisked into a hole in the animal's back and taken off to some evil lair.

Fantastic as these stories were, they were easy to believe in the atmosphere of old Zululand. "At night," wrote Leslie, "while sleeping, something came to the door of the hut and tried to open it. Grout (my Zulu) and I got up and, on looking through the door, saw an animal which our fears at once magnified into an isiDawane. Grout got an assegai and ran it through the door when a great howl convinced us of our mistake. Notwithstanding, I knew what nonsense it was, I confess I was rather frightened."

The lords of these bogeys were of course the witch doctors. Although they had somewhat lost their power in Mpande's benevolent reign they were nevertheless something to be reckoned with. Leslie records a description of one of these creatures.

"I have never in my life seen such a horrible-looking being as this woman was. In height she was about the middle size, and very fat. From her ankles to the calf of the leg was wrapped round with the entrails of a cow, or some animal of the kind, filled with fat and blood. Then came the usual petticoat, made of hide, secured and embroidered with lions' and leopards' teeth, snakes' bones, beads, round bulb-looking things, little buck horns, and such-like savage bijouterie; round the loins was one mass of entrails, snake skeletons, medicine bags, roots, human and other teeth, brass buttons and wire.

"The body was tattooed all over, and smeared with red and black earth; round the neck was a repetition of the above 'ornaments'. The hair was long and smeared with all sorts of abominations, with a stuffed snake round the forehead by way of decoration; a leopard skin hung down her back, with the grinning physog showing over her head, and the head of the snake peeping with a startling lifelikeness, out of its mouth and, o ye gods and little fishes, didn't she sm-ell-ahem!"

In this environment Leslie developed his business. When he returned to Durban from his first trip of seven weeks he had traded his stock of £50 worth of goods for 78 head of cattle, as well as having paid his porters. With cattle then worth about £2 a head his trip had yielded a profit of £156.

With this money Leslie acquired a wagon and a larger stock of goods on the pay-next-Christmas principle, and returned to Zululand. He was delighted with his new comfort. Henceforth he could ride instead of walk; and when it rained, instead of miserably sheltering for days in some bush, he could lie snug in his wagon reading the few books he carried or blowing castles in the air from his pipe.

In company with traders such as Bob Forbes, Leslie developed an extensive trade and hunting business. From Mpande he and a partner secured sole hunting rights to an extensive tract of country along the Phongolo River. There they established a headquarters and employed about fifty Zulu elephant hunters to scour the bush in search of ivory and game.

Leslie, meanwhile, traded and revelled in the hunting himself. The spirit of the wilds brooded over Zululand in those days, and if she lured many a man to wander down her silent glades of adventure to his death, the victim consoled himself that at least life had been full and worthwhile to the very end.

Leslie found each day different. Some were hot and sweltering, some still and others seeming full of menace. There were the hard, shimmering days before the first rains, and then the beautiful freshness, the crystal clarity that followed the rains, when the ten thousand hills of Zululand rolled away in front like a green and purple dream.

Game was still so plentiful that it seemed like great herds of cattle over the country. Gazing from the overlooking hills, whichever way one turned, there were herds of sturdy buffalo. The graceful impalas went leaping and jumping through the grass. The sociable herds of zebra and wildebeest stood watching your approach and then rushed off, with the wildebeests swishing the legs of their calves with their tails in order to bring laggards into line, an antic from which the Zulus acquired their habit of carrying a wildebeest tail with them on long journeys, for they considered that an infallible remedy for weariness was to swish their legs with one of these magic stimulants.

In this area Leslie and his hunters once trapped a herd of 300 buffalo in a deep pool of the Phongolo. They shot scores of them before the rest escaped and every Zulu within a radius of 50 miles hurried there to feast on meat.

Leslie's progress to fortune in Zululand was not without trouble. Adjoining his hunting ground, just across the Phongolo, was the area occupied by the redoubtable Conraad Vermaak, a grant from the Swazi king. There were frequent clashes between the hunters employed by Vermaak and Leslie. One day two of Leslie's hunters, wandering along the banks of the Phongolo, encountered Vermaak. He invited them to his house, where he fed them, pumped them of information concerning Leslie's plans, then seized their guns, thrashed them, and drove them away.

Leslie couldn't take this incident lying down. Prestige with the Zulus was at stake. He kept quiet for a month, hunting as usual, and then suddenly raided Vermaak's area. He surrounded the farmhouse by stealth and then sent a small party of Zulus to the place, armed only with spears and a story that they were in search of a runaway girl.

Vermaak was mending a gun, just inside his own door, when the Zulus arrived. One of his sons was lounging about but the others were away. Little by little the Zulus edged in, crying to one another, meanwhile, to come and see how guns were made. Others of the party disposed themselves about the son, as though conversing with him. Suddenly, at a given signal, both parties poured upon the men, while one or two guarded Mrs Vermaak.

The old woman put up a tougher scrap than the two men together. She seized a spade and held everyone at bay until the rest of the party arrived. Then, in the face of numbers, she surrendered. Leslie and his Zulus then seized 21 head of cattle as compensation, enjoyed a hearty meal on the house, and then vanished into the bush leaving Vermaak to curse.

Adventuring about in northern Zululand Leslie heard much of Tongaland. It was a favourite hunting ground for many of his Zulu hunters. In it they could do much as they liked. The Tongas were always considered a cowardly lot by the Zulus and the hunters would impudently occupy their best kraals, eat their food and seize their women. Any mild protest was met by shooting or thrashing. The consequence of this treatment was that the Tongas would scatter into the bush at the merest rumour of the presence of Zulu hunters.

Impressed by the stories he heard of Tongaland, Leslie resolved upon a pioneer trading visit to the country. In May 1871 he sailed up to Lourenço Marques from Durban on a little schooner. From Lourenço Marques he proceeded up the uSuthu River in a half-decked, lateen-rigged boat. Nine expert Tonga boatmen navigated the river for him, rowing away rhythmically and singing the songs of the river.

It was a fascinating journey, for the uSuthu is a noble river, broadly flowing and navigable for 35 miles for vessels drawing not more than six feet of water. Leslie watched the ever changing river scenery glide by, the mighty flatness of Tongaland, the majestic forests, the reeds, mangroves, and the teeming river life of hippos, crocs and strange birds and fish.

The only thing wrong with the journey was the mosquitoes. "As the birthplace of mankind was Asia, so, I believe, the birthplace of the mosquito-kind must have been upon the uSuthu," wrote Leslie. "From there, I believe, as they increased and filled the country, they spread over all the world, but none of them leave the spot, so long as there is room to fly."

Noziyingili, the Tonga king, had his capital about 20 miles from the nearest river landing point. It consisted of about one hundred huts arranged into a rather slovenly village to which was appended the ingenious name of Gcinamacebozwi (where all falsehoods end), which was perhaps a bit doubtful. Its principal marvel was an ancient dwarf, 33 inches tall and with a pair of ears as large as a donkey's.

Leslie took some cloth and a five gallon keg of rum as a present to the king. Noziyingili was by repute very fond of rum. He sent his induna to meet Leslie and gave him a comfortable hut a short way from the capital. The keg of rum was then placed on the head of the strongest Tonga queen and carefully carried to the capital.

Leslie bedded down and tried to sleep, but he didn't have a chance. There was a tremendous uproar in the capital. The Tongas drank and shouted, sang and quarrelled all night until the five gallons were finished. They were great rum drinkers. "They will give even their life for rum, since they care not though they die if they only die drunk," reflected Leslie with a tired sigh at four o'clock in the morning.

The next morning Leslie did his business as quickly as possible. He had been told that the king was drunk from noon till early morning the next day and all interviews had to be conducted in the morning. Apart from this weakness for rum, Leslie found the Tongas to be an industrious crowd with ivory, hides, agricultural produce and other items to trade for the usual blue and striped Salempore cloth, blankets, brass wire, hatchets, picks, guns and lots of rum.

For seven months Leslie roamed around Tongaland. His hunters scoured the country and his whole enterprise yielded rich dividends. The Tongas even had much money to pay, for many of them tramped down to Natal to labour on the estates and brought their wages back with them.

In September 1871 the schooner *William Shaw* sailed up the uSuthu River to pick up Leslie's goods and bring fresh supplies. While anchored in the river, loading, the ship was seized by a party of Portuguese. The affair became a subject of lengthy diplomatic exchanges, but Leslie got no satisfaction from the matter.

On 21 December 1871 he left the Tonga king's kraal and walked down to Durban. From there he returned to England and, after surviving all the perils of Africa, he died the following year when only 34 years old, which was strange. Behind him, in Zululand, the storm clouds were blowing up over the political horizon, and the hunters' moon which had shone so brightly for so many years, was soon lost forever behind the murkiness of strife and upheaval.

TWENTY

The Valley of
a Thousand Hills

The beautiful Valley of a Thousand Hills, where the Mngeni River goes swirling downwards on its journey to the sea, is a changeless place: full of moods and colours; of mists and mirages and hazes; of solitude and silence and a certain brooding savagery, hiding there among the hills as a last relic of that wilderness which was once all Natal.

In numberless years, this vast valley has changed not at all. It remains today a place haunted by bitter memories of cannibals, of raids and tribal feuds which perpetuate themselves each year in faction fights and endless quarrels.

Along the southern edge of the valley European man settled and developed his civilisation, like an exotic tree imported from overseas, flourishing in the African setting only with constant care and reinforcement.

First it was the road leading from Durban to Pietermaritzburg which brought man to the verge of the valley. Then the grandeur of the scenery, the healthiness of the heights, combined with the accessibility which the road provided, induced man to settle along the wayside in homesteads and villages.

The first road, the so-called "Old Dutch Road", left Durban by way of Congella, Umbilo and Sea View. Sea View had originally been the home of Robert Dunn, who first came to Durban with his family in 1836. He was trampled to death by an elephant in 1847 and, with the death of Mrs Dunn four years later, the family had broken up. Young John Dunn then wandered off to Zululand, where he acquired so much fame as a white chief.

The homestead itself remained as a landmark for many years. "The property is beautifully situated," E. Feilden, a settler, said of it, "but the house, a long, low, dark place, is choked with trees, damp and dismal." Oranges and lemons, dates, pawpaws and coffee bushes all grew there in such abundance that they choked themselves to death. The atmosphere of decay they gave the place made it seem perpetually to mourn the family who had built it.

Past Sea View, the road twisted up through the hills, over the Bellair farm of John Hillary to the area of modern Malvern. This pleasant spot, in the 1890s had among its residents one of the best-known characters in Natal. His name was Colonel J.H. Bowker, a keen naturalist, renowned raconteur and opinionated correspondent to newspapers.

Bowker settled in what was known as Upper Malvern in 1892 and built a rambling house, which he called The Cedars. The place had a glorious garden and he turned it into a wildlife sanctuary, full of birds and friendly little animals.

One of the birds was a turkey buzzard (ground hornbill) which had been a pet since it had been a chicken and behaved like a tame dog. It roosted in the Colonel's room and was habitually petted and accustomed to being fussed over.

A story about this bird tells us that the Colonel was once sick and could take no notice of it. The buzzard was most perturbed at this lack of attention. Leaving the sickroom, it shortly returned with a bullfrog which it deposited next to the Colonel as a gift.

The Colonel still took no notice of the bird. In some dudgeon, the buzzard went off again and returned with a fat lizard. With this gift in its beak, it danced up and down beside the bed. There was still no response from the Colonel.

The bird stalked thoughtfully out of the room and vanished into the bush. A couple of hours passed. Then the buzzard came racing into the room, bursting with pride and wild excitement. In its beak was a wriggling snake. This certainly fetched the Colonel. He was out of bed like a shot. The bird was most distressed when its present was summarily despatched and the corpse removed in a dustpan.

Bowker was famous for a type of story known as "Bowkeriana". A typical example concerned the Colonel on a naturalists' expedition in the great Thukela Valley. He was leading a pack-horse laden with food and camp equipment. Following a path through the dense bush, they encountered a mighty python with its tail around a tree. It swallowed Bowker, horse, food and equipment.

So large was the python that Bowker was able to make progress. He led his horse along, past some bones and porcupine quills. On reaching the tail, the traveller made his way out and escaped. The python, meanwhile, relaxed to digest its meal. It woke up several weeks later to find itself starving.

Bowker, of course, was not the pioneer of the Malvern area. Frederick and Cecil Barker had been in Upper Malvern since the early 1880s, while Doctor Barber, a nephew of Bowker, was settled in his home of Ivanhoe.

Bowker died in October 1900. In 1904 a railway halt was opened, with the official name of Bowkers, but was known more popularly as "Soap Box Siding". There was no platform and, the trains being high, most passengers arranged to have their servants carry soap boxes to the place to act as steps for detraining. The engine driver whistled as he approached the place and a whole procession of soap-box carriers would be seen running out of nearby houses. In 1911 the new Union Government asked that a different name be selected for the place, to avoid confusion with the older Bowker's Park in the Cape. The siding was then named Escombe, after the Honourable Harry Escombe.

Beyond the Malvern area the old road climbed to the farm

Salt River, originally granted in October 1847 to Andries Laas. Laas subsequently sold it to the Milner brothers, who subdivided the farm into 18 sections, which then passed into the ownership of various persons.

Archibald Murray obtained some of the land in 1849 and established the Wayside Hotel as a staging post on the road. In 1850 his land was surveyed into a township, and this was called Pinetown, in honour of Sir Benjamin Pine who had replaced Martin West as governor when the latter died on 1 August 1849 in Pietermaritzburg.

Later suburbs of Pinetown were Ashley, named by its original owner after his birthplace in Kent; and Sarnia, named by the first owner, Captain Drake (a descendant of Francis Drake) after the place of his origin in England.

Pinetown soon established itself. By 1855 it had a population of 151 residents, although the area around it was still sufficiently wild for Captain Drake to shoot a black-maned lion on his Sarnia farm at the end of October 1854. On the same farm there was some excitement in 1894, when Frank Stephens reported that he had discovered gold there. Zulu alarms were also so common in the early fifties that the residents built a fortified bank and ditch around Murray's Hotel as a central place of retreat, known generally as "Fort Funk".

In December 1854, two Hollanders from Java arrived in Durban with the intention of growing indigo in Natal. The two men were T.C. Colenbrander and W. van Prehn. They met Murray from Pinetown and entered into partnership with him. They built a small factory on the Mbilo River, at the foot of Cowie's Hill, and staffed the place and the indigo farm with Javanese workmen whom they had brought with them.

Van Prehn had an attractive house with Javanese servants. At Pinetown, Colenbrander's subsequently famous son, Johan, was born in 1856. The indigo business did not flourish. The enterprise came to grief in a legal wrangle, in which only the lawyers won. Van Prehn then left the country in April 1857, very enraged with Murray, while Colenbrander remained and later settled on the north coast. Murray got into serious financial trouble over the lawsuit. In July 1857 most of his Pinetown properties were sold to the Rev. J.L. Crompton, who converted the old hotel into his residence and led a retired life there, much suspected of being a Papist by the prim nonconformists of the day.

At Pinetown the more direct road from Durban, over the Berea, joined the Old Dutch Road. William Stanger surveyed this alternate route properly in 1849, and it was soon developed into the main link with the interior, for the Old Dutch Road suffered from severe gradients. At the top of the Berea hill a toll gate was eventually erected in 1886, and for fourteen years all vehicles were mulcted of 2s. 6d. and pedestrians of 6d., in order to help pay for the hardening of Durban's roads and pavements. Beyond the Berea the road passed several well-known estates, such as the Clare estate of the Clarence family; Cato Manor, the farm of G.C. Cato, and the settlement of New Germany.

Beyond Pinetown the combined roads climbed on up Field's Hill and across the fine farm named Richmond, which was granted to William Swan Field in 1851 for services rendered as Collector of Customs and Magistrate of Durban. His brother, John, later took over the place and, in 1866, his daughter Elizabeth married a certain William Gillitt who had come out with his parents as an emigrant in 1849.

Gillitt bought the adjoining farm to that of his father-in-law and this he called Emberton, after his family's home at Emberton in England. A portion of this farm, known as Hill Crest, was subsequently leased for residential purposes.

Gillitt gave a third place name to the Durban-Pietermaritzburg road. When the railway came, Gillitt's station was named after him. Later, the Railway Department obtained rights to water from one of his dams, and in exchange they built a siding called Emberton, at which any passenger train would stop for the convenience of his family. The farm was noted for a fine stone wall, laboriously built around its boundaries over a period of years by Gillitt and a couple of Africans.

Beyond Hill Crest comes Botha's Hill and from there, for some miles, the road dawdles along the very edge of the mighty valley, exciting the appreciative traveller with superb views of this vast scene. Who it was who first called the place "The Valley of a Thousand Hills" remains unknown; the name came into general use only after the Anglo-Boer War. Before that the valley passed under a variety of names and, although its present title seems so aptly obvious, it nevertheless needed a touch of genius to devise it.

One of the earliest explorations of the valley was also one of the most interesting. On 10 January 1893 two young men, Messrs Foley and Marianni, reached Durban after travelling the whole length of the valley from Pietermaritzburg in two 16-feet canoes. The journey took them seven days of adventurous travelling, with plenty of upsets and misadventures; but it yielded them unforgettable memories of the most secret reaches of the valley in the heyday of its wildness.

Beyond the railway stops of Alverstone, named after Lord Alverstone, who visited Natal in 1903 on an immigration commission, and Drummond, named apparently after Sir F.C. Drummond, another immigration organiser of the 1870s, the road twists on across the narrow ridge of Inchanga (*ntshangwe* is the Zulu name for a long-bladed knife or a sharp ridge).

Cato Ridge is the first place of consequence on these heights. It consisted at first of small rented farms on the estate of G.C. Cato. Towards the end of 1912 these farms were offered for sale, the original tenants having the first option, and the place as we know it today came into existence.

From Cato Ridge there is an alternative way to Durban, down the valley of the Mlazi River, which nowadays is followed by the main railway line. Only sidings and signalling stations line the route, except at Mariannhill, where stands the renowned religious edifice of the Mariannhill Monastery.

This Mariannhill Monastery had its beginning at the Chapter General of the Trappist Order held at Sept-Fons in France in 1879. Bishop Ricards requested the assembled abbots to found a monastery in his diocese of South Africa, and R.P. Francis, prior of a Turkish monastery, agreed.

On 28 July 1880, Prior Francis arrived in Port Elizabeth with a party of monks and made his way to Dunbrody, the proposed site for the monastery. After two years, however, it was decided to move elsewhere, and, on 24 November 1882, 20 monks under Sub-Prior Dom Joseph, journeyed up to Natal.

After a preliminary stop at the Bluff, with the Fathers of Mary Immaculate, they selected the site of Mariannhill as the scene of their future activities. By the end of the year, all their brethren from Dunbrody had joined them and the new monastery was underway. Today it is a renowned educational organisation. Although the way of life of some of its inmates certainly seems strange to laymen, the work done in industrial training, in agriculture, and schooling, is undoubtedly good.

Beyond Cato Ridge lies Camperdown. The founder and original owner of this place was one John Vanderplank, and of him there is a romantic tale. In the early 1800s Vanderplank, an Englishman of Dutch extraction, migrated to Tasmania as a shipbuilder. He enjoyed some success and returned to England to marry the girl of his dreams, Louise Whitechurch, who was waiting for him.

Instead of marrying, however, they quarrelled. The girl married somebody else, while Vanderplank sailed away in his ship, the *Louise*. In the course of trading he visited Natal, shortly after the Weenen massacre in 1838. He liked the place and decided to remove there, in order to wipe out all traces of his shattered dreams in Tasmania.

Returning to Tasmania, he collected his belongings and also some seeds of the wild black wattle shrub which, in Australia, was noted only for its rapid growth and usefulness as a windbreak or hedge.

Back in Natal, Vanderplank acquired the farm which he

named Camperdown. There he settled, planting his black wattle seeds as a hedge around his homestead. His first homestead certainly needed all the shelter it could get. It consisted of a large packing case. From this establishment, secure beneath the lid, he would at times open fire on marauding leopards and hyenas.

In time, Vanderplank naturally built himself a more substantial home. Many travellers stopped to enjoy hospitality that became proverbial, and the sturdy, quick-growing wattle trees around his home were remarked upon. The strangeness of the fact that they grew so well in Natal, while in their Australian home they seemed stunted, attracted much attention. Seeds were obtained from Vanderplank for the asking, and soon a trail of wattles was growing as windbreaks on nearly every farm, from Camperdown to Rustenburg in the old Transvaal. None of the planters, least of all John Vanderplank, had the slightest notion of the real value of the tree for anything other than firewood.

In time Camperdown farm naturally went through the mincing machine of real estate. In December 1865 the *Natal Mercury* reported, "The plans of this new Camperdown township may be seen at the Exchange Rooms. There are many streets, all of which are, in accordance with what we regard as a very silly and snobbish custom, called after the leading officials of the colony."

Everything was done to induce people to settle at Camperdown. Smallholdings were offered to eligible farmers for five years free of rent, with extensions of twenty years, at 2s. 6d. an acre a year. A few, like William Thrash, jumped at this offer, but the majority of people thought the place too betwixt and between Durban and Pietermaritzburg. In 1870 J.W. Mathews found it to consist of simply "two or three homesteads and a third-rate roadside inn." It remained in that innocent state for many years.

Beyond Camperdown lay the old farm of Uys Doorns. Nowadays, the village of Thornville stands on the site of the former farmhouse and subsequent shop and canteen, renowned for its hospitality when it was the last staging post before Pietermaritzburg.

There were many staging posts and roadside inns scattered along the road between Durban and the capital. Especially when the settlers came did these places flourish, for a whole stream of people made their way along the road and all needed accommodation at night, as it took from three to four days to do the journey by wagon or on foot.

Many of the inns were crude, while others were extremely comfortable. Carbo Fisher's hotel, near Camperdown, consisted of three large wattle-and-daub huts enclosing a hollow square. There were four stumps in the floor, with a packing case lid to act as table. The bed was made up of sticks, with a mattress stuffed with grass or seaweed. Candles were the only lights, until cheap paraffin was introduced at the beginning of 1860.

Most of these inns kept an excellent table, but some were atrocious. For the stranger, selecting shelter for the night, it was very much of a lucky dip. J.D. Holliday has described an arrival on a cold wet night at one of these smaller hostelries. The establishment consisted of two rooms, divided from each other by a partition of cloth. Accommodation for travellers was apparently one stretcher with a stuffed hay pillow, a solitary cotton sheet and no mattress. To make things colder by comparison, the host's marital couch was well covered with a splendid kaross as well as blankets.

The household retired to bed. The shivering traveller listened to the snores of the host and his wife until it became intolerable. Then he worked his arm through the cloth partition, caught hold of the kaross and eased it gently off the bed. With this warm booty he wrapped himself up happily and slept till past sunrise.

When he awoke, the guest found himself looking up into the scowling face of the host. He did some quick thinking. Then he sat up with feigned pleasure and thanked the host profusely. "I don't know which of you it was," he said, "who slipped to my bed in the dark and covered me with this kaross, but it was most kindly." With an oath the host stormed out of the room in search of his wife.

Because of the heavy traffic along the road it was easy for ramshackle establishments to skim off a small trade for themselves. A stream of wagons passed their doors. Especially after the discovery of diamonds and gold in the interior, so many farmers found it most profitable to put their wagons on the road that it seemed as though the entire male population of Natal had turned into transport riders.

The wagons travelled singly, in groups, or big batches of a dozen or more. It was a picturesque sight to see them go by with their varied loads – all the goods desired by the lusty commercial and mining appetite of young South Africa.

A fascinating crowd were most of these transport men. Their tales of mishaps and adventures, told at night in the roadside canteens, were crammed with all the incident, excitement and restlessness of mankind. Farmers, adventurers, runaway sailors, well-educated emigrants, rogues, remittance men – all were represented in that varied throng.

Handling a whip was considered to be the true hallmark of experience and skill among this company. The callow newcomer could never handle the 20-feet lash without getting it tangled into a knot. The real expert could perform almost miraculously. Wild Bill Leathern, the most famous of the transport men, could flick the necks off a dozen bottles in a row, or send a shilling flying off the ground with the point of a lash.

Leathern, the doyen of his kind, had been born in Grahamstown in 1827, the son of 1820-settler parents. The family removed to Natal in 1842, and young Bill was apprenticed to Joseph Cato as a carpenter. After a year he left and joined his father in a butchery business. Then he started transport riding, and over the years developed an extensive business with several wagons on the road.

Apart from his great strength and skill with a whip, Leathern was renowned for one particular feat. He used to jump off a moving wagon, whip up the two after-oxen, dart under the *trektouw* between the next row, whip them up, then dive under the *trektouw* between the next pair and so on, until he had looped-the-loop right up the entire team. Oddly enough, in a tough company, Wild Bill was an absolute teetotaller. He died in Pietermaritzburg in 1913 at the ripe old age of 86.

Apart from the wagons of the transport riders, heavily laden going up (at about 1s. 9d. per ton per mile); empty, or filled with skins or biltong coming down; there was much variety in the traffic along the road. Occasionally, a military convoy would pass, enlivened, maybe, by a band marching at the head. Long files of cavalry would jingle past as well; magnificent, perhaps, in the uniform of the 17th Lancers (The Death or Glory Boys), with their pennants flying and the gleaming steel of their lances.

Odd novelties in the way of vehicles would attract much attention. G.C. Cato had a smart, high, two-wheeled sulky. The Governor travelled in a swanky turnout with a military escort. In 1879 the funeral cortege of the unfortunate Prince Imperial passed: a long, sadly impressive affair, winding down to Durban with massed military bands playing the "March of the Dead". The following year, in April, the bereaved ex-Empress Eugenie journeyed along the way in a closed carriage, to view the place of her son's death and provide a sort of final epilogue to the whole miserable business of the Anglo-Zulu War.

The first coach service between Durban and Pietermaritzburg did not start until 1860. In Pietermaritzburg, one J.W. Welch had set himself up with a rickety, unsprung Crimean wagon as a public transport. Welch had been a professional coach driver in England. When railway construction ended his occupation, he removed to South Africa and recommenced business.

By day, Welch busied himself in carrying loads of bricks and other goods. At night he would cover his wagon with a tent, put seats inside it and convey noisy parties of young people to balls, "obeying," as he put it, "the doctor's usual instructions to be well shaken while being taken."

From this beginning, Welch conceived the idea of a service to Durban. John Dare, his driver, was busied for some time in building a suitable vehicle and breaking in horses to pull it. At last, big advertisements appeared in the press. On Easter Monday, 1860, the bus *Perseverance*, with room for 20 passengers at 30s. a head, would leave the bus office in upper Church Street at 6 a.m. and arrive in Durban that evening.

The usual snags complicated final preparations. "Either a wheel was missing," wrote Welch, "the *disselboom* not fixed, or some other tarnation disarrangement caused a postponement till Easter Tuesday, and then the horses, smelling some good forage at a gentleman's stable at Pinetown, bolted sharp round a corner, carried away a lump of his house, wrecked the bowsprit part of the bus, and didn't get into Durban until Wednesday."

Thenceforth, once a week, the bus journeyed down to Durban and back, doing the trip in about twelve hours. After some time (and several financial difficulties) the service was increased to twice a week, then three times a week, and then a daily service with a new bus, the *Prince Alfred*, taking turns with the old *Perseverance*.

Then a rival service, run by George Jessop, entered the picture in April 1868 and a price war developed. Jessop reduced the fare to 15 shillings; Welch promptly lowered his fare to 10 shillings; Jessop lowered his again to 5 shillings; Welch then threw in a free dinner at the halfway house known as the Royal Hotel run by his wife near the present railway stop of Alverstone. The free dinner broke Jessop. He gave up the fight and Welch was left with the monopoly. The addition of a post-cart express to the service took place at this time, to replace the original Zulu runners who had been carrying the mail for the past 15 years.

A journey by this coach line was generally considered to be comfortable by overseas standards. Old Welch was an experienced whip, but when his sons took over the service deteriorated.

Anthony Trollope, the famed writer who arrived in Durban in August 1877, has described a typical journey for us.

The coach was driven by a coloured man, whose mastery over the four jibbing, opinionated horses was complete and superb. The coach started full and the passengers were informed that one place was booked by somebody climbing on further up the road. The passengers sneered at this. Then, when the extra man appeared at one of the stages it was not a gentleman only, but a gentleman with the biggest, smelliest fish in his arms that Trollope had ever seen or smelled – short of a dolphin. It was a 45 pounder, announced the man proudly. It was his luggage, he had booked his place and must be carried with his impedimenta.

The man endeavoured to deposit the fish on the footboard, but the two passengers sitting there beside the driver indignantly kicked it off. The man became angry. The fish, he said, was worth £5 and had to go to Pietermaritzburg that day. The passengers informed him it obviously should have gone two days before. They gave the driver a nudge with a five shilling tip, the horses received a clout, and off rumbled the coach.

The man with the fish put up a shout. He ran along in the dust behind. Then, catching hold of the back of the vehicle, he clambered on and sat with his feet dangling over the edge, holding his fish in his arms, while its smell steadily enveloped the coach and left a trail behind that brought every tomcat to the doors of the houses as they clattered past.

For the rest, the journey thrilled Trollope, experienced globetrotter that he was. The food was good. "I never saw a better coach dinner put upon a table," he wrote; and the scenery was magnificent, the mass of hills in the Mngeni valley looking "as though they had been crumbled from a giant's hand."

So the highway cavalcade rode past, the hurrying post-carts doing the journey in six hours, the lumbering stage-coaches and the laborious, dawdling ox-wagons. Often, rows would develop if an ox-wagon blocked the road. Generally the wagons travelled at so leisurely a pace that both driver and *voorloper* would climb aboard for a nap and leave the leading oxen to pick a way patiently along the road.

Then along would come a post-cart, its driver blowing his bugle and emitting a stream of curses, rousing the wagon men in a flurry as they tried to turn their vehicle out of the way at the side of the road. Then, a final exchange of abuse and the post-men would gallop off to make up for lost time, blow-ing their bugle to warn the ostlers at the staging posts to have fresh spans ready. So the journey would go on: a quick change of the old sweating team with their heaving flanks, a loud "all aboard", and a scurry of the male passengers from the depths of the bar.

The coming of the railway was the ruination of much that was picturesque. The blacksmiths' shops, the hostelries, the restless personalities; all disappeared beneath the steel road. They left only memories of themselves behind: wayside ghosts, still sitting beneath the shade of the kaffirboom trees, while all around them comes the roar of the passing motors, the whine of the tyres on the bituminised road, the whistle of the trains – and only the misty beauty of the Valley of a Thou-sand Hills remains to man, as yet untouched.

TWENTY-ONE

Pietermaritzburg

Pietermaritzburg in the 1850s was a much pleasanter place than Durban. At the height of the emigration wave Durban was very much of a boom town, while Pietermaritzburg remained tolerably tranquil in its setting of hills. Most of its business sharks had removed to Durban to feed on the emigrants, and the capital was the cleaner for it.

It was a neatly built little town; an outpost where civilisation merged with the wilderness; a last stepping stone to the interior, where prim traders and conservative civil servants sought to lead conventional white-collared lives, while all around them bustled the noisy, colourful panoply of the Africa of the hunters and adventurers.

If Pietermaritzburg was the political centre of Natal, then its market square was the centre for the adventurers. Every wagon was entitled to outspan there and disgorge its cargo of produce, hunting trophies and sun-bronzed humanity, while all around stood the stores and business establishments, primly watching the agitation on the square like ladies at a boxing match – not quite approving, but nevertheless hoping that a portion of the excitement might come their way in the form of trade.

Each day started with the shrill crowing of hundreds of roosters, for every wagon carried a hen-coop slung between its wheels. The African camp servants would then crawl out of bed, and the crackling of wood would announce that the fires were alight. Coffee and morning toilets would then occupy the Europeans, while their servants rolled up the bedding, and their wagon-drivers collected the oxen and horses and drove them off in long files to graze on the commonage.

By 8 a.m. all was ready for the day's business. The ringing of bells and the shrill cries of the auctioneers announced the beginning of the sale of livestock, draught animals, and the goods of those wagons whose owners had decided to offload them in Pietermaritzburg.

All day the animation continued. Some parties, preparing a trip into the interior, would be busy obtaining their equipment in the shops. Others would be arriving from long journeys, their wagon tents torn and patched; the men, weatherbeaten fellows with rifles over their shoulders, bunches of long white ostrich feathers in their hats, and always followed by a few battle-scarred, dusty-looking dogs.

"I saw one cart on its way home after such an expedition," wrote E. Mohr, a German hunter and explorer who came to Natal in 1869, "with a lion about five months old, which had been taken young and tamed, in a clumsy cage at the back; whilst from the front, near the driver's seat, a young hartebeest antelope, or kamma, looked wonderingly out with its large, intelligent eyes upon the confusion in the streets. Side by side with the reserve oxen, horses and goats of the caravan, marched several gnus and a young Cape buffalo."

In the evenings, the market square was doubly fascinating. It was alive with campfires, the wagon-men lolling around them. Every dark street was a menace to the pedestrian, with some stray ox lying chewing its cud in the middle of the way.

Supper over, and their valued oxen resting in two long, double rows in front of the shafts, the Europeans would visit one another. In the wandering, Bedouin-sort-of-life led by these people, they picked up information from every part of the country, and in these evening meetings they traded suggestions and knowledge with one another. The elephant hunt-

317

ers commanded the most respectful attention. They were the social giants of this company. They were the adventurers with the greatest experience, men to whom antelopes were merely to be eaten, lions simply vermin, and the only quarry worthy of a sportsman's shot, the mighty elephant.

Around this picturesque throng Pietermaritzburg lived and had its own thoughts, ambitions and intrigues. The town had matured considerably since its republican days. By 1852 it had a population of 1508 Europeans, and there were 443 dwelling houses, mostly attractive little places with thatched or tiled roofs, although some had already been inflicted with the hideous corrugated iron which was then in the process of being introduced to South Africa.

Management of the little town was vested in five municipal commissioners elected in March 1848 and consisting of W. van Aardt, A.T. Caldecott, P. Ferreira, P.J. Jung and Doctor B. Poortman. John Steele became the first town clerk. Their powers were limited, but they busied themselves with the supply of water, the health of the town, and the improvement of its streets. Only in 1854 did the town attain the status of a proper borough, with its own mayor and council and a seal displaying an elephant and the Zulu name for the place – Umgungundhlovu.

A variety of businesses and shops had been established. The first hotel, the Crown, had been opened in February 1849, by William Platts. He went bankrupt and removed to Durban, went bankrupt again in his second hotel, the Trafalgar, and then joined the army and was killed in the Crimea; but behind him a whole string of hotels sprang up in Pietermaritzburg to cater for the settlers and travellers.

Grocers, butchers, tailors and all the other tradesmen were well established. By 1854 there were 26 shops in the town and business was brisk. Blacksmiths, carpenters, wagon-makers (turning out stout wagons for £100 each), millers and candle-makers made up the industrial section of the population.

Social life in the town was rent by petty squabbles and stupid snobberies between the military garrison and government officials on the one hand and the merchants and tradespeople on the other. Within the two main sections there were further subdivisions, generally caused by the women's feuds over some absurd point of social precedence or fancied snub.

The government officials, largely a crowd of juniors or failures sent up from the Cape or out from England to occupy what were really minor posts in an unimportant colony, made up for their insignificance by their pomposity. The upper, official, social circle had the reputation of being made up largely of bores and snobs, and the place was considered by visitors to be one of the most clique-ridden townlets in the empire.

As in Durban, there were few entertainments. The military occasionally indulged in amateur dramatics, and now and then some itinerant entertainers would put in an appearance. They were invariably enthusiastically received, although their performances were vile. If one of the visitors had any trace of glamour to him, like one Ali-Ben-Sou-Alle, an Irishman posing as a Moor in 1859, he carried all female hearts before him as if by storm.

Religious squabbles provided the residents with much distraction and agitation. Pietermaritzburg had long been partial to this type of argument. Back in the republican days when the first Dutch church had been opened on 15 March 1840, old Erasmus Smit, a Voortrekker himself, had ministered there, although he had never been ordained. After much ill-feeling, Sarel Cilliers removed the pulpit in protest. The American missionary, Daniel Lindley, then replaced him, and old Smit was pensioned off.

The classic Natal church row, however, developed in 1855 with the arrival of Bishop John William Colenso, appointed two years previously to the Episcopal See of Natal. Colenso brought his family and a body of clergymen with him and immediately became involved in a complex series of quarrels.

Colenso, known to the Africans as Sobantu (father of the people), was a man of considerable personality; deeply sincere but extremely opinionated, and as stubborn as a mule. Quarrels of ritualistic procedure and church management flared up all over his diocese. In Durban, a rude, surpliced effigy of Colenso was burned in public by a gang of youths.

Church meetings – usually dignified affairs with frock-coated, bearded gentlemen discussing matters of management – became lively, to say the least. Fathers of families and pillars of society pulled one another's beards, brought actions of assault and brawled over obscure points of ritual, of which the wise layman should properly know little and care less.

The question of financing church affairs was one of the major bones of contention. The churchwardens rented the pews (in opposition to the wishes of the Bishop) and financed affairs that way. Durban was as much stricken by these quarrels as Pietermaritzburg. One church council meeting after another "degenerated into a babel and a brawl," remarked the *Natal Mercury*, "the result entirely of the constant interruption, speeches, and interpolations of the Reverend Mr Crompton."

The quarrelling gradually mounted in a crescendo of ill-feeling. In July 1857 a fanatic by the name of Patrick Carnegy laid a sensational charge against Archdeacon McKenzie, one of Colenso's supporters, accusing him of unnatural offences against an African boy. After much filth and mudslinging, the case was thrown out and Carnegy was arrested for perjury.

The climax came in October 1862 when Colenso published his *Critical Examination of the Pentateuch*, presenting his conclusion that these books were forgeries and that Deuteronomy in particular was a pious fraud. There were screams of rage at this. Colenso was accused of heresy. In November 1863 he was tried in Cape Town and his ecclesiastical superior, Bishop Gray, sentenced him to deposition. Public outcry resulted and when the sentence was read in the Natal churches many of the laity walked out.

In London, the Privy Council pronounced against Bishop Gray's action and Colenso was re-established by law as Bishop of Natal. Bishop Gray then retaliated by excommunicating

The bush-covered lowveld of Zululand. In such a setting a young Senzangakhona met Nandi, Shaka's mother.

The Sentinel, brooding darkly above the snow-covered plateau of the Mount-aux-Sources Amphiteatre.

The valley of the Thukela River, traditional border between Natal and Zululand

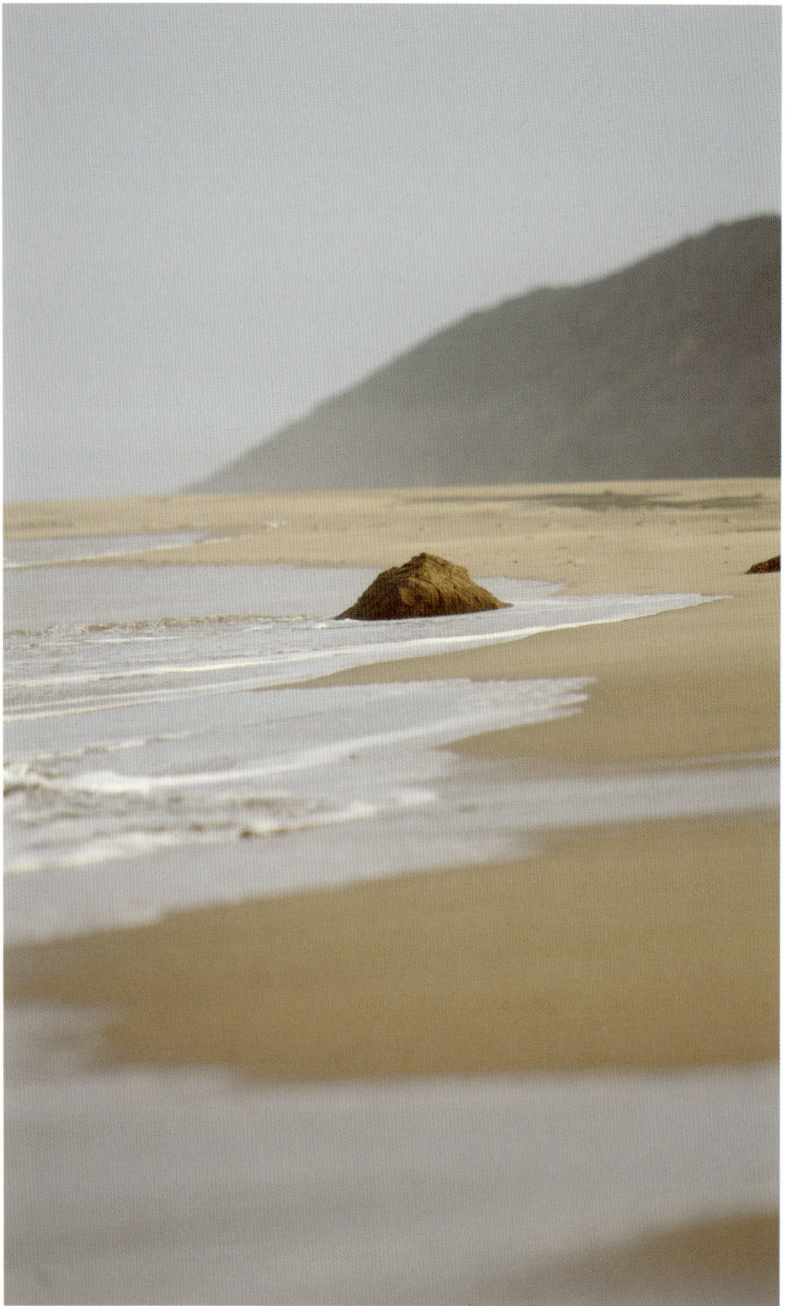

The golden sands of the Natal coast where many found adventure and others came to grief.

Colenso immediately after his return to Natal in November 1865 after successfully pleading his case in England.

The churchwardens of St Peter's Cathedral served notice on Colenso that he was not to preach, as was his intention, on the coming Sunday, 19 November. The cathedral doors were locked and the church plate removed. Colenso secured a court interdict forcing the wardens to open the cathedral.

An ignoble and idiotic war then followed between Colenso and the wardens, led by the Dean, the Very Reverend J. Green. Rival services were held and sabotaged by flooding the cathedral with water, hiding keys and tampering with the organ. Innumerable court actions were fought and interdicts served. When Colenso eventually established his legal position beyond further argument and Green was ejected from the Deanery, a dissenting church known as the Church of the Province of South Africa was formed, and its own Bishop, W.K. MacRorie, was consecrated in 1867. It had its own Pietermaritzburg cathedral of St Saviour's. Thenceforth the quarrel gradually died away, like water going off the boil, changing from hot to warm and then to cold.

This unseemly religious squabble brought the Anglican Church into considerable ill-repute and shook Pietermaritzburg to its social foundations. Side by side with it, the endless feuds of the officials continued. The streamlets of water meandering down Pietermaritzburg streets, the enormous gardens with their flowers, vegetables and fruit, the cool houses with their shady verandas, might all contribute to give the town an air of tranquillity; but beneath the surface a fever raged.

Few of the officials were exempt from these bickerings. The technicians, such as William Stanger the surveyor, were the best of the bunch, for they were kept too busy to indulge in quarrels. In any case Stanger, who had come to Natal fresh from exploring the Niger River and was well pickled with tropical diseases, died in Durban on 14 March 1854. John Bird was appointed Acting Surveyor General in Stanger's place until the following year. Then he resigned and Doctor Peter Cormack Sutherland, who had originally set up a medical practice in Durban on his arrival in Natal in 1853 and the following year been engaged as government geologist, was appointed to the position.

Martin West, the Lieutenant Governor, had been reasonably well liked, but he was an unimaginative, stodgy type of civil servant, without any ambition save that of eventual retirement. His successor, Benjamin Pine, who assumed office on 19 April 1850 was not much better. Politically, in fact, Natal was in the doldrums before the settlers came to change things.

A government made up of half-pay army officers, acting as junior civil servants to departmental heads disappointed in promotion elsewhere, could hardly be expected to be progressive.

Many of the settlers, on the other hand, were intelligent men who had played their part in politics in England. They soon found the rule of civil servants to be intolerable and political movements such as the Natal Political Association were formed in Pietermaritzburg to agitate for some measure of self-government.

The newspapers soon became a partisan in the matter, and the *Natal Witness* especially was guilty of violent personal antagonism towards individuals of the government, particularly Governor Pine. Another newspaper, the *Natal Independent*, run by James Archbell, the former Wesleyan missionary, crusaded for Pine and editorial abuse was frequent.

In 1845 Natal had been entirely separated from the Cape in its government. Then, in November 1856, when John Scott arrived in Natal to relieve Pine as Governor, he was just in time to observe the first elections to a Legislative Council. The British Government had bestowed upon the colony a new charter, making provision for representative institutions and, although their powers were limited, and many restraining strings were held by the Governor, it was still a big step forward.

February 1857 saw the first elections for the new Legislative Council. There was much excitement and high feeling at the hustings all over the country, and bitter criticism of the British Government's native policy.

The question of native policy was, in fact, the principal bone of contention between the British Government and the colonists. Nearly all the colonists had their interests vested in farms, which needed labour. The relatively benevolent feelings of the British Government towards the Bantu people found no responsive chord of sympathy in Natal.

The highly contagious, recurring, economic disease of using cheap and ever cheaper labour, was picked up by settlers almost as soon as they landed. They resented the existence of native locations where, in their reasoning, the tribespeople wasted their time and the soil by laziness and primitive agricultural methods. The settlers wanted the means of extracting labour from these social backwaters and they found the British Government standing between them and their desires.

The constant platform of the local politicians, then, was that distant London could have but a hazy idea of Natal's domestic problems. Although politically immature, they clamoured for what they were pleased to call "'sponsible government".

To this clamour, the British Government made but reluctant concessions. It was afraid that the local politicians were not, as they claimed, identifying themselves with the country in their demands. Rather, with an ingenious twist often seen in political manoeuvres, it was suspected that they identified the country with themselves. In this way their business desires became, to their minds, the needs of the country, and anybody criticising this naive assertion was blandly accused of being unpatriotic.

The Legislative Council was a reluctant concession by the British Government to the popular clamour. It assembled in Pietermaritzburg's government schoolroom on 23 March 1857 for the first time, and was officially opened with all pomp and ceremony by the Governor on the following day.

To a salute of 21 guns the Governor arrived, escorted by all the local bigwigs, dressed as impressively as they could manage. The ladies, of course, made the most of the affair as a variety of colonial fashion parade and henceforth, in fact, going to "the house" to listen to the regular evening debates became a major social entertainment.

The "house" itself was a big thatched barn of a place, with huge windows staring down at the members from white-washed walls. The 15 members, with Donald Moodie as the Speaker, sat comfortably in armchairs around a large horse-shoe-shaped table and performed their duties with dignity and scrupulous attention to parliamentary convention.

The Assembly became the battleground between the local politicians and the government over many issues, but especially the ever-recurring native question and the constant demands for a greater degree of responsible government.

The native question was complicated, in British eyes, by the fact that the 120 000 Africans then in Natal paid a greater tax contribution to the government than the Europeans. Nevertheless, they had no representation at all and looked to the British Government for some protection against the colonists.

Years of bickering followed. The colonists advocated the breaking up of most of the locations to satisfy land-hungry Europeans, and as the complete method of forcing the Africans to go out and work. They justified this by pointing out the gross abuse of the soil being practised in the locations.

The Africans were pastoralists rather than agriculturalists. Endless tribal disturbances in past years had given them no chance to settle down, while the debilitation of tropical diseases, bilharzia and fever, had left them a legacy of cultural lethargy. Now, with the roaming life of raids and migrations necessarily over, they were floundering about, making a hopeless mess of agriculture. With no spark of initiative in themselves to put them on the road to progress, and little desire by the Europeans to help them on to anything other than the pittance of a labourer, their prospects were miserable. To top it all, the complete stagnation in the locations gave the natural increase in population no avenue of employment in any industries consequent on progress, and pressure on the unfortunate, eroded location lands simply increased year by year.

The quarrel went on and on. Occasionally, some outbreak of trouble in one of the locations would stir up the whole issue. Africans have always loved cattle raids, and periodically some character would find covetousness for a neighbour's livestock getting the better of him. Trouble also flared up in March and April 1857, when the chief Sidoyi of the Ntlangwini tribe, living in the middle reaches of the Mkhomazi valley, launched a series of raids upon a neighbour after a brawl at a wedding. The government was forced to intervene. Shepstone swept along the riverbanks with some force, confiscated most of the offending tribe's cattle and deposed the chief. Eight Africans on all sides were killed during the course of operations. A few months later another petty chief, Matyana, of the Klip River area, became involved in some rather barbarous murders over witchcraft. When he refused to appear before a court, Shepstone went to see him. A row developed and 25 of Matyana's men were killed. The chief escaped to Zululand. Both affairs provided a storm in a teacup for the Pietermaritzburg political parties, and the clamour that the locations were getting out of control was added to the general plaint.

Then occurred a much more serious outbreak. Living along the banks of the upper Bushman's River was the Hlubi tribe, under a chief with the odd name of Langalibalele (the sun is hot) whose original home had been in the modern Utrecht area. He and his people had been settled in their new location in December 1849, in order to act as a buffer between European farms and the predatory Bushmen cattle raiders of the Drakensberg.

Like the Europeans of Natal, the Hlubi young men became attracted to the diamond fields, not only because of the wages, but because irresponsible diggers, urgently wanting labour, were offering rifles in lieu of money. These weapons were of the gaspipe variety, capable of doing more harm to the user than the target, but their presence in accumulating numbers caused considerable alarm in Natal.

In 1873 a demand was sent to Langalibalele for his tribe to register their guns. He refused. An involved quarrel then commenced between the chief and the government. The culmination was the despatch of a punitive force with orders to bring the Hlubis to heel, their guns to the scrap heap, and Langalibalele to gaol.

The Hlubis fled at the approach of the military. Driving their cattle before them, they followed the Bushman's River up to the Drakensberg. Then they trudged up to the heights, through the pass ever since known as Langalibalele Pass.

Behind the Hlubis the pursuers came galloping: a Major Durnford in command of a party of military and a Mr Allison in charge of 500 native levies. From a distance, they saw the straggling mass of humanity and cattle winding up the face of the mountain range. They decided to intercept them. Allison led his men around to what was found to be a non-existent pass marked as Champagne Castle Pass on the maps. Meanwhile, hidden in valleys, the mounted carbineers rode to the nearby Giant's Castle Pass and scrambled hurriedly up, until they reached the Basutoland plateau.

By the time the 33 carbineers and their native levies had reformed and galloped around to the head of the Langalibalele Pass, the chief and most of his tribe had already made good their escape into the bleak mountain jumble of the Basutoland highlands. Several thousand head of cattle, however, were intercepted; and possession of this agreeable booty distracted the livestock-conscious minds of the young volunteer farmers.

Then, while Durnford was discussing matters with the indunas, in the midst of the confusion of bewildered cattle, soldiers and herdboys, some of the young Hlubi warriors apparently surrounded the Europeans. A Sergeant Clarke suddenly shouted out that they had been betrayed. Both cattle and carbineers stampeded and the Hlubis opened fire. The Europeans galloped headlong back down the pass, not stopping until they considered themselves safe in the lowlands again.

Up on the plateau, the Hlubis moved on into Basutoland with their cattle. After a few hours all that remained of the fray at the head of the pass were the bodies of three carbineers – Robert Erskine, Edwin Bond and Charles Potterill – with two of their African allies, Elijah and Katama. They still lie sleeping there, in the windswept silence of the great heights, 8800 feet up, with a mound of stones and a cross alone to mark the tragedy of that day, 4 November 1873.

There was a tremendous outcry in Natal about this affair. The Hlubis were declared to be outlaws and serious threats of vengeance were shouted abroad. The Hlubis, meanwhile, trekked on and reached Leribe in the Caledon valley, where they hoped to find sanctuary with some of their chief's relatives. Instead, Langalibalele and 91 of his men were induced to surrender on 11 December 1873, while the rest of the Hlubis hiding in the mountains were gradually ferreted out – surrendering or being shot, and their bones littered parts of the desolate moorland on the roof of South Africa.

A ridiculous trial followed. According to the prevailing system of ruling the tribespeople, all trials were conducted under native law by the Supreme Chief (the Governor or his appointed deputy). Accordingly, Langalibalele's accusers were also his judges, and the whole business was hardly fair or sound in law. The chief was not even allowed a counsel.

On 9 February 1874 Langalibalele was sentenced to banishment for life. Then the fun began. Bishop Colenso and his family had been a thorn in the side of the officials in Natal ever since the reverend gentleman had arrived in the colony. The fact that a thorn in the side was certainly needed for that moribund body did not make it any the less painful to them.

Now Colenso took up the cudgels on behalf of Langalibalele. He had always interested himself in the tribespeople, doing his best to aid them and shelter them from the mercies of what he considered to be the more reactionary of the colonists. He was occasionally wrong in his opinions but more often right, but in any case the unflinching obstinacy and irritating emotionalism with which he adhered to his beliefs made him many enemies.

By defending Langalibalele, he outraged half Natal and had all Pietermaritzburg by the ears. To defend an African who had been condemned for responsibility in the deaths of European soldiers must have taken much courage on Colenso's part. By doing so he certainly shook up the local officials.

There were almost as many casualties in the government as the troops had sustained. The British home authorities took the affair to heart, after much agitation by the Bishop and various bodies in England. The Lieutenant Governor, Sir Benjamin Pine, was recalled from his second term of office in Natal. Langalibalele was reprieved from his banishment to Robben Island and eventually, in 1887, after a stay in Cape Town, allowed to return to Natal. The old autocratic native administration, established by Shepstone, was brought to a sudden end after serving its purpose reasonably well for the past 30 years. Henceforth, jurisdiction in serious cases passed to a proper Native High Court, while administrative control was gradually delegated to a host of minor officials.

This intervention on the part of the British Government was a further source of irritation to the local politicians. It remained, in fact, the principal bone of contention in Natal right up to Union. The local politicians never had the locations completely at their mercy. The locations were eventually transferred to the Natal Native Trust, virtually the Executive Council, which had to administer them to the advantage of their inhabitants. The farmers had to depend on the wages they offered to draw workers from the location areas or private properties, such as those of the Natal Land and Colonisation Company, where they squatted and were fleeced of intolerable rentals by some pretty notorious land shark organisations. Rackets such as these combined with normal taxation and the backwardness of the locations to squeeze labour out. Over the years, more and more Africans became available for work, and the modern system of Natal's economic life steadily emerged.

TWENTY-TWO
Colonial days

The native question was not the only source of squabbling in colonial Natal. Running a close second was the question of railways, and on this matter there was most bitter contention in Pietermaritzburg.

The first railway in Natal was the product of private enterprise. Early in 1859, a company was formed to construct a railway from the Point to Durban town. After much quarrelling over the site for the terminus, construction was eventually started and Natal watched its progress with fascination.

The arrival of the first locomotive (in pieces) was a great event. Not that it was much of a locomotive. It was a 24 horsepower affair which, like some small-sized human beings, made up in noise for what it lacked in strength.

Henry Jacobs assembled the engine with its head facing the Point, and it ran in this way, always returning in reverse, for there was no turntable. Jacobs became the driver, and on 23 June 1860 he took it on its first run. With the chairman and directors of the company standing proudly on the footplate, the engine hauled a goods train down to the Point, to the accompaniment of cheers and whistles.

On the 25th there was a ceremonial opening, with soldiers on parade, schoolchildren singing "God Save the Queen", and hordes of excited Africans. The little engine, smartly painted green and with plenty of copper pipes for driver Jacobs to keep clean, almost burst with pride. It fumed, fussed, whistled and filled the driver's cab full of steam, smoke, coal grit, grease, and swear words when somebody got burnt on the hot pipes.

Thenceforth the train ran three times a day whether the engine worked or not, a span of oxen pulling the train if the engine was indisposed. Fares were one shilling first class and sixpence second class for the two-mile journey.

This pioneer railway system stimulated Natal's appetite. Agitation for an extensive network, and particularly a link between Durban and Pietermaritzburg, became a topic of political argument. The trouble was finance. After the boom years of emigration, economic affairs in Natal had rapidly deteriorated. The overberg trade collapsed with the Basuto War. The Zululand trade was quiet, and there was much competition from Lourenço Marques. Crops failed in bad seasons of drought and by 1865 there was a major depression.

In Pietermaritzburg, several respected institutions went bankrupt. Every newspaper was full of the insolvencies of small businesses. The Colonial Bank of Natal, the Commercial and Agricultural Bank and the Natal Fire and Insurance Trust Company all went out of business in 1867. The Treasury returns showed an alarming deficit. Unemployment was common. It was certainly a hard time to finance railways but, nevertheless, private interests stirred.

Several concerns were formed in the hope of constructing a railway to the interior. The most ambitious project was that of the Natal Central Railway Company, formed in 1863 in London. Its secretary, F.B. Elliot, a suave, immaculately dressed man, spent much of his time in Pietermaritzburg promoting the ideas of his firm by entertaining and flattering politicians. Eventually, a concession was drawn up by the Legislative Council, making land grants and giving financial aid on such generous terms that the Imperial Government promptly vetoed the entire business, to the intense annoyance of not a few Natalians, who regarded this as gross interference and still another proof that Natal needed "'sponsible government".

During the Depression years, the only real railway development came with the opening of a four-mile extension of the railway from Durban to the quarry on the banks of the Mngeni River. This extension, opened on 25 January 1867, was built for the express purpose of conveying rock to the harbour works, but it was at least a hopeful sign for the future.

With the return of general prosperity in the early seventies, railway ambitions revived. Once again a group of financiers appeared on the scene with the so-called "Wellbourne Scheme", and gulled the Legislative Council into offering them 2 500 000 acres of land for nothing, an annual subsidy, and a ten-year monopoly on all steel and iron in the colony. Once again, this scheme was too much for the Imperial Government. It was vetoed, and once again Natal simmered under the fancied harsh frustration of its railway hopes.

At last, with the increased revenues consequent upon a return to prosperity, and guided by the British Government's advice, the Natal authorities decided to commence construction themselves.

The whole route of the future line was carefully surveyed in 1873. Three surveyors did the job: Kemp tackled the portion from Durban to Karkloof; Carige continued from Karkloof to Colenso; and Arrot Browning selected the route from Colenso, over the Drakensberg into the Free State. By July 1873 most of the surveys were finished and work started on the proposed routes for the north and south coast lines, surveyed by Paterson and Kemp respectively.

On 1 January 1876, the first sod was turned in Durban for the line to Pietermaritzburg. The Lieutenant Governor of the day, Sir H.E. Bulwer, performed the ceremony with great pomp. There was a large concourse of spectators, a triumphal arch, a grand luncheon, a children's treat, a volunteer inspection, fireworks at night and letters to the newspapers afterwards complaining of the fire hazard. Thence onwards, the progress, difficulties, and troubles of the construction joined Bishop Colenso and the Langalibalele affair as the major topics of conversation in Natal.

The contractors, Messrs Wythes and Jackson, portioned out most of the work to subcontractors. Labourers were imported from Mauritius and the line made steady progress, not only through the endless hills of Natal but through a welter of public argument as to the route, the gauge, the number of curves, position of stations and quality of rolling stock. In fact, the whole construction was considered a sort of open season for public criticism.

The Government had bought the original six miles of line in Durban for £40 000. One of their first tasks was to root it all up and change the gauge from 4 ft 8½ in. to 3 ft 6 in. which they had decided to use.

The first big engineering task was the construction of the bridge over the Mbilo River, which was opened at the end of August 1877. For the rest, construction was the usual hard slog of digging, blasting and filling. The line certainly had a rugged bit of country to traverse; in fact many people had doubted the possibility of a railway at all. Within 73 miles the line had to climb from sea level up to 2218 ft at Pietermaritzburg, the whole route twisting through an involved jumble of hills.

"How the railway is to drag itself up and round all these thousand-and-one spurs running into one another, with no distinct valley or flat between, is best known to the engineers and surveyors who have declared it practicable," wrote Lady Barker in 1875, and she voiced the doubts of many.

Nevertheless, the steel road did climb up. On 4 September 1878 the line was opened to Pinetown, and on 24 March 1879 it reached Botha's Hill. Rains held up construction at times and two or three engines were engulfed when embankments collapsed, but otherwise the whole project was proceeding extremely well.

The first stations on the line were Umbilo, Bellair, Malvern, Northdene (named after one of its earliest residents, George North), Pinetown Bridge, Pinetown and Botha's Hill. As the line advanced, so the transport men receded before it, establishing forwarding agencies at each of the successive railheads.

The coaching men made a last few pounds by charging the full Durban-Pietermaritzburg rates from each of the railheads, right until 1 October 1880, when the line was opened to Camperdown. Then public annoyance at being mulcted started to mount and they reduced the fare by half.

With one more station by the way, Richmond Road (later Thornville), together with several watering points, twelve bridges, one tunnel, many steep embankments and a 90-feet viaduct at Nchanga which swayed on windy days, the line at last reached Pietermaritzburg and was officially opened on 1 December 1880.

The arrival of the railway at Pietermaritzburg was certainly one of the most momentous events in the history of the town. It was a social occasion which attracted nearly every inhabitant and gave its notorious social cliques a glorious opportunity to snub one another while the women paraded like peacocks in their finery.

Not that Pietermaritzburg's social set had no grievous setbacks. Occasionally, a nice juicy scandal would rock it to its foundations. In May 1877, for instance, a Mrs St George, a great socialite, was arrested for falsity and fraud. She was sentenced to six months in gaol as final settlement for having lived on borrowed money for some time.

Again, the Reverend St Charles Frederick Cawkill Barker, of some fame in the Transvaal at the Pilgrim's Rest goldfields, came to grief in the same year and got six months for fraud. He was hardly out before he was in again, in 1882: this time doing three years' hard labour for falsity. Another well-known fraud was the self-styled "Lady Avonmore" alias Mrs Yelverton, the central figure in a sensational Irish divorce action of 1858. In Pietermaritzburg she earned part of her living as a writer of scurrilous material for the *Natal Witness*. She died unlamented in 1881.

However, despite these scandals and the endless trouble from what was called the "social pest" (a long series of vicious assaults on European females by Indian and African males, particularly in 1886), which made life most insecure, the people of colonial Natal were prim and great sticklers for convention. They dressed conservatively in the stuffiest European fashions, permitting no relaxation at all on account of the warm climate of Natal.

Attempts were even made to impose fashion on the tribespeople. Laws were passed threatening penalties for those who entered towns dressed only in their traditional skins. In this connection, we are naively told by one Charles Hamilton, that at the bridge leading to Pietermaritzburg over the Msunduze River, in the middle 1860s, could be witnessed "a very extraordinary scene. An old man sits on the bridge, and earns a respectable livelihood by letting old trousers and other garments to the Kaffirs at moderate charges." The customers received the trousers on their way in (hired at the rate of sixpence a day) and then returned them on their way out.

European fashions were catered for on more conventional lines. Business was established by a number of haberdashers, such as Richard Harwin in Durban, whose corrugated-iron emporium sheltered among its cloths and laces two young assistants, T.M. Harvey and B.W. Greenacre. In after years these two went into business together. By means of good sense and, it is whispered, an odd spot of gunrunning, they laid the foundations for their subsequent prosperity and renown.

Not that gunrunning was considered too heinous an offence. People traded in anything in those days and one advertisement, published on 5 May 1858, during the Boer-Basuto War, announced:

"To Boers and others. For Sale, two new long Four-pounder Guns, on carriages complete with a quantity of Round Shot and Grape. Apply to J.D. Koch."

Whether these guns, in Boer or Basuto hands, would be more deadly than the social snub is unknown. The upper set certainly had their greatest opportunity for trying out their powers in 1860, when the 16-year-old Prince Alfred made a formal royal tour of South Africa.

The most ridiculous social jostlings occurred on that occasion. The general atmosphere of emotionalism was as thick as a triple-coloured ice-cream. The young prince travelled overland from the Cape, escorted by Sir George Grey, the Governor. On 3 September he rode into Pietermaritzburg and found himself flattered by banners bearing such words as "Thou Royal, we loyal."

After digesting effusions such as the above, shaking hands all round, listening to addresses of welcome, dancing with a few of the select, planting trees, presenting colours, watching an African war dance, and laying the foundation stone of the new town hall, he rode down to Durban.

The Durban people did their best to outdo Pietermaritzburg, both in the length and hysteria of their addresses and the extravagance of the ladies' gowns. What the young man thought of it all is sadly not on record. The thing he probably most enjoyed about Durban was his manner of leaving the place. On 6 September 1860, he was stowed aboard the train and Driver Jacobs then obliged with a record-breaking run to the Point of "two minutes and forty seconds, a speed of something less than forty miles an hour, the fastest journey that South African soil has yet seen."

The foundation stone for Pietermaritzburg's new town hall was left behind by the Prince to lie in respected isolation for years. The Depression of the 1860s put an end to many of Natal's projects, and the new town hall was one of them. Among the very few public works completed in this dreary period was the 81-foot-high lighthouse erected on top of the Durban Bluff, 211 feet above sea level. It was built of steel parts sent out from Britain and was opened on 23 January 1867 by Lt Col John Bissett, who was acting as Lieutenant Governor of Natal until R.W. Keate, the new Lieutenant Governor arrived in May of that year.

The construction of this lighthouse, the first in Natal, had been an urgent necessity for some time. There was a slight similarity between Durban Bluff and Isipingo Bluff, a few miles down the coast, and more than one ship had almost come to grief as a result of misidentification. One of these escapades gave Natal almost as much to talk about as the visit of the Prince.

On 29 June 1857, a rakish, heavily armed schooner named the *Minnetonka* arrived off Durban and anchored far out in the roadstead. Her captain, an American named John Ward, reported that they had been in want of stores and had landed the mate and a boat's crew of five men at the mouth of the Mlazi River, having mistaken Isipingo Bluff for Durban. The boat had been smashed on the rocks and its crew were walking up the beach.

The whole atmosphere of the heavily armed ship seemed so sinister and she had such an ugly-looking crew, that the port men hurriedly tumbled back into their boat, murmuring something about having to attend to a fictitious man-o'-war schooner in the bay.

At this, the newcomers became as alarmed as the men of the port boat. They hauled up their anchor and within a couple of minutes they were off. When the mate and his companions came up the beach it was found that they spoke only Spanish. When they were told, through an interpreter, that their ship had abandoned them, they broke out into violent abuse. They confessed that the ship was a slaver from Havana, bound for Cape Corrientes, and was searching for human cargo on the way. For the rest, only bad language rewarded further questioning.

Many other sensations disturbed the tranquillity of those colonial days. The Bushmen raided again and again from their sanctuaries in the Drakensberg. If autumn was the time for falling leaves in Europe, in Natal it was the time for Bushmen. They relied on the poor pasturage and harsh winter conditions of the mountaintops to prevent any determined pursuit. From the source of the Thukela to the source of the Mkhomazi was a happy hunting ground for them. They would slip down and, with no fences to hinder them, they would select a fine herd and get a good 24 hours' start before the theft was even noticed.

Their technique was always the same. They would drive the cattle along the most appalling and secret paths, over narrow ledges and up the beds of rivers in order to hide the trail. At the most precipitous places a Bushman would go ahead and smear cow dung about, in order to fool the animals into the belief that others had passed that way and therefore it must be practicable for them.

Every frontier farmer had heavy losses. In December 1848, 250 head of prime stock were rustled from Marais's farm, right under the nose of the military post on the Bushman's River. Three months later 200 head vanished from the farm of H. Ogle. So it went on, from one end of the colony to the other.

The farmers were at their wits' end. Commandos were raised to ride against the Bushmen almost every year, but they were most difficult to track. Many of the robbers were sheltered by the Mpondomise tribe in the Transkei, who received a share of the loot in return. The Bushmen would raid from the Drakensberg, and then make their way over the mountains and around the back to their protectors in the Transkei.

In an effort to curb the raiders, small military outposts were established in the 1850s, such as Fort Nottingham, built in the middle of the infested area by the Nottingham Regiment (the Sherwood Foresters). Against such skilfully erratic raids, however, there was little that fixed garrisons could do. The regular soldiers were soon withdrawn. Cape coloured guards replaced them but, in the monotony of garrison life, these soon degenerated and passed their time in gambling or endlessly squabbling among themselves over smuggled drink. The Bushmen simply raided on.

Robert Speirs was one of the farmers who suffered most. In 1851 his best herd was swept off and two of his herdboys were killed. The following year the same raiders swept down to the farm Boschhoek. They stole 150 head of cattle from the chief Lugaju, then living there. The chief collected 300 of his men

337

and set off in pursuit. Near the sources of the Mkhomazi, in the middle of the path, they came upon the head of a baboon stuck upon a stick. Fearful of witchcraft, the Africans turned back.

Pursuing the Bushmen was always hazardous. Captain Lucas, who led many of the pursuits, tells of how he and a party of Cape Mounted Riflemen trailed one band. They followed the path until their supplies ran out. By then they were deep in the foothills of the mountains and close on the heels of their quarry.

In the night they bivouacked around a fire, with their saddles arranged about them as a small-scale laager. That night Lucas was uncommonly nervous. Giving way to his fears, he crawled to each of his men in turn. It was a pitch-dark night. He ordered them all to move quietly out of the circle of saddles. It was fortunate that they did. In the morning they found 25 poisoned arrows within the circle, all shot silently by some Bushman in the darkness of the night.

Of course, the Bushmen did not always get away with it. In May 1868 they raided the Cathkin area and looted much livestock from the tribespeople there. The Africans pursued them and managed to recover some of their animals near the sources of the Orange River.

News of this success stimulated the depressed Europeans. The following year, when the Bushmen raided several farms, a commando was raised. Captain Allison was in command. With 11 Europeans and 200 Africans, he rode to the top of the mountains and followed a trail "made visible by the remains of game and occasionally the relics of slaughtered beasts."

This time the Bushmen had become careless from their long immunity. They were overtaken near the sources of the Orange River. Seventeen Bushmen were killed and seven women and children captured, along with 60 horses. The rest escaped with a crowd of their Basuto allies, but the band was well scattered before the commando returned home on 19 October 1869.

This was not the end of the business by any means. In April 1870 the raiders were busy around Fort Nottingham, but each year their numbers slowly decreased. Not only the European farmers, but the Africans as well, shot them on sight. The chief, Dumisa, was particularly active against them. In July 1872, when they seized 17 of his horses including his favourite pony, he pursued them to the valley of the upper Orange River. He surrounded their fire one night, surprised them, killed eight men and women and took two women captive. In this fashion, by yearly instalments as it were, the Bushmen of the Drakensberg were wiped out until in the end nothing remained of them save a few pictures painted on their cave walls – and a few curses in the memories of the farmers.

The greatest of all the excitements of those early colonial days started in August 1852. On the 15th of that month the 234-ton *Sir Robert Peel*, a schooner-rigged screw steamer, arrived in Durban at the commencement of the first regular mail service from the Cape to Natal. A special half-holiday allowed most of Durban's population to go down to the Point the following day to watch the little steamer, drawing nine feet of water, come in safely across the bar.

Then the mailbags were opened and in them was the first news of the discovery of gold in Australia. It was bad news for struggling Natal. Thenceforth, with every ship men, singly or in parties, started to sneak away to Australia. Entire firms, such as J. Millar & Co., decided to remove bodily to the new field of riches, although mature consideration induced them to remain. Lawyers, clerks, mechanics and farmers all went off, including Mr Geddes, the sexton of Durban, who considered that his talents for digging would be more profitably employed in the goldfields.

As a counterbalance to this drainage of manpower, in February 1853 the government offered rewards for the discovery of coal in Natal, while private firms, envious of Australia's boom, offered £1000 to anybody who discovered gold. A fair amount of prospecting activity commenced with the promise of these rewards.

Rumours of discoveries of gold in the Cape, Transvaal and Free State, made the people of Natal all the more excited. The usual optimistic claims were made. Fannin claimed to have found both coal and gold on his farm Dargle in April 1854. All over the country traces of coal were found and the search for these deposits soon superseded the more nebulous gold.

For over ten years, gold-prospecting fell into abeyance. Then, in 1866, two parties of prospectors started to rummage around the country once more. The Depression was then in full swing and many hoped for some find of gold to save the colony from bankruptcy. Even Theophilus Shepstone joined in the search and, in August 1867, claimed to have discovered copper on the Mkhomazi River, seven miles above the point of tidal rise.

The government shared the general hope in a mineral discovery. On 24 September 1867, it offered a reward of £1000 to anybody discovering payable gold, together with aid for prospectors in the shape of loans of wagons and tools. A flood of reports of gold, coal, silver, copper and other metals started to come in, all sent by optimistic souls who knew nothing about geology but misinterpreted odd rock formations on their properties.

Ancient African smelting places, discovered at Mfume and the Mlazi River, increased the excitement, and gold and coal became the chief topics of conversation in Natal. Then, at the end of 1867, came the first stories from the Transvaal of Carl Mauch's gold discoveries at the Tati River and in Rhodesia. Men started to drift out of Natal and head for the north, with picks and shovels packed on top of their knapsacks.

Among those who stayed to prospect in Natal was George Robert Parsons. With some companions, he wandered down the south coast, panning the various rivers. Then the big news came. On 3 August 1868 he reported a find of gold in the Mthwalume River. Fourteen days later one of his partners, Walter Compton, claimed to have found gold in the Mahlo-ngwa River. In this way the south coast gold rush started.

Parsons went off to Pietermaritzburg with his find of gold – exactly one speck. He applied for aid and, on 24 August, the government granted him an advance of £40 a month for two months, to allow him to continue work.

The whole of Natal was excited at this news. Local farmers started to dream of soaring land values, while from all over the colony men started to gravitate towards the Mthwalume River.

To add to the excitement, in November 1868, Charles William Steward announced a find of gold in the rugged country around the Nyembe hill, near the junction of the Thukela and Mzinyathi rivers. Another rush of hopefuls took place in this direction, with a syndicate in Durban and the Greytown Mineral Prospecting Company floated to finance activity on the new field. Resolute gold-seekers such as Edward Button, George Parsons, W. Marshall, Antonia Moriss and Ludwig Schwikkard all busied themselves in this area, while several parties of Government officials and idle spectators gathered to watch Steward sink the shaft which he was certain would lead to fortune.

More and more gold traces were found. George Sides reported finds in the Fafa River, while the enterprising George Parsons found colour in nearly every river of the south coast, from the Mzumbe to the Mphambanyoni. Gold there certainly was in this part of the world, but the problem was to locate it in payable quantities.

The richest traces were found along the tributary of the Mthwalume known as the Little Mngeni. A small alluvial flat on the banks of this stream became the scene of great activity. Several separate groups of diggers laboured there. None of them knew much about gold and their methods varied considerably. One party dug a capacious shaft; another group rummaged around in the bush; a third group sat waiting for somebody else to find something.

Under government patronage, Parsons's group dug a water-race to allow them to sluice the flats and thoroughly expose the anticipated gold. A fifth group of diggers led by Captain Augustus Lindley, on its way to the Rhodesian fields from England, also arrived there and left some descriptive record of the rush.

"In many places," wrote Lindley, "'we succeeded in obtaining *the colour* in very minute particles, but so trifling in quantity as to be quite unworthy of further attentions." They explored every stream within a radius of 15 miles, splashing about in the waters and sending the birds flying with the sound of their picks and the clatter of their pans.

The scene of the rush was extremely beautiful. A rolling, green sea of hills and bush tumbled down towards the coast, with rivers threading their way tortuously from inland. Every slope was aflame with the brilliant scarlets of the kaffirboom trees. Wild flowers danced in the arms of the wind. Strange table-topped mountains such as the mighty uMsigazi (the commanding one) looked down on the valleys in serene detachment, sometimes echoing the voices of those few Africans who had in past years found sanctuary from the terror of Shaka in this lovely wilderness.

The prospectors had their camps by the banks of the Little Mngeni, among the acacia trees which gave the stream its name, at a spot where the waters spread out "to form a wide and charming pool off the end of the flat, round which it took a sharp bend before joining the Mthwalume." At this pool, deep and cold, the best traces had been found; and there, for some time, the work went on. There was much hunting and immense eels could be caught in the pool when the diggers wanted relaxation.

Other parties came to the scene of the discovery, all eager to make their fortunes. A number of Australians had arrived in Durban, attracted by sensational newspaper stories of Carl Mauch's discoveries in the north. In February 1869, 30 of these Australians decided to prospect the south coast. They explored the whole area as far south as the Mzimkhulu, but found nothing payable.

The best find made by the Australians was on the tributary of the Mzinto River, known as the Mhlangwa. At this place three of the Australians – Alick (Scottie) Jarvis, Charles Redmond and Jenomie Carter – remained after the rest of the party had gone off in disgust. Working near the head of the stream, they succeeded in recovering ten ounces of gold, but over so long a period and with so much hard work that it was obviously unpayable.

The rush at the Little Mngeni also petered out. Parsons got his water-race going, but after weeks of sluicing only twelve grains of gold (worth about half-a-crown) had been recovered. The whole affair was a disappointment. Men started to drift away for the Transvaal. By November 1869 there were only nine men still working in the area, and they were dispirited. In two years of hard work on the south coast, a total of about one hundred diggers had produced about 20 ounces of gold, mostly from the Mhlangwa stream, on the farm named, optimistically, Golden Valley by its owner M. Crowley.

The Australians, particularly, were much soured by their disappointment. In a Durban bar they encountered one south coast prospector who excitedly claimed a rich discovery. Asked to show a sample, he displayed so minute a grain of gold that it blew away when someone breathed on it. The Australians picked the optimist up and threw him in the horse-trough.

The Australians also went to inspect Steward's discovery in the Thukela area. For some time they rummaged around in the bush and heat, finding quite a few mambas, tantalising traces of minerals and, on the islands in the Thukela, several hot springs as well as the ruins of stone walls erected by the Lala tribespeople.

They visited Steward and found him still trying to prove his find. By that time the man was working at the bottom of quite a deep hole. After inspecting his samples, the visitors told Steward that if he dug any deeper he'd probably reach Australia, but that was all. They abandoned the place in disgust.

That was the end, for the time being, of the first excitement over gold in Natal. Indisputable traces of the metal, however, had certainly been found and many people in Natal remained hopeful. In June 1873 the well-known Thomas Baines, on behalf of the South African Goldfields Company, prospected along the banks of the Thukela. Together with C.F. Osborne he visited Steward's abandoned workings on the Nyembe hill, cleared the shaft of dead reptiles, and collected samples. There was quartz with traces of gold but nothing payable. Baines and Osborne wandered off but others persisted in the search, and among these was Fred Markham, an enthusiast from Greytown, a place notably infected with gold fever in those days of reports of great alluvial discoveries in the Transvaal.

In 1886 the persevering Markham found good colour when he panned the Mfongosi (river of rushing noises), a tributary of the Thukela which lies twisted up like a brown snake in a valley wilderness of its own.

There was an immediate rush to the valley when Markham spread the news of his find. By August 1886 there were 80 other prospectors camped along the river, killing mambas and rummaging around for gold. On 9 August a gold commissioner by the name of A. Muirhead was appointed to control the field and it developed with all the speed and excitement and hope of a proper gold rush.

By November there were 35 companies and syndicates busy in the valley. Dams, water races and machinery were being dug or set up all along the swift-flowing river and much hard work was put in there. The whole length of the Mfongosi seethed with activity. Many different reefs were found and all given names in customary mining fashion, such as: The New Sheba, The Sunrise, Molly's Luck, Golden Crown, The Good Hope of H.T. Davies, The Better Still, and Hidden Treasure.

A stream of hopefuls made their way towards the place and found that most of their energy and enthusiasm was exhausted in trying to reach it. An atrocious road, made up of a confusion of footpaths, connected the place with Greytown. It led first to the edge of the valley, where a wise man named Bell decided he'd go no further but would find his gold where he was, and so opened a store and canteen which he called The Oasis.

From the pub the track dropped down into the valley by means of the notorious Devil's Staircase. At the bottom a rickety punt was set up to ferry persons across the river for one shilling a trip, and beyond it lay a wilderness of thorn bush, heat, snakes and bad language.

By December 1886 Mfongosi was a rowdy village of 50 shacks; a number of stores, such as Ford's Osborn Store; a few hotels and canteens, including Fry's Hotel, the Pioneer Hotel, H. & T. Davies' Gum Tree Hotel; and the establishments of several tradesmen, such as Harper's Bakery.

A regular, twice-weekly post had been organised and stores were being dragged in by oxen to the tune of candles at one shilling each; brandy, seven shillings a bottle; gin, four shillings and threepence; and castor oil a shilling.

Some 2000 claims had been properly registered and a regular diggers committee of 15 members had been elected, with A.H. Manning as secretary.

Ladies came to join their husbands and a sociable, cheerful sort of life was led by all. By January 1887 Mfongosi could stage its first race meeting, with three hundred Europeans present, a thousand Zulus and one newspaper correspondent. "The scene was most picturesque and charming," he wrote, "being laid on the eastern bank of the Mfongosi River under some great trees. The ground was good and everything tended to ensure us the successful meeting we had. There were about three hundred people on the course and I only noticed six cases of drunkenness, all of which were of a mild and good-natured description."

An even more remarkable thing about Mfongosi was its rate of growth. By March 1887 the town consisted of about two hundred shacks, with four hotels and many shops lining a main street which was assuming impressive proportions. There was even a soda-water manufactory commencing business.

The village was situated at the junction of the Mfongosi and Manziwayo streams and it had as its centre the office of the gold commissioner. This individual was a government one-man band. He acted as policeman, JP, postmaster, sanitary inspector, district surgeon, and public whipping boy for all complaints. His most important function was as registrar of the claims, 150 x 300 ft each, for which the diggers paid a prospecting licence of ten shillings each month.

Around this capital of the Thukela some seven hundred European prospectors radiated in the greatest rush the valley ever knew. No less than 20 different crushing mills were erected along the Mfongosi River, and to cater for all the inhabitants two clubs were built. One was the Working Man's Club, under the presidency of R.P. Watson, while the other was a stylish place consisting of "quite a jolly little room where one can see all the Durban papers and many English ones. It is passably furnished and boasts, in addition to a piano, a framed photograph of the Queen, the only lady admitted into the Club."

All this enterprise was built entirely on hope. An undoubted strike of gold had been found and nobody doubted that the mills, once they began working, would be able to turn out the gold. There was quite a race to see which mill would be working first and the day of the initial crushing was a holiday for the entire valley.

All the prospectors gathered outside the mill door. Beer was downed and speculation as to the yield was rife, with bets being made and everybody very merry. The day wore on and the mill quietened down. Suddenly the door opened and the manager of the concern, with a face as black as thunder, strode out, shouldered his way through the crowd, and walked hurriedly away. The crowd was dumbfounded. Then they started clamouring at the door. "What was the result?" they shouted. Presently came the sullen reply. "Practically nothing," and that was the end. There was some gold all right, but in small quantities and so refractory that no known method would extract it from the quartz into whose secure keeping nature had entrusted it.

By November 1887 Mfongosi was a ghost town with deserted shacks, hotels and shops. Expensive machinery was abandoned to the mambas; the shops were given to the rats. The club was closed and the Indian waiters made tracks to other parts. The tennis court had its first weeds, and by the river, beneath the trees, a spirit named Hope sat with its head on its knees and wept.

The excitement at Mfongosi had attracted many prospectors to the adjacent area. In the middle of 1887 one of them, C. Tatham, claimed that he had found gold at Msinga (place of open clearness) and the Golden Eagle Mining Company was formed to work it, with no success.

Further away, around the Nondweni stream, another strike was made later in 1887. About 20 reefs were uncovered there and given the usual romantic names, such as Ned's Luck, Maggie's Fortune, and Forget-me-Not. This find also proved a disappointment. In the same year, on the south coast, R. Parker claimed to have found gold on his farm three miles beyond the Mkhomazi River; and there was much excitement when a quartz reef was discovered by H. Palmer and J. Pearse on the old Golden Valley farm. A Durban syndicate was formed by H. Greenacre and F. Reynolds to prospect the reef, and once again a number of prospectors turned their attention to the south coast.

The village of Umzinto was crowded out by some 300 visitors, and the supposed South Coast Fields once again became the talk of Natal. Frank Reynolds had already been running the Umzinto Gold Prospecting Company for the past few years, with George Pigg acting as prospector on the farm Esperanza. Now he turned with great energy on the Golden Valley prospects. The Golden Butterfly Mine was opened at Umzinto and by 1888 a 50-foot shaft had been sunk. Though, following Barberton custom, extravagant claims of ore yields of 13 ounces to the ton were made, nothing resulted.

At nearby Dumisa, the first battery in Natal, a five-stamp affair, was ceremonially opened by Sir Arthur Havelock, the

Governor, on 20 October 1888. For the next ten years there was a fair amount of activity by individual miners, mostly working claims with small profit around the battery at Dumisa. Many traces of gold were found, and even a few small diamonds on Nyangalezi farm. The rivers, also, continued to tantalise many people with their gold traces. In January 1902, one concern, the Natal Gold Dredging Syndicate, planned to take over all the gold-bearing rivers and dredge them thoroughly but, as from the Mzinto hopes, nothing resulted from this scheme.

The Dumisa mine, worked at intervals by various persons, was the only one of all the Natal gold mines ever to show any real profit, and it was small enough. Between 1907 and 1909 it recovered gold valued at £3711 for its owners, Messrs Egan and Foye. Recoveries such as that were enough to show that Natal had some gold and to provide the local people with curios and a small experience of those wild hopes and bitter disappointments which make up the stormy history of gold mining all over the world.

TWENTY-THREE
The road to the interior

Howick Falls

The hunters and adventurers generally considered that the best thing about Pietermaritzburg was the road out of it. The town with its quarrels, snobberies and politics, irritated them. They bought, or disposed of, their goods there and then wandered off, finding little about the place to talk of in future campfire gossips, save one or two of its peculiarities, such as the 13-feet pet python kept in 1897 by Phipps, the owner of the Corner Canteen. It had the run of the pub and was the only known living thing which could drink two quarts of beer at a draught.

From Pietermaritzburg, the road to the interior followed the old wagon track blazed by the Voortrekkers. First of all came the long, hard pull up the slopes of the town hill (Zwartkop) and over World's View to the heights, 2500 feet above the level of Pietermaritzburg. This hill was a notorious pull for oxen and the abakwaMpumuza tribe, living on its slopes under the well-known chief Teteluku, who died in June 1899, were often called out to help heave a struggling wagon onwards.

In the early days of Natal all roads were atrocious. Hardly anything was ever done to them – except damage. Rain turned them into ribbons of mud; bridges were non-existent; and years had to pass before the scars, left on the landscape by the wheels of the wagons, were healed over with a hard scab of macadamised surface.

The inns were like the roads. In parts they were fair, but mostly they were bad; and at first there were so few on the road to the interior that the government was forced to turn host itself. A chain of straw huts was erected along the roadside at the Mngeni ford, Stinkhoutrand, Bushman's River, Bloukrans River, Little Thukela, Great Thukela and Venterspruit. These huts were left under the care of African headmen, who had orders to accommodate wayfarers and sell them milk, eggs and fowls.

Four miles from Pietermaritzburg, a small hostelry named the Travellers' Rest, run in 1875 by a man named Jones, provided travellers with a stopping place during the steep pull. The first outspan proper, however, was the well-known Kettlefontein (called kwaKhehlelifantini by the Africans) on the farm Groenkloof.

The old name has nowadays been forgotten as a popular landmark. The district itself, one of the fairest in all Natal, is known rather from the presence of the renowned Hilton College, which today stands there as one of South Africa's best-known schools.

In the days of the old transport riders there was of course no such place as Hilton College. It was only in 1860 that Gould Arthur Lucas, one-time officer in the British garrison and subsequently in the Natal magisterial service, purchased a portion of the farm originally known as Ongegund. This farm had been bought in 1853 by Joseph Henderson who had named it Hilton, doubtless after one of the several Hiltons in the British Isles. On his portion of this property, called Upper Hilton, Lucas intended to settle in his old age.

Then, at his magisterial post in Ladysmith, Lucas met the Reverend W.O. Newnham. The two men organised a village school in Ladysmith in 1868, but the venture did not flourish. Newnham disliked the climate, and the predominantly Dutch-speaking community was not keen on the English type of public school.

Accordingly, in January 1872, the school reopened for its

new term in a new home. Newnham removed the entire establishment from Ladysmith to Upper Hilton farm, which he considered climatically ideal and conveniently near a greater concentration of potential pupils. The old farmhouse, built in republican days, was converted into the school; and from this simple origin grew the great Hilton College of today.

Beyond the Hilton area, the road to the interior made its way through a pleasant land of undulating hills, richly grassed and watered, and so beautiful to the eye that many a transport rider felt his heart yearn for possession of those fertile acres.

Through this land there goes swirling, with many an eddy and a million reflections, the waters of the Mngeni. It is a land of waterfalls, for the Mngeni and its tributaries go tumbling down through gorges and precipices on their journey to the sea. Of these waterfalls there are innumerable stories. Like beautiful sirens, they have lured most travellers into at least a moment's admiring pause, while a surprising number have given their lives to the call of the waters.

In former times the road forded the Mngeni across the flat ledge of rock immediately above the fall known to the Africans as kwaNogqaza. This waterfall, actually 305 feet high, although usually claimed to be 60 feet higher as a result of an early misprint in survey figures, had an evil reputation from the very beginning because of the number of human beings carried over its brink. Innumerable Africans in past years, and 17 recorded individuals in recent times, have been killed by this sinister waterfall.

The area around the waterfall was first settled upon as a home by the well-known Wesleyan missionary, James Archbell. On 2 April 1849 he secured three magnificent farms in the shape of Oatlands, Woodlands and Stocklands, and his personal enthusiasm for the scene of his retirement attracted many fellow members of his church to settle in Natal.

The main ford across the Mngeni in republican days was known as Allemans, but by 1850 the route had been altered slightly to the more convenient, if far more dangerous, ford immediately above the waterfall. This spot became increasingly important as the road to the interior developed into an arterial highway. The government, accordingly, following the advice of their 1847 commission, obtained from Archbell a portion of his farm as a site for a village.

This village was named Howick, after the Northumberland home of Earl Grey, the British Colonial Secretary of that time. On 23 November 1850, erven were put up for sale and there was a brisk demand. All the erven were sold, for the site was good and the village promised to become a place of some consequence on the main highway.

There was already one inhabitant in Howick before the sale, and the place was well known long before the village was ever started. Charles Barter, who travelled along the road to the interior in October 1851 has left us a description of the place.

It was, he said, "a favourite resort of the pleasure seekers of Maritzburg, who disturb the solitude with noisy picnic parties, and help to fill the pockets of Old Lodge, a quondam ship's purser, who keeps a small house of entertainment on the bank, and a punt for crossing the river in times of flood. For this last office he is paid by the government, whose servants he is bound to ferry over in case of need."

Lodge, in his way, was quite an unhappy figure, for one of the first recorded tragedies of Howick Falls concerned his own son. On 16 January 1851, a farmer had arrived at the fording place. The river was in flood, but he needed to cross over to the other side.

Lodge rowed the farmer safely across in his ferry boat, while the man's two horses were given to a coloured servant and Lodge's own 12-year-old son to ride across the river. The coloured man crossed safely, but the horse young Lodge was riding lost its footing near the middle of the river.

The current rolled the animal over and over, while the boy held on to its mane. About three feet from the brink of the fall the boy lost his hold. The horse managed to save itself and got ashore, but the boy was carried over the falls. For many years afterwards the cairn of stones which marked his grave at the foot of the waterfall was an object of interest to travellers, and the story of his death was told around many a campfire on the highway to the north.

Lodge himself did not remain in Howick. A certain George Holgate, who had bought property at the first village sale, replaced him as ferryman and district postmaster. He and a Mr Dicks were for long the sole residents of the place.

The slow growth of the village was little to the liking of Mr Holgate. On 7 March 1857, he memorialised the government with a plaintive protest. "More than six years have elapsed," he wrote, "since these promising circumstances (siuation [*sic*], government promises of water and a bridge) induced memorialist and his neighbour, Mr Dicks, to settle at Howick. Yet the village is still unsupplied with water. There is no bridge over the river, the traffic is rapidly on the decline and there is no chance of any additional inhabitants. If the erven were now brought into the market by the unlucky proprietors, memorialist is of opinion there would scarcely be a bid for them." Mr Holgate, in short, considered he had been *had*.

Nevertheless, despite Holgate's pessimism, Howick did grow. In 1869 when Thomas Baines passed that way, he found it to be a pretty township "with its neat, substantial little church, its inn and other houses showing here and there through the dark foliage of tall Australian gum trees".

The ford still had an evil reputation. The first bridge built across it had been washed away, and although most travellers paused to see the falls, they usually did so with a shudder. "A somewhat melancholy interest attaches to these falls," wrote Baines, "for, owing to the proximity of the drift, and its occasional dangerous condition, persons who once miss their footing have little opportunity of recovering it and none of swimming out, before they are at the verge of the falls. Several have been swept over within the last few years."

The increase in traffic along the road, consequent upon the discovery of diamonds and gold in the north, brought further victims to the waterfall. One of the most famous accidents occurred on 12 March 1870. A Dutch farmer was fording the river in a wagon. The river was in flood but, even though the ferryman had his red danger flag flying, the farmer persisted in attempting a passage.

The oxen soon found themselves out of their depth. Down the river they were carried, dragging the wagon after them. Fortunately, an outstanding rock halted them just at the edge. The waterfall, however, was not to be denied its victim entirely. An African wagon-boy lost his nerve and tried to jump for the shore. He slipped, fell into the river, and was carried over the fall. The farmer watched him vanish, stoically shouted: "Trek!" to the floundering team, and managed to draw his wagon out to safety.

Stories such as this spread the fame of Howick far and wide. Visitors flocked there from all over and it became a favourite holiday resort. By 1877 Lady Barker could write: "Howick appears to be all hotel, for two have already been built and a third is in progress. A small store and a pretty wee church are all the other component parts of the place."

The waterfall, of course, remained the principal pride of the place, but the atmosphere as well was a pleasant change in summer from the sultry heat of the coast. "It is certainly an enchanting change from Pietermaritzburg," went on Lady Barker, "were it not for the road which lies between – at least it is not a road at all. What is the antithesis of a road, I wonder – the opposite of a road? That is what the intervening space should be called."

Every few years some fresh tragedy gave the waterfall additional renown. On 20 January 1881 a transport rider named Mathew Whitridge dined too well in one of the Howick inns. Returning across the river to his wagon late at night, he was carried over the falls and killed.

Ten years later, on 31 January 1891 while a party of military were encamped at Howick, a sentry, Driver Burn of the Royal Artillery, disappeared from his post at night. His body was subsequently found at the foot of the waterfall.

Ten years later, on 8 August 1901, a carpenter named Joe Hudson tried to wade across the river just above the falls. He was carried over and killed. By that time, of course, there was a bridge over the river. It was a cumbersome wooden affair, built in the 1870s and generally expected to wash away in every flood since then. A new and stylish three-span bridge was opened on 7 November 1903 by Sir Henry McCallum, the Governor; but even this failed to save people from the lure of the waterfall and two weeks later there occurred one of the best known of all Howick's tragedies.

On 24 November 1903 an unfortunate Indian woman, while washing clothes in the river, was carried over the waterfall. The body struck a projecting ledge of the face of the fall, about 80 feet down. From there it bounced to another ledge, 150 feet from the summit and about 10 feet to the left, clear of the main body of water.

On this second ledge the body lay, plainly visible and apparently quite irrecoverable from above or below. All manner of schemes were advocated for its removal, from dynamite to a round of artillery fire, but none seemed likely to succeed.

Then Gunner Mapleson of the 78th Battery, in camp at Howick, volunteered to do the job. He had formerly been a steeplejack and his plan was to have himself lowered on a plank seat, covered with a roof to protect him from the water. A derrick was constructed and after a couple of trial attempts, with a sack as passenger, Mapleson was at last lowered down.

It was a hazardous venture. Falling rocks, projecting ledges, precariously growing trees and the force of the water all combined to shake the plank cage severely. Eventually, the cage, half obscured by spray, stopped on a sloping mound above the ledge where the body lay. Mapleson scrambled to the body, fixed a spare rope to it and then to the relief of the 300 spectators, was hauled safely up again. The body was brought up immediately afterwards.

All these tragedies had so far been accidental but, on 27 October 1906, James Kerr made the discovery that the waterfall had possibilities as a means of committing suicide. He threw himself over the top and thus started a particularly unhappy sequence of events.

A whole series of suicides took place at Howick. One of them, on 4 June 1937 provided a similar problem to the death of the Indian woman. A schoolmaster named James Bell jumped to his death and his body was also caught on a ledge, 140 feet down. A member of the Maritzburg Fire Brigade had to be lowered to retrieve the corpse.

Another celebrated accident occurred in November 1940. As a result of reading a newspaper account of an imaginary dive over the falls, a young student named Charles Booker decided to emulate the feat. Egged on by the bets of irresponsible friends, he dived and was killed. Divers were used in an effort to recover the body, but they had difficulty in operating in the obscurity of the brown Mngeni waters. Sharp rocks obstructed them and giant eels twisted past in the gloom 30 feet down. All they found were some old wagon wheels originally rolled over the falls as a protest against injustice by a group of disgruntled blacksmiths' apprentices who had gone on strike. The body floated to the surface of its own accord some time later.

So the sorry tale of Howick Falls continued. On 18 August 1941, Beryl Jordan, a young Pietermaritzburg girl, jumped to her death. Five years later, on 30 May 1946, a student named E.M. Valey attempted to climb the precipice beside the fall. He fell and died of his injuries three days later.

The following year, on 25 February 1947, an electrician named Joseph Walsh was swimming in the river. He was carried over the falls and killed. Then, on 4 December of the same year another Pietermaritzburg girl, Margaret Lister, took a taxi to the falls and jumped to her death. In 1951 an Indian girl also committed suicide there while, on 15 February 1952, the body of an Indian known as Passing Show was found at the foot of the fall. A gang of drug-runners and burglars was accused of throwing him over, as he had threatened to expose them. After a sensational trial two members of the gang, Brian Duncan and Puther Khan, were convicted and sentenced to death on 17 October 1952. On 26 January 1954 Cecil Hosking, a Maritzburg plumber, threw himself over the falls, and on 24 March 1958

Mrs Doris Reed committed suicide in the same way, while on 17 April 1965 the body of Raymond Borain, a welder who had been ill for some time, was found in the pool below the falls.

Howick is not the only waterfall in what is really a land of waterfalls. The village of Howick, in fact, like a proud father, sits beside the highway and boasts to passing traffic of no less than four beautiful waterfall daughters. Each of them is widely different in mood but each of them, in some strange way, is tainted with tragedy.

Cascade Falls is the smallest of the quartet. It is a tumbling rush of water, cascading down 83 feet to a rippling little pool. A friendly, playful sort of waterfall, Cascade can also be treacherous. About 1944 a young man, John Taute, tried to climb down it. He fell, struck a ledge and eventually died of his injuries.

Cascade Falls occurs in a tributary of the Mngeni known as iGobongo (the hollow thing). After tumbling down Cascade it races on, increasing in size as it travels and then, like a white phantom, it forms the 123-feet-high Shelter Falls. Shelter Falls is an adolescent beauty, with the dreamy, self-centred detachment of its age and type. Like its sisters, it too has claimed its victims. On 19 April 1897 a girl, Mary Fynn, daughter of the pioneer, Henry Francis Fynn, tried to climb a rock in order to carve her initials. She slipped and fell into the pool at the foot of the fall. A male member of her picnic party, Alfred Kinsey, from Port Shepstone, dived in to rescue her. Both were drowned.

The siren Howick Falls is the third in the quartet of waterfalls, whose eldest member is a comely, 343-foot-high matron known as Karkloof Falls. Karkloof has a small infant waterfall, about 30 feet high, just above it. This infant, it seems, had inherited all the qualities of its seniors. About 1885 a farmer named William Woodhouse was fording the river above the small fall. His horse tripped and threw him. The horse scrambled out, but the man was washed over the fall, which thenceforth was known as Woodhouse Fall, in memory of the tragedy.

Karkloof Falls has also claimed its victim. In September 1938 three young men tried to climb the precipice to the right of the actual fall. They were almost at the top when one Dean Griffiths put his hand on a loose rock. He fell and was killed instantly.

The river and range of hills known as Karkloof took their name from the long, steep valley through which the road from Howick climbed towards the interior. About 1845, as the story goes, a Dutch farmer was travelling along the road in a heavily laden Cape cart. As he crossed the valley, his horses took fright, swerved and overturned the cart. Nobody was hurt, but the wreck of the cart remained for years as a landmark and gave the name Karkloof (the valley of the cart) to the place. The entire district between Howick and the Mooi River became known as the Karkloof district, and it has always been a beautiful area in the green setting of the sweeping midlands of Natal.

Many people settled in this pleasant land. One of the most interesting was John Goodman Household, the son of an 1850 British settler. In the early 1870s, Household conceived a desire to fly. Roaming among the hills of his beautiful homeland, he watched the birds gliding over the valleys, the eagles soaring on the updraughts, the rock pigeons and the swallows so evidently thrilling to that last sweeping flight, done just for the love of it in the cool before sunset.

Household shot a vulture, carefully measured its wingspan and, in relation to the bird's weight, worked out the proportions of a glider to carry him. Working with bamboo, a few steel tubes, oiled silk and paper, Household completed his first glider about 1871. The pilot's seat of this contrivance, like a swing, was suspended from the wing on four ropes.

This first glider refused to fly. Household thereupon built a second glider. With this contrivance completed, the pilot and his brother, Archer, assisted by some Zulus, trundled it one moonlit night to the top of a ravine. Everything had to be done in secret, for fear of public ridicule and parental displeasure.

After much effort the glider was at last launched from the

cliff edge and away into the evening shadows soared the intrepid Household, skimming the tops of trees, climbing to nearly 300 feet, crossing the valley, three-quarters of a mile wide, and then attempting a landing on the far side.

Unfortunately, the controls of the glider were crude, it sideslipped, stalled and crashed into a tree top. Household was catapulted out into a pool of water and broke his leg. The glider was wrecked and while the unfortunate pilot was confined to bed, the heap of twisted metal and fabric was dumped in a loft. Household's parents saw to it that he never repaired it and after a while the historic glider was thrown on to a garbage heap and forgotten. Thus ended what was almost certainly man's earliest attempt to fly in Southern Africa.

Apart from the Households, other settlers in the Karkloof area were the Shaws, Barters, Trotters, Proudfoots, Parkinsons and, of course, several families from republican times. George Curry, a retired sergeant-major from the British garrison, was a well-known settler who has left his personal name as a place name. He established a staging post on the road to the north at Houtbosrand. This hostelry, known as Curry's Post, became the first centre of the district. Three repair shops were erected there, two hotels for travellers, and a blacksmith's shop for wagons. A couple of stores were also established, and in its day Curry's Post was quite a busy spot, until the railway and a relocated road left it all alone in the countryside.

James Methley, who settled on the beautiful Shafton Grange farm, was another of the early settlers. He had met Captain Allen Gardiner in England and from him heard the fascinating story of the lost silver mines originally worked by the Lala people in the Thukela Valley. Methley spent much of his time searching for these mines, only to learn, in the end, of the miserable fate of the miners and the complete obliteration of all traces of their works.

John King was another man to settle in the Karkloof area. He arrived from Perthshire in Scotland in October 1849. He refused his original Byrne allotment and, after a six months' spell of work in Pietermaritzburg, he acquired from Petrus Potgieter a farm named Wilde Als Spruit. This farm King renamed Lynedoch and in May 1850 he and his family were taken up to the place in Potgieter's wagon and dumped down upon the veld.

King's brother-in-law, James Ellis, bought a neighbouring farm which he named Balgowan after the village in Scotland. The two families settled down to the task of building wattle-and-daub houses, while they lived in home-made tents. Both families were extremely Scottish, and it was a Natal joke that their African servants all learned English with a Scottish accent.

The whole area was still completely wild and undeveloped. An occasional elephant was still found in the Karkloof bush and the last lion in the district was not shot until about 1856, when an old male was killed in the deep gully of St Ives Hill, near Lions River.

It was on the farm Boschfontein, near Balgowan, that one development occurred of particularly pleasant consequences for Natal. In 1882, John C. Parker, of Tetworth farm north of Howick, wrote to the editor of *The Field*, asking for advice on the introduction of trout. Sir James Maitland, of Howicktown Fishery, promptly replied with a present of 10 000 ova.

This first shipment sent to Tetworth farm was a failure. The following year, Maitland sent 10 000 more ova, but these also died. Interest had been aroused, however, and in 1889 Cecil Yonge, Legislative Council member for Pietermaritzburg, obtained a government grant of £500 for the introduction of trout and salmon to Natal.

A committee of three men – J.C. Parker, C.A.S. Yonge, and Lt Col H. Vaughan – was formed to manage the enterprise. The farm Boschfontein was selected as the hatchery. Hatching boxes and filters were erected. In March 1890, 30 000 ova were imported from Dumfries. Many of these ova hatched out successfully and in May 1890, the first 1500 fry were released in the Bushmans, Mngeni and Mooi rivers.

Each year after that more ova were imported, until most of the suitable rivers were stocked and many Natalians started to experience the quiet joys of wandering along the banks of a pleasant stream, and that special thrill which comes when the angler "touches" a big one and, with sportsman's tackle, fights him into the frying pan.

The lives the early farmers lived by the side of the original road to the interior were simple in the extreme. They were all friendly, homely people who enjoyed listening to one anothers' troubles and getting together occasionally for dinners, or for hunts which were notable more for bad shooting than anything else. Beyond that, there were only old newspapers to read, letters to write and anticipate, and occasional marketing visits to Pietermaritzburg to provide a break in monotony.

Everything was new. People were roughing it in all manner of shacks, sleeping on the floor if they could not build their own furniture, and learning by hard experience all the snags of farming in an area for which nobody even knew the best crop or type of livestock. New diseases puzzled them and conversations were concerned mainly with opinions on suitable crops and the causes of horse-sickness, scab in sheep, and suchlike.

Jackals and wild dogs were another problem, and all these farms were so situated that the Drakensberg watched them from the horizon like a line of gathering storm clouds, full of threats of Bushmen raids.

Beyond Curry's Post, the original road wound up to the top of the Karkloof. In 1875 Theodore Taylor had a small hotel there, sitting huddled in a bleak situation, swept by the Drakensberg winds and all alone in the night, the mists and the rain, with just a dim light peeping out into the darkness.

From there the road went on to the old farm of J.N. Boshoff, known as Mooi Rivier. Boshoff, a highly intelligent man who became President of the Orange Free State, had certainly picked a fine spot for his Natal home. It lay in one of the most fertile parts of Natal, and the ever-flowing river, with its miles of shady banks lined by green willows, fully justified its name of the Mooi (beautiful) River.

Where the road forded the river, John Whipp had an inn and store in the 1860s, and he it was who became the first inhabitant and human foundation stone of the future village. Beyond his store the road went on through the hills, around a bend; and then before it lay the valley of the Bushman's River, dotted with acacias and guarded by a small fort built upon a hill, first occupied at the end of December 1847.

On 16 December of that year, the government had announced its intention of establishing a seat of magistracy at the Bushman's River. On the strength of this announcement and stimulated by the presence of a garrison, the first inhabitant of the future village, a man named Flory, made all haste to settle in the place.

Charles Barter, who visited the place in October 1851, has described it and its first inhabitant. "On the further bank," he wrote, "was a solitary little cabin in which, however, the spirit of trade was actively at work, making for itself a fresh starting place from which to spread over the whole of this now desolate region.

"Here as spruce a shopkeeper as ever stood behind a London counter, with a large-eyed, theatrical-looking wife and one or two thumping babies, had established himself, and, monopolising the custom of the little garrison with that of chance travellers, was already doing a business which would be considered very decent in a country town in England."

Flory was not alone for long by the banks of the Bushman's River. Abram Nickson came and established a hotel; the inevitable blacksmith also arrived and a village grew up. By 1863 the place was important enough to deserve a name, and the earliest settlers met to choose one. B.J. Wilkes, Robert Ralfe, W.F. Moore and several others were at that meeting. After due discussion over a pot of beer, it was decided that they could do no better than name the place Estcourt, after Thomas Henry Estcourt, an English parliamentarian who had sponsored the immigration of many of the original settlers in the place.

By 1866 Estcourt consisted of twelve houses, with the original store, hotel and magistrate's office standing slightly apart, down by the wagon drift. The original magistrate still lorded it over the place. He was John MacFarlane, a great character, known as iNdaba ineSilevo (the law with a beard) to the Africans, on account of the colossal whiskers on his face. The flood of travellers who passed through Estcourt on their way to the diamond and goldfields all knew him as a most imposing figure. If gaols were the natural consequence of civilisation, then he at least gave the process of going to one a cloak of dignity.

Estcourt, like all the roadside villages, flourished on the backs of the passing traffic. The great rush to the Transvaal goldfields gave tremendous impetus to stores, hotels, blacksmiths and other tradesmen. By September 1876 Estcourt had 120 European inhabitants, eight stores, one church, one school, two doctors, three hotels, two canteens, three blacksmiths, three wagon-makers, one tailor, one lawyer and a selection of government officials.

The towns along the roadside were not content to allow all the excitement about gold to pass them by. Nearly all the roadside centres staged their own gold rushes at various times. Even sleepy little Howick thrilled with excitement once, when a local storekeeper named Hosking reported gold in the gorge at the foot of Howick Falls. Wagons raced off to Pietermaritzburg to secure prospectors' licences, and the farming community caught the fever. The whole gorge was soon smothered in claim pegs but, apart from providing fuel for subsequent fires, the pegging yielded nothing save mica fragments.

Mooi River also had its excitement in July 1852, when coal was reported on Boshoff's farm; but the greatest sensation was in Estcourt. In October 1886 some enterprising soul claimed to have found gold on the town lands. Estcourt went wild with excitement. Claim pegs were so thick and tempers so heated that there was danger of a conflagration, until disappointment caused the whole thing to fizzle out like a veld fire in the rain.

The town settled back to its habitual way of making a living: serving the farmers and travellers. People who found the monotony beyond them simply stepped into the passing stream and were carried away. Edwin Woods, one of the first storemen, was one of these. He packed up not only his goods but his double-storied corrugated-iron shop as well and carted the whole affair up to Johannesburg, where it became Dickinson & Woolf's Haberdashery Store.

Beyond Estcourt, the road to the interior went on to the Bloukrans River, where a Scotsman named MacDuling farmed, with a fat, comfortable Dutch wife and twelve children. The first staging post proper on the road, however, was a total of four-and-a-half hours' ride from Estcourt, where the road forded the Thukela River at Commando Drift. About 1852, a trader named Vause settled at this place. He bought up the only farmhouse there, opened a shop and named the place Colenso, in honour of the opinionated Bishop of Natal. Three years later erven were sold to the public and on 19 May the place was proclaimed a town. The Africans, in their fashion, gave the place a different name: eSkipeni (the place of the boat), because of the ferryboat stationed there.

At this place in 1871, there stood the British Hotel, run by Captain Dickinson, "the most gentlemanly landlord on the road," and a village of a dozen or so houses and businesses had grown up to supply the travellers delayed there by the river. The first bridge, the Bulwer Bridge, was opened only in October 1879.

By this time, travellers to the interior had made up their minds whether they were bound for the Transvaal or the Free State. If the latter was their destination, they branched off to the north-west and made their way towards the purple wall of the Drakensberg. These last miles of the journey through Natal led through a land but sparsely populated. Only old, ruined stone huts and cattle kraals spoke of a former African population, in times before Shaka and his raids.

Few Europeans had settled in this area. John Coventry, with his four strong sons, made his home there in 1869 and named the district Acton Homes, after his original home at Iron Acton, near Bristol; but there were few others.

One celebrated inn, however, was also built beside the highway on this last stage to the Drakensberg. This establishment, run by a host named Dodd, was named the Dew Drop Inn. Thomas Baines, who stayed there in 1869, has described the place. It had, he said, "a name which the reader will see conveys also an invitation to the passer-by, the host having rather a varied talent in the line of catchword advertisements.

"Mr Dodd had a young baboon, tame enough to drink beer for the entertainment of visitors, of course out of *their* glasses. His walls were hung with about a dozen chromo-lithographs, and some old oil paintings not by any means second-rate, and decidedly not first. These had cost him, if I remember rightly, £470; and I offered to stay a fortnight and paint him a dozen more for the same amount, but soon found, as indeed I had guessed from the first, that his picture gallery was all he had been able to get from a bad debt."

After the Dew Drop Inn came the Tent Hotel, at the very foot of the Drakensberg. From there the road wound upwards for 2000 feet, the whole zigzag course of the mountain pass being made more apparent by the white-covered wagons scattered along it.

The pass the road followed to reach the Free State was not one which the Voortrekkers had used. In 1856, when the Natal Government first built a proper road pass over the Drakensberg, it was constructed along a route suggested to them by Frans van Reenen, a former Cape Town man who had settled on Sandspruit farm at the foot of the pass. The pass he discovered, relocated slightly in 1926, has remained the principal route to the Orange Free State ever since.

From its summit, the travellers to the interior could pause to rest their weary oxen and look down for a little while on the fair land of Natal, stretched out like a vision beneath them. To most, this stupendous view was simply something at which to marvel. Others, more perspicacious, were wont to wonder at the past and future of the land, remembering its climate and delightful scenes, the kindness of its settlers, the simple problems of their lives, and the way the road had wound and climbed and twisted through a land of ten thousand hills.

TWENTY-FOUR

Clouds on the horizon

Mpande, in his old age, was much beloved by his people. Although Cetshwayo was generally acknowledged as the real power in Zululand, nominal obedience and immense respect were accorded to the old king from everybody, including his impetuous son.

Mpande was a fat old fellow in the last months of his reign. He was very fond of gossip and enjoyed the visits of European traders. "He enquired about all the doings and wonders of the white man," Leslie wrote, describing an interview, "and after about half-an-hour's talk, gradually dozed off to sleep, when I left him to enjoy his siesta.

"The old King is wheeled about in a little wagon. He never walks, although I am inclined to think he might do so; but I should not like to *lay the odds* on his ability, as, from his enormous obesity, it would be rather a difficult matter at the best to carry the Habeas Corpus Act into operation with him."

So Mpande went his way in his bumpy little wagon, while his people kow-towed and ran in front removing stones and sticks, and crying out the praises of their king. He died peacefully on 18 October 1872, one of the very few of Senzangakhona's famous children to have the comfort of dying both a natural death and one which was generally lamented by everyone who knew him.

Mpande was buried in the traditional royal manner. He

366

was wrapped in an ox-hide and seated in a special tomb excavated at the head of the cattle fold at Nodwengu kraal. His two personal attendants and the two youngest of his wives were strangled and buried with him for company. The tomb was then closed in with slabs of stone and piled with earth. Cattle were slaughtered in sacrifice. Guards then watched over the tomb until two expected signs were seen – a little snake and then a big snake – to denote that Mpande's spirit was contented.

The period of mourning then ended and the time of the *Nqina Yehlambo* (the cleansing hunt) arrived, when the warriors had to wash their spears in blood. The bush of Zululand was well ransacked for game. Countless antelope and other animals were slaughtered, but the Thulwana regiment found more than it bargained for. In the bush, at the junction of the two Mfolozi rivers, a great hunting ground of that time, the warriors flushed a black rhinoceros which was a renowned specimen of its kind.

This rhino was known to have killed three women some time back. Now the warriors went against him for vengeance. He didn't have to be provoked for long. He came hurtling out of the bush like a battering ram. There was a hectic fight. After 20 minutes the rhino was dead with some one thousand spears in his hide. On the ground around him lay four of his attackers killed and 20 more wounded.

After his long wait Cetshwayo was at last able to enter into his own. His Zulus, after 32 years of peace, were prosperous and numerous and famed as the greatest Bantu tribe in Southern Africa. Cetshwayo was both conscious and proud of this fact and in exchange his people took him to their hearts, for he was a man possessed of all the strength and intelligence which they expected from their king.

The coronation was the occasion of an immense spectacle. In August 1873 Cetshwayo, with his followers, set out from his kraal of eSiqhwagini on the Mlalazi River. He made his way in a royal promenade over the hills and valleys, towards the kraals in the centre of Zululand. The whole nation mustered to greet him. All along the way groups of plumed warriors and gaily bedecked women rallied to his party until it swelled into a mighty concourse.

John Dunn was much in evidence as Cetshwayo's confidant. He was in charge of Cetshwayo's carriage and drove it with great skill all the way, although Cetshwayo preferred to walk the distance in the midst of his people.

As the party travelled it hunted. The whole length of the mighty Mhlathuze valley was systematically beaten. Each of its great forests, such as the Mandawe, the Lukholo and the Ludukaneni (place where you get lost) was ransacked for game, and at night the whole valley was alive with campfires and merriment and feasting on venison.

The first big camping spot was at Mkhindini. From there the concourse shifted to the Mthonjaneni ridge where it was arranged that the northern Zulus would rendezvous with Cetshwayo. From there the party removed to Makheni. The Zulus were divided into three great groups. Cetshwayo and his followers from the south formed one group. The followers of the northern chiefs Hhamu and Mnyamana formed a second group, while the renowned fighting chief Zibebu headed the largest party of all.

An enormous human circle was formed and there was a steady firing off of blank cartridges, a good few individuals getting burnt in the press when guns were fired off too close together.

Nobody knew quite what to do, for there was no precedent to follow in the matter. A ceremony of sorts, however, took place in the centre of the circle. Masiphula, Mpande's old Prime Minister, crowned Cetshwayo, and then a spectacular session of dancing, feasting and flirting with the girls took place. For three days the people celebrated and indulged in a feast of national hysteria.

Cetshwayo had sent a message to Natal, asking the government to send representatives to his coronation. He expected

Theophilus Shepstone, the Native Administrator, to come and in the delay he withdrew to the kraal known as the Mlambongwenya (crocodile river) kraal near the drift over the Ntukwini river. There the Zulus completed their feasting and then started to disperse.

Eventually Shepstone arrived, with an impressive entourage consisting of such well-known individuals as the explorer Thomas Baines and Lewis Reynolds, the sugar planter. A sizeable escort of soldiers accompanied the party.

Shepstone pitched his camp about three miles from the kraal and Cetshwayo walked over to see him. They held a long conference in Shepstone's tent while their two praise-singers tried to outdo each other in bawling out praises in front of the tent until they very nearly came to blows.

Inside the tent several matters were discussed. The Zulus had many complaints about Boer boundary encroachments, relations with Natal and the activity of the missionaries in Zululand. Cetshwayo was not in favour of the religious. He admitted that the missionaries were good men but considered that their doctrines were for white men only. "A Christian Zulu is a Zulu spoiled," he said, and he would be glad if the missionaries all left the country. He had many objections to them; one was the habit the missionaries had of insisting (on what biblical directive he knew not) that all converts throw off Zulu costume and dress themselves up in some European's cast-off trousers, thus converting themselves from well-appointed individuals in attire nobody need be ashamed of into something a cross between a dilapidated tramp and a clown.

Eventually Cetshwayo agreed that those missionaries in the country could remain, but he wanted no more. He requested a close alliance with the British and then Shepstone raised the matter which interested him most, facilities for native labour recruitment in Tongaland. The Zulus would have nothing to do with labour on the Natal sugar plantations, but the Tongas were keen workers. After some discussion Cetshwayo agreed to the appointment of John Dunn as labour agent for Tongaland at a salary of £250 a year.

The next day, Monday, 1 September 1873, Shepstone crowned Cetshwayo. A large marquee was pitched, and decorated inside with blankets, shawls and the various presents Shepstone had brought to Cetshwayo from the government.

Outside this tent Shepstone spoke to the grandees of the Zulu nation and such commoners as were still present. He proclaimed that there should be no more indiscriminate bloodshedding and that there should be no condemnation without open trial. Only the king was to have the power of death.

Cetshwayo was then led into the tent and dressed up in a scarlet mantle and head-dress. A throne was erected for him outside and to the accompaniment of a 17-gun salute from the artillery and a rousing medley from the army band he was proclaimed king by Shepstone.

The next day there was a final meeting and then Shepstone left. He had been much impressed by Cetshwayo. "Cetshwayo is a man of considerable ability," wrote Shepstone in his report. "He has much force of character, and has a dignified manner; in all my conversations with him he was remarkably frank and straightforward, and he ranks in every respect far above any native chief I have ever had to do with."

In this auspicious manner Cetshwayo became king. The whole ceremony had gone extremely well. The only incident had occurred when a grass fire had swept into the camp. In the confusion sundry individuals indulged in a spot of looting. One petty headman stole a case of two dozen bottles of chlorodyne in mistake for gin.

Back at home this individual experimentally dosed his wives with some of the liquid to see if it would make them gay or sad. It made *him* sad. When they fell sick he was discovered and Cetshwayo had him put to death as the first person to suffer that extreme penalty in the new reign.

Cetshwayo settled down to his new responsibilities. His first task was to erect a new capital for himself. This was sited close to Mpande's old Nodwengu kraal in the Mahlabathini basin, and on completion it was named uluNdi or oNdini (the heights), the name by which the Zulus know the Drakensberg range.

While Ulundi (as it came to be known to Europeans) was being constructed, Cetshwayo took stock of the royal cattle. For a week some 100 000 head of cattle were herded before him and redistributed among his own military kraals. This giant cattle show had unfortunate results. Lung-sickness spread among the cattle from a few infected specimens, and within two years almost half of them died.

Many thousands of cattle were also traded to gunrunners, for Cetshwayo was keen on his Zulus being well armed, and there were many Europeans in Natal and Portuguese East Africa who were prepared to supply him with anything he needed. The Natal authorities did their best to control this traffic, and such offenders as could be caught, such as John Mullins on 16 October 1878, were given six months' gaol time and a fine of £100.

Sodwana Bay was a favourite gunrunners' landing point. The local Tongas were always impressed into carrying the cargoes into Zululand, and as payment for labour was generally overlooked, they naturally disliked it. When they became somewhat refractory over the matter, Zibebu was sent there with an army, and they were knocked about a bit to bring them, if not to reason, at least to docility. In the process of this operation a small section of the Zulus was caught in a bog and knocked about slightly itself by some Tonga spear and rock throwers.

The guns the Zulus acquired were turned to immediate effect against the game-animal world, or such remnants of it as still existed after the onslaught of the Europeans. Cetshwayo made some effort at preventing the final destruction of elephant and buffalo by issuing an edict proclaiming them royal game, but by this time there were precious few left to protect, and his Zulus had to have some target for their lethal sports.

Shortly after his coronation, Cetshwayo wanted to release the pent-up spirits of his warriors by allowing them to raid

Swaziland. John Dunn wrote a letter for him to the British asking for permission. Shepstone, however, on 22 October 1874, replied with an official refusal. The only campaign which Cetshwayo launched in the years after his coronation was a minor affair conducted on the quiet against Sambane and his people on top of the Lubombo and intended as a rebuke for the murder of Dingane. Sambane hid in the bush and suffered little damage.

One vicious fight flared up among Cetshwayo's own followers. Shortly after his accession, Cetshwayo granted permission to girls to marry men of two of his regiments, the inDlondlo (the vipers) and uDloko (the fierce men), aged between 37 and 40 years. These middle-aged bachelors had to find wives from girls of the inGcugce (the deprivers) age group, and a complication immediately arose. The girls had been waiting so long that most of them had already given their hearts to men younger than the regiments allocated to them.

A stream of complaints poured in to the king. He resolved to be firm in the matter. The nation had to be shown that his word was law. In 1876 he gave an order that all inGcugce girls unmarried or married to men younger than the regiments allocated to them were to be killed and the property of their parents confiscated.

There was a certain amount of changing of affections. Instead of men searching for wives, Zululand was covered with girls frantically rummaging the country in search of middle-aged husbands. At the end of the allotted time about ten girls were killed, but the rest had either become wedded, fled the country with their lovers or, in the case of a few, committed suicide.

There was an unfortunate sequel to this affair. At the time of the ceremony of the first fruits, at the end of 1878, two years after the memorable "Marriage of the InGcugce", the long, simmering ill-feeling between the disappointed young lovers and the older men who had got the last laugh, and the girls, came to a head.

Dunn and Cetshwayo were sitting at Nodwengu kraal

watching the regiments performing their part of the ceremony, when Dunn noticed a scrimmage taking place at uluNdi,
about one-and-a-half miles away. The young men of the newly
enrolled inGobamakhosi (the tamers of chiefs) regiment had
attacked the older Thulwana regiment of headringed (married) men who had compassionately married some of the girls
from the inGcugce.

Cetshwayo attempted to stop the fight, but the jealous
young men were beyond control. Every headringed man
who came near them was attacked. The centre of the fight
took place at Dunn's camp. When he returned to it at night he
found the place a shambles. It was draped with corpses, and
his tents, clothing and food were sprayed with blood. About
seventy men were killed in the fight, and the hyenas had a rich
feast that night.

Above this Zulu pattern of life, with its storms in a beer-
pot, the clouds were steadily blowing up over the boundaries
– and troubled boundaries they were. Ever since Cetshwayo
had promised to give the Boers land east of the Blood River in
return for the surrender of his brothers there had been a simmering dispute.

The Zulus had sent a stream of protests to the British about
Boer boundary encroachments. In 1870 the British agreed to
arbitrate in the matter, but political changes prevented it. Then,
on 25 May 1875, the Republic proclaimed the disputed area as
being definitely its territory. A commission was appointed to
register land claims in the territory and to throw out the 15 000
Zulus who lived there.

Cetshwayo was enraged. He instructed his Zulus to tear
down the Boer beacons, and on 3 April 1876 he instructed
Dunn to write a letter to the British denying the entire Boer
land claim. Shepstone was at first sympathetic to the Zulu version, but after his ill-conceived annexation of the Transvaal, he
found it politic to change his opinion in order "to protect a civilised settlement against a brutal invasion of established rights".

This double-crossing worked Cetshwayo up to fever heat.
There was much sabre-rattling on both sides of the frontier.

Eventually, in February 1878, the Lieutenant Governor of Natal, Sir Henry Bulwer, suggested a commission of arbitration. This suggestion being agreeable to all sides, the Attorney General of Natal, Michael Gallway; the Secretary for Native Affairs, J.W. Shepstone; and Colonel A.W. Durnford settled down to examine the mass of claims, intrigues, double-crossings and hard lying which form the ingredients of most boundary quarrels.

Apart from this long-threatening boundary dispute, there was a rapid and alarming deterioration in the friendly relationship which had existed between Zululand and Natal for so many years. The principal cause of this deterioration was that demon of high politics which has been the troublemaker in most international quarrels and has invariably remained incomprehensible to the mass of people, obscured behind a veil of newspaper hysteria and deliberate propaganda.

The year 1878 was one of general wars between European and African. In the Transvaal the Pedi tribe of chief Sekhukhune was being subdued. In the Cape the Xhosas and their allies were making a last bid to challenge the power of Europeans. The British Government began to regard the Zulus, the strongest of the remaining independent tribes, as a fountainhead of these troubles. All other tribes in Southern Africa looked to them and their independence as an inspiration and were wont to indulge in wishful thinking by saying that the Zulus would help them in their struggles, or that the Zulus were going to throw all Europeans out and make all Africans free again.

Sir Bartle Frere, the British High Commissioner, had been sent to South Africa to promote confederation. Under him the miserable failure of the Transvaal annexation was forced through, and to him an independent Zululand was not only contrary to his hopes, but an actual threat to them. On the issue of furthering high politics he had long resolved to destroy Zulu independence. From him the British army in South Africa, through its commander-in-chief, General Thesiger, became infected with the idea that, as war with the Zulus was a possibility, it must, in professional soldiers' dictum, be prepared for as though it were a certainty. Accordingly, with the ending of the war in the Cape, troops were steadily concentrated in Natal and the messes were full of speculation and boasting by subalterns as to the chances of a tilt at the renowned Zulu power.

The Natal colonists themselves became confused. A fear of the Zulu power had always been present deep in their hearts, but they had got along well for so many years that they possessed no active animosity. The sugar planters were the only group to have any lurking desire for war. The prospect of a defeated Zululand was attactive to them as it held some hope of a new source of chronically scarce plantation labour. The independent Zulus had hitherto never been prepared to leave their homes for work in foreign parts.

Steady warmongering on the part of the politicians, their professional soldier servants and by the missionaries, however, gradually prepared general public opinion for future events.

The missionaries played an important part in this preparatory "cold war". Their efforts at converting the Zulus had not met with conspicuous success. After 27 years of labour the Norwegians had nine mission stations, with 100 Zulu converts. The English church had four stations, with about 20 converts, and the Hanoverians had five stations, with little other result for their efforts than an unpleasant reputation.

The whole Zulu national way of life was opposed to the form of Christianity advocated by the missionaries of that time. To the Zulu, a man owed sole allegiance to his king, and to nobody else. He was, in duty, bound to give military service and obey the slightest order, even if it led to death.

The few converts the missionaries made were suspect to the Zulu nation. The Zulus said that they were mainly criminals, runaway women, witches or other rascals who had found sanctuary with the missionaries as a way of avoiding their responsibilities and punishments.

Sensational stories in Natal newspapers, which Cetshwayo suspected were contributed by missionaries, also brought about mutual ill-feeling. These stories, mainly of Zulu atrocities, with the usual ingredients of slaughtered babes in arms, were mostly plain nonsense penned by individuals who knew not the fifth commandment.

Against this rising tide of propaganda there were very few voices raised in defence of the Zulus. Bishop Colenso made some attempt and pointed out the absurdity of the more extravagant press reports and the irresponsibility of those disgruntled individuals who claimed that the godless despotism of Cetshwayo must be overthrown by a recourse to war, as a prerequisite of Christianity.

But feelings became more and more inflamed. In 1877 rumours had grown that Cetshwayo intended killing all Christian converts. One convert was in fact killed near the Hanoverian station at Nyezane on the grounds of being a witch. A few days later another was killed at Eshowe. The rest took fright and bolted into Natal, leaving the missionaries high and dry with no congregation whatsoever.

For another year the missionaries stuck it out. Then they decided in conference to abandon the country, and by the beginning of May 1878 the whole crowd had removed into Natal, where they occupied themselves in writing a stream of complaints to the newspapers and the government.

The Boundary Commission, meanwhile, had struggled on towards a conclusion. Sir Bartle Frere and Theophilus Shepstone were both certain of the outcome before the commission even sat. Frere, in fact, regarded it as merely an opportunity "to clear up and put on record in a form calculated to satisfy Her Majesty's Government an answer to all doubts as to the facts and equity of the question."

Shepstone thought of it as merely a way of confirming the Transvaal claim on "evidence the most incontrovertible, overwhelming, and clear."

Some surprises were in store. The commission was an honest affair. "Probably we shall have much trouble in getting out the truth, but out it shall come," wrote Durnford in a letter to his mother. Hearings started at Rorke's Drift on 7 March 1878, and day after day the commissioners sifted evidence. Around their heads whistled a mass of influences and alarms, but they kept remarkably to the point.

On 2 April Durnford wrote to his mother: "You will hear that as all missionaries have left the country, it is war. All bosh! These missionaries are at the bottom of all evil. They want war so that we may take the Zulu country, and thus give them homes in a good and pleasant land. They have not been turned out. They came out of their own accord. The Zulus do not want them, and I for one cannot see why we should cram these men down their throats."

By 21 April the commission had completed its task, and in July its findings were submitted to the government. Months had to pass, however, before the findings were published.

Meanwhile, many influences for and against war wrestled for supremacy. John Dunn was doing his best to keep the air clear. After Cetshwayo's accession he had largely abandoned his carefree hunting life and settled down to the serious business of advising Cetshwayo and managing the recruitment and transportation of Tonga labourers to the sugar plantations, for which purpose he erected a chain of rest huts all the way from Tongaland to Natal.

Dunn had persuaded the Natal authorities to grant him two permits for the purchase of a total of 250 guns for Cetshwayo, on the grounds of reinforcing the authority of the king, and would have obtained more but for an outcry in the Natal press. The arming of the Zulus had then fallen to the lot of the gunrunners. Many people in Natal thenceforth regarded Dunn as being the principal culprit, although, apart from the two official purchases, there is no evidence of his ever having become involved in the unsavoury business of gunrunning.

Dunn did his best, by means of letters to the press, to the government and to the Aborigines Protection Society, to stave off the approaching war. He had a genuine affection for the Zulus and a great regard for their customs. He, of all Europeans, saw Zululand in the last days of its glory. He saw the last great harvest festival ever destined to be performed, and in 1877, when a severe drought reduced the country to hardship, he witnessed the rain-making magic of Cetshwayo.

He saw the black oxen Cetshwayo kept for these occasions sacrificed on the ancestral graves, while the army chanted its supplication. "Strange to say, they had not been gone an hour," wrote Dunn, "when, although there had been no sign of rain, the sky became overcast with heavy clouds, and as soon as they reached Mpande's grave and solemnly commenced the deep and impressive national chant, the rain began to descend, and continued for about a week. I was so much surprised at this that I wrote a letter to the *Colonist* stating the facts of the case, and saying that if a congregation of whites had prayed in church for rain and it had descended from God in answer to their prayers, the matter would have been alluded to as an additional illustration of the wonderful efficacy of prayer. If this holds good with one, why not with the other? They are both creatures of a Great Creator."

Against Dunn's good work several other contentions arose along the frontier. On 26 July 1878 two wives of the border chief, Sihayo, fled across the frontier into Natal with their lovers. One of Sihayo's sons, named Mehlokazulu, promptly led a party of about one hundred armed Zulus in pursuit. They captured the women, dragged them back across the river frontier and executed them.

This affair was regarded by Sir Bartle Frere as being most serious, although Cetshwayo declined to regard it as such. He considered it the act of a hot-headed youth seeking to avenge a cuckolded father. He offered to pay a fine of £50 instead of handing the culprits over, but Sir Bartle Frere simmered over it for some time.

A short while later a surveyor named Smith, accompanied by a trader named Deighton, was inspecting the road from Greytown down to the Thukela near Fort Buckingham. This road led straight to the river and was regarded most suspiciously by the Zulus, who considered it as being built by the military as a threat to themselves.

The surveyor and his companion got themselves on to an island in the river on what the Zulus considered to be their side of the boundary. A Zulu frontier guard thereupon arrested them. They were detained for about one-and-a-half hours and closely questioned as to the purpose of the new road. Then a Zulu officer arrived and the two Europeans were released. Much fuss was made about this episode in Natal.

As always, war fever was infectious. Additional British troops were sent to Natal, and news of their arrival alarmed the Zulus. They concentrated extra men on their frontier. The British, in turn, took alarm, and their troops were moved closer to the frontier to be ready to meet any invasion. Rumours were bandied across the Thukela like a tennis ball in a match.

Traitors started to plan treacheries and opportunists looked for chances of personal gain. One renegade Swazi prince named Mbilini, who had fled from his own country into Zululand some time back and had been a nuisance ever since, added to the general embarrassment by raiding into Swaziland, killing men and seizing women.

The result of these frontier affairs was the appearance of still more British troops. General Thesiger, just become Lord Chelmsford on the death of his father, busied himself in systematically collecting information on Zululand and drawing up a campaign.

Chelmsford's battle plan was based on the simultaneous invasion of Zululand by a number of separate columns, all converging on uluNdi. For this purpose roads were prepared and bases were constructed along the Thukela River. Early in November 1878 a fort was constructed at the Lower Thukela Drift, close to the ramshackle hotel maintained there by an old soldier named Smith.

A detachment of sailors landed from the HMS *Active* on 19 November and were sent up to garrison this fort by their Commodore, F.W. Sullivan. The fort was named Fort Pearson, after Colonel Pearson, and the sailors made themselves comfortable there with fowl coops and vegetable gardens.

Native levies were also raised in Natal to support the regular troops, and all preparations were completed. Meanwhile, the findings of the Boundary Commission had been kept a close secret. Some hint that its findings favoured the Zulus reached Cetshwayo, and he anticipated the publication by building a kraal in the disputed territory and another in the north at Luneberg. Fresh alarms among the Europeans in Natal followed these acts.

Then, at last, messengers were sent to Cetshwayo informing him that the findings of the Boundary Commission would be announced on 11 December 1878 at the Lower Thukela Drift. Three Zulu indunas were sent to the meeting, and Shepstone, in company with several government dignitaries, came to meet them.

The meeting was held under an awning spread beneath a large fig-tree just below Smith's hotel. First came the boundary award. It had been a most complete slap in the face to Sir Bartle Frere. Some of the findings, indeed, were startling. After wading through a mass of evidence, the commission had found that not only was the Boer claim to land east of the Blood River at fault, but in fact their ownership of the land west of the river was, far from being a grant, nothing more than permission to graze stock given to one Cornelius van Rooyen and five friends in 1854. These individuals had settled on the grazing rights, attracted others, built houses, claimed the land as their own, and established the Utrecht Republic.

Then, in June 1860, this Republic had formed a commission whose object was to regulate matters between them and the Zulus and, if possible, obtain more land. Both Cetshwayo and Mpande, at various times and for their own purposes – Cetshwayo for the surrender of the refugee princes, and Mpande for support against Cetshwayo – had promised to yield up land to this commission, but beyond these promises nothing definite had ever been completed. The Republic had never occupied the disputed area or had jurisdiction over its Zulu residents. Cetshwayo had welshed on his promise once the refugees had been handed over, and in any case the land was not his to give. Mpande had first promised, and then backed out when he patched up relations with Cetshwayo. All the Republic had as evidence of its claims was a variety of documents, signed by sundry Zulus, all making confused and vague promises of land, some day.

Sir Bartle Frere was hard-pressed by this finding, but he had to publish it. The disputed area east of the Blood River was recognised as belonging to the Zulus, although Europeans already resident there were to be allowed to remain under British protection. The land west of it, up to the Drakensberg, in view of its long occupation by Europeans and their establishment of a government there, without dispute by the Zulus, was henceforth to be regarded as indisputably under the Republic.

With this finding the frontier dispute as a cause of war fell away. Sir Bartle Frere, however, had an alternative up his sleeve. After Shepstone had read the award, the Zulus were presented with an ox, and everybody retired for lunch. Then, in the afternoon, a second gathering was held and the Zulus were presented with an ultimatum.

The ultimatum was a lengthy affair drawn up by Frere and based largely on misinformation and prejudice poured into his brain by high policy, alarmists, Zulu refugees and sundry disgruntled European missionaries, hunters, and would-be labour recruiters.

It stated in detail the various boundary quarrels and demanded the surrender of the Swazi renegade, Mbilini, for his raids across the Phongolo into Transvaal and Swazi territory. It detailed the raid into Natal by Sihayo's sons, and demanded their surrender and a fine of 500 head of cattle.

The ultimatum then complained that Cetshwayo's promises to Shepstone at the coronation had not been fulfilled. It demanded that fair trials be instituted and indiscriminate blood-shedding ended. It demanded that only the king have the power of the death sentence, and complained that all Zululand lived in fear on account of mass executions.

It struck at the very heart of the Zulu way of life by complaining of their military system. It demanded the abandonment of the traditional military system, whereby all young men were called up to serve the king for a number of years and could only adopt the headring and marry when he gave permission as a reward for service.

It complained that the existence of this army made all neighbours insecure. It demanded that the regiments be dispersed, the men allowed to marry when they pleased, and the army only mustered subject to British permission.

It demanded that all missionaries be allowed to return to Zululand, and that a British Resident be appointed to reside with the king and see that the ultimatum be properly carried out, and to supervise in any dispute between Zulus and Europeans. Thirty days were given to Cetshwayo to accept the ultimatum, which naively ended on the note that by its acceptance the king would have contented subjects.

This ultimatum made war inevitable, for no self-respecting nation could accept such blatant intervention in its domestic affairs without a fight.

The Zulu indunas listened to it in astonishment. "Have the Zulus complained?" asked one, when the ultimatum stated that the nation was suffering "so much hardship and so much misery" from the oppression of the military system. Another induna remarked that their nation surely had as much right to maintain an army as the British. They asked for an extension of the time limit by ten days, but this was refused.

The meeting broke up. That night the indunas slept at John Dunn's Mangethe residence, four miles from the Lower Drift. He was in a quandary about the whole matter. The Zulus were suspicious of him, for many looked upon him as a spy, and the young warriors were already shouting abuse at him.

Cetshwayo sent a message to him telling him to "stand on one side" if fighting came, but he was in a difficult position. He crossed the Thukela and saw Chelmsford. The general was disinterested in Dunn's protests that there was no need for war. He blithely underrated the Zulus, and his principal concern seemed to be to provoke hostilities. "The only thing I am afraid of is that I won't get Cetshwayo to fight," he told Dunn.

Dunn said: "Well, my lord, supposing you get to his kraal and he won't fight, what will you do?" Chelmsford answered: "I must drive him into a corner and make him fight." He advised Dunn to bring all his followers across the river, where they would be cared for.

Accordingly, on 30 December 1878, Dunn's followers collected at Mangethe. From there they went to the Thukela, and for two days Dunn struggled to get them and their livestock safely across a flooded river. On the other side they were disarmed and sent to a location between the Mvoti and Mhlali rivers, where they settled down as comfortably as possible in the face of much uncertainty. Because of this move the Zulus ever afterwards regarded Dunn and his followers as being traitors, while the Natalians, who had always regarded him as a renegade, retained their opinion of him. Dunn, poor man, had no alternative to the course he took. He had wished for neutrality, but Chelmsford had ordered him either to join the British forces on the Natal side or accept the consequences.

With Dunn's removal, the only European left in Zululand was a young Hollander named Cornelius Vijn, who was trading there. All the other European traders had fled the country, so he was doing particularly good business and was loath to leave. He traded until the last minute, and then, when things deteriorated, he asked Cetshwayo to protect him. With his goods he was placed in a kraal near uluNdi, and there he remained in safety through all the bitter months that followed.

The ultimatum, meanwhile, had been carried to Cetshwayo by word of mouth. There was much discussion over it in uluNdi. The Zulus were not disposed to listen to threats. They were not cowards, and if the British army was superior to theirs, it was a matter for trial. Frere had calculated that the idea of free marriage would cause the Zulus to desert their king. He thought they were unhappy under conscripted military service. This was a fallacy based on inaccurate information. The Zulu army was the cream of the country. To be in it was the test of manhood, and every youth dreamt of being enrolled, of serving his time honourably and of being distinguished in the end by the coveted reward for service – permission to marry and the consequent mark of the headring.

To ask Cetshwayo to end this ingrained system within 30 days would have been like asking the Victorian Britons to become nudists overnight. Cetshwayo in reply agreed to surrender Sihayo's sons and pay the various fines. He stated that Smith and Deighton had been arrested on an island on the Zulu side of the river, and in any case they had been quickly released. He asked for longer time to discuss the other demands with his people.

This request was refused. Everything was ready for war. Chelmsford had decided that three separate columns would invade Zululand. One, the right-hand column, was to operate from the Lower Thukela Drift under the command of Colonel Pearson, and a heavy pont was assembled at the drift and its hawsers fixed on both sides of the river on 6 January 1879.

A second column under Colonel Glyn was to invade Zululand from the drift where James "Jem" Rorke had originally run a store, which had lately been taken over by the Reverend Otto Witte on behalf of the Swedish mission. At this place, known as *kwaJim* to the Zulus, a barrel raft was made to supplement the existing pont.

A third or left-hand column under Colonel Wood was to invade Zululand from the north at the hill known as Bemba's Kop, from the chief of that name.

The right and left columns both mustered 2000 mixed troops. The centre column had 1600 European troops and 2500 native levies. Chelmsford planned that this column would strike the main blow and, from headquarters at Helpmekaar, he intended to accompany it on its raid to uluNdi.

So the days passed, with the troops waiting impatiently and watching the enigmatic Thukela River as it swept down to the sea. At dawn on Sunday, 12 January 1879, the invasion of Zululand began.

TWENTY-FIVE
Thunderclap

iSandlwana

Confronted by the British three-pronged invasion of Zululand, Cetshwayo and his advisers adopted a straightforward counterplan. Two holding forces were detailed to harry and delay the right and left British columns. The main Zulu army, about 14 000 strong, under the command of Ntshingwayo kaMahole Khoza, left the Nodwengu kraal, after praying at the grave of Mpande, on the afternoon of 17 January 1879, and headed straight for Lord Chelmsford's central column, which, their spies had rightly informed them, was the principal threat.

The British right column, in the meantime, had poured across the Lower Thukela Drift, with the boisterous Naval Brigade leading the way. On the opposite bank they erected a fort, which was named Fort Tenedos, after the HMS *Tenedos*, from which vessel many of the sailors had come.

Oxen pulled the pont across the river three times an hour, and by 15 January Colonel Pearson had sufficient men on the Zulu side to allow a reconnaisance for nine miles without sign of opposition.

Then, at dawn on 18 January, Pearson commenced his advance. He led his men without opposition to the *Nyezane* (place of willow trees), where they arrived at eight o'clock on the morning of 22 January. They were following the normal wagon route to the kwaMondi mission station. Before them

385

the track left the coastal plains and started to climb the green-blue hills of Zululand.

The troops settled down to breakfast. A few Zulu scouts were seen on the hills, and Pearson ordered his native contingent to drive them away. The contingent rushed up the hills willingly enough, but immediately encountered heavy rifle fire. They retreated hastily, losing five Europeans and three Natal natives in the process.

Pearson hastily drew his force up on a knoll. From its summit they discovered a mass of Zulus working around and trying to get at the long trains of supply wagons.

Shells and rockets were hurled at them; then the sailors charged with a will and a yell and drove the Zulus away. By 9.30 a.m. the fight was over. Ten men had been killed on the British side and sixteen wounded. The Zulus had lost about three hundred men.

From this battlefield the troops marched on the next morning, and without further opposition they reached the kwa-Mondi mission station at Eshowe. It was their intention to use it as a supply base for an advance on uluNdi.

The Eshowe mission was a pleasant place, sitting on the high hills and looking at the view. It consisted of a small church, parsonage, school and a few outhouses, all built of brick, with thatched roofs, and the whole hidden away among plantations of orange and gum trees. A gorgeous natural forest grew all around, while close to the church a streamlet babbled pleasantly to itself about such things as shade and coolness on a summer's day.

The whole establishment was precisely as the industrious Norwegians had left it. The soldiers threw up an entrenchment around it. With some reluctance they cut down such surrounding trees as could afford cover for the enemy, and distant outbuildings were blown up. It was not an ideal military site, but its buildings were invaluable as stores and hospital, and its geographical situation was excellent for Pearson's purpose.

The northern column, meanwhile, had left its camp on the Blood River at Bemba's Kop on 10 January and marched down the river. The column rummaged around the country for some days, without any sign of Zulus, and Colonel Wood met Lord Chelmsford close to Rorke's Drift.

The column then removed to the kraal of a petty chief named Thinta, who had surrendered, and there they built a fort named Fort Thinta, on the upper reaches of the White Mfolozi River. From this base they patrolled the surrounding countryside, seeing many Zulus but without precipitating an engagement.

The central column commenced its invasion at dawn on 11 January. In the teeth of mist and drizzly rain the troops were ferried across the Buffalo River, and by evening the whole force, with its impedimenta, was bivouacked in Zululand. For some days they busied themselves in rummaging about the country in search of cattle. They had one minor brush with Zulus in the Batshi valley, where they captured 413 head of cattle and killed 30 Zulus, with a loss of two of their native levies.

Then, on 17 January, Lord Chelmsford rode to an isolated hill which glowers over a rather bleak and windswept stretch of country a few miles from Rorke's Drift. Sandlwana was the name of this hill, a curious name for a curious hill, for it means literally "something like a small house", the name given to the second stomach of a cow, which it is said to resemble in appearance and shape.

Chelmsford selected the east side of this hill as a camping spot as it was the best available in the locality. On Monday, 20 January, the central column advanced to this place from Rorke's Drift. A snug enough camp was made in the shadow of the curious hill, and Chelmsford set out to examine the surrounding countryside, without sighting any Zulus. No effort was made to fortify the camp in any way. The wagons were all engaged on transport and a laager was considered unnecessary.

The entire surroundings of Sandlwana, although rugged, were completely bare of trees or any appearance of cover for a large body of men. The Zulu general, however, was manoeuvring his army with great skill. With a fringe of spies thrown out in front, it felt its way through the valleys and over the ridges, like an ant army feeling its way with its antennae.

On the 20th, the day the British made their camp at Sandlwana, the Zulu army reached the nearby Siphezi hill. Their plan was to out-manoeuvre the British force and attack it by surprise on the flank as it advanced, for Cetshwayo, learning from past experience, had strictly ordered them never to attack a fortified camp.

From his bivouack below the hill, Ntshingwayo watched the British through the eyes of his spies. Early the next morning these spies informed him that two British forces had sallied out from the camp to patrol the country. Appreciating that the British camp would be weakened by the absence of these two parties, Ntshingwayo sent his army off. One regiment after another slipped away to a new position in a rocky, bushy little valley, only about five miles from Sandlwana and at the foot of the Ngquthu hill.

The two British reconnaisance parties sighted Zulus, but only in small groups, in transit to their new camp. The reconnoitering British force, under Major Dartnell, saw one of the regiments on the march and sent to Chelmsford for reinforcements. When these were refused, Dartnell bivouacked his men on the Ndlagazi heights for the night in order to watch the Zulus.

Dartnell reported having seen so many Zulus on the move that he informed Chelmsford, who agreed to join him the next morning. At 4 a.m. on 22 January, therefore, Chelmsford marched out of the Sandlwana camp with part of his force and went to join Dartnell. Before he left he sent a message to Colonel Durnford, who was stationed at Rorke's Drift, ordering him to advance, reinforce the Sandlwana camp, and take command of it in the General's absence.

All that night the Zulu army had lain in its valley, absolutely quiet and without fires. The strength of this army lay, indeed, in its discipline: it moved like a machine, in its mobility, for it travelled far and fast without transport; and in its ability to conceal itself in a minimum of natural shelter. Added to these qualities were its remarkable system of spies, and the courage of its men.

In the Zulu camp the spies reported to their general that Chelmsford had marched out to join Dartnell. Ntshingwayo was appreciative of his good fortune, but he was in a quandary. The diviners had warned him that it was the day of the new moon and unpropitious. Ntshingwayo therefore ordered his army to lie down and sleep. They would attack at dawn the next day. Meanwhile a will-o'-the-wisp force was detached and ordered to lead Chelmsford's reconnaisance away on a dance across country.

At 10 a.m. Colonel Durnford arrived at the Sandlwana camp with a force of native levies. He was immediately told that a body of Zulus had been seen in the north-east. He sallied out to investigate, leaving the camp behind him to carry on with its duties.

Then fate took a hand in this game of hide-and-seek. About noon a troop of Sotho levies, under Lieutenant Raw, came upon a herd of cattle. Following it to the top of a rise, they saw the Zulu army about one mile away, at the bottom of a valley, sitting at ease. On seeing they were discovered, the Zulus immediately sprang up and a regiment advanced to attack.

The Sothos opened fire and fell back. The shots riled the Zulus. The regiment swept on and, one after the other, the rest of the units of their army rose up and joined the combat. Ntshingwayo was nonplussed at first. Then, realising that the die was cast, he ordered one of his commanders, Dabulamanzi, to take two regiments of about 3600 men to seize the road to Rorke's Drift behind the camp.

The main army went on after the retreating Sothos. Like a flood-tide the Zulus swirled down the valleys and over the crests, a vast mass of men, their skins and feathers waving in the air, their officers marching in the front.

The scattered British scouting groups did what they could. Some raced back to camp. Others, like a walker on the beach when the tide comes in, found themselves trapped by eddies and waves.

Durnford rallied his men along a large donga at the foot of the camp. On the plain before them the Zulu host manoeuvred expertly into the traditional central chest and enveloping wings. Their drill completed, they advanced and were met by a hail of bullets.

The Zulu left horn, attacking Durnford's section of the line, found the fire so hot that it lay down in the grass and sheltered behind its own dead. In the sudden pause Durnford withdrew his men to the camp, where cooks, officers' batmen, quartermasters and others of their ilk still stood at their duties, wondering what to do.

The native levies had a shrewder idea as to what was happening. They started to melt away and head for the nearest horizon. The Zulu host, meanwhile, had drawn up into battle order, but they were encountering a most galling barrage. Rifle and cannon fire were pouring into their ranks.

Seeing their left horn sheltering in the grass, the main host was tempted to follow suit. They dropped down, and with the disappearance of their targets, the British soldiers stopped firing uncertainly. Then, in the sudden silence, one lone Zulu voice was heard. "*UHlamvana bul' umlilo kashongo njalo,*" it said, making a play on one of Cetshwayo's praise names. "The Little Branch of Leaves that extinguished the veld fire gave no order such as this."

As one man, the host jumped up. Hitherto they had travelled in absolute silence. Now they first whistled and then shouted out in a hoarse, ferocious, exultant cry. At this, the remaining members of Durnford's native contingent turned and fled, leaving a vast gap in the British lines. Through this gap the Zulus poured, and in an instant all was confusion.

There was a wild tangle of white and black bodies. The Europeans did not panic, but they were badly confused. Chelmsford had left the camp like a textbook model of British manoeuvres. There were no defences, no ammunition carriers, and most of the ammunition was still in the wagons in tightly-screwed cases.

The soldiers fixed their bayonets and fought it out. There were innumerable personal combats. Under the wagons and behind the stones isolated soldiers tried to hold out. One tall man jumped on a wagon with a revolver and held all at bay until someone shot him.

It did not last long. The soldiers saw death; it was primeval and savage, but it was also brave and honourable in its way, and if one has to die, it is better to die at the hands of men than cowards. By 2 p.m. the camp was a shambles, the only European survivors were those who had managed to slip through the Zulu lines and race away towards the drift over the Buffalo River, known ever afterwards as Fugitives' Drift.

Behind them, the jubilant Zulu army ransacked the camp, drinking and looting everything the warriors could find, dressing themselves in soldiers' uniforms and eagerly seizing all guns and ammunition. Around them lay the corpses of 806 British soldiers, along with 58 of their officers and 470 of the Natal native levies. About 1000 Zulus were battle casualties.

Meanwhile, the two regiments commanded by Dabulamanzi had been engaged in cutting off fugitives. Thus busy chasing soldiers they were gradually led on towards Rorke's Drift.

The buildings of the Oscarberg Swedish mission there were garrisoned by one company of British soldiers under Lieutenant Bromhead. They had camped close to the two stone mission buildings and had converted the church into a storeroom, while the parsonage acted as a hospital. A detachment of the Natal Native Contingent was also there, and the senior officer was Lieutenant Chard, of the Royal Engineers.

At 3.15 p.m. Lieutenant Adendorff and a carabineer galloped in with the news of Sandlwana. The carabineer rode on to Helpmekaar with the news, while the Rorke's Drift garrison was mustered and put to work, hastily fortifying their camp with parapets of mealie bags and biscuit tins.

The noise of battle rapidly approached. Soon after 4 p.m. the native contingent panicked and fled the place. Eighty British soldiers of the garrison and 35 sick men in the hospital, with a few others to a total of 139 men, were left in the fort.

Shortly afterwards, about a hundred Sothos who had been guarding the line of communication to Sandlwana, rode in. They refused to stop, and instead rode hell-for-leather towards Helpmekaar. Then, about 4.30 p.m., the two Zulu regiments came into sight.

The Zulus had already forded the river. They approached the buildings from the rear, and about 600 men hurtled up to within 50 yards of the south breastwork of mealie bags before heavy fire checked them. They pulled off and tried again on the north-west corner, but once again heavy fire drove them back.

The main body then lined the overlooking hill and sent a hail of bullets into the little fort. Under cover of this fire some of the Zulus crept up close to the walls, and soon they were firing on one side, while the British held out on the other.

Thus attacked, from above and in front, the British suffered severely. At about 6 p.m. they fell back behind an inner retrenchment of biscuit boxes. The Zulus had been trying to force their way into the hospital. Eventually they threw lighted brushwood on to the thatched roof and it went up to the heavens in flames. Most of the sick inside were helped out, but some were burnt to death when the flaming thatch fell upon them. A few had to batter a hole through the wall to escape.

By darkness the defenders, behind their biscuit boxes, were completely surrounded. All night they fought, eventually being driven into the last shelter of the cattle kraal. If it had been dark the Zulus would have overwhelmed them, but the hospital burned all night and its red glow provided light to see and fire.

It was a hard fight. The flash of guns, the dull glint of spears, a confused noise of firing and cursing and screaming and crackling wood, and the two young lieutenants cheering their men on.

About 4 a.m. Dabulamanzi pulled his regiments back to lick their wounds, and the battle was over. Four hundred Zulus had been casualties. Fifteen British soldiers had been killed and most of the survivors had been wounded.

Chelmsford, meanwhile, had been gaily pursuing the will-o'-the-wisp force sent to lure him away from camp. Several messages had reached him from Sandlwana warning him of the presence of Zulus. From ten miles away his officers had observed the camp through telescopes without seeing anything unusual. He was so certain that the country was deserted of Zulus that he pushed on.

When the Zulus eluded him he selected the site for the next camp and despatched a messenger to Sandlwana, ordering the troops there to send up the baggage of the forward units.

About 12.15 p.m. there was a distant sound of cannon fire and the eyes of some of the Zulu scouts just captured, began to dance. The officers hurriedly climbed to a hilltop and viewed the camp through their glasses. Everything appeared to be in order, with no sign of Zulus. They continued interrogating their prisoners.

A battalion of native troops, under Commandant Browne, had been sent to check on the lines of communication. They rode towards the camp until they heard a sudden uproar of firing. Then a mass of Zulus appeared across the path. Browne despatched a hurried message to Chelmsford: "For God's sake come back; the camp is surrounded."

This message was carried to Chelmsford's senior A.D.C., Major Gossett. He scoffed at it. He carried it to Chelmsford and then returned with no other comment than that original orders were to be carried out and the campsite be changed.

About 2 p.m. Chelmsford decided to return to Sandlwana. With his staff and bodyguard he rode leisurely back, letting the tired horses walk all the way. At 3.30 p.m. the camp was five miles away.

Then a man rode up on a stumbling pony. He gave them the news. It was like a thunderclap. The bringer of evil tidings was Commandant Lonsdale. He had sallied out in the morning on patrol, lost touch with his men, and then ridden back to camp, fagged out. Then, ten yards from camp, he discovered that what he thought were British soldiers were really Zulus, dressed up grotesquely in red coats and engaged in looting the tents. Lonsdale turned his horse and escaped in a hail of bullets.

Chelmsford listened to the story, dumbfounded. "I can't understand it," he exclaimed in bewilderment. "I left a thousand men there this morning." The fact that he had been completely outmanoeuvred by the Zulu general never occurred to him.

Messengers were immediately sent to recall the troops. Chelmsford advanced slowly on the camp, marking time to allow the main body to join him.

At 6.30 p.m. the combined force was mustered. They moved forward towards the camp in the dusk, each man numb and sick with the feeling of catastrophe. They reached the camp at about 8 p.m. The place was like a butcher's shop after hours. Everywhere was the smell of death. Nothing moved. The Zulu army had disappeared as silently as it had come.

Chelmsford bivouacked on the neck, the troops sleeping miserably in blood, while the darkness blanketed a nightmare which their imaginations only vaguely comprehended. On the horizon, from Rorke's Drift, came an ominous glow.

At 4 a.m. Chelmsford marched his column down the road to Rorke's Drift. It was littered all the way with corpses. But when they reached the drift they found the Zulus gone and the remnants of the garrison busy removing the thatch from the parsonage as precaution against further attack. The Union Jack still moved, albeit somewhat limply, in the sultry morning breeze – a breeze that was strong enough to carry a hearty cheer when the garrison saw them approaching.

Far away, among the ten thousand hills of Zululand, the Zulu army was going home, laden with booty, each man helping along some wounded comrade. Thunderclaps are sharp but short.

TWENTY-SIX

Storm over Zululand

The immediate effect of Sandlwana was immense. The British army in Natal lost its prestige and offensive potential at one blow. The whole of the transport and equipment of the central column was wiped out. Eight hundred rifles, over 400 000 rounds of ammunition and two cannons were dragged off to uluNdi by the Zulus as booty.

Chelmsford, a badly-shaken man, returned to Pietermaritzburg to face a storm of criticism from the press and the public. Innumerable post-mortems on the battle were held all over the world and many ingenious theories attempted to explain away the disaster by pinning the blame on this or that subordinate officer, such as the unfortunate Colonel Durnford, who had been killed trying to defend a camp left defenceless by its supreme command.

The effect of the disaster on Natal was considerable. Lieutenant General Sir William Butler, the Assistant Adjutant General, saw it from the inside. "The state of confusion within Natal could scarcely be exaggerated," he wrote. "To the extreme of overconfidence which had, indeed, been the primary factor in the disaster of Sandlwana, had succeeded the dread of a Zulu invasion. You will usually find that the term 'picnic' at the rising of the curtain upon one of these little wars is readily changed to 'panic' before the conclusion of the first act."

Forts were hastily thrown up at towns most remote from the Zulu frontier, and the wildest rumours found credence the further they travelled. The Zulu army itself had dispersed to its kraals, but the Natalians were not to know this. They imagined it like a leopard, waiting to pounce. In reality the individual soldiers were busy healing their wounds as well as their primitive medicine allowed; in recounting their exploits; and in fondling their loot of uniforms, blankets and knick-knacks, while the widows and relatives of those slain lamented the dead with misery and tears.

The tactical result of the Sandlwana disaster on the British invasion battle plan was to stall it completely. The right-hand column was busily engaged in fortifying Eshowe when news reached it of the disaster. In a telegram to Pearson, Lord Chelmsford ordered him to use discretion as to whether he remained at Eshowe or retreated.

Pearson decided to remain. He had ample food for two months and the place was strong enough to stave off any attack. He doubly strengthened the encampment with wagons and earthworks. All non-essential native contingents and mounted men were sent back to the Thukela, and Eshowe was left with a force of 1339 Europeans and 355 Natal natives as a besieged garrison.

The Zulus around the place made no effort to take it by storm, but they showed themselves in increasing numbers. Any doubts the garrison had as to whether they should remain or not were settled for them by inability to leave even if they wished.

The troops therefore settled down to an easy enough time. They busied themselves in strengthening the fort and playing games for exercise, while the two bands with them played at intervals each day.

The Zulus sat in the forest around the fort, listening to the music and watching proceedings with interest. Their presence provoked innumerable false alarms, especially at night. Most of the minor casualties of the garrison came from hitting their heads against the floors of the wagons under which they slept when night scares, especially in the first two weeks of the siege, brought the men tumbling out of bed.

On one of these occasions a furious fire was directed on a moving figure in the moonlight. It was subsequently discovered to be a pair of sailor's breeches which had been left to dry on a bush. It was discovered well riddled with holes the next morning.

Beyond these alarms, the only events were the arrival of occasional native messengers, who slipped through the Zulu lines and brought the garrison depressing details about Sandlwana, or hopeful tidings of approaching relief.

The left-hand column, under Colonel Wood, meanwhile was the only really active force against the Zulus. From its little Fort Thinta the column raided in all directions, destroying kraals and seizing cattle. A fort and strongpoint was built on the slopes of Nkambule hill. From it raids were launched against the resolute Swazi renegade prince, Mbilini, who was in charge of Zulu forces in the neighbourhood.

This British column had some success. Mbilini's strongpoints in the caves along the Ntombi River were scoured, and on 4 March, Hhamu, one of the principal Zulu chiefs in the north, saw fit to flee from Cetshwayo and surrender to Colonel Wood with about 700 of his followers.

These successes were sprinkled with some reverses. The most serious of these occurred early in March, when a supply convoy of wagons set out to reach a small garrison stationed at Luneberg.

This convoy had a rendezvous on the Ntombi River ford with an escort under Captain Moriarty, sent out from Luneberg to meet it. The river was in flood and a laager was made there, pending the lowering of the water level. A few wagons had managed to ford the river before it became impassable, so the force was divided into two.

At about 4.30 a.m. on 12 March a Zulu force of about 800 men crept down through the mist upon these two groups of wagons. They slipped in among them and did bloody work. Captain Moriarty, 62 of his soldiers and 17 transport men were killed. The remnants of the British party fled from the place, leaving the Zulus to thoroughly ransack the wagons before vanishing with their loot.

The principal Zulu stronghold in the area was the great flat-topped mountain named Hlobane. Mbilini lived upon this mountain and the Zulus regarded it as being the watchdog of their northern approaches. The constant raiding activity of the British column around it riled the Zulus, and provoked them into what was really the major battle of the war.

At uluNdi, Cetshwayo had received the news of Sandlwana with delight, but he was still full of foreboding for the future. Time after time he sent off messengers asking that peace discussions be started, but nothing resulted. Then the constant news he received of British preparations for resumption of the invasion and the activity of the left-hand column induced him to summon his army for service again.

The Zulu command at first intended to send the army against the garrison at Eshowe, but Mbilini was pressing in his reports of British activity in the north. Accordingly, when the army was marshalled again at the Nodwengu kraal Cetshwayo had it doctored by three Sotho witch doctors and, under the command of Mnyamana Buthelezi, it set off for the north.

Colonel Wood, meanwhile, had determined on raiding the Hlobane Mountain itself. For this purpose he divided his force into two. The one section, under Lieutenant Colonel Buller, set out at 4 a.m. on 28 March and clambered up the north-eastern end of the mountain. On the way Zulu snipers peppered them with shots, and three men were killed and many horses wounded.

The Zulu outposts were well entrenched in caves and, firing from these shelters, they did considerable damage. Colonel Wood, leading the second section and following in Buller's path, had his horse shot dead under him and two of his men killed.

They found the mountaintop to be a vast, undulating meadow, three miles long by about one-and-a-half miles wide. Buller and his men discovered a herd of about 2000 head of cattle there and were busy rounding them up when, looking over the edge of the mountain, they discovered the Zulu grand army approaching from the south-eastern horizon.

The garrison of the mountain had also rallied and were making things hot for the raiders. Buller hastily completed collecting the cattle, but promptly had to abandon the entire herd, for the only path by which they could make a retreat was down the western face and was exceedingly steep.

The British started to scramble down, while the Zulu snipers crowded along the top of the mountain and fired upon them. Cursing and dragging their horses, the British slithered down, leaving a trail of corpses behind them. Piet Uys, leader of a Boer contingent, and 17 Englishmen were killed on the retreat.

Another party of cattle raiders at the base of the mountain got themselves cut off by the approaching Zulu army. Retreating in haste, they ran into a trap set for them by the garrison of the mountain. Fifteen officers and 79 European soldiers were killed, and so were many of the native levies that the rest, disgusted at the incompetency displayed by some of their officers, deserted. Eventually of a force of 800 men only 50 remained.

Among the Europeans engaged in this fight was a young Frenchman named Ernest Grandier. Separated from his fellows in the uproar, he was felled by a rock thrown at his head. When he came round he was pinioned with thongs and, with much abuse, he was forced to run to Mbilini's kraal on a ledge on the south side of the mountain.

There he was brought before Mbilini. The whole kraal was full of bustle and noise, while Mbilini, a determined and tough-looking character, sat surrounded by about fifty of his officers.

Through an interpreter, Grandier was questioned about the traitor, Hhamu, and about future British plans. By his somewhat flamboyant, home-made uniform they evidently thought him an officer of high rank.

Eventually he was taken to a hut, bound to a heavy log, given some milk and maize, and left until morning. The next day he was stripped naked and sent off under guard to Cetshwayo, as a sign of Mbilini's victory.

For four days Grandier trudged through the hills of Zululand, clad in nothing else save his pocket handkerchief. Arriving at uluNdi, Cetshwayo saw him on 4 April and thoroughly questioned him about Hhamu and the British invasion. An effort was then made to induce him to join with Cetshwayo's armourer, a half-caste Portuguese known as Mqali, who was trying to get the cannon captured at Sandlwana into working order.

When Grandier refused, after ten days at the Zulu capital, he was sent back to Mbilini with two guards. On the way, while the party was sleeping, Grandier managed to grab a spear. He stabbed one of his guards to death and drove the other away. Grandier then walked on, hiding by day and travelling by night, until he was picked up by a British patrol.

The Zulu grand army had left for the north under strict orders from Cetshwayo not to attack any entrenchments, but to pass them by. His plan was to force the British to attack the army by pretending an invasion of European territory, and thus draw the soldiers out of fortified positions. The army, however, was in an aggressive mood. Their success at Sandlwana had gone somewhat to the heads of the warriors and they were of the opinion that, armed with the rifles they had captured, they could overwhelm any European camp of reasonable size.

At his Nkambule fort, Colonel Wood was in an excellent position. To add to his advantage, early on the morning of 29 March a Zulu deserter brought him the warning that the army intended to try an attack on him that afternoon. Wood planned accordingly. He gave his men an early lunch and then posted them beside open boxes of ammunition. Cracking Cockney jokes and chewing biscuits, they waited.

At 1 p.m. the Zulus arrived. They intended to surround the fort and subdue it by overwhelming rifle fire. The main body attacked the outlying cattle kraal and easily overwhelmed it. This was their undoing. Pleased with their success, they re-formed. Their General reckoned that the army had disobeyed orders once and been successful. He resolved to repeat the process.

For five hours the Zulus attacked the fort. Then they tried one last great charge. They were thrown back, and a shiver seemed to run through them. Then they turned and fled. In their army of about 17 000 men they had an estimated 2000 casualties. The British force of 1998 men suffered 25 casualties all told, including 18 killed.

This battle of Nkambule was the real decisive battle of the Anglo-Zulu War. The Zulu army was completely depressed. Cetshwayo was aggrieved and enraged at the defeat. He blamed and threatened to kill the commanding officer for dis-obeying orders, but there was nothing he could do about the defeat. All Zululand mourned the fallen, while men with fear-some wounds limped or crawled to their homes. The country was full of pessimistic talk and odd rumours that the Europe-ans had apes and lions to help them, and that they cut off the heads of the killed Zulus to send to Queen Victoria.

Chelmsford failed entirely to appreciate the nature of the Nkambule battle. A victorious conclusion to the war was his for the asking after the battle, but entirely lacking any infor-mation as to happenings in Zululand, and with a very hazy idea of things in general, he plodded along with painstaking preparations for a grand mass attack.

From the excess of careless optimism before Sandlwana, the army had changed to an excess of caution, and the nervous complaint known as "the jitters" was common. False alarms and scares were everyday occurrences. There is one story of a nervous quartermaster officer of comfortable proportions.

This gentleman was having a swim in a river far behind the front one afternoon. At the nearby camp the native contingent, armed with muzzleloaders, was under orders to fire them off that afternoon – a periodic routine in order to prevent the charges from getting too stale. No sooner was the fusillade discharged into the air than the quartermaster was seen racing for camp, dressed in nothing but a revolver, which he held in his hand and fired over his shoulder.

Another result of this nervousness was that most men slept in their uniforms, in order to be ready for the inevitable night alarm. From this treatment, together with the effects of rain and thorns and the absence of regular replacements, clothing had but a short life. The men, and particularly the officers, improvised all manner of uniforms for themselves, made up of bits and pieces of every colour and description. Some of them only needed a few candles to complete the illusion of a Christmas tree.

Vast reinforcements poured into Natal after Sandlwana. Troops from all over the Empire were despatched post-haste. Even the navy rallied to the emergency, and Commodore Richards, of the West African squadron, sailed to Durban and landed a naval brigade, which he commanded in person.

Chelmsford had as his immediate objective the relief of Eshowe. For this purpose a sizeable force was concentrated at the Lower Thukela Drift. Communication with the besieged garrison was established by means of a heliograph at the drift and an improvised looking-glass at Eshowe, and it was confirmed that they had ample food for the present.

The garrison was naturally short of luxuries. Towards the end of the siege an auction of goods found in the baggage of the surplus men Colonel Pearson had sent back to Natal before the siege yielded 20s. a pound for tobacco; 12s. for a tin of sardines; 25s. for a bottle of pickles; and £7 10s. for a ham.

There were few events. On 1 March the garrison sallied out in an attempt to destroy the military kraal, under Dabulamanzi, about eight miles away, on the hill known as Ntumeni (place of bitter apple trees). They reached the kraal and burnt some of the huts, but were well peppered all the way home by snipers in the trees and long grass.

From the middle of March, sickness began to appear in the camp and heavy rain reduced the prescribed area in which the men lived to something resembling a large pigsty, both in odour and appearance.

The only real pastime, apart from games such as whist, quoits and cricket, was to stand around the signallers, listening to them spell out the messages which everybody hoped would announce the departure of the relief column.

At last, after several false alarms, the relief force started from the Lower Thukela Drift on 29 March 1879. It consisted of 3390 Europeans and 2280 native levies, with 122 wagons carrying supplies.

Chelmsford proceeded with extreme caution and used a troop of scouts raised by John Dunn to spy the land out. Large parties of Zulus were observed in the neighbourhood, and he took no chances. On 1 April the troops camped about 300 yards from Gingindlovu kraal, which was burnt down, and there, the following morning, Dabulamanzi led a Zulu force of about 10 000 against them.

Chelmsford's men, this time, were sheltered in a secure laager. The Zulu attack was futile from the start. Dabulamanzi exploited such cover as there was, but withering fire from the British never gave the Zulus a chance. They suffered some 1200 battle casualties in 40 minutes, while British casualties were only 9 killed and 52 wounded.

The battle of "Gin, Gin, I love you" (as the soldiers called it) took place on a fine, clear morning, with the Eshowe garrison eagerly watching the whole affair from their fort. The next morning at 8 a.m. Chelmsford sent off a flying column, and at 5 p.m. a war correspondent named Charles Norris-Newman of the *Standard* was the first to ride into the fort, bubbling over with laughter at his contemporaries of *The Times* and *Cape Argus*, who got stuck in a bog.

The garrison, during the ten weeks' siege, had lost four officers and 27 men from sickness, while about 120 were in hospital. When the last of the relieving force, the 91st Highlanders, arrived at Eshowe at midnight, with their bagpipes in full cry, the garrison had enough food left to give them a hearty meal, and the siege ended in a general celebration.

On 5 April Eshowe was evacuated, and the Zulus immediately set it on fire. The retiring force was followed all the way back, and, in their nervousness, while bivouacked at the old imVuchini mission, a false alarm was raised. Five outlying European pickets and nine of John Dunn's scouts were shot in the dark in a panic of mistaken identity. Apart from this incident the force reached the Thukela in safety.

Chelmsford prepared for his second invasion of Zululand with the most elaborate care. His heavily reinforced command was rearranged entirely. Two divisions were formed. The 1st Division, based on the Lower Thukela Drift, was under the command of Major General Crealock. His orders were to establish advance strongpoints up the Zululand coast and destroy the military kraals there as a diversion, while the 2nd Division attacked uluNdi from the north.

The 1st Division built Fort Crealock on the Matigulu River and Fort Chelmsford on the Nyezane. A telegraph line was constructed to the latter fort, and an army of 250 ox-wagons proceeded to stock the forts with enormous supplies of food.

The Zulus did not interfere with this laborious task. Enteric fever killed three officers and 68 men of the division, while an average of ten oxen died each day as there was little food and the constant passage of wagon convoys destroyed all available grazing.

The problem of supply had given the British command some concern. One suggested solution was that the navy discover a landing point somewhere along the coast, and this, if it could be found, would be an ideal base. Accordingly, on 5 January, the *Active* and the *Tenedos* had cruised along the coast, under the command of Commodore Sullivan. They explored the whole coastline as far as the mouth of Lake St Lucia, and eventually, about 15 miles north of the mouth of the Thukela, they discovered a shoal running parallel to the shore, with still water behind it.

Stormy water forced the ships to abandon the survey, but when the gale blew out they returned on 13 January, and both promptly ran aground on a reef ever since known as the Tenedos Reef. Some damage was done to both vessels, while the *Tenedos* herself had to return to Simonstown for repairs.

The 455-ton gunboat, *Forester*, under Lieutenant Commander Sidney Smith, was then detailed to make the survey. In the middle of April the little craft went up on its first trip. She took soundings at various spots, and while thus engaged, a party of Zulus appeared on the beach and opened fire. The ship replied with a few shots from her big guns, and this type of ship-shore engagement became quite common during the course of the survey.

The *Forester* found a usable landing point a short distance above Point Durnford. They named the place Port Durnford, and their satisfactory report induced the army to use it as a supply point. Another result of the survey activity of the British navy was the naming of the mouth of the Mhlathuze River. The indentation there was named Richards Bay, after Commodore Frederick William Richards, of the West African station, who had come to Natal to aid Chelmsford. In after years, when this officer, after a distinguished career, became Admiral Sir Frederick Richards, First Sea Lord of the Admiralty, the bay was sometimes known as Port Sir Richards.

By 13 June the 1st Division was concentrated at Fort Chelmsford. From there the men moved to the Mlalazi River, at a place they named Napoleon Hill after the Prince Imperial. Port Durnford was inspected by Commodore Richards and found to be merely an open, sandy beach, but the surf broke with less than its usual north coast violence there and Richards decided that it was practical.

A pont was thrown across the Mlalazi River, with Fort Napoleon to protect it. To this place, on 26 June, messengers came from Cetshwayo, carrying a tusk and asking for peace, but Crealock referred them to Chelmsford.

At Port Durnford another small fort was built, named Fort Richards and, on 30 June, the HMS *Forester* with two transports, a tug and surfboats, arrived from Durban and the first stores and mules were landed upon the beach.

The balance of Chelmsford's command had been concentrated into what he called the 2nd Division. Command of this division was given to Major General Newdigate and its headquarters were at Landman's Drift on the Buffalo River. Chelmsford accompanied this division and among his staff was the impetuous and handsome young Prince Imperial of France, who had come to South Africa with the general flood of reinforcements, after Sandlwana.

On 31 May the division crossed the Blood River and made a camp on the Thelezi hill. From there, on the morning of 1 June, a reconnaisance was sent to find the next camping site. This party consisted of the Prince Imperial, Lieutenant J.B. Carey and six European troopers.

They rode on happily enough, through country which had already been searched for Zulus and found to be empty. At about 3 p.m. they arrived at a small kraal near the Tshotshozi stream. There they offsaddled and brewed coffee while their horses rested.

At about 4 p.m. their guide reported that he had seen a Zulu come over the hill. The horses were promptly caught and saddled. The Prince gave the order to mount, and as he spoke a volley was fired into them by a number of Zulus who had crept up through the long, surrounding grass.

The surprise was complete. The horses bolted with the startled troopers. The Prince was in the act of mounting. His horse shied and bolted while he ran beside it, trying to mount. The Zulus fired from the kraal. One trooper was hit in the back and fell. The guide and another trooper had been stranded at the kraal by their bolting horses. Both were killed.

Lieutenant Carey and the four surviving troopers galloped on across a nearby donga before they recovered their wits. They reined up and looked behind them. They saw the Prince's horse galloping riderless away. Concluding that the Prince must have fallen and not knowing the strength of the attackers, the troopers rode back to camp to report.

The next morning a strong party was sent to the kraal. They found the two troopers lying dead in the grass. In the donga lay the body of the Prince. He must have run there, emptied his pistol at his pursuers and then been stabbed to death. The body was carried back to camp, preserved as best the army doctors could, and then sent to England. Lieutenant Carey was later court-martialled on a charge of misbehaviour before the enemy, but was found not guilty.

With this initial misfortune to dishearten it, the 2nd Division continued its advance into Zululand. On 5 June it reached the Nondweni stream and built a fort there named Fort Newdigate. While busy completing the fort, three Zulu envoys met Chelmsford and terms of surrender were discussed. Chelmsford demanded, in addition to the original ultimatum, the restoration of all loot from Sandlwana and a token laying down of arms at the British camp by one Zulu regiment.

While the Zulus were considering these demands the division moved on to the Phoko valley, where they built one of their inevitable forts, this time named after Major General Marshall. While busy building this fort, on 7 June, Chelmsford learnt of the penultimate result of Sandlwana. He was to be relieved of the supreme command and Lieutenant General Sir Garnet Wolseley was to take his place on arrival from England.

This news shook Chelmsford and spurred him on somewhat. He groped off across Zululand with his division, practising the most extreme caution and leaving a trail of forts behind to guard communications. There was nothing the troops hated more than to be left behind to garrison one of these little forts. Towards the end of the campaign there were more men doing guard duty in them than were engaged in actual hostilities. Long after the war was over a legend grew up in the British Army that somewhere in Zululand the garrison of one of these forts had been forgotten, and with the passing of the years had become a tribe of its own.

All these garrisons had to be supplied and fed. A vast army of 2500 wagons and carts was engaged on this task. Some 27 000 oxen and 4500 mules were employed on haulage and mortality among these animals was fantastic. The oxen, particularly, had a cruel time of it, with heavy loads, no roads, steep gradients and poor grazing. The oxen had a negative revenge when they appeared on the menus. Their beef was the principal food, and it was as tough as the thorn trees.

On 27 June the division climbed past the hill known as Ntaba Khathazo, where the *khathazo* plants (*Alepidea amatybica*), used as a specific against colds, grow, and proceeded to camp on the Mthonjaneni heights. There three more messengers came from Cetshwayo with two tusks, 150 head of cattle and a request for peace written for the chief by Cornelius Vijn.

Chelmsford repeated the original conditions for peace with minor modifications. Then, while the Zulus went back to Cetshwayo, he packed all his stores into a laager on Mthonjaneni and, on 30 June he led his division down into the valley of the White Mfolozi. He had learnt that Wolseley intended to displace him from the Zululand theatre entirely and he was keen on enjoying some victory before ignominious dismissal.

Another fort was built on the White Mfolozi and still another appeal was received from Cetshwayo begging for peace. In reply Chelmsford once again moderated his demands and gave the Zulus a time limit up to noon on 3 July.

Many Zulus were seen across the river and their temper was evident when they forcibly prevented messengers of Cetshwayo from driving a propitiatory gift of a herd of the famous white cattle to Chelmsford.

No reply was received from the Zulus by the expiration of the time limit. A British reconnaisance unit was sent across the river and, in the process of gaining information, three of its men were killed and four wounded. On the same day a sharp telegram was received from Wolseley, objecting to Chelmsford's division of his army into two completely independent sections and threatening to put "things in order" as soon as he arrived.

It now became a do or die effort on the part of Chelmsford. At dawn on 4 July he crossed the river with 4160 Europeans and 958 native levies, while 529 Europeans under Colonel Bellairs remained in the White Mfolozi fort as guard.

Chelmsford formed his men into a hollow rectangle. The native contingent, ammunition and stores were placed inside. The whole force then advanced along a route selected as a result of the previous day's reconnaisance.

The Zulus, meanwhile, were mustering in the hills. They had little spirit for the coming encounter but had decided to make some show of resistance. When the British formation was about one-and-a-half miles from uluNdi the Zulus surrounded it in a great circle. They gradually contracted until they were within range and general fire commenced.

Again and again the Zulus tried to close with the British on various fronts, but they never drew nearer than 30 yards. Then they lost heart and began to waver. At 9.45 a.m. Chelmsford ordered the 17th Lancers out. They drove the Zulus off, uluNdi was burnt, and the troops removed to the Mbilane stream nearby to have lunch. By 4 p.m. they were back at the fort on the White Mfolozi. They had lost 12 men and 88 were wounded. The Zulus lost about 1500 men from a total force of about 17 000.

Next day the troops marched back to Mthonjaneni and there, sitting in some sort of triumph in the wet and mud of a torrential downpour, Chelmsford decided to resign and return to England in as much glory as he could expect from the latest battle. The Zulu army, meanwhile, had dispersed and Cetshwayo had vanished.

Wolseley was left with the task of clearing up the debris. After an abortive effort to land at Port Durnford in rough weather, on 2 July, he had eventually ridden overland from Durban and joined the 1st Division on 7 July. He found that its total contribution to the Anglo-Zulu War was the burning down of the old eMangweni and oNdini military kraals. On 23 July, Wolseley disbanded the Division, most of its troops being embarked at Port Durnford.

Wolseley busied himself in accepting the surrender of various Zulu chiefs. After disbanding the 2nd Division he retained light mobile forces, and from Fort Albert at the kwaMagwaza mission and Fort Victoria near the White Mfolozi, they rummaged the country, rounding up guns, accepting surrenders and building sundry strongpoints as a precaution against further unrest.

Cetshwayo, after watching the battle for uluNdi from the hills in the south-east, had fled to the kraal of his prime minister, Mnyamana, on the Sikhwebezi River. From there he removed to the hills in the north and sent Mnyamana and Cornelius Vijn, who had accompanied him, to the British with a message saying that he was prepared to surrender.

However, when Vijn returned with a promise of good treatment, he found that Cetshwayo had moved to a small kraal on the river known as the Mona (the spoiler) where he was pondering his future.

Vijn told him to surrender but the king demurred. Sitting in a ramshackle hut, he said he was afraid that he would be shot. Vijn tried to persuade him but Cetshwayo was firm and Vijn was sent back to Wolseley with information to that effect.

Then an exciting hare and hounds chase began, which the troops generally referred to as "Catchwayo".

Vijn, for a promised £500 reward, led a party of Dragoons to the kraal where he had last seen Cetshwayo. They reached the kraal at 1 p.m. on 14 August, after making enough noise on the journey to frighten a railway engine, let alone a nervous Zulu. Cetshwayo had heard them coming five miles away and had run for it.

From there, for days they followed a will-o'-the-wisp, with the tribespeople misleading them with conflicting directions. All Zululand seemed to be inscrutable and a first-class wild goose chase took the British to the most inaccessible kraals. By the time the search ended, some troops, working on certain information, were searching in the bush of the Mhlathuze valley, one hundred miles away.

On 26 August, however, information was received that Cetshwayo was in the Ngome forest, at the kraal of a man named Dwaza. Laboriously making his way to the top of the Ngome range, Major Marter and his men looked down the precipitous western slopes into a narrow valley about 2000 feet below.

There they saw the kraal. They sneaked down into the valley. By 3 p.m. they arrived near the kraal. In a concealed hollow they mounted their horses. Then they raced up around the kraal, taking it completely by surprise.

In the kraal they found Cetshwayo and 17 companions. All were arrested and the party moved off in triumph. On the way four of the prisoners attempted to escape. Two were killed while two got away. The following day, 31 August, a mule-cart picked up Cetshwayo at the Ndaza kraal and he was removed to uluNdi. From there he was sent to Port Durnford, where he was embarked on the *Natal* and despatched to banishment in Cape Town.

That was the end of the Anglo-Zulu War. Seventy-six officers, 1007 European soldiers and 604 native levies had been killed on the British side, while 17 officers and 330 men had died of diseases. Seventy-eight men received the Victoria Cross. The Zulu casualties will never be known but they must have been around 6000 men.

By the end of September 1879 the last detachments of the British Army had left Zululand with their baggage. Durban became chock-a-block, with the bars doing a roaring trade. In the general confusion one story put the finishing touch to the war.

Lieutenant General Sir William Butler informs us that just before one crowded transport sailed, the captain received orders to delay a while, as six soldiers found to be insane during the course of the war were being sent on board under escort, for consignment to a British lunatic asylum.

The captain, nervous at losing a tide, waited impatiently. Presently a boat containing the new passengers put off shore. On the transport a mass of men of different units, many already demobilised, lined the sides, having a last look at Durban. The boat reached the side of the ship; the lunatics, still in their uniforms, scrambled up the ladder and immediately vanished into the crowd.

There was complete consternation. The shore escort wanted to get back home and the captain wanted to sail. The escort furnished such descriptive details as they remembered and rowed back to the shore, while on board the ship's officers held an emergency conference with the military.

For fear of starting a general panic, news of the occurrence was kept a close secret. A select corps of observers was enrolled from men known to the officers, or wearing decorations, and these were sworn to secrecy and detailed to watch different portions of the ship.

All the way to Cape Town the observations went on. Any man sitting apart in the throes of seasickness found himself suspiciously regarded. At frequent intervals some man would be tapped on the shoulder and led to an inspection panel of the ship's doctor, captain, and an army officer.

By the time the ship reached Cape Town there were 26 men in detention. The authorities were alarmed. Obviously there must be some mistake and, if anyone of the men happened to be the son of some person of importance, there might be unpleasant consequences.

Accordingly, urgent demands were made from Cape Town for someone to come from Natal who could positively identify the lunatics. An asylum orderly was hastily sent down. He found that none of the men detained were the lunatics. On the contrary, the six men wearing long service medals and innocent expressions had all been engaged on the search for themselves and had been the most conscientious in reporting others as madmen.

So the Anglo-Zulu War passed into history: a rather sorry affair, with little to commend it. A war provoked by a straightforward act of aggression or frankly aggressive in itself can be regarded unemotionally and the causes dispassionately examined. But when the war, as is so often the case, is cloaked in unctuous hypocrisy; when the name of the Lord is self-righteously invoked as justification for man's knavery; then one is left with a nasty taste in the mouth. And so it was with this war, whose combatants fought so bravely and where heroism was common.

TWENTY-SEVEN

The thirteen kinglets

Winning the Anglo-Zulu War was one thing; devising a workable peace was something else. Wolseley was deluged with all manner of suggestions as to what to do with the country. Eventually, on 1 September 1879, he announced that he intended to partition Zululand into thirteen districts. Each district was to have an independent kinglet ruling over it, with the only connection a loose sort of allegiance to Britain.

News of Wolseley's decision astounded most people who knew the Zulus. John Dunn wrote in his diary:

"The so-called settlement of Zululand was the maddest piece of policy ever heard of. The Zulu people, after their defeat, naturally looked upon themselves as subjects of the government. They would willingly have allowed themselves to be moulded into any shape. The country ought to have been annexed and brought under British rule at first, without sending Cetshwayo away."

Instead, Wolseley set about selecting his thirteen kinglets. His natural choices were mostly people whom the Zulus considered to be traitors or renegades, as they had served the British; and for this service they were rewarded by appointment to high position.

Thus were the seeds of boundless discontent sown and of the most bitter of contentions the whole stormy history of Zululand ever produced.

Each one of the kinglets had to put his mark on an agreement. In it they recognised the British victory and the supreme power of the Queen. They agreed to respect the boundaries of the areas allocated to them. They were to end the traditional military system; their men were to be allowed to marry when they pleased. Migrant labour was to be encouraged, the sale of arms and ammunition prohibited and fair trials instituted, with a British Resident to act as supreme arbitrator in all quarrels.

W.D. Wheelwright was appointed as first British Resident, with his seat on the slopes of Nhlazatshe Mountain, and around him he had thirteen wards who were about as amenable to order as a pride of lions at a kill.

One of the best known of the kinglets was a Sotho named Hlubi, who had been given his high appointment as a reward for services during the war. He received the lands of the former chiefs Sihayo and Matshana, near Sandlwana.

Further to the north, touching on the Ngome forest, the renegade chief Hhamu who had gone over to the British during the course of the war, secured a substantial area. Next to him, to the east, a man of entirely different calibre was established as a kinglet. This individual was named Zibebu and he was one of the most remarkable personalities Zululand ever produced.

Zibebu was the grandson of a man named Sojiyisa, whose precise relationship to the Zulu royal family had been a matter of some contention and scandal. Sojiyisa, who was certain only of his mother's name, built himself a kraal which he named kwaMandlakazi (place of the mighty seed) and his followers became known from the name of his kraal.

Zibebu had never been over friendly with the Zulu royal house, although he had fought with distinction against the British in the Anglo-Zulu War. Many slurs were constantly being cast at his parentage, and political disagreements between himself and Cetshwayo had been common. Even the name of his capital kraal, Banganomo (the disputed aristocrat), perpetuated the memory of an old quarrel, when Cetshwayo had insisted that an individual named Sikizane be appointed induna of the kraal, much against Zibebu's will.

Even better known than Zibebu was, of course, John Dunn. Dunn, in reward for his war services, was given the largest of all the thirteen portions of Zululand, from the Thukela to the Mhlathuze River, and from the sea up to the Mangeni River in the west, where his area adjoined that of the Sotho kinglet Hlubi.

Dunn reigned supreme in this vast area, as a sort of great white chief. At his old headquarters of Mangethe on the farm he named Moyeni (the windy place), Dunn re-established himself with his numerous wives and followers. There he enjoyed so much publicity and fame, consequent to his unique position, that for some time he was deluged beneath a shoal of letters. These supplications came from persons all over the world who claimed to be related; in the form of long-lost sisters, mothers or, in the case of one most persistent woman from Ireland, a wife deserted by him 36 years before.

Dunn set to work to administer his area with considerable sense and resolution. A hut tax, first of 5s. and then of 10s. a hut, was levied on his subjects. Licences were demanded from all traders and with the proceeds roads were made. His territory was managed with all the care of a squire's estate in England.

Dunn lived well, hunting and fishing at his favourite resort, Mthunzini (shady place), and raising cattle. He was renowned for his hospitality. His capital of Mangethe was quite an establishment, consisting of five well-built houses, an office and a gaol. His chief wife, Catherine, lived there, as well as a European secretary and a European tutor named Gilling, who had the task of educating his family.

One of the houses at Mangethe was a guest house, and it was generally occupied by some friend, traveller or big game hunter, attracted there by Dunn's hospitality, his excellent table, wines, and inexhaustible fund of hunting stories.

One of the visitors, B. Mitford, has described Dunn as he was in 1880:

"He is a handsome, well-built man about five feet eight in height, with good forehead, regular features, and keen grey eyes; a closely cut iron-grey beard hides the lower half of his bronzed, weather-tanned countenance, and a look of determination and shrewdness is discernable in every lineament. He was neatly dressed in plain tweed suit and wideawake hat.

"In manner he is quiet and unassuming, and no trace of self-glorification or bounce is there about him. He has a reputation for reticence and doubtless his success is in great measure due to the fact that he knows how and when to hold his tongue."

To aid him in controlling his area, Dunn appointed three European magistrates. One Martin Oftebro was stationed at the western end of his territory, at a place named Nsingabantu (look at the people). Two other magistrates, E.A. Brunner and Frank Galloway, were established on the eastern side of Dunn's land, and with their aid he kept his people under firm control. All traffic in liquor was forbidden and even missionaries were made to toe the line of his authority.

The taxes Dunn and the other kinglets levied on the itinerant traders had the immediate effect of forcing those restless individuals to establish themselves in one spot and build permanent stores, for it became unprofitable to wander about the country and be constantly mulcted of tax by every authority.

In this way, the first proper stores came to Zululand. They were rough and ready establishments, generally made of wattle and daub, in the shape of an oblong. Inside they were divided into two, a counter of packing cases in one half and rows of shelves on the walls. The whole place would be festooned with trade blankets, Salampore cloth, coloured handkerchiefs, rolls of tobacco, buckets, sheath knives, beads, brass wire, looking glasses, tin pannikins, three-legged pots, cleavers, straps, hats, military surplus clothing, umbrellas and a thousand other oddments.

The other side of the partition was the trader's bed-sitting room, with a rough table, an old newspaper for a cloth, some jam stains, a mattress on a home-made bed, a few packing-case seats, some bacon rinds and a million breadcrumbs on the floor.

The first storekeepers were an interesting crowd. Herbert Nunn was one of the earliest. He established himself in the territory of Hhamu and became his confidant and adviser, and at the same time made a fair amount of money by working a timber concession in the Ngome forest.

John Eckersley was another of the early traders. He had a store at Banganomo, while Thomas Peachey and Cornelius Vijn both had stores scattered around the country.

By far the best known of all the early traders, however, was Johan Colenbrander, one of the most resolute frontiersmen ever bred in Southern Africa.

At the time of the appointment of the thirteen kinglets, Colenbrander was a pleasant-looking young man in his early twenties. Dressed in rough buck-skin clothes, with a dark beard and bronzed complexion, boots and spurs, a revolver in a holster and a formidable clasp knife suspended from his belt, he looked every inch an adventurer. A deep weal across his forehead, received from the spear of a cattle raider, made him look even more rugged than he really was. With a partner named Grosvenor Darke, he had trading interests in northern Zululand and was the particular friend and adviser of Zibebu.

For a short time, after the so-called settlement of Zululand, there was the uneasy peace that comes before a storm. Underneath the surface there was a seething mass of discontent. All sorts of intolerable anomalies had been perpetuated by the partition. Proud chiefs, such as Mnyamana, Cetshwayo's former prime minister, had been reduced to the status of vassals to people they considered as traitors, such as Hhamu.

Ndabuko, haughty brother of Cetshwayo, had been placed under the social outcast Zibebu, whereas previously he had been second only to the king. The kinglets were also keenly aware of the changes in social position, and they made the most of them. Hhamu eyed Mnyamana's cattle and then demanded 1400 head as compensation, for stock which he claimed had been seized when he absconded to the British.

Zibebu, likewise, was no laggard in collecting cattle from the wealthy grandees, and his demands for full homage so riled Ndabuko that the latter slipped off to Pietermaritzburg in May 1880 to petition for the return of Cetshwayo. When Ndabuko returned home, Zibebu fined him for absence without leave, and this was a pill of bitterness which Ndabuko could never swallow.

The British Resident, W.D. Wheelwright, was well aware of what was brewing in Zululand. Realising that the terms of his appointment established him as simply the eyes and ears of government, with no voice or power, he resigned and was replaced in March 1880 by Melmoth Osborn. The new Resident received some slight addition to his power, by being appointed a magistrate over all British subjects in Zululand, on 14 September 1880.

Trouble soon came. Just north of Dunn's boundary lay the territory given into the charge of an old and rather weak kinglet named Mlandela. In July 1881, an adventurer by the name of Sitimela suddenly appeared in this area and announced himself as being the grandson of the renowned Mthethwa chief Dingiswayo.

Adjoining Mlandela's area was another partition under the rule of an avaricious old drunkard, named Somkhele, who lent his support to the pretender. Mlandela promptly fled to Dunn for protection. Dunn packed the old man into a wagon and carted him back to his kraal, where they found the pretender happily engaged in winning the favour of the people by distributing Mlandela's cattle.

The two sides glowered at each other for a while. Osborn hastily went up to see what all the trouble was about and, on 27 July, ordered Sitimela to disperse his army. When he refused, Dunn, Zibebu and other elements loyal to the British, were called upon to restore order by force. Zibebu was anticipating an attack on his own country, but he sent off 500 of his best warriors under the command of Johan Colenbrander who, in thus serving the chief, set an unfortunate precedent as a white belligerent in the current troubles.

It wasn't much of a fight. Some of Mlandela's men went to see if Sitimela was dispersing his army, on 31 July. They were chased away and ten were killed. Dunn and Colenbrander promptly mustered their combined force and chased Sitimela along a course marked by the bodies of 200 of his followers, ending at an indeterminate point somewhere beyond the horizon. Sitimela was never seen again.

So ended the first clash in the lands of the thirteen kinglets. It was just a curtain raiser for what was to follow. The whole of Zululand seethed with threats and rumours. Dunn's area was the only part retaining any semblance of peace. The white chief was optimistically planning a prosperous future and the construction of a harbour on the coast. The only future the other kinglets saw was death, preferably for somebody else.

Loud complaints were coming from the grandees that Zibebu and Hhamu were taking all their cattle. On 31 August 1881, Sir Evelyn Wood, Governor of Natal, visited the ramshackle little British Residency at Nhlazatshe. English prestige at that time was at a low ebb after the defeat by the Transvalers at Majuba, and his first task was to try and explain away the military setback.

At a meeting held at Nhlazatshe, Sir Evelyn did his explaining, and then turned to affairs in Zululand. He proposed the imposition of a 10s. hut tax throughout Zululand, so that British authority could be reinforced and roads could be made. Referring to current troubles, he ordered Hhamu to return half of the 1400 cattle seized from Mnyamana, while Zibebu was also ordered to restore one third of the cattle he had seized from Ndabuko.

This meeting and its awards only made matters worse. Hhamu refused point-blank to return any cattle, while Zibebu promptly expelled Ndabuko from his lands. With Mnyamana and others, Ndabuko withdrew to the territory of another of the 13 kinglets, Mfanawendlela, next to Hhamu's lands, and plotted vengeance.

In Hhamu's territory there was one particularly militant group called the abaQulusi – living in the valley of the Bivane

River. Their chief had formerly been the custodian of Cetshwa-yo's personal medicines. The odd name of abaQulusi (the people of the naked buttocks) came from the abaQulusini kraal established by Shaka. He gave it that name because the local people made a costume which exposed their behinds to the cooling breezes. Shaka's aunt Mkabayi was the first governor of the kraal. She repaid her nephew's trust by conspiring with his other brothers to assassinate him. She had the reputation of being a veritable virago. These abaQulusi resisted Hhamu's authority to such degree that, on 2 October 1881, he attacked them and drove them away into the Transvaal.

All Zululand was in a sorry state, with no other prospect than anticipation of war. The lack of an overruling central authority was apparent to everyone. John Dunn, on 30 September 1881, had actually written to the British Resident, proposing himself as supreme chief. Osborn was inclined to agree that such an individual was necessary, although he did not think Dunn was a satisfactory applicant for the post.

Over in England, a new British liberal government had been made painfully aware that the adventures of their predecessors, in various parts of the world, were coming home to roost with a vengeance. So far as Zululand was concerned, they received a constant stream of appeals that, as the Anglo-Zulu War had been unjust, the new government should restore Cetshwayo, thus making amends and solving the political tangle in Zululand in one stroke.

Cetshwayo, all this time, had been in exile in Cape Town. After a preliminary detention in the castle he had been removed to comfortable quarters at the Oude Molen, an old Dutch building opposite Mowbray railway station. There he whiled away his time in the company of three Zulu men and four women, while an interpreter named R.C. Samuelson, taught him to write, and prepared for him a detailed defence and an appeal to be allowed to visit England.

This appeal was eventually granted in September 1881 and, escorted by Henrique Shepstone, Cetshwayo sailed to London. He was a great success in England. He was well-mannered and dignified, and London society delighted in entertaining him. He was invited to dinners and taken to pantomimes and shows, where the buxom chorus girls of the day reminded him of the Zulu beauties in his harem.

Shepstone togged out his charge in striped trousers, frock coat and necktie and promenaded him around London to see the sights. The usual London crowd gathered outside his residence, standing there for hours, gaping at the place in hopes of seeing the famed Zulu king. Cetshwayo at first took this for a combination of stupidity and rudeness, but Shepstone explained to him that it was an old English custom. Accordingly, every few hours, Cetshwayo had to go to an open window and bow, while the crowd shouted "Hurrah!"

The round of social visits and all the appeals and requests had their due effect. On 9 January 1883, the *Briton* anchored off Port Durnford, and the following morning Cetshwayo was returned to Zululand, along with a lot of impedimenta, souvenirs of London, and a vast collection of curs and hounds of sundry breeds, which had attached themselves to his person during the course of his exile.

There were very few Zulus on the beach to welcome him, although larger numbers met him on his journey up to uluNdi. Among those who did meet him, however, was Mahlangeni, the last great bard of the Zulus. He made up for the otherwise moderate welcome by bawling out the king's praises for a solid three hours, starting off with an imitation cock-crow at dawn and carrying on without a break.

Preparations for the return of Cetshwayo had only emphasised antagonisms. The kinglets, who had tasted uneasy independence for the past couple of years, were all summarily deposed. Instead of thirteen partitions, Zululand was divided up into three sections.

In the north Zibebu was left in independence, but his area was much reduced in size in order to remove dissident grandees, such as Ndabuko, from under his rule. Cetshwayo was to rule the second big section, while a third section, made up of the lands of Hlubi and John Dunn, was reserved under British control, as a home for all elements unwilling to be under either Zibebu or Cetshwayo.

There were very mixed feelings at this new political set-up. John Dunn was bitterly disappointed. His area had been well run and now, for no direct reason, he was deprived of his power without compensation save a few hundred pounds to be paid to his magistrates as consolation for the loss of their jobs.

At his reinstatement, on 29 January, Cetshwayo saw how mixed were the feelings of his people. Hhamu failed to put in an appearance. Zibebu came merely to see Theophilus Shepstone, who had escorted Cetshwayo up from Port Durnford with a detachment of Dragoons.

Still, Cetshwayo settled down. He rebuilt his old uluNdi kraal, reappointed Mnyamana as Prime Minister and around his person were rallied his immediate following: the uSuthu; the Buthelezi people of Mnyamana; and the Mgazini people, who unfortunately dwelt in Zibebu's area.

For the rest, Zululand was in ferment. The British had established Henry Francis Fynn as Resident with Cetshwayo, while Melmoth Osborn became Resident Commissioner in the Reserve area. His headquarters were at Eshowe, near the site of the old kraal once kept there by the ill-fated chief Mashongwe Sibiya, who had his eyes put out by Shaka and who, by some, is supposed to have left his name to posterity in the form of Eshowe.

To support Osborn, a force of 50 Zulus was raised in April 1883 under the command of Inspector G. Mansel. It was officially called the Reserve Territorial Carbineers, better known as the Nongqayi (the restrainers). Unfortunately the force had little power to restrain anything save disturbances in its own area and northern Zululand was left to ferment on its own.

Zibebu and his white advisers were doing some hard thinking. Acts of violence were increasing all around his territory and it was pretty obvious that a fight was brewing. Being the man he was, Zibebu took the bull by the horns. He assembled his army and commenced beating down all treacherous elements in his area.

This was a sure sign to Zibebu's enemies that it was time to move. Near the Ngome forest a considerable force was marshalled, around the middle of March 1883. From there this force, about 5000 strong, invaded Zibebu's territory. The warriors tramped up to the Nxongwana (hill of the little clump of bushes), and there burnt down Zibebu's Nkungwini kraal, without much opposition.

Then they marched up the Msebe valley, towards Banganomo and there, on 30 March, they met their Waterloo. Zibebu only had a thousand men, but he was a first-class leader and his adviser, Colenbrander, had quite a touch of military genius. The two concealed their men in the dense grass of the valley and set a trap. The invaders fell right into it.

They could not see Zibebu's army and had no idea of its strength. They only knew that various portions of their force had been suddenly attacked. They promptly panicked, and each man fled for his life. It was a blind rush through the grass for safety. In the crush Zibebu lost ten men, but about two thousand of his enemies were killed.

The invaders seemed to have gone mad. One man was discovered standing in the grass, holding his shield before him and stabbing at the air as though in conflict. He simply did not see the astonished group who surrounded and watched him for a little while. Eventually somebody stuck a spear through him.

Zibebu was delighted at the result. After chasing the invaders home and sending an official complaint to the British, he sallied out and raided the uSuthu area in the valley of the Black Mfolozi, burning kraals and looting to his heart's content.

All the British could do was to reprove Cetshwayo for allowing his force to attack Zibebu in the first place. Beyond that the uSuthu were left to lick their wounds and prepare for the next round. They mustered their strength and set out to attack

Hhamu, but he retired into the wilds of the *Ngoje* or *Ngotshe* (place of precipices), and held all at bay.

An endless uproar of murders and outrages went on in northern Zululand. On 14 July Cetshwayo's army once more invaded Zibebu's territory. It was simply a raid this time, and many huts were burnt and women carried off before Zibebu could retaliate.

Zibebu was enraged at the business. He secretly mustered his full force at his Kuvukeni kraal and set off along secret paths for uluNdi.

At his capital, Cetshwayo was in conference with the leaders of his people. All his grandees were present, discussing plans for subduing Zibebu. On the night of the 20th they went to bed, contented with the preparations they had made.

All that night Zibebu led his army through the bush. With him rode three Europeans: Grosvenor Darke, John Eckersley and J. MacAllister, all traders of northern Zululand, who had lost heavily from the uSuthu raids, and were bent on vengeance. His adviser, Johan Colenbrander, led a parallel diversionary raid in case it was necessary to rescue Zibebu's main force from any difficulties.

At dawn on the 21st Zibebu was five miles from uluNdi. There he marshalled his men, assigned them their tasks, and set out to surround Cetshwayo's followers.

Cetshwayo's followers discovered the attack too late. At 8 a.m. Henry Fynn saw the uSuthu army sallying hastily out of the kraal. They charged up towards the attackers, but within half-an-hour they were running back, scattering like a swarm of bees. The slaughter was great. "All the principal headmen were killed," wrote Darke in the *Natal Advertiser*. "Sekethwayo, Ntshingwayo, who had commanded at Sandlwana, Hhamu, Mbopha, and many others. Being all fat and big-bellied they had no chance of escape; and one of them was actually run to earth and stabbed by my little mat-bearers."

Fifty-nine notables were killed in that attack and immense booty was captured. Looting uluNdi was a fascinating business. Besides the usual impedimenta found in kraals, there were loads of goods and presents belonging to Cetshwayo. Flamboyant uniforms, top hats, coloured umbrellas, rings, gold studs, silk shirts, ornamental cups and mugs and signed pictures of royalty; all these were gleefully seized by Zibebu's men and paraded about in triumph. The whole kraal, of about one thousand huts, was burnt down.

In the confusion Cetshwayo had disappeared. Jumping on a decrepit horse, he had sought to escape. His horse had given in and he had hidden in a clump of bush. There he was discovered by a section of Zibebu's men. They saw his figure among the leaves and threw their spears at him. He was wounded twice in the thigh. He called out to them, telling them who he was. Out of respect they dressed his wounds and then allowed him to escape.

Leaving Fynn to take charge of his people and to restrain Zibebu from killing everyone, Cetshwayo fled deep into the Nkandla forest where he found sanctuary with the chief Sigananda in a lonely kraal at the foot of the waterfall in the Mhome gorge.

Zibebu continued his victorious career. With his white allies, he attacked Somkhele in the middle of August 1883 and drove him into the Dukuduku bush, with the loss of his primest livestock and women.

In his forest retreat all Cetshwayo could do was send a stream of protests and complaints to the British, through the medium of a European named William Grant, of the Aborigines' Protection Society, who acted as his secretary and adviser.

The whole country was in uproar and outrages of every kind were a daily occurrence. The British were in a complete quandary. They attempted to persuade Cetshwayo to go down to Eshowe, but he refused even to see the British Resident in the forest.

All the British could do in the uproar was to protect themselves by means of a small earthwork fort, built in October 1883 by Lieutenant Yolland at Eshowe, and watch proceedings from there. They gave no active support to either of the contestants and their only policy was a confused series of remonstrances to both parties.

As usual it was Zibebu who started the next act. Seeing that Cetshwayo refused to leave the forest, Zibebu ostentatiously marched his force up to Babanango. At the same time Fynn managed to see Cetshwayo and at last prevailed on him to go to Eshowe for sanctuary.

Cetshwayo removed himself on 15 January 1884, and settled down in his old Siqhwagini kraal, while the government pondered the problem of what to do about him. For once the resolute Zibebu played no part in the next move. At 4.30 p.m. on 8 February 1884, Cetshwayo died peacefully in his hut from fatty disease of the heart. After much uncertainty, he was buried in the Nkandla forest near the Mhome gorge on 23 April. He at least had found a solution to his problems, and by his death allowed others to seek for a way of escape from the chaos.

JOHAN COLENBRANDER

TWENTY-EIGHT

Dinuzulu

Cetshwayo's heir was his young son Dinuzulu (the satisfier of the Zulus). In the ominous quiet that followed the death of his father, the young man looked about him in bewilderment. Zululand was in ruins; kraals were burnt and cattle and crops wantonly destroyed, with all that peculiar bitterness of feeling which belongs entirely to a civil war.

Cetshwayo's supporters were mostly refugees, hiding in bushes and caves, sniping at Zibebu when they could and reviling him and his white advisers all the time. Zibebu was busily engaged in breaking up every concentration of hostile persons he could discover. The British were still floundering about uncertainly, torn between the local officials' desire to end the chaos by imposing authority and the vacillating, disinterested policy of the home government. John Dunn was seeking to pull a plum out of the pie by offering, against cash payment of £4000, to restore order in Zululand by force. There seemed no ray of hope anywhere in a dark land.

In this predicament, Dinuzulu received a message from a group of Boers. They had been watching Zululand affairs with interest and had formed their own opinion of them. The Zululand troubles were reviewed in a report by P.J. Joubert, the Transvaal Superintendent of Natives, on 9 January 1884. He summed them up as follows:

"After the war between the English Government and the

Zulus in 1879, Zululand was divided into several small states of chieftainship. This, of course, was done to divide the nation against itself and to weaken it, or to cause the one tribe to extirpate the other. This policy soon bore fruit."

If this, indeed, was British policy it was to bear fruit they little expected. The Boer message to Dinuzulu was an offer of support. They guaranteed to establish him as undisputed chief if, in return, he would reward all those who aided him with farms.

It was a tempting offer and the two Boer messengers, C. Meyer and J.F. van Staden, were pressing. Dinuzulu discussed the matter with Mnyamana. Both were nervous, for Cetshwayo had occasionally dabbled with the idea of enlisting Boer aid, but always put it off with the argument that once in they would never get them out.

Now, however, there seemed to be no alternative. So, in the end, Dinuzulu climbed into the trap between the two messengers and rode off with them to Wakkerstroom in the Transvaal.

News of this development spread throughout Southern Africa. Land-hungry farmers, younger sons not sure of an inheritance and all manner of adventurers rode post-haste to offer their service to Dinuzulu. On 1 May 1884 a committee, the Committee of Dinuzulu's Volunteers, was formed and a letter was sent to Hhamu and Zibebu, informing them that Dinuzulu was in the Committee's hands and ordering the chiefs to lay down their arms.

Two days later the commando crossed into Zululand and camped at Tintwa's Kop on the Black Mfolozi, eight miles south of modern Vryheid. With reinforcements constantly streaming in, they then removed to the Ngwibi Mountain and held a conference at a site they called Salf-Laager. An agreement was drawn up with Dinuzulu, in which he agreed to make land grants in exchange for being restored to power.

On 21 May, Dinuzulu was crowned king. In the presence of about 8000 Zulus, four of the Boer leaders climbed on to a wagon with Dinuzulu. They made him kneel. Then, placing their hands on his head, they swore to protect him against his enemies as long as he observed the conditions of the alliance.

News of these ominous developments put Zibebu into a panic. His erstwhile friends started deserting him and edging in the direction of Dinuzulu. He gathered all his people and livestock at Banganomo and sent off urgent appeals to the British, but they still took no action. Colenbrander endeavoured to raise a mercenary force in Natal to reinforce Zibebu, but without means there was little which he could do.

The local authorities were seriously perturbed, but they were helpless. On 5 May Zibebu instructed John Eckersley to write his last letter to Osborn.

"The chief begs me to say that he does not know if this messenger will reach you or not as the roads are all stopped by the uSuthu party. Should this one get through it will be the last, and then, he says, that he does not know what will become of him, as the whites are interfering; if it was only the Zulus he would know what to do. He always depended on you, his father, for help; and thought that when he died, you would be near at hand. He begs to say that fighting against whites he does not like, but he will never give in to the Boers; he will be killed by them first. He says that he *konzaed* (paid tribute) to the British, and he still intends to do so to the last. The Boers are now at the Ntabankulu, and they intend to go direct to the oNdini (uluNdi) kraal, where they intend to place Dinuzulu, and then they mean to fight with Hhamu and us."

Osborn sent the letter to the Natal Governor who, in turn, on 19 May 1884, sent it to the British authorities with a letter of his own, which summed up the feeling of the local officials.

"It is impossible to read this letter without a feeling of the most painful regret for the position in which that chief is placed by the action of the Boers, a regret which with me is intensified by the knowledge that in the unhappy conflicts and disorders that have afflicted the Zulu country the past twelve months, the offence has not been with him but with those whose object it was to destroy him, and all whose attempts he had hitherto prevented by the force of his personal character and by his great capacity for command; by the conviction that his sentiments towards us are those of true loyalty and friendliness; and by the persuasion that if we had but consented to take over the rule of Central Zululand we should have found in him a powerful supporter in our objects of restoring order, of maintaining the integrity of the Zulu country, and of building up a peaceful and contented native community."

Apart from expressing sentiments such as these, all the British would do was protest to the Boer republics. Both denied all knowledge of the projected invasion of Zululand. It was essentially a fillibustering campaign on the part of private individuals, and beyond the control of either the Transvaal or Orange Free State.

Zibebu searched around desperately for allies. He tried John Dunn, but the white chief refused to budge. Johan Colenbrander rode hastily down to Natal and inserted an advertisement in *The Times of Natal* for Tuesday, 13 May 1884.

"All able-bodied men of good character who can ride and shoot well are required at once. Applicants must be prepared to provide their own horse, carbine, etc., such as they may require for field service. Satisfactory remuneration offered. For further particulars apply A.B.C.D. Times Of Natal."

At the Thukela, Colenbrander raised a small force of eight Europeans and two coloured men, known as the Stanger Disreputables, and with these he attempted to reach Zibebu, driving a number of horses he had bought in Natal. The whole country, by then, was in conflict and Colenbrander found his way effectively blocked by the uSuthu. In the end he had to disperse his pocket army and, on 8 June 1884, he abandoned Zululand and went back to Natal.

Fighting was taking place all over the country. Two uSuthu armies, led by Bejana and Somkhele, were effectively neutralising John Dunn by seemingly threatening to invade his territory. On 2 June Hlubi was attacked by another diversionary force. The British at Eshowe were effectively bottled up by

Dabulamanzi, who had aggressively roamed around the reserve territory all through May and even attacked the camp of a British force sent against him on 10 May.

All these were minor diversions. The big show was taking place in the north. Over 400 Boers had already poured into Dinuzulu's camp, to support him and receive arms. Early in June the force moved against Zibebu. There were 5000 of Dinuzulu's men, about 500 mixed African auxiliaries from the Transvaal, 15 European adventurers led by a German named Captain Schiel, and 100 Boers led by Lucas Meyer.

Before this force, Zibebu retreated eastwards. His Banganomo kraal was abandoned to the invaders. Zibebu retreated down the Mkhuze River, until he reached its pass through the Lubombo, where the renowned Ghost Mountain keeps guard over the river passage.

At the foot of the mountain, between it and the river, Zibebu selected his battlefield. Among the long grass and bush, his army turned at bay like a wounded buffalo and sullenly awaited the approaching enemy. True to his habit, he attempted an ambush of his enemies by concealing one of his detachments on the bank of the river, so that they could suddenly appear behind the Boers in the midst of the attack.

Meyer led his men towards the spot with extreme caution. On 5 June they reached the place. Schiel was leading the advance guard when there was a burst of rifle fire. Meyer was about to advance in force to the spot when an accident happened, which possibly proved decisive. Some excitable member of Zibebu's ambuscade accidentally fired his gun and betrayed their position.

The Boers turned on the ambush and Zibebu's men were forced to come into action immediately. The whole valley echoed with the staccato rap of the guns and the conflicting war cries of the opponents, the lusty "*Washesha*" (we hurry) of Zibebu's men, and the deeper "*uSuthu*" of Dinuzulu's party.

Describing the fight afterwards, Zibebu told Osborn that:

"The uSuthu advanced in the Zulu way, with breast and

two horns. The Boers were behind, urging the uSuthu on, threatening to shoot them if they retreated. The enemy, on getting to within a few hundred yards, began the attack on me by the Boers opening fire. They were on horseback when they fired, keeping up a heavy fire all the time.

"When the enemy was within a short distance from us my force met it and the fight took place. The left wing of my force closed with the right wing of the enemy, and drove it back in confusion on to the breast. While this was going on, the Boers, having taken up a favourable position, opened a heavy flank fire on my men, and it soon became impossible for them to stand it and they gave way; they retreated, pursued by the Boers who shot down many in their retreat!

"The uSuthu, too, pursued. My force ran to the Mkhuze, and while crossing this river very many of my men got killed by the enemy, as the river was deep and the drift not very practicable. My force retreated across the Mkhuze, where all our families and cattle had been placed for safety. The enemy kept up the pursuit until late that day, when the uSuthu retired to the battlefield; the Boers remaining at some wagons belonging to traders that were stationed at the Mkhuze."

Thus ended the battle of Ghost Mountain and the scramble for farms began. After spending a few days looting cattle, the Boers retired to their main camp on the Ngwibi hill. There the uSuthu army was disbanded and the Boer pay-off began.

There were over 800 applicants for farms. The committee was somewhat embarrassed by all the applicants, for there was hardly enough vacant land in Natal and Zululand put together to satisfy such a crowd. They announced, accordingly, that only men who had joined the commando before 10 June would be entitled to full 4000-acre farms. About 500 men were eligible for this. The other 300-odd applicants would have to be content with "half-farms".

A great registration of names took place, and for over a month they argued the toss about politics and farms, while the Zulus were left to their own devices. Eventually, on 5 August, at a new laager named Boom Laager on the Hlobane Mountain, a proclamation establishing the New Republic was issued and Lucas Meyer appointed as president. The town of Vryheid (liberty) was laid out as a capital and the survey of farms began.

Sixteen men were appointed as an inspection group to lay out farms. Among them were such well-known men as Louis Botha, Jack Andrews, Dirk Uys, the three Emmett brothers, Tom Kelly, the five Hendersons and others. Their instruments of survey consisted of a compass and a pair of crossed iron bars.

With these instruments, they would ride a horse for 20 minutes at a speed of 100 yards a minute. Then the crossbar was brought into use and a course laid at right angles. A beacon would be erected at each corner. In this way the 16 men surveyed themselves right across Zululand until they reached the sea. The fever season came, with them still working, but gin mixed with blue gum leaves and faith kept them healthy. Then they found that they had been overgenerous in the survey. There wasn't enough land in Zululand. So they had to do the survey all over again and reduce the sizes of the farms.

At Lake St Lucia, the Republic decided to lay out a township, which it was hoped could be developed into a trading outlet. The proposed port was named Eugenie after the Empress of France, mother of the unfortunate Prince Imperial. The German trading firm of Luderitz was interested in this proposition and one of its agents, Augustus Einwald, in November 1884, visited the lake with Alfonso Schiel.

Einwald publicly claimed to have bought Lake St Lucia, and 100 000 acres of land adjoining it, for £50 worth of trade goods. He ceremoniously annexed it to Germany and this, of all things, woke the British up to what was happening in Zululand. In December 1884 they hastily sent the HMS *Goshawk* up to St Lucia Bay. On the 18th Lt William Moore hauled up the Union Jack, and much excitement and some diplomatic exchanges followed between Britain and Germany.

The New Republic also continued to regard the lake as its own, and D.J. Esselen was sent over to Europe in the middle of 1885 to secure recognition of his state and its title to St Lucia. He ridiculed both the German claim and the British annexation, which had been repeated in July 1885 when the cruiser *Moor* sailed up. On this occasion a boat had attempted to land but was swamped in the surf. Four men were drowned and the survivors forced to tramp down the coast until they reached John Dunn.

The Zulus, meanwhile, saw their whole country being steadily beaconed off as farms, the farmers' appetites increasing with every acre they received. All the Zulus could do was protest. They had no leaders worth their salt and the few Europeans, such as Colenbrander and Darke, who could have given them some guidance, had been so ruined during the Boer invasion that they had abandoned the country and wandered up to Swaziland, where living was still pleasant. Zibebu was a helpless refugee, living under British protection near Eshowe.

In January 1886 the Zulus sent a petition to the British Queen asking for help, and in April they made a second appeal. As a result, the British asked the New Republic to send a deputation to Durban to discuss matters. The meeting was a complete failure. The deputation refused even to discuss anything to do with Zululand's independence or a restriction of their boundaries. To them the Zulus were now a nation of squatters, living on Republican territory and subject to taxes and manual labour.

On 4 May Dinuzulu again complained to the British and informed them that even the sacred heart of Zululand – the royal graves in the valley of the Mkhumbane – was being desecrated and the traditional Zulu guardians driven away by Boer settlers.

Early in October, Dabulamanzi sought to protest about the Boers' behaviour, and was shot dead for his pains. Dinuzulu's uluNdi kraal, built on Nhlazatshe Mountain, was also burnt down.

Once again war seemed in the air and, on 18 October, the British held another meeting with the Boers. This time some agreement was reached. The Boers were to abandon their protectorate over Zululand and a boundary was agreed upon, substantially establishing Zululand as it is today. It excluded from Zululand that area regarded as the cradle of the Zulu race. The Boers received most of the land they wanted except St Lucia, but at least a portion of the country was saved for the Zulus. The nearest the Republic got to the sea was a wedge of land, running down between the Mkhuze and the Phongolo rivers to the Lubombo Mountains.

The Zulus protested at the whole agreement, but there was nothing they could do. On 4 December 1886 the Boundary Commission began its work, and by 15 January of the following year the whole thing was settled. Then, on 5 February 1887, Osborn informed the Zulus that their portion of the country was to be a British protectorate. While they were still digesting this news, the British Government, on 9 May 1887, decided to annex the country entirely. The Governor of Natal was to act as its Governor and the laws of Natal were applicable.

On 21 June 1887, Melmoth Osborn was appointed to be Resident Commissioner and Chief Magistrate of Zululand. The whole of Zululand had already been divided up into magistracies. Eshowe became the capital of Zululand and a magisterial post under A.L. Pretorius was established in the Nkandla district. Major McKean was sent to Nquthu; J.L. Knight was sent to the Mthonjaneni district on 6 April 1887, and established himself at a seat first known as Mfule, on the farm of W.J. Orlett, and which was later roughly surveyed as a township under the name of Melmoth.

In the south A.J. Shepstone was sent, in July 1887, to establish the Lower Mfolozi magisterial district, eventually defined on 6 December. Its seat was at first on the eMbabe (bitter) River but eventually, after several changes, fixed in 1894 at Empangeni.

In the north the new status of Zululand was proclaimed at

Nkonjeni, eight miles north of uluNdi, on 7 July and Richard Addison was introduced to those chiefs who were present as magistrate over what was to be called the Ndwandwe district. Dinuzulu ignored the entire proceedings and stayed ostentatiously away.

Zululand failed to settle down under the new order. A greater degree of control came to it, but Dinuzulu kept aloof and rumours were current of approaching trouble with him. Meanwhile, traders built their stores and a flood of applications for land grants poured in from Europeans who impatiently waited for the government to decide on a policy of settlement.

A few roads were also built, for communications were excessively difficult. The only existing roads were just the hunters' and traders' tracks. The only arterial routes consisted of the ancient coastal track and the so-called Rathbone's Road. This road was blazed in November 1885 by the trader Thomas Rathbone, on behalf of Durban merchants who wished to trade with the Barberton goldfields. It led through the western edge of Zululand, past Mthonjaneni, uluNdi and Magudu, to Swaziland and the Transvaal, and was in fair condition and general use. Another transport rider, Peter Marcus, blazed a second goldfields road up the coast in 1887. His road, known as Marcus Road, became the Zululand main coast road of to-day; running up to Somkhele, Hluhluwe, Mkhuze, across the Phongolo at Glen's Drift, and then off across Swaziland to Pigg's Peak and Barberton.

Meanwhile, friction between Dinuzulu and the British steadily increased. Dinuzulu ignored the new administration entirely and attempted to direct the affairs of his people as though there was no other government. A major clash was inevitable. It came when a man named Mfokazana was sentenced to death by Dinuzulu for witchcraft. A party of men was sent to execute the sentence.

Mfokazana was discreetly absent when the killing party arrived, but his wife was put to death and his cattle seized. The magistrate of the Ndwandwe district protested and demanded that the cattle be returned. Dinuzulu, as usual, ignored the government message.

Osborn then proceeded to the Nkonjeni seat of the magistrate and summoned Dinuzulu to appear before him on 3 September. Still Dinuzulu ignored the message. Osborn then fined him 30 head of cattle for contempt and a force was sent to seize them, together with the cattle Dinuzulu had seized from Mfokazana. There was no resistance, the occupants of Dinuzulu's uSuthu kraal simply maintained a hostile silence while the police sorted and drove off their cattle.

When the police left, Dinuzulu called a meeting of the uSuthu and it was resolved that he proceed to Vryheid to appeal for aid from the Boers. On his return he spread the rumour that once again a commando was to be sent to aid him, this time against the British.

The annoyed British Resident summoned Dinuzulu to Eshowe. After some hesitation he went on 14 November 1887. Osborn gave him a good lecture: "Dinuzulu must know," he said, "and all the Zulus must know, that the rule of the house of Shaka is a thing of the past. It is dead. It is like water that is spilt on the ground. The Queen rules now in Zululand and no one else." Dinuzulu listened in silence. He was fined 50 head of cattle and then informed that the government had decided to allow Zibebu to return to his old home, as a counterweight to any trouble with the uSuthu.

Addison was instructed to remove the seat of his magistracy to a point sandwiched between Dinuzulu and Zibebu. The spot chosen was on a high, wind-swept ridge known as kwaNongoma (the place of the diviner), and, on 18 November 1887, Addison and 50 men of the Nongqayi arrived there and commenced the erection of a few buildings. The site of the magistracy was the point where Rathbone's Road from the south met the track coming up from Somkhele's area on the coast. The place was at first named Vuna, from the nearby river, but, in the course of some months, when it was found that the Zulus preferred the name of the ridge, it became officially known as Nongoma.

On 3 December Zibebu and 700 of his followers arrived in the district from their exile in the south. His return unleashed a flood of ill-feeling. His old lands had been occupied by the uSuthu and their crops were green. They refused to abandon them. Addison had a nightmare time trying to restrain Zibebu from kicking the uSuthu out, while he ejected them properly and gave them compensation for the loss of their crops.

Sullen resentment greeted all these developments. Zibebu continued rebuilding his old Banganomo kraal in an electric atmosphere, which threatened to explode at any moment. Dinuzulu slowly mustered his forces and prepared a stronghold on the mountain known as Ceza (the chipped one). War rumours were whispered in all the kraals.

The year 1888 saw the start of trouble. In March one of the uSuthu headmen, Nkowana, attacked and killed two of Zibebu's men; and cattle raids became common as Dinuzulu's army decided to feed itself on Zibebu's livestock.

Then one of the uSuthu chiefs, Mthumbu, threatened with eviction from Zibebu's area, refused to move and declined to appear before the magistrate. A warrant was issued for his arrest and Sub-Inspector Osborn, with eight policemen, marched to the uSuthu kraal to demand the surrender of the chief and two other recalcitrants. They found a regiment 1000 strong grinning at them over the kraal fence. The policemen made a formal demand and then discreetly withdrew.

Troops were hurriedly requisitioned. Dinuzulu was also busy, collecting reinforcements in Boer territory. It appeared to the British that the only course open was to arrest him and his principal adviser Ndabuko, and warrants were accordingly made out on a charge of cattle theft.

On 1 June the British force attempted to put the warrants into effect. A mixed force of 140 soldiers and 64 policemen set out from Nkonjeni, and made for the store of D. Louw at Mfabeni. There they rendezvoused with 400 Zulu allies, provided by Mnyamana, and the following day the mixed force set out for Ceza Mountain.

Reaching the place, the government force found itself faced by about 1800 Zulus. The uSuthu immediately charged and a hot little fight resulted, until the government force was compelled to withdraw with a loss of two men killed. The government men had not come expecting a major battle, so they returned to Nkonjeni for food, ammunition, and instructions.

The uSuthu were jubilant and commenced raiding in all directions. The trader, D. Louw, was murdered for having guided the government troops, and his son Klaas was also killed at his store on the Vuna River on 6 June. All around the country supporters of Dinuzulu, such as Somkhele on the coast, began to move restlessly, and Tshingana at the mountain then known as Hlophekhulu (the great white one) near uluNdi, went into open revolt and embarrassed British communications by cutting the road to the south.

At Nongoma, Sub-Inspector Osborn garrisoned a rough, little earthwork fort with 35 Zulu policemen. Mrs Rosetta Louw (widow of Klaas Louw), and her 12-year-old daughter, Catharina, took refuge there, along with a few other Europeans. Zibebu was requested to march to the place to reinforce it and, with his men, he encamped on the Ndunu hill, about half a mile from the fort.

To this place, on the night of 22 June 1888, Dinuzulu sent his army by stealth and along little-used paths. At the magistracy the garrison passed a peaceful night. Then, at 6 a.m. the next morning, the sentries reported a large body of men advancing on the north side of the camp. The 50 occupants of the fort – policemen, Europeans and native court messengers – were quickly alerted and Zibebu hurriedly drew up his men.

Then the uSuthu appeared over the hill, about 1200 yards from the fort. They divided into two, with one section of about a thousand men advancing menacingly on the fort while the larger section of about 3000 made for Zibebu.

Zibebu had about 800 men to confront this force. The

uSuthu charged down upon him with a rush. For a moment the Mandlakazi held firm. Then pressure told and they broke and fled hotly pursued by the uSuthu for two-and-a-half miles. About 200 of Zibebu's men were killed in this clash and 40 of the uSuthu. The force advancing against the fort was simply a diversion. The warriors approached to a distance of about 600 yards and then wheeled off as soon as the defenders opened fire.

When news of this attack reached Melmoth Osborn at Nkonjeni, he decided to evacuate Vuna, as he had not the men to spare for its defence. Accordingly, the following day, 24 June, Major McKean marched up to Vuna, and at 1 p.m. Addison and the garrison, with Zibebu, were escorted back to Nkonjeni. Behind them the triumphant uSuthu burnt the little magistracy down and news of the victory spread throughout Zululand.

Trouble started to break out all over the country. Traders were attacked in isolated places and their goods looted. At the Mhlathuze River one trader, Cecil Tonge, was murdered, while another was killed on the Lower Mfolozi.

Despite the general unrest, troop reinforcements were rapidly concentrated in the north and the end soon came. At noon on 2 July 1888 a mixed government force, about 2000 strong, attacked the Hlophekhulu fortress. It was a hot, little fight while it lasted. The uSuthu, led by Tshingana, resisted stubbornly from rocks, ravines and bush, but they were routed at a cost of two Europeans and about 63 native levies.

Tshingana escaped in the uproar and fled to Dinuzulu at Ceza. The news he brought of his defeat and the evident presence of the army in strength in Zululand sobered the uSuthu considerably. Over 2200 soldiers were scattered about the country and in the face of this force Dinuzulu, on 5 August, packed his bags and fled into the New Republic, burning his huts at Ceza and leaving the place deserted.

On 6 August the army re-occupied the Vuna magistracy, finding the whole place just a pile of rubble and charred debris from the burning of Addison's house.

This was the end of the affair. The army did a general promenade through the country, overawing the minor rebels, but there was no more opposition. Somkheles's renowned fortress in the Dukuduku forest was thoroughly searched by Captain Baden-Powell, but not a man was found there.

At Vryheid, Dinuzulu and his leaders sought to surrender to the Boers, but when this was denied them they, one by one, returned to Zululand and surrendered.

Dinuzulu caught the train at Elandslaagte and went down to Pietermaritzburg on 15 November. There he went to Bishopstowe, where the family of the late Bishop Colenso (who had died on 20 June 1883) sheltered him. The following day he surrendered to the police.

An involved trial at Eshowe followed on 16 October 1888. It was full of legal wranglings and quarrels, with much mudslinging and sensational newspaper stories. At the end Dinuzulu, Ndabuko and Tshingana were all found guilty of high treason and sent to St Helena Island to serve their respective sentences of 10, 15 and 20 years.

A commission then proceeded to delineate the boundary between the uSuthu-Mandlakazi tribes and the northern area of Zululand was closely studied to facilitate its future administration. As part of the general change J.Y. Gibson was sent to Vuna as magistrate and under him the name of the place was finally changed to Nongoma.

To facilitate control, a new magistracy was also established near Glen's Store, on 1 April 1892, and named Hlabisa after the tribe living there. Exactly six years later, on 1 April 1898, a second magistracy was established under C.A. Wheelwright, in the Mahlabathini area, at a place ingeniously known as Mashonengashoni (that which disappears without disappearing, something which remains in view for a long time). Ever since, the northern areas have been among the most tranquil in all Zululand.

TWENTY-NINE
Northern frontiers

The northern frontier districts of Natal, as we have seen
in the preceeding chapter, have played an intimate and
somewhat uproarious part in the story of Zululand. Like
all frontier lands they were always a resort for the adventurous. Well watered, spacious, and with superb pasturage, they
made an excellent home for a rugged, almost Wild West-like
community, and those pioneers who settled in the area, mainly of hardy Voortrekker stock, treasured their independence
and were Republicans to the core.

The story of the abortive Klip River Republic has already
been told. After the collapse of this pocket state, Andries Spies
and some of the more resolutely republican of his fellows decided to remove to an area where they could shake off British
administration. Accordingly, a party rode up to see Mpande,
the Zulu king, and had no difficulty in obtaining from him,
in exchange for 100 head of cattle, grazing rights in the area
between the Buffalo and the Blood rivers.

This permission to graze stock was granted in 1854 to Cornelius van Rooyen, Andries Spies, Christian Klopper and others.
On the strength of their permit, a number of farmers settled
in the area and formed a republic, with Spies as *landdrost*, Van
Rooyen as field cornet, and Klopper as commandant of everybody save his wife, who was a renowned strong-woman, fond
of challenging visiting males to wrestle and always ending by
throwing them over her shoulder.

This republic was named Utrecht (the outside meadow) after the ancient city in Holland. Its inhabitants settled down to quarrel with one another in good old trekker style, and to develop a capital for themselves which, by 1862, was a rather dreary little town of about 20 houses, a church built in 1854, one hotel serving bad gin out of a teacup, and a courthouse furnished simply with a chair, table and a set of stocks. Constant rumours of wars with the Zulus plagued the place and gave life in this 20-miles-wide and 40-miles-long Republic a permanent sense of insecurity.

The area of the former Klip River Republic, between the Thukela and the Buffalo rivers, consisted of a great plain full of sweet and waving grass, green in the summer, golden in the winter. It was deceptive country, seemingly open, and yet an army could lose itself among the hillocks sprinkled over the plain, each covered with acacia shrubs and flowering mountain aloes.

In October 1848 steps were taken to administer the area and establish a capital. On the 2nd of that month, the Lieutenant Governor of Natal appointed John Bird to the task of surveying the area and acting as magistrate over what was proclaimed, three days later, as the Klip River district. Bird's immediate task was to select a site for the proposed town and, after due examination, he established himself on the farm of Van Tonder, close to the great flat-topped landmark of Mbulwana (the hill of mountain aloes).

Bird made his headquarters in the thatched cottages on Van Tonder's farm and busied himself in laying out the proposed town. With this task completed, he was recalled to his normal survey duties in Pietermaritzburg and replaced on 4 December 1849 by James Melville, as full-time magistrate of the district.

The site was confirmed by all as being well adapted for a district centre. It was proclaimed as a town on 20 June 1850 and a few huts were put up to house the magistrate, his staff and force of 25 African policemen. William Allerston was appointed constable of the place at £4 a month, and was glad to get that princely salary in those times.

"I was there about seven months with my family," he wrote, "and a pretty hard time we had of it. There were four houses of wattle and daub when we went up. There had been a fifth, but it had fallen down the day before our arrival. In order to obtain food supplies, I had periodically to walk to Estcourt, bringing the provisions home on my back."

In July 1850, Lieutenant Governor Benjamin Pine rode up to inspect the place. He named it Ladysmith, in honour of Sir Harry Smith's wife, and in order "that it may be a suitable partner for the Dutch settlement of Harrismith on the further side of the Drakensberg".

After this, the town went ahead. George Winder arrived in September to open the first store; water furrows were dug; and by 1854 the place had 23 houses and was on the way to what it has become today: a long, broad street, with a town on either side of it. In those days it consisted of little more than the street!

The town had many sensations and excitements in its early years. On 26 August 1854, £340 of public money was reported missing from the home of the magistrate, Captain Johannes Struben. Struben was a most popular man, but much scandal resulted from the disappearance of this money and eventually he removed into the Transvaal.

The town's greatest excitement came in 1860. Living in the Klip River district was one of the best-known characters in Natal, Johannes Hendrik de Lange. De Lange or "Hans Dons", as he was sometimes called, had played his full part in the history of Natal and Zululand, and his personality was most romantic. Charles Barter has left a good description of the man as he was in 1851. Barter had stuck with his wagon at the foot of the old Quagga Pad Pass (Bramhoek Pass) and eventually enlisted the aid of a local farmer in order to hire extra oxen. The farmer was Johannes de Lange.

"He was clad in a narrow striped jacket," wrote Barter, "such as footmen in England occasionally wear, and trousers of black corduroy, his hat was tied up in a many-coloured handkerchief, and at his side hung a huge powder-horn.

445

"His moustache and whiskers were united, and both were snow-white and his countenance was more expressive and less stolid than those of most of his countrymen, while his frame was that of a tall, powerful man.

"Hans de Lange, for such was his name, was altogether a very fine-looking old fellow, and did not belie the character which he bears of a brave man and a keen sportsman, and especially of a daring and successful lion hunter."

At the end of November 1860, an African named Ncatya broke into a new farmhouse being constructed on De Lange's property and molested a young Fingo housemaid. The maid identified the man and De Lange took him off to the police. On the journey De Lange and his prisoner apparently came to blows. De Lange killed the man and then, fearing the consequences, he concealed the body and reported that the man had escaped and run away.

Some of De Lange's farm labourers, however, carried the story to the police. De Lange was arrested and charged with murder. There was tremendous excitement in the district at this. People talked about rescuing him by force; and on all sides it was said that a local jury would never convict him, for the shooting of an African in those times and parts was hardly considered to be murder.

G.A. Lucas, the Resident Magistrate at that time, had the unpleasant task of conducting the preparatory examination. De Lange was committed for trial and, as Lucas had nervously reported the feelings of the public, he was secretly removed to Pietermaritzburg and his trial scheduled for 20 February 1861.

The accused man, however, rightfully petitioned that he should be tried in Ladysmith. It would be more advantageous to the defence, as the local jury would be familiar with the scene of the crime and all witnesses could be easily obtained. The petition was granted, and on 20 February 1861, he was tried in Ladysmith before the Second Puisne Judge, H. Lushington Phillips, and a jury consisting of W. Lazenby, J. Watson, J.L. Labuscagne, B. Nel, C. Pieters, A. Krogman, G. Potgieter, J. Potgieter and J. Labuschagne.

The trial lasted for three days. At the end, a majority of eight of the jury found him guilty of murder and the judge, accordingly, passed sentence of death. This sentence was confirmed by the Governor and caused a considerable sensation in Natal.

The law, in those days, could hardly have been called gentle. Sentences were severe and all executions since the first one in Natal on 15 June 1852, when two Africans had been hanged in Pietermaritzburg, were conducted in public. The sensation about De Lange's case lay in the fact that, for the first time, a European had been found guilty by his fellows and was to hang for killing an African.

The whole business aroused intense public feeling. Rumours spread that Mpande was sending an army to stop the execution on the grounds that De Lange was his friend and captain, with full rights to shoot any African.

The local Ladysmith people imposed a complete boycott on proceedings. In the gaol, doors were left open deliberately by sympathising warders, but as a matter of honour De Lange declined to escape.

None of the officials wanted to have anything to do with the execution. Hangings are disgusting things at all times; and the officials also feared repercussions from De Lange's friends.

The usual hangman was a convict named Scheepers. He jumped out of the wagon while being taken up to Ladysmith for the execution and hid himself until the affair was over. Thomas Phipson, the sheriff, feigned sick and passed the job on to his chief constable, White, who refused point-blank to do it. Eventually an underling named Moore, assisted by a malefactor from the Ladysmith gaol, was ordered to perform the execution.

Moore was a complete amateur and very frightened. The townspeople ignored him. They refused to supply timber or rope. Moore and his assistant had to rig up a crude structure and make a grass rope themselves.

Lucas, the magistrate, was in a complete panic over the matter. He advised Moore to gallop away from Ladysmith as quickly as possible after the execution, for fear the population would lynch him. This advice naturally put Moore into a fine state of nerves and, inevitably, he made a complete mess of things.

At 6.30 a.m. on 26 March 1861, Moore tried to do his best. Fortunately, the public ignored proceedings and there were no spectators. The rope broke once and the unfortunate old man had to experience the horror a second time, with the grass rope doubled. The business ended with the thud of hooves as the hangman galloped away.

For the purposes of law, order and effective administration, the Klip River district was far too large; and the insecurity associated with De Lange's execution duly impressed itself upon the authorities. They decided to divide the district into two sections, and, on 5 December 1862 the new magistracy was constituted, with Philip Allen as first magistrate.

In any case there was a natural division of the old Klip River district, in the rugged shape of the range known as the Biggarsberg to Europeans and as oNdini (the heights) to the Africans. This range with the long, bush-covered 5862-foot Hlathikhulu (mountain of the great forest) as its highest point, lay like a wall across the frontier lands. North of it lay a bleak and undulating grassy plain with an occasional hillock, rolling up to the frontier with the Transvaal.

The new district was one of varied climate. Floods were common, but so were droughts; and the rivers were erratic streams such as the Ngagane (unexpected one), the Ncandu (small flow), and the Ngogo, onomatopoetically named from the noise of its current gurgling over the stones.

The selection of a site for the capital of this new district involved much argument. The required site was on the main road to the Transvaal, but it had several disadvantages. The water supply was uncertain and there was no building stone or convenient timber for use as fuel. This latter deficiency gravely perturbed the surveyor, Doctor Sutherland, when he visited the place in February 1863.

Sutherland was aware, however, that there was coal in the

vicinity; but, for some strange reason, he thought it improbable that "the supply from that or any other source will materially affect the industry of the inhabitants except so far as in a very few cases it may be sufficient to serve for blacksmiths' work of a local character."

Despite the objections to the site, a sale of erven took place in the new town on 16 March 1864. The sale, held outside the recently-built courthouse, was well attended, as the district had an excellent reputation for its grazing and hunting. Objections to the actual site of the town continued. Droughts and floods, which inundated the place, alternated so rapidly that by some the town was said to be amphibious.

The new town was named Newcastle, in honour of the then Colonial Secretary, the Duke of Newcastle, and in January 1865 the commercial life of the place started when F. Steel opened the first store. By that time there were 40 Europeans living in the town and 365 in the district.

It was strange that Sutherland, a man renowned for his geological knowledge, should so casually dismiss the known coal deposits in the new district. Ever since the days of the trekkers' commando against Dingane, it had been known that coal was of common occurrence in the area.

Fanners used to send wagons for loads of fuel from surface outcrops. At the time of the founding of Newcastle, Peter Smith of Talana farm, near the present town of Dundee, was already mining surface deposits on his farm and sending wagon-loads for sale on Pietermaritzburg's market square. This was the actual beginning of the coal industry in Natal.

This Natal coal marketed by Peter Smith excited considerable interest. John Gavin made comparative tests between it and imported coal in his *Caledonian Foundry*; and William Crowder, an analytical chemist, proved the local product to be just as good as the best British coal. Public meetings were held to discuss the prospects of a new Natal industry, and a deputation was sent to the government in 1867, asking for a commission on coal to be established.

Several wagon-loads of coal were sent down to Durban, for trial in ships and trains. The survey ship, *Hydra*, experimented and the results were favourable. J.A. Lodge, the engineer in charge, in his report on 28 May 1868 stated: "It is my opinion that if the Natal coal can be obtained free from earthy matter, it will be equal to the best qualities of Welsh coals."

The Durban tug also tried Natal coal and found it serviceable. There was, however, considerable opposition on the part of vested interests in England to the development of a local bunker supply. The Natal Government had no funds at that time of Depression for the large-scale geological survey essential to any development; and when it approached the British Government for aid in the matter the project was quietly shelved for a few years, the local coals being dismissed as inferior.

All through the Depression years of the late 1860s, the northern frontier areas had a dreary time. Progress was halted, trade was dull, and the only excitement came from periodic uproars along the border. In June 1865, during the Free State-Basuto War, a band of Sothos, led by Letswane, raided along the top of the northern Drakensberg and invaded Natal up to Van Reenen's farm on the Sandspruit.

In the general alarm, the Natal Frontier Guard was called out from Ladysmith on 28 June. They found that the Sotho had looted the farmhouse of a settler named Wilkie and then ridden back up the mountains, leaving a trail of feathers from stolen pillows and mattresses.

The Frontier Guard climbed up the Drakensberg, to the top of Bezuidenhout's Pass at Bingham's farm, but the Sotho had vanished. Five Dutch transport men – Piet Pretorius, his three sons, and Andries Smidt – had been killed at the top of Van Reenen's Pass; and all wagons were examined to see whether they contained Boers or British.

The Sotho chief, Molapo, apologised for the invasion of Natal by his overimpetuous followers and offered compensation. The frontier quietened down again although, in October

1865, a band of cattle rustlers, exploiting the troubled times, swept down Van Reenen's Pass and raided the surrounding farms for livestock.

The most troubled frontier was that of the former Utrecht Republic. The security of tenure of this pocket republic (by then attached to the Transvaal) was hazardous, and there were constant bickerings between land-hungry Boers and the Zulus over farms which projected more and more into Zululand.

In March 1861 Cetshwayo, the Zulu Crown Prince, as we have seen, signed a document promising to give the Utrecht farmers a slice of land which would extend their Republic up to a line from Rorke's Drift to the Phongolo River. The document stated that in exchange the farmers would hand over some cattle and two of Cetshwayo's rival half-brothers, who had fled to Utrecht for sanctuary.

The farmers sent the refugees and cattle to Cetshwayo and started to beacon off their new boundaries. There was an immediate protest from Mpande. Cetshwayo had no right to make a land grant involving the homes of about 15 000 Zulus and the nation repudiated any such agreement. This was the start of a boundary quarrel which dragged on for years, with all the irritation of an open sore.

The quarrel gradually reached a climax. On 25 May 1875, the Republic proclaimed the disputed area as being definitely its territory. A commission was appointed to register land claims and eject resident Zulus. The Zulus tore down survey beacons as fast as they were put up and things looked ugly.

As usual in such troubled times, opportunists started to provoke hostilities for their own advantage. Among these individuals was a Swazi renegade prince named Mbilini, who lived under Zulu protection in the harsh wilderness along the middle Phongolo River. He stirred things up by means of sundry frontier outrages and when, in January 1877, Cetshwayo summarily ordered all European settlers in the disputed area to leave, Mbilini started to reap a rich harvest in loot from deserted farmhouses.

The Republicans withdrew into Utrecht town and held excited meetings. Appeals for support were made to the Transvaal Government but this was refused, as the people of Utrecht had consistently declined to pay war or railway tax to the central government ever since they had joined their state to the South African Republic.

In the end Utrecht itself raised a commando of 26 Europeans and 50 Africans, under Field Cornet J. Ferreira. They tracked Mbilini to his fortified cave stronghold and besieged it; but want of resolution allowed the troublemaker to escape, leaving only a few deserted kraals for the commando to destroy.

The Utrecht Republic had thrown in its lot with the South African Republic (Transvaal) in January 1856, when C. Steyn had been sent down to become *landdrost* of the district. When the British Government took over the Transvaal in the first annexation, it also took over the long-drawn-out Utrecht boundary dispute. From general sympathy with the Zulus, they switched over to aggressive support of the old Republican claim.

In February 1878, however, a full-scale commission of arbitration discovered that not only was the Republic's claim to land east of the Blood River at fault, but it had no valid title to the original ground of the Utrecht Republic itself. This was a rather awkward discovery and could have proved embarrassing, but the Anglo-Zulu War of 1879 smothered all these boundary squabbles and the affair was forgotten.

In 1884 a new development occurred in the frontier lands. Zululand was then in its hopeless state of civil war, with the young king, Dinuzulu, completely unable to establish his authority. A number of farmers in the Orange Free State and the Transvaal had been watching this chaos with interest. A few of them saw an opportunity favourable to themselves, and in March two messengers, C. Meyer and J.F. van Staden, rode in to see Dinuzulu, offering him European support, provided he would reward all those who aided him with farms. It was a tempting offer. After much anxious deliberation, the young king climbed into the trap between the two messengers and rode off to Wakkerstroom in the Transvaal. What befell him there has already been told.

Suffice to remind the reader here that the committee certainly restored Dinuzulu to his country but failed to restore the country to him. In fact, they kept it. On the victorious return of their force to Boom Laager at Hlobane, they hammered out the draft constitution for what was called the New Republic and set out to find a site for their capital. This was surveyed in October 1884 by H. Maarschalk, named Vryheid (liberty), and proclaimed a town on 12 November 1884.

A proper republican government was constituted, with Lucas Meyer as Acting State President, while Jan C. Pretorius became Commandant General. A Volksraad was also elected and an inspection group appointed to survey farms.

For the next 21 months, the Republicans quarrelled steadily with one another over who was to be president and whether they should remain independent or join Natal or the Transvaal. Eventually, a motion was passed in the Volksraad asking the Transvaal to annex the New Republic. This merger took place on 21 July 1888, after one of the shortest, noisiest and most abusive histories any republic ever had.

In the rest of the frontier areas of Natal, meanwhile, great events were taking place. The long-desired geological survey of the coalfields had taken place in 1880. F.W. North did the job and his report was most exhaustive. Workable surface coal, computed at 2 073 000 000 tons, was found over 1100 square miles of the frontier districts, while some of the deposits on the farms named Dundee and Coalfields were exceptionally rich. Minor deposits were found in Weenen and Umvoti and a few delusive deposits on the North Coast; but it was on the frontier that the real fortune lay.

North's report was a revelation to many, but to Peter Smith it was merely confirmation of his own ideas. All through the years, since 1862, he had been mining coal. Using primitive methods and ox-wagon transport, by 1881 he had mined some 7000 tons of coal and had big ambitions for the future.

After the disturbance of the Anglo-Transvaal War in 1881, Smith started to develop his plans. With Dugald Macphail, who lived on the nearby farm named Craigside, and Charles Wilson, he laid out a town in 1882, on the farm known as Dundee. This town of Dundee became the centre of the coal area, and by 1896 had grown to such an extent that it received local government.

The whole prospect for Natal coal was improving. On 5 June 1886, the first full train-load of coal arrived in Durban. The train was decorated for the occasion and came bowling merrily into the station, to the cheers of the population. In the following month the first substantial order for bunker coal came, from Sir Donald Currie's Castle Packets Co. One hundred tons were ordered from the Elandslaagte Mine for the SS *Melrose*, and the order was considered to be a landmark in Natal's history.

Smith set out to develop coal-mining in a large way. In January 1889, through his exertions, the Dundee Coal & Estate Company was formed to work Smith's Talana farm. Benjamin Greenacre became chairman of the company and capital of £50 000 was subscribed locally. This was the first commercial coal-producing company in Natal. The first sod in the shaft was turned in June 1889; and the first output was in October of the same year when 84 tons of coal were produced.

Numerous other companies were soon formed. The old hostility from overseas-vested interests, who were frightened of losing the profits of exporting bunker coal to South Africa and India, was overcome by the shipping companies themselves. E.J. King of the Bullard King Line backed the Dundee Company; and his line was the first to adopt Natal coal in large and regular supplies for bunker purposes. J.T. Rennie, Son & Co. followed suit and backed the second company to be formed, the Elandslaagte Colliery. Thenceforth, Natal coal came into general use.

In such fashion did the great coal-mining industry of northern Natal commence. All that was needed to complete the modern economic pattern of life in the old frontier districts was the coming of the railway.

The railway line, in fact, was groping up through the hills from Pietermaritzburg. It was a laborious piece of construction, with severe gradients, aggregating a total vertical climb of about two-and-a-half miles between Durban and the intended terminus on the Transvaal border.

Not until 21 June 1886 was the line opened to Ladysmith. By that time there was a clamouring demand for it. A constant stream of fortune seekers was pouring along the road to the north, crowding the hotels if they had money, or the hedges if they hadn't.

Each successive terminus of the railway, as it pushed inland, became a busy railhead. Then, when the line reached onwards to the next point the prosperity would vanish, the village would be left behind and passengers travelling through would wonder what maintained its population.

Ladysmith, in January 1890, had about 2000 inhabitants and was the most bustling place in Natal, except for Durban. "I suppose there is not at the present moment a town on the face of the earth with an equal population half so busy," wrote the *Natal Advertiser*. "It is literally bursting with traffic. Its stores and sheds are full of goods; its hillsides covered with unyoked oxen; and its roads and squares and streets thronged with rumbling wagons going and coming."

About 2500 wagons passed through the town each month in those days. The townspeople were pessimistic about the expected Depression when the railway moved on, but the local farmers prayed for the event. The passage of all these wagons reduced the veld on either side of the road and around the town to an absolute wilderness, and all the grazing was consumed as though by locusts.

Most of the traffic was destined for the Barberton goldfields. The enterprising Welch had started a coach service for passengers and mail; and with all the traffic, the usual string of inns and canteens had sprung up along the road to the north.

Three hours' ride, or 20 miles away, at the Sundays River stood the *Fox and Geese*, a hostelry which exposed to the elements a horribly executed painting depicting the incident said to have given the place its name: a pair of artillerymen, from a detachment under Captain Fox, making free with some poultry belonging to mine host.

Another three hours' ride brought travellers to Allen's Halfway House, at the Biggarsberg. Four more hours and the coach arrived at the Ben Lomond Hotel, and by 5 p.m., twelve hours after leaving Ladysmith, the travellers pulled up at the Salisbury Hotel in Newcastle. The 71-mile road was in chronically bad condition. A passenger, travelling along it in April 1887, complained to the newspapers that he saw only one road gang working during the whole journey; and its European overseer was stretched out on the veld, fast asleep.

The railway was pushed on as quickly as possible. There was, in fact, a keen race between the Natal, the Cape and the Lourenço Marques lines, for the commercial profits of being first to serve the Transvaal. On 12 September 1889 the line was opened to what was at first called Biggarsberg Junction, but subsequently renamed Glencoe. A branch line, from there to the Dundee coal mines on Talana farm, was opened on 29 March 1890 by the Governor of Natal. In the same year, the separate division of Dundee was created.

On 15 May 1890 the line was opened to Newcastle, and all that lay between the railway and its terminus was the Drakensberg range. The two railway passes over the Drakensberg, to the Orange Free State and the Transvaal, were constructed simultaneously. After being surveyed, work on the Van Reenen railway pass started on 7 November 1889 when, in the presence of many notables, Sir Charles Mitchell, the Governor, turned the first sod to the thud of a 21-gun salute.

The line had to climb 2236 feet in the 38 miles from Ladysmith to the diminutive village of Van Reenen at the summit of the pass. Construction lasted until 19 November 1891, when the line was opened as far as the village; at that time a miserable place consisting of "about four small wood-and-iron buildings. One of these is a hotel, one a blacksmith's shop, and one a native truck store." This line reached its terminus at Harrismith, 60 miles from Ladysmith, and it was opened jointly by President Reitz of the Orange Free State and the Governor of Natal on 13 July 1892.

The line to the Transvaal had already reached its destination. The final 36-mile stretch from Newcastle climbed 1493 feet to its terminus on the border, at a place named Charlestown, after Sir Charles Mitchell the Governor. The line, a total of 318 miles from Durban, was opened on 7 April 1891 by Paul Kruger and the Governor of Natal. The final climb up the Drakensberg was done by a tedious series of zigzags and reversing stations, with a tunnel bored through Laing's Nek.

The terminus remained at Charlestown for some time. The Natal merchants had hoped for a quick link with the Transvaal, but strategy made the South African Republic proceed first with the link to Lourenço Marques. In the delay Charlestown rapidly became a town, with all the bustle of a railhead. Only on 3 February 1894 was a treaty signed, under which the line was to be carried through to the great market of the Witwatersrand.

On 11 October 1895 the last bolts were ceremonially driven in at Heidelberg and the 494-mile line from Durban to Johannesburg was finally completed. Thence onwards, the economic life of the northern frontier districts of Natal settled down to a pattern of stock-farming, coal-mining and transport, consolidated after the Anglo-Boer War when Vryheid and Utrecht were incorporated in Natal. This area supplied all South Africa with food, warmth, power and transport of such quality and importance that it ranked as one of the most prosperous and vital in the country.

THIRTY

The Drakensberg

Ampitheatre

W hen you journey up along the road to the interior, away from the sultry coastlands of Natal, you see before you, as though on the edge of the world, a range of mountains, serene, aloof and purple in the sky. Above these mountains the great, white thunderclouds go tumbling, while beneath them, like offspring clustered around their mother's skirt, a myriad of infant rivers go gurgling downwards on their journey to the sea.

This is the Drakensberg, the legendary abode of dragons and the scene of a host of tales of mountain adventure as wild as the peaks themselves. Just who it was who first named the range the Drakensberg (dragon mountains), is unknown. The name was in use before the Voortrekkers came to Natal. Probably it was some superstitious tribal African in the Cape, telling a story to a European traveller in the days of old, who mentioned some legend of a dragon in the mountains and so inspired the name.

At all events, belief in the existence of this mountain dragon persisted for many years, and its home was said to be in an enormous cave. Even in 1877 the belief was still current. In the Bloemfontein *Express* for 26 April of that year, appears the story of an old farmer and his son who claimed to have seen the dragon: a huge snake the thickness of a wagon wheel, with two wings and a forked tail. It was flying at a considerable height and was several hundred feet long.

Legends apart, the geological story of the formation of the Drakensberg is sensational enough. In the beginning, science tells us, when the great continent known as Gondwanaland was shattered by some global upheaval, it left among its fragments the shape of South Africa: a lump of basaltic lava, resting on a base of miscellaneous sediment.

The clouds came over this arid, high-lying mass and precipitated a deluge of water. Rivers were formed and, with voracious appetite, they bit into the parent mass and wore it into valleys and ravines. Confronted by the relentless appetite of the waters, the mass of basalt began to dwindle. It retreated backwards at the rate of about one foot in 250 years, and left Natal behind as an undulating and fertile scar, 100 miles wide.

Basutoland alone remains of this once all-enveloping mass. Bored into from within by the Orange River, and relentlessly attacked from the east by the river system of Natal, this last island of basalt is slowly disintegrating and its eastern frontier is ever moving westward.

From the surrounding plains and downlands, the central, triangular-shaped basalt island appears as a mountain range – the Drakensberg from the east, the Maluti from the west – with the apex of the island at Mont-aux-Sources. Its wide base is broken open raggedly in the south-west and is drained by the Orange River.

More than one mountaineer has clambered eagerly to the top of the island edge and expected to see beyond a view as breathtaking as the one behind him. Instead, the climber is confronted with the bleak summit plateau of the island – a waterlogged soggy jumble of desolation in summer, a frozen waste in winter – stretching off in solitude.

All down the hundred miles' sweep of the eastern wall of this rock island there lies a world of pinnacles and gorges, of caves and precipices, with the grandest features invariably occurring at the source of the greatest rivers. There it is that erosion has wrought especial havoc on the rock face, and has

459

worn spectacular and, often fantastic, shapes into the face of the mountains.

To the Africans living in the eastern lowlands, the rock face of the basalt island was known originally as uKhahlamba (a barrier, as though made of up-pointed spears). In latter years variations of the root *ndi* (*uluNdi* or *oNdini*) meaning "the heights", have become alternative African names; while the Sotho, who have a different aspect of the rock island, call its eastern face Dilomo Tsa Natala (the cliffs of Natal).

The most remarkable portion of the Drakensberg face is, without doubt, the area known generally as the Mont-aux-Sources Amphitheatre. This comprises the sharply delineated, 10 740-foot-high peak known as the Sentinel, which actually terminates the high mountain wall in the north; the 10 000-foot-high curved line of the escarpment, known as the Amphitheatre; the 10 280-foot-high Eastern Buttress; and the actual peak of Mont-aux-Sources, a hillock summit 10 822 feet high, perched on top of the Amphitheatre plateau.

In the old days, the Sotho hunters found herds of eland grazing on this Amphitheatre plateau and accordingly, named it Phofung (the place of the eland). Then, in 1836, while exploring the mountain roof of Basutoland, the two French Protestant missionaries, T. Arbousset and F. Daumas, penetrated to the escarpment edge of Phofung. They found the sources of so many rivers there that they named the plateau the Mont-aux-Sources (mountain of sources).

This unique plateau of Mont-aux-Sources is a geographical marvel. On it lies the Beacon Buttress where the borders of the Free State, Natal and Basutoland meet; and from any commanding point not only those three territories may be seen, but on a clear day, portions of the Transvaal and the Cape are visible as well.

The Thukela River has its source on the slopes of the actual Mont-aux-Sources summit. Within a stone's throw of this spring lies a second source, that of the Elands River. For a while the two streamlets flow side by side, separated by a low, boggy ridge.

Then the streams veer off in opposite directions. The Thukela plunges down the eastern face of the Amphitheatre in a tremendous waterfall, leaping and splashing down in a series of cascades and falls to the lowlands 6000 feet below, eventually reaching the Indian Ocean. The Elands River veers off in the opposite direction. It, too, drops off the edge of the plateau in a spectular fall. Then, leaving Mont-aux-Sources far behind, it meanders off across the central plains. It joins the Vaal River and through it feeds the great Orange, ending its journey in the west, in the cold Atlantic Ocean a thousand miles away.

Immediately behind the western side of Mont-aux-Sources' summit a third river, the Khubedu, tributary of the Upper Orange, finds its source in this gigantic mountain sponge.

On the south-eastern side a fourth stream springs to life. This stream, the Eastern Khubedu, once twisted around and joined its western namesake, but at some time the ever-retreating rock face overwhelmed its course. Now, most of its flow tumbles over the edge as the Ribbon Falls and rushes away to Natal. Only a trickle manages to sneak around and escape from the voracious Thukela, whose erosion was responsible for depriving the lordly Orange of this one of its many sources of water wealth.

Through the centuries, this river piracy has continued. One after the other, the sources of the upper Orange tributaries have been overwhelmed; and the streams they fed have dwindled slowly from bustling rivers in broad valleys to struggling streams sunk deep in topographical clothing now much too big for them.

From the Mont-aux-Sources' summit there is a most stupendous view. The whole fair land of Natal lies spread out in infinite detail and beauty before one, with the rivers linking the hills together like silver strings supporting a necklace of jewels.

The rugged foothills reaching up to the rock face have been the setting for as many stories and legends as the Drakensberg itself. In the old days when the mountain mass acted as a

461

stronghold for the Bushmen the farms lying in the immediate shadow of the mountains were in endless uproar.

The farm Tugela Hoek, originally owned by Adriaan Olivier, was one of the most troubled of these frontier farms. There is a story that Olivier, after years of depredations by the Bushmen, was driven nearly to distraction. He secured all his livestock at night, but the little men of the mountains still plagued him and eventually carried away his best bull.

This was the last straw. Olivier dug a deep pit at the usual entrance to his cattle kraal, while a new gate was made at the back. With devilish glee Olivier furnished the pit with steel mantraps, covered it carefully and left it for the Bushmen. That night he was aroused by a stream of Bushmen clicks, clacks and curses. With the dawn, Olivier was satisfied to discover two Bushmen securely lodged in the pit. One was already dead and the other he shot.

Six miles from the old Olivier homestead lies a mighty cavern, 200 feet deep and 550 feet from corner to corner. A waterfall tumbles over the cavern mouth and tradition tells that it was a resort of cannibals under the chief Sidinane.

Another cave nearby had more pleasant associations. In the 1860s there was a flourishing timber-cutting industry in the mountains. The woodcutters were a rough crowd of mixed nationality whose common characteristic was a love of liquor. There was a track over the mountains to the Orange Free State from Olivier's farm. This track crossed the mountains at a pass known as Sungubala (where you overcome a difficulty) and along it the woodcutters tramped to secure supplies of Cape Smoke and Square Face Gin from a frontier store. On the way back the shopper would meet his cronies in a small cave by the pathside, called Flask Krans, and there indulge in celebration. The cave was an old Bushman retreat and its walls were well covered with paintings.

There is one curiously poignant story about this Sungubala pass. Living on the farm Kilfargie, in the shadow of Cathkin Peak, was a young man named Robert Hope Moncrieff, who had settled there in February 1863, shortly after his arrival in Natal. Moncrieff was a lonely character with little, save hope, among his assets. John Dobie, an itinerant sheep dealer of the day, visited him on his farm and found him to be a "tall young fellow living in the very roughest style, a kaffir hut and not a morsel to eat. Would not like to live like that if I were to get the whole of Natal, but he seemed to fancy it and think he was doing a heavy trick!

"Had a drink of coffee and gave him a smoke, which he relished amazingly, and after yarning a while turned in all standing, he having only one blanket which I positively refused to take, and we lay down on the hard floor. Poor fellow, when he thought I was asleep he got up and spread the blanket over me."

Towards the end of 1863 Moncrieff started to build a house for himself, as his farm was flourishing. Needing labour, and hoping to trade saddles in Basutoland, he rode off just after Christmas. He climbed the Drakensberg up Sungubala Pass. Near the summit flows the Manzamnyama (black waters) stream and there he offsaddled to rest and eat. While he sat beside the stream four Africans came by and, envying him his fine new saddles, they killed him and stuffed his body into a hole.

Four years later, when the disappearance of the young man had been almost forgotten, there was a beer drink amongst the Africans at Emmaus Mission. As part of the entertainment on such occasions, one of the drunkards started to thrash his wife. Among the spectators was an African policeman. He heard the woman say, protestingly, "If the white men knew what you had done you would not thrash me." The interested policeman later interviewed the woman privately and the whole story of the murder was divulged. The end of the matter came with the visit of the public executioner to the Estcourt gaol.

A few years after this affair, in 1871, when the stream of traffic from Natal to the diamond fields created a demand for a new Drakensberg road pass, the old path was improved into a passable road which served as an alternative to Van Reenen's Pass. It was then named Oliviershoek after Adriaan Olivier who at that time still lived at its foot.

Two other Drakensberg farms of historical interest are Goodoo and Dooley. On them one of the woodcutters, Dooley by name, had his headquarters. Later they were used for stock and eventually, in 1903, Goodoo farm was purchased by Walter Coventry. It was during his time that the idea was first conceived of attracting holidaymakers to the mountains. In 1906, W.F. Clayton, the Natal Government Minister for Agriculture and Lands, proclaimed the unoccupied area adjoining the mountains as a national park. A Committee of Management was formed, but lack of funds crippled the scheme.

The foundations for the future park, however, were laid. The Surveyor General had marked off the Crown lands there as a reserve. The Natal Government Railways Publicity Department was invited to send a photographic team there. A party went up and laboured in very wild country to some effect. Thenceforth, every railway carriage and guidebook on Natal carried a photograph of the Mont-aux-Sources area, and this brought it well into the public eye.

Shortly before Union, however, the government decided to abandon the scheme and sell the land. Fortunately, a public-spirited member of the Management Committee, Colonel J.S. Wylie, bought the 10 200-acre property. After Union he sold it back to the government, on agreement that it would be retained for all time as a recreational area for the people of South Africa.

For administrative purposes, 2740 acres of Native Trust land were added to the park, and the two farms, Dooley and Goodoo, were bought from Walter Coventry in 1919. On Goodoo, a Mr and Mrs F.C. Williams had already opened a small mountain hostel, and this simple farmhouse was made into the first climbers' resort with Coventry as the first lessee. Colonel Wylie, aided by a committee of mountain enthusiasts, controlled the policy and destiny of the 14 902-acre park.

Only twelve guests could be accommodated in that first hostel, but the place rapidly became famous for its scenery and climbs. Coventry was an energetic man, and he busied himself in laying out the first bridle paths and building a passable road for motor transport to the hostel.

Things were primitive in those days. Most visiting cars got stuck in the ford across the Thukela. The closets were in the bush and midnight users often found a puff adder in prior occupation. Mrs Coventry had views on liquor, so there was much surreptitious drinking in the barn. If anybody fell sick, no doctor was handy. Mrs Coventry would dust off a great, old-fashioned doctors' book. She would browse through it, comparing symptoms aloud until the patient's hair stood on end, although her treatment always ended the same way – one tablespoon of castor oil.

Some first-class climbing was done in those days. The celebrated Tom Casement, who ran the old Free State climbers' hostel of Rydal Mount, accompanied by his famous Sotho guide Mlatu, often brought parties over as far back as 1908. Mont-aux-Sources was thoroughly explored, and on 17 October 1910, W.J. Wybergh and a Mr McLeod were the first to climb the Sentinel, while on 13 June 1913, Father A.D. Kelly and J.G. Millar climbed the inner tower of the Eastern Buttress. The same two climbed the outer tower on 10 July 1914, and by the end of the First World War the northern end of the high Drakensberg was well known.

An ever-increasing stream of climbers and campers was visiting the mountains. In 1910 a Drakensberg Club was formed, with Judge Broome as first president. It provided much more publicity for the mountains, but it came to grief during the First World War. All that is left to remind us of this early society is the name Broomehill, given to the hill in the park in memory of the club's president, who first beaconed it before the war.

At a public meeting held in Pietermaritzburg on 15 April 1919, with the Natal Administrator in the chair, a new club, the Natal Mountain Club, was formed. Within a year it had

150 members and the first annual outing went to Kranskop. In July of the next year the annual outing made its first regular camp at Mont-aux-Sources, and this large-scale influx marked the beginning of major developments in the park.

Accommodation in the hostel was increased to 70 and, on 1 November 1926, Otto Zunckel took over the lease of the place. For years his name was synonymous with the Drakensberg. He had the knack of running his hostel with all that atmosphere of good fellowship and adventure which means home to the mountaineer. In his time the park enjoyed probably its most active climbing period.

Parties were out on excursions all day and every day, and few remained to idle their time waiting for morning tea, or for the bar to open. The celebrated Zulu guide, Charlie Sentinel, conducted so many people to the top of the Sentinel and became so renowned that even overseas newspapers carried news of him when he once slipped on a climb and suffered some bad cuts.

Walter Coventry had built the bridle path to the top of the Mont-aux-Sources plateau in 1924. A stone hut was built up there by the Mountain Club and opened at Easter 1930 by Mrs Botha-Reid. Ever since, a constant stream of visitors has stayed there and enjoyed the thrill of standing on those great heights to see the dawn break, and watch the shadows of night creep back to their lairs in the cold valleys of the inner mountains.

The future of the Natal National Park was now assured, with only one setback. On 10 December 1941 the hostel was burned to the ground. The new hostel, opened in the middle of 1943, was altogether a larger and more modern building, and it was there that the British Royal Family stayed in March 1947 and gave to the park the full title of the Royal Natal National Park, which it bears today.

Since then, it has gone from strength to strength. Trout have been introduced to the rivers, wildlife had increased under protection, and the gorgeous forests of yellow-wood and stinkwood recovered from the depredations of the early woodcutters. As for climbing, the last great peaks in the area have been conquered. In April 1935 the Amphitheatre Wall was climbed by a party led by D.P. Liebenberg, while the most sensational of all the Mont-aux-Sources climbs, the Devil's Tooth, was first extracted from the list of unclimbed peaks in August 1950, when D. Bell, P. Campbell and E.H. Scholes managed to wriggle their way to its summit.

South of Mont-aux-Sources lay the wild area inhabited by the Ngwaneni tribe. These people, a ruggedly independent crowd of wanderers, have played an uproarious part in the story of Southern Africa. They first settled in the Mont-aux-Sources area about 1818, seeking sanctuary from the endless disturbances in Zululand. They were not left in peace for long. The nightmare of a Zulu raiding army appeared on the horizon. In panic, they packed their belongings and clambered over the Drakensberg to the high veld plains.

For years, the Ngwaneni led a robber existence in the Caledon River valley, despoiling the resident Sotho tribes of their cattle and belongings. They gained rich booty, but their success was the cause of their own undoing. The Zulus heard of their achievements and the claws of Shaka reached out for a share.

Once again the Ngwaneni and their chief, Matiwane, had to flee. About June of the year 1828 they poured down the escarpment edge into the lands of the Thembu tribe in the Cape, leaving Basutoland behind them. Once again they started looting and killing, but this time they came to grief. The British garrison at Grahamstown, labouring under the delusion that the raiders were Zulus, sallied out and, after some fighting, completely routed the Ngwaneni.

The tribe was dispersed. Matiwane, a lonely and weary man, fled back the way he had come with only a handful of supporters. The compassionate Moshoeshoe, forgiving the depredations of the Ngwaneni, offered Matiwane sanctuary, but the old chief went on. He tramped back a thousand miles, to the very fate he had for so long sought to avoid, and his road was milestoned by the relics of those he had himself destroyed.

In Zululand Shaka was dead and Dingane was on the throne. To this savage monarch, Matiwane appealed for shelter. Dingane gave him a village for a while, but then fate complicated the picture. One of Matiwane's sons, Hlathi, became a favourite of Dingane. One night, while visiting his father, he was taken ill and died, and Dingane's councillors blamed Matiwane.

The king summoned the old chief before him. "Where are all your people?" he asked. "All that I have left are with me now," replied the chief. "Then take them away," Dingane said to his executioners, and on the hillock ever since known as kwaMatiwane the old chief died, with sticks forced up his nostrils to his brain.

Matiwane's proper heir, Zikhali, escaped the holocaust. He fled to Swaziland with a few followers and found sanctuary with Sobhuza, the Swazi king. Fresh troubles awaited the young man there. Nomlalati, daughter of Sobhuza, fell in love with Zikhali. She invited him to a feast in her hut one night. When it was time for the guests to leave, the princess ordered Zikhali to remain.

The young man asked her what she wanted. "You will sleep here," she said. He expostulated. She was putting him in danger of death. She simply replied that if he tried to leave she would call out that he was violating her, then he would be killed anyway. He stayed!

Rumour of this scandal soon reached Sobhuza and he was enraged. Zikhali's death was arranged, but his sweetheart warned him. With nine followers he fled in the night and went back to Zululand. There, Dingane had heard of the escapade and was amused. He established Zikhali as tributary chief over the relics of the Ngwaneni tribe and allowed them to return to their former home. After a spell on Daniel Bezuidenhout's farm, under the Thintwa Mountain, where the scattered tribe once again rallied around their new chief, Zikhali led them to the area south of Mont-aux-Sources. Nomlalati slipped away from her father and joined her lover there, and in the afternoon shadow of the Drakensberg the Ngwaneni people once more prospered. Zikhali and his love lived to a ripe old age. He died in December 1863, leaving Nomlalati's son, Ncwadi, as his heir.

The first Europeans to settle in this area arrived in 1847, when the Reverends C.W. Posselt and W. Gulden-Pfenning of the Berlin Mission Society established the Emmaus Mission for the Ngwaneni tribe. In January 1850 the Reverend C. Zunckel took charge of the place, and his family have ever since been among the best-known European inhabitants of the area.

European farmers also started to settle in the district, and in the early 1870s Captain Allison made his home at the border post of Oliviershoek, where he acted as JP for what was subsequently proclaimed as the Upper Tugela Division. Allison's home, in those days, was something of an oasis on the long road from Estcourt, over Oliviershoek Pass, to the Free State; and anyone wishing to visit the mountains invariably made the most of his hospitality.

The first village in the area came to life only in 1897 when a few shops and houses were built by the banks of the Thukela on the farm Kleine Waterval, owned by a retired sea captain named Wales. In 1903 this conglomeration of store, police post and post office, received the name of Bergville, and today it is a quiet, rustic little centre, sitting beside the river, listening to its gurgling, and watching the cloud shadows playing with the Drakensberg.

The second village in the area, Winterton, came into being only in 1905. Three farms – Nooitgedacht, Kerkplaats and Deeldrift – were purchased by the government and a weir was built across the Little Thukela to allow for irrigation. A settlement was then established; first named Springfield but renamed Winterton in 1910 after H.D. Winter, the Secretary for Agriculture.

The mountain wall which looks down upon this area south of Mont-aux-Sources contains some of the most beautiful crags and summits in the whole Drakensberg. The Africans know the area as Mweni (the place of fingers) for erosion has worn the grey face of the mountains into an intricate maze of columns and spires, reaching up to the clouds as though they were stalagmites or icicles of rock.

This stretch of the Drakensberg lies in the area of the Ngwaneni reserve and is proscribed for Europeans. The first climbers to explore it were A.H. and F.R. Stocker of the Alpine Club. These two climbers who explored many of the Drakensberg peaks in 1888, are ranked as the doyens of Natal mountaineers.

Today the Mweni area is just as they found it, with no roads or development at all to open it up to an appreciative world. The mountain queen of the area and, indeed, of all the Drakensberg, is the 10 225-foot-high peak first climbed by the Stockers on 20 June 1888. They called it Unumweni Castle (the castle of fingers) and it was well named, for the summit of this lovely mountain is decorated like a queen's crown. Innumerable spires and serrated edges ornament the top, while on the northern edge there looms up, like the point of a guardian spear, a sharp pinnacle known as Mponjwana (the horn).

Immediately behind Unumweni Castle, the Orange River has its source in a boggy sponge. In front of it, like attendant pages to the queen, loom up the smaller, but spectacular, twin peaks known as the Inner and Outer Mweni Needles. The Outer Needle, 9625 feet high, was first climbed in July 1921 by K. Cameron and D.W. Bassett-Smith; while the 9500-foot-high Inner Needle first bowed its head to the mountaineers in May 1943, when A.S. Hooper, P.B. Fenger and L. Burton managed to reach the top.

Next to Unumweni Castle (sometimes misnamed The Rockeries) looms her knight-at-arms and guardian, the greatest rock mass in the Drakensberg. This 10 320-foot-high giant the Stockers tried to climb, but failed. They named it Segwana Cirque, although modern mountaineers know it generally as The Saddle. Like most Drakensberg peaks, its summit is easily accessible from the Basutoland plateau, but from the Natal side, first climbed in 1924 by O.K. Williamson and D.W. Bassett-Smith, it is an ascent of some magnitude.

The southern end of the Mweni area is marked by a ridge of mountains projecting from the main range into Natal and known to the Africans as abaMponjwana (the ridge of horns). This ridge contains some of the best-known peaks of the Drakensberg.

At the eastern extremity of the ridge, projecting well into Natal, stands the familiar mountain bulk of the 9856-foot-high Cathedral Peak. In past years this mountain was generally known as Zikhali's Horn, after the Ngwaneni chief who lived at its foot. Just who changed the name to Cathedral Peak is unknown; but when it was first climbed in July 1917 by D.W. Bassett-Smith and R.G. Kingdon it already had its new name.

Owing to its projecting position, there is an unequalled panorama of the face of the Drakensberg from the summit of Cathedral Peak. The mountain itself presents little similarity to a cathedral, unless the latter structure had been well bombed, but next to it stands a peak whose sharply defined shape unmistakably deserves the title of The Bell.

The Bell, 9575 feet high and regarded as one of the most sensational of Drakensberg climbs, was first "tolled" on 17 January 1944 by Hans and Else Wongtschowski. The same ridge also contains the oddly shaped group of rocky outcrops collectively called the Chessmen and the Inner and Outer Horns, 9898 and 9872 feet high respectively.

The Inner Horn was first climbed back in 1925 by a party under the leadership of H.G. Botha-Reid, while the Outer Horn was first climbed by D.P. Liebenberg, Doctor Ripley, H.G. Botha-Reid and F.S. Brown in July 1934.

Along the southern slopes of this Ridge of Horns, the river named Mlambonja (the river of the dog) flows from its source at the foot of the main mountain wall. In the valley of this crystal river several farms were originally surveyed. In 1936 one of these farms, named Inhoek, was bought by Philip van der Riet, and he soon realised the superb holiday possibilities of this portion of the mountains. He established a hotel and, in

December 1939, received his first guests. Today the Cathedral Peak Hotel is probably the best known of all the mountain holiday resorts.

The Cathedral Peak area has tremendous variety in its surrounding mountains and foothills. Great government forestry projects and experiments are slowly covering the approaches to the mountains with trees. The sensational Monzali's Forest Road, built by the Forestry Department and G.R. Monzali, the well-known Italian contractor, provides a scenic drive of remarkable beauty which reveals a sweeping panorama of the rugged face of the mountains.

Southwards from the Ridge of Horns there are several peaks of interest. The curiously shaped Qolo la Masoja (ridge of the soldiers), known also as The Organpipes, and the 10 570-foot-high bulk of Cleft Peak are prominent landmarks.

Cleft Peak was first climbed in 1936 by D.P. Liebenberg and Doctor Ripley. It is a climb which can be as easy or difficult as the climber chooses, according to which route he selects. Slightly detached from the main wall, however, are two peaks of which each has only one way up, and that is the hard way!

One of these peaks, The Pyramid, 9276 feet high, was first climbed in 1936 by Brian Godbold and a party. The second of the difficult pair, The Column, ranking as one of the stiffest of all South African climbs, was conquered on 9 December 1945 by George Thomson, climbing alone and watched with bated breath by experienced climbers who had long shared the view of their fellows that the peak was too hazardous to be worth it.

South-east of the Cathedral Park area, there looms up the great cornerstone of the Drakensberg: Cathkin Peak. This 10 438-foot-high giant has been delegated by nature to the task of swinging the mountain wall around more to the south. In the process, Cathkin Peak is left so much exposed that it seems to dominate the range for miles, and the Africans have named it, in keeping with its overwhelmingly masculine character, Mdedelele (make room for him), a name often given to a bully.

Cathkin Peak received its European name from David Gray, who called his farm at its foot after Cathkin Braes near Glasgow. Gray was jointly responsible for another of the Drakensberg names. In 1860, a Captain Grantham of the Royal Engineers was busy on a military survey of Natal. In the course of inspecting the Drakensberg, he visited Gray and the two men decided to climb Cathkin Peak.

Cathkin is no easy scramble, but a climb in D-category. The two men were both amateurs. Two-thirds of the way up, they decided they had had enough. They settled down to rest and to lighten their loads by drinking a bottle of champagne they had optimistically brought, to celebrate the first successful climb of Cathkin Peak.

On removing the bottle from the haversack, however, it was found to be half empty. A certain amount of argument followed. Both men had taken turns to carry the haversack and neither would admit to having stolen a drink. Eventually they ended the quarrel by blaming it on the mountain, and they decided to rename Cathkin Peak "Champagne Castle".

For years, maps of Natal marked the mountain as Cathkin Peak or Champagne Castle. Only much later was the confusion ended, when the survey department transferred the new name to the hitherto unnamed 11 072-foot-high summit on the main face of the mountains opposite Cathkin Peak.

Cathkin Peak, because of its detached prominence, was for long considered to be the highest mountain in the Drakensberg. Several attempts were made to climb it before the summit was at last conquered. The Stockers tried to climb it on 12 August 1888, but they failed. They had already, in April 1888, reached the top of Champagne Castle by following the pass known as Gray's Pass up the gorge at the northern end. From the summit, the Stockers immediately saw that Cathkin Peak was well below them; and that the highest point in the mountains appeared to be on a spur projecting into Basutoland, a few miles south from Champagne Castle.

The Stockers did several other climbs in the area. On 24 May 1888, they climbed the north peak of the Sterk Horn, and on 19 August of the same year they conquered the more difficult South Peak.

There were several other climbing attempts on Cathkin Peak during the next few years. Despite the observations of the Stockers, the popular idea still persisted that Cathkin Peak was the highest point, and the honour of being the first to climb it was eagerly sought after. Many renowned climbers of past years, such as George Amphlett and W.J. Wybergh, made attempts on Cathkin, but bad weather and the remoteness of the area, together with the difficulty of the climb, contrived to keep the mountain inviolate.

Then, on 12 September 1912, G.T. Amphlett, Tom Casement, W.C. West and Father Kelly attacked the mountain. They found the easiest way up the southern gully at the rear of the mountain, and had no difficulty in reaching the summit. There they were rewarded with a magnificent view, but had the mortification of finding that what was fondly imagined to be the highest peak was in reality only a minor summit.

To them, it also seemed that the highest Drakensberg peak was on the spur projecting into Basutoland. Nothing seems to have been done to confirm this, however, until 1938 when Colonel William Park-Gray, grandson of David Gray, and J. van Heyningen, the forester of the Champagne Castle area, climbed to the top of the range with a spirit level.

From Champagne Castle, they easily confirmed the fact that the Basutoland peak was certainly higher than anything on the actual escarpment. The two men tramped to it and left upon its summit a cairn of stones with a bottle containing their names. The African name of the peak was Makheke, and its height, established some time later, was 11 355 feet. Two other high points were on the same spur as Makheke, and these – *Mafadi*, 11 320 feet, and Ubutswane, 11 265 feet – were also higher than anything on the actual edge of the escarpment.

In March 1951 another party, led by Desmond Watkins, explored the mountains south of Makheke and found the highest of all Drakensberg and, indeed, of South African peaks, in the shape of the 11 425-foot-high Ntaba Ntlenyana. This peak, 14 miles south-west of Giant's Castle, lies near the head of the Mohlezi Pass at the source of the Mkhomazi River. Like Makheke, it is some miles into Basutoland from the edge of the escarpment and is invisible from Natal.

From the Natal side, the mountain wall in the Champagne Castle area is full of spectacle and novelty. Apart from Cathkin Peak and Champagne Castle, this court of the mountain kings is crowded with almost as many characters as the establishment of human royalty. Just to the north of Champagne Castle is the strange ridge known as the Dragon's Back – an oxtail affair of joints and crags – culminating in the oddest of all Drakensberg peaks, the 7992-foot-high Ntunja (the eye), also known as Gatberg; with a great hole bored by nature immediately underneath the summit, so that it stares out over the surrounding countryside like a one-eyed giant.

Behind Cathkin, like a sinister power behind a princely throne, is hidden a peak of evil climbing reputation, the gaunt 10 700-foot-high Monk's Cowl. This peak, first climbed in May 1942 by H. Wongtschowski and a party, was conquered only after it had caused the death of Richard Barry on 28 January 1938 in one of the surprisingly few climbing accidents of the Drakensberg, considering the crumbling nature of the rock.

In the eastern shadow of Cathkin lie two holiday hotels: Cathkin Park, founded in 1929 by Carter Robinson on his farm of that name, and Champagne Castle Hotel, founded about 1930 by H. Martens, on the mountain farms of Heartsease and Woestyn.

Curiously enough, several finds of gold have been claimed in this area. In November 1891 J.T. Howe reported gold on a spur of Cathkin Peak, while in February 1892 there was quite a rush to the Phutini valley where J.M. Sayman had made a find. Nothing worthwhile resulted.

South of the holiday resorts of Cathkin Peak there lies a particularly beautiful stretch of the mountains. For 20 miles the mountain wall maintains a steady height of 10 000 feet, with prominent points rearing their heads still further upwards.

The Njesuthi Twins, 11 182 feet high (at the source of that quaintly named stream, the Njesuthi (well-fed dog), The Thumb, Bannerman, and a flat-topped nameless mountain,

10 936 feet high, all look down serenely from these great heights. At the end of the 20-mile stretch looms one of the great landmarks of Natal, the 10 868-foot-high bulk of Giant's Castle.

Giant's Castle, like Cathkin, has the task of acting as a cornerstone of the mountain wall. It is there that the rock face is swung so sharply south-westwards that Giant's Castle is left exposed, as though it marks the end of the entire range, when viewed from either north or south.

To the Africans, Giant's Castle is known as iNtabayikonjwa (the mountain at which one must not point). The name reflects a superstition common along the Drakensberg, to the effect that pointing at an exposed mountain will bring bad weather. A slight variation on the idea is applied to the smaller, 6852-foot-high Ntabayikonjwa in the foothills near Cathedral Peak. It is said that a woman who points at this mountain will marry a man living upon its slopes.

The name of Giant's Castle was originally applied by Captain Allen Gardiner to the small, castle-shaped mountain further south, near modern Underberg. In May 1865, however, when Doctor Sutherland, the Surveyor General, went down to establish the southern boundary beacon of Natal in the Drakensberg, he saw fit to displace the old name. To Giant's Castle proper, he applied the name of Garden Castle, in honour of his mother whose maiden name was Garden. The older name was henceforth applied to the great cornerstone of the main mountain wall.

From earliest times, the Giant's Castle area was a great resort of antelope. Hartebeest and eland were particularly numerous. The foothills of the mountains provided magnificent grazing grounds, with rich grass, cool, invigorating winds and the coldest and clearest of streams. The upper reaches of the Bushman's River were great strongholds of the animals, and in turn became a favourite resort; first for Bushmen, who covered the caves with their paintings, and then for European hunters.

These hunting parties were the first to explore the area

thoroughly. One of them, led by Bob Speirs and Augustus Bouill in February 1864, was the first to climb the Giant's Castle. The party was caught in the rain on the summit and returned home wetter if wiser men; but many others followed in their footsteps.

The uproar about the Langalibalele Rebellion made the area still better known. After the trouble, it was decided to seal off the frontier by blocking all the mountain passes. John Fannin, the surveyor, examined the numerous Giant's Castle passes in detail. Then Colonel A.W. Durnford and a detachment of the 75th Regiment were sent up to the mountains. For six months, in 1874, they laboured at the task of blowing up the passes right along the Drakensberg from Oliviershoek to Giant's Castle. Before their departure in September, the regimental cook carved the number of the regiment, "75", into a great boulder above their camp, close to the source of the Bushman's River.

In the years after the rebellion, hunting party after party visited the Giant's Castle area, until its once prolific animal life was almost annihilated. Then, in 1903, it was proclaimed that some 50 000 acres in the area were to be established as a game reserve. Sydney Barnes was appointed as first game conservator, and on 9 November of that year he journeyed up to take charge of the place.

The area was completely wild at that time. Not even a pathway led the traveller to his destination, and for months Barnes lived in one of the old Bushman caves. Shooting in the area was prohibited in 1904, and in 1907 the boundaries of this Giant's Castle game reserve were defined.

Barnes, meanwhile, had built himself a house in that beautiful mountain land and settled down to a lonely but happy open-air sort of life: chasing poachers, marauding leopards and jackals; inspecting the boundaries; counting eland; fighting the grass fires; cursing a toothache; and whiling away the lonely hours when rain and snow kept him close to home.

Mystery occurred in those days as well. Ranger Barnes kept a diary, and in it, on 12 January 1906, occurs the entry: "The

Reverend C.C. Bates arrived on a visit to me." For a few days the routine reports follow and then on 31 January comes the entry: "Bates went out after breakfast and did not return."

Behind that terse remark lay a night of anxiety. A storm had started in the afternoon and all through the dark hours the rain came pelting down. The next day thick mist blanketed the mountains, but all day Barnes and his African rangers groped about the wet valleys, searching for the missing man.

They followed his track to near Giant's Castle and then lost it. All the next day it rained, but still they searched. At seven o'clock on the following morning a fox terrier named Nip, who had accompanied the Reverend Mr Bates, came cringing through the kitchen door, half-starved and frozen.

The rangers tried to follow Nip's tracks, but once again the rain had obliterated everything. The search went on day after day and, indeed, at desultory intervals for years afterwards, for the minister had carried a valuable gold watch with him.

Ranger Roden Symons, who took over from Barnes in September 1906, added a final postscript to the story in the diary.

"The search for Mr Bates failed," he wrote. "Nothing was ever found of his body. During the nine years I was in charge here I found several skeletons, but they were most probably those of rebels killed in the Langalibalele Rebellion. I personally think that Mr Bates was benighted at the foot of the mountain and taking refuge in one of the numerous dry watercourses, died of exposure and the body was washed away by the floods on 2nd February."

Roden Symons left in 1915 and his assistant, Philip Barnes, took over the park. For 32 years he remained there, guiding the place through the years of infancy, as a father does his child; protecting it from occasional raids of wild Cape hunting dogs, the numerous onslaughts of poachers, and killing over 600 jackals in the course of his service.

In December 1947, Edward Thrash took over from the retiring Philip Barnes, and later Philip Barnes's son became the warden of this most pleasant place. Roads have been made and accommodation built for visitors. Superb scenery and climbing, fine fishing in the rivers, a variety of game animals, rhebok, duiker, grysbok, klipspringer, bushbuck, and over 1500 of the magnificent mountain eland, maintained in their natural state of freedom, all combine to preserve in this portion of the Drakensberg something of the atmosphere of those past years, when the mountain wall was the last frontier of adventure of the fair land of Natal.

Giant's Castle

THIRTY-ONE

The North Coast Road

O f all the roads of Natal, the North Coast Road is undoubtedly the most romantic. It was the road first
blazed by the Zulu warriors, by the old ivory traders
of Port Natal, and by the host of wanderers who made their
way northwards to Zululand in its golden days of trade and
adventure.

At first, few of this passing throng cared to turn aside and
settle by the way. To most, the north coast of Natal was just an
intervening 50 miles of hills and river valleys between Durban and the Thukela River frontier, beyond which lay so much
promise of game and gold, of novelty and chance of fortune.

Among the few who settled on the north coast in the early
days was one who was destined to shape not only its history,
but that of all Natal. His name was Edmund Morewood. He
had been an early settler during republican days at Durban,
where he had held the appointment of harbour master and
superintendent of customs until the second British occupation.

Morewood had then become manager of an experimental cotton plantation on the Mdloti River, on the north coast.
There, he commenced experiments to find a suitable cotton
crop for the coastal districts of Natal. Among the few other settlers on the north coast at this time it so happened that there
were several former sugar planters from the island of Mauritius. Hard hit by the temporary collapse of sugar prices in

1847 they migrated to Natal and, like Morewood, tentatively experimented with crops.

Among these immigrants from Mauritius there was frequent speculation about sugar prospects in Natal. An indigenous variety of cane, known as *impha*, flourished and was eaten with relish by the Africans, but its sugar content was so low as to be uncommercial. Nevertheless, speculation continued, and in September 1847 the Durban firm of Messrs Milner Brothers, who maintained a trade with Mauritius, made a trial importation of a cargo of seeds and shoots of various Mauritian and Réunion Island crops. Included in the cargo were 40 000 tops of an inferior variety of sugar cane, known as "Mauritius red cane".

This mixed cargo was sold by auction, and a number of people experimentally planted the cane. The Milner brothers disseminated such information about the cultivation of the cane as they had been able to glean on the islands, and all Natal watched the experiment with interest. "What a change would come over the spirit of affairs here," wrote the *Natal Witness* wistfully on 22 October 1847, "if, instead of the useless *iMpha* – sweet cane – a like quantity of the genuine plant were raised and manufactured."

The following year, one of the best known of the north coast's early settlers, Ephraim Frederick Rathbone, arrived from Mauritius. He was interested to see the luxurious growth of the patches of cane imported the previous year, and was very full of the matter when he journeyed up to the Mdloti River to become an overseer on the Cotton Company's estate, under Edmund Morewood.

Rathbone made Morewood interested in sugar; and from a small patch of the imported cane, growing on the farm of Mr Pell at the Mngeni River, he secured some tops to plant an experimental five acres on the Cotton Company's ground in February 1849.

The Cotton Company, however, was not interested in sugar. The project would have languished but, late in 1849, Morewood left the company to take up a farm of his own named Compensation, between the Thongathi and Mhlali rivers. He had become personally interested in sugar. In October of that year he removed the growing cane to his own farm and, with such funds as he possessed, he struggled to prove sugar as an economic Natal crop.

Rathbone replaced Morewood as manager of the Cotton Company, until that enterprise went bankrupt in 1850. He then became one of the greatest of the Zululand traders. By 1852 he was so friendly with Mpande that he received a grant of the first farm in Zululand to be given to a European, the so-called Mauritius farm, on the Msunduze River. He remained there until 1862, when Cetshwayo ordered him to leave, then he removed first to the Umvoti district and afterwards to Utrecht.

Morewood, meanwhile, struggled on with his sugar experiments. In 1850 he built a crude sugar mill, the first in Natal, and with this he managed to produce the first sugar from his first crop in 1851. The little mill could only handle about twelve gallons of juice an hour but its product was certainly good sugar. This success set many hearts beating at a faster rate. Compensation farm became a focal point of interest. Innumerable visitors journeyed up the north coast to the place, to view the beginnings of Natal's sugar industry. Hospitality was a strain on Morewood, for he was a bachelor. He had little on his farm save an untidy house, a galvanised-iron sugar manufactory and very well-tilled fields.

Cane from Morewood's plantation was carried all along the coast of Natal. In addition, tremendous publicity was given to the north coast as an ideal sugar-growing area, and many new settlers hastened to obtain farms.

The enterprising Morewood had also discovered coal on his farm. On the side of a cliff, overhanging the sea, there was a vein of visible coal. Morewood used this coal as fuel for his sugar mill, and great interest was aroused. In 1852, John Bird the surveyor was sent up by the government to examine the deposit, and six wagon loads were sent to Durban to be tried out on the mail steamer. In January of the following year, a government boring appliance was sent up to prove the deposit.

Morewood was so certain of approaching success for his efforts that he went to England to raise financial aid. Unfortunately the coal on Compensation proved very inferior. Its discovery, however, had at least interested many people in new mining possibilities for Natal. In October 1852, an engineer named Sowerby was sent out from England to prospect for coal. He claimed finds of coal and many other minerals and metals, especially in the Klip River area of the north; and in the following year five specimens of Natal coal were exhibited to the Manchester Chamber of Commerce in England, but nothing resulted immediately, for the deposits so far found were, like the coal of Compensation, very poor in quality.

The sugar industry, on the other hand, went ahead at a great rate. One plantation after another was commenced. In July 1853, M. Jeffels of the Sipingo area imported the first proper sugar mill and plant; and by 1855 sugar was being produced on a commercial scale, with a third mill at Springfield, that of the Natal Sugar Company of J.B. and H. Milner, adding its output to that of the first two establishments.

The industry had no easy beginning. Transport was nonexistent and roads along the coast were atrocious. Occasional floods also did great damage. In April 1856 most of the young cane plantations were half washed away and the mills, all established near the banks of rivers, suffered grievous damage. In the four days' downpour, from the 12th of that month, 27 inches of rain fell. The Mngeni River came down 20 feet high, and for a few days Durban was part of its mouth.

"The Springfield Plantation, three miles from Durban, was under water," wrote Bishop Colenso. "The current rushed through the mill with a depth of nine feet and an impetuosity which enabled it to carry the heavy pans of the boiling battery clean out of the masonry. During the height of the flood, a large elephant was swept past the mill, struggling with the stream and sounding a furious alarm with its trumpet."

To many, the problem of plantation labour seemed to be the greatest stumbling block in the establishment of sugar. There was an immediate clamour that some measure should be introduced to import cheap and plentiful labour.

To a number of those in the sugar industry, this clamour of labour scarcity was unreasonable. "During many years' residence here in Natal," wrote Morewood to the *Natal Mercury* on 18 January 1853, "I have never experienced such a want and could name many persons who are in the same position. The plain fact is that those who treat the natives properly can at all times secure the number of servants they require, and the cry of 'want of labour' is almost exclusively raised by persons who either cannot afford to employ servants or expect unreasonable returns for small pay and cheap food."

However, the craze for cheap labour had already warped the outlook of Natal planters too much for them to approach such a problem with foresight. They pointed out that they were establishing the industry in the face of the fact that sugar could be dumped in Natal by foreign growers at a price uneconomic to local farmers. Therefore, cheap labour and tariff protection were imperative. Those who considered that any industry established on such a basis could turn out more bitterness than sweetness for the country, were soon shouted down.

One petition after another was sent to the Governor, praying for aid in the labour problem. The government duly investigated the question of overseas recruitment. In the end, on 16 November 1860, the barque *Truro* arrived in Durban with the first load of 341 Indian labourers, mainly Hindus, recruited from the Madras Presidency.

Durban welcomed them half curiously, half fearful of such Asiatic bogymen as cholera or plague. The Africans just stared at them, with surprise and some antagonism. They promptly named them abakwaMnanayi, from their nasal speech, and smiled at their appearance.

They were certainly an exotic crowd. The *Natal Mercury* described the event. "As the swarthy hordes came pouring out of the boat's hold, laughing, jabbering, and staring about them with a well-satisfied expression of self-complacency on their faces, they hardly realised the idea one had formed regarding them and their faculties.

"They were a queer, comical, foreign-looking, very Oriental-like crowd. The men, with their huge muslin turbans, bare, scraggy shin-bones, and coloured garments; the women with their flashing eyes, long, dishevelled, pitchy hair, with their half-covered, well-formed figures, and their keen, inquisitive glances; the children with their meagre, intelligent, cute and humorous countenances mounted on bodies of unconscionable fragility, were all evidently beings of a different race and kind from any we have yet seen either in Africa or England."

It was the start of a new epoch in Natal. Nineteen other immigrant ships followed, bringing 6000 Indian labourers. The planters were delighted. The Indians were under contract at ten shillings a month for the first year. This was increased each year, until the labourer received a maximum of 14 shillings a month in the fifth year. At the end of five years' service, the labourer was free of his contract and could do as he pleased. Naturally his pleasure was not to continue working for 14 shillings a month. The free tickets which the planters were obliged to offer back to wretched conditions in India were also not much in demand. As early as 1856, Baboo Naidoo, an interpreter and high-caste man, had opened the first Indian store in Natal. It was in Field Street, Durban, and sold Asiatic condiments and delicacies.

Morewood's enterprise had certainly popularised the Natal north coast. As for himself, he recovered nothing from his labours. Short of capital from the start, he spent what little he had in establishing sugar cane as a practical crop. Then he went bankrupt before he could enjoy any legitimate reward. He left Natal and removed to South America.

By 1870, the Natal north coast supported a busy and prosperous community on its sugar plantations. The railway terminus was still at the quarry on the south bank of the Mngeni

River. The North Coast Road crossed the river at two alternative fords: one, near the mouth, known as George's Drift, after the ferryman there; and the second, higher up, named Morewood's Drift, after E. Morewood.

Beyond the river stood a small hostelry, kept by a host named Allen who ran a bus service of sorts three times a week up to Verulam. The road was the usual mixture of mud, rocks and ruts. Travelling along it was still a hazardous affair. There were still hippos in the Sea Cow Lake of the little Mhlanga River. Hyenas, jackals and various other small animals were plentiful.

An occasional lion was still heard at night, although the last was supposed to have been shot in 1854. In July of that year, a large black-maned lion had killed an ox on Springfield Flats and for some months kept the countryside in terror, until it was eventually killed in Pinetown. In the general panic, J.C. Fielden claimed to have shot another lion in the Stella Bush, but this was found next morning to be one of his own oxen.

The road twisted northwards through a patchwork of farms. Coffee, arrowroot and sugar were all being grown, and there were many fine estates. One of the best known in these parts was that of Thomas Duff. He had first arrived in Natal with his father, John Duff, in 1850. After farming unsuccessfully at Verulam, he had become a Zululand trader and then in 1860, settled down to farm and trade in the area of the Mhlanga (reedy river), at what became known as Duff's Road.

Another farm in the vicinity was one established by Thomas Watkins. His first attempts at growing sugar had been totally destroyed in a fire. The new farm, replanted in the ashes of the old, he named Phoenix; and it prospered somewhat more lastingly than the previous venture. North of Phoenix lay the settlement of Mount Edgecombe, apparently named after the seat of the Earl of Mount Edgcumbe in Cornwall. Its best-known settler was William Campbell, who arrived in Natal in June 1850 and in due course settled in the area on a farm which he named Muckleneuk.

Verulam, the capital of Victoria County, had become a separate magistracy on 23 May 1852. At that time it was a tranquil little place, with a pretty church smothered in honeysuckle, four stores, a library, a steam mill, two blacksmiths, two bakeries, two butcheries, two chemists, three inns, a saddler, a shoemaker and a tailor. The magistrate of the county lived there, as well as the county member to the Council, a district surgeon, a lawyer and a minister-schoolmaster. It was then the stronghold of Wesleyanism in Natal and a busy centre for the sugar, coffee, cotton and tobacco plantations around it. Its best-known inhabitant at the end of the century was an odd man named Alexander Mclean, reputed to be an illegitimate offspring of English royalty and sent out on a remittance after making an attempt to assassinate Queen Victoria. He was also said to have the secret of some great mineral discovery in Natal, but although several people tried to prise this out of him, he went to his grave in silence and poverty.

A continuous succession of plantations lay between Verulam and the Thongathi River. There was no village of Tongaat then. It grew later, with the coming of the railway, and became a hamlet only in 1930 and a township in July 1945; but the area was settled by such well-known individuals as George Marcus, who had come to Natal in 1849 from Ceylon and started a cotton farm.

Beyond the Thongathi River lay Morewood's old Compensation farm and the area once favoured by the Zulus for military barracks. Their capital kraal of Dukuza lay where Stanger stands today. At the site of one of these barracks, named Mdumezulu (where the heavens thunder) a magisterial post had been established in 1850 with C.H. Williams as the first official. The place was then generally known as Williamstown, but after the departure of the magistrate the name Umhlali came into use from the river flowing through the district, which took its name of *mhlali* from the number of monkey-orange trees (*Strychnos spinosa*) growing on its banks.

Another military kraal was that of kwaHlomendlini (place of the home guard regiment) established by Dingane. The site of this kraal, overlooking the Tete stream, was subsequently included in a farm named, for some reason, Shaka's Kraal, two miles from the present village of that name. In the vicinity of this place there were many great estates: A. Coqui had the first steam mill there; T. Reynolds had his Oatlands plantation nearby, while Stephen Gee founded his famed Saccharine Estate in the same period.

North-west of Shaka's Kraal, away from the main road, lay both the Riet Valley Estate of the Cotton Company and Glendale, a village first settled at the beginning of 1869 as a centre for farmers with estates in the hot valley of the Mvoti River. The old mission station of Groutville, back on the North Coast Road, was still running very well, with its central church and school and some 55 cottages occupied by African converts.

Stanger, in 1870, was non-existent. Only two years later was the magistracy, then known as the Tugela Division of Victoria County, removed there from Umhlali. A large African hut served as the magistrate's office. In March 1873 the Surveyor General, Doctor P.C. Sutherland, laid out a town around this simple magistracy, over the scars of Shaka's former capital, and named the place Stanger, after his late predecessor. The first grant of an erf was made to H.K. Bill on 18 October 1873. By 1877 there were 52 Europeans living there.

The land between Stanger and the river known as the Nonoti from the *mnono* trees (*Strychnos henningsii*) growing there was occupied by T. Colenbrander, who settled in 1859, after his unfortunate indigo-growing experiment at Pinetown. He brought out 80 settlers from Holland and erected a big house and a sugar mill, but the settlement, named New Gelderland after Gelderland in Holland, did not flourish. By 1880 it consisted of little more than a hotel, a one-storied building, with a thatched roof and a proprietor whose bills had the reputation of being as picturesque as his establishment.

One of the most interesting of all the settlers north of Stanger was Alexander McCorkindale. Originally he had been a traveller for a cotton machinery firm. He visited Natal in August 1850 on business and was so impressed with the place that he decided to immigrate.

In April 1856 McCorkindale returned to Natal with a party of 150 settlers, including 22 boys from English reformatory institutions. McCorkindale received a grant of 8000 acres beyond the Nonoti River and endeavoured to form an industrial settlement there. Depression defeated his plans, however, and his settlers gradually dispersed throughout Natal. Most of the reformatory boys did very well for themselves.

McCorkindale himself went up to the Transvaal and embarked upon another ambitious scheme which he called New Scotland. He planned a port, Port Corkindale, at the mouth of the uSuthu River, but died of fever on Inyack Island on 1 May 1871 while waiting for the ES *Tysden* to arrive with building materials.

Another well-known settler in the area was Liege Hulett. Born in Sheffield in 1838, he landed in Durban when he was 19 and became a chemist's assistant in Pietermaritzburg. He then leased a farm in the area surveyed by John Moreland (Mount Moreland), built a house, brought his parents and three sisters out from England and commenced farming. After struggling for some years, managing a cotton farm for a company at Driefontein and trading in Zululand, Hulett eventually bought the farm he named Kearsney, after the hamlet near Dover. There he planted coffee and tea when the government imported seed experimentally in March 1877. Eventually he started planting sugar, erecting his first mill at Tinley Manor in 1903 and developing his interests until Hulett and sugar became almost synonymous in Southern Africa.

Beyond the Nonoti lay the area of the Zinkwazi River. This was the frontier area of Natal, and the well-known Captain Joshua Walmsley, the border agent, had his residence, Chantilly, at a strategic position on the road. A small hostelry kept by Dickens, and the home of Jack Hill, the ferryman, were the last buildings on the North Coast Road before the great Thukela River marked the border with Zululand.

Many well-known Zululand traders had their homes in this frontier area. Herbert Nunn, John Hill, Percocks, Cook, Downing, D.C. Toohey, who had first arrived in Natal on the cutter *Circe* early in 1835, and several others lived there.

Transport was the greatest problem for these early settlers on the north coast. Some attempt was made to solve the problem by developing a small port at one of the river mouths. In October 1864 a tug was sent up from Durban to investigate possibilities; and both the surveyor, Doctor Sutherland, and W. Bell, the Durban Port captain who carried out the inspection, considered that loading could be done with surf boats at several points between Durban and the Thukela.

Other people had more ambitious ideas than just a beach landing place. In 1863 David Smith came out to Natal to re-investigate coal possibilities. He tested the Compensation deposit but found it useless. He then went up to the Biggarsberg area of northern Natal and was so enthusiastic over the deposits there that he planned a major mining industry, with a railway down the Thukela Valley to the coast and a terminal coaling station at the mouth of the Zinkwazi River. Unfortunately, Smith had no money and his schemes languished.

Railway construction on the north coast started only after the completion of the line from Durban to the Transvaal. On 21 August 1878 the line was extended from the Mngeni River to the Avoca farm, and on 1 September of the following year it was opened to Verulam, where it remained for some years.

Eventually, the Natal-Zululand Railway Company secured a concession in 1896 to carry the line on from Verulam to the Zululand border. The route had already been surveyed in 1890, but the expense of all the essential river bridges had delayed construction. In the years of delay Verulam, as the railhead, had grown rapidly and had become a place of consequence. On 21 July 1882 it had elected its first Town Board, with T. Groom as chairman.

On 3 December 1897 the line was at last opened as far as Tongaat, which had its civic birth as a row of tin shanties on the side of one dusty road. On 9 August of the following year, the line reached out for 22 more miles to Stanger. The last north coast section, to the Thukela River, was opened on 1 December 1898. The line was 66 miles long and it was served by one train a day, which left Durban at 7.15 a.m. and took seven hours of dawdling to complete the journey.

Generally, life on the north coast in those days was as exciting as the speed of its trains. Only occasionally did it have some diversion. On 8 June 1897 the 447-ton Norwegian barque *Trygve* was brought to anchor near the mouth of the Zinkwazi River, after being much battered by weather. The crew tried to land, but their boat capsized and six men were drowned. The ship was washed up on the beach and provided the north coast with much salvage and sensation.

More excitement came in December 1889, when a Mr Ritchie claimed to have discovered gold at Shaka's Kraal. This was a complete disappointment, but in August 1903 another discovery was made, on the two farms Lynton and Hopeful in the Mhlali-Shaka's Kraal district. A small-scale rush took place over this find, over 50 claims were pegged, boreholes were sunk and company promoters left for England to raise capital. Some reports claimed assays of over 500 ounces to the ton, but the whole affair soon petered out. If there was any gold there, it was what the prospectors had lost.

Another excitement came in October 1906. A dredger named the *Octopus* left Durban on 13 October, bound for Australia. She immediately struck a storm and by the next morning the firemen were up to their knees in water. The crew abandoned the craft in two boats and after six hours of rowing they reached the beach at the Mhlanga river mouth. The one boat, with Captain Ogilvie aboard, capsized while trying to land about one-and-a-half miles north of the river and his wife and two children were drowned. The second boat reached the beach at Mhlanga Rocks and all her crew landed safely after one upset. The *Octopus* herself later drifted on to the rocks higher up the coast and left her plates to rust there for many years.

Several extremely interesting developments have occurred along the north coast, particularly of an educational nature.

In 1885 a Catholic missionary, the Reverend Louis Mathieu, founded Oakford on a farm bought from a Mr Oaks on the Mdloti River. On 2 April 1889, with the aid of eight Dominican sisters, he started a school which today is one of the best-known establishments on the coast.

Fifteen years later in 1904, the famed Ohlange Institute was founded by Doctor John Dube in the Nanda hills. Dube, a Pastor of the American Board of Missions, had visited America and been much influenced by the work of Booker T. Washington.

When he returned to Natal, Dube resigned his mission post and founded his institute. It is unique in that it is African-controlled, although its teachers are paid by the government. It is a school which educates pupils up to matriculation standard, and has academic, commerce, trade and agricultural sections. Holding 700 pupils and a staff of 30, the building and all the plant were erected and are maintained by Africans. Dube himself was a brilliant man, who not only founded the institute and the Natal Native Congress but also started the newspaper *Ilanga Lase Natal*, and was the first African to be awarded the degree of Doctor of Philosophy by the University of South Africa. He died in 1946.

Another interesting establishment was the Phoenix Settlement. In 1893 the earnest young lawyer, Mahatma Karamchand Gandhi, was sent to South Africa from India to participate in a Transvaal lawsuit. On the train inland from Durban he was ordered out of the first class section on the grounds of his colour. He spent a cold night on the Pietermaritzburg railway station cogitating on the meaning of racial prejudice. This experience was the great turning point of a momentous life.

After settling the lawsuit out of court, Gandhi decided to make his home in Natal and aid his fellow Indians who were to be debarred from the vote in Natal's first responsible government. For the next 21 years Gandhi was a powerful figure in the world of the South African Indian and his experiences influenced much of his future career and the formulation of the famous doctrine of *satyagraha* (passive resistance).

Trains seemed to play a particular part in the life of Gandhi. Reading Ruskin's *Unto The Last* on a train one day, he determined to mould his life in accordance with its teachings. He established the Phoenix Settlement in the Nanda district. It was a farm settlement where all workers drew the same wage and produced in spare time the influential newspaper *Indian Opinion*. When Gandhi returned to India in 1914, he left a trust to manage the settlement.

Two years after Gandhi's departure, the renowned African prophet and faith healer, Isaiah Shembe, founded his village of ekuPhakameni (place of spiritual uplift). Shembe had been born in the Drakensberg about 1869. At an early age he began to have visions. He claimed divine guidance, became a faith healer and preached throughout most of South Africa. Eventually, he settled in Durban in 1911 and formed his Nazarite Church.

Shembe then bought 38 acres of land in the Nanda district and founded ekuPhakameni. He died on 2 May 1935, leaving his son, Johannes Galilee Shembe, to carry on control of an all-African religious movement, notable for its spectacular ceremonies and four big festivals each year, in January, April, July and September. Shembe's grave at ekuPhakameni has become a shrine for the movement, one of the most active of all African churches.

Today the north coast is one of the most important economic areas in Natal. Since Morewood's pioneering days the sugar industry has developed into an immense activity. From the 1860s, when there were 27 small sugar mills turning out about 2000 tons a year, the industry has become highly organised on the north coast with giant mills at Doornkop, Glendale, Gledhow, Shaka's Kraal, Melville, Tongaat and Mount Edgecombe all combining to produce some 600 000 tons of sugar a year; nearly half of the total output of South Africa.

Administratively, the area has developed along with its population. Inanda became a separate administrative post back in 1851, when L.E. Mesham was sent there, and in 1854 promoted from Assistant to the first full Resident Magistrate of the place. Several other new magistracies have been established since then. In 1894, the Norwegian mission station of Maphumulo (the place of rest) became an administrative seat. W.R. Gordon, last of the border agents, transferred his activities there as first magistrate from the old, so-called Insurance Office, first established by Captain Walmsley.

In January 1890 F.E. Foxon had been sent to eMbumbulu (the place of the round knoll), to open a Native Administration Office. In 1894 this office was removed to the high Ndwedwe (narrow table land) lying between the coastal plains and the beautiful valley of the upper Mdloti River. There it remains today, looking at what is without doubt one of the most superb views to be seen in South Africa.

Of the older places, Stanger became a town on 13 October 1920 and a borough on 1 August 1949, while the old farm of Darnall started its growth in July 1940 by becoming a village with a Health Committee of its own. So the north coast has grown and changed. The romantic old road still winds through its hills, although tar macadam covers the former surface of mud and ruts, and bridges carry the traffic without hindrance over the slippery fords which once caused so much delay. All around, the hills still tumble down towards the sea, but their old carefree costume of flowers and bush has gone for ever. Only endless miles of sugar cane wave today, where once the game animals, the Zulu armies, the ivory traders and restless adventurers roamed unchecked.

THIRTY-TWO
Misty hills

T he misty hills of the Natal midlands are as beautiful and gentle and as full of moods as the face of a maiden. How often, in the course of my journeys, have I caught my breath at the loveliness of some fleeting facet of their nature. I have seen them in their spring costume of wild flowers and soft green grass; in summer, lazy and carefree, like good-natured giants playing chequers with the shadows of the clouds; in autumn, when the grass is golden and whispers legends to the winds; and in winter when the hills are sleeping and the Dragon Mountains guard them from dim and distant purple heights.

The story of the human beings who settled among these hills is varied – full of humour, achievements, personal tragedies, hopes, trials and disappointments. Let us roam at will among these midland hills and watch the human play enacted in their green setting, for it provides both a diversion and a study of all the good and ill of which man's nature is capable.

The Natal midlands were first settled by Europeans in republican times, and a patchwork of farms, mostly oversized and little worked, spread out among the hills. With scattered population there was little call for towns, and it was only when the British came and the 1850 immigrants arrived that rural administrative and trading centres were needed.

So it was in the Umvoti district of Natal. In the report published on 29 December 1847 by the Government Commission engaged upon the division of the country into magistracies, the Umvoti district was first visualised, and a district centre planned at the old wagon ford across the river, but some years went by before any positive steps were taken.

Then, in 1850, Thomas Oakes surveyed a town on the farm of L.J. Nel, and on 31 December 1853 a meeting of residents in the district was called to decide upon a name for their proposed centre.

The meeting decided to call the place Pretorius, after Andries Pretorius. However, the government refused to allow this as Pretorius had borne arms against the British. Instead, a tentative name already fixed to the plan by the surveyor was adopted and the place was henceforth called Greytown, in honour of Earl Grey, the renowned British statesman and Colonial Secretary.

The following year, on 24 June 1854, the district of Umvoti was proclaimed and G.G. Kelly was appointed first Resident Magistrate. Almost the first thing he did was to find coal on Van Rooyen's farm, and a wagon-load was mined and sent off for tests to local blacksmiths. It was inferior coal, unfortunately, and nothing came of the discovery.

Despite this early disappointment, Greytown grew into a pretty little place, lying in a hollow – a congregation of houses and trees gathered around a church. By 1861 there were 16 houses and two stores – Handley's and Player & Wheeler's. A square, stone, loopholed enclosure, with walls 250 feet long and 7 feet high, surrounded the thatched courthouse and served as a protective fort for the district.

A minister and schoolteacher were in residence, as well as the magistrate, and the town was an independent, sunny sort of frontier place, much given to Zulu alarms and quick on the trigger. Water furrows down the street brought a drinking supply occasionally flavoured by a dead dog, but there was little sickness.

The first crops in the district were wheat and maize, while

a few ostriches were also kept down in the thorn country; but nobody made a fortune. The only money, in fact, resulted from trade with Zululand, while Ephraim Rathbone and his sons occasionally went up as far as Swaziland, where they traded with the chief, Mswazi, at his Hoho kraal, in 1864.

Of this trade there is an old story. In the early 1860s a young officer, Captain McLean, arrived in Greytown with a small cannon packed among his belongings. He wanted to go up to Swaziland to hunt, and he had learnt from Rathbone that the Swazi chief would give anything for guns. The cannon, however, was confiscated by the local magistrate and for years it was used to announce the arrival of the mail and to salute any suitable public occasion.

An increasing number of settlers arrived in the district and among the most interesting was Louis Botha, second son of the Botha of Botha's Hill overlooking the Valley of a Thousand Hills. This Louis Botha settled in the Greytown area on the farm Onrust, and married the local reigning beauty, Minnie van Rooyen. She presented him with 13 children, of whom the eighth, born on 27 September 1862, was a boy named Louis, destined to become the renowned General Louis Botha whose name is part of the history of Southern Africa.

Another noted character of the district was Pastor Louis Harms, who founded the Hermannsburg Mission in September 1854. This was the Natal headquarters of the Hanoverian Missionary Society, sponsored by the congregation of Hermannsburg in Germany. In November 1856, the Reverend H. Hohls commenced a school in conjunction with the mission. In its day this school was one of the best known in Natal.

The Greytown fort saw many excitements. The slightest alarm of a Zulu invasion across the nearby Thukela River would bring the farmers trooping in with their families; and the fort would be a lively place, with grubby children running about, eating bread and jam, playing Zulus and soldiers while the young bloods made the most of the opportunity to inspect the girls.

Some people, in fact, regarded these alarms as a form of entertainment. One afternoon some of the young officers stationed at the place decided for a lark to sound the alarm, a large bell hung on a tree. People were soon streaming out of their houses and down the street to the fort. Mrs George Newmarch had a mother's help named Hetty. She promptly complicated proceedings by flopping out on the sofa and having hysterics. Nobody knew how to bring her round. Then bluff uncle Edward Newmarch arrived. "Call the kitchen boy. Put her into the wheelbarrow and he can wheel her to the fort," he said. Hetty recovered!

Granny Plant, another great local character, came bustling down the street with a large umbrella and a huge armful of teapots, gridirons, frying pans and what-not, while her kitchen servant followed in the rear, laden with food supplies, including a couple of alarmed roosters under each arm.

Halfway to the fort one of the officers, laughing so much he could hardly speak, stopped the perspiring old woman and told her it was all a joke. She promptly dropped all her impedimenta except for a frying pan, and with it she beat him over the head.

Zulu alarms, it is true, were generally false; but the settlers among the misty hills had many real troubles and the greatest of them all were the Bushmen. Of these relentless cattle raiders, there is one story often told in the farmhouses of old Natal.

In March 1862 there was a big raid on James Speirs's farm of Mount Park, in the Fort Nottingham area. Seventy-five head of cattle and 15 horses, including a thoroughbred stallion, vanished. James Speirs's nephew, Charles Speirs, also suffered losses. Neighbouring farmers all rallied to help and by noon on the day of the raid they were off on the trail.

The farmers galloped up to the sources of the Mngeni River. Ten miles further on they came across a Bushman's horse, caught in a swamp and stabbed to death. In a fearsome gorge they reached the Msinga River and camped for the night. The next morning they started off again and found, to their chagrin, that the trail was beaconed for them by the carcasses of

Speirs's cattle, wilfully stabbed to death as they became exhausted: cows in calf, yearlings, two-year-olds, then the bull – as they tired so they had been hacked to death, rather than abandoned for their rightful owner to recover. Then came the climax. In a wild ravine, past the Lotheni River, they discovered the rest of the cattle lying in a ghastly heap of mutilated carcasses. The Bushmen had evidently felt themselves too hard pressed and had rid themselves of the handicap of the cattle.

This callous slaughter enraged the farmers. They arranged for help from Lugaju, the chief of the location established at Mpendle (the exposed place), as a buffer against the Bushmen. Ten days later, 24 Europeans and 14 Africans gathered under Captain Proudfoot and made their way to the place where the cattle had been butchered.

For two days rain held the party up in such a dreary camp that they named it Mount Misery (later Lotheni Pass). Then the clouds cleared and they set out along the trail. For two-and-a-half days they rode north-west. Then the trail veered south-west for another two-and-a-half days, and then switched to the east, leading them in a wide circle.

After eight days of hard riding they were at the source of the Mzimkhulu River. All they had seen of the Bushmen during this long ride were a few abandoned shelters and some exhausted horses, left behind with horribly sore backs.

Then, on the eighth day, they spotted a Bushman on horseback about one mile away. There was a rush to give chase. Racing down a steep slope, the Bushman's horse tripped and fell. The Bushman scrambled up and fled for a swamp, with his pursuers splashing in after him.

As the Bushman ran he continually jabbed behind him with a spear. Then Robert Speirs caught up with him, jumped off his horse and pinioned the Bushman to the ground. He was taken prisoner and kept by Captain Proudfoot for three years on the farm Craigie-Burn, at Karkloof. Eventually he died of tuberculosis. Doctor Sutherland, the surveyor, later dug up his bones and presented them to the Edinburgh Museum.

During this chase, an unfortunate accident had occurred. Thomas Hodgson, one of the farmers, had been accidentally shot through the thigh by one of his comrades. It was a murderous wound and the bone was completely shattered. They did what they could for him, binding up the wound and building him a small shelter.

Two-thirds of the party pushed on after the Bushmen. They used their prisoner as a guide, driving him on with a thong around his neck. They reached the Bushmen encampment at the top of the Drakensberg, but only in time to see eight women and children slipping off on the other side of the ravine.

The disappointed farmers returned to camp. Four men were then delegated to remain and care for Hodgson, while the main body returned home. Robert Speirs was one of Hodgson's four guardians. Roaming around, he became separated from the others. He was caught in rain and forced to shelter for the night in one of the Bushmen's caves.

The next morning, in pouring rain, Speirs returned to the camp. He found it deserted. A heap of stones was piled up in the form of a grave. Speirs prised off a few stones and found Hodgson's body buried underneath. Everything else was gone, including Speirs's horse.

In a tearing rage, Speirs set out to follow his comrades' trail, certain that he would find them waiting for him somewhere. He walked until sunset, firing off an occasional signal shot. It rained most of the time and Speirs was soaked to the skin.

He walked all night through the rain to avoid freezing to death and then rested in the warmth of the morning sun. During the night he had lost the trail and for the rest of the journey he found his own way. He had no food or blankets and hardly any powder for his gun.

For food, Speirs killed a few birds and ate them raw. One day he killed a dassie, the next day he lived on bulbs, and so it went on. Grasshoppers, "not bad at all, but scarce and hard to catch," appeared on the menu. Again, he noted: "I saw an ants' nest on the top of a bush by the banks of the Mkhomazi River. I took it down and fed on the ants for four days."

Some days he was cheerful, on others pessimistic. Once he scratched his will on the rock of a small cave, but despite his foreboding, he at last struggled into Dumisa's kraal at Mpendle. There he was kindly received and a messenger was sent on to his farm. The walk had lasted for 14 days.

There were many recriminations over this affair between Speirs and his former companions. In after years the old man became a renowned bore in Natal. He always insisted on telling and retelling the story of his hardship to all and sundry, adding many aspersions on those of his companions who had deserted him. The name Hodgson's Peak, on the 10 688-foot-high Drakensberg Mountain where Hodgson died, reminds us of this old misadventure.

The whole south-western border area of Natal at this time was an untamed jumble of hills and valleys. Richmond remained the frontier village, and the road which led through it to the southern frontier of Natal was notorious for its gunrunners and smugglers.

It was said that Natal's respectability ended at Richmond. The village certainly marked the end of official communications in the colony. African runners connected the place with Pietermaritzburg until 1872, and then a post-cart service was started by Henwood. The place had all the appearance of a frontier town – a scattering of shops and canteens, a dusty road and the little coach clip-clopping in every second day, with its horses covered in sweat and as thirsty as a pair of troopers.

As the last staging post before the long journey to the Cape, Richmond was generally crowded with wagons, its commonage full of grazing transport animals and horses rolling about in the dust of its streets in order to rid themselves of the prickly perspiration from their travels.

South of Richmond, the road wound through the hills to the hot valley of the Mkhomazi River. There a ferryman kept a rough accommodation house. John Leask, an argumentative ex-sailor, had the place in the 1880s and was generally credited with shooting the last crocodile of the Mkhomazi in October 1895 when he killed a specimen 6 ft 3 in. in length. By that time he had long since left his position as ferryman-innkeeper. Peter Weldon had succeeded him, only to lose his job in 1889 when the Josephine Bridge (named after the wife of the Colonial Engineer, Lt Col A.H. Hime) was opened. Further on at the border post on the Mzimkhulu River two brothers, Thomas and Joseph Hancock, maintained a customs office in the early days.

The only other Europeans resident in the area were a few renegades such as Thomas Huron, who led a band of coloured cattle rustlers from a hideout in the Drakensberg, and some gunrunners. The Africans resident in those parts were an equally unruly crowd of bandits and refugees. A renegade Sotho named Lisawana had a pack of mixed cattle rustlers working from the mountains, while the chief, Mdegane, was also involved in sundry frontier escapades of a dubious nature. A solitary traveller in this area ventured at his own risk. Edgar Bucknall, a young man trading for mealies, disappeared entirely somewhere near the junction of the Mzimkhulu and the Pholela (cool river) and only a few of his possessions were ever found, scattered among the tribespeople.

Of the gunrunners, several were colourful characters. Yorky Walker, Jim Shaw, Rudd and Andrews were all heavily involved in the business. With guns of the gaspipe variety fetching up to six oxen each, it was a most profitable occupation and there was little chance of discovery.

There is one story of the government's seizing a great store of illicit guns from a trader. In order to destroy the guns, the authorities laid them on the ground side by side and drove a wagon over the barrels. The gunrunner was left awaiting his summons and ruefully surveying the wreckage – or so the authorities thought. Instead, he collected the weapons, hammered them out slightly and then sold them at a higher price than normal to his clients, with the guarantee that they could shoot around corners.

This frontier area had originally been settled by farmers in republican days, but the cattle raiders had driven them away. As the area quietened down in the 1860s however, farmers started to return. Doctor Calloway of Springvale Mission Station purchased a farm in the area he named Highflats, and men such as Thomas Stuart and Robert Gold soon settled there as neighbours.

In July 1860 two brothers, Captain C.G. Helps and Doctor G.G. Helps, received grants of the two farms, Landsdown and Ellerton. They built a residence named Landsdown House, and near them a trader named Williams started a store. The area then formed part of the Upper Umkomaas magisterial district; but on 13 March 1876 it became a magistracy of its own, with H.C. Campbell establishing a first official residence in a converted stable on Landsdown farm.

After some minor changes of address, a Mrs John Grant, who had bought Landsdown farm, eventually presented the authorities with a building site. The surveyor, G. Williams, laid out a town in July 1878 around this spot, and the place was named Stuartstown after Martinus Stuart, the district magistrate. The following month, three wattle-and-daub shacks were erected for the magistrate and a public sale of erven was held at the Landsdown Hotel, the first hostelry in the district.

The name Stuartstown did not last long. Martinus Stuart was killed at the battle of Ngogo while serving with Colley, and his name meant little to the new generation. The African name for the marshy stream upon which the town stood, Ixopo (eXobo), was adopted instead.

Some interesting people settled in this district at various times. In the valley of the Mkhomazi, Herbert Rhodes started his career in South Africa as a cotton farmer on Stainton. His younger brother, the famous Cecil Rhodes, came out to Natal on 1 September 1870 and settled on the nearby Lions Kloof, until the discovery of diamonds in Kimberley took them both off – the one to fortune, the other to a miserable death on the shores of Lake Nyasa.

The first settlers in the district had to be a rugged crowd to stand up to the frontier cattle raiding. Their methods were as tough as those of the raiders. Sheep stealers were shot out of hand and the corpse was left on the veld, with a dead sheep tied to it as a warning. When the man's relations came in search of the missing party there were no questions asked.

The social centre for this rural community was the old hotel first started by Robert and William Gold in 1878, and by them named Off Saddle. Of this hostelry there are many stories. One of them tells us how John Chaplin drove up to the hotel one afternoon in a one-horse gig.

Now, his horse was notoriously stubborn – and so was Chaplin. When Chaplin tried to leave, after three hours in the bar, the horse refused to budge. Chaplin decided to sit it out. He had dinner sent to him and he ate it in the gig. Afterwards, a small table was carried out and one of Chaplin's cronies, McMinn, got into the gig with a pack of cards and started a poker game which went on until 3 a.m.

This was too much for the horse. With a jerk he started off, upsetting table, cards, money, McMinn and several empty bottles. For about five miles the horse hurtled towards the horizon. Then Chaplin got him under control and drove him quietly home. Ever afterwards the horse was most obedient!

North-west of the Ixopo area, the hills gradually piled up like the waves of a petrified sea breaking on the cliffs of the Drakensberg. Each year farmers penetrated deeper into this area, and soon stores and the beginnings of villages grew up to serve them. Back in March 1865, Doctor Sutherland had surveyed a town at the place known as Dronkvlei from the semi-poisonous grass growing there, which seemed to make grazing animals lightheaded. Nothing developed at this place until some time later, in March 1905, when the area was thrown open for settlement and renamed Creighton, after the family name of Lady McCallum, the wife of the Governor.

Donnybrook, north of Creighton, took its name from the farm of Robert Comrie; but the principal centre of this new district grew up in the shadow of the 6832-foot-high mountain known as amaHwaqa (the frowning one). The land around this gloomy peak was settled in the early 1880s, and in 1885 the government put up a few buildings for native administration. On 1 January 1889 this nucleus of a town became the seat of magistracy for the new Ipolela Division; and the following year the first erven were sold in what was thenceforth called Bulwer, in honour of the Governor, Sir Henry Bulwer.

The area west of Bulwer up to the Drakensberg was the last portion of Natal to be settled. Damp and bitterly cold in winter, it had never been occupied even by the Africans, and only cattle raiders from Basutoland ever wandered through it.

Then, in 1886, R.W. Cockerell secured government permission to mark out a farm for himself, which he named Fondeling. Other settlers quickly followed suit, but for some time they all had a miserable time in their new homes. Communications were non-existent and the nearest market was one hundred miles away in Pietermaritzburg.

Stock farming, sheep, and transport riding kept the settlers alive. Cockerell started growing potatoes, but prices were so low (five shillings a bag) that it was hardly worth taking a crop all the miles to market.

The centre of the district consisted of one store, built by Michel and Benast under the slopes of the 6247-foot-high mountain known as Hlogoma (the place of echoing noises). At the time of the abortive rebellion of Le Fleur, in Griqualand East, the settlers petitioned the government to establish a proper village, with a fort for their protection.

A small commission was accordingly sent up by the government to investigate the matter. To the annoyance of the settlers this commission rejected the store site. It was on private property and under the mountain, with a consequent loss of military value. Four miles north, however, there was a block of Crown land suitable for a village and this, to the disappointment of many, was duly selected as the village site and named Himeville, after Sir Albert Hime.

In 1902 W.H. Acutt was appointed as first magistrate to the new district, and a gaol, store and hotel were erected. The champions of the former centre of Underberg, however, refused to accept the new village and a curious rivalry commenced. Their first choice continued to grow up unofficially and most irregularly on private ground. To complicate the matter, in 1917, when the railway sent a branch line groping up through the hills from Donnybrook, it ended for some reason at Underberg, and left little Himeville sitting a few miles away, like an officially dressed-up wallflower languishing at the commercial dance.

Several other villages came to life among the misty hills. Mpendle became a magistracy on 1 July 1894. Twenty years previously, a post office named Mid-Illovo had been established on the farm of A. McCullough, in the area of east Richmond. John Jardine of Stoney Hill farm had been the first to settle in this area, where the remnants of the old eMbo tribe lived around their stronghold of the Ngilanyoni (bird's gizzard) Mountains.

The more northerly portion of the land of the misty hills, meanwhile, had continued its quiet life. In the 1860s, the road from Pietermaritzburg through this area was the usual rough affair. Past Otto's Bluff and the well-known Upper Saxony farm of Petrus Ryno Otto (who had established himself there after migrating from the Cape in 1841) the road went on to the Mngeni River, where a rough hotel existed, a one-roomed affair, consisting of a bar with enough space on the ground to stretch a few mattresses.

A second hotel run by Garbutt, stood at the Sterkspruit. It was larger than the first and such hospitality as it could offer was often in demand. The Sterkspruit was a notorious stream. It often came down in vicious floods, and in February 1864 it managed to carry away the Second Puisne Judge, Lushington Philips, with cart, horses, luggage, and robes. He escaped, but lost everything he had with him.

Greytown remained the only village in the area. To the Zulus it was known as Mgungundlovana (Little Pietermaritzburg), for it was the first European town they encountered if they visited Natal on any business.

Watching over the Zululand road was a small fort named Fort Buckingham, which was erected by the military in July 1861 at Kranskop. A bigger fort, named Fort Cherry, subsequently replaced the first structure; and it was from there, in 1879, that Captain A.M. Montgomery set out and became the first ever to reach the summit of that great watcher over the Thukela Valley: Kranskop.

For years after the Anglo-Zulu War, the only excitement to disturb the equanimity of the Greytown area came from the Natal Mounted Police stationed thereabouts, who were notorious for fights and were generally considered to be the curse of the district.

One incident in the early 1870s did cause a sensation in Greytown. Hanging outside the local Dutch Reformed Church was a fine bell, cast by J.E. Biebeer of Hamburg back in 1861 after a public subscription by all the people of Greytown.

This bell was supported on poles and was rung for both the Dutch and Anglican services, as the latter church had no separate bell. Complications developed in this amicable arrangement when the Anglicans rang the bell while the Dutch were holding service and disturbed them.

Much ill-feeling and dispute arose. The Dutch Reformed Church minister was a Scotsman, the Reverend James Turnbull, noted as a hard drinker and straightforward talker. He and the Anglican minister could reach no agreement over the bell; and opinion became so inflamed that, about 1873, five local men decided to steal the bell and thus stop further friction.

Major Menne, F. Hill, Joe Short, Tom Thrash and Mr Crabbe, assisted by a tame Bushman, did the job one night. The bell completely disappeared. The whole town was ransacked but not a sign of it could be found.

A reward of £50 was offered for the return of the bell, and this alarmed the conspirators. There was a danger that their Bushman accomplice might talk, so on New Year's Eve they removed the bell from its hiding place, gave it a good ring at midnight, and buried it.

The midnight ringing provoked another intensive search, but for 70 years nothing more was seen or heard of the lost bell. The conspirators released a rumour that before the last of them died they would reveal the hiding place, but in any case it was in such a position that it would automatically be discovered one day. None of the conspirators ever did talk, but on 13 April 1946 building excavations in the garden of H. Holst unearthed the old bell. It was still in perfect condition and after a good polish it was taken back to the Dutch Reformed Church, where it hangs and rings today.

For some reason, Greytown people have always been keen on mining. In 1868, when gold was first discovered in the Thukela River valley, a tremor of excitement went through the village. After this, Greytown people played a major part in prospecting the valley; and it was a local man, Fred Markham, who started the rush to Mfongosi in 1886.

The village, at this time, had grown somewhat, and the *Natal Witness*'s special correspondent, on his way to report on the gold rush, has given us a description of Greytown in 1886.

"Upon the first night of my arrival here," he wrote, "I succeeded in falling over a heap of rubbish in the street and having nearly dislocated my neck, I concluded there was a municipality, as my experience has so far been that this sort of thing only occurs where there is a corporation. I find, however, that I was mistaken, as there is neither a corporation nor town board.

"There are a magistracy, a bank, a masonic hall, several stores, and the usual proportion of churches. I am told there are also hotels but would strongly advise intending visitors to bring tents and cooking utensils as the accommodation offered is positively disgraceful.

"The court house, gaol, and telegraph office are all together and readymade justice is dispensed by an ever-popular and sensible magistrate who, while having the hearts of the people, might be improved upon as a lawyer.

"The postal arrangements are a discredit to the Colonial Government. Post is received tri-weekly and is carried by a post-cart which enjoys monopoly of passenger and parcel carriage, which is shamefully abused.

"On the whole, however, Greytown, with its picturesque cottages nestling among the tall gumtrees and surrounded by high hills, is a sweet little town, and visitors will find its citizens exceedingly kind and hospitable."

The excitement about the Mfongosi gold strike soon subsided. In its place, Greytown produced a sensation of its own. In May 1889, the Reverend T. Taylor and Mr Shapley were out walking one afternoon. Reaching a small waterfall "at Burrups" the parson wanted to get to the bottom. "He found little difficulty in doing this," said the old report. "He tumbled down some twenty feet in less than half that number of seconds."

Sitting up in a daze at the bottom, the parson found himself half deluged by a shower of silver ore. News of this shook the whole district. There was an immediate rush and the locality was soon pegged out. Nothing ever resulted except disappointment.

The trouble with the district was that nobody had as yet discovered its most profitable crop. There was a well-knit agricultural community with a society which had been active since the 1850s, but each man favoured a different crop and nobody had any hope of great prosperity in the district unless there was a lucky strike of gold. Yet the area was so pleasant it seemed as though it must inevitably become wealthy some day, so the people had patience and waited.

J.D. Holliday visited the village in the late 1880s and wrote his comments: "Greytown – very nicely situated in the county of Umvoti, surrounded by a rich district, and likely to become a thriving place. Some time back attended a sale there, but having no bell, called the people together by rattling a saucepan with a knobkerrie.

"A dance being got up after the Agricultural Society's dinner, in the evening, the only music procurable was the whistling of one of the company, whilst another kept time by hitting a glass with a spoon. Lights going out, a general demand was made by the landlord of the hotel to know who were going to lodge there; to each of those who replied in the affirmative a blanket was pitched, and they took up their quarters, some on chairs, some on tables and others underneath them. You might take choice of your spot, anywhere under the roof, for the small charge of two shillings."

The solution to the problem of a suitable crop for the Umvoti district was reached in the pleasant waterfall land of Howick. We have already seen how John Vanderplank introduced wattles to Natal. Among the farmers who planted them was G.M. Sutton of the Howick district. Sutton had planted them for the usual general utilitarian purposes, but by accident he noticed the strong, stringent, acid taste of the liquid between the outside wood and the bark of the trees.

Sutton experimentally packed off a bundle of bark to London for tests. No one in London was particularly interested. The bundle lay neglected in a Thames warehouse for twelve years until, again by chance, an analytical chemist tested it and immediately discovered the high tannic acid content.

In October 1887, Sutton shipped ten tons of bark to London for sale. This was the first commercial export of wattle bark from Natal, and it had a ready sale at £7 a ton. The following year Sutton published a pamphlet detailing his experiments in growing wattle, and this was the foundation of the industry.

All over the hilly midlands of Natal, where the mist and rainfall made conditions ideal for wattle-growing, the farmers started to become interested. There were, of course, many doubters. Planting wattles in quantity was a hazardous undertaking. The trees had a notably detrimental effect on springs and streams and it was considered that plantations would ruin a farm.

Farmers in the Umvoti district were interested, but they held back. Then Frederick Angus, of Ravensworth farm near Dalton, took the plunge. He had tried many crops which had all failed. Now he ploughed the whole place up. "What are you doing?" a visitor asked in alarm. "Planting wattles," replied Angus. "You'll ruin the farm," said the visitor in horror. "It's already ruined me," said Angus dryly, "so I might as well ruin it." He went on planting. Soon the whole district was covered in trees.

The beginning of the wattle epoch in the Umvoti district changed its whole economy. In 1896 a railway line was surveyed from Pietermaritzburg to Greytown. At the beginning of 1898 constructional work began, and on 25 July 1900 the line was opened to Greytown.

Several new villages developed. Kranskop was laid out as a town in 1894, with the name of Hopetown, but this was soon changed in order to avoid confusion with Hopetown in the Cape. It was connected to Greytown by a branch line on 23 February 1914.

From the early 1890s, the Umvoti district and the midlands have had a life dedicated to the wattle trees. Greytown has grown – first to a town in 1897 and then to a borough in 1915, with J.C. Becker as first Mayor. There have been a few setbacks. On 29 March 1918 a whirlwind practically wrecked the town and in 15 minutes brought about £10 000 worth of damage; but all through the midlands of Natal, where the hills hide their summits in the cold, white mists, the coming of the wattle tree has wrought a mighty change.

From Greytown to Ixopo, from the Zulu frontiers to the frontiers of the Cape, the green trees grow. They clothe the hills with a gown of forest – sometimes sedate, sometimes gay with yellow blossoms, but always having something of that cheerful tranquillity which seems to be the nature of those who live among the rolling hills of the misty midlands of Natal.

THIRTY-THREE
Down in the South

Down in the south, for 100 miles from Durban to the frontiers of the Cape, there lies a sunny coastline of blue lagoons; of fifty river mouths and 50 streams; of countless bays and rocky promontories where the breakers pound, boiling and tumbling and spreading themselves out like fine lace on the golden sands.

There is one particular marvel of this friendly coast – the coming of the sardines. Each year, in immense shoals of a hundred million fish or more, these little pilchards make their appearance on their annual migration; and the south coast residents, normally a mild-mannered, easy-going crowd, are caught up in a wave of excitement and seized with the urge to become fishermen.

The migration of these pilchards is a miracle of nature. Nothing much is known of them for certain, but it seems probable that they deposit their eggs beyond the mudline, in deep water, south of the Cape. Swimming north up the warm Agulhas Current the hatched fry reaches a point some 50 miles off the Pondoland coast.

At that stage, some physical change in the two- and three-year-olds induces them to leave the warm Agulhas Current flowing to the south, and approach the cooler water close to land at Port St Johns.

They make a landfall off the lighthouse at Port St Johns between 7 and 10 June each year. At this season the water temperature off Port St Johns is 17 °C to 18 °C, which appears to be the pilchards' ideal.

They follow water of this temperature up the coast, coming closer to land or keeping further out in a manner most irksome to anglers, but determined entirely by cold or warmth. A cold freshet from a river can send them miles out, but a warm shore current can bring them into the breakers and up on the beach.

Tens of thousands of diving birds circle over the vast, seething shoals, while a white cloud of birds lies heaving upon the water, having gorged their fill. Barracuda, kingfish, salmon, garrick, mussel-crackers, and a dozen other varieties of big fish feed around the verges, fearful of swimming into the centre in case the masses of pilchards suffocate them.

Behind the big fish come the sharks. Leisurely schools of porpoises cruise majestically around, while upon every coastal vantage point the anglers crowd. Some encamp upon favourite places night after night, like seals securing lodging on the rookery. In the general crush (if the temperature brings the sardines in) thousands of yards of tackle become entangled and lost, hooks are a menace, and feelings run high in the infectious mania of something for nothing.

With coastal fishing deteriorating each year, as a result largely of the eroded silt brought down by the rivers burying the fish foods, the passing of the sardines is the angling event of the Natal year.

Travelling about 40 miles a day, in a dozen or more shoals, each following the other, the pilchards go north as far as Durban. There, at the end of June, they turn about and swim back down the coast to the Cape far out to sea. At the end of the year they swing south from there. They spawn in the rich, floating meadows of the ocean which lie between the Cape and East London; and the whole remarkable cycle takes place all over again.

Just who was the first European to appreciate the excitement of the sardine shoals is unknown. We have seen how the shipwrecked Portuguese explored the coast, and how the ivory traders, such as Fynn and Ogle, settled there in isolated encampments. Dick King, too, made his fantastic journey down King's Way to the Cape; and Captain Smith led his men laboriously up along the beach. All these may have known of the marvels and the beauty of the coast, but, intent on some specific objective, they went their historic way leaving no comment.

An individual who certainly had the leisure to enjoy the coast in the early days was a certain eccentric named Charles Hamilton. This curious soul arrived in Durban in January 1864. He roamed around the country for some time, eventually becoming practically destitute and earning an honest penny in Pietermaritzburg by manufacturing pork sausages under the trade name of "Mrs Hamilton's Sausages".

Hamilton trekked down the south coast in his wanderings. He found a chain of Englishmen settled there, all living in crude little huts and shelters, but all exceedingly hospitable. It was a lazy, detached life that they led. Hamilton recommended it to younger sons and literary gentlemen with large families.

He arrived at Umzinto in time to attend a regular race meeting, patronised by punters from all along the coast. Hamilton, it would seem, lost most of his remaining money at the Umzinto races. He sold his wagons and such of his oxen as had survived disease, old age, or the bookies, and turned native, settling by the banks of the Mzimkhulu River to wait for his next remittance from England. He found the Africans most hospitable.

"A comfortable hut was allotted to me," he wrote, "and, having done with the only remains of civilisation – money-making – I resigned the fragments of what had been European clothes, and dressed myself as a Kaffir. I hope no indelicacy will be attached to this confession. I wore skins of animals tied round my waist, in sufficient quantities for all purposes of ordinary clothing; and large banana leaves were sewn together by the sympathising girls of the kraal to prevent the sun from scorching my back and shoulders, as my skin was not yet as capable of the same endurance as that of the natives."

For ten months Hamilton lived (by African standards) the life of a millionaire. He hunted, fished and lazed around, living on the proceeds of the sale of his draught animals. He was the only European within miles of the Mzimkhulu, and the banks of the river teemed with game.

He danced and drank beer and feasted on venison, until eventually he tired of it all and wandered up the coast to the Fafa River, until he met some European settlers, dressed himself "like a Christian" again and went back to Pietermaritzburg to make sausages and collect his remittance.

Let us examine the south coast in detail, as Hamilton must have found it in 1864. From Durban to the Mlazi River the country was almost in its original state of wildness. At Clairwood, then known as Clairmont, the owner of the estate, W.R. Thompson, was struggling to grow coffee and sell stands in a village which G.C. Cato had surveyed for him in August 1852. Beyond the Mlazi, in the fertile alluvial flats of the river known as iSipingo, Dick King had been awarded a 6000-acre farm as some reward for his great ride.

King was a good-natured, simple, bushy-bearded man and he soon split up his so-called Isipingo farm and sold most of it piecemeal to various settlers, who all went in for sugar. Among these farmers were some well-known men, such as M. Jeffels who imported Natal's first commercially made sugar mill in 1852; and several other energetic individuals, such as Lawrence Platts, E.P. Lamport, Smart, Babbs, Atkinson, Burkett, Mack, and some score others.

The leader of the local planter's community was Daniel de Pass. He had originally made his money from the Cape guano islands. Arriving in Natal, he had bought up several of the subdivided portions of Dick King's estate and named the combined farms Reunion.

De Pass was a great experimenter, and it was fortunate for Natal that he had the money and inclination for the work.

When the inferior type of cane first introduced to Natal became rotten with disease, he imported a number of varieties from all over the world. Among a batch from India was one bundle of cane tops identified only by the letters U.B.A. on a half-obliterated label. This cane grew phenomenally well and was so resistant to disease that the Natal sugar farms were soon replanted from this one original bundle. Nowadays other varieties of cane are replacing the old U.B.A.; but in its day it, and Daniel de Pass of Reunion Estate, were the saviours of the industry.

Beyond the Mbokodweni (Umbogintwini) River, as far as the Mkhomazi (Umkomaas) River, lay a reserve for the Africans, and development in it was negligible. The Adams Mission Station on the aManzamtoti was active and maintained a resthouse for passing travellers, but there were few Europeans in residence in the area besides the missionaries.

A handful of Africans tried to go in for sugar on their own account. Two of them, Nembala and Nwayana, erected a small mill for themselves at the aManzamtoti; but they later went bankrupt. The rest of the activity in this area consisted of a store run by MacDougal on the Lovu (Illovo) River, while in 1862 a Mr Pearce established a tiny wattle-and-daub inn on the south bank. When he died, his widow married a Mr Poss and continued the trade, while his son, William Pearce, later went in for sugar and, in 1890, started the great Illovo Sugar Mill.

Beyond the Lovu lay the reserve of chief Mnini, of the Luthuli tribe. It was an unspoilt, beautiful area, and through it the old road twisted laboriously over the hills and valleys. Three rivers came down to meet the sea in this area and formed lagoons which seemed to invite the passer-by to pause a while to fish and swim. They were the Msimbazi, the Mngababa (river of jealousy), so named because the Luthuli tribe were envied their possession of the area around the river by those who were jealous of its fertility, and the Ngane (the infant) a tiny river all on its own, which never had much water in it.

Beyond this infant river lay the broad, brown Mkhomazi,

its banks richly covered in the greenest of cane. A Mr Peddie had his farm on the northern banks of the river, where the road dropped down from the overlooking heights in the most notorious gradient and mud slide on the whole coast.

The drift over the river had an evil reputation. A punt was maintained there by a ferryman named W.H. Reynolds, who took passengers over at one shilling per head. Wagons had to be dragged onto the punt by two oxen, while the rest of the team swam across, leaving four Africans to manhandle the unwieldy craft after them.

Crocodiles were always present. William Ulyate claimed to have shot the last of these reptiles only in 1868, at Crocodile Bend, while hippopotami were common until 1860. A unique sight was seen at the drift in 1861, when a herd of oxen were swimming the river and a large crocodile jumped on to the back of one of them.

South of the punt lay John Mackenzie's Craigie-Burn estate, the earliest sugar plantation to be started south of Isipingo, back in 1855. Other settlers in the area were Captain H. Maxwell of Canonby Estate, and Lewis Reynolds. The centre of the area lay on the hilltop overlooking the ford from the south. There Greenacre had a store, and a ramshackle little inn offered accommodation to travellers. Two miles further on stood the courthouse and offices for what was called the Lower Umkomaas magistracy of the district, named by its settlers Alexandra, in honour of the then Princess of Wales. This magistracy had first been centred at Umzinto, but in 1859 it had been removed to Mkhomazi with Henry Francis Fynn as magistrate.

There was no village of Umkomaas in those days. Instead, Captain Maxwell had named the area of the river mouth Port Scott, in honour of the Governor. Maxwell had surveyed the mouth of the Mkhomazi in June 1856 and found it wide and never less than six feet deep. He considered that the river was navigable for vessels of up to 60 tons for 15 miles inland, and several places along the banks were suitable for development as ports.

These harbour possibilities intrigued the planters all along the south coast. The greatest handicap to their farming came from the complete absence of transport facilities, and everyone welcomed the shipping prospects.

A small company, the Alexandra Shipping Co., was formed; and in March 1861 the *Natal Mercury* carried the following interesting advertisement:

"For Port Scott. Umcomas.

—

The Screw steamer,
NATALIE

Captain W. Anderson

will leave for the above Port on Monday the 25th March at 6 a.m. A limited number of passengers only can be accommodated. Return tickets £2. 2s.

It is expected that the vessel will return on Wednesday,

the 28th inst.

For freight or passage apply
M'ARTHUR, MUIRHEAD & CO."

The arrival of the ship was a matter for great local excitement. As big a crowd as the neighbourhood could muster, gathered for the occasion. The *Natalie* arrived at low water and loitered around until the bar deepened with the change of tide. Then Captain Anderson turned his little craft into the breakers and, with a heave and a couple of rolls, she crossed the bar into the broad basin of the river.

"Though the work of a few minutes," wrote the *Mercury* correspondent, "it was an anxious time, and as the cheers of those on shore mingled with our own, none but those who have realised the situation can appreciate the exultation we all experienced as the anchor dropped and we felt we were really safe, and had tested the much debated problem of entering, for the first time, Natal's only navigable river."

Two days were spent in celebrating, loading up a cargo of mango poles, and marking the channel with flags to facilitate further visits. On a conspicuous rock was painted: "25th March arrived Screw Steamer *Natalie*". Then, at 3.45 p.m. on the 28th, the little ship sailed safely out again, to the complete astonishment of one crocodile watching from a sandbank.

This good beginning, unfortunately, did not last long. The *Natalie* traded with the Mkhomazi until 11 August 1861. Then, laden with 800 bags of sugar, she struck on the north-east spit at the river mouth, veered over against some rocks and sank. After much hard work, she was eventually refloated and, in January 1862, she sailed up to Durban for repairs under her own power.

South of the Mkhomazi lay the area occupied by the Hlongwa tribe, with an American mission station as its centre. On the coast, between the two rivers named after the tribe (the Hlongwa and Hlongwana) Bernard Schwikkard had received the grant of a farm which he named Clansthal, after his wife's ancestral home in Hanover.

Two-and-a-half miles off the coast from Clansthal lay the Aliwal Shoal, a first-class shipping menace, one mile long and three-quarters of a mile wide, first observed at the end of 1849 by Captain James Anderson of the immigrant barque *Aliwal* when he narrowly avoided a collision with it. After Anderson's report on the shoal, made in January 1850, Captain F. Skead was commissioned to examine it in 1859, the authorities having apparently waited nearly ten years to see whether the shoal would prove itself dangerous by causing the loss of some ship. No warning sign of the shoal was erected for a few more years, until real tragedy eventually forced the official hand.

South of Clansthal lay the mouth of the Mphambanyoni River. At this place, in November 1860, the first township south of Durban had been laid out by the surveyor Adams and named Scottburgh, in honour of Governor John Scott.

There were high hopes for this town, although nobody had so far settled there. In July 1860, Captain Grantham of the Royal Engineers, in the course of his military survey of Natal, had been favourably impressed by the harbour possibilities of the place. The local sugar planters, even more troubled by transport problems than their Mkhomazi contemporaries, had leapt at the idea. They promptly named the shallow bay at the river mouth Devonport, and planned to build a jetty there and arrange for shipping.

The farmlands around Scottburgh, down to the Mzinto River, were settled by a particularly enterprising crowd of men. Among the pioneers there were: Brander of Umsuny Lodge; E. Johnson of Ida Vale; Higham; W. Brown; J.H. Turton; Pigg; C. Dacomb; James Arbuthnot, on his well-known Umzinto Lodge Sugar Estate; Sinclair; Eaglestone; W. Moodie; and several others, such as John Rennie, near Park Rynie, on which fine estate the district held its sports and races every year.

In this area, in 1858, the first public sugar company in Natal, the Umzinto Sugar Company, had entered into a grant of 9000 acres along the Mzinto River. In February 1858 the manager, Crawford, had arrived in Durban from Java with the first Asiatic labourers to be brought into Natal. With their aid the company planted cane and, in March 1861, opened a substantial sugar mill which had been dragged piecemeal down from Durban in wagons.

The nucleus of a village was growing up at Umzinto. A Mr Pearse had opened a small inn and the Reverend J. Barker was in charge of a fair-sized congregation. On 6 October 1860 the residents formed a committee to erect a school, and were sufficiently community conscious to turn out at intervals with their employees and struggle to improve a road, the vileness of which was a constant bone of contention between themselves and the government.

By 1865 Umzinto was recognised as the centre of the Alexandra district. In December of that year the magistrate, W.J.

Moodie, removed from the Mkhomazi back to Umzinto, and the village, with a gaol and other buildings, became his seat. In the same year, Charles and George Knox established their Ballarat Store and Inn, and the usual quota of blacksmiths and other tradesmen soon appeared at the village.

South of Mzinto, between the rivers known as the Nkhomba and Nkhombana, so called from the palm trees of that name (*Jubaeopsis caffra*) growing there, Pennington had his estate with his two sons, James and John. Old Pennington went out hunting on 10 February 1865 during which he wounded a leopard at sunset. He returned to the spot the next morning. As he did so the leopard charged out and mauled him most grievously. When his sons ran down to help, they were attacked as well and wounded. The old man died in great agony.

The sons continued to run the estate. They opened a wagon-building shop at what became known as Pennington and went transport riding along the coast. A portion of their estate was subsequently sold to Sir Frank Reynolds, and this Umdoni Park, where the *mdoni* (water-myrtle trees) grow, was later donated as a holiday residence for the prime ministers of South Africa.

South of the Penningtons' estate lay a river originally known as Malangeni, from the Malangeni tribe who had lived there. Legend says that in olden times this river was the haunt of numerous water creatures, hippos, iguanas, and crocodiles.

Among these creatures there dwelt a particularly renowned crocodile which, by reason of its man-eating characteristics, brought the whole river into evil repute. Like a diviner, this crocodile was said to have the ability to *smell out* its victims, no matter where they were fording the river.

The legend tells us that Shaka and his army were once bivouacked by this river and a number of the warriors were attacked by this odious monster as they washed. Shaka thereupon decided to hunt down the crocodile in vengeance, so that he might possess the skin of so renowned a creature.

The crocodile was eventually killed, but its name, iSezela (the one who smells out), lingers on over the river as a memory of the past.

Beyond the iSezela a smaller river, known as the Ndesingane from a type of herb grown there, much sought after by herbalists, twists down to the sea. South of it lay the fine Nil Desperandum estate of one of the most remarkable personalities ever to settle on the Natal south coast – John Bazley.

Bazley, like many more of the south coast settlers, had originally farmed at Richmond. Hard times and setbacks in that area had driven him out. Governor Benjamin Pine, a friend of Bazley's, had suggested the coast to him in 1860 and had recommended "Nil Desperandum" as the name of his new home.

Bazley himself was an engineer, and his whole 600-acre estate reflected his immense energy and ingenuity. Fittingly, he had been the first to start a mill on the south coast. He was ever to the fore in district matters – building roads, planning and executing public works, writing letters to the newspapers, and exposing abuses – a big, burly, cheerful sort of man who would tackle anything for the love of seeing it done. Among his most successful activities was the production of seven strapping sons.

Bazley's neighbours were people such as Joyner, J. Few, and the American missionary, the Reverend Mr Stone. Across the Fafa River, the last and most southerly farmer was George Compton, on the banks of the Mthwalume River. Just across the river, higher up its course, the Reverend H.A. Wilder had his mission, and in the early 1860s this was the last European outpost.

South of the Mthwalume lay nothing save the hills and the bush and scattered African kraals. Eleven rivers of note threaded their way through this luxurious wild, each with its name and several with a legend of some old event.

The first river south of the Mthwalume is the iNamfu (the sticky one), so named from a type of tree growing there whose bitter-tasting sap was used to make bird-lime.

Next comes uMakhosi (the river of the chief). Of this river, the local Africans say that in the golden age of legends a certain chief was wont to sit upon its banks. The scenery of the river pleased him and he decreed the place to be his own. No man dared to swim or fish in it, and in the course of years the fish grew so bold that they played upon the surface of the waters, leaping and basking for all men to see.

South of the Makhosi comes a river with the derogatory name of uMfazazane. Of it, legend tells that a certain woman was washing there when labour pains overcame her. Contrary to all social taboos, she gave birth to a child on the banks of the river. To mark this unfortunate social offence the river was thenceforth named uMfazazane (the river of the contemptible woman).

Next in the list of rivers is the uMhlungwa (the river of the division) where Shaka was said to have divided his army into two sections while on his journey to raid the Pondos. Beside the riverbanks, there still lies a stone on which Shaka is said to have stood when he made his selection.

South again lies the uMzimayi River (the home of cattle), the name originating from a *hlonipha* word, *izimayi* (cattle). Then comes the Mzumbe and beyond that the quaintly named iNjambili – two streams, big and small, running very fast towards the sea, like two dogs coursing parallel to each other after an antelope. Where the rivers meet, the Africans say, the two dogs have caught the antelope they chase. The sea is the antelope they have sought. That is how the name iNjambili (the two dogs) originated.

Next comes iKhotshwana, whose name indicates a small stream, dried up and covered in long grass. Beyond it is the uMhlangakhulu (river of many reeds) and south again is the Mtentweni, on whose banks grow the spiky type of grass which gave the river its name. Beyond it is the Mzimkhulu, which marked the boundary of the Alexandra district and, for many years, the frontier of Natal.

Only a few isolated events disturbed the equanimity of this old frontier area of Natal. On 27 July 1852, the 600-ton barque *Hector* was run ashore at a point between the Mthwalume and Mzumbe rivers. She had sprung a leak out at sea. Six of her crew were drowned when she was run ashore, and the cargo of rice and sugar she was carrying from Batavia to Bremen littered the beach for miles. The survivors found hospitality with the Reverend Mr Wilder and were sent to Durban by ox-wagon.

Sixteen years later, at the end of August 1868, a vicious rainstorm struck the south coast, bringing the rivers down in floods 25 feet high. At the height of the storm, on 30 August, the 535-ton barque, *Ambleside*, was wrecked between the mouths of the Mtentweni and Mzimkhulu rivers. Fortunately, no lives were lost, but the beach was strewn with a cargo of 2850 bales of cotton and linseed on its way from India to Liverpool. Five hundred and eighty-two of the bales were salvaged and sold by auction on the spot, with considerable profit.

Oddly enough, the next wreck on the coast occurred at almost the same spot. On the night of 6 October 1871, during a thick fog, the 1001-ton *Defiance* landed on the beach about two miles north of the Mzimkhulu river mouth. The captain and six men sailed up to Durban in the ship's boat, while the rest of the crew got safely on to the beach.

The cargo of the *Defiance* consisted of 5750 bales of cotton and wool, bound from Bombay to Liverpool. Like its unfortunate predecessor, the *Defiance* was put up for auction and, influenced by the profits from the last wreck, £1000 was bid for the rights of salvage. John Bazley received the contract to do the work; and his son William was employed on the task, assisted by ten members of the original crew.

The wreck was securely wedged about 100 yards from the shore, and it was planned to recover the cargo and ship it back to Durban on the *Congune* (the new name for the *Natalie* of Mkhomazi harbour fame). Young Bazley, a great man for dynamite, blew the wreck open with a 400-lb. charge; but the cargo was found to be rotten, with bales stuffed with waste, and the whole thing had to be abandoned after only 300 bales had been salvaged.

These wrecks, and the gold rush to the Mthwalume and Mzinto areas, were the only notable events along the south coast in the Depression years of the 1860s. At the beginning of the decade a European population of 864 had been settled along the coast, cultivating 788 acres of cane. By the end of the decade, the dreariest in Natal's history, the population had been reduced by two; and this stagnation remained until a return of prosperity in the seventies stirred the Alexandra district into its present prosperous and pleasant form.

iSezela

THIRTY-FOUR
Alexandra

During the Depression years, the problem of transport in the Alexandra Division received considerable attention. In June 1862 the Colonial Engineer, Patterson, surveyed the coast and reported favourably on harbour possibilities for the Mkhomazi, Mphambanyoni and Mzinto rivers. At the mouth of the last-named river was a beach which many of the neighbouring settlers, such as Arbuthnot, considered suitable for loading coasters; and they had every intention of trying out the project as soon as prosperity returned.

In September 1862 the Lieutenant Governor and his staff travelled down the coast, examining the harbour possibilities all the way to the Mthamvuna River, where they visited the curious fossil relics found on the nearby beach.

As a result of these visits, the government authorised work to provide harbour facilities in the Mkhomazi. A sea and river wall was constructed of rubble and mangrove poles, and two townships were surveyed on either side of the river mouth. They were named North and South Barrow, and the first 40 lots in the latter township were auctioned in Pietermaritzburg on 12 December 1865.

The harbour works had been completed by then but, pending the construction in England of a special coaster for river sailing, no further ships had called. When the river coaster *Gnu* eventually arrived at the end of the year, it was found to have too deep a draught, and the Mkhomazi harbour remained unused.

The Depression dragged on, and the south coast settlers just managed to keep out of bankruptcy. The Umzinto Sugar Company was having a particularly thin time of it, and even tried silkworm culture as a means of staving off approaching financial troubles. Even the irrepressible John Bazley was hard hit, although, in 1868, he hopefully claimed to have discovered coal somewhere near his estate.

All progress was halted. South Barrow township remained deserted except for Saunders, the government poundmaster, who had been ordered to move there as its first inhabitant from his former centre near the drift. As for the harbour, £2500 had been spent there – but only the crocodiles used it.

A few settlers arrived in the area. Near Durban, E.P. Lamport started his Merebank estate. On the hill above the aManzamtoti a Mrs Jones opened an inn, while Stafford and Fyvie leased ground on the Mngababa River in the Mnini Location area.

The Mkhomazi was still sorely in need of a bridge, but a new ferryman, N. Nelson, did his best to carry over some 1200 tons of sugar a year, as well as all the necessities of trade. His wife had opened a comfortable inn for travellers on the north bank of the ford. The best-known inhabitant of the Mkhomazi at this time, however, was a cunning and very large crocodile, who had given every traveller in the district a scare at some time or another.

South of the Mkhomazi, the Landers brothers had started an estate at Renishaw (named after Renishaw village in Derbyshire), and C.R. Sinclair had a flourishing farm in the Mphambanvoni valley. Umzinto was in the doldrums, with the sugar mill rusting and the sugar company's estate a bankrupt grave of its £40 000 capital. Later, Lewis Reynolds bought it and re-developed the estate into eventual prosperity, with a great mill opening at Esperanza in 1883.

The sign of the ending of the Depression came in 1873 when the railway from Durban to Isipingo was surveyed, and at long last a suitable coasting vessel was found for the Mkhomazi harbour. This little steam lighter, the *Anthony Musgrave*, made her maiden voyage from Durban to the river on 8 August 1873. Under Captain Hynes, she had no difficulty in crossing the bar and steaming merrily up to Port Robinson (the farm Craigie-Burn, then leased by G.E. Robinson). There she discharged 14 tons of cargo and loaded 30 tons of sugar before returning safely to Durban.

The *Anthony Musgrave* commenced a regular trade with the Mkhomazi after that. Unfortunately, like the old *Natalie*, she soon came to grief. On 19 November 1873 she struck the rocks at the mouth of the river and had to be beached. The wreck was eventually sold for £120 in 1875.

This was a serious disaster for the whole south coast. Ox-wagon transport was scarce and expensive, for most wagons were away on the goldfields in the Transvaal. In April 1874 the settlers held a meeting to discuss their predicament and resolved to invite the harbour master of East London, Captain G. Walker, to advise them on the problem of the river ports.

Walker inspected the coast the next month. He recommended Scottburgh as being much more suitable than the Mkhomazi as a port. On this recommendation the settlers formed the South Coast Landing and Shipping Co. and chartered the cargo boat, *Alexandra*, to trade between Durban and Scottburgh.

Steel cables attached to buoys were laid at Scottburgh, and on 7 August 1874 the *Alexandra* made her first successful call. She picked up a full cargo, and a 29-ton cutter, the *Phoebe*, also started a trade with the place, although she was wrecked there on her second visit and it took three months to repair her.

In any case, Port Scottburgh was itself soon wrecked. The wagon owners along the coast deliberately reduced their charges by 25 per cent to ruin the shipping. As the shipping was hazardous, the planters preferred the wagons. The warehouses, surfboat and wire warps at Scottburgh were left to rust, although several small coasters such as the 100-ton *Adonis* and the 41-ton *Annie* visited the place occasionally, and a company styled the Alexandra & Victoria Shipping Co. Ltd struggled to keep the trade alive until 1877 when it went bankrupt.

The biggest sensation on the coast at this period came on 16 May 1875, when the 314-ton schooner, *Tonga*, becalmed near the mouth of the Lovu River, was carried by the current and a sudden sea breeze on to the rocks about one-and-a-half miles north of the river mouth.

The crew and five passengers all reached the shore safely in the ship's boats, although the steward had to be shot and wounded when he became troublesome in the general panic.

The *Tonga* carried a fine cargo of mixed groceries. She was bought at auction for £650 by Sydney Turner, and a gang of Africans under a Mr Forte busied themselves in salvage. The party camped upon the beach and erected a small store at a streamlet ever since known as Winkelspruit (store streamlet).

The salvage was extremely successful and the whole beach was soon piled with groceries. People from all along the coast journeyed to attend sales there and at Price & Chapman's Lower Illovo Store. In 1900, when the government sold the first plots there to Romer Robinson and W. Wyndham, and they brought down the old Durban Yacht Club building as the first house, the name Winkelspruit was applied to this simple beginning of a village. It was later picked up by the railway, in the form of Winkelspruit, for a siding there in 1903.

The endless coast problem of transport was partly solved on 10 May 1878, when the twin-screw, 47-ton, schooner-rigged vessel *Somtseu* arrived in Durban on her maiden voyage from England. This hardy little steamer built for T.N. Price, especially for the tricky coastal trade, was destined to become the best known of all small craft plying a trade from Durban. She was 90 feet long, 17-and-a-half feet in beam and drew only 4 ft 9 in. of water.

The *Somtseu* made her first coastal voyage on 19 June 1878, when she sailed down to Scottburgh and towed back to Durban the old surfboat which was rusting there on the beach.

Henceforth, all possible river ports were visited by this enterprising vessel, and the completion of the south coast railway as far as Isipingo on 15 January 1880 meant that coastal transport problems were considerably eased.

The Mkhomazi was the most hazardous of all the river ports. The *Somtseu* visited the place regularly in 1881 and 1882 to remove sugar crops, and always had a close shave in crossing the bar. In October 1882 she was stranded, to the inconvenience of the entire coast, and remained stuck fast for five months. Eventually she was refloated with the aid of 20 spans of oxen, and was surely one of the few ships ever to depend on that form of motive power.

The efforts of the *Somtseu* attracted others to the coast trade. In May 1883 the coaster *Zulu*, arrived in Durban from England and, on the 26th of the month, commenced her coastal career by sailing to Park Rynie, where it was planned to establish a landing point at what was called Mtshitshiwana Bay from the uMtshitshiwana (the streamlet of young girls).

In all these years of shipping activity, the Aliwal Shoal had almost been forgotten. In March 1883 a staff with a triangle had been erected at Greenpoint as a warning, but there was no light of any description.

Then, at 8.20 a.m. on 20 May 1884, the 2066-ton steamer *Nebo*, on her maiden voyage with a cargo of 4500 tons of railway material for Natal, hit the Aliwal Shoal, tore a large hole in her bottom and sank in deep water. The *Duart Castle* happened to be nearby and she saved all the crew. Thousands of railway sleepers were washed up on the beaches for miles along the south coast. This disaster induced the authorities to send the HMS *Sylvia* down the coast in July 1884 to survey the shoal, and new beacons were erected on the shore.

A second depression in the middle 1880s gave the coast another setback, but in 1886, with some prosperity returning, a new shipping venture, the Umzinto Shipping Co., was formed. This enterprise obtained special lighters and hired the steamboat, *Carnarvon*, to tow them down to the mouth of the

Mzinto River on 22 June 1886. There, 60 tons of sugar was successfully loaded and one new portlet was added to the coast, where regular visits were made thenceforth by the *Carnarvon*, the *Somtseu* and the *Lion*.

A wharf with a storehouse was built at the Mzinto and, although legal squabbles between the planters and the African Boating Co., who ran the ships, were a handicap in 1889, Port Umzinto flourished for some years. In 1891 the Umzinto Steamship Co. brought out a 100-ton coaster of its own, the *Gertie*, which traded to Port Umzinto for some time. Like all the other river ports, however, Port Umzinto was extremely hazardous. In January 1892 the two lighters used there for loading purposes were both washed up on the beach near Park Rynie in rough weather and nothing seemed able to move them. The shipping company went bankrupt in March 1892 and Port Umzinto fell into ruin. The advent of the railway was keenly anticipated by all, and the river ports were nothing but a precarious transport improvisation until the arrival of the dependable iron road.

Oddly enough, the wreck of the *Nebo* prepared the coast for another wreck. The 749-ton Italian barque, *Fidia De Genoa*, sailed from Moulmein for Falmouth in May 1889, with a cargo of teak logs. On the journey she ran into heavy seas, sustaining much damage and a serious leak.

The crew struggled to keep her afloat until they could reach Durban. On 18 July 1889 they made a landfall and saw the newly erected beacons on the shore, marking the Aliwal Shoal. As these beacons were not marked on their maps, they thought they had overrun Durban. Despairing of keeping afloat much longer, they ran the ship ashore on the north side of the Mkhomazi mouth. The captain and one seaman were drowned, but the rest of the crew reached the beach safely.

As a result of this disaster, the authorities were at last stimulated to beacon the Aliwal Shoal area properly. On 20 February 1892, two attended lights were brought into use. They were erected on iron structures at Scottburgh and Mahlongwa

Head, and were arranged so that they showed a red light when a ship was in the dangerous vicinity of the shoal. The situation of the two lights was reported all over the world.

The great event on the coast in this period of the 1890s was, of course, the coming of the railway. On 14 June 1894 the Legislative Council passed a bill to allow the extension of the south coast line from Isipingo to Park Rynie. Carl Hall did the survey for the new line in the same year, and A. Middleton received the contract on 18 June 1895 for the £93 000 construction. By the end of 1895 construction work was well in hand.

There was much controversy over this south coast line. Most people felt that it would never pay for itself. From Isipingo to the Mkhomazi, the line passed through an almost unpopulated countryside, and the whole construction seemed to be for the exclusive convenience of the isolated sugar planters at Umzinto.

Nevertheless, construction went on, measured more by the number of bridges built than the miles of rail. Tin shanty sidings were erected at stations named Amanzimtoti, Illovo and Illovo Beach, and at 7.55 a.m. on 22 February 1897, the first train pulled out of Durban with *Umkomaas* on its indicator.

A merry party of 50 people travelled down in this first train, a 90-ton affair of two goods trucks, two passenger trucks and a brake-van, drawn by a diminutive Dubs-type engine. The scenery was wild and beautiful. The little train ran jauntily through green bush and along golden sands, while the blue ocean laughed at it and a host of rivers came tumbling down hurriedly, like the Africans, to watch it pass.

The terminus was on the north bank of the Mkhomazi River. A bridge, 825 feet long, was still under construction and during the delay two survey parties located the proposed line from Park Rynie to Port Shepstone. W. Brockbank worked from Park Rynie and G. Holgate from Port Shepstone. The two parties met at the Mzimayi River on 3 March 1897. Comparing notes, they found that 23 rivers would have to be bridged, aggregating 6420 feet in bridges. The total cost of the 38-mile line from Park Rynie to Port Shepstone was estimated to be £216 000.

On 1 December 1897, the 40-mile line from Durban to Park Rynie was opened by D. Hunter, the Assistant General Manager of the railways. It was a great day for the coast, and also the final death-knell for the river ports. The two Aliwal Shoal lighthouses were decked in flags and a cheering crowd greeted the first train at Park Rynie at 1.4 p.m. [sic], after its three hours and 49 minutes' journey.

Journeys along this early line were hardly comfortable. All trains were mixed, and at nearly every station the engine would detach itself and fuss about shunting goods while passengers fumed impatiently.

Still, the railway transformed the coast economically and every new mile of construction was welcomed with delight. The Bluff railway was opened on 13 June 1898 to the station named Wests, after Sam West, who had founded his well-known hostelry on the Bluff in the 1870s. King's Rest, another station on this line, took its name from the presence in the vicinity of the grave of Lieutenant J.S. King.

The main south coast line pushed on down the coast steadily. On 8 August 1900 it was opened as far as Mthwalume, while a branch line from what was at first called Alexandra Junction reached out to Umzinto railway station, built on the site of the old Umzinto sugar factory which, by then, had been replaced by Esperanza.

It was a pity that bluff John Bazley had died back in February 1892. As an old assistant to George Stephenson, builder of *The Rocket*, he would have enjoyed the excitement of the opening of the line and would have been interested in a construction which had as its engineering highlight one-and-a-quarter miles of bridges, the longest of which was a 24 span, 725-feet affair over the Fafa River.

On 20 March 1901 the railway was opened to Mzumbe, and on 26 July of the same year it at last reached its terminus on the north bank of the Mzimkhulu River.

The final opening was a big event. All the local dignitaries were present. The Governor, Sir Henry McCallum, made a suitable speech; all the stations along the line were decorated; and thenceforth one train a day left Durban at 10.5 a.m. [*sic*] and arrived at the terminus at 3.50 p.m.

The terminus, called North Shepstone, consisted of a siding and loading stage on the north bank of the river. Plans for a bridge further up the river – in order to allow ships to use the lower portion – were already made, along with schemes to carry the line on to Harding.

The coming of the railway to the coast and the facility it gave to communications, attracted innumerable new settlers, and over the next few years the nuclei of several new villages were established.

Umbogintwini, 15 miles from Durban, had its start in 1909 when Kynoch's explosive factory was established there, close to the Mbokodweni River.

Amanzimtoti, three miles further south, received its first hotel early in 1898. It was the inevitable wood and iron building and was burned down in May of the following year. It marked the start, however, of Amanzimtoti as a holiday resort, and by 1902 the place had grown to the dignity of having its first stationmaster. In 1928 it was taken out of the Native Reserve by the Department of Lands, surveyed as a township, and included in the general Southern Umlazi Health Board area. In September 1934 the village obtained its own Health Board under J.M. Hutchinson, and with 774 European inhabitants it was second only to Port Shepstone on the south coast. In September 1952 Amanzimtoti became a municipality.

Doonside, 19 miles south of Durban, started off as a siding named Middleton, after the constructor of the line. In 1910 at the time of Union, the postal authorities requested that the name be changed to avoid confusion with the older Middleton in the Cape. It so happened that at that time W.A. Dicker, a Devonshire-born man, had a house on the hill overlooking the station, which he had named Lorna Doone, after R.D. Blackmore's famous book. On his suggestion, the name of Doonside was adopted.

Warner Beach, one mile further south, started in 1910 when the government surveyor, T.A. Warner, surveyed it as a settlement for pensioners and people who had suffered in the Depression. Smallholdings of ten acres, on the beach side of the present railway line, were distributed for use as market gardens; but the land was next to useless. It subsequently developed into a minor holiday resort and residential area.

Karridene, 24 miles from Durban, took its name from W. Karri-Davis, the Rand mining magnate, who built there a recuperative centre for phthisis sufferers. This was burned down, but the name continued.

Umkomaas continued to be called South Barrow until 1924, when the present name came into use. For years the place had been a village only on the maps of the surveyors. Apart from the poundmaster only William Ulyate settled there, in a shanty where the railway station stands today. With the arrival of the railway, the place awoke somewhat from its torpor. The district post office was moved there from its former site near the old deserted Lower Umkomaas magistrate's office. Robinson opened the first store in 1901, and in 1902 the first Town Board was formed under H. Brown. The present railway bridge across the mouth of the river was opened on 21 July 1948.

Scottburgh's use as a port was not entirely ended by the railway. The vicinity of the nearby Aliwal Shoal was noted for its fishing. In November 1898 a Mrs Hunt of Durban sent a fishing boat down to Scottburgh, intending to station it there.

This pioneer boat proved leaky and had to return to Durban. A Durban syndicate, headed by a boatbuilder named Brophy, then entered the field. They built eight boats, each 36 feet long and 6 ft 4 in. in the beam; and these, with a crew of eight men in each, were stationed at Scottburgh. The first one, the *Marianne*, sailed down in January 1899. It foundered within a week, but the rest of the fleet prospered. Other Durban interests sent boats down to Scottburgh and about 80 tough fishermen busied themselves there, with a giant Norwegian named Vos acting as their lord and master. The lighthouse at Scottburgh was transferred to Port Shepstone in 1905 and, from September of that year, a new lighthouse at Greenpoint (Clansthal) kept watch over the Aliwal Shoal.

Park Rynie developed somewhat when it was the railhead. Its port facilities were also used and in 1915 Park Rynie Whales Ltd had a whaling station at the place, with a landing pier and a very tough company of whalermen.

Like the name of Middleton, the name Alexandra Junction also had to be changed at the time of Union, for there was, of course, a much older Alexandria in the Cape. The name was then changed to Kelso, the name of the adjoining farm whose owners, first the Cook family and then S.J. Abrams, had family connections with Kelso in Scotland.

Hibberdene, 63 miles from Durban, took its name from C. Maxwell-Hibberd, one time Postmaster General of Natal, who settled on a farm at what was originally known simply as Mhlungwa, from the nearby river. Among its earliest residents were C.J. Stewart, who opened a store and hotel, and Stott, who started a rope factory which subsequently developed into the S.A. Cordage & Spinning Co.

Umzumbe, four miles further south, had its biggest event in 1891 when the Reverend A.D. Noyes started the Fairview Mission Station. For the rest, estate agents and land speculators have cut up holiday resorts in numerous areas and inflicted them with place names, mostly in horrible taste and completely out of keeping with their environment.

The coast has had few excitements in past times. Shipwrecks have occasionally provided local sensations. On 2 November 1893 the Norwegian barque *H.C. Richards*, carrying a cargo of deal, struck the Aliwal Shoal and received a bad hole. Her crew managed to sail her as far as the mouth of the Lovu River, where they were forced to run her ashore when she became waterlogged. There, they patched her up with a sail stretched over the hole, and with the aid of a tug and their pumps, managed to get her safely up to Durban.

Nine years later, on 19 August 1902, the Italian barque *Espero* went ashore near the mouth of the Mzumbe River. She was a vessel of 909 tons, laden with railway sleepers on the way from Java to Cape Town. The crew all escaped safely, but the ship was a total loss and the seas around it were littered with so many floating sleepers that they were actually proclaimed a danger to navigation.

The south coast, for some reason, seemed to be the Waterloo for ships carrying railway material. On 31 May 1905 one of the worst storms ever recorded, hit the coast. At its height, two days later, the German sailing ship, *Trichera*, was wrecked between Scottburgh and Park Rynie. The captain and eight of the crew were drowned and 80 000 sleepers for the Cape Government railway were littered along the beach.

Apart from these shipping sensations, the south coast has led a tranquil life down through the years. Holidaymakers have discovered each bay and lagoon, and innumerable hotels and lodging houses have grown up to contribute towards what has become the principal industry on the coast. Retired settlers have also contributed their numbers to the permanent inhabitants. Although most of these old-timers have grown a bit cross-eyed, watching rates with one eye and progress with the other, the south coast still remains one of the pleasantest and most genial areas in all of Southern Africa.

THIRTY-FIVE
Alfred

S outh of the Mzimkhulu (the great home of all rivers) there lies a pleasant 30 miles of sunny coast and countryside, stretching down with infinite variety to the Mthamvuna River and rolling gently inland through green hills and forest and palm trees for 50 miles, to the 7422-foot-high range known as iNgeli (the broken precipitous mountains).

Sixteen rivers flow down to the sea along the coastline and each has its ancient name and legend. South of the Mzimkhulu lies the umBango (the disputed one), the frontier, in days of old, between two contentious clans.

Next comes the river known as iBoboyi, from a type of grass growing along its banks, much used in making mats. South again lies iZotsha River, where the Zotsha clan settled in olden days. Then comes the umHlangeni (the river where the reeds grow), and south of it flows iVungu, the river onomatopoetically named from the sound of the wind rushing through its gorges.

Beyond iVungu lies the river iNkhongweni (the place of entreatment); an odd name derived, so the Africans say, from an old complaint that the local tribespeople were parsimonious to travellers and always refused beer or food unless especially entreated.

South again flows iBilanhlola (the marvellous boiler), so named because certain pools in this river appear to bubble and boil and swirl as though by magic, or the disturbance of some strange animal stirring in their depths.

Next comes umBizana (the place of little pots), so named because of the small potholes worn into the rocks along the river's course. South again, flows umKhobi (the river where the wild vines [*Rhoicissus rhomboidea*] grow). Then comes um-Hlangakhulu (the great reedy river), and beyond that the iMphenjathi, whose name is derived from a reedy type of grass growing there.

Next comes iKhandandlovu (the place of the head of an elephant), an old elephant stamping ground, the tribespeople say, which was beaconed for many years by the skull of an elephant.

Four more rivers lie southwards from iKhandandlovu. They are iThongasi, named after the headman Thongasi Susha; another Boboyi River; then the saNdlundlu (named from the hill shaped like a hut); and finally the great Mthamvuna (the reaper of mouthfuls) sunk deep in its gorge, forming the end of this pleasant stretch of coast.

In the old days this area was called No-Man's-Land. It lay wedged between the Natal border on the Mzimkhulu and the frontiers of Kaffraria on the Mthamvuna.

The first Europeans to settle in the area were, of course, the Fynns; but apart from them and their coloured offspring and African followers, the land was for many years scantily inhabited, with few events save the beer-drink brawls of the tribespeople to disturb its peace.

One event of those times occurred on 7 September 1852, when the 681-ton *Fairfield*, on a voyage from Calcutta to Liverpool, was blown on to the shore near the mouth of the Mbango River. Seventeen men were drowned but seven survivors managed to reach the beach in pouring rain. Fortunately, the few Africans resident there were hospitable and gave them food, shelter, and a guide up the coast to Durban.

Beyond unfortunates such as these shipwrecked men, an occasional trader on his way to Pondoland, or the visit of some party (such as that of the Lieutenant Governor in September 1862) to view the fossils on the beach south of the Mthamvuna, this No-Man's-Land was left untouched. The fact that the area was of potential value, however, was generally known. In December 1865 Colonel Bissett, then Acting Lieutenant Governor, journeyed down to No-Man's-Land with a party and formally annexed it. On 1 January 1866 a large concourse of Africans as well as Adam Kok and 150 of his followers from Griqualand gathered at Gun Drift on the banks of the Mthamvuna.

At this meeting, it was announced that No-Man's-Land had been annexed as from 13 September of the previous year. The Union Jack was then run up and suitably saluted by means of two small cannon, brought for that purpose by Adam Kok and Colonel Bissett. The gubernatorial party, which included J.W. Shepstone and Dr P.C. Sutherland, spent some time exploring the new district. The mouth of the Mzimkhulu had already been loosely named Port Shepstone, while the new district was named Alfred County in honour of Prince Alfred.

One of the objects of greatest interest in the area, especially to Doctor Sutherland, the surveyor, was a deposit of marble on the north bank of the Mzimkhulu. Back in 1864, two American missionaries, Robbins and Bridgeman, had been shown this deposit by the Africans who knew it as amaHlumvu. They took samples to America, where tests showed it to be carbonate of lime; but not quite realising its worth, they did nothing else.

The annexation party, however, took a sample of the marble back to Pietermaritzburg, where it excited much interest. Several plans were set afoot to exploit the deposit and develop the river mouth as a port of export. In April 1866 Dr Sutherland returned to the area with a Mr Jesse Smith, and did some extensive prospecting in an effort to secure big blocks to send overseas.

From the time of annexation Alfred County started to develop. From an administrative point of view, Lieutenant H.K. Wilson was appointed first magistrate on 6 January 1866, and the site of his magistracy was selected on the banks of the Bo-boyi River, about ten miles inland from the mouth of the Mzi-mkhulu.

This place was at first called Alfred, and by June 1866 several shacks had been erected by the magistrate and his staff. Later the place was renamed Murchison, in honour of Sir Roderick C. Murchison, the renowned geologist, to whom the marble samples had been sent for inspection in England.

By September 1866 the European population of Alfred County consisted of eleven individuals. At the ford about three miles above the mouth of the Mzimkhulu, Sydney Turner had settled. He planted coffee there, opened a store, conducted a fishery at the mouth of the river, and had a punt which he used as a ferry at the rate of 7s. 6d. per wagon and 1s. per person. Two sawyers, Ford and McKenzie, had also settled there, under licence to cut stinkwood and yellow-wood trees.

Several other people were attracted by the idea of settling in the new area. Even Colonel Bissett had thought it so beautiful that he purchased a farm near the Mzimkhulu and reserved it for his retirement.

John Hargreaves also settled there on a farm, and in March 1868 Archibald Sinclair arrived from his earlier home on the Mphambanyoni River. It was a languid, sub-tropical sort of place in those days. Sinclair built himself a shack and a boat. "I had no money," he wrote in after years, "and arrived with my gun and blankets as my sole worldly possessions and made my first money by ferrying kaffirs at sixpence each. There was then plenty of buck to be had for the shooting and plenty of fish in the river.

"When I first came here great shoals of king fish and salmon used to come in regularly. I have seen a shoal of king fish stretching from the entrance to three miles up the river, making a broad dark line in the water, and all large fish forty pounds and over."

Sinclair named his sugar farm Ambleside, in memory of the shipwreck, and on it he erected a small ox-mill, bought on easy terms from the American missionary at Mzumbe. With this contrivance, he manufactured treacle to sell to the Africans and some sugar for sale to the traders.

Other settlers wandered into the place. Lewis Reynolds came, bought a farm and offered a £50 bonus to anyone who would open the river for shipping. An old sailor named George Anderson also arrived and commenced fishing for a living, while another newcomer in those early days was the Reverend P. Stoppel. He established a mission just south of the Mzimkhulu and named it Marburg, after his home town in Germany. Six different trading stations had also been established in the county by 1870, including that of C. Knox at Murchison and two at the Mzimkhulu ford.

Murchison was not prospering. Wilson had gone. The only memento of himself he left behind was his name on Wilson's Cutting, on the old road leading to Murchison. His successor, H.C. Shepstone, had hardly settled in the little village with its total of three houses before the capital of the county was changed, in 1873, to a position closer to the troubled Griqua border. It was at a new village named Harding, after Walter Harding, the Supreme Court Judge.

By April 1873 this new centre consisted of one store, managed by R.N. Acutt for Ballance & Goodliffe, and a few African huts. "One of those Kafir huts," said the *Natal Mercury* in May 1873, "does the work of a much larger edifice, for the police, post office and canteen are all held under the one roof, Mr McKenzie being the policeman, Mrs McKenzie postmistress and hotel keeper. When the magistrate's house is built, and the public offices, Harding will then have a more town-like appearance. Of course every place must have a commencement, but I am afraid it will be a long time before this place is any size, or goes ahead."

Nevertheless, by January 1877 it had grown sufficiently for A. and H. Downes to open an inn.

Murchison soon became a ghost town, with only one or two gumtrees to mark the site of the former village. The only commercial activity in the country was at the Mzimkhulu ford, where Moss had become the ferryman. A couple of storemen, such as Muller, made a fair livelihood, while Bob and Jim Wooley and Sinclair were prospering with sugar estates. The marble deposits had hardly been touched. In 1875, a Mr Caldwell went there and made several kilns of lime from the marble for use by the sugar refiners, but that was all.

One sensation did occur at this time to disturb the tranquility of this peaceful part of the world. At 2.30 a.m. on 22 March 1878, the 287-ton barque *Ivy* hit the beach about four miles north of the Mthamvuna river mouth. It was a clear night in calm weather. The mate swam ashore with a line and by its aid Captain Orr and his crew got safely on to the beach, with the loss of only one man, who was washed overboard.

The next day some Africans appeared on the scene and treated the survivors very kindly, giving them food and shelter and an English-speaking guide to take them to the nearest Europeans, who in turn passed them on to the magistrate at Umzinto.

The *Ivy* had been on her way from London to Durban, with a large cargo of liquor. The wreck was securely wedged on a tongue of rock about 60 yards from land and at low water she was almost high and dry.

Every African within a radius of five miles of the wreck was drunk for weeks, and their huts were stacked with bottles. The wreck was put up for auction at Umzinto on 4 April. A Mr Lawson bought it for £220 and William Brickhill, with seven Europeans and 30 Africans, were employed salvaging.

A block and tackle was rigged, while at low tide files of Africans walked to the ship and carried hundreds of cases of gin, brandy and beer on to the beach.

On 14 June the salvaged cargo was auctioned on the beach. The place, by then, resembled a combination of a bar after a free fight and a grocery store in eruption. Charles Knox of Umzinto was in charge of the goods, and he had a hard time looking after everything.

Knox told the workmen they could drink as much of the loose liquor as they liked, but they could not broach any cases. Shoe Smith, a well-known character from Pondoland, was there, along with every other hard case within a radius of a hundred miles. One morning Smith broached a case in defiance of orders. Knox strode up to the man. "Two pounds cash or pull your coat off." Smith paid!

"A few nights after this," wrote Knox, "one of Smith's Pondoland friends, three sheets in the wind, kept throwing loose bottles on the roof. I called for volunteers to help me. There was a main topsail on the grass. I then had the man thrown on his back and tied his legs to one set of reef points and his arms to another. This stopped any further opening of cases for the rest of the time."

A big crowd of traders attended the auction. Free liquor was provided on a lavish scale and the *Natal Mercury* correspondent reported that everybody, even the African labourers, was "rather top-heavy". Stealing was not tolerated. "One ill-looking Griqua caught in the act of stealing a case of gin, was caged in an empty crockery crate until Mr Knox let the bird out, and, declining to prosecute, gave him a couple of lifters with the toe of his boot."

The merriment at the sale added substantially to the prices. "All the buyers present," went on the correspondent, "were exceedingly merry, and bidding went up seemingly as if they did not know where they were standing, for they advanced prices, regardless of transport, which to Durban would be 12s. 6d." The wreck itself was broken up and sold for £35, to a buyer who stated he was going to build a church out of the pieces.

In 1877 the well-known Aiken brothers – James, William and David – moved from their sugar plantation, Maryland at Ifafa, to the Mzimkhulu, where they settled on the estate Ruthville. They were a most energetic family and in their new home they interested themselves in sugar, tea, lime and marble. The problem of transporting the products of the district to Durban also occupied their attention, and it seemed that, apart from one ledge of rock, there was nothing really to prevent the development of the Mzimkhulu river mouth as a port.

The Aikens of course, knew the Bazley family; and young

William Bazley had already visited the Mzimkhulu back in 1871, while on a hunting trip. In 1879 David Aiken invited William to visit the river again and discuss the opening of its mouth. Bazley made an estimate and drew up a plan of work, which was submitted to the government. However, official assistance was refused, for experience with other river ports such as Mkhomazi, had been unfortunate. All the government would do was to say that it had no objection to any private attempts.

The Aiken brothers then contracted to pay William Bazley £500 if he succeeded in removing the rocks. Aided by his brother Edward and some Africans, Bazley laboured on the river for several months, occasionally turning his energies in other directions, as in March 1880, when he thought he had discovered gold in the vicinity.

The work went well and in due course the Aikens invited T.N. Price, owner of the coaster, *Somtseu*, to visit the river and inspect its possibilities. His findings were favourable and on 7th May 1880 the little *Somtseu* left Durban with a general cargo, on her first voyage, to what the newspapers suggested should be called Port Bazley, but what was, of course, officially known as Port Shepstone.

The following morning, Saturday 8 May, the *Somtseu* arrived off the river, with a lighter in tow. Some of the crew and the owner, Price, landed in a boat to inspect the channel, and then Captain Jewitt turned the little *Somtseu* into the mouth and headed for the river. As they came across the bar the skipper became alarmed at the speed. He tried to slow down, but the lighter, carried in by the tide, shot ahead. The towing hawser wrapped around the *Somtseu*'s screw and, unmanageable, the coaster ran on to the beach.

On the following Monday the *Somtseu* was manhandled off the beach and up the river, where she was examined at low tide on a sandbank. Fortunately, she was not very damaged. The enterprising Bazley improvised a patch of planks, rope, tar and oakum; and with this over the hole, like a pirate with an eyeshield, the little coaster limped back to Durban for repairs.

Despite the accident, Port Shepstone had been proved a practical harbour and it was an event of some importance. Port St Johns was being developed by the Cape, and the Natal merchants had felt themselves at a grievous disadvantage in the competition for the Kaffrarian and Griqualand trade. Now, however, a regular shipping service to Port Shepstone reduced transport rates from Durban by half, and the whole economic picture changed.

Even prospects of working the marble deposits improved with transport facilities. In June 1880 the *Adonis*, which relieved the *Somtseu* while she was being repaired, brought out several marble blocks to be shipped to England as samples by the Aiken brothers.

The opening of the river mouth was without doubt the most important event which had occurred in the district. While Alfred County was still excited about the affair, one more incident occurred to mark 1880 as a year of events. At 10.30 p.m. on 6 November, the 249-ton brig *Leading Star*, loaded with deal from the Baltic for Durban, hit the beach near the mouth of the Mzimkhulu. It was a calm night and the ship's dog did his best to warn the crew, but the eight men were all asleep. They woke up in time for four of them to swim ashore. The rest, including the captain, were drowned.

There was a boom throughout the whole of Alfred County after the opening of the river to trade. More and more people came to settle. General Sir John Bissett, after serving with increased honours overseas, returned to settle on the farm he had bought when he was Acting Governor of Natal. With him he brought 15 young men as immigrants, and at the end of 1880 they were all settled along the lower Mzimkhulu, planting sugar, coffee and tea.

Another well-known settler of the time was H.T. Bru-de-Wold. He was a Norwegian, who had deserted from his country's navy by diving overboard in Durban harbour. After wandering around for a while, he had eventually been employed by John Bazley at Ifafa. There he had married one of Bazley's daughters and then removed to Mzimkhulu. In after years, he had an honourable military record in the Anglo-Boer War and Bambatha Rebellion, eventually holding the rank of colonel. Even little Harding showed signs of increased prosperity. By the beginning of 1882 the village had three stores, a barracks for 25 Natal Mounted Policemen, the quarters of the magistrate, Major J. Giles, four private houses and a brand-new hotel, the Southern Cross, in course of construction by H. Downes.

The Mzimkhulu mouth, of course, remained the busiest centre in the county. Long wagon trains left there for Pondoland and Harding, carrying the trade goods brought in by the coasters. William Bazley had entered government service and was busy constructing roads, blasting away the Zingolweni cuttings, and generally making himself useful while his plans for improvements to the port were considered by the authorities.

There was still no Port Shepstone, except in name. The centre remained at the ford, where stood about eight houses and a ramshackle hotel named The Enterprise. All Crown land around this centre was surveyed and, on 11 October 1881, the first government land sale took place in the district and 22 farms and plots were sold. At the beginning of 1882, as an additional economic development, the Aikens started to quarry marble from the so-called Marble Delta at the confluence of the Mzimkhulu and Mzimkhulwana. They shipped the blocks to Durban for use as tombstones, using flat-bottomed boats to convey the marble to the river mouth.

Early in 1882, the Legislative Council at last voted £10 000 for the establishment of a harbour at Port Shepstone. Then William Bazley set to work with a will, blasting away rocks and building a wall on the south side of the river in such a position that tidal and flood water would be channelled and would scour the entrance clear, instead of spreading out and allowing a bar to form.

Bazley worked hard and enthusiastically on this harbour project. Using a diving dress, he did all the underwater work himself. Diving in shallow water is always rough. Sharks annoyed him and once a big dog almost killed him by persistently clambering on to his head every time he tried to reach the surface.

A story from this period tells us that when Sir Henry Bulwer, the Governor, inspected the Port Shepstone works, some joker told him to stay clear of Bazley because he always carried dynamite in his pockets. The same joker told Bazley that the Governor was deaf and any explanations of harbour works should be shouted into his ear.

When the two men met, it was a constant business of the one slipping away and the other following up. Relations at length became so strained that the joker had to intervene and explain matters.

Bazley did his work extremely well. His breakwater, built entirely of stone, ran eight feet above high-water mark for 500 feet. Its only disadvantage was a rather sudden curve to the northward, which made navigation difficult, especially in bad weather. This curve had been adopted to discharge the river current at right angles to the beach and thus keep cutting away at the spit of sand growing in from the north. In this respect the wall was entirely successful.

The need for a proper town at the mouth of the river was increasingly apparent. In November 1881 the local inhabitants, now amounting to about one hundred people, petitioned that the land originally reserved for a township on the south bank should be properly laid out as a town.

The need for this was all the more imperative as an organised immigration of settlers from Norway was expected the next year (1882), and temporary huts for their accommodation were already being erected.

In May 1882 Doctor Sutherland went down to Port Shepstone. He surveyed the lands for the Norwegians and, on 16 May, he started laying out Port Shepstone as a town. A sale of the first 36 lots was arranged, to be held on the 28th of the following month, and all 36 lots were sold at an average price of £25 each.

Alfred County was certainly progressing. A Lower Umzimkulu District Association had been formed by residents, to work for a school, a Port Shepstone magistracy and other social amenities, including a doctor. The need for the latter was imperative. On 24 June 1882 one of the best-known men in Natal, Ephraim Rathbone – the adventurous Zululand and Swaziland trader who had settled at the Mzimkhulu when Utrecht, his former home, had been handed back to the Boers – died a most miserable death. Seventy years of age, he accidently cut his knee with an axe while working on his new farm. With no doctor available, all the local people could do was watch him die in considerable pain.

The biggest single population increase in Alfred County came in August 1882, with the arrival of a party of 246 Norwegians. Back in 1878, Marburg had been laid out as a settlement area for a number of German families. Opposition from the German Government had prevented the immigration of the would-be settlers; and the London agent of the Natal Government, W. Peace, had gone to Norway in seach of immigrants.

The Natal Government offered one hundred acres to each settler, at seven shillings and sixpence an acre, payable over ten years. Thirty-eight families were selected, while the Reverend Emil Berg of London agreed to join them as their pastor. He was a Norwegian who could speak English, and as an individual he was ideally suited for the post, being a hardworking man, patient and honest.

The immigrants left Norway on 10 July 1882, and on 26 August they arrived at Durban aboard the 1822-ton *Lapland*, bringing with them £4000 cash and 150 tons of personal goods. At Durban they drew lots for their farms and then, two days later, they sailed down to Port Shepstone in the *Lapland*, with the *Somtseu* acting as tender.

The voyage from Norway had been very pleasant. Three children had died on the way out, but the rest all reached Port Shepstone in good spirits at 7.40 p.m. on 28 August. The *Lap-*

land anchored off what at first appeared to be a dark, uninviting shore. Soon, however, the people of Alfred County came down to the beach, waving lanterns in welcome, while the irrepressible William Bazley fired off five charges of dynamite in celebration.

The ship replied with some rockets, while on shore a big bonfire was lighted. Three cheers were shouted from the beach and returned by the immigrants. Then a farewell concert was improvised on the ship, while the music floated off across the waters to the people of old Port Shepstone sitting listening on the beach in the moonlight.

The sailors also joined in the singing, beneath the light of the ship's lanterns, and there were several last fond farewells in the shadows. In the midst of the jollification the little *Somtseu* arrived tooting its whistle and receiving a welcome of more rockets, gunshots, and charges of dynamite from Bazley. Then, with a last "Auld Lang Syne", the ships dropped off to sleep.

At 5 a.m. the next morning everybody was astir. Unfortunately, the sea was running high and the *Somtseu* could not get into the river. The lighter had to be warped out along the cable. The immigrants were then packed down below in batches and were given a wild three-quarter of an hour while the lighter was hauled to the shore by hand along the warp.

On the beach 500 African warriors, led by Mduka and Jim Fynn, presented a dance in full feathers and war paint to entertain the Norwegians; but seasick, wet, cold, fed up and far from home, most of them were more alarmed than amused.

After days of irritating delay, while the sea hampered the unloading of their goods, the settlers were at last dispersed to their new homes. There they settled down – a good, hardy, cheerful crowd – to do the work of life. They became some of the sturdiest and best of all the miscellaneous peoples who make up the total of the South African nation.

THIRTY-SIX

The coast of dreams

Margate's monster

The golden coastline of Alfred County, from the beginning, was the coast of dreams. It was there, of all places in Southern Africa, that the sea seemed so blue, the whitening breakers so cool and inviting, the lagoons so languid, and the air so full of warmth and laziness that it was easy to forget the outside world with its toils and troubles. There, it was easy to sleep in the shadows of the tall palm trees, or fish, or wander casually down the golden sands like a beachcomber on some tropic isle.

Not that the inhabitants of Alfred County did not work hard. It was given to their guests of later years really to enjoy the beauty of the coast. The pioneers had to work and plan, and experience all those conflicting successes and disappointments which are the foundation stone of every human story.

At the end of 1882 there were 600 Europeans living within six miles of Port Shepstone; and they were a homely, friendly crowd. The Norwegians and the older British settlers were mixing well. It was certainly fitting that the first romance developed between young William Bazley and Miss Martinison, eldest daughter of one of the newcomers.

It was a real gala day in Port Shepstone when those two married on 6 December 1882. Pastor Emil Berg was delighted to perform the ceremony, and the whole settlement was *en fête*. At the ford the couple were met by the two port whaleboats,

551

with their crews smartly dressed in white. General Bissett read them an address. Then, in Bazley's boat, they were towed by the whaleboats down the broad and noble Mzimkhulu River, while from the sides echoed the roar of the dynamite explosions which Bazley loved so well.

In those days, Bazley had his home on the north bank of the river. Later, he built an astonishing sort of house on the summit of a hill on the south bank of the river, with a stupendous view over land and sea. There were 20 rooms in this house, including a lofty reception room, four bathrooms, and a 100-yard veranda, 12 feet wide. Around this house Bazley planted indigenous trees. In it he collected fossils and books, for he was a great reader and scholar, a man of considerable mental and physical activity and a renowned Zulu linguist.

So life went on in the pleasant land of Alfred. The only people, in fact, who ever disliked the place were the occasional crews of wrecked ships. One of these wrecks, on 30 April 1883, was the 232-ton Dutch brig, *Vrijheid*. Laden with coconuts, she was sailing for the Cape when a storm overwhelmed her. The crew of ten were forced to abandon her 24 miles out to sea from the Mbizana river mouth. They rowed to the beach safely and from there were guided up to Port Shepstone by an old beachcomber, known as Staunsellar, who had been wrecked himself a couple of years back and had liked the coast so much that he had stayed there.

Port Shepstone harbour, at that time, was becoming busier by the month. The Natal Shipping Co. was formed to manage the trade, and a new 101-feet-long twin-screw coaster called the *Lion* was brought out from England in February 1883 to join the *Somtseu* in a fortnightly service from Durban. A diminutive screw tug, the *Sir Garnet*, was stationed permanently in the river, and a pilot and coxswain named Bill Sayers was installed as a hard-swearing, hard-working general factotum of the river.

A fishing enterprise was also started with a small steamer, the *Commodore*, employed by a local syndicate. More settlers from Europe arrived in July 1883, when 56 Germans, "a hearty lot of people of the peasant class," were settled around the Reverend Mr Stoppel's Marburg Mission. By September 1883 there were 246 Norwegians, 175 Britons and 112 Germans settled in the district, farming or trading.

The traders were unfortunately having a thin time of it. Men such as T. Batstone, who managed Hill & Howell's store at the Mzimkhulu ford (Batstone's Drift) were all experiencing the grievous Depression which racked Natal in the middle 1880s. At its worst, in 1884, even the shipping service was largely curtailed, and many of the settlers were driven away in search of work.

Three of these exiles were Inguald and Bernhard Nilsen and Zefanias Oslen. They wandered up to the Witzies Hoek area of the Orange Free State. There, while working, they grew so homesick for Norway that they built a four-and-three-quarter-ton boat, 20 feet long, 7 feet wide and four-and-a-half feet deep. They named it *Homeward Bound*, dragged it down by ox-wagon to Durban in March 1886, and announced it as "from Witzies Hoek, Orange Free State, for London Bridge".

The *Homeward Bound* was certainly the only deep-sea craft ever to hail from the Orange Free State. The three Norwegians, all middle-aged "old salts", sailed in her from Durban on 2 May 1886. Her passage to England was watched with intense interest and anxiety all over the world. She arrived safely in Dover on 28 March 1887 and by that time was so famous that she was removed bodily to the Crystal Palace and placed on public exhibition.

The last years of the 1880s marked a return to prosperity in Natal. So far as Port Shepstone was concerned, this meant a revival of the coastal trade and increased importance which resulted, on 20 April 1889, in its establishment as the seat of a new magistracy named the Lower Umzimkhulu Magisterial Division.

In 1893 Port Shepstone was declared a full fiscal port and the second harbour of Natal, with F.H. Staunton in charge of a customs house. There were big plans for its development. A new training wall was to be built, which would straighten the channel and, it was hoped, allow bigger craft to enter the river.

Up to that time (1893) £23 000 had been spent on the harbour, and the original object of allowing small coasters to enter the river had been fulfilled. Although river navigation remained hazardous, coasters such as the *Somtseu* and *Alfredia* could sail six-and-a-half miles up stream, as far as the first rapid at what was known as St Helen's Rock, after Helen Sinclair who had been the first female to climb it. Beyond that point, only barges and rowing boats could venture.

Marble was being worked extensively by the Aikens at that period, while several people were burning lime. Another group of local people had formed a new shipping enterprise, The Port Shepstone Shipping Co., and were busy building a schooner named *Sobantu* (Bishop Colenso's African name).

The great trouble with Port Shepstone was always the unreliability of the river. In winter, or in years of drought, the mouth would be entirely blocked up and all trade would be dislocated, with tons of sugar, marble and other cargo left to wait for weeks on end, unless ox-wagons were obtained for transport.

The winter of 1894 was particularly bad. The mouth was completely blocked. A warp was laid outside to allow a barge to load ships at sea, but the whole affair was so hazardous that very little shipping was done until the end of the year. Even after the summer rains, the river continued to give trouble. The Port Shepstone Shipping Co. fitted out an old, 47-ton lighter as a ketch, with the name of the *Pioneer*, and introduced her to the trade in February 1895; but even this rusty tub had to wait two weeks for a spring tide to allow her to cross the bar.

Still people persisted with what was really a hopeless problem. The river was silting up so fast from soil erosion along its catchment area that no dredging or construction could ever have lasting effect. One tiny ship was built at Izotsha by Haajem at this time and launched in May 1895 with the name of *Norman*. She relied on sail and a hand-turned propeller, and traded between Durban and Port Shepstone until October 1895, when a gale blew her from her Durban anchorage and wrecked her about five miles north of the mouth of the Mvoti River. Three of her crew were drowned.

Another, and more famous, wreck of this period was that of the 1976-ton, four-masted, steel sailing ship, the *Fascadale*. This ship was from Java, bound for Lisbon with a cargo of sugar. At 2.30 a.m. on 7 February 1895, when most of her crew of 28 were fast asleep, she ran straight on to the rocks, just to the south of the mouth of the Mbizana River and about 125 yards from the shore.

For some time the crew tried to reach the shore, but heavy seas prevented them. Two men were drowned in the attempt, while one reached the shore. Then the steamer *Norham Castle* arrived. She sent her boat over and the chief officer, Frank Whitehead, managed to swim to the wreck with a lifeline. Along this line the crew were saved, while five others swam to shore. Altogether four men, two monkeys, half-a-dozen cockatoos, a dog and two cats were listed as missing in this wreck.

Work at Port Shepstone harbour went on. W.B. Kinsey was the engineer in charge. While he busied himself on the new training wall, commenced in 1897, the *Snipe*, a small dredger, battled to keep the river open; but over all the shipping activity hung the knowledge that the railway was coming and, inevitably, the port was doomed.

One event of this period was the passing of the perky little *Somtseu*. This famous coaster, actually a most uncomfortable sea boat which took ten hours of tossing to do the Durban-Port Shepstone journey, was nevertheless a firm favourite on account of her dependability. She was sold in 1897 to a Portuguese firm in Lourenço Marques, her former owners replacing her with a new 90-ton coaster named the *Umzimvubu*, which arrived from London in March of that year.

All through the year cargoes of lime, marble, tea, cotton, sugar and fresh fruit were taken out of Port Shepstone by the coasters, and all the goods of trade were brought back in return. The *Pioneer, Umzimvubu,* and the 24-ton *Sobantu* when she was launched in October 1897, all laboured on this task, while a little tug named the *Premier* had the task of bumping across the bar with a lighter when the water was too low to allow the coasters to enter.

The well-known name of the *Somtseu* was not long absent from the coastal trade. In 1898 a 32-ton ketch named *Somtseu* was launched and was extensively used on the Port Shepstone-Durban run. Oddly enough, the approach of the railway brought a temporary boom in coastal shipping. Land values and enterprises were all flourishing in anticipation of the arrival of the railway, and the coasters had to bring in the necessary materials for houses and other construction.

The Port Shepstone Shipping Co. went so far as to build a new 140-ton steel coaster named the *Penguin*. She was built in Durban from parts sent out from England. She made her maiden voyage in August 1898, replacing the rusty *Pioneer*, which had thus far made 85 trips to Port Shepstone.

The *Penguin* had two cabins for passengers, and these were sorely needed. The *Umzimvubu*, that year, had been transferred entirely to the Port St Johns run, leaving only sailing vessels for Port Shepstone. As these would take 70 hours to sail to Durban on occasions of contrary winds, the plight of passengers can be imagined.

Another vessel used on the Port Shepstone run during this swansong of the coasters was a ketch named the *Harry Mundahl*. She made several visits. Then, at 5.30 p.m. on 30 January 1901, she was wrecked near the mouth of the Mtentweni River. Her crew of ten all got ashore safely, but the ship and her cargo of lime and sugar for Durban were a total loss.

The railway reached its terminus on the north bank of the Mzimkhulu on 26 July 1901, and this marked the end of the coasting service. The new harbour works were still being completed, but the trade was over. The *Penguin* thenceforth traded to Port St Johns, while the old *Pioneer* sailed to East London and was eventually lost with all hands in a storm there in June 1902. The little *Penguin* also came to grief in August 1904, while engaged in an effort to salvage the *Dorothea* treasure.

During these years, when most of the interests of Alfred County were concentrated on its transport problems and the growth of Port Shepstone, first as a port and then as a railhead, the life of the rest of the district had been quiet.

Few events occurred to disturb the normal passage of time in a rural and isolated community. One sensation occurred on 30 October 1898, when a well-known European farmer named James Kay was brutally murdered on his farm, *Glenalvon*, near iziNgolweni. The murderers were a group of African herbalists who decided to kill Kay in order to obtain ingredients (*muthi*) for magical purposes from his body. All the culprits were duly caught and hanged.

The European population of Alfred County was still scanty and widely scattered over the country. There were, however, some interesting characters among these early settlers. Back in 1883, for instance, Alfred Eyles had established a mission near the hill known as Ntsaba (the lookout) at the mouth of the Mbizana River. His establishment, a wattle-and-daub shack run as a mission for the Society of Friends, was the first European house in that area.

Eyles later obtained a farm in the vicinity which he named Outlook, after the hill. This name was later changed to South-broom, after Southbroom Hall, the family home in Wiltshire. Later, in 1933, a township with the name of Southbroom came to life on the farm site, and today it is a favourite resort noted for its lagoon and golf course.

A year after the arrival of Eyles, a police constable named Christopher Sanders was sent down from Harding to establish a coastal police post known as Imbezana, which would control the area from the Mthamvuna to Ivungu.

Sanders had a wild area under his charge in those days. Shortly after his arrival, he was patrolling the Mthamvuna River when he found a small African girl who had been living in the bush like a wild animal since her parents had been butchered in a tribal fight two years before. Sanders took her to a friendly kraal and had her adopted. She was named Nogusa, and eventually grew to be a beautiful girl who brought her adopters 13 head of cattle as lobolo.

Apart from the usual faction fights and cattle rustling, the only troublesome element in Alfred County consisted of a scattering of European gunrunners living along the Mthamvuna River frontier. Shoe Smith was one of the best known of these – a curious character, often to be seen sitting by the banks of the Mthamvuna reading.

Harry Spencer, Donald Coutts, the well-known Mitchell family and, in 1904, Arthur Crompton, were all early traders in Alfred County. One of the best-known characters in the business was Peg Leg Clark, who retired from the sea and built a store near the frontier which he named Braemer, after his last ship. Peg Leg was a kindly character, and memory of his personality and stories of his ways still linger among the Africans along the southern frontiers of Natal.

Mixed farming was practised on one or two farms, but lack of communications was a hopeless handicap. In 1902 the Alfredia Wattle Co., managed by Emil Zierau, started planting the first wattles in the county on the Murchison Flats, but for some time this venture was just an experiment.

No matter what the crop, the question of transport was dominant, and this was nowhere better demonstrated than on the grassy plateau known as the Oribi Flats, after the sprightly little antelopes which once abounded there. This Oribi Flats area was a completely isolated tongue of fertile land, separated from the rest of the world by the vast ravines of the Mzimkhulu River on the north and the Mzimkhulwana on the south.

In 1907, a number of Norwegians from Marburg settled on the Oribi Flats and started to farm. They were immediately affected by the problem of transport, more so than any of the other settlers in Alfred County, and the story of the way in which they overcame the difficulty makes interesting reading.

First of all, the settlers naturally tried the government for aid. The narrow-gauge railway from Port Shepstone to Harding was being built at the time, and the Oribi Flats settlers attempted to persuade the government to alter the route of this line, to bring it on to the flats. Screams of rage from settlers at iziNgolweni and Harding effectively prevented this development.

A road was the only possible method of communication. Four settlers thereupon set to work and located a route through the deep Oribi Gorge. A government road surveyor was then requested to examine the route; but this worthy, after being stranded in the river, reported the route as being unpractical.

Nothing daunted, the settlers, led by Peter Skorpen and Gustav Lehr, collected £22 amongst themselves and cut a track through the bush along the route. A government surveyor then reported on it, but the authorities considered the project too expensive. The settlers were left to collect £150 among themselves and commence work. Another £150 was contributed, and then the government granted them a subsidy of a pound for every pound collected.

In 1917, a 12-feet-wide track through the gorge was completed. This was later widened to 16 feet, and at least the settlers had some form of communication, although they longed for a wider and better road. Then a government party visited the Oribi Gorge to inspect its possibilities as a nature reserve. The settlers saw their opportunity.

As the government party was driving up out of the gorge, a secret signal sent Rupert Larkan down the road with a vast load of wattle bark on a rickety lorry. Halfway up the precarious one-way track, the officials were horrified to encounter the unwieldy lorry. They had no choice. After some hard language, they had to descend the steep gradient in reverse in order to allow the lorry to pass. The Oribi Gorge road was remade, widened and surfaced within a year.

The first use of the beautiful coast of Alfred County as a holiday resort was naturally made by its own inhabitants. Edward

Stafford, the transport rider from Stafford's Post, Harding, built himself a holiday shack among the red sand dunes near the mouth of the Mthamvuna. His shack was later enveloped by the sand; but then T.K. Pringle bought up the area and named it Banner Rest, for it was there that he intended to "strike his banner" and retire. Pringle also planned a township, named Kennington after himself (Ken), but this name he changed to Port Edward, in honour of the then Prince of Wales.

Further up the coast, a number of German families had settled in the years before the Anglo-Boer War. Among these was Walter von Baumbach, who planted fibre on the farm named Munster by the government surveyor, after the resort in Ireland.

Another German settler of those times and parts was Otto Strauss, who claimed to be a brother of Johann Strauss the composer. Strauss grew pineapples on the farm Jericho. He was an independent sort of character, walking around barefoot and making his own clothes out of canvas – very stylish and waterproof! He lived in a corrugated-iron shanty by the banks of the Mphenjathi River and, before the Anglo-Boer War, induced a nephew of his to emigrate from Germany and join him. Strauss went up to Durban to meet the young man. Not being inclined to pay hotel bills, he accommodated himself in a storage field of large, new drainpipes. After welcoming his nephew, he took him there as well for a night. Strauss claimed the pipes were comfortable and the curvature was good for the spine.

A neighbour of Strauss's was Ludwig Steinaecker, a diminutive, bumptious little man who had wandered down to the Alfred County from South West Africa, where he had got into some trouble with his government. Steinaecker managed the farm of Charles Reed, near Ivy Bay, where the old *Ivy* had been wrecked. Later, he sickened of the solitude and removed to Marburg as a barman in the local pub. Then came the Anglo-Boer War. Steinaecker joined the British army, and the story of his curious adventures with his "Forty Thieves" is worth reading in the history of that conflict.

Surveyors and land speculators have inflicted many hideous place names on the Alfred County coast. The ugly name of Ramsgate, applied to the farm at the mouth of the Bilanhlola River, was one of these surveyor-given names. Its first inhabitant came in 1922 when a globe-trotting painter, writer and violin-maker named Paul Buck discovered the place with its lazy, blue lagoon. He named it Blue Lagoon, and there he settled to breed tropical fish and lead the pleasant, dreamy sort of life which was characteristic of the coast in those carefree days.

Just north of Ramsgate, the sterile imagination of the surveyor had imposed another imported name on a farm. This farm, named Margate, was purchased in 1919 by Hugh Ballance from a Mr Manning for £466. Ballance fancied the place for its beautiful beach and congenial scenery. It had all the ingredients for a holiday resort; the swimming was safer than most other beaches in Natal, there was a shallow lagoon which was ideal for children, there were rocky outcrops for fishermen, and romantic stretches of the Khongweni stream, where pathways twisted through a shady forest and water lilies slept upon the surface.

Ballance cut the farm up into half-acre plots and planned a township named Inkongweni. The place did not develop with any speed. Communications were bad and the Alfred County coast was little known. Still, a few settlers arrived. In March 1921, a former market master of Johannesburg named Gillett built the first rondavel on one of the plots. His arrival was prophetic of the future, when Margate was destined to develop into something like a seaside suburb of Johannesburg.

What the place needed to start it off properly was publicity, and in 1922 it first reached the notice of the world when countless millions of newspaper readers were jolted out of their breakfast apathy and sent in search of Margate on the map after reading a most curious story.

"On the morning of 1st November," wrote Hugh Ballance to the world's press, "I saw what I took to be two whales fighting with some sea monster about 1,300 yards from the shore. I got my glasses and was amazed to see what I took to be a polar bear, but of truly mammoth proportions. This creature I observed to rear out of the water fully twenty feet and strike repeatedly with what I took to be its tail at the two whales, but with seemingly no effect."

The battle continued for three hours, after which the whales made off, leaving the monster floating on the water inert. It was washed ashore that night on the beach beyond the hill known, for some reason, as Tragedy Hill. It was a monstrous thing, "forty-seven feet long, ten feet in breadth and five feet high. At one end it had a trunk about fourteen inches in diameter and five feet long. At the other end was a tail two feet thick and ten feet long. This horror was clothed in snow-white hair and seemed to be devoid of blood."

For ten days the creature lay upon the beach, and a span of 32 oxen failed to budge it. Meanwhile, all the world was talking about Margate and its monster, and puzzled scientists were preparing to journey to the place to make an inspection. Then, a spring tide did with ease what 32 oxen had failed to do. Overnight the carcass vanished and left only a most intriguing mystery for innumerable writers to publicise and discuss.

The spring tide, in fact, had been most fortunate for Margate's publicity. Had the carcass remained, some prosaic scientist would doubtless have dismissed the whole business for what it probably was – just the half-putrefied body of a whale, the blubber stringy and white and half detached, with shapeless masses lying around like a fancied trunk, or legs or tail – and that would have been the end of Margate's first publicity.

Instead, the place went on. Ballance sold it to a New Zealander of Scots descent, with the South African-sounding name of J.J. Erasmus. Erasmus was a vigorous man, with a considerable amount of that sense of business which is characteristic of many of the inhabitants of the place today. Despite the handicap of bad roads and non-existent amenities, he proceeded resolutely with the scheme of development.

By 1924 there were six buildings in Margate, including one hotel, the Dol Marina, on the site of the later Marina Hotel.

Erasmus had bought a bus to bring visitors to the place from the Port Shepstone railhead but, despite this convenience, a visit to the coast of Alfred County in those years still required pioneering spirit.

"We heard from friends how nice it was," wrote Mrs John Reid, "but they also warned us there were no shops. So we loaded up a tremendous saratoga trunk with groceries and went off by train to Port Shepstone.

"Mr Erasmus' bus met us at Port Shepstone and it was quite an adventure travelling down the track to Margate. It was about twenty miles long, and it took four hours to cover, fording about eleven rivers, with the driver wrapping canvas around the engine to keep the water out.

"It got dark and started to rain before we arrived at Margate, and on the last hill the bus broke down, probably owing to the weight of our luggage. So we had to slosh through the mud to the cottage we had hired. The place was dark and dead and we weren't exactly thrilled, but in the morning we saw how beautiful it all was, and in the golden sunlight it was different.

"There were very few people there and it was quite a social call when even the milkman arrived, a farmer named Mr Lane. There were only four other women living in the place. Mrs Murphy was the oldest, with Mrs Green, Mrs McGee and Mrs Ardon.

"So far as the beach was concerned we had it entirely to ourselves for the whole month of December. No wonder we came back next year, and the year after, and then stayed for good."

So Margate grew. By 1932 there were about one hundred permanent residents, and on 11 February 1932 its first Health Committee was formed. From this civic start, it has progressed through the inevitable storms in a council chamber over such matters as water-supply, sewerage, lighting, and all the other quarrels which have ever made village management a lively affair. In 1948 the place received its first Town Council, and

today it is a bustling holiday resort, more characteristic perhaps of overseas specimens of its kind than any other place in
Southern Africa.

Since the visit of its celebrated monster, Margate's beach
has provided mankind with a great amount of happiness. In
its setting of lala palms and banana plantations, the whole of
this tranquil coast has become a holiday land. Apart from the
inevitable drownings, a few shark attacks, and the wreck on 21
June 1947 of the 120-ton fishing vessel *Ivanstan* on the rocks of
Margate's Tragedy Hill, Alfred County has seen spectacular development of its resorts, with innumerable seaside townships
laid out by property owners and speculators. With nature in
this part of the world so generous and accommodating, even
the most ill-conceived and tasteless of these projects tend, after
a while, to be assimilated into the luxurious background of a
coast which ranks with the loveliest areas on earth.

THIRTY-SEVEN
Empire of the trees

A s a complete contrast to the mild coastal lands south of the Mzimkhulu, Zululand has a hot and troubled northern frontier along the feverous banks of the Mkhuze; a sullen, muddy, typically African river with its tangle of shrubbery and its spectral fever trees, watching their own reflections in the sinister pools haunted by the lurking death of the crocodiles.

The Mkhuze was so called from the aromatic trees of that name (*Heteropyxis natalensis*) growing along its banks and used from time immemorial for medicinal tea and perfume and whose excellent timber has provided the fencing for many a cattle kraal. Rising on the slopes of the Hlobane Mountains, the Mkhuze flows eastwards through the Lubombo range and then veers sharply south to pour its quota of water, hippos, and crocodiles into the vast reservoir which Europeans call Lake St Lucia but the Africans know simply as eCwebeni (the lagoon).

North of this river frontier there lies a beautiful wilderness of trees growing over a flat and spacious wild. For 3500 square miles this green empire reigns supreme. It is full of sand, bogs, lakes and dozens of shallow, enchanted little lakelets haunted by reflections and ripples which warn of the evil concealed within. These placid waters lie spilled out into the flatness by the Phongolo River when its flood waters stir it, like the appetite of the brown python it resembles, from lethargy into destructive activity.

Marulas and acacias, of numerous varieties, form the population of this forest empire and their monarchs are the wild fig trees. The Phongolo, particularly, nurses a magnificent company of these giants. There is a Tonga saying: "The Phongolo will never be found without a fig tree", meaning a man will never lack a crony, and certainly there seems to be a congenial alliance between the two, the one providing water and the other shade along the many miles of dark African waterway.

This empire of the trees is bounded on the west by the Lubombo. To the east it stretches for some 25 miles and then peters out with strange abruptness into a belt of lala palm trees. The dividing line roughly follows an ancient, sand-enveloped river called the Mosi swamp (from the *umusi* reeds), a thin line of bog which runs all the way across this wild from St Lucia to Lourenço Marques.

Beyond the palm trees lies a belt of undulating open land covered with lush, green, sour grass, waving in the breezes, covering the sandy soil like a sea with scattered island clumps of lala palm, wild bananas, or shrubbery.

Next follows a thin line of coastal forest, a tall wall of sand dunes built by nature as a dyke to keep the sea out of the flatlands, then a stretch of glistening beach and rocky fishermen's promontories jutting out into the languid blue of the Indian Ocean.

In places this line of dunes has opened and allowed the sea to remain in what was once its own, or closed up too tightly and blocked proper drainage from the rear. The result has been the lakes of Tongaland. In the south a solitary streamlet, aptly known as Sodwana (the little one on its own) busies itself in draining a swamp which in turn drains one of these lakes; a small specimen of its kind called Ngobeseleni, as still as death, full of crocodiles and set around with a dense and oppressive jungle of trees and shrubs.

Further north lies a vast and intensely blue sheet of water,

23 square miles in extent, and encircled by a beach of shining white. The Africans call this place iSibayi (an enclosure with no visible outlet). Once again their name is aptly chosen, for the marvel of this 92-feet-deep reservoir of drinkable water is that no rivers feed it and no outlet allows its waters to pour into the ocean, 50 feet below the level of the lake, through the narrow coastal sand dunes. Sibayi must be fed by powerful underground seepage and direct rainfall only, for it maintains its level in spite of immense evaporation.

The chain of lakes still further north, known to Europeans as Kosi, have a connection with the sea and as such are salt with their level approximating to the high-water mark. Hlangwe (the reedy one) is the African name for the greatest of this chain of lakes. Five miles long by three-and-a-half miles wide, and touching 160 feet in its deeps, it lies only five feet above sea level with a narrow saddle in the sand dunes known as Mbange Nek alone separating it from the sea.

Linked to Hlangwe is a smaller lake, oKhunwini (the place of firewood). Beyond it is the third in the chain, uKhalwe (the distant one), and from it the chain of lakes reaches the sea through an estuary known as eNkovukeni from the "up and down" tidal action of its waters.

All these lakes are full of fish. Sibayi is noted for its barbel, upon which the crocodiles feed; but the Kosi lakes are rich in sea-pike, grunter, bream and a host of other sea fishes which have made their way into its depths and adapted themselves to the diminishing saltiness of each successive lake, from the 35 per cent salt of the sea to the 3,31 per cent of Hlangwe.

Crocodiles and hippos abound in all the waters, while tiger fish lurk in the rivers and pans. Over 200 different species of birds wing through the air – hornbills, kingfishers, black storks, cattle egrets, Cape sea eagles, ospreys, louries, red cormorants, flamingoes, pelicans, wild duck and geese; and as monarchs of this land of the birds, the magnificent vulturine fish eagles whose favourite haunts are the Kosi lakes.

Game animals as well have found a paradise in this wilderness. Rhino, blue wildebeest, kudu, inyala, many other antelope, lions and elephants have all wandered through the trees and, especially on the so-called Makhathini flats below the Lubombo, they traditionally congregated in vast numbers.

The human beings who came to this wilderness were never numerous. In the south a few minor clans wandered in, like driftwood washed up by tribal upheavals far away. Way back in about 1750, a member of Malandela's party, Manzi, quit the society of the future Zulus and wandered up to the shores of Lake Sibayi, where he settled with some followers and founded a tiny tribe which survived by becoming vassals to the more powerful Tembe-Tongas.

Other odds and ends joined these so-called Manzis. Wizards – especially unsuccessful ones – were frequent colonisers of new lands when their old became too hot to hold them. One Funjwa, known as Mabaso (the fire kindler) was of this breed, and he, becoming entrenched in the land of his refuge, towards the end of the eighteenth century attracted to himself a crowd of Tongas who became known as the Mabasos.

A third group inhabiting this land called themselves the people of Zikhali. They came into the Tonga wild as refugees in the time of Dingane, people originally of the Mangwaneni tribe, and found a place for themselves among the sand dunes and lala palms south of the great lake of Sibayi. There, as we shall see, with their contemporaries they duly played a minor part in the curious Tongaland story.

The featured human players in this wild were naturally the Tongas themselves. Their presence gave the land its name, although as in the case of so many African tribes, it was a name foreign to themselves. It was one indiscriminately applied by the Zulus as a generic name to everybody dwelling north-east of them, who remotely appeared to fall by language or custom into the tribal group of Portuguese East Africa where, far up in the north, some Tongas proper dwell who, doubtless unknowingly, have lent their name to the southlands.

The self-avowed name of these people of the Tonga wilderness is Tembe, the name of a renowned chief of theirs who lived far back around the 1550s. They were a tribe distinct in themselves with their own language, customs and peculiar skills. Generations of living in a steamy hell of malaria and bilharzia had given them a notably stunted physique. They were a timid people with no ambitions of military renown; the men partial to their wives, or numbers of them; experts at brewing tasty alcoholic drinks from lala palms and marula berries; and with brains well pickled in the resultant product.

They were busy agriculturists, manufacturers and pedlars. They worked copper and iron and wood and ivory into artistic products and patiently carried their wares, along with later European trade goods including the domestic cat, deep into the bush of Southern Africa in search of profit in barter.

This chief, Tembe, according to tradition, led his people down from the north where they seem to have been splinters from the great Karanga tribe of Rhodesian fame. Settling around the bay of Lourenço Marques they prospered somewhat and, in the nature of man, increased their numbers, quarrelled among themselves and divided into two branches; the one remaining on the Tembe River and the other removing to a river Europeans have misnamed the Maphutha after their fractious chief Mabudu.

It is this latter section of the tribe which is of particular interest to us. It was this section principally which migrated down into Tongaland. During the reign of the chief Makhasana, particularly around 1825, several groups moved south. Two of these groups were led by minor princes, sons of Makhasana, named Makhane and Ndumo. Their names still linger over the areas in which they settled: Makhanes Drift and Ndumo Hill dominating the present game reserve, with its chain of lakelets such as Nyameti (Munyamati) (the place of brak water) and Mvutshini (the place of hippos) each in a setting of reeds, with its waters full of tiger fish and crocodiles and a laze of hippos at every turn.

These human invaders found the empire of the trees to be a hard place for a living. It was infested in parts with the tsetse fly and haunted with mosquitoes. It was riddled with malaria and blackwater fever and it was hot and humid, and subject to drought with but scanty surface water. The trees were kindly enough to them with wild fruits, and the lala palm with its sap. The game, until it was thinned out, provided meat but, except in the alluvial valley of the Phongolo, the soil was meagre.

The only cultivation the Tonga agriculturists could apply to this wild was the wasteful technique known as "shifting cultivation" – burning a patch of bush and then exploiting to exhaustion the relatively rich humus mixed with wood ash before the farmer moved on to repeat the process on another patch of virgin forest.

This process of constant burning, setting alight the forest with happy-go-lucky extravagance and depending on the heavy dews at night to put the fire out, gave rise to the first name by which Tongaland was known to Europeans: Terra dos Fumos (the land of smokes).

The first known European to make a home in Tongaland was a German named G. Bruheim, known as Madevu to the Africans. During the reign of Noziyingili, the grandson of Makhasana, this solitary European put in an appearance, married one of the chief's daughters and commenced trading.

Noziyingili died on 20 July 1877, leaving a minor son Ngwanase as heir and the widowed queen, a Swazi princess named Zambili, to act as regent. It was during her rule that Bruheim attained much influence in Tongaland and secured the first concession: a scrap of paper purporting to give him possession of the Kosi chain of lakes.

It was at about this time that Europeans first became actively conscious of the strategic value of Tongaland with the possibilities of harbour development at Kosi. Several appraising eyes were cast on this one desirable feature of the Tonga wilderness and the tribespeople were shaken out of their customary preoccupation with the delights of lala palm wine by the activities of several European parties of adventurers.

The British had already made some moves in the direction of Tongaland. As early as 1822, when Owen led his survey along the coast, he had attempted to stake a claim over the Lourenço Marques area and a desultory quarrel with Portugal over this manoeuvre had persisted for years. Eventually the quarrel had been sent to arbitration and in 1875 Marshall MacMahon of France awarded Portugal the bay and all lands south, down to the present Natal-Mozambique border.

This ingenious decision, arrived at by a Frenchman working with some mapmakers in Paris, left the area south of the arbitrary border open for British penetration. The British, however, guided by Owens's negative report on that part of the world, regarded Tongaland as being simply a feverous backwater which could safely be left to its own devices with no danger of any rival power finding a base there. As we shall see, as soon as anybody found anything of value in the Tonga wilderness, the British attitude sharply changed.

The effect of the MacMahon award on the Tonga people themselves would have been comic if it wasn't pathetic. Far away in Paris a politician in striped pants sat down and drew a sharp line straight through their tribal possessions while they sat drinking lala wine, quarrelling over women and scratching themselves in the sun. Nobody took the trouble to inform the Tongas of the profound change in their territorial possessions. Accordingly, when the Portuguese, after a few years of inertia, started demanding taxes on account of the Tongas now being their subjects, there was a certain amount of surprise.

On 20 May 1887 Zambili sent Bruheim and two Tonga notables down to Pietermaritzburg to see the British Government. On 17 June they told their troubles to an amused Sir Arthur Havelock. The Portuguese were demanding taxes and burning down huts in half of the Tonga lands north of the Maphutha River when payment was refused. The Tongas said they wanted a treaty with the British. According to them they had always been tributary to the Zulus but now that Zululand belonged to the British the Tongas were prepared to pay tribute to them. They requested a British resident and support of the 12-year-old Ngwanase as Tonga king.

The Government was quite agreeable to a treaty and on 6 July 1887 it was provisionally signed. The treaty recognised the desire of the Tongas to become British subjects without actually granting them this status. It prohibited the Tongas from signing any treaty or from having correspondence with any European power without British sanction. In return Britain guaranteed peace and friendship.

In order finally to ratify this treaty, the British, on 12 September 1887, sent C.R. Saunders, D.G. Giles and a party of 25 Zulus up to visit the Tonga queen. It was a fascinating journey that they made. They used wagonettes, crossing Rorke's Drift and going up to Vryheid. From there they followed the Swazi traders' road for 30 miles before branching off to the Ngome forest. Then across the Mkhuze River to Marcus Road which led them up across the Phongolo and into the thick bush known as Golela (gathering place of animals), used as a hunting ground by the then ruling Nyawo chieftain Sambane.

About 20 miles north of the Phongolo the party left their wagonettes at the foot of the Lubombo. They climbed to the top of the mountain ridge, struggling up a steep path to the chief Sambane's kraal. He welcomed them hospitably, showing them the sights of his land, including the grave of Dingane at the edge of the Hlathikhulu forest. He claimed all the top of the Lubombo, from the Phongolo to the Ngwavuma, as his tribal land.

Sambane claimed to be a British subject and told the interested party that for the last three years he had paid taxes to one Mtshakela (J. Ferreira, Republican Native Commissioner of Wakkerstroom) who he thought was the British representative.

From Sambane the party followed the Phongolo to its junction with the uSuthu and then down that mighty river to the Tonga royal kraal, Mfihlweni (place of concealment), about 50 miles south-west of Lourenço Marques. They arrived on 11

October and spent some days explaining the treaty and signing it in company with the grandees of the Tonga nation.

They were the first European visitors to the Tonga domain to take any deep interest in the country and its scenery and make a report on their observations. They found the land still teeming with game – elephants, buffalo, rhino, hippos, wild pigs, baboons and antelope sported through the forest glades. The Tongas were rapidly diminishing the game by means of muzzle-loading guns sold to them for £2 to £3 by the Portuguese. The guns were of the type with a kick like a mule and belched forth such a cloud of smoke with each shot that the firer had to run about six feet aside before he could see if he'd hit anything. Nevertheless, with their aid the Tongas became good shots and lived well on venison and their famous lala palm wine.

The Tongas were industrious and although enervated with malarial fever and bilharzia, they were skilled at basket making, carving in ivory, horns and wood, fashioning earthenware, and even making a sort of cloth from the fibrous bark of the wild fig trees mixed with a variety of wild cotton. They made canoes out of tree trunks and were expert fishermen, constructing complex fish traps and organising great communal fish drives, long lines of fishermen wading through the lakelets driving the fish into the shallows, with much excitement when an occasional crocodile broke through the line to escape.

Saunders had been instructed to visit the great lake Europeans knew as Kosi and which recent rumour painted so favourably as a possible port. However, his whole party was stricken with fever and he had to content himself with enquiry. He immediately learnt that the Tonga knew not the name of Kosi, but by his descriptions they guessed he meant the great lake of Hlangwe and of it they told him what they knew.

Then the homeward journey began. The party went back the way it had come to the waiting wagons and with these followed the Marcus Road (substantially the modern North

Coast Road) all the way to the eMbabe River where Arthur Shepstone had his seat as resident magistrate of the Lower Mfolozi.

Zambili had told Saunders that several Europeans had lately visited her with various schemes. The Swaziland concession mania was then in full swing and an overlap of money-mad adventurers from that country had found their way into Tongaland. The well-known Dr Somershields had secured a mineral concession on the east side of the Lubombo. A Mr Grantham was also rummaging around and a Mr Lamont Thompson was trying to get a farm. All these individuals had been shown the draft British treaty and been sent away.

There was one most persistent adventurer in Tongaland. He was Colonel William Jesser Coope and his particular scheme was to develop a port somewhere on the Tongaland coast, link it by railway to Swaziland and exploit the known coal deposits on the western side of the Lubombo.

With this object in view, Coope explored the whole of the Tongaland coast on behalf of what was known as the Mapootaland Syndicate. Using a small steamer, the *Marguerite*, drawing three-and-a-half feet, he cruised along the coast sounding all the bays and attempting, without success, to enter the Kosi lakes. Then he returned to London to prompt his financial backers into greater support of his schemes.

Meanwhile a first-class row was developing between the British and the Transvaal Republic over Saunders's treaty. The Republic also had its eyes fixed on the Kosi lakes as a possible point for their much desired outlet to the sea. The Saunders Treaty had blithely included as Tongaland all the area north of the Mkhuze River and between the Indian Ocean and the Lubombo Mountains.

The Republic protested against this on 30 January 1888. They pointed out that the Nyawo and Mngomezulu tribes living along the Lubombo were certainly independent of the Tonga. A portion of their people lived in the Transvaal and paid tax. According to the Republic their Native Commissioner at Wakkerstroom, Joachim Ferreira, had collected tax from the Transvaal overflow of Sambane's people ever since 1885 and both the Nyawos and Mngomezulus had pressed so frequently to be taken into the Transvaal that a draft treaty had already been drawn up to that effect.

At this information the British sat up and took notice. They informed the Republic that whilst the Nyawos and Mngomezulus were certainly independent of the Tongas, they were both vassals of the Swazis. Mbandine, the Swazi chief, in fact had already portioned out most of the Mngomezulu lands as mineral concessions to Alexander Meikle. Neither of the tribes, therefore, was entitled to independent negotiations with foreign powers.

Aware for the first time that there must be something of value in Tongaland, if only because other people wanted it, the British hurriedly decided to extend a protectorate over the country if the Tongas still wanted to be British subjects. Lt Col Martin at that time happened to be journeying up to Lourenço Marques by sea in order to be present at a delimitation of the Swaziland boundary. He was instructed to visit the Tongas, investigate the general tribal position and particularly to look into the rumoured value of the Kosi lakes.

Martin went down from Lourenço Marques to see the Tonga queen. He did not have the time to explore the country, so he contented himself with enquiries. He was unimpressed by what he heard of Kosi. According to the Tongas it was but a shallow lake with only an occasional very light draught trading vessel able to slip across the bar.

He reported on 21 July 1888 that Ferreira had sought permission from the Tongas to make a road from Kosi to the Transvaal and that Colonel Coope had wanted a similar concession. He confirmed that the Lubombo tribes were certainly independent of the Tongas. Another discovery of his was that the name Tonga was a Zulu name implying a contemptible and subject people. The Tongas, however, did not object strenuously to the name and henceforth it was confirmed in official use, although the Portuguese continued to refer to this southern section of the Tembe tribe as the Maputas of Maputaland.

The redoubtable Colonel Coope, meanwhile, had returned in full force to Tongaland. Accompanied by a crowd of toughs from Swaziland, he rode through the length and breadth of the country in August and September 1888. He levied taxes and extracted from each petty chief a 99 years' lease over their lands. Using the notorious Charlie du Pont of Swaziland as an interpreter, he informed the various tribes between the Mkhuze and the Tongas proper that they had all been placed under him. They had to sign a paper (the 99 years' lease) without knowing what it contained, although Du Pont told them it was simply to say that they were now protected by the British queen. As a final grim jest, Coope appointed Charlie du Pont as magistrate over the tribes and instructed them in future to take their troubles, and taxes, to him.

Coope and a civil engineer named Ridley Henderson then went to Sodwana Bay. They surveyed the place in October 1888 and optimistically planned a major harbour there. They named the lake Lake Johnstone and laid out wharves and a town of the first magnitude.

Coope was nothing if not an optimist and chancer. Just how he imagined he could construct a harbour out of the shallow stream, the rank swamp, and the feverous little lake is unknown. Nevertheless, he certainly planned it. Returning to civilisation, he collected together a small party consisting of T.R. Bangay, a Mr Boast and ten Africans. These he packed into the cutter *Nellie* and sent up to Sodwana Bay early in February 1889 as the start of his projected settlement.

There was much publicity in England about this venture and several questions were asked by the Lords of the Admiralty as to how so reputedly excellent a natural harbour could have been overlooked in the surveys.

The survey vessel *Stork* under Commander Pullen was hastily sent up to examine the matter. This vessel arrived off Sodwana on 20 February 1889, and found under the bluff hill south of the river mouth a corrugated-iron shack and a flag-staff flying the Red Ensign.

A surf boat came off from the river mouth and Bangay came aboard, very much in need of provisions. From him the survey men learnt the history and intentions of the settlement. Then they commenced a survey. They were disgusted: "Mr Ridley Henderson's inspection would appear to have been made from the deck of a Durban to Delagoa mail steamer and re-turn," wrote Pullen in his report.

There was no harbour or any prospect of one ever being made. To connect the lake to the sea would cost an astronomi-cal figure and then, without complex locks, the lake would promptly drain away, for it was far above sea level.

The next day the naval party abandoned the place, leav-ing Coope's settlers sitting on the beach fishing for food in the solitude. On several occasions supplies were sent up for them but each time the sea was too rough to land. Then Boast died of fever. Bangay and the Africans, reduced almost to starva-tion, loaded up their surf boat with their belongings, hoisted some trade blankets for sails, and made their way down to Durban before a stiff breeze. On 11 April 1889, they ran their boat ashore on the back beach of Durban and headed for the nearest food. That was the end of the Sodwana Bay settlement.

THIRTY-EIGHT

Tongaland

Lake Isibayi

The beautiful wilderness of Tongaland is a tranquil place, where stillness reigns and the pagan spirit wanders, alone and free, down green and silent glades. No great human wars have raged through its tangle of trees and no single event occurring there has contrived to shake the world. Obsessed with the endless struggle for existence in a hard land, beset with mosquitoes, the tsetse fly and bilharzia, with enterprise smothered by heat and humidity, the human inhabitants have made little history.

Nevertheless, a fascinating collection of characters have made a home there, among the acacias and lala palms, and the story of their lives, merged into the story of Tongaland, makes a curious and oft times romantic tale.

Charlie du Pont was about the most notorious of these Tongalanders. After the collapse of Colonel Coope's Sodwana Bay settlement, Du Pont remained as the last, lingering relic in Tongaland of the Mapootaland Syndicate.

The irrepressible Charlie continued exercising his powers as a magistrate for some little while and his ideas of justice were ingenious.

In July 1889, for instance, one of the chiefs, Fokothi, complained that Sambane had looted girls and cattle from him. Du Pont first of all received a fee of £5 10s. from Fokothi, and then, with three other European toughs and some Swazis, he rode up to see Sambane.

After a few threats, Sambane gave up eight of the girls and 19 head of cattle. Du Pont took them back to Fokothi. "Now the parents must pay five head of cattle to redeem each girl," he said. After some complaint the cattle were collected and handed over. Du Pont released six of the girls, all very young. The other two were marriageable. These two, Du Pont announced, he intended to marry and returned the ransom of five head of cattle to their parents as lobolo. Then, extracting another £9 from the chief for his services, he returned to his hideout on top of the Lubombo, near Stegi.

One result of Coope's search for a harbour was that the British Government, in December 1888, published an addition to their original proclamation of 19 May 1887, making Zululand a British possession. The old proclamation had loosely defined the northern border of Zululand as being Tongaland. Now it was proclaimed as containing the areas of the petty tribes living south of Lake Sibayi and in whose lands lay the presumed harbour of Sodwana. Tongaland was said to lie north of their lands.

A note was sent to Zambili, informing her of the new boundary and expostulating with her because she had recently sent an army to raid cattle in what was British territory. The Tongas were a bit flabbergasted at this move. Bruheim wrote a letter of protest for them, claiming the Mkhuze as the traditional boundary, but this was rejected.

The Tongas then, in April 1889, sent a deputation down to Pietermaritzburg and appealed for redress "as to the way in which our country has been divided and taken away from us and given to the Portuguese without our knowledge and consent. More than half our country is cut off." Cynical now of European "protectorates", the Tongas asked to be released from their treaty of amity with the British and be left to do "as they think is the best for the country and the Tonga people."

This request was rejected. A similar deputation of protest was sent to the Portuguese. This deputation actually sailed to Portugal in February 1889, but their appeal, made in May in Lisbon, met with a like fate. In this appeal the Tonga queen suggested that the Portuguese rather take over the whole country than have it split in half and the Tongas crushed by two powers instead of one. The Portuguese simply informed her that the question was closed. In order to settle the issue of boundaries, Saunders was sent off once more to Tongaland on 22 July 1889. He visited the petty tribes between Sibayi and the Mkhuze, collected taxes and set up boundary beacons, although the Tongas sent a formal protest.

Saunders then pushed on to the Lubombo Mountains. He immediately ran into a spot of trouble. Since his last visit, the Transvalers had been busy in those parts. They now had an outpost on top of the Lubombo, at Njanos' Hill, where a Hollander, an ex-naval officer named H.F. van Oordt (Ntanyana), was established in a small stone house with a cellar underneath to act as a gaol. In this curious outpost of civilisation he lived in such style as he could manage, always dressing in full naval regalia when he tried cases. He was an odd character, very fond of gin and of some literary talent, for he had a book on West Africa to his credit. On the Lubombo he was linked with the outside world solely by a steep and narrow path, aptly known as Manamathela (persistence), just to the south of the Nyawo place of execution, iSiwa Sabathakathi (cliff of the wizards), marked as the Devil's Dive on modern maps.

When Saunders and his party passed along the top of the Lubombo, Van Oordt protested that they were trespassing and seeking to influence the Republic's native subjects against their country. The Republic had surveyed the area in the first half of 1888. According to Van Oordt, both the Nyawos and Mngomezulus were eager to give their country away to the Republic, which hoped, by such territorial acquisitions, to secure access to a navigable stretch in the uSuthu or Phongolo River. In February 1889, T.W. Ferreira and F.A. Lammerding had actually secured two petitions signed by the Nyawo and Mngomezulu chiefs, requesting that they be annexed by the Transvaal.

In the game of power politics the Republic had offered, on 4 May 1889, to barter all their claims to Bechuanaland and Rhodesia in exchange for Swaziland and Tongaland, but the British would have none of it.

Saunders persisted with his investigation. He returned to Eshowe, where he was magistrate, on 20 September 1889, and wrote a long report. He considered that all the petty tribes wedged between the Tongas and the Zulus were formerly tributary vassals of the Zulus and, as such, legally part of the booty after the conquest of Zululand by the British. He recommended that the whole crowd be absorbed into Zululand and two new magistracies be created to control them.

Acting on this report, the British, on 15 February 1890, annexed the lands of all the remaining petty tribes in the south, ruled by such chieftains as Manaba, Fokothi and Mjindi. The fate of the Nyawos and Mngomezulus was left in abeyance, pending settlement of a few doubts that, as they had prudently paid tribute to the Swazis as well as the Zulus, they might legally be Swazi subjects.

In order to facilitate the administration of the newly acquired territories, a magisterial seat was established on a healthy site, high on the top of the Lubombo range, and Saunders was appointed Assistant Commissioner and Magistrate on 12 August 1890.

This place, named Ubombo from its mountain situation, looked out like an eagle from its eyrie, over all the flat vastness of Tongaland. A lonely little place on those silent, windswept heights, Ubombo became an outpost from which the British empire of those days watched the unattached areas to the north.

Five years passed. All sorts of odd adventurers wandered into Tongaland, thinking they would find the elusive spirit of fortune hiding in that poverty-stricken land. One concern, the Tongaland Exploration Company, was formed to exploit the concessions originally obtained by Gustav Bruheim and Dr Oscar Somershields back in May 1888. These concessions were most comprehensive and purported to give the company exclusive rights to Kosi Bay and a strip of land along the Portuguese border, to provide a corridor all the way to Swaziland.

Several other groups also claimed to have obtained similar rights and one of these adventurers, George Bell McCreedy, was actually hawking around his concession to Kosi Bay, offering it to the Transvaal Republic and to the Germans.

All this activity was duly reported to the British Government. As a result, immediately after the Republic took over Swaziland, they at length decided to move and clarify the confusion about the lands of the Lubombo. In March 1895 they ordered Saunders once again to journey up to the Lubombo, annex all the petty tribes resident there and make arrangements for their administration as part of Zululand. He was also to visit the Tongas and remind them that they were under British protection.

Saunders was again stationed at Eshowe at that time. On 25 April he started his journey to the north and at Ubombo rendezvoused with an escort of police under Captain Bell-Smythe which, 51 strong, was large enough to command respect from both Boer and African living along the top of the Lubombo.

With this force Saunders reached Sambane's Gazini kraal, near the Hlathikhulu forest, and camped about 400 yards away. Sambane visited him and expressed his compliance with the absorption of his territory. At 10 a.m. the following morning of 13 May 1895, the Union Jack was run up, the escort fired a royal salute and the 300 Africans present dutifully replied with a resounding *bayede* (hail). Saunders then removed to Sambane's kraal Kwaliweni (place of refusal) where he planned on establishing a police post for the district.

That afternoon Van Oordt arrived and made a formal protest. News of the British annexation had been received by the Republic with considerable annoyance. Van Oordt stated that Sambane had already given his country to the Republic. The chief was then called in for questioning. He acknowledged having signed some papers but claimed that he had been browbeaten into doing it by Ferreira.

The chief, with a shrug of his shoulders, stated that the question of who should annex his country really did not concern him. Whatever he said would not be taken into much account. He had not asked for either Britain or the Transvaal to annex his land. He would prefer to be independent but, if both countries insisted on annexing him, then it was a quarrel between them. With that he withdrew.

Saunders left a detachment of police at Kwaliweni, under Sub-Inspector Peirce. With the rest of his party he climbed down the western wall of the Lubombo to join the wagons which had trekked through the bush from Ubombo. The united force then went on to the river known as the Ngwavuma, from the trees of that name (*Pseudocassine transvaalensis*), whose bark is used medicinally for stomach troubles.

They climbed to the top of the Lubombo at the river pass. On the summit a site for their camp was selected, at a place known as Mthombeni (place of the *mthombe* or wild fig tree) to the Africans. Saunders considered it to be most central and convenient for the future administration of the Trans-Phongolo Territories and, from his arrival there on 19 May, he spoke of the place as Ingwavuma and regarded it as destined to become the seat of magistracy.

From this centre, Saunders went up to Mbikiza's kraal and, on 25 May, he hoisted the Union Jack there. On 27 May he was at the kraal of the chieftainess Mdlaleni and for the third time the ceremony of annexation was performed. Then, for a change, he journeyed off into the empire of the trees with his escort and the surveyor L.M. Altern to visit Ngwanase, the Tonga chief.

There, at the Mfihlweni kraal, on 30 May 1895, Saunders made a formal declaration of a Protectorate over Tongaland. The Tongas were friendly enough, although much grieved at the way in which their country had been divided between the Portuguese and the British. They wanted to know exactly where the boundaries lay and once more repeated that they would prefer their whole country to be annexed, rather than it should be divided by an arbitrary line.

Saunders warned the Tongas against granting concessions to Europeans and, whilst their domestic politics would remain unchanged, he explained that the Governor of Zululand, as from 18 May, had been appointed Special Commissioner for Tongaland and was to be approached through the magistrate at Ubombo. Saunders then returned to Ngwavuma, on 3 June, and commenced erecting the wattle-and-daub shacks which were to be the office and residence of himself and his successors at this remote and lonely little place. The few Boers living along the top of the mountains soon left and removed into Republican territory, while Richter, the first storekeeper and a somewhat objectionable sort of individual, closed down his store near Van Oordt's old residence and moved elsewhere. So the new order came to the Lubombo.

The next event in the story of these northern lands started in Tongaland proper. During their wars with the Shanganes in 1894, the Portuguese asked the Tongas to aid them. Bruheim induced Ngwanase to raise an army and led it to aid in the defence of Lourenço Marques.

The Portuguese armed the Tongas. They promptly turned back for home with their guns leaving, as they thought, the Portuguese to be blotted out by the Shanganes. On their way home the Tongas looted a few stores and generally made mortal enemies of the Portuguese.

Ngwanase and Bruheim quarrelled noisily over this behaviour for days. Eventually the Tongas drove Bruheim away and all his property was seized. Ngwanase considered that Bruheim had been responsible for the trouble. He offered the Portuguese money in compensation for the damage, but the Tongas had offended them beyond repayment.

As soon as the Shanganes had been subdued, the Portuguese turned on the Tongas. Saunders had told Ngwanase to address himself to the Ubombo magistrate when he had any complaints, and he soon had many. On 25 January 1896 a letter was sent in, with a terse message. "I am in the bush. I am in the bush because the Portuguese want to catch me."

Another letter followed. "I am in great trouble about the Portuguese because they want to fight with me, unless myself I don't want to fight with the white police so I ask the Queen to be mercy on me because I am in great trouble. Please be kindly to receive me with whole my land. I want to be under the British Government as my father used to be."

What had happened was that a Portuguese officer, Captain Albuquerque, and 35 soldiers, on 22 January 1896 had been sent to arrest Ngwanase as retribution for the damage and intransigence of the Tongas during the Shangane war; and in 1895 when they had also looted stores and demanded tribute from the storekeepers.

The Portuguese occupied the Tonga capital kraal of Mfihlweni without a fight while Ngwanase fled pell-mell across the border into the British zone to a slovenly little kraal named Phelindaba (the end of the matter), which he had built on his periodic visits to the southern section of his domains. Behind him, the Portuguese set up a new puppet chief of their own, named Mpobobo, and commenced levying taxes as a sign of new authority.

H.W. Stephens, the magistrate at Ubombo, went up hastily to the border to find out what was happening. He reassured Ngwanase of British protection. As a result, the chief removed with about 60 followers, including his secretary, a Tonga by the name of Izaak Tembe who had worked in the Cape and been educated at Lovedale, to the Ubombo magistracy on 3 March 1896. There, at a site about ten miles away in the flats, he was allowed to settle, pending the decision of the British Government as to the fate of his country.

The decision was soon made. On 27 May the government decided to return Ngwanase to his Phelindaba kraal, with an escort of Zululand police under Sub-Inspector C.C. Foxon to reside with him and administer Tongaland as a protectorate, with the laws of Zululand in force.

On 26 June, Foxon and Ngwanase arrived at Phelindaba. Foxon set to work at defining the boundary by means of a string of beacons following the parallel of the junction of the Phongolo with the uSuthu. Using dugout canoes, he explored the rivers and shallow lakes. At the Madingi store, run by

Louis von Wissel and Ernesto Finetti, he met the Portuguese captain and a friendly talk soon cleared up border problems and threatened clashes. Talking to each other in Zulu as a common language, they agreed to restrain the Tongas on their respective sides of the boundary from cattle raiding.

Peace then returned to the Tonga wilderness. The Tongas left their hiding places in the bush and returned to their kraals, with their country finally divided into two camps, each with its own chief. British Tongaland was legally established as a protectorate by an order in Council, dated 29 June 1896. Foxon became the British Resident. After thoroughly exploring the country, he established himself near the Manguzi forest at a site generally known as Maphutha, which he considered to be the healthiest in the country.

This post of Maphutha was the loneliest outpost in South Africa. The only Europeans in the whole territory, apart from Foxon and his staff, were a trader named H.J. Coetzee who had a store about ten miles from Phelindaba, and Von Wissel and Finetti, whose Madingi store, doing a roaring trade in rum, was on the Portuguese side of the uSuthu River, about two miles south of the Phongolo junction.

Von Wissel and his partner used the uSuthu as a waterway for bringing their goods up from Lourenço Marques. When the uproar in the country subsided, they established a store at Ngwavuma; supplies for this place being ferried up the Phongolo to a point three-and-a-half miles above its junction with the uSuthu. Five tons were carried at a time, on a boat 30 feet long, with a draught of two feet.

Foxon remained in such official glory as his post allowed for some time. When Tongaland was annexed to Zululand on 27 December 1897, Foxon was appointed magistrate of the district. Then, in August 1899, the Maphuthaland office was closed down and Tongaland lost what identity it still possessed by being merged with the Ngwavuma district.

Ngwavuma, meanwhile, had grown into relatively the most important centre for the northern districts of Zululand.

Remote and quiet, it nevertheless had its occasional excitements. On 7 July 1898, for instance, Bhunu, the Swazi chief, with 18 followers and a European adviser, Thomas Rathbone, sought sanctuary there from legal troubles with the Boers. He was detained at Ngwavuma, pending negotiations, and eventually returned to stand trial in Bremersdorp.

Then came the Anglo-Boer War. Joachim Ferreira, who had worked so hard to get the lands of the Lubombo for the Republic, finally had a chance of vengeance for the frustration of his hopes. On 28 October 1899 he led a commando up to the top of the range at Kwaliweni. From there they rode towards Ngwavuma, cutting the telegraph line on their way.

There were about 250 men in the commando. The Ngwavuma magistrate, B. Colenbrander, decided it was 250 too many. On 29 October he evacuated the place and retired with his staff into the bush of Tongaland, eventually making his way safely to Ubombo. Behind them, the commando set Ngwavuma alight and systematically destroyed the place, before they abandoned it to the wind and rain.

Ngwavuma remained deserted until January 1900, when the trader E. Finetti returned. He found the place in ruins, with bullet holes riddling every water tank and even 17 holes in the village's patent shower bath. Then, in a letter describing the damage, Finetti sorrowfully related the greatest loss of all.

"The demijohn of dop I buried is gone and there is only one kraal from which they can have seen me hide it."

The dop stealers were not the only people on the Lubombo to take advantage of the white man's absence during the war. One ingenious individual named Moses, an African secessionist missionary, moved into Van Oordt's old storehouse. There he set up shop with a cunning plan of soul saving which attracted mainly young females to his banner.

Around the establishment of this prophet, a considerable number of women encamped themselves. Moses had discovered in Van Oordt's house a perfect sanctuary for his activities. The place was just on the Transvaal border and neither the police of Natal nor Swaziland could interfere to secure the return of runaway women to their legitimate homes and owners.

Before the war, the Republican Government had proclaimed as a game reserve seven farms in the narrow wedge of the Transvaal lying between Natal and Swaziland. In 1903 the British reproclaimed this area and a Major Fraser was appointed as warden.

This Major Fraser was a strapping man of 48 years, six feet tall, broad in beam and with a flaming beard and temper. He had soldiered for 25 years in India, where he had become an expert in whisky drinking, reading *The Field* and scoffing at newspapers and civilisation.

Fraser came out from uneasy retirement in Scotland to take up his appointment as game warden. He duly arrived at Van Oordt's stone house, which was destined to become his headquarters, and found a church service in full swing, with hymns being sung by Moses' flock to the tune of a mouth organ.

There was some hard talking between Fraser and Moses. Fraser had some difficulty, 'tis said, in explaining that by "Game Sanctuary" four-legged animals and not women were indicated. After some debate, Moses at last was ejected and Fraser took up his abode in the little house, with its serene view over the bushveld.

As a reserve, this strip of land, some four-and-a-half miles wide by 20 miles long, was useless. A few kudu and some impala were the only resident animals of any account. Fraser was soon withdrawn and removed to the north, where he became one of the most celebrated characters in the story of the Kruger National Park. The Phongolo Reserve was deproclaimed and was soon shot out entirely.

In the years following the Anglo-Boer War, many other human characters came to the lands by the banks of the muddy Phongolo. Rubber attracted many of the newcomers. In 1905, Messrs Lepper and Pennington obtained a lease over 600 square miles of Tongaland for the purpose of exploiting the wild Landolphia vines, and a first shipment of rubber was sent away in October 1907.

Fever, however, took heavy toll of the workers. Arthur Menlove, who was trying to develop rubber possibilities in the Ngwavuma district, died of fever in December 1906 and many others were driven away.

The so-called Tongaland Rubber Corporation nevertheless persisted, with its headquarters at Maphutha. A steam launch was used for transport on Lake St Lucia and some efforts were made to use the waterway of the Phongolo, but heat, solitude and mosquitoes drove many away who found insufficient consolation in the meagre wealth of Tongaland.

Among those who remained was one of the best known and respected of all Tongalanders – Charles Eastwood. Eastwood was an ex-member of the Natal police, having served as a prison gaoler for many years at Estcourt and Ngwavuma.

In 1917 he resigned and, in partnership with E. Lehman, he started a chain of stores with headquarters where a pont crosses the Phongolo, at the place named oThobothini, from the groves of the willowy *thobothi* trees which grew there and were used so much as laths in hut building.

At this place Eastwood settled and lived the life of a traditional English gentleman in the wilderness. He was always immaculately dressed in the whitest of white ducks, and his hospitality was renowned. No traveller was ever allowed to pass without a meal, or drink, or rest, in his amiable company. Although he was the target of much chaff on account of his mild eccentricities, his death from fever on 28 July 1923 bereaved all Tongaland. For years travellers still looked for his familiar white-clad figure, while they waited for the lazy pontmen to ferry them across the river. And perhaps he still lurks there, at ease in the shadow of the wild fig trees, for he loved the place, on account of its wild beauty, and was well loved himself as a good fellow.

Among the other traders who came to Tongaland in the years around the First World War, was J.D. Smythe who ran the store at Phelindaba for Harrison & Co. and later established himself in the south as the largest trader in the Ubombo district.

Partner to Smythe at Phelindaba was a bad-tempered old Scotsman named Angus "Jock" Grant, and of him there is a story. Grant, 'tis said, had a remunerative sideline in buying up diamonds brought back to Tongaland by returned mine labourers. Through this trade Grant accumulated a fine collection in two preserved-fruit jars. Then a Hebrew commercial traveller undertook to market the diamonds. Jock cautiously gave one jar, but found he had not been cautious enough, for the traveller was seen no more. Rumours of police investigation for I.D.B. then alarmed Jock. He buried the second jar in the Mosi swamp, and there it still lies, despite sundry efforts to locate it since Jock died of a combination of blackwater fever and alcoholic remorse.

Brian Browich, who managed Harrison & Co.'s store at Maphutha, was another well-known Tongalander of the period. Von Wissel and Finetti were also still busy trading. At Ndumo they had established a store and acquired three farms when the government surveyed a block of 23 farms down the west bank of the Phongolo, in the former lands of the Nyawo and Mngomezulu tribes.

No other farms were handed out from this block, as the suitability of the area for European settlement was doubtful. Von Wissel attempted to work his farms, but without success. Then, in 1919, Richard Rutherfoord arrived and bought the Ndumo farms and store from Von Wissel, thus founding the present wide interests of his family in Tongaland (Ndumu Limited).

Rutherfoord tried farming, but the cotton slump ruined him. He then abandoned farming at Ndumo and concentrated on trading. The three farms were eventually sold to the Agricultural Development Corporation in 1946. This organisation planned to grow rice, but the only crop was a sheaf of debts. Then, in February 1948, Wilfred Needham came out from England. He acquired a controlling interest in the company and, as Managing Director, settled down to develop the place, in the teeth of droughts, pests, forest fires and all the other troubles which beset anyone struggling to do something new in the wilderness of Africa.

Apart from the traders and this one lone farming enterprise, there has been some mission activity in Tongaland. In 1911 the Wesleyan Church erected a mission at Ngwavuma under the Reverend C. Poulsen. Poulsen did regular tours of the Tonga lowveld and, in 1913, he erected a shack at Kosi Bay to shelter him on his periodic visits.

In 1917 this Kosi Bay shack was turned into a proper mission by the Reverend D.E. Carr and named the Threlfall Memorial Mission, in memory of William Threlfall who, back in 1822, had sailed up to Lourenço Marques with Captain Owen to establish a Tongaland mission. Fever had driven Threlfall away to a brutal death in Namaqualand, but now his name returned to the first field of his choice. It was to this mission, on the shores of Kosi Bay, that the well-known medical worker, Miss Hanschen Prozesky, came in 1925, and in the years leading up to the Second World War became one of the best-known figures in Tongaland.

The police force has also added its quota of personalities to the Tongaland story. The Tongaland police posts rank with the loneliest outposts in Southern Africa. Mseleni, on the tip of Lake Sibayi, was a particularly solitary post. Evil memories haunt the ruins of this old station, for it was from there that four of its staff went boating on the lake on 25 August 1910. A sudden squall blew up. The boat capsized, and Sub-Inspector Wright Ingle and Trooper Wolhuter were drowned. The rest of the party managed to swim to the shore.

This Mseleni post was particularly noted for its loneliness. It is said that two young men stationed there once battled long and unsuccessfully for transfer. Eventually it was discreetly noised abroad around police headquarters that the two men had gone mad. The District Officer went up hurriedly to inspect. On arrival he found one man sitting in a tree crowing like a rooster. The other was sitting on a table in the living room fishing. Both were transferred.

591

Nowadays the Mseleni police post is just a memory. In 1936 the post was transferred to the place known as Mbazwana, from the headman Mbazwana Zikhali who used to live there. This Mbazwana in latter years became an important point in the lowlands east of the Lubombo as the centre of an extensive experiment in afforestation, which was likely, judging by its initial success, to have had profound effects on local economy later on.

Little else has happened in Tongaland in the years up to the present. Locusts attacked the place in force between 1933 and 1935. Alternate floods and droughts have brought annual variety to the climate, and periodic revivals of interest in the development of Kosi Bay as a port have kept Tongaland in the news.

All manner of expeditions and visitations to Tongaland have at least kept the local inhabitants amused, if productive of little other result. The Kosi lakes and even lonely little Sodwana have been surveyed and resurveyed as possible harbours, but the beautiful, green wilderness of Tongaland remains in much the same solitude as it has enjoyed for twice ten thousand years. In it a multitude of birds live happily, the hippos and fat crocodiles laze in those shallow lakelets which, set around with fever trees and the wild figs, are linked together like a strangely sinister necklace of fever, heat and death by the ever-restless, ever-dangerous, never predictable waters of the Phongolo.

CHAPTER THIRTY-NINE
Natal and Zululand

In 1888, at the end of the long drawn-out Zulu troubles, Natal and Zululand were able to take stock of themselves and look forward to a period of peaceful development. So far as Zululand was concerned, its status as a British protectorate guaranteed it a degree of law, order and stability, but little stimulation to social change or progress.

Man simply attempted to resume his traditional way of life, the Zulu matrons tilling the fields while the youths herded cattle and their fathers drank beer and diverted themselves in the usual cattle raids and brawls over girls.

Europeans resumed trading and hunting. The golden age of big game was long past, but it was still profitable to hunt such animals as hippos. Each hippo yielded about £25-worth of tusks, as well as commercially valuable skin and fat and, for the hunter's table, its lips and other tender parts of its anatomy. Such hunters as Charles Toohey and Gerrard Colenbrander made a good profit at this period from hippos, especially in Lake St Lucia, and lived very well, with fine fishing and their camp tables groaning beneath loads of sweet potatoes, *maas* or *umlaza* (thick milk), beer, partridge, guineafowl, wild duck and other good things of veld and vlei.

The prospectors also resumed their search after the elusive mineral wealth of the land. With so many gold traces to beguile them, it was inevitable that there would be finds, excitements, and many disappointments.

One of the prospectors, named Staniland, made a strike in the Thukela Valley on the Nsuze stream which flows through the ruggedly beautiful country below the heights of the Nkandla. Quite a rush took place to this find and on 27 March 1890, Melmoth Osborn, the Resident Commissioner of Zululand, ceremoniously opened a battery for this so-called Lower Nsuze Goldfields. This place became the centre of prospecting activity for the Thukela Valley, but the prospectors had no luck. By March 1891 the Staniland mine was in liquidation. Albert Bremer, of Swaziland fame, tried to run the place for a while, but it was one of those mines where it was far easier to lose gold than mine it. The whole Nsuze area gradually fell into decline.

In 1892 only 786 ounces of gold were produced in Zululand as the total result of the labours of about 270 prospectors working in the Thukela Valley and at Nondweni. One of the most persistent of these workers was Natal's pioneer aviator, J.G. Household, who operated mainly in the Msinga area, at the junction of the Thukela and Buffalo rivers, where he unearthed, with some small profit to himself, a patchy reef he called the Golden Dove.

There was certainly gold in Zululand but it was not only difficult to find but, through chemical complications, refractory and hard to work. Then, in October 1892, Thomas Denny, John Dalton and Scott Paulson appeared on the scene with a new hope for mining in Zululand. The three men were members of a syndicate formed to acquire and develop mines whose ore was of a refractory nature. The syndicate had rights to a recovery process patented by the Thwait-Denny Syndicate of London; a process said to be able to extract gold from a well-worn Egyptian ten-piastre note, let alone from Zululand ore.

The so-called Denny-Dalton Syndicate had capital and confidence. Early in 1893 it acquired several Zululand mining properties and by March had erected a plant on the farm Malta. The energy of this syndicate was a stimulant to the whole local mining activity. With hope pinned on the patent recovery process (invented by Thomas Denny and financed by John Dalton) innumerable little properties such as the Enterprise and the Three Sisters mines on the Nondweni field and in the Thukela Valley were developed to the point of waiting for the syndicate to provide with its plant a practical gold extraction process.

All through 1894 the syndicate worked on, erecting plant and accumulating ore. A town was laid out on Malta farm and the syndicate took options on several prospects and mines, while many others planned on becoming tributary in exchange for rights to the use of the recovery process.

The big test of the first large-scale crushing in the patent plant was scheduled to take place in April 1895. The whole of Natal and Zululand expected big things and with bated breath awaited the results. It was a complete failure and a second crushing in May 1895 confirmed the result. Thomas Denny died in July 1895 from the bitter disappointment of the whole fiasco. His two sons, H.S. and G.A. Denny, attempted to retrieve something from the mess, but there was really nothing much which they could do.

The entire Zululand gold-mining activity went into depression. The total amount of gold recovered by 264 prospectors in 1895 was only 268 ounces. By 1896 even the most stubbornly optimistic of these men were bankrupt and the only lingering activity was in the Nondweni area where a few properties, such as the Three Sisters, contrived to show some faint promise.

One prospector who did manage to bring a significant change to Zululand was David Brown, owner of the Darnall farm in Natal. Hearing of the discovery of the renowned Sheba Reef at Barberton in the Transvaal, he set out to walk up Marcus Road in order to try his luck.

North of the Mfolozi River he entered the lands of the old chief Somkhele who, when drunk enough, liked to claim the ownership of all Zululand. What he did own was probably the largest herd of cattle in the whole country. During the recent years of turmoil, many people had sent their livestock for sanctuary into the vastness of the Dukuduku forest and paid Somkhele tribute for grazing rights. Apart from these tributes, many of the cattle owners had been killed in the disturbances and their heirs failed to claim the livestock. Vast herds had thus fallen into the hands of Somkhele and riches had gone somewhat to his head. His son, on account of a complicated birth, had been given the rather extraordinary name of Mthubuthubu (he who was pummelled out). The name, in the form of Mtubatuba, was later applied to a railway station near his home.

Brown went to pay respects to Somkhele. Near Nomathiya, the kraal of this pocket despot, the prospector observed an outcrop of anthracite coal. Brown kept the discovery a secret for some time. His heart was set on gold but when he was disappointed in his hopes of sudden fortune, he mentioned the anthracite discovery to James Liege Hulett in Natal.

A diamond drill was sent up to test the extent of the discovery. The results indicated a major deposit and in consequence there was formed a syndicate composed of Brown, Hulett and Arthur Reynolds. On 8 April 1893, this syndicate applied for a lease of the athracite area and a concession to construct a railway line from the Thukela River to the proposed mine. A provisional fifty years' concession covering the mine and line was granted to the syndicate on 11 August 1894. The line was to be completed by 1903. It would be built under official supervision and worked by the Government who were to keep 59 per cent of gross revenue and retain the option of purchasing on due notice. Thomas Reynolds took over the portion of the concession covering the railway and construction was scheduled to commence as soon as the north coast line was completed from Durban to the Thukela. Great hopes were attached to this projected railway, for many individuals had schemes of development in Zululand but the atrocious lines of communication with Natal made any such ideas abortive.

In Natal itself, this year 1893 was notable as seeing the climax of the movement towards responsible government. Since the first elections for the Legislative Council in 1857, there had been steady pressure from Natal for increased government powers. The British Government responded by making an occasional concession in respect of the strength of the Legislative Council. Originally, it had consisted of twelve elected and four official members. However, by 1873 this number had been increased to 15 elected members and five officials.

The responsible government movement was hardly appeased by these concessions. Especially after the Langalibalele trouble, there was a rapidly increasing clamour for an overhaul of the existing administrative body.

In 1875, Sir Garnet Wolseley was sent out from England as temporary Governor of Natal, with a comprehensive commission to investigate affairs in general. In Natal much was expected of Wolseley's visit, but once again all that resulted were more additions to the Legislative Council, increasing it to 15 elected and 13 official members.

Natal was bitterly disappointed, but it took some years for the colonists to marshall their strength for an assault on the pinnacle of self-government. There was much disagreement amongst themselves about the matter, but in 1890 the election to the council returned a majority of four members in favour of responsible government, and full-scale negotiations with the British authorities were immediately commenced.

There were many people, even in Natal, who doubted whether the colony was ready for self-rule. These diehards, styling themselves the Conservative Party, fought the whole issue on the grounds that Natal was immature; that it would be unable to defend itself without a recourse to the type of burgher law produced in the republics; and that it would be unable to raise loans for public works.

A bitter quarrel resulted over the whole question. John Robinson and G.M. Sutton, leaders of the Responsible Government Party, went to Britain in 1891 to confer with the British Government on Natal affairs, and eventually it was determined to put the matter to the test of a general election in Natal.

The hardest fought election ever held in Natal took place in September 1892. After all the noise and abuse, when the new council assembled, to the dismay of the Responsible Government Party supporters, the Conservatives held a majority of four members and promptly passed a resolution "that the house did not consider it desirable to consider the question of responsible government."

However, four of the election results were in dispute on account of irregularities. By-elections were held, and after intense excitement the Council which met in May 1893 for the 14th and last of its sittings, had a Responsible Government Party majority of three men. On 11 May this majority passed a motion approving responsible government. The British Government assented to the measure and at long last, in September 1893, the first proper elections were held for a Natal House of Assembly of 37 elected members. An Upper House, or Legislative Council of eleven members, was to be nominated by the Governor.

On 19 October the new Parliament of Natal was opened by the Governor, Sir Walter Hely-Hutchinson. The old stalwart of responsible government, John Robinson, became the first Prime Minister, and a vigorous political programme of development in matters relating to transport, police and other departments was undertaken. There were also several serious problems to confront.

In 1896 rinderpest swept into Zululand from the north. In an effort to prevent it spreading into Natal, the government closed the frontiers to animal-drawn traffic and the need for rail communication with Zululand became even more apparent.

The year 1896 was also bad for drought and the Zululand Government, importing sorely needed mealies, was forced to charter the 100-ton coaster *Gertie*. In November of that year she took two cargoes of mealies up to Port Durnford. The cargoes were unloaded by means of a lighter and a warp, and stored in sheds on the beach. The expense, however, was such that sheds were then built at the Thukela ford where Stephen Bond had run a ferry and hotel since the 1860s. The wagons were unloaded on the Natal side, then the load of mealies was ferried across and reloaded into wagons on the Zululand side. The desirablility of a proper Zululand harbour had long been apparent to the government. Port Durnford was at best but a wretched sort of place where cargoes were handled more by luck than anything else. Some opinion favoured developing the Mhlathuze lagoon as a harbour, with the railway line from Somkhele ending there. The idea was to construct a first-class naval coaling station in the lagoon, and in July, August and September 1897, a detailed hydrographical survey was made of the place by Lieutenant L.B. Denham.

The Mhlathuze lagoon had long been a favourite hunting resort. Its broad expanse of water, seven to nine feet deep; its diminutive islands such as Hippo Island; and its mouth, generally open to the sea, made it one of the most striking natural harbours in all Southern Africa. It had always teemed with fish and wild life. Hippos and crocodiles were especially numerous. It was there, indeed, that John Dunn killed a crocodile of record-breaking size for Southern Africa.

Hunting hippos one day, he was standing in the reeds, with his legs apart over a hippo track covered with about four feet of water. Feeling a movement, he looked down into the water and saw this mammoth crocodile coming towards him. He fired into its throat three times and killed it. It was 22 feet long.

Lieutenant Denham and his party were enthusiastic at the results of their survey, but imminent political changes forced the government to shelve the idea. The British Government had decided to hand Zululand over to Natal, and the Natalians were more concerned with developing Durban than in finding a rival harbour elsewhere. They also were somewhat preoccupied with more pressing matters.

There was increasing anticipation of war in the north between Great Britain and the Transvaal. The fiasco of the Jameson Raid at the end of 1895 had been the first sign of serious trouble. In the midst of this crisis a trainload of refugees from Johannesburg jumped the rails nine miles north of Glencoe on 31 December 1895. Thirty-eight people were killed when the engine couplings broke and the carriages overturned on a curve. This disaster brought home to Natal the unpleasant fact that, personal feelings notwithstanding, a fight between the British Government and the Transvaal Republic would inevitably bring tragedy to all of Southern Africa.

Politically, there was a growing tension in Natal. On 13 February 1897, Sir John Robinson resigned as Prime Minister of Natal on grounds of ill-health, and Harry Escombe who replaced him, soon ran into stormy political seas. From 1895 onwards there had been a general public uneasiness about the continued immigration of Indians into Natal. By that time there were already as many Indians as Europeans in the colony, and in November 1896 a union had been formed to try to stop the further influx. Demonstrations were held in Durban and immigrant ships were picketed. By then it was generally realised that the irresponsible importation of an entirely alien community into Natal by sugar planters motivated simply by a desire to exploit cheap labour for their own profit, was a matter not to be suffered any longer by the public.

The planters had already been unwillingly driven by public pressure to the commonsense idea that, if they wanted to import cheap labour, it was at least up to them to return it home again after exploitation and not dump it on the rest of the community for assimilation. Free Indian immigrants, however, were still pouring into the colony, attracted by formerly indentured workers who were now prospering in liberty and were bringing in their relatives and friends.

In January 1897, there was a climax to this public hostility when two ships, the *Naderi* and the *Courland*, arrived with nearly 600 free immigrants. One of those who landed from these ships was M.K. Gandhi, returning from a visit to India. He was mobbed and kicked by the angry crowd who regarded him as the dominant spirit among the Indians. Only the intervention of Mrs Alexander, wife of the local police superintendent, who sheltered the stunned Gandhi with her parasol, saved him from possible serious injury.

Escombe had to placate the public and steer through Parliament a bill calculated to stop further Asiatic emigration. At the same time, the government was sorely pressed by the outbreak of rinderpest. For months, the Natalians had watched the approach of the dreaded cattle disease through the Transvaal and hoped it would miss them. Then, in July 1897, there was an outbreak on a farm a few miles from Dundee. Eighty head of cattle were immediately shot in an effort to eradicate it, but the disease cropped up all over Natal. It was like the sparks of a veld fire carried by a gale, setting fresh flames alight all over the colony. Before the gale passed and the flames died of their own accord, half the livestock of Natal had been wiped out.

In the midst of these troubles and a developing financial crisis, the second general election was held at the end of 1897. The Conservatives, who had for so long opposed responsible government, now found themselves returned to power. H. Binns became the new Prime Minister, and his party had to readjust its whole approach to administration and settle down to manage an independent country. Zululand was an addition to their problems.

The last months of 1897 were occupied by the British Administration in officially washing its hands of Zululand. Dinuzulu and his fellow exiles were returned to Durban on 30 December 1897, and on the same day Zululand was officially annexed to Natal. As a preliminary to this, Tongaland had been annexed to Zululand on 22 November 1897, in order to present Natal with a unified administrative area. Several conditions were attached to the final annexation. The most important of these were that the existing system of land tenure be maintained for five years, with no grants of land to be made; and a joint Imperial and Colonial Commission to be appointed in the meanwhile to delimitate sufficient and inalienable reserves for the Zulus.

Everything seemed ready for immense development in Zululand. The completion of the railway would synchronise with the expiration of the restriction on European settlement in the country. Innumerable schemes were afoot for various projects. Eshowe, where the first sale of town erven had taken place in September 1892, two years after its survey, hummed with excitement and hopes. A newspaper, imaginatively named *The Sausage Wrap*, commenced publication there in March 1899, and the town's population of officials, traders and wagon builders all had high hopes of a new epoch.

Then the Anglo-Boer War came and all projects were shelved. Zululand was affected more by the general economic chaos than by anything else. There was little fighting in the country itself. Apart from their raid on Ngwavuma, the Boer forces, on 28 April 1901 attacked Mahlabathini. They seized much livestock thereabouts, but the little garrison of 20 men of the Natal Field Force held out on Nkonjeni Nek with a loss of five killed, and the Boers soon withdrew.

The Zulus themselves were little interested in the white men's quarrels. Only on the north-western frontier were they at all involved. There, in the Vryheid area, the chief Sikhobobo's people were much harried during the prolonged period of guerilla operations by parties of Boers in search of provisions.

One small commando in particular succeeded in riling the Zulus at the end of April 1902. In retaliation, on 6 May, the Zulus gathered secretly and proceeded to the place known as Holkrans, where they knew the commando was in laager in a cattle kraal.

The Zulus surrounded the laager, planning a surprise, but one of them prematurely fired a gun. The Boers jumped for their arms in the dark and opened fire. The Zulus lost 200 of their men, but in the darkness they crept in and practically wiped the commando out, killing 56 Boers and taking three prisoners.

In Natal the war reached its first great climax with the

Boer invasion, the Siege of Ladysmith and many other actions which are best read in their proper setting of the whole story of this most tragic sequence of events. So far as the people of Natal were concerned, the war, although uneasily anticipated for the past few years, came as a profound shock. Their own relations with the Overberg republics had been excellent. In 1898 a customs union with the Cape Colony and the Orange Free State Republic had been innovated while trade with the Transvaal was booming.

Still, the war came and there was nothing they could do about it. Sir Henry Binns, the Natal Prime Minister, who was friendly to President Kruger, unfortunately died just before the outbreak of the war and his successor, Colonel Albert Hime, was more of a firebrand in the cause of British Imperial expansion. A degree of patriotic emotion was whipped up by means of accusations of disloyalty to Queen and flag for all those who had misgivings and suspicions about the motives of the coming conflict, and the people of Natal were well confused about issues by the time the war actually broke out. Their government plunged heartily into the fray but popular enthusiasm remained lukewarm and hardly one out of five of the able-bodied men in Natal volunteered for service.

Developments in both Natal and Zululand during the war were naturally minor. The irrepressible gold prospectors carried on with their endless search. In September 1901, one group, the Kranzkop Prospecting Syndicate, announced a rich find in the Thukela Valley, but it never came to anything. Another concern, The Southern Cross Gold Dredging Syndicate, was floated in Durban in March 1902, for the purpose of dredging the Zululand rivers for gold. Machinery was sent up to the Mfule River in May 1902, but nothing was ever extracted except mud and, as the Zululanders had more than sufficient on their roads, the syndicate showed no profit.

Besides delaying the Zululand railway, the war had also held up plans of opening the country for European settlement. The long-delayed Delimitation Commission was only appointed on 1 August 1902, after the clamour of land-hungry Europeans had reached a crescendo.

The Commission consisted of Brigadier Sir J.G. Dartnell and C.R. Saunders of Tongaland fame. The two commissioners were instructed, especially after some representation by European sympathisers with the Zulus, that their first duty was to provide liberally for the tribespeople and to consider not only existing requirements but also to allow for a natural increase in population.

The Commission set to work carving up Zululand, and certainly no building excavator ever had a more attentive audience. All manner of land-hungry individuals watched the activities of the Commission with the closest interest. Most of the would-be Zululand settlers appeared to be labouring, as the Commission's report put it, "under the impression that all the Commission was required to do was to indiscriminately throw open the whole of the lands suitable for European occupation, irrespective of the interests of the natives occupying those lands, who in fact, had hardly been considered as a factor in the settlement. It is also noticeable that in all the published criticisms on the settlement, not a voice appears to have been raised in the natives' interests."

The Commission generally did its work well. It was naturally expected to pick out the eyes of the country for European settlement, but the Zulus were left with a respectably sized portion of their homeland and unlike the Swazis, were never reduced to the status of a nation of squatters living on European-owned farms.

A mass of work confronted the Commission at the start of the task. Mission, trading, tribal rights and claims had to be examined. After 17 months of work, Dartnell retired on the grounds of ill-health, and R.H. Beachcroft replaced him. Another 18 months of work followed before the Commission's report was finally tabled by the Prime Minister of Natal before the Legislative Assembly on 7 June 1905.

One of the numerous responsibilities of the Commission

had been to allocate the descendants of John Dunn a reserve of 10 000 acres. Dunn, after one of the most curious lives ever led in Southern Africa, had died on 5 August 1895 at his home at Mangethe. He was 61 years of age at the time and the records of the Moyeni Mission, established near his home in 1895, as the first Roman Catholic mission in Zululand, show that he left 49 wives and 117 children. There were also innumerable followers and retainers, including several Europeans who were married to his children.

None of Dunn's sons were strong enough in character to replace their father. His four chief indunas carried on in control of his area and reported direct to the magistrate at Eshowe. Later, the Mlalazi district was formed with an assistant magistrate in charge, and the area of the Dunns came under him.

Dunn had left a fair amount of wealth in cattle for his dependants, but the rinderpest which came the year after his death, swept away most of this fortune. Under this blow, and with no central figure to bind them together, his followers disintegrated. Most of the Dunns scattered into towns in search of employment but, for the family as a whole, the Delimitation Commission set apart the so-called Dunn's Reserve, between the Thukela and the stream known as the Nyoni (the place of birds).

While the Commission was busy in Zululand there were many schemes afoot for the eagerly anticipated coming development of the country. One of these schemes was a revival of interest in the possibility of a harbour somewhere along the coast. The idea was made doubly attractive during the Anglo-Boer War, when the absorption of the two Republics seemed imminent, and it was considered that the harbour and rail facilities of Durban would prove inadequate for the coming demand.

The great lagoon of the Mhlathuze River once more entered the news. It appeared to be the most likely place for a harbour and, from a railway point of view, presented the shortest straight line from the coast to Volksrust and the Transvaal.

Accordingly, the Zululand coast was most carefully examined in 1902 by a party of surveyors under Cathcart W. Methven. In August of that year the surveyors visited the Mhlathuze lagoon and, at the end of October, the tug *Richard King* steamed up to Richards Bay and made detailed soundings.

Methven was much impressed by the Mhlathuze lagoon. The vast sheet of water was nearly double the size of Durban lagoon and he considered that it could certainly be made into a port. For £800 000 he considered that an entrance with a training wall could be made on the north end of the long, narrow spit of land which divided the lagoon from the sea. The existing eight-foot channels could be dredged, and there was an excellent site for a township on the high ground overlooking the lagoon.

With Lake St Lucia, Methven was not impressed. He found the whole lake and estuary badly silted up in September 1902, and had difficulty in finding any place deeper than five feet. "Very extensive entrance works would be necessary and constant heavy dredging operations to keep the mouth open," he wrote in his report.

The chief interest of Lake St Lucia, indeed, lay in its wild life. The place was teeming with birds and the islands were the resort of vast numbers of crocodiles. Hunters, such as Colonel Addison and T.C. Colenbrander, still found great sport there and the crocodiles had recently, on 26 March 1902, been responsible for killing a missionary named Lindfield. This unfortunate individual was in the process of wading across the shallow water towards the Mount Tabor Mission. The crossing was the traditional way across the lake, but the tribespeople always made a point of fording it in a body to scare the crocs. The missionary failed to take this precaution.

So far as the whole idea of a harbour in Zululand was concerned, the ruling Conservative Party was defeated in 1903 and the Responsible Government leader, G.M. Sutton, who became the new Prime Minister, had no enthusiasm for any such project. The Utrecht and Vryheid areas had just been added to Natal at the end of the Anglo-Boer War and he was pre-occupied there, and in dealing with post-war problems and the clamours of an Assembly now increased to 44 members to cater for a new and greater Natal.

Nothing, therefore, came of Methven's survey. The Natal election, in fact, had largely been fought on the issue of a Zululand harbour and the decision was that Durban could cater for the Transvaal and also for Zululand when it was linked up by rail.

The Zululand railway, meanwhile, was steadily pushing north. On 18 July 1902, the 1340-foot, 16-span bridge across the Thukela at Bond's Drift was opened. Then, on 17 September 1903, the Governor of Natal opened the Zululand line to its terminus at Somkhele, and from thence on, a train left Durban each morning at 8.30 and puffed and fussed its way through Zululand until it reached Somkhele at 9.15 that night. The time of arrival was more or less a guess on the part of the railway.

It was an odd little line at first. For 170 miles it trailed through a wilderness with nought save a few Zulus to watch its progress. Apart from one or two isolated storemen, there were no Europeans living in all those miles of bush. Optimistically the railway had scattered a number of sidings along the way, each with a stretch of cinders for a platform and a name board, but most of them were as busy as a graveyard, and in its first year of operating the line showed a loss of £48 917.

Of one of these Zululand sidings there is a tale. It appears that a certain couple were induced by some wags, whose friendship did not persist for long afterwards, to book their honeymoon journey up to Port Durnford. Accommodation, space and no disturbance from anyone, the wags assured them. So up the Zululand line the couple travelled. The train duly stopped and they bundled out with their baggage. "Village must be on the other side," said the bridegroom, as the couple waited for the train to pull out. A Zulu found them the following morning sleeping among some bags. They returned to Durban by the next available train.

The coal mine at Somkhele commenced operations shortly after the opening of the railway line. If a journey to the place was a dreary business of twelve hours of bouncing and banging through drab coastal bush, with no comfort, food, or drink, but infinite dirt and monotony, then ultimate arrival at Somkhele was a fitting and miserable climax.

Somkhele, when reached at night, was a dark, windswept platform, with a tin shanty, one swinging paraffin lamp and a sardonic stationmaster to collect tickets and wonder what any strangers were doing there.

The mining settlement consisted of about twelve shanty buildings and a few tents. A small corrugated-iron hotel consisting of three bedrooms and a bar had been brought up bodily from Mthwalume on the Natal south coast, and this was the most pretentious building in the place.

By daylight Somkhele looked worse, if anything. It lay in a monotonous mixture of hills and clumps of bush. A shimmering heat haze was generally the only moving thing to be seen.

About 12 Europeans and 150 Zulus were employed in the place, working under a mine manager named Grainger who was typical of his kind, an individual of 40 who looked 80. Most of the staff were generally down with fever and it was one of those places where a man valued his soul next to a quinine tablet.

The mine itself was a primitive place. Owned by an organisation styling itself the Zululand Collieries Company, it consisted of two pits, burrowing about 400 feet into the ground and periodically vomiting black lumps of coal. The coal deposit was of such quantity that the owners reckoned there was enough to last for 250 years of working. Qualitatively the coal, unfortunately, was inferior and difficult to burn.

Inclined shafts, with the inevitable coco-pan rails, led down into the mine, a dreary affair of flickering candles, dripping water, the odour of perspiration, hard work and a floor made up of a horrible goo of oozing, black mud. Shift work went on day and night and, as a result, a maximum of 35 tons of coal were mined each day and poured into the waiting railway trucks, down a long, clattering, iron trough, held up by timber staging.

At 5 a.m. each day the train quit Somkhele with a puff of relief and headed for Durban. On the way the engine driver generally left his locomotive to the fireman and passed the time playing cards with the passengers. Refreshments were carried by each passenger in his suitcase and were well wrapped up in bottles. At the Thukela bridge a tent on the platform supplied bully beef to the hungry, but by that time most of the passengers were more in need of spiritual solace than nourishment. Durban, even in February, seemed a haven of cool comfort when the train steamed in on its last gasp, some time in the dark hours.

In April 1904 the Natal Government took over the railway from the company for £725 000. The line had been a dead loss ever since its opening. A stream of European settlers was arriving in Zululand to take up the farms allocated by the Delimitation Commission, but it would be many years before their joint efforts produced an economic activity strong enough to support the railway and only a government could afford to subsidise it during the time of waiting. Somkhele, with its output of 35 tons of coal a day, could hardly pay for a train a week, let alone a worthwhile service.

Many projects, however, were definitely afoot. As early as 1901 tests had been made of Zululand rubber, and samples sent to London were well received. Sugar, however, was the main preoccupation from the very start. Two areas along the coast had been opened up for Europeans. The first extended from the Mandeni stream up to the Mhlathuze River and the second from the Mhlathuze to the Mpangeni stream, where the Norwegians had rebuilt their mission on a new site after its destruction in the Anglo-Zulu War and where, in 1894, after many changes of site, the Lower Mfolozi magistracy had at last fixed its seat.

To serve these two settled areas the government, in 1905, invited proposals for the establishment of a sugar factory in Zululand. Liege Hulett tendered and was accepted on 9 August 1905. He then built the first sugar plant in Zululand, on the Matigulu River, and this commenced operations on 6 August 1908.

The area north of the Mhlathuze selected Empangeni as its "capital". A village was established there in 1906 and in 1913 George Armstrong's Zululand Sugar Milling Company erected a sugar factory at the place. This factory was really responsible for Empangeni's development to township status, which it achieved in 1913 – a pleasant little place, lying on the top of a hill, like an inhabited island in a sea of sugar cane.

Such then was the manner of the construction of the Zululand railway. The construction anticipated Zululand's development, and by this anticipation facilitated the work of the pioneers. Freed from those crippling worries of transport under which so many others have laboured in areas where the railway belatedly followed progress, the Zululand settlers set to with a will at clearing the bush, planting their crops and establishing the industries which today support the line to the north.

FORTY
Bambatha

On the southern border of Zululand, along the precipices overlooking the mighty valley of the Thukela River, there lies a forest known from its ruggedness as the Nkandla (a place of exhaustion). It is a forest of immense antiquity and majesty. Giant trees, festooned with creepers, reach upwards to the sky. Shadows, dark and cold, fall downward with a million silver beams of light, while on the ground lies the soft, dank springiness of countless centuries of humus.

Leopards, bushbuck, monkeys and mambas haunt this forest. It is a place full of secrets and legends of hidden caves and hiding places, where silver streams torture themselves to twist a way through the shadows; and ghosts dwell there, the legends say, finding sanctuary in forgotten glades and the most silent portions of the forest, such as the Ziwojeni, whose trees seem so still they must surely be enchanted.

There are ten main sections to this forest, each with its own atmosphere and name, such as Dukuza (where you get lost), leNdlovu (place of the elephants), iBomvana (the little red place), and kwaVuza (place of the dripping one). In the centre of them all lies the very heart of the forest, a deep and sinister gorge, one-and-a-half miles long and shut in all around by great 2000-foot-high mountain walls. Through it a streamlet called the Mhome (the drainer), flows, tumbling headlong into the gorge over a cliff and then rushing out as if to escape from so dark and fearful a place.

This forest, so beautiful and noble, was the scene of a curiously vicious human conflict, which reached its climax and unhappy end there.

The tree of bitterness which Man's passions sprouted in the Nkandla forest had its roots in a mound of old discontents. Ever since the Anglo-Zulu War, a variety of disasters had combined to disturb the tribes of Southern Africa. Locusts in 1895; rinderpest in 1897; the Anglo-Boer War at the turn of the century; and then East Coast Fever sweeping through the country, preceded by confusion and panic and followed by enforced deterioration of living standards among the pastoral tribes.

Progress in Natal and Zululand at the same time was hamstrung by petty political squabbles and a developing financial crisis. Then, in 1905, a coalition ministry under C.J. Smythe took office. It was this government, confronted by a budget deficiency, which imposed a poll tax on all adult males in the colony.

The Natal tribes were ripe for trouble at this period and hardly likely to welcome a poll tax of £1 a head. In the last months of 1905 the magistrates all over Natal were busy holding meetings and explaining the new tax. They encountered an ominous reception. Grumbling and open abuse were heard at nearly every meeting.

All through Natal rumours spread that the ancestral spirits were ready to support a rising against white authority. As a sign of preparedness to follow the spirits, all white fowls had to be killed, all European-made cooking utensils discarded, and all pigs destroyed or sold. So many pigs were placed on the market on this order that the current price dropped to one shilling an animal.

Discontent spread from one kraal to another. The very mode of life of the tribal Bantu was given to the spreading of distortions. Having no newspapers, they depended on hearsay, and if the mood of the people favoured prejudice, then any rumour supporting that feeling was readily believed. All manner of mystics, village halfwits, witch doctors and prophets found it profitable to spread stories of omens and signs of their ancestors' wrath at the burdens of the Bantu. Secret commands were whispered for all manner of preparations by rumoured order of such personages as the king of the Basuto, Dinuzulu; or Mujaji, the Rain Queen of the LoBedu.

Actual collection of the poll tax started on 20 January 1906. Three days before, a farmer named Henry Smith was stabbed to death on the veranda of his house at Umlaas Road after he had induced his farm workers to pay the tax in advance. This murder was the start of a series of unconnected outrages all over the country.

The most serious of these early outbreaks started at Henley on 7 February. When the magistrate of the Mngeni area was collecting tax, the local chief, Mveli, warned him that a party of 27 of his tribe from the Richmond district was on a nearby hill, armed with spears and looking for trouble.

After confirming this report, the magistrate ordered 14 European policemen to proceed the next day and arrest the armed party. The policemen, under Sub-Inspector Sidney Hunt, made their way to Trewirgie farm near Byrnetown, and there they identified and handcuffed two of the wanted men.

An angry crowd of Africans gathered around the policemen and demanded the release of the two men. A clash soon occurred. Hunt was in front of his men. He was stabbed to death, while Trooper G. Armstrong was forced into a donga and horribly cut up.

The rest of the policemen retired into the evening mist, taking with them a wounded sergeant, who died later. Nine Africans had been shot in the uproar. There was a general alarm in Natal after this affair. Rumours reached Richmond that thousands of armed warriors were advancing on the town. As the only defence of the place consisted of a maxim gun with no ammunition, there was, to say the least, some uneasiness.

Martial Law was proclaimed in Natal on 10 February 1906, and a force of about 1000 men, led by Lieutenant Colonel Duncan McKenzie, was soon concentrated in the area. By then, most of the rebel Africans had retired into some bush about five miles from Nelsrust. McKenzie and his men, supported by the local chief, Mveli, swept through the troubled area, arresting suspects and generally restoring order. There were several minor scrimmages, but by 5 March all the rebels, with their leader, Mjongo, were under arrest.

Twenty-three of the rebels were court-martialled in Richmond between 12 and 19 March. Twelve of the accused were sentenced to death, while the rest received terms of imprisonment. The twelve condemned men were publicly shot in Richmond on 2 April, after some legal argument with the British Government over the sentences had been settled.

There were several other smaller, unconnected outbreaks in Natal. After settling the Richmond affair, McKenzie left on a general military promenade around the colony. Ixopo and Highflats were visited without incident, save that at night isolated individuals could be heard shouting warsongs from hilltops, and rumours of future trouble were rife.

From Highflats, McKenzie took his men down to the south coast. The tribe under Charlie Fynn seemed in the mood for trouble. When the Magistrate, J.L. Knight, had endeavoured to collect tax at Mthwalume the tribe had staged a demonstration. They had hurled abuse at the Magistrate and refused to listen to him, although Fynn had endeavoured to restrain them.

McKenzie and his men arrived at Umzinto on 15 March, and the rebels soon buckled up. Fynn was summoned to appear with his tribe. A fine of 1500 head of cattle was imposed and all dissident headmen were arrested. There was no more trouble on the south coast.

Another disturbed area was in the Maphumulo district on the north coast. The chief, Ngobizembe, and his followers had received their Magistrate, R.E. Dunn, in most truculent manner when he had tried to collect the tax at Allen's Store on 22 January. He had been told to shut up when he had tried to speak and a crowd of young warriors had done a war dance around him.

On 24 February, a mixed force under Colonel Leuchars marched into the area from Stanger. The rebels were summoned to appear at Allen's Store. When they failed to show up, the chief's kraal was shelled for 20 minutes at dawn on 5 March and was afterwards burned down. The chief was arrested in a neighbouring kraal and fined 1200 head of cattle and 3500 goats.

For the time being, this ended the matter on the north coast. The tribes paid their tax and seemed subdued. One searchlight put the whole district into a state of nerves when a story went around that it was a big eye sent up into the air in order to look down into the kraals and spy on the Africans.

The centre of disturbance then moved up to the Greytown district. Living among the acacias in the valley of the stream known as the Mphanza (the sponger) was a recently deposed petty chief named Bambatha. He had been the chief of the small Zondi tribe, and his capital kraal of Mkhontweni (the place of the spear) was a centre noted for its beer-drinks and faction fights.

Bambatha was a man about 40 years of age, of violent temper and considerable personal resolution. He had already been in trouble on several occasions for faction fighting and cattle thieving, and with the imposition of the poll tax he became most pugnacious. He refused to pay and, on 22 February, a rumour reached Greytown that Bambatha was preparing to attack the place. The population immediately took shelter in the town hall and most of their African servants fled to the bush. Nothing happened!

Bambatha was summoned to appear in Pietermaritzburg, but he refused. When a police patrol was sent to arrest him, he fled with his wife and two children into Zululand and henceforth became the central figure and principal leader of the whole poll tax rebellion.

Zululand, up till then, had been an uneasy spectator of the Natal troubles. The Zulus were no more enthusiastic at paying the tax than anybody else. In their perplexity most of them looked to Dinuzulu for leadership. Many chiefs sent messages to him, asking for guidance. In reply he simply told them that he could do nothing. Early in January, he made his own followers pay the tax. Forty-five other chiefs paid up, leaving 16 chiefs unwilling and awaiting events. At this stage Bambatha arrived and made his way to Dinuzulu, at his uSuthu kraal.

At Dinuzulu's kraal a secret consultation was held. Dinuzulu was in a difficult position. His official status in Zululand since his return from St Helena was simply that of a district chief, with no other power over Zululand than the influence of his family name.

On the strength of this name, the rest of the independent district chiefs frequently approached him for his advice or blessing and in the troubled times many individuals came to him. Being looked upon by them as a sort of father, it was hard for him not to play the part. Properly, as a salaried government induna, he should have arrested Bambatha when that adventurer approached him for his blessing on the revolt. Instead, Dinuzulu sympathised with him in private. He undertook to shelter Bambatha's family; and two minor followers of Dinuzulu named Ngqengqengqe and Chakijana joined Bambatha as a sign of moral support.

Thus strengthened in his purpose, Bambatha returned to his old haunts in Natal. On 3 April he raided the kraal of his uncle Magawababa, who was acting as regent of the tribe, and kept the old man prisoner for a short while. The whole district fell into uproar. Police and troops were concentrated there and outlying European residents were gathered into Greytown. While thus engaged in escorting three women and a child from Keat's Drift, a police force under Colonel Mansel was ambushed on the night of 4 April.

Groping their way along the road to Greytown, under a half moon, the policemen suddenly found themselves surrounded by a dense mass of Africans. There was a hot little fight in the moonlight for a quarter of an hour. Firing from behind their horses, the 151 policemen drove the attackers back into the bush and then rode on, followed by a stream of abuse and bullets. Three Europeans were killed, four wounded and one was missing as a result of the encounter.

A mixed force under Colonel Leuchars was mustered as quickly as possible and sent down from Greytown in search of vengeance. On 9 April they surrounded Bambatha's kraal and bombarded it, but he had vanished. They searched the bush, but all they found was the body of the man, Sergeant Brown, who had been missing after the ambush. The body was badly mutilated, sundry parts having been removed for purposes of witchcraft, while his upper lip and moustache had been carried away as an omen with which to enlist more rebels.

Bambatha meanwhile had slipped across the Thukela and made for the Nkandla forest. Living there, in his kraal of Nhlweni (the place of the pauper) as head of the Cube tribe, was an old family friend named Sigananda. This tribe, some 4300 strong, was of Lala origin, traditionally workers in iron and principal spear makers to the Zulu royal house, to whom they were intensely loyal. They lived in the forest and their particular stronghold was in the Mhome gorge, where Sigananda had his capital kraal at the foot of the waterfall.

Bambatha and his men encamped in the gorge, while Sigananda, an old man of 85, argued with his headmen about what they were to do. Some said Dinuzulu was behind it all, others that Bambatha was just an outlaw. A message was sent to Dinuzulu, asking for guidance, but he evaded the issue, saying it was no concern of his. Other neighbouring chiefs also remained aloof from appeals for aid.

However, Sigananda decided to join Bambatha. He summoned his people to arms and the forest became full of menace, war cries and excitement disturbing the silence of the trees. The witch doctors had a special magic which was said to make the warriors impervious to European bullets. They were instructed to abstain from women and sleep on the bare ground. Then, with their mouths full of the magic medicine, they were taken to the top of the mountain known as Ndundumeni (the place of the summit.) There they all spat the medicine in the direction of the enemy and cursed the white race. Then they removed in a body to Cetshwayo's grave, deep in the forest, where they camped, praying to his spirit for aid.

The Natal Government, meanwhile, had summoned all loyal Africans to oppose Bambatha and a demand was sent to Siganada for his surrender. At the bleak little magisterial seat for the Nkandla district, Mpandleni (the bare place) a considerable force of mixed troops was concentrated and all preparations made for war. Each of the four South African colonies contributed men to the campaign, and some 2100 soldiers were gathered into what was called the Zululand Field Force, under the command of Colonel Duncan McKenzie.

All sorts of outrages were occurring in the surrounding country. Stores were being looted and several minor skirmishes took place between the gathering troops and the rebels. To add to the uproar, on 3 May, H.M. Stainbank, the magistrate of Mahlabathini, was shot dead while on a tax-collecting tour on the south bank of the White Mfolozi River.

By 5 May there were enough troops on hand to stage an offensive operation. Colonel Mansel led a mixed force of 910 men through a portion of the forest. They made their way off the main road and down the ridge known as uBobe, aptly named from the dense tangle of its vegetation.

On the ridge, the force was charged by about one thousand rebels. They attacked with absolute fearlessness, confident in the witch doctors' medicine. Bambatha watched the action from nearby and the last seen of him was when he galloped off on a white horse to find the witch doctors, for the whole affair was a bitter defeat for the rebels. Sixty of them were killed and many wounded, while only three of Mansel's force had been hurt. Even worse for the rebels was the blow to their morale. What Bambatha did to the witch doctors is unknown but, like a few other generals, he had a warm time of it himself the next morning, when a crowd of bereaved women threatened to tear him to pieces.

For the next few days McKenzie rummaged about the country with his force and reconnoitred from the top of the Mpandleni hill, which looks out over all the ruggedness and greenness of the Nkandla to the pale blue of the Indian Ocean, 50 miles away.

The 16th of May was the date set for the first big operation. McKenzie resolved to attack the rebels' camp at Cetshwayo's grave. For this purpose he divided his force into three sections, each to converge on the grave from a different direction.

At 5.30 a.m. the troops set off. The main column, under McKenzie, set out from Mpandleni and filed down the same steep *ingoqongo* (twisted) spur which Shaka had once followed in his fight with Zwide. In the bush at the bottom the excited men surprised a number of rebels and the sharp rat-a-tat of the maxim guns sent them scattering, leaving much livestock behind.

On through the forest the attackers swept, burning kraals, rounding up cattle and searching for rebels in each gorge. By the time they reached the grave they had captured over 2000 head of mixed stock. At the grave they had a rendezvous with the other columns and set to work burning the crude huts which formed the deserted camp of the rebels.

Cetshwayo's grave was an oval mound about 12 feet long, 10 feet wide and 15 inches high. It had been scrupulously protected by a relative of Sigananda's and as a result a taboo copse had grown up around it, infested by so many snakes, especially fat puff adders which had found sanctuary there, that sightseeing troops were driven ignominiously out.

The combined force of 1700 Europeans and 2000 native levies, camped about half a mile south of the grave at a little stream they subsequently named Stinkfontein, for the place was far from being hygienic.

They remained there for some time, destroying huts and crops in the neighbourhood and hopefully waiting for the rumoured surrender of Sigananda, who had sent an emissary with a white flag to see the colonel. After several days of time-gaining procrastination on the part of the rebels, McKenzie decided on a fresh move. With his men, he started searching through the wilderness for Bambatha, following a series of rumours which took the weary troopers on many a wild goose chase, from the depths of the Nsuze valley to the tops of the windswept Devil's Gorge, where the slightest slip meant death and one pack-horse fell a thousand feet.

Bambatha was always one step ahead of them and his followers were as elusive as fortune. On 29 and 30 May, for instance, the troops searched for him through the Thathe gorge. It was the type of adventure to which they had become accustomed. The troops moved cautiously along the bottom of the gorge while snipers attempted to shoot them from hideouts in palisaded caves on the sides and, when picked out themselves, crashed headlong down hundreds of feet of precipice. About 60 rebels were killed and 400 head of cattle captured, but of Bambatha there was not a trace.

Then, on 1 June, McKenzie launched a major attack on the famed Mhome stronghold. Two guns and some pom-poms were placed on the overlooking "Gun Hill" dominating the gorge, and for an hour they peppered the place with shots, unfortunately hitting a couple of their own side in the process.

The troops scrambled down the sides of the gorge and then vanished into the bush at the bottom, as though they had been swallowed. The only resistance came from scattered snipers who mortally wounded one European trooper. The whole gorge was swept, up to the cave at the foot of the waterfall, but no sign of life was found, other than 300 head of cattle.

Sigananda's deserted kraal went up to the heavens in flames but Bambatha persistently refused battle against so large a force and the forest hid him as effectively as it did its ghosts.

Two days later the troops set off on another search for the rebels. Working from the Bomvana ridge, they set out to rummage through the Dukuza forest. It was a wearisome business, pushing through a dense tangle of forest with alertness dulled after hours of heavy going and then a sudden emergency. Captain E.G. Clerk has described it well.

The force was strung out in a long line, with one European – three African levies – one European – etc. They made their way forward and soon saw fresh tracks in the ground, indicating a large force of men. Soon they came in contact with a small party of rebels. In the excitement the line straggled into groups.

The men pushed on and found six rough huts which they destroyed. In the huts was some loot from stores. The party under Clerk went on cautiously across a donga. Suddenly an African stepped out of the bush about 40 paces away. He raised his rifle and fired at the men. Immediately the whole forest became alive with rebels. It looked like an overturned beehive.

"They must have been lying down till the shot was fired," wrote Clerk. "They yelled 'uSuthu' and charged at us. I turned to call to the men, only to find out the native levies were running for their lives. I shouted to the men to move back and rally in the donga lower down.

"Knowing that unless the centre were checked in some way, the enemy would cut us up before we could get back to the donga, I emptied my carbine into the main lot. This checked them for a minute or two and I took advantage of it to run after the men. While doing so I slipped another cartridge into the breech of my carbine and had just succeeded in doing so when I ran into another lot of the enemy who had charged between the donga and myself. I fired five shots at them with my revolver. They broke and left, as I thought, a clear line to the donga where I could hear Fraser's voice calling out 'Here we are, Sir.'

"Just then a native rose from the low bush in front of me. He had a stabbing assegai and some sort of weapon. He raised the assegai but as he did so, I snapped at him the last shot in my revolver and he fell. As he fell, another native appeared suddenly on my left – I think he had been behind a small tree. He was within stabbing distance before I noticed him. I had no time to aim my carbine, merely being able to swing it up and parry his thrust. The assegai just grazed my right eyelid and I thought my eye was out as the blood almost blinded me.

"Catching my foot in something I fell but succeeded in throwing myself right over and again faced my adversary. Swinging my carbine forward I pulled the trigger with my little finger. The shot struck the man in the chest and he fell forward past me.

"Recovering my footing I ran down and leaped into the donga where the others were. The rebels seemed to surround us immediately and I had succeeded in firing only about two shots when Alexander staggered forward crying out, 'Oh, my God, pull this out, pull this out,' referring to an assegai which had been driven into the middle of his back. Someone pulled the assegai out and he sank down and died immediately.

"Almost immediately afterwards, Hawkins staggered forward and sank against the east bank just on my right, with two assegais in his back. He remained in a crouching position and, from the peculiar sound, I knew his lung had been injured. Once he cried to someone to shoot him and put him out of his misery.

"Just as he fell, I felt a shock through my left upper arm, which caused my hand to lose its power. Owing to this, I dropped my carbine. Stooping quickly to pick it up, I found that my left hand was useless and that I could not grasp anything. The little finger only retained its normal power. I seated myself on a root and, raising the carbine with my right hand, succeeded in loading it by gripping it between my knees. I fired it with the little finger of my left hand.

"Shortly after I was wounded I heard Homes say, 'Ah, I've got it.' A bullet had gone through his thigh. He, however, continued firing, leaning against a tree. Woolnough had already been wounded in the ankle, and was lying close by the bank. Flynn had blood streaming from wounds on the face, but Fraser, though in a very exposed position (with a white shirt on) suffered no injury whatever."

The group was in a tough spot. Three times the rebels charged them and three times they were beaten back. Then reinforcements rushed up and the rebels fled. Five Europeans had been killed and nine wounded but the bodies of 140 rebels lay scattered in the bush.

So the drives went on, each with its excitements but none productive of any decisive result. More reinforcements arrived, but the rebels were too well informed by their spies to be caught in any trap.

Then, at last, at 9.30 p.m. on 9 June, a deserter from Siganda's people gave McKenzie the information that Bambatha, with the bulk of his men, was meeting Siganda in the Mhome gorge that night. It was a great opportunity and McKenzie made the most of it.

In the darkness he marshalled his men and they slipped off through the shadows of the sleeping forest. Three troopers, C.W. Johnson, G.O. Oliver and W. Deeley were sent with a message to the force stationed at Cetshwayo's grave, instructing them to bottle up the entrance to the gorge. The three men galloped for 15 miles through the forest, along twisting paths haunted by shadows and glinting eyes, with trees pulled across their way as barriers and strange figures starting up from campfires in alarm as they raced by. At 1 a.m. they reached the Grave Camp and gave the officer in charge, Colonel Barker, the message.

Barker roused his sleeping force and they set out in dead silence. At 4 a.m. they reached the mouth of the gorge and saw about 60 campfires burning, some 1000 yards into the gorge. The column halted and Barker quietly prepared them for battle.

McKenzie, meanwhile, had led his men as quickly and silently as possible over hair-raising ridges, until they blocked the upper end of the gorge and all possible pathways up the sides. Bambatha and his men were completely bottled up.

The fight started with the first light of dawn. The whole valley became alive with flashes, guns spitting out into the shadows like fireflies doing a dance of death.

623

It was a massacre. The rebels sought refuge in every patch of bush in the Dobo (valley) forest, on the floor of the gorge. A few managed to escape by clambering up precipice sides or hiding in secret caves, but the majority died. One of their principal leaders, the chief Mehlokazulu, was shot dead by Sergeant Rundle, while 500 of Bambatha's followers were killed during the day-long battle. Only three Europeans were killed and eight wounded.

Bambatha had been trapped with the rest. He tried to escape by crawling in the water up the Mhome stream. He was unarmed and dressed in just a shirt. Two of the African levies saw him in the water and attacked him with their spears. He fell into the water with them on top of him. Then an African policeman ran up and shot him through the head. His attackers left him lying there, without realising who he was.

After a night's rest, McKenzie marshalled his jubilant men and set to work beating through the forest, in order to hunt down the surviving rebels before they could reorganise. Many isolated groups were flushed from hiding places in gorges such as the oFeni (crack) and the forests on the range of mountains, known as the Qhudeni (place of the cock).

While they were thus engaged, Sigananda surrendered and was taken into captivity at the Nkandla magistracy. On 14 June the troops were searching through the bush of the Thukela Valley when a message reached them that the body of Bambatha had been identified in the Mhome gorge. Resounding cheers echoed from the ancient precipices of the valley that afternoon, for to the troops the death of the dashing Bambatha seemed the end of their task.

And, indeed, it was all over in the Nkandla forest apart from surrenders, courts-martial and captures. To facilitate identification, Bambatha's decomposing body was decapitated and the head taken to the magistracy where it was roughly preserved and shown to anyone who doubted his death. Later it was taken back and buried with the body, on the right bank of the Mhome stream.

All that remained for the troops was the task of settling a few minor disturbances elsewhere. These were principally in Natal, in the Mvoti and Maphumulo districts and in the thorn bush below the mighty bulk known as siwaSembuzi (the precipice of the goats) which, with the range of hills on the opposite side of the valley known as Khangelani (the lookout), watches over what is probably the most spectacular view in all Zululand.

On 19 June, a convoy of wagons was travelling from Stanger to Maphumulo. It ran into an ambush and one of the two European police escorts was killed. The second European, Sergeant Knox, escaped with a spear wound and ran the seven miles to Maphumulo to report.

Then the bloodshed began all over again in Natal. A party of Natal Mounted Riflemen rode out and found the wagons already looted. They followed the tracks of the raiders and surprised about 400 men at the kraal of chief Ndlovu ka Timuni. About 180 of the Africans were shot dead and the rest driven into the bush with their chief.

A whole series of outrages then took place in the jumbled mass of hills between the Mvoti and Thukela rivers. Stores were looted and traders killed. Several nasty tragedies took place. Oliver Veal, an official in the Public Works Department, was riding through the area on a push-bike and was captured near the Mvoti River. After a mock trial, he was killed and his body was hacked up for medicinal purposes.

The military force from the Nkandla forest was hurriedly transferred to the new trouble centre. The store at Thring's Post became the headquarters for operations. The army was rallied there by McKenzie from all troublefree centres. On 1 July a mixed supply column of 22 wagons under Major Campbell, escorted by 135 men and a dog, was making its way to the headquarters. The dog was an old black mongrel who had attached himself to the column and was under a sort of suspended sentence of death for worrying sheep.

About 7 p.m., when the hills were resting in the cool winds of evening, the column approached a corrugated-iron store known as Macrae's. As they passed the store, the dog stood still, ruffled his hair, and growled in the direction of a plantation on the right.

The soldiers became suspicious and prepared their weapons. Suddenly, a mass of about 900 Africans sprang out of the grass, with a noise like a flock of guineafowl rising. They charged forward, screaming out the familiar war cry: *"uSuthu! uSuthu!"* (the name of the royal faction in Zululand).

The soldiers poured volley after volley into the charging men. About 40 of the attackers were killed in three successive attempts to overwhelm the troops. Then they turned tail and fled. One soldier had been mortally wounded and the black dog had been shot dead by his own side while he was trying to return from barking at the ambuscade. After bivouacking for the night, the convoy reached Thring's Post safely the next day.

The principal chief involved in the new Natal rising was Meseni of the Qwabe tribe, whose kraal Mthandeni (the place of love), at the junction of the Mvoti and Nsuze rivers, was the rebels' principal stronghold. After a number of minor clashes, the army eventually launched an attack on this place on 3 July.

The kraal lay in a deep and rugged valley, with the renowned 2699-foot high bulk of isiThundu Mountain looking down in sombre silence on the doings of man. A day of hard fighting ended in the capture of the kraal. About 400 rebels were killed in the attack, and the mutilated body of the unfortunate Oliver Veal was found in the kraal. Meseni escaped into the bush, but the whole rising was soon over.

For ten more days the troops searched the bush of the Mvoti and Thukela river valleys, rounding up prisoners, killing a few rebels, and dispersing a resistance which never had much resolution. One after the other, the rebel leaders were wiped out. Matshwili and 547 of his followers were killed on 8 July in the ziNsimba (valley of genets), while the Thukela Valley was scoured in search of the elusive Meseni and Ndlovu. Both these chiefs, after hiding in the scenic wonderland below the siwaSembuzi (precipice of the goats), eventually slipped across the Thukela River and surrendered in Eshowe.

Courts-martial and gaol sentences marked the final end of a vicious little affair. Bambatha's much publicised rebellion had proved little more than an armed protest by a small section of the Natal Bantu and a few very minor groups in Zululand. Not more than 11 000 Africans had been involved in the risings. Of them about 2300 had been killed by the military, while 4700 received gaol sentences ranging from six months to two years. Twenty-five of the leaders were deported to the island of St Helena.

Sigananda died in the Nkandla gaol on 23 July and the whole affair would have ended with only a few stubborn souls hiding in the wildest parts of the country and an occasional murder such as that of the chief Sitshitshili, who had remained loyal to the government and was shot dead by an indignant rebel.

During the numerous trials implications were made against Dinuzulu. Especially was it said that, although he had taken no active part in the trouble and, indeed, had actually offered the use of his regiments to the government, he was in reality behind the whole movement. When Sitshitshili was murdered it was whispered that Dinuzulu was taking secret vengeance on all loyal chiefs and, when the officer in charge of investigating the murder, Sergeant Wilkingson, was fired upon through the window of his bedroom, strong police patrols were sent to Zululand.

Then, on 3 July, Bambatha's wife surrendered at Mahlabathini. To the interested police she reported that she had been sheltered all this time by Dinuzulu and had not been told that Bambatha was dead.

At Pietermaritzburg the woman told a long story to the authorities about how Dinuzulu had stimulated her husband into revolt. She told them of the two men he had given to

Bambatha as a sign of his support, and of his regiments being prepared for war and armed with guns smuggled in from Lourenço Marques.

Acting on this report, preparations were made to arrest Dinuzulu. Troops were concentrated at Gingindlovu and, on 3 December, martial law was proclaimed. The plan was to march the troops up to Dinuzulu's uSuthu kraal, but he forestalled them on 9 December by surrendering voluntarily at Nongoma. From there, he was sent to Maritzburg to stand his trial. Behind him, in Zululand, the military searched his uSuthu kraal. They found it to be but a dilapidated weed-grown place, with no rebels or arms to be found. About 400 guns were surrendered or found in all Zululand and, by the beginning of 1907, the only remaining rebels were a few diehards who had found a precarious sanctuary around the junction of the Black Mfolozi and Mbekamuzi rivers.

The preliminary examination of Dinuzulu started on 23 December and lasted seven months. He was then committed for trial on charges of high treason, public violence, accessory to murder, sedition and contravention of the Firearms Act.

His trial started on 3 November 1907 at Greytown. In the local town hall 95 witnesses appeared for the Crown and 68 for the defence, to the tune of 6148 pages of evidence.

Chakijana was tried first and given seven years' imprisonment. Jombolwana, tried for the murder of Sitshitshili, was sentenced to death. Dinuzulu, after a most careful trial lasting four months, on 3 March 1908, was found guilty of high treason on the grounds of harbouring Bambatha, his wife, and other rebels. He was found not guilty on all other counts but was sentenced to four years' imprisonment and a fine of £100.

He was deposed from his position as a government induna and district chief and his uSuthu kraal was dismantled. He was first imprisoned at Newcastle. Then, after Union, he was banished to the farm Rietfontein, eight miles from Middelburg in the Transvaal, where he was allowed to live a reasonably free life, on an allowance of £500 a year, paid to him for subsistence.

That was the end of the Bambatha Revolt; the misnamed, so-called Zulu Rebellion. It was but a sorry affair at best, which brought only fresh unhappiness to the very people who had used it as a sign of their own discontent. Like most wars, it righted no wrongs and did no good. It simply provided a release for all the pent-up resentments, frustrations and annoyances which had plagued the Natal Bantu for some time. With a variety of apparent oppressions in the shape of government, stock diseases and climatic troubles, they had simply selected the most tangible one to fight against – white authority – and had suffered grievous hurt in the process.

FORTY-ONE

Roads across the wilderness

Bambatha's rebellion was a notable point in the story of Natal and Zululand. In its tragic way it was the last stirring of the old times when all the country had been the hegemony of Shaka and his Zulu army and killing was the normal means of protest or punishment.

It was after the rebellion that civilisation finally replaced savagery in the affairs of the country. Isolated individuals – stalwarts of the old order – might continue to resist change but for the majority, the restless, moody giant of the wilderness was bound down ever more by barbed wire fences; by roads; by cultivation; and by signs reading "Trespassers will be prosecuted".

Repercussions of the Bambatha rebellion on Natal's domestic life were considerable. Apart from the alarm and financial cost of the military operations, the dislocation of commerce was a sad setback. General public dissatisfaction caused the downfall of the government in 1906 and F.R. Moor became the new Prime Minister charged with responsibility for restoring affairs to prosperity, and guiding Natal through the period of growing excitement about the idea of closer union which was to result in the formation of the Union of South Africa.

Several events of interest and importance occurred during

this period of transformation. In Zululand there were very significant changes. Probably the most important was the commencement of afforestation by both the government and private interests. As early as 1905 the Natal Government had established an experimental plantation at Empangeni. Eucalyptus and other trees were planted with such success that survivors still growing from that early experiment near Empangeni have reached a height of up to 180 feet.

Another trial plantation was started in 1914 at Port Durnford; again with such success that seven years later a vast afforestation scheme, mainly comprising eucalyptus, was commenced there. The success of pines, mainly of the *Caribaea* variety, gave still greater momentum to afforestation. One after the other, vast plantations were commenced. Kwambonambi and Dukuduku, both started in 1930, were two of these enterprises. Today all along the high rainfall area of the coast, there lie vast belts of green trees with forestry stations and sawmill settlements dotted along their length, like islands in a pleasant sea of cool shadows and whispering leaves.

Private enterprise followed in the lead of the government Forestry Department. Along the misty verges of the hills wattles were planted; dense green patchworks of trees, splashed with vivid yellow in the blossom season and sending such a perfume drifting through the air that the shade of old Zulu himself must surely sit up at times and take a sniff.

An extract factory was eventually opened at Melmoth in August 1926, to process the bark of the wattles, and the straggling little village found itself and its economy largely dominated by the trees and the men who grow and process them. As a culmination to the developing industry based on trees, large paper and rayon factories were built in 1952 at the place known as Mandeni, from the streamlet of that name where the *munde* trees (*Euphorbia tirucalli*) grow.

Mining also added its quota of interest to Zululand's economy. Such is the geological nature of the country that pockets of gold and other minerals and metals were constantly being discovered. In 1906, particularly, there was much excitement.

In March of that year A. Middleton discovered a reef which he named the Rebellion Reef, at the foot of the Ntumeni range, on the banks of the Matigulu River. Over 200 claims were pegged. Eshowe residents formed the New Year Syndicate to work their claims but, like most other strikes in Zululand, the reef petered out and left only disappointment behind.

Still, mining activity persisted. The Tugela Mining Syndicate was busy at Mfongosi in 1909 and tin was being mined at Melmoth in the same year, with some little success. Later, discoveries of asbestos and other base minerals also combined to keep the miners, if not happy, at least busy and eager for more.

Prospectors wandered through the country, exploring and re-exploring practically every square foot. Each man was a character, and one of the best known at this time was Old Man Bettinson. He was a large, shaggy specimen of his kind and had roamed, in his time, if not all over Zululand then at least into every pub.

One day Bettinson arrived at Melmoth in a state of great excitement. In the pub he told his cronies that he had found a natural spring of paraffin. He had been riding through rough country and, reaching what he took to be a pool of clear water, he had dismounted for a drink. Plunging his face into the pool, he had found it to be of a peculiar flavour, which he diagnosed as being natural paraffin.

There was some ribald comment at this. It was said by some that Bettinson had long ago forgotten what water tasted like. Maybe the pool was simply stagnant? Bettinson, however, stuck to his guns and his enthusiasm was infectious.

There and then, in the pub at Melmoth, the Bettinson Natural Paraffin Springs Company was formed, a chairman was elected, a board of directors appointed and Bettinson given 1000 vendor shares.

The next morning Bettinson set out to guide the shareholders to the spring. His associates were a rather short-tempered crowd following the night's celebration, and after riding for a while in the sun it did not pay for anyone to be facetious.

They picked their way for hours through heavy country,

climbing up and down ravines and plunging through thorny shrubs. As the day wore on the rosy hopes began to fade.

By midday, aspersions were being cast at old Bettinson. It was being said that he was unfamiliar with (a) the country, (b) paraffin and (c) the truth.

About 5 p.m. the old man confessed himself lost – and so was the party. There was a certain amount of bad language. They returned to Melmoth the next morning!

Another minor venture of the beginning of Zululand's new era was a persistent effort to exploit the wild rubber of the landophia vine. In the north the Zululand Rubber Co. was busy in the years before the First World War, and their perky little steam launch on Lake St Lucia was a familiar sight.

One source of persistent activity in Zululand came from the wrecks along the coast. Since the days of the Portuguese the shores of Zululand had been well littered with fragments of shipping disasters. Apart from the Portuguese, in more recent times such disasters had occurred as the wreck of the 401-ton German steamer *Emin*. Sailing from Durban to Lourenço Marques at the end of December 1891, this vessel vanished on the way and only scattered wreckage on the Zululand coast was ever found.

Three years later, at 1 a.m. on 28 January 1896, a 271-ton Portuguese-owned steamer named the *Saxon* was wrecked off Kosi Bay. Fortunately the night was calm and nobody was drowned.

The following year, on 16 October 1897, the 1375-ton *Clan Gordon* came to grief on the south end of the Tenedos Reef, off the Mlalazi river mouth. Again, fortunately, nobody was drowned. The master, Captain Wakeford, had his certificate suspended for three months.

The next year, 1898, saw one of the most remarkable wrecks ever known upon the coast of South Africa. On Monday night of 31 January 1898, an old, leaky tub named the *Dorothea* was abandoned at sea about five miles east of the ledge of rock known as Cape Vidal. The ship was a barque, recently bought in Lourenço Marques by a Doctor Kelly of Johannesburg and was being sailed down to Durban by a scratch crew under Captain H. Mathisson.

There was no loss of life, the vessel had just leaked itself into a sinking condition. The crew abandoned it in two boats and were picked up by passing steamers. The *Dorothea* drifted on to the shore and sank. That would have been the end of the matter, but soon a most sensational story was whispered around the world.

According to this story, the *Dorothea* was originally the *Ernestein*, which had first arrived in South African waters in 1896 with a general cargo from Hamburg. At Cape Town the ship had been found leaky. After discharging her, it was found that a cargo of acid had spilt out and eaten into her hull. She was repaired and then sold for £800 to a Mr Camp of East London, in order to defray expenses.

Camp sent her to the South Seas to carry a cargo of copra to Antwerp. Then she brought a cargo of Baltic railway sleepers out to Lourenço Marques. On entering the harbour, she struck a reef and the Captain had to run her ashore. There she was unloaded and then taken into the river, where she was sold for £75 to a Mr Pitt as a hulk.

For over a year she lay mouldering on the beach. Then a Johannesburg syndicate, headed by Doctor Kelly, bought her, ostensibly for fishing purposes. She was put under the American flag and renamed the *Dorothea*. A Captain Vibert patched her up and then she sailed for Durban, in order, so the syndicate announced, to be repaired.

But rumour told a different story from this public announcement. It was said that illicit gold buying on the Witwatersrand had been proceeding on a fantastic scale. The Johannesburg syndicate was heavily involved in this racket. The syndicate members had bought the ship in order to smuggle their loot out of the country, and some 120 000 ounces of gold were reported to have been concealed among the ballast in her holds.

This story soon produced results. Three months after the wreck, Captain Charles Gardiner, commander of the salvage ship *Alfred Noble*, sailed up to investigate the wreck on behalf of the Natal Government. He located it with its masts still above the water, but seasonal bad weather prevented him from doing anything about it.

Then, very furtively, in June 1899, an expedition was sent up the coast in a small steam fishing boat named the *Nidaros* and commanded by the same Captain Wakeford who had lost his certificate at the wreck of the *Clan Gordon*. The trip was financed by a syndicate of the original owners and some leading shipping men of Durban. A surfboat, diver and proper crew were provided.

The expedition found the wreck and, to the diver's intense excitement, he found some pigots of yellow metal lying among the timbers. Wild with excitement, he was hauled up and the pigots examined. They were found to be copper. Then, on a second visit, the salvage men lowered their surfboat and anchored it above the wreck. While they were working, however, a heavy sea struck the surfboat, capsized it, and four men were drowned, including the diver and Captain Wakeford.

The next month, on 25 July 1899 the tug *Hansa* commanded by the same Captain Vibert who had repaired the *Dorothea*, sailed hastily up the coast. An overland expedition had left a few days earlier to provide a shore party.

At the wreck, the *Hansa* lowered her surfboat but it was promptly capsized and lost. She returned to Durban for another boat but, back at the wreck, she found the weather too bad and abandoned her efforts until the next winter season, when the seas could be expected to be calmer.

The Anglo-Boer War came as an awkward distraction to the treasure seekers. Nevertheless, despite it, in December 1899, a small 29-ton vessel, the *Countess of Carnarvon*, was chartered by a syndicate headed by a Mr Hall. Captain J.P. Nansson commanded the vessel and good divers were employed, but again the results were disappointing. All the syndicate said they found were some curios, but the mere fact that something had been found kept men all down the coast dreaming of the *Dorothea*'s treasure, and syndicates were planned as far away as the sleepy little port of Kowie.

The next attempt came on 22 July 1901 when Captain George Vibert sailed up again, on a pocket-sized salvage steamer named the *Fenella*. Again the only result was disappointment, and seasickness for one of the policemen who had been sent up by the government to scrutinize the doings of the salvage group.

In 1903 the Honourable Thomas Hassall decided to make an attempt. He chartered the steam tug *Ulundi* and, with government support and an expert diver, he left Durban in December 1903. Again only failure resulted from the search.

Next to enter the lists came the small 247-ton coasting vessel, owned by C. Smith & Co. of Durban, and named the *Penguin*. On 13 August 1904, this hopeful little steamer sailed out, commanded by J. Jorgenson and with a well-fitted party on board led by a Scandinavian named C.E. Frees. Off the Mhlathuze the expedition encountered very heavy seas. The hatches were soon stove in and they were forced to abandon ship. Eleven men were drowned and the poor little *Penguin* went down eight miles from the shore, with all her diver's kit and stores. The survivors had a grim 40-hour battle without food and water in their open boats before they reached the beach.

The promoters of the *Penguin* expedition were not deterred by the disaster. At the end of October 1904 they sent a second ship, the *Good Hope*, up to Cape Vidal. A sizeable land party went up as well, and on the beach they erected two large marquees and several bell tents, while two divers worked from surfboats.

While they worked, a large company, the Dorothea Treasure Trove Syndicate, was launched in the Transvaal in December 1904. Sir Edward Murray was the chairman and a prospectus optimistically described the gold as consisting of 120 000 ounces, packed in twelve boxes and three leather bags, all placed at the foot of the foremast and covered with six inches of cement. Nothing of this treasure was ever reported as having been recovered by the company.

Many more companies came and went, the one optimistically following in the bankrupt path of the other. One of the largest was a £25 000 concern in 1906, styled the S.A. Salvage Co., which planned to salvage not only the *Dorothea* but also several other wrecks, through the medium of Captain Gardiner and his ship the *Alfred Noble*, which had, some years before, examined the site of the Cape Vidal lost treasure.

But the sea seemed to laugh at all these efforts, and the laughter was never more cynical than on 12 March 1908, when the 6242-ton *Newark Castle* was wrecked about three miles north of Point Durnford, while on the way to Lourenço Marques. Three people were drowned and the ship was abandoned.

The wreck was well above water, close to the shore and easy to reach. It was bought for £575 by the Johnstone Syndicate and it seemed that they had bought a bank.

Part of the cargo of the ship consisted of 750 000 five-rupee notes, being conveyed to Mauritius in six steel boxes. Two of these boxes were broken open in the wreck, and the Zululand beach for miles was littered with 250 000 of these notes. The syndicate salvaged the other four boxes, with £33 000 worth of notes, but the British Government promptly demonetised the banknote issue and the money had no value save for use as wallpaper.

So far as the *Dorothea* was concerned, as an almost last hope came the Dorothea Barque Treasure Trove Syndicate Limited of 1908. It was organised by one of the keenest of all the *Dorothea* salvage men, S.E. Hall. A crack diver named S. Abramson spent six weeks on the job at Cape Vidal around November 1908. He found nothing save wood and anchor chains, half buried in the sand.

The *Dorothea* still lies beneath the green waters at Cape Vidal, with nought save the wreckage of the companies, their rusting chains, poles and debris, lying on the rocks to mark the spot. Her anchor and chain, recovered by one of the salvage parties and left as a sign for others, lie there as well, but beyond that, and some broken human hopes, there is nothing to be found save solitude, and no sounds or movement save the wind and the birds and the waves on the beach.

Several notable events also occurred in Natal in the period after Bambatha's rebellion. Among these was the Glencoe Colliery disaster on 13 February 1908, when 12 Europeans and 63 Africans were killed in an explosion.

In the same year, 1908, political excitement over what was called the Closer Union movement reached a climax with the meeting of a national convention in Durban on 12 October, followed by a subsequent meeting in Cape Town when the Draft Act of Union was prepared.

There was inevitably much contention over such a far-reaching measure. The Natal Parliament approved of the draft, subject to amendments, on 30 April 1909; and on 10 June the matter was put before the electorate in the form of a referendum. At the count 11 121 people voted for acceptance of, and 3701 rejected the idea of Union.

Six days later, the Natal Parliament met to pass an address to the King, praying that the Act of Union might be put into force. On 21 September 1909 this Act received Royal assent, and so there was an end to the independent political life of Natal.

Thenceforth, the old Colony of Natal and its sister, Zululand, with their beautiful hills and golden beaches, merged their identity with the composite body of the Union. The romantic company of raiding Zulu armies, ivory traders, Voortrekkers, British settlers, and all the odd characters with their diverse personalities and fortunes have said their piece and one by one slipped silently to rest. All their hopes and schemes, their sacrifices and triumphs, were like tears upon a child's face, having lingered but a little while and then been lost in sleep.

Today Natal and Zululand remain as lovely as they ever were, and physically but little changed by all man's enterprise. Only that intangible spirit of the wilds in some places seems to have been driven away, and in its place the ten thousand hills are haunted ever more by countless phantoms of the past.

Select bibliography of works on Natal and Zululand

Ashe, W. 1880. *Story of the Zululand Campaign*
Baldwin, W. 1863. *African Hunting*
Barker, Lady M. 1877. *Year's Housekeeping in S. Africa*
Barter, C. 1852. *Dorp and Veld*
Barter, C. 1866. *Alone Among the Zulus*
Behn, M. 1932. "Klip River Insurrection" (Thesis)
Binns, C.T. 1963. *The Last Zulu King*
Bird, J. 1888. *Annals of Natal*
Bosman, W. 1907. *The Natal Rebellion*
Boteler, T. 1835. *Narrative of a Voyage*
Brooks, H. 1876. *Natal*
Brookes & Webb. 1965. *A History of Natal*
Bryant, A.T. 1929. *Olden Times in Zululand and Natal*
Bryant, A.T. 1949. *The Zulu People*
Buchanan, B. 1941. *Natal Memories*
Bulpin, T.V. 1961. *The White Whirlwind*
Bulpin, T.V. 1965. *Lost Trails of the Transvaal*
Burgess, A.S. 1934. *Unkulunkulu in Zululand*
Butler, Sir W. 1911. *Autobiography*
Campbell, E.D. 1951. *Birth and Development of Natal Railways*
Cheesman, E. 1946. *By the Roadside*
Chesson, F. 1879. *The War in Zululand*
Clements, W.H. 1936. *The Glamour and Tragedy of the Zulu War*
Colenso, F.E. 1880. *History of the Zulu War*
Colenso, J.W. 1855. *Ten Weeks in Natal*
Coupland, R. 1948. *Zulu Battle Piece*
Cox, Sir G.W. 1888. *Life of J.W. Colenso*
De Vos, P.J. 1945. *Dunns of Zululand*
Dobie, J.S. 1945. *South African Journal*
Drummond, W.H. 1875. *Large Game of South Africa*
Dunn, J. 1886. *Cetewayo and the Three Generals*
Durnford, E. 1882. *A Soldier's Life*
English, E.F. 1949. *Birth of a South African Village*
Eyre, C.J. 1932. *Dick King*
Fannin, N. 1932. *The Fannin Papers*

Feilden, E. 1887. *My African Home*
Francis, G.E. 1929. *Historical Ixopo*
Fynn, H.F. 1950. *Diary of H.F. Fynn*
Gandhi, M.K. 1927. *Autobiography*
Gandhi, M.K. 1928. *Satyagraha in South Africa*
Gardiner, A. 1836. *Narrative of a Journey to the Zoolu Country*
Gibson, J.Y. 1911. *The Story of the Zulus*
Gray, C.J. 1936. "Records of Early Search for Gold in Natal" (Thesis)
Grout, L. 1862. *Zululand*
Haggard, Sir H.R. 1888. *Cetywayo and his White Neighbours*
Hamilton, C. 1870. *Sketches of Life and Sport*
Hattersley, A.F. 1936. *More Annals of Natal*
Hattersley, A.F. 1938. *Pietermaritzburg Panorama*
Hattersley, A.F. 1938. *Later Annals of Natal*
Hattersley, A.F. 1940. *The Natalians*
Hattersley, A.F. 1950. *British Settlement of Natal*
Hattersley, A.F. 1951. *Portrait of a City*
Henderson, W.P. 1904. *Durban*
Holden, W.C. 1854. *History of the Colony of Natal*
Holden, W.C. 1866. *Past and Future of the Kaffir Races*
Holliday, J.D. 1890. *Dottings on Natal*
Holt, H.P. 1913. *Mounted Police of Natal*
Ingram, J.F. 1895. *The Colony of Natal*
Ingram, J.F. 1899. *The Story of an African Seaport*
Isaacs, N. 1836. *Travels and Adventures*
Kermode, W. 1882. *Natal*
Kirby, P.R. (ed.) 1955. *Andrew Smith and Natal*
Klein, H. 1955. *Winged Courier*
Kotze, J.D. (ed.) 1950. *Letters of the American Missionaries*
Krige, E.J. 1936. *Social System of the Zulus*
Kuper, H. 1960. *Indian People in Natal*
Leslie, D. 1875. *Among the Zulus and AmaTonga*
Lindley, A. 1872. *After Ophir*
Lloyd, W. 1881. *Defence of Eshowe*
Ludlow, W.R. 1882. *Zululand and Cetewayo*
Lugg, H.C. 1949. *Historic Natal and Zululand*
McIntyre, J. 1957. *Origin of Durban Street Names*
Mackenzie, P. 1946. *Pioneers of Underberg*
Mackeurtan, G. 1930. *Cradle Days of Natal*
Macmillan, W.M. 1937. *Durban*
Malherbe, J. 1965. *Port Natal*
Mason, G. 1855. *Life with the Zulus*

640

Mathews, J.W. 1887. *Incwadi Yami*
Mitford, B. 1883. *Through the Zulu Country*
Mohr, E. 1876. *To the Victoria Falls*
Molyneux, W.C. 1896. *Campaigning in South Africa*
Montague, W.E. 1880. *Campaigning in South Africa*
Moodie, D.C. 1886. *John Dunn*
Moodie, D.C. 1879. *History of the Battles*
Morris, D.R. 1965. *Washing of the Spears*
Nathan, M. 1937. *Voortrekkers of S. Africa*
Ndongeni. 1905. *Story of Dick King's Ride*
Newman, C.L. Norris. 1880. *In Zululand with the British*
Norbury, A. 1880. *Naval Brigade in South Africa*
Owen, Rev. F. 1926. *Diary*
Owen, W.F. 1833. *Narrative of Voyages*
Palmer, M. 1957. *Indians in Natal*
Plaisted. 1758. *Journal*
Powell, W.J. 1895. *Precis of Information*
Preller, G. 1920. *Voortrekker Mense*
Preller, G.S. 1937. *Andries Pretorius*
Ritter, E.A. 1956. *Shaka Zulu*
Roberts, B. 1965. *Ladies in the Veld*
Russell, G. 1899. *History of Old Durban*
Russell, R. 1903. *The Garden Colony*
Samuelson, L.H. 1928. *Zululand*
Samuelson, R.C. 1929. *Long, Long Ago*
Schimlek, F. 1953. *Mariannhill*
Shepstone, S.W. 1937. *History of Richmond*
Shields, C.S. 1939. *Life of John Dunn* (Thesis)
Shooter, J. 1857. *The Kafirs of Natal*
Shuter, C.F. 1963. *Englishman's Inn*
Slater, E. 1962. *Isipingo*
Smail, J.L. 1965. *Historical Monuments and Battlefields*
Smith, E. 1949. *Life and Times of D. Lindley*
Spender, H. 1916. *General Botha*
Stevenson-Hamilton, J. 1937. *South African Eden*
Stuart, J. 1913. *History of the Zulu Rebellion*
Theal, G. 1886. *Republic of Natal*
Theal, G. 1897. *Records of S.E. Africa*
Theal, G. 1922 *History of South Africa*
Trollope, A. 1878 *South Africa*
Van Warmelo, N.J. 1938. *History of Matiwane*
Vijn, C. 1880. *Cetshwayo's Dutchman*

Walker, E. 1948. *The Great Trek*
Walmsley, H.M. 1879. *Zululand*
Watson, R.G. 1960. *Tongaati*
Watt, E.P. 1962. *Febana*
Welch, S. 1946. *South Africa under King Manuel*
Welch, S. 1948. *South Africa under John III*
Willcox, A.R. 1956. *Rock Paintings of the Drakensberg*
Willcox, A.R. 1963. *Rock Art of South Africa*
Wood, A. 1962. *Natal Past and Present*
Wood, W. 1840. *Statements Respecting Dingaan*

Bird Collection, Natal Archives
Cape Almanac
Cape Mountain Club Annual
Daily Tribune
Davis Natal Directory
Huisgenoot, Great Trek Issue, 1938
Imperial Blue Books
Magisterial District Records
Natal Advertiser
Natal Agricultural Journal
Natal Mercury
Natal Mountain Club Annual
Natal Witness
South Coast Herald
Times of Zululand

Index

Active, HMS 379, 404
Adams, Dr N. 137, 177, 220, 229
Addison, R. 437, 438, 439, 441
afforestation 592, 631
Aiken brothers 544–546
Alexandra 517, 520, 523, 525, 526
Alfred County 540, 541, 546, 549, 550, 551, 557–561, 563, 564
Alfred, Prince 334, 540
Aliwal Shoal 510, 530, 531, 533, 535, 536
Alverstone 307, 313
Amanzimtoti 532, 534
Ambleside 524
Amphitheatre 460, 461, 467
Annabella 248
animals, game 10, 15, 71, 72, 87, 97, 245, 274, 479, 494, 568
apprentice system 208
Archbell, Rev. J. 204, 322, 351, 352
arrowroot 228, 486
Ashley 305
assassination attempts 110, 112, 421, 487
avocadoes 229

Babanango 58, 427
baboons 49, 264, 573
amaBaca 67
Baines, T. 344, 353, 365, 369
Baldwin, W. 261, 262, 268–274, 279, 288, 293
Balgowan 360
Bambatha 547, 615–618, 620, 623, 624, 627–630, 638
bananas 9, 228, 514, 564, 566
Banganomo 415, 418, 424, 430, 432, 439

Bantu 15, 16, 20, 29, 36, 41, 46, 139, 323, 367, 612, 613, 627, 629
Barker, Col 623
Barker, Lady 354
Barker, Rev. F.C. 333
Barracouta 77
Barter, C. 271, 352, 362, 445
Batstone's Drift 99, 104, 553
Bazley, J. 238, 522, 524, 527, 533, 547
Bazley, W. 524, 545, 547, 548, 550–552
beads 34, 43, 45, 49, 82, 83, 86, 119, 126, 149, 272, 290, 294, 297, 417
Beaulieu 237, 238
amaBedhlane Mountain 26, 29
Bees Kommando 183
Beje 96, 97, 99, 100, 115
Bele people 20, 63, 65, 104
Bellair 106, 303, 332
Berea 130, 139, 140, 244, 245, 289, 306
Bergtheil, J. 229, 234
Bezuidenhout, D. 151, 152, 156, 171, 212, 215, 468
Bezuidenhout's Pass 151, 222, 290, 450
Biggar, A. 140, 164, 169, 170, 173, 175
Biggar, R. 134, 163
Biggarsberg 137, 138, 170, 181, 448, 456, 490
bilharzia 11, 17, 324, 569, 573, 578
Binns, H. 601, 603
Bissett, Lt Col J. 335, 540, 541, 546, 552
Biyela people 19
umBizana 539

Blijde Vooruitzicht 144
Blinkwater Mountain 25
Blood River 172, 173, 182, 373,
    380, 381, 386, 406, 443, 452
Bloukrans 152, 163, 350, 364
Boboyi River 121, 122, 539, 541
Boers 142, 149, 154, 155, 169, 182,
    185, 209, 239, 285, 286, 295, 334,
    373, 428, 430, 432–436, 438, 442,
    450, 451, 549, 584, 587, 602
Boesmansrand 167, 176, 180
Bonaventura 42
Bongoza 173–175
Boshoff, J.M. 167, 189, 205, 361
Botanical Gardens 252
Boteler Point 78
Botha, L. 187, 434, 497
Botha, P.R. 187
Botha's Hill 187, 307, 332, 497
Boundary Commission 376, 380,
    436
Bowker, Col J.H. 303, 304
Braemer 558
Brazilia 194–196, 208, 209, 211
British Government 135, 137,
    145, 150, 168, 207, 208, 215, 219,
    322–324, 328, 331, 374, 436, 450,
    452, 571, 579, 582, 585, 597, 598,
    600, 614, 637
Bromhead, Lt 391
Brown, D. 595, 596
Brown, J. 164, 196
Bruheim, G. 570, 571, 579, 581,
    584
Bryant, Rev. J.C. 220
siBubulungu 24, 134
Buchanan, D. 227, 228
buffaloes 19, 25, 259, 262, 269
Bulawayo 57, 71, 84, 92, 93, 100
Buller, Lt Col 398, 399
Bulwer, Sir H.E. 331, 374, 505, 548
Bulwer 505
Bushman's River 166, 188, 222,
    225, 325, 326, 337, 350, 362, 476,
    477

Bushmen 11, 15, 16, 20, 29, 52,
    68, 99, 116, 134, 190, 215, 220,
    225–227, 325, 336–339, 361, 462,
    476, 498–500
Buthelezi people 19, 58, 93, 423
Byrne, J. 233, 234, 236, 237, 240,
    359
Byrnetown 238, 613
Cabane 103
Campbell, W. 486
Camperdown 308–310, 333
Cane, J. 89, 91, 99, 107, 112, 114,
    115, 118, 119, 121, 133, 138, 153,
    162, 163, 252
cannibals 65, 66, 70, 103, 137, 138,
    229, 302, 462
Cape Vidal 78, 633, 636, 637
Cascade Falls 357
Cathedral Peak 471, 472, 476
Cathkin 242, 338, 462
Cathkin Peak 462, 472–476
cattle rustling 220, 451, 502, 558
Cato, G. 187, 196, 200, 202, 247,
    250, 255, 306, 307, 312, 515
Cato Manor 306
Cato Ridge 307, 308
Cawood brothers 121, 123
kwaCekwane 29, 65
Cele people 25, 68, 69
Celliers, C. 169, 170–172
Centaur 42, 43
Cetshwayo 185, 278, 280, 281,
    283–288, 291, 366, 367, 369,
    370–373, 375–378, 388, 390, 397,
    398, 400, 401, 406, 408, 410, 411,
    414, 415, 418, 419, 421–429, 451,
    482, 618, 619, 623
Ceza Mountain 439–441
Champagne Castle 473–475
Champion, Rev. G. 137–139
Chard, Lt 391
Charlestown 457
Charters, Maj. 168, 169, 175, 245
Chelmsford, Lord 379, 382–385,
    387–390, 393–396, 401–409
Chunu clan 19, 64–66

Cindaneni people 28
Clairwood 515
Clan Gordon 633, 635
Clansthal 519, 536
Cloete, Commissioner H. 218, 224
Cloete, Lt Col A.J. 204–207
coaches 312, 314, 315, 333, 455, 456, 501
coal 8, 177, 182, 214, 330, 339, 340, 363, 448–450, 453, 454–457, 482, 483, 527, 574, 596, 599, 608, 609
coffee 82, 185, 228, 254, 293, 303, 317, 486, 487, 489, 515, 541, 546
Colenbrander, J. 418–420, 424, 425, 430, 431, 435
Colenbrander, T.C. 305, 606
Colenso 181, 331, 364
Colenso, Bishop J.W. 252, 319–321, 327, 328, 331, 376, 442, 483, 554
Collis, J. 116, 117, 127, 130, 135, 214
Collison, F. 213, 232, 233
Comet 164
Committee of Dinuzulu's Volunteers 429
Compensation 241, 482, 483, 487, 490
Conch 203, 204
Congella 89, 169, 178, 197, 198, 202, 205, 302
Coode, Sir J. 249
Coope, Col W.J. 574–576
cotton 229, 230, 235, 480, 487, 489, 503, 524, 555, 573, 590
Coventry, W. 464–466
Cowan, Dr 50
Cowie, Dr A. 112–114
Cowie, W. 165, 176, 194, 203
Crealock, Maj. Gen. 404, 406
Creighton 504
crocodiles 10, 24, 61, 70, 264, 269, 273, 293, 501, 517, 519, 521, 522, 527, 565–567, 569, 573, 592, 599, 606
Curry's Post 359, 361

Da Gama, Vasco 30, 31, 49
Dabulamanzi 389, 391, 393, 402, 403, 432, 435
Dalton 242, 510
Dambuza 129, 146, 180–182
Danskraal 181
Dargle 242, 340
Darke, G. 418, 425, 435
Darnall 494
isiDawane 296
De Beer's Pass 151, 222
De Pass, D. 515, 516
De Natalier 216, 218, 227
Debe people 25, 26, 28, 46, 64, 69
Defiance 524
De Lange, J.H. (Hans) 174, 178, 223, 265, 445–448
Delegorgue, A. 177, 181, 182, 185
Delimitation Commission 603, 605, 609
Denny-Dalton Syndicate 594
Depression 331, 335, 340, 450, 455, 525–528, 535, 553
deserters 132, 139
Dingane 57, 69, 108–113, 115, 117–125, 127–132, 134, 136–140, 142, 143, 145–150, 152, 153–156, 159, 160, 163, 166, 167, 169, 172, 173, 175–184, 186, 188, 189, 212, 280, 287, 295, 372, 449, 468, 487, 568, 572
Dingiswayo 50, 51, 54–56, 58, 59, 63, 419
Dinuzulu 428–430, 432, 435, 437–442, 452, 453, 601, 613, 616, 617, 627, 628
Dlamini 16, 20
Dlanyoka 25
Donnybrook 504, 506
Doonside 534, 535
Doornkop 152, 158, 493
Dorothea 557, 633–635, 637
Drakensberg Mountain 8–11, 20, 21, 26, 39, 63, 68, 69, 99, 113, 123, 125, 134–137, 139, 142–146, 150–154, 160, 165, 167, 187, 188, 190,

195, 210, 213, 216, 219, 220, 222–224, 226, 242, 290, 325, 326, 331, 336, 337, 339, 361–365, 371, 381, 445, 450, 456–461, 463–467, 469–477, 479, 493, 500–505

Dronkvlei 29, 65, 504

Drummond, W.H. 260, 262, 274–277, 307

Dube, J. 492

Duff, T. 257, 288, 289, 486

Dukuduku forest 23, 426, 442, 596, 631

Dukuza 105–107, 110, 112, 487, 611, 620

Dumisa 68, 347, 348

Dundee 181, 449, 453, 454, 456, 601

Dunn, J. 280–285, 291, 292, 303, 368, 369, 372, 373, 377, 378, 383, 403, 414–417, 419–421, 423, 428, 431, 435, 599, 605

Durban 24, 30, 36, 42, 117, 132, 135, 150, 176, 179, 202, 244–255, 401, 411, 412, 454–457, passim

Durban Bay 8, 201

Durban Bluff 9, 38, 335

Durban harbour 9, 203, 245, 246, 248, 546

Durban lagoon 41, 67, 606

Durnford, Col A.W. 374, 376, 377, 388, 389, 390, 395, 477

Eastwood, C. 589

Eckersley, J. 418, 425, 430

elections 322, 597, 598

elephant hunting 68, 92, 100, 115, 116, 261, 265, 293

elephant tusks 43, 84, 99

Elizabeth and Susan 102, 106, 112

Emberton 306

Emmaus 463, 469

Emin 633

Empangeni 71, 131, 287, 436, 610, 631

entertainment 118, 128, 155, 189, 251, 253, 319, 324, 365, 463, 498

Escombe 304

Escombe, H. 304, 600, 601

Eshowe 53, 60, 71, 131, 287, 376, 386, 396, 398, 402–404, 423, 426, 427, 431, 435, 436, 438, 442, 581, 582, 601, 605, 627, 632

Espero 537

Estcourt 152, 362–364, 445, 463, 469, 589

Eugenie, Empress 312, 434

executions 84, 111, 147, 156, 184, 253, 285, 293, 381, 447, 448

Fafa River 341, 515, 522, 533

Fairfield 539

Farewell, Lt G.F. 79, 81, 83–92, 98, 107, 112, 114, 115, 117, 118, 214

Fascadale 555

Ferreira, J. 452, 572, 575, 587

fever, malarial 286, 573

Fidia de Genoa 531

Field, W.S. 250

first fruits ceremony 137, 295, 372

flying glider 358

Fort Napier 212

Fort Nottingham 337, 339, 498

Fort Pearson 379

Fort Tenedos 385

Fort Thinta 387, 397

Foxon, C.C. 585, 586

Fraser, Maj. 588, 621, 622

Frere, Sir B. 374, 376, 378, 380, 381, 383

Fugitives' Drift 391

Fumos 381, 570

Fynn, D. 122, 550

Fynn, Frank 120, 121

Fynn, H.F. 79, 81–92, 95, 98–102, 104, 105, 107, 112, 113, 117, 119, 120–122, 283, 357, 423, 425–427, 514, 517, 614

Fynn brothers 112, 115, 119–122, 539

Gandhi, M.K. 492, 493, 600, 601

Garden Castle 134, 476

Gardiner, Capt. A.F. 127–132, 140, 143, 145, 146, 149, 159, 164, 250, 359, 476
Gasa 21, 22, 60, 62
Gatslaager 166, 167
Ghost Mountain 22, 62, 432, 433
Giant's Castle 11, 21, 136, 326, 474, 476–478
Gibbs, Lt C.J. 220
Gillitt, W. 306, 307
Gingindlovu 283, 284, 403, 628
Glencoe 456, 600, 638
Glyn, Col 384
gold 73, 305, 311, 339–348, 353, 363, 475, 491, 508, 509, 594–596, 634
Golden Valley 343, 347
Golela 572
Good Hope 41, 42, 636
Grandier, E. 399, 400
Green, B. 113, 114, 125
Greyling, A. 144, 151, 152, 176
Greytown 344, 378, 496, 497, 506–509, 511, 615–617, 628
Grosvenor 89
Grout, Rev. A. 137, 220, 296
Groutville 220, 448
Gun Drift 540
gunrunners 371, 377, 501, 502, 558
Gwayi people 28

Hamilton, C. 334, 514, 515
Harding 534, 542, 547, 557, 559, 560
Harding, W. 218, 221, 225, 229
Harry Mundahl 556
Havelock, Sir A. 347, 571
Hector 524
Hermannsburg 497
Hewetson, Rev. H. 162
Hhamu 368, 397, 399, 400, 415, 418, 420, 421, 423, 425, 429, 430
Hibberdene 536
Highflats 503, 614
Hillary, J. 303

Hill Crest 306, 307
Hilton 350, 351
Hime, Lt Col A.H. 502, 505, 603
Himeville 505, 506
Hippopotami 115, 517
Hlambamanzi (Jacob) 80, 85, 118
Hlabisa 442
umHlangakhulu 523, 539
umHlangeni 538
Hlathikhulu 184, 448, 572, 582
Hlobane 398, 434, 453, 565
Hlogoma 505
Hlongwa people 24, 67–69, 519
Hlophekhulu 440, 441
Hlubi tribe 20, 50, 63, 325–327, 415, 416, 423, 431
Hluhluwe River 269, 289, 291
Hodgson, T. 500, 501
Hodgson's Peak 135, 501
Hogg, P. 200, 265, 266, 274, 292, 293
Holkrans 602
Holstead, T. 89, 90, 112, 118, 134, 146, 149, 155
Homeward Bound 553
horse races 252
Household, J.G. 358, 359, 594
Howick 352–358, 360, 363, 510
Howick Falls 28, 352, 356, 357, 363
Hulett, L. 489, 596, 609

Ilanga Lase Natal 492
Illovo 42, 516, 529, 532
immigration 168, 222, 231, 233, 234, 242, 307, 362, 548–600
iNanda 26, 271, 493
Inchanga 307
Indian Opinion 493
Indians 333, 484, 485, 492, 600
Indigo 228, 305, 488
Ingwavuma 583
iron mining 73, 74, 331
Irons, W.J. 234
Isaacs, N. 90, 92, 93, 98, 99, 106, 107, 112, 115–118, 120, 214

Ivanstan 564
ivory 37, 41, 76, 79, 89–92, 97, 99, 118, 118, 192, 228, 268, 290, 569, 573
Ivy 543, 560
Ixopo 28, 503, 504, 511, 614

Jacobs, H. 329, 335
Jargal, H. 229, 252
Jervis, Capt. H. 175, 176
Jobe 49, 64, 137, 138, 142, 143, 170, 181, 226
Job's Kop 65, 138, 143
Johanna 41
Julia 79, 81, 82, 88–90

ukangel' amaNkengane 89
Karkloof 28, 234, 331, 357–361, 499
Karkloof Falls 357, 358
Karoo system 8
Karridene 535
Keate, R.W. 335
Kearsney 489
Kelso 536
Kerkenberg 144, 150
Kettlefontein 188, 350
uKhahlamba Mountains 460
eKhambathini 26
Khandandlovu 539
kwaKhangela 131
umKhobi 539
iKhotshwana 523
Khoza, Ntshingwayo 385
Khumalo people 19, 96
King, R. (Dick) 125, 134, 135, 159, 164, 169, 200, 201, 203, 250, 514
King, Lt J.S. 79, 80, 81, 90–92, 94, 98, 100, 106, 116, 159, 214
King's Rest 533
King's Way 514
Klip River 20, 223, 224, 325, 444, 445, 448, 483
Klip River Republic 443, 444
Kosi lakes 38, 567, 574, 575, 592
Kranskop 48, 61, 162, 163, 181, 466, 507, 511

labour 323, 325, 328, 369, 484, 600
Ladysmith 181, 350, 351, 445–447, 450, 455, 457, 603
lala palms 9, 564, 566, 568–570, 573, 578
Lala people 16, 22–25, 29, 30, 49, 51, 67, 73, 74, 343, 359, 617
land grants 330, 429, 437, 451
Landman, C. 164, 173–175, 206
Langalibalele 19, 325–328, 331, 477, 478, 597
Langeni people 22, 52, 53, 57, 58, 120
Leading Star 546
Leathern, Wild Bill 311, 312
Legislative Council 322, 323, 330, 331, 360, 532, 547, 597, 598
eLenge Mountain 65
leopards 157, 237, 264, 309, 396, 477, 521, 611
Leslie, D. 294–301, 366
Levant 192
Leven 77, 78
Lidgett, J. 234
lighthouses 335, 512, 533, 536
Lindley, Rev. D. 141, 177, 319
lions 135, 197, 259, 261–263, 270, 272, 297, 318, 401, 415, 568
Lister, W. 228
locations 217, 220, 323–325, 328
locusts 455, 592, 612
Lourenço Marques 33, 34–41, 43, 51, 77–79, 81, 93, 100, 113–115, 120, 139, 203, 211, 215, 265, 290, 299, 330, 456, 457, 555, 566, 569, 571, 572, 575, 584, 586, 591, 628, 633, 634, 637
Lovu River 68, 220, 237, 529, 536
Lubombo 8, 17, 20, 21, 40, 113, 183, 266, 274, 290, 372, 432, 436, 565, 566, 568, 572, 575, 579–584, 587, 592
Luneberg 380, 397
Luthuli people 24, 82, 516

Mabasos 19, 568
Macingwane 64, 65
MacMahon award 571
Madikane 65
magistracies 221, 436, 494, 496, 581
Magudu 21, 182, 437
kwaMagwaza 287, 410
abakwaMagwaza people 22
Mahlabathini 184, 370, 442, 602, 618, 627
Makhasana 569, 570
uMakhosi 523
Malandela 17, 568
Malangeni 24, 521
Malvern 303, 304, 332
Mandeni 609, 631
kwaMandlakazi 415
Mangethe 285, 382, 383, 416, 605
mangoes 229
eMangweni 52, 278, 283, 284, 286, 410
aManzamtoti 105, 220, 516, 527
Maphumulo 68, 494, 614, 625
Maphutha 569, 571, 586, 589, 590
marble 540, 541, 543, 544, 546, 547, 554, 555
Marburg 104, 542, 549, 553, 558, 560
Marcus Road 417, 572, 573, 595
Margate 561, 562, 563
Margate monster 561, 562, 564
Mariannhill 307, 308
Maritz, G. 151, 152, 158, 159, 160, 167, 176
Maritzlaager 166, 167
Markham, F. 344, 508
Mary 79, 90, 93, 159
Mashonengashoni 442
Matabele 123, 138, 140, 142, 159
Mathambo 281
Matigulu River 22, 53, 132, 177, 284, 404, 610, 632
Matiwane 58, 63, 467, 468
Matyana 325

Mauritius 228, 241, 250, 332, 480–482, 637
Mazeppa 177, 199, 200, 202
eMbabe 436, 574
Mbazwana 592
Mbekamuzi 93, 265, 628
Mbilini 379, 381, 397–400, 451, 452
Mbilo 8, 76, 82, 197, 305, 332
eMbo 16, 20–22, 25, 29, 49, 506
abakwaMbonambi people 23, 24
Mbubu 28
Mbulazi 278, 280, 281, 283, 287, 288
Mbulwana 444
eMbumbulu 494
McCallum, Sir H. 335, 534
McCorkindale, A. 488, 489
McKenzie, Lt Col D. 613, 614, 618–620, 623–625
Mdloti River 26, 68, 69, 87, 184, 222, 229, 234, 480, 481, 492, 494
Mdumezulu 67, 135, 487
Melmoth 60, 436, 631–633
Merebank 527
Methven, C.W. 249, 606, 607
Meyer, L. 237, 432, 434, 453
uMfazazane 523
amaMfengu people 67
Mfolozi River 37, 54, 106, 269, 367, 595
Mfolozi River, Black 23, 109, 183, 260, 268, 424, 429, 628
Mfolozi River, White 23, 59, 106, 173, 174, 184, 387, 408–410, 618
Mfongosi 344–347, 508, 509, 632
Mfume 141, 340
Mgazini people 19, 423
Mgungundlovu 110, 112, 127, 128, 134, 139, 140, 143, 145, 146, 152–154, 172, 175, 176, 178, 184
Mhlali 69, 178, 383, 482
Mhlanga 486, 491
uMhlangakhulu 523, 539
Mhlangana 108, 110
Mhlangwa 342, 343

Mhlathuzana 67, 188
Mhlathuze River 17, 22, 32, 37, 53,
  57, 60, 61, 74, 84, 138, 286, 289,
  405, 416, 441, 605, 609, 610, 636
Mhlungwa 536
Mhome 426, 427, 611, 617, 620,
  623, 624
Mid-Illovo 506
Milne, J. 248
Minerva 238
mining 311, 344, 348, 449,
  453–455, 457, 483, 490, 508, 535,
  594, 595, 608, 631, 632
Minnetonka 336
missions 132, 137–141, 147, 177,
  201, 220, 279, 287, 375, 386, 456,
  457, 494, 519, 591
Mitchell, Sir C. 456, 457
Mjilo people 28
Mkhomazi River 28, 35, 39, 67,
  116, 135, 201, 222, 336, 338, 340,
  347, 474, 500, 501, 503, 516, 526,
  528, 530, 532, 545
Mkhumbane 18, 52, 56, 57, 71,
  110, 435
Mkhuphane 73
Mkhuze River 78, 182, 271, 432,
  572, 574
Mlalazi River 22, 98, 287, 367, 405,
  406, 633
Mnambithi see Klip River
Mngababa 141, 516, 527
Mngeni River 25, 28, 64, 69, 180,
  202, 252, 302, 331, 351, 483, 506
Mngomezulu clan 183, 574, 575,
  580, 581, 590
Mnyamana 93, 368, 398, 410, 418,
  420, 423, 429, 440
Mocke, F.G. 210
Mona River 410
Moncrieff, R.H. 462, 463
kwaMondi 287, 385, 386
Mont-aux-Sources 459, 460, 461,
  464–469
Moodie, D. 218, 324

Mooi River 21, 67, 222, 242, 358,
  360, 363
Moor, F.R. 35, 319, 630
Moordspruit 158
Moreland, J. 233, 237, 489
Morleys Bank 78
Morewood, E. 204, 229, 480–487,
  493
Mosi swamp 566, 590
mosquitoes 11, 23, 78, 113,
  268–271, 286, 300, 570, 578
Mount Edgecombe 486, 493
Mount Sargeaunt 25
Mountain Club 465, 466
Moyeni 416, 605
Mozambique Current 8, 9
Mpande 177–184, 212, 213, 223–
  225, 256, 266, 278–280, 285–287,
  295, 366, 380, 381, 447–451, 482
Mpandleni 618, 619
Mpaphala 24
Mpendle 499, 501, 506
Mphambanyoni River 29, 105,
  201, 341, 519, 526, 541
Mphanza 615
Mpofana River 21, 222
Mqangqatho 71
uMsigazi 342
Msonginyathi River 25
Msuluzi 152
Msunduze 22, 26, 70, 132, 334, 482
Mtentweni 523, 524, 556
Mthamvuna River 29, 48, 526,
  539, 540, 557, 558
Mthethwa people 50–56, 58, 419
Mthonjaneni 18, 57, 60, 173, 368,
  408, 409, 436, 437
Mthubuthubu 596
Mthunzini 416
Mthwalume 525, 533, 608
Mthwalume River 68, 340–342,
  522, 524
Mtshezi River 21, 152
uMtshitshiwana 530
Munster 560

Murchison 541, 542, 558
Mvoti River 25, 125, 178, 222, 225, 625, 626
Mweni 470, 471
Mzilikazi 96, 115, 122, 123, 145, 146, 150, 153
uMzimayi River 523, 532
Mzimkhulu River 29, 35, 39, 89, 105, 123, 502, 514, 533, 544, 552
Mzinto River 40, 342, 520, 526, 531
Mzinyathi River 19, 20, 50, 341
Mzumbe 67, 103, 341, 523, 524, 533, 537, 541

Natal Government 365, 450, 464, 549, 609, 618, 631, 635
Natal Parliament 638
Natal Table Mountain 28, 70
iNamfu River 522
iNanda 26, 271
Nandi 52–55, 100–102, 105
Napier, Sir G. 168, 179, 189, 190, 207, 208, 214–216
Natal Cotton Co. 229
Natal Mercury 251, 309, 484, 518, 542, 544
Natal Witness 226, 227, 322, 333, 481, 508
Natalie 518, 519, 524, 528
native policy 323
Ncandu 448
Ncapayi 190, 191, 193
Ncome River 170
Ndabankhulu 106
Ndaka River 20
Ndesingane 522
uluNdi 370, 373, 379, 383, 384, 386, 395, 398, 400, 404, 409, 411, 422, 423, 425, 430, 435, 437, 440, 460
oNdini 410, 430, 448, 460
Ndlela 110, 138, 146, 160, 182, 183
Ndlovini people 26
Ndondakusuka 163, 181, 280, 281, 283, 288, 294, 295

Ndongeni 200, 201
Ndumo 569, 590
Ndwandwe people 21, 58–63, 95, 96, 102, 437, 438
isaNdlundlu 120, 121
Ndwedwe 494
Nebo 530, 531
Nelsrust 237, 614
New Gelderland 488
New Germany 230, 254, 306
New Republic 434, 435, 441, 453
Newark Castle 637
Newcastle 449, 456, 457, 628
Newdigate, Maj. Gen. 406
newspapers 140, 194, 223, 239, 248, 254, 290, 303, 322, 331, 361, 375, 376, 456, 466, 522, 545, 588, 612
Ngagane 448
Ngcobo 24
Ngcwanguba 104
Ngeli
Ngilanyoni 506
Ngogo 448, 503
Ngoje 425
iziNgolweni 122, 557, 559
Ngome forest 19, 96, 100, 115, 411, 415, 418, 424, 572
Ngotshe 425
Ngoye forest 285
Nguni people 16, 17, 19, 22, 29, 49
Ngwanase 570, 572, 583–585
Ngwaneni people 19, 63, 65, 467–471, 568
Ngwanyane River 20
Ngwavuma River 113, 183, 184, 290, 572, 583, 584, 586, 587, 589, 591, 602
Nhlanyanga valley 138, 143
Nhlazatshe Mountain 18, 415, 435
Nieuwejaars Spruit 175
Njambili River 48, 49, 104, 162, 523
Njesuthi River 21, 64, 475
Njilo people 26
Nkambule (battle) 400–401

Nkandla (district) 436, 618, 624
Nkandla forest 60, 74, 426, 427,
    611, 612, 617, 619, 624, 625
Nkhomba 521
kwaNkosinkulu 18
Nkulwini 25
Nkwenkwe 18
No-Man's-Land 539, 540
Nodwengu 285, 289, 367, 370,
    372, 385, 398
kwaNodwengu see Nodwengu
kwaNogqaza 28, 188, 351
kwaNomnyali 99
Nomsimekwana 70
Nondweni 347, 407, 594, 595
Nongalazi 163
Nongoma 439, 440, 442, 628
Nongqayi 423, 438
Nonoti River 68, 488, 489
Noord 43
Northdene 332
Norwegians 279, 375, 386, 548,
    549, 550, 551, 553, 558, 609
Nossa Senhora da Atalaya 40
Noziyingili 300, 570
Nsimbini 99, 122
Nsuze 74, 594, 620, 626
Ntaba Khathazo 408
Ntabakayikhonjwa see Blinkwa-
    ter Mountain
Ntambo people 28
Ntlangwini people 67, 116, 135,
    325
Ntaba Ntlenyana 474
Ntlozi people 23
Ntsaba 557
Ntshele people 28
Ntshingwayo 385, 388, 389, 425
Ntumeni 402, 632
Nunn, H. 418, 489
Nyakamubi 107
Nyamvu people 25
Nyasane people 29
Nyavu people 26, 27, 70
Nyawo clan 183, 184, 572, 574,
    575, 580, 581, 590

Nyezane 376, 385, 404
Nyoni 605
Nzimakwe people 29
Oakford 492
Octopus 249, 491
Oftebro, Rev. O. 287
Ogle, H. 82, 89, 91, 112, 115, 121,
    133, 135, 162–164, 169, 202, 212,
    337, 514
Ohlange Institute 492
Ohrig, G.G. 194, 195
Olivier, A. 462, 464
Oliviershoek 464, 469, 477
Oribi Flats 558, 559
Osborn, M. 419, 421, 423, 430, 432,
    436, 438–441, 594
Otto's Bluff 65, 506
Owen, Capt. W.F. 77, 79, 81, 139,
    140, 145–147, 149, 150, 153, 155,
    156, 159, 162, 591
Park Rynie 520, 530–533, 536, 537
Parsons, G.R. 340, 341, 343
passes 10, 142, 143, 151, 167, 188,
    456, 477
pawpaws 228, 303
Pearson, Col 379, 384–386, 396,
    402
Penguin 556, 636
Pennington 521, 588
Perestrelo, M. 35, 38
Pescaria 36, 38
oPhathe 173
Phoenix 486
Phoenix settlement 492, 493
isiPhofu 29
Pholela River 502
Phongolo River 20, 21, 40, 113,
    138, 182, 183, 266, 273, 274, 285,
    290, 297, 298, 381, 436, 437, 451,
    465, 566, 570, 572, 580, 585, 586,
    588, 589, 590, 592
Pietermaritzburg 28, 180, 183,
    176–180, 187–191, 195, 208–212,
    221–229, 223, 316–321, 349, 419,
    442, 444, 511

pilchards 512, 513
pineapples 228, 560
Pine, Sir B. 305, 322, 328, 445, 522
Pinetown 245, 305, 306, 313, 332, 486, 488
Point, the 9, 90, 169, 197, 200, 202, 204, 205, 236, 241, 246, 329
Point Durnford 78, 637
poll tax 612, 613, 615
Pondos 29, 30, 43, 64, 88, 89, 91, 103–105, 121, 123, 124, 136, 191, 192, 523
Pont, C. du 576, 578, 579
population 40, 41, 51, 71, 134, 169, 223, 225, 230, 232, 242, 243, 251, 253, 305, 311, 318, 324, 339, 364, 447, 454, 455, 493, 495, 525, 541, 549, 557, 566, 602, 604, 615
Port Durnford 405, 406, 410, 411, 422, 423, 598, 599, 607, 631
Port Natal 79, 81, 83, 84, 87–100, 102, 106, 107, 109, 112, 114, 117, 126, 130, 132, 141, 143, 144, 154, 168, 169, 175, 177, 187, 192, 194, 195, 232, 236, 480
Port Edward 560
Port Shepstone 357, 532–534, 536, 540, 545–557, 559, 563
Portuguese 32, 35–39, 51, 100, 113, 120, 124, 571, 573, 576, 579–586, 633
Potgieter, H. 151, 152, 160, 161, 164, 360
Prehn, W. van 305
Pretorius, A. 167, 169, 170, 173, 175, 182, 183, 189, 190, 193, 197, 198, 204, 205, 211, 496
Prince Imperial 312, 405, 406, 434
prospectors 340, 342, 344, 346, 347, 363, 491, 593–595, 603, 632

abaQulusi people 420, 421
Qwabe people 18, 22, 24, 50, 60, 114, 118, 286, 626

railways 329, 330, 533
Ramsgate 561

Rathbone, E.F. 228, 481, 482, 497, 549
Rathbone, J. 280
Rathbone's Road 437, 438
rebellion 477, 478, 505, 547, 615, 627, 629, 630, 632, 638
religious squabbles 319, 321
Renishaw 527
Rensburg Spruit 158
Responsible Government Party 596–598, 601, 606
Republic of Natal 179, 180–193, 207
Retief, P. 143–146, 148–154, 156, 157, 159, 160, 172, 173, 176, 181, 182, 187, 212, 214
Réunion Island 228, 481
Reynolds, L. 369, 517, 527, 542
rhinoceros 99, 258, 273, 367
Rhodes, Cecil & Herbert 503
Richards Bay 405, 406
Richards, Com. F.W. 402, 405
Richmond 237–239, 501, 506, 522, 613, 614
rinderpest 598, 601, 605, 612
Rio de Medaos do Ouro 37
Rio de Natal 41–44, 76, 80
Robinson, G.E. 251, 528
Robinson, J. 597, 598, 600
Rorke's Drift 285, 376, 387–389, 391, 394, 451, 572
Ross, J. 100
Rowland's Macassar oil 102, 107
rubber 588, 589, 609, 633

iSabuyazwi 72
Sacramento 40
Saint Albert 39, 40
Saint Benedict 35, 38
Saint Jerome 31, 32
Saint John 31, 32, 34–36, 40, 45
Saint John the Baptist 40
Saint Lucia, Lake 23, 37, 38, 78, 79, 213, 266, 268, 270, 271, 274, 292, 405, 434, 565, 589, 593, 606, 633
Saint Thomas 38

Salisbury 79
Salisbury Island 159, 164, 200
Sambane 184, 372, 572, 575,
    578–579, 582
Sand River 20
sandstone 7–11, 63
Sarah Bell 245
sardines 204, 236, 402, 512, 513
Sarnia 305
Saunders, C.R. 572–574, 580–584,
    604
Saxon 633
Scott, J. 322, 519
Scottburgh 105, 519, 520, 528, 529,
    531, 535–537
Schreuder, Rev. H.P.S. 279
Sea View 197, 281, 302, 303
Seluku people 24
siwaSembuzi 625
Sentinel 460, 465, 466
iSezela 522
Shaka 7, 9, 52–65, 67, 69–75, 77,
    78, 80, 82–89, 91–112, 115, 146,
    148, 192, 214, 221, 278, 342, 364,
    421, 423, 438, 467, 468, 488, 491,
    493, 521, 523, 619, 630
Shaka's Kraal 488, 491, 493
Shwawu people 28
Shelter Falls 357
Shembe, I. 493
Shepstone, T. 175, 218, 220, 221,
    223, 244, 245, 340, 369, 370, 372,
    373, 376, 380, 381, 423
shields 72, 85, 115, 128, 129
eShongweni 69
eShowe 286
Sibaya, Lake 8
iSibayi 567
Sibiya people 19, 423
Sidoyi 325
Sigananda 426, 617–620, 623, 624,
    627
Sigonyela 143, 149, 151–154
Sihayo 378, 381, 384, 415
silver 73, 340, 359, 509

Siphingo River 9, 69
Sir Robert Peel 339
Sitimela 419, 420
slaving 41, 115
Smellekamp, J. 194, 195, 208, 211,
    215
Smit, E. 150, 186, 319
Smith, Dr A. 122–124
Smith, Sir H. 226, 250, 445
Smith, P. 449, 453, 454
Smith, Shoe 543, 544, 558
Smith, Capt. T. 191, 192, 196–204,
    206, 217, 514
Smythe, C.J. 612
Sobantu 319, 554, 556
Sodwana Bay 39, 371, 576–578
Sokana people 23
Somkhele 419, 426, 431, 437, 438,
    440, 442, 595, 599, 607–609
Somtseu 244, 245
Somtseu 529–531, 545, 546, 549,
    550, 552, 554–556
Soshangane 60, 62, 96, 105, 106,
    265, 266
Sotho 183, 389, 398, 415, 450, 460,
    467
Southampton 204
Southbroom 557
Speirs, R. 337, 477, 499, 500, 501
Spies, A. 222–225, 443
Stanger 97, 220, 487, 488, 490, 494,
    615, 625
Stanger, W. 217, 221, 249, 306, 321
Stavenisse 43
Steenkoolspruit 182
Steinaecker, L. 560
Steward, C.W. 341, 343, 344
Stocker, A.H. & F.R. 470, 473, 474
Struben, Capt. J. 445
sugar 37, 250, 369, 375, 377, 480–
    489, 493, 494, 515–517, 519, 520,
    524, 527, 528, 530–533, 541–544,
    546, 554–556, 600, 609, 610
sugar cane 127, 184, 481, 485, 610
Sundays River 456

Sungubala 462, 463
survey 38, 43, 77–81, 217, 351, 405, 434, 436, 444, 450, 451, 453, 471, 473, 530, 532, 576, 577, 599, 602, 607
Susha people 29, 539
Sutherland, Dr P.C. 322, 448, 449, 476, 488, 490, 499, 504, 540, 548
uSuthu River 266, 273, 299, 301, 586
Sutton, G.M. 510, 597, 606
Swazi people 20, 21, 138, 184, 185, 298, 379, 381, 397, 451, 468, 497, 570, 572, 575, 578, 581, 587, 604

tea 229, 466, 489, 544, 546, 555, 565
Tembe 100, 568, 569, 576
Tenedos 379, 404
Teteluku 349
Thekwini 24
Thembus 29, 64, 104
Thintwanyoni 151
oThobothini 589
Thongasi 29, 539
Thongathi 25, 69, 83, 140, 178, 222, 482, 487
Thornville 309, 333
Thring's Post 625, 626
Thukela River 36, 48, 61, 132, 163, 181, 213, 222, 223, 280–282, 294, 364, 379, 384, 460, 480, 489, 491, 497, 508, 596, 611, 625–627
Thuli people 67
Thulwana regiment 185, 367, 373
utokoloshe 48
Tonga 529
Tonga people 22, 23, 38, 49, 78, 259, 272, 273, 299, 300, 301, 369, 377, 566, 568, 569, 570–592
Tongaat 487, 490, 493
Tongoland 33, 37, 40, 51, 78, 100, 106, 113, 266, 272, 273, 299, 300, 301, 369, 371, 377, 566, 568, 569, 570, 571, 574–576, 578–592, 601, 604

Townshend 91, 112
trade 33, 36, 38, 41–43, 51, 79, 87, 113–118, 134, 168, 177, 187, 192, 240, 250, 287, 481, 492, 553, 603
Tragedy Hill 121, 562, 564
transport riding 241, 311, 505, 521
Trichera 537
Trollope, A. 314
trout 360, 466
Trygve 491
tsetse fly 17, 268, 570, 578
Tshaneni Mountain 21

Ubombo 581–585, 587, 589
ukutekela 16
ultimatum 381–383, 407
Umbogintwini 28, 516, 534
Umdoni Park 521
Umhlali 487, 488
Umkomaas 197, 503, 516, 517, 532, 535
Umzimvubu 555, 556
Umzinto 347, 514, 517, 520, 521, 527, 530, 531, 532, 543, 614
Umzumbe 536
Underberg 476, 505, 506
Utrecht 95, 285, 325, 380, 444, 451, 452, 457, 482, 549, 606
Uys, D.C. 161, 434
Uys, P.L. 124, 125
Uys, Piet 160–161, 223, 399
Uys Doorns 187, 309

Valley of a Thousand Hills 9, 25, 26, 70, 188, 302, 307, 315, 497
Vanderplank, J. 308, 309, 510
Van Reenen's Pass 450, 451, 464
vegetation 9, 273, 618
Veglaager 167
Venable, H. 138
Vermaak, C. 298, 299
Verulam 234, 235, 237, 486, 487, 490
Vijn, C. 383, 408, 410, 418
isivivane 103, 147
Vlug Kommando 161

Volksraad 178, 186, 189, 191, 193, 195, 205, 209–212, 216, 222, 453
Voortrekkers 142, 147, 156, 159, 160, 165, 179, 180, 185, 209, 219, 226, 290, 349, 365, 458, 638
Vryheid 73, 429, 434, 438, 442, 453, 457, 572, 602, 606
Vuna 176, 438, 440–442

Walmsley, Capt. J. 281–283, 291, 489, 494
War, Anglo–Boer 307, 457, 547, 560, 587, 588, 602, 605, 607, 612, 635
War, Anglo–Zulu 312, 401, 410, 411, 413–415, 421, 452, 507, 609, 612
War, First World 465, 589, 633
Warner Beach 535
Waschbank River 20
waterfalls 9, 25, 48, 188, 351, 352, 353, 354, 355, 357, 426, 461, 462, 509, 510, 617, 620
wattles 61, 90, 308, 309, 510, 511, 558, 559, 631
Weenen 172, 188, 222, 226, 308, 453
Welch, J.W. 312–314, 455
Wen Kommando 175, 181
West, Lt Gov. M. 217–219, 224, 225, 250, 305, 322, 474
Wests 533
Westville 229
whales 28, 105, 196, 561, 562
Wheelwright, W.D. 415, 419
White, Elephant 266, 268, 270, 271
wildebeest 10, 38, 136, 263, 264, 272, 298, 568

William Shaw 301
Wilson, Rev. A. 138
Winkelspruit 529
Winterton 181, 469
witch doctors 22, 40, 93, 264, 296, 398, 612, 617, 618
Wolseley, Lt Gen. Sir G. 407–410, 414, 597
Wood, Col 384, 387, 397–400
Wood, Sir E. 420
Wood, W. 146, 155, 156, 163
wrecks 31, 38–41, 44, 196, 247, 525, 536, 552, 633, 637
Wushe people 28, 65

Xholo people 28, 89
Xhosa tribe 20, 103, 104, 124, 245, 374

Yolland, Lt 426
York 242

Zambili 570, 571, 574, 579
zebras 38, 263, 298
Zelemu people 26
Zibebu 368, 371, 415, 416, 418–420, 422–432, 435, 438–441
Zietsman, J. 209, 211
Zikhali, M. 468, 469, 568, 592
Zinkwazi River 25, 489–491
Zizi tribe 20, 21, 63
iZotsha River 538
Zulu people 19, 22, 55, 56, 58–60, 64–67, 69–73, 80, 82, 96 passim
Zulu regiments 99, 392, 407
Zunckel, O. 466
Zwartkop 28, 349
Zwide 58–60, 62, 64, 87, 95, 96, 619